A Reader
for
Writers

Edited by

Collin Craig

Staci Perryman-Clark

Nancy C. DeJoy

Michigan State University

 **Primis Online**

Boston   Burr Ridge, IL   Dubuque, IA   New York   San Francisco   St. Louis
Bangkok   Bogotá   Caracas   Lisbon   London   Madrid   Mexico City
Milan   New Delhi   Seoul   Singapore   Sydney   Taipei   Toronto

A Reader for Writers

1 2 3 4 5 6 7 8 9 0   QSR   QSR   0 9 8

ISBN-13: 978-0-697-78322-6
MHID: 0-697-78322-7

Primis Senior Manager: Cathleen Mattura
Primis Systems Manager: Donna DeBenedict
Primis Sponsoring Editor: Joan L. McNamara
Cover Design: Maggie Lytle
Printer/Binder: Quebecor World

Contents

Lived

Literacies

Gloria Anzaldua (1942–   ) was born in Jesus Maria of the Valley, which is located within Texas's Rio Grande Valley. Anzaldua earned an M.A. from the University of Texas at Austin in 1973. She has taught at the University of California at Santa Cruz, Georgetown University, and Colorado University. Her books include the collection of essays and poems, *Borderlands/La Frontera: The New Mestiza* (1987), several children's books, and a novel, *La Prieta* (1997). Among other distinctions, she has won a National Endowment for the Arts fiction award and the Sappho Award of Distinction. "How to Tame a Wild Tongue" is taken from *Borderlands*.

How to Tame a Wild Tongue

Gloria Anzaldua

"We're going to have to control your tongue," the dentist says, pulling out all the metal from my mouth. Silver bits plop and tinkle into the basin. My mouth is a motherlode. 1

The dentist is cleaning out my roots. I get a whiff of the stench when I gasp. "I can't cap that tooth yet, you're still draining," he says. 2

"We're going to have to do something about your tongue," I hear the anger rising in his voice. My tongue keeps pushing out the wads of cotton, pushing back the drills, the long thin needles. "I've never seen anything as strong or as stubborn," he says. And I think, how do you tame a wild tongue, train it to be quiet, how do you bridle and saddle it? How do you make it lie down? 3

"Who is to say that robbing a people of its language is less violent than war?"
—Ray Gwyn Smith[1]

I remember being caught speaking Spanish at recess—that was good for three licks on the knuckles with a sharp ruler. I remember being sent to the corner of the classroom for "talking back" to the Anglo teacher when all I was trying to do was tell her how to pronounce my name. "If you want to be American, speak 'American.' If you don't like it, go back to Mexico where you belong." 4

"I want you to speak English. *Pa' hallar buen trabajo tienes que saber hablar el inglés bien. Qué vale toda tu educación si todavia hablas inglés con un* 'accent,'" my mother would say, mortified that I spoke English like a Mexican. At Pan American University, I, and all Chicano students were required to take two speech classes. Their purpose: to get rid of our accents. 5

Attacks on one's form of expression with the intent to censor are a violation   6
of the First Amendment. *El Anglo con cara de inocente nos arrancó la lengua.* Wild
tongues can't be tamed, they can only be cut out.

OVERCOMING THE TRADITION OF SILENCE

> *Abogadas, escupimos el oscuro.*
> *Peleando con nuestra propia sombra*
> *el silencio nos sepulta.*

En boca cerrada no entran moscas. "Flies don't enter a closed mouth" is a saying   7
I kept hearing when I was a child. *Ser habladora* was to be a gossip and a liar, to talk
too much. *Muchachitas bien criadas,* well-bred girls don't answer back. *Es una falta
de respeto* to talk back to one's mother or father. I remember one of the sins I'd recite
to the priest in the confession box the few times I went to confession: talking back
to my mother, *hablar pa' 'trás, repelar. Hocicona, repelona, chismosa,* having a big
mouth, questioning, carrying tales are all signs of being *mal criada.* In my culture they
are all words that are derogatory if applied to women—I've never heard them applied
to men.

The first time I heard two women, a Puerto Rican and a Cuban, say the word   8
"*nosotras,*" I was shocked. I had not known the word existed. Chicanas use *nosotros*
whether we're male or female. We are robbed of our female being by the masculine
plural. Language is a male discourse.

> And our tongues have become
> dry   the wilderness has
> dried out our tongues   and
> we have forgotten speech.
> —Irena Klepfisz[2]

Even our own people, other Spanish speakers *nos quieren poner candados en la*   9
boca. They would hold us back with their bag of *reglas de academia.*

OYÉ COMO LADRA: EL LENGUAJE DE LA FRONTERA

> *Quien tiene boca se equivoca.*
> —Mexican saying

"*Pocho,* cultural traitor, you're speaking the oppressor's language by speaking English,   10
you're ruining the Spanish language," I have been accused by various Latinos and

Latinas. Chicano Spanish is considered by the purist and by most Latinos deficient, a mutilation of Spanish.

But Chicano Spanish is a border tongue which developed naturally. Change, 11 *evolución, enriquecimiento de palabras nuevas por invención o adopción* have created variants of Chicano Spanish, *un nuevo lenguaje. Un lenguaje que corresponde a un modo de vivir.* Chicano Spanish is not incorrect, it is a living language.

For a people who are neither Spanish nor live in a country in which Spanish is 12 the first language; for a people who live in a country in which English is the reigning tongue but who are not Anglo; for a people who cannot entirely identify with either standard (formal, Castillian) Spanish nor standard English, what recourse is left to them but to create their own language? A language which they can connect their identity to, one capable of communicating the realities and values true to themselves—a language with terms that are neither *español ni inglés*, but both. We speak a patois, a forked tongue, a variation of two languages.

Chicano Spanish sprang out of the Chicanos' need to identify ourselves as a dis- 13 tinct people. We needed a language with which we could communicate with ourselves, a secret language. For some of us, language is a homeland closer than the Southwest—for many Chicanos today live in the Midwest and the East. And because we are a complex, heterogeneous people, we speak many languages. Some of the languages we speak are:

1. Standard English
2. Working class and slang English
3. Standard Spanish
4. Standard Mexican Spanish
5. North Mexican Spanish dialect
6. Chicano Spanish (Texas, New Mexico, Arizona, and California have regional variations)
7. Tex-Mex
8. *Pachuco* (called *caló*)

My "home" tongues are the languages I speak with my sister and brothers, with 14 my friends. They are the last five listed, with 6 and 7 being closest to my heart. From school, the media and job situations, I've picked up standard and working class English. From Mamagrande Locha and from reading Spanish and Mexican literature, I've picked up Standard Spanish and Standard Mexican Spanish. From *los recién llegados,* Mexican immigrants, and *braceros,* I learned the North Mexican dialect. With Mexicans I'll try to speak either Standard Mexican Spanish or the North Mexican dialect. From my parents and Chicanos living in the Valley, I picked up Chicano Texas Spanish, and I speak it with my mom, younger brother (who married a Mexican and who rarely mixes Spanish with English), aunts and older relatives.

With Chicanas from *Nuevo México* or *Arizona* I will speak Chicano Spanish a   15
little, but often they don't understand what I'm saying. With most California
Chicanas I speak entirely in English (unless I forget). When I first moved to San
Francisco, I'd rattle off something in Spanish, unintentionally embarrassing them.
Often it is only with another Chicana *tejana* that I can talk freely.

Words distorted by English are known as anglicisms or *pochismos*. The *pocho* is   16
an anglicized Mexican or American of Mexican origin who speaks Spanish with an
accent characteristic of North Americans and who distorts and reconstructs the language according to the influence of English.[3] Tex-Mex, or Spanglish, comes most
naturally to me. I may switch back and forth from English to Spanish in the same
sentence or in the same word. With my sister and my brother Nune and with Chicano
tejano contemporaries I speak in Tex-Mex.

From kids and people my own age I picked up *Pachuco*. *Pachuco* (the language   17
of the zoot suiters) is a language of rebellion, both against Standard Spanish and
Standard English. It is a secret language. Adults of the culture and outsiders cannot
understand it. It is made up of slang words from both English and Spanish. *Ruca* means
girl or woman, *vato* means guy or dude, *chale* means no, *simón* means yes, *churo* is sure,
talk is *periquiar*, *pigionear* means petting, *que gacho* means how nerdy, *ponte águila*
means watch out, death is called *la petona*. Through lack of practice and not having others who can speak it, I've lost most of the *Pachuco* tongue.

CHICANO SPANISH

Chicanos, after 250 years of Spanish/Anglo colonization have developed significant   18
differences in the Spanish we speak. We collapse two adjacent vowels into a single
syllable and sometimes shift the stress in certain words such as *maíz/maiz, cobete/cuete*.
We leave out certain consonants when they appear between vowels: *lado/lao,
mojado/mojao*. Chicanos from South Texas pronounced *f* as *j* as in *jue (fue)*. Chicanos
use "archaisms," words that are no longer in the Spanish language, words that have
been evolved out. We say *semos, trufe, baiga, ansina*, and *naiden*. We retain the
"archaic" *j* as in *jalar*, that derives from an earlier *h*, (the French *halar* or the Germanic
halon which was lost to standard Spanish in the 16th century), but which is still found
in several regional dialects such as the one spoken in South Texas. (Due to geography, Chicanos from the Valley of South Texas were cut off linguistically from other
Spanish speakers. We tend to use words that the Spaniards brought over from
Medieval Spain. The majority of the Spanish colonizers in Mexico and the Southwest
came from Extremadura—Herrian Cortés was one of them—and Andalucia.
Andalucians pronounce *ll* like a *y*, and their *d*'s tend to be absorbed by adjacent vowels: *tirado* becomes *tirao*. They brought *el lenguaje popular, dialectos y regionalismos*.[4])

Chicanos and other Spanish speakers also shift *ll* to *y* and *z* to *s*.[5] We leave out   19
initial syllables, saying *tar* for *estar*, *toy* for *estoy*, *hora* for *ahora* (*cubanos* and *puertor-*
riqueños also leave out initial letters of some words). We also leave out the final syllable such as *pa* for *para*. The intervocalic *y*, the *ll* as in *tortilla*, *ella*, *botella*, gets
replaced by *tortia* or *tortiya*, *ea*, *botea*. We add an additional syllable at the beginning
of certain words: *atocar* for *tocar*, *agastar* for *gastar*. Sometimes we'll say *lavaste las vaci-*
jas, other times *lavates* (substituting the *ates* verb endings for the *aste*).

We use anglicisms, words borrowed from English: *bola* from ball, *carpeta* from   20
carpet, *máchina de lavar* (instead of *lavadora*) from washing machine. Tex-Mex argot,
created by adding a Spanish sound at the beginning or end of an English word such
as *cookiar* for cook, *watchar* for watch, *parkiar* for park, and *rapiar* for rape, is the result
of the pressures on Spanish speakers to adapt to English.

We don't use the word *vosotros/as* or its accompanying verb form. We don't say   21
claro (to mean yes), *imagínate*, or *me emociona*, unless we picked up Spanish from
Latinas, out of a book, or in a classroom. Other Spanish-speaking groups are going
through the same, or similar, development in their Spanish.

LINGUISTIC TERRORISM

> *Deslenguadas. Somos los del español deficiente.* We are your linguistic nightmare, your   22
> linguistic aberration, your linguistic *mestizaje*, the subject of your *burla.* Because we
> speak with tongues of fire we are culturally crucified. Racially, culturally and linguis-
> tically *somos huérfanos*—we speak an orphan tongue.

Chicanas who grew up speaking Chicano Spanish have internalized the belief   23
that we speak poor Spanish. It is illegitimate, a bastard language. And because we
internalize how our language has been used against us by the dominant culture, we
use our language differences against each other.

Chicana feminists often skirt around each other with suspicion and hesitation.   24
For the longest time I couldn't figure it out. Then it dawned on me. To be close to
another Chicana is like looking into the mirror. We are afraid of what we'll see there.
Pena. Shame. Low estimation of self. In childhood we are told that our language is
wrong. Repeated attacks on our native tongue diminish our sense of self. The attacks
continue throughout our lives.

Chicanas feel uncomfortable talking in Spanish to Latinas, afraid of their cen-   25
sure. Their language was not outlawed in their countries. They had a whole life-
time of being immersed in their native tongue; generations, centuries in which
Spanish was a first language, taught in school, heard on radio and TV, and read in
the newspaper.

If a person, Chicana or Latina, has a low estimation of my native tongue, she   26
also has a low estimation of me. Often with *mexicanas y latinas* we'll speak English

as a neutral language. Even among Chicanas we tend to speak English at parties or conferences. Yet, at the same time, we're afraid the other will think we're *agringadas* because we don't speak Chicano Spanish. We oppress each other trying to out Chicano each other, vying to be the "real" Chicanas, to speak like Chicanos. There is no one Chicano language just as there is no one Chicano experience. A mono-lingual Chicana whose first language is English or Spanish is just as much a Chicana as one who speaks several variants of Spanish. A Chicana from Michigan or Chicago or Detroit is just as much a Chicana as one from the Southwest. Chicano Spanish is as diverse linguistically as it is regionally.

By the end of this century, Spanish speakers will comprise the biggest minority   27
group in the U.S., a country where students in high schools and colleges are encour-aged to take French classes because French is considered more "cultured." But for a language to remain alive it must be used.[6] By the end of this century English, and not Spanish, will be the mother tongue of most Chicanos and Latinos.

So, if you want to really hurt me, talk badly about my language. Ethnic iden-   28
tity is twin skin to linguistic identity—I am my language. Until I can take pride in my language, I cannot take pride in myself. Until I can accept as legitimate Chicano Texas Spanish, Tex-Mex and all the other languages I speak, I cannot accept the legitimacy of myself. Until I am free to write bilingually and to switch codes without having always to translate, while I still have to speak English or Spanish when I would rather speak Spanglish, and as long as I have to accommodate the English speakers rather than having them accommodate me, my tongue will be illegitimate.

I will no longer be made to feel ashamed of existing. I will have my voice: Indian,   29
Spanish, white. I will have my serpent's tongue—my woman's voice, my sexual voice, my poet's voice. I will overcome the tradition of silence.

> My fingers
> move sly against your palm
> Like women everywhere, we speak in code. . . .
>   —Melanie Kaye/Kantrowitz[7]

"VISTAS," CORRIDOS, Y COMIDA: MY NATIVE TONGUE

In the 1960s, I read my first Chicano novel. It was *City of Night* by John Rechy, a gay   30
Texan, son of a Scottish father and a Mexican mother. For days I walked around in stunned amazement that a Chicano could write and could get published. When I read *I Am Joaquín*[8] I was surprised to see a bilingual book by a Chicano in print. When I saw poetry written in Tex-Mex for the first time, a feeling of pure joy flashed through me. I felt like we really existed as a people. In 1971, when I started teaching High

School English to Chicano students, I tried to supplement the required texts with works by Chicanos, only to be reprimanded and forbidden to do so by the principal. He claimed that I was supposed to teach "American" and English literature. At the risk of being fired, I swore my students to secrecy and slipped in Chicano short stories, poems, a play. In graduate school, while working toward a Ph.D., I had to "argue" with one advisor after the other, semester after semester, before I was allowed to make Chicano literature an area of focus.

Even before I read books by Chicanos or Mexicans, it was the Mexican movies   31
I saw at the drive-in—the Thursday night special of $1.00 a carload—that gave me a sense of belonging. "*Vámonos a las vistas*," my mother would call out and we'd all—grandmother, brothers, sister, and cousins—squeeze into the car. We'd wolf down cheese and bologna white bread sandwiches while watching Pedro Infante in melodramatic tear-jerkers like *Nosotros los pobres*, the first "real" Mexican movie (that was not an imitation of European movies). I remember seeing *Cuando los hijos se van* and surmising that all Mexican movies played up the love a mother has for her children and what ungrateful sons and daughters suffer when they are not devoted to their mothers. I remember the singing-type "westerns" of Jorge Negrete and Miguel Aceves Meía. When watching Mexican movies, I felt a sense of homecoming as well as alienation. People who were to amount to something didn't go to Mexican movies, or *baíes* or tune their radios to *bolero*, *rancherita*, and *corrido* music.

The whole time I was growing up, there was *norteño* music sometimes called   32
North Mexican border music, or Tex-Mex music, or Chicano music, or *cantina* (bar) music. I grew up listening to *conjuntos*, three- or four-piece bands made up of folk musicians playing guitar, *bajo sexto*, drums, and button accordion, which Chicanos had borrowed from the German immigrants who had come to Central Texas and Mexico to farm and build breweries. In the Rio Grande Valley, Steve Jordan and Little Joe Hernández were popular, and Flaco Jiménez was the accordion king. The rhythms of Tex-Mex music are those of the polka, also adapted from the Germans, who in turn had borrowed the polka from the Czechs and Bohemians.

I remember the hot, sultry evenings when *corridos*—songs of love and death   33
on the Texas-Mexican borderlands—reverberated out of cheap amplifiers from the local *cantinas* and wafted in through my bedroom window.

Corridos first became widely used along the South Texas Mexican border during   34
the early conflict between Chicanos and Anglos. The *corridos* are usually about Mexican heroes who do valiant deeds against the Anglo oppressors. Pancho Villa's song, "*La cucaracha*," is the most famous one. *Corridos* of John F. Kennedy and his death are still very popular in the Valley. Older Chicanos remember Lydia Mendoza, one of the great border *corrido* singers who was called *la Gloria de Tejas*. Her "*El tango negro*," sung during the Great Depression, made her a singer of the people. The

everpresent *corridos* narrated one hundred years of border history, bringing news of events as well as entertaining. These folk musicians and folk songs are our chief cultural mythmakers, and they made our hard lives seem bearable.

I grew up feeling ambivalent about our music. Country-western and rock-and-roll   35
had more status. In the 50s and 60s, for the slightly educated and *agringado* Chicanos, there existed a sense of shame at being caught listening to our music. Yet I couldn't stop my feet from thumping to the music, could not stop humming the words, nor hide from myself the exhilaration I felt when I heard it.

There are more subtle ways that we internalize identification, especially in   36
the forms of images and emotions. For me food and certain smells are tied to my identity, to my homeland. Woodsmoke curling up to an immense blue sky; woodsmoke perfuming my grandmother's clothes, her skin. The stench of cow manure and the yellow patches on the ground; the crack of a .22 rifle and the reek of cordite. Homemade white cheese sizzling in a pan, melting inside a folded *tortilla*. My sister Hilda's hot, spicy *menudo*, *chile colorado* making it deep red, pieces of *panza* and hominy floating on top. My brother Carito barbecuing *fajitas* in the backyard. Even now and 3,000 miles away, I can see my mother spicing the ground beef, pork, and venison with *chile*. My mouth salivates at the thought of the hot steaming *tamales* I would be eating if I were home.

SI LE PREGUNTAS A MI MAMÁ, "¿QUÉ ERES?"

> "Identity is the essential core of who
> we are as individuals, the conscious
> experience of the self inside."
> —Kaufman[9]

Nosotros los Chicanos straddle the borderlands. On one side of us, we are constantly   37
exposed to the Spanish of the Mexicans, on the other side we hear the Anglos' incessant clamoring so that we forget our language. Among ourselves we don't say *nosotros los americanos, o nosotros los españoles, o nosotros los hispanos*. We say *nosotros los mexicanos* (by *mexicanos* we do not mean citizens of Mexico; we do not mean a national identity, but a racial one). We distinguish between *mexicanos del otro lado* and *mexicanos de este lado*. Deep in our hearts we believe that being Mexican has nothing to do with which country one lives in. Being Mexican is a state of soul—not one of mind, not one of citizenship. Neither eagle nor serpent, but both. And like the ocean, neither animal respects borders.

> *Dime con quien andas y te diré quien eres.*
> (Tell me who your friends are and I'll tell you who you are.)
> —Mexican saying

Si le preguntas a mi mamá, "¿Qué eres?" te dirá, "Soy mexicana." My brothers 38
and sister say the same. I sometimes will answer *"soy mexicana"* and at others will
say *"soy Chicana" o "soy tejana."* But I identified as *"Raza"* before I ever identified as
"mexicana" or "Chicana."

As a culture, we call ourselves Spanish when referring to ourselves as a linguis- 39
tic group and when copping out. It is then that we forget our predominant Indian
genes. We are 70 to 80% Indian.[10] We call ourselves Hispanic[11] or Spanish-American
or Latin American or Latin when linking ourselves to other Spanish-speaking peoples of the Western hemisphere and when copping out. We call ourselves Mexican-
American[12] to signify we are neither Mexican nor American, but more the noun
"American" than the adjective "mexican" (and when copping out).

Chicanos and other people of color suffer economically for not acculturating. 40
This voluntary (yet forced) alienation makes for psychological conflict, a kind of dual
identity—we don't identify with the Anglo-American cultural values and we don't
totally identify with the Mexican cultural values. We are a synergy of two cultures
with various degrees of Mexicanness or Angloness. I have so internalized the bor-
derland conflict that sometimes I feel like one cancels out the other and we are zero,
nothing, no one. *A veces no soy nada ni nadie. Pero hasta cuando no lo soy, lo soy.*

When not copping out, when we know we are more than nothing, we call our- 41
selves Mexican, referring to race and ancestry: *mestizo* when affirming both our Indian
and Spanish (but we hardly ever own our Black ancestry); Chicano when referring
to a politically aware people born and/or raised in the U.S.: *Raza* when referring to
Chicanos; *tejanos* when we are Chicanos from Texas.

Chicanos did not know we were a people until 1965 when Cesar Chavez and 42
the farmworkers united and *I Am Joaquín* was published and *la Raza Unida* party
was formed in Texas. With that recognition, we became a distinct people. Something
momentous happened to the Chicano soul—we became aware of our reality and
acquired a name and a language (Chicano Spanish) that reflected that reality. Now
that we had a name, some of the fragmented pieces began to fall together—who
we were, what we were, how we had evolved. We began to get glimpses of what we
might eventually become.

Yet the struggle of identities continues, the struggle of borders is our reality still. 43
One day the inner struggle will cease and a true integration take place. In the meantime, *tenemos que hacerla lucha. ¿Quién está protegiendo los ranchos de mi gente? ¿Quién
está tratando de cerrar la fisura entre la india y el blanco en nuestra sangre? El Chicano, sí,
el Chicano que anda como un ladrón en su propia casa.*

Los Chicanos, how patient we seem, how very patient. There is the quiet of the 44
Indian about us.[13] We know how to survive. When other races have given up their
tongue, we've kept ours. We know what it is to live under the hammer blow of the

dominant *norteamericano* culture. But more than we count the blows, we count the days the weeks the years the centuries the eons until the white laws and commerce and customs will rot in the deserts they've created, lie bleached. *Humildes* yet proud, *quietos* yet wild, *nosotros los mexicanos*-Chicanos will walk by the crumbling ashes as we go about our business. Stubborn, persevering, impenetrable as stone, yet possessing a malleability that renders us unbreakable, we, the *mestizas* and *mestizos*, will remain.

ENDNOTES

1. Ray Gwyn Smith, *Moorland Is Cold Country*. Unpublished book.
2. Irena Klepfisz, "*Di rayze aheym*/The Journey Home," *The Tribe of Dina: A Jewish Women's Anthology*, eds. Melanie Kaye/Kantrowitz and Irena Klepfisz (Montpelier, VT: Sinister Wisdom Books, 1986) 49.
3. R.C. Ortega. *Dialectología Del Barrio*, trans. Hortencia S. Alwan (Los Angeles, CA: R.C. Ortega Publisher & Bookseller, 1977) 132.
4. Eduardo Hernandéz-Chávez, Andrew D. Cohen, and Anthony F. Beltramo, *El Lenguaje de los Chicanos: Regional and Social Characteristics of Language Used By Mexican Americans* (Arlington, VA: Center for Applied Linguistics, 1975) 39.
5. Hernandéz-Chávez xvii.
6. Irena Klepfisz, "Secular Jewish Identity: Yidishkayt in America," *The Tribe of Dina*, 43.
7. Melanie Kaye/Kantrowitz, "Sign," *We Speak in Code: Poems and Other Writings* (Pittsburgh, PA: Motheroot Publications, Inc., 1980) 85.
8. Rodolfo Gonzales, *I Am Joaquín/Yo Soy Joaquín* (New York, NY: Bantam Books, 1972). It was first published in 1967.
9. Kaufman 68.
10. Chávez 88–90.
11. "Hispanic" is derived from *Hispanis* (*España*, a name given to the Iberian Peninsula in ancient times when it was a part of the Roman Empire) and is a term designated by the U.S. government to make it easier to handle us on paper.
12. The Treaty of Guadalupe Hidalgo created the Mexican-American in 1848.
13. Anglos, in order to alleviate their guilt for dispossessing the Chicano, stressed the Spanish part of us and perpetrated the myth of the Spanish Southwest. We have accepted the fiction that we are Hispanic, that is Spanish, in order to accommodate ourselves to the dominant culture and its abhorrence of Indians. Chávez 88–91.

Keith Gilyard (1952–) received an M.F.A. from Columbia University and a doctorate of education at New York University. He is a poet, essayist, and editor, and a Distinguished Professor of English at Pennsylvania State University. Known for his research on language and literacy instruction for people of color and his emphasis on language's interrelation with social conscience and politics, he has been in demand as a writer and lecturer for three decades. The most recent of his five books is *Rhetoric and Ethnicity* (2004), and he has edited and co-edited another four. In 1992, his memoir *Voices of the Self: A Study of Language Competence* won an American Book Award. He was inducted into the International Literary Hall of Fame for Writers of African Descent in 2002.

FIRST LESSONS

Keith Gilyard

Some events come before the memory. Completely beyond the veil of vagueness. Just no way to recall. The only knowledge I have of the times came through eavesdropping. I could not deal with direct questioning because it was clear that made me a bug. Try to open up the past and I would get shrugged off with stares like roach spray. So I just kept listening and observing and drawing my own conclusions, trying to get a sense of what the pre-memory was all about. That's important to me because it's a part of life too and it's a lot like the wind, you know, you can't see it but it can kick your rump pretty good if it blows hard enough.

1

I hit the scene uptown in 1952 on a Sunday afternoon. I think I started out as a good reason for all to be happy, but there was a curious error on the take-home copy of my birth certificate. In the space where the name of the father belongs my own name was written in. His was left off the document altogether. That error, however committed, was my first omen.

2

I hadn't yet cut a tooth when I received omen number two. A fire broke out in our apartment. Started in back of the refrigerator. My mother detected it first, yanked my one-year-old sister out of her bed, snatched me up from the crib, and hustled on outdoors. She didn't bother to arouse her husband/my dad. It's a blessing he managed to get out on his own. I've always thought that was a horrible thing for her to do although by the time I heard the story, with the influence I was under, I felt he probably deserved it. And I have chuckled

3

about the event on numerous occasions since. But at other times I have pic-
tured my father lying dead in a robe of bright yellow flames and felt my own
palms moisten with fear. There was no doubt something cruel going on in our
little world.

The signs persisted like ragweed. Sad events that would be revealed to me   4
in tale. The tale of the perfectly thrown frying pan, you know, it's more feisti-
ness than I would like to see in a woman of mine. Sherry and I were, in one
sense, beneath it all. Down on the floor knocking over and spilling everything.
But we also assumed a role in the power play as it was we who became its center. Mama took that battle also; as far back as we can remember we had the distinct impression that we belonged to her exclusively. We were her objects of
adornment and possession, always dressed for compliments. Pops could get no
primary billing in that setup. When I think back now to my earliest remem-
brances I sense him only as a haze in the background. And even as I reel forward again and he begins to crystallize for me, it's quite some time before he
appears essential. Moms, on the other hand, was ranked up there next to sun-
light from the beginning.

That's a long way to come from Ashford, Alabama. Way down by the   5
Chipola River. Little Margie, with stubbornness her most celebrated trait.
Might as well whip a tree, they would say, if you were figuring on whipping her
for a confession. At least you spare your own self some pain. And she was real
close to her few chosen friends. If she liked you she could bring you loyalty in a
million wheelbarrows. Labeled "good potential," she worked far below it. Skated
her way through school. Folks have camped just outside her earshot for years
whispering, "She's smart so she could do better if. ..."

Ammaziah, though bright, didn't have a chance to skate through school.   6
He had to work on a farm northeast of Ashford, going up toward the Chatta-
hoochee. "He's just a plain nice man" is the worst thing I have ever heard anybody outside of our own household say about him. And I guess it would be hard
not to like a big and gentle Baptist with a basic decency who could hold his
liquor and had a name you could make fun of.

He liked to watch all the horses run and all the New York women too.   7
Couldn't lick either gamble. He hadn't developed enough finesse for the big
town. I know he tried hard at times but whenever he put together two really
good steps irresponsibility would rear up and knock him back three. He couldn't
be any Gibraltar for you.

All this going on around our heads. The big folks. Both destined to be   8
enshrined in the best-friend-you-could-possibly-have hall of fame, provided
they could keep each other off the selection committee. But they still hung out

together. Hadn't fully understood the peace that can crop up here and there amid the greatest confusion. And right in the middle of 1954 came daughter number two. Judy ate well and slept a lot, then less, and grew to be a good partner to knock around with as we caromed off the walls of the Harlem flat and tumbled forward.

In the early reaches of memory events swirl about like batches of stirred leaves. No order or sequence. I remember we had two pet turtles. One had a yellow shell. The other's was red. We kept them in a bowl with a little plastic palm tree and tiny cream-colored pebbles. Sherry fed them and I poured in the fresh water. Well the turtles were a bit frisky. They often climbed out of the bowl and we had to overturn tables and cushions and chairs to find them. I don't recall how many times we went on this chase but it was all over one morning when they were found under the sofa with their bellies ripped open by rats. For a long time afterward I would associate rats with turtlemeat first, rather than cheese, which I guess isn't exactly a good start toward a high IQ.

So the turtles died early on. But I can't tell you whether that was before the back of my head was split open on the front stoop. There was a bunch of us out there preparing to run a dash down 146th Street. Victory wasn't the main thing in these races. Just please don't come in last or you would be the first one to get your mother talked about and everything. I had poor position inside along the rail next to this chubby girl, but as we came thundering past the front of the building I began to pull away from her. I was getting away from the last spot for sure when she reached out and pushed me down. My head banged hard into the edge of a concrete step and the blood started dripping down the back of my neck and I started screaming like crazy. Then I had to get shaven bald in one spot and look like a jerk so I could get patched up right. But that was better still than being last. I mean I had heard Pee Wee Thomas, who was in school already, tell Tyrone that the reason he was so slow was because whoever Tyrone's father was had to be slow too not to have been able to get away from Tyrone's ugly damn mama.

There was a babysitter we went to sometimes down on Seventh Avenue. Her name was Janine and she had boy-girl twins, Diane and Darnell, who were a few months older than Sherry. She was real nice and let us drag our toys all over the house, but whenever her husband, Butch, would come home early in the afternoon she would round us up quickly and herd us into the kids' room. We were under strict orders not to come out and of course we didn't. But she never said anything about peeping. The first time was at Darnell's suggestion. We crept up to the door and cracked it with the stealth of cat burglars. I couldn't see over Sherry and the twins so I crouched to the floor and never did

get a look at the action. Darnell almost burst out laughing and we retreated to
the farthest corner of the room. We sent Judy off to play with some blocks.

"What is they doin Sherry?" I whispered as I took a seat atop Darnell's   12
wagon.

"Oh you so stupid Keith."   13

"Well I ain't see so good."   14

"Oh you just so stupid. Tell him Darnell." She and Diane were giggling.   15

"No you Sherry."   16

"No Darnell you."   17

"It's your brother. You 'pose to."   18

"I can't. I don't know for real."   19

"You know for real."   20

"No I don't."   21

"Then why you laughin?"   22

"I was laughin at you." And they all started laughing at each other. Then   23
Darnell came and whispered in my ear: "They doin nasty."

"NASTY OOOOH NAS–." Darnell clamped his hand over my mouth.   24
"You gotta be quiet Keith or we can't go no more."

I was quiet. And got to go many times before I decided, or was it Diane who   25
decided, that we could do some nasty of our own. But we announced our intentions first and Sherry squealed and Janine gave both of us a spanking. Barely
five, I was mad I had to wait.

I remember one Saturday we were coming home from the beauty parlor   26
with my mother. I had on my cowboy get up, six-shooters at my sides. We were
walking well up in front of her as usual, trained to stop at the corner. That
morning, however, I took it into my head to go dashing across Eighth Avenue
on my own. I think I saw my father but I'm not sure. I know I didn't look for
any traffic lights. I tripped about halfway across and couldn't get to my feet
again. I was struggling hard but my coordination had deserted me. Like scram-
bling on ice. There was a screeching of brakes and then the most gigantic bus
imaginable was hovering over me. I still couldn't get the feet to work together. I
was somehow yanked from under the bus, dragged the rest of the way across the
street and, with my own pistols, beaten all the way up the block. It was a fierce
thrashing and there were folks out there imploring my mother to stop. But verbal support was all I received. Wasn't anybody out there going to risk tangling
with Moms. I have never fallen in any roadway, nor been pistol-whipped, since.

One evening we were digging into some fruit cocktail after dinner and   27
heard a great ruckus out in the hallway. The cops were chasing these two drug
addicts and they were headed for the roof. "They's junkies I know" said a man

across the hall. Sherry had mentioned something about junkies to me before, but when the police paraded them down the stairs stark naked with their hands cuffed behind their backs it was the first time I had a good opportunity to see what they actually looked like. It was somewhat disappointing, however, for they looked just about like everybody else.

I was bringing a loaf of bread home from the store when I saw this gray dog getting his neck chewed off in a dogfight on the corner. I dropped my bag to go save him and was trying to push my way through the circle of gamblers and spectators when this huge man hoisted me up onto his shoulder. He thought I merely wanted a better view. Before I could figure a way to get down another man rescued the dog, though he was cursing the poor animal, and green bills changed hands around the circle.

Sherry had gone off to kindergarten and I decided to give Judy a sex change operation while our mother was asleep. I slipped her into a change of my clothing as I kept reassuring her. "You know it gon be more fun. You know it right?" She was properly willing. We had to roll the pants up at the bottom and her feet couldn't make it down into the toes of my sneakers but we could live with that. But we were dissatisfied with her hair. Such soft long braids. Boys get away with that now but not in '57.

"You gotta cut it."

"Then I be a boy Keith? I finish that I be a boy?"

"Yeah you'll be one. It gon be more fun too."

Scissors please. She wouldn't cut it in one fell swoop like I wanted her to do. She started nibbling at the edges. Tiny dark patches falling gently to the floor. As she became more relaxed, however, she began to clip at a faster pace and made a clearing on one side all the way to the scalp. I was urging her to clip even faster, "go head Judy go head," when Sherry came charging into the apartment, saw what was taking place, let out a long and soulful "Oooooooooh I'm gonna tell Ma," and ran into the other room to awaken her. I began to sweat.

"You made me" Judy accused.

"No I didn't and you gon git in trouble and git a beatin too."

"You made me."

"I did not."

"Yes you did."

"I DID NOT." I had to get loud to prove my innocence. Moms was already approaching fast like an enraged lioness and I wanted no part of her fury. She slashed me across the legs with her strap and cast me aside. I was getting off light. Unbelievably so. But Judy got it all.

Maybe I could have stood up for Judy, but by then I was taking the vast   40
majority of the whippings in the household. So I guess I figured what the heck,
Judy could stand to share some of the weight. She may have become a trifle less
eager to pursue my ideas of fun but I was sort of growing bored with running
around the house with her all morning anyway. I mean Sherry was bringing
home books and fingerpaintings all the time and making kindergarten seem like
the hip thing.

It was all right I suppose. Artwork and musical chairs and fairy tales. The   41
biggest kindergarten thrill for me, however, was the chance to come home
along Eighth Avenue unescorted. Sherry didn't get out until three o'clock and
my mother didn't embarrass me by picking me up like I was a baby, so every day
I had a three-and-a-half-block distance to negotiate as I pleased. Or at least I
took it that way.

Some of us would go scampering along the Avenue. Anything could hap-   42
pen out there. The side streets were tall and narrow with hallways no more
interesting than our own. But Eighth Avenue, well, that was the real world. We
stuck our noses into the barber shop, the shoe repair shop, the fish market, the
bars. The conversation was mostly baseball and whores. Willie Mays was clearly
the Prince of Uptown, and the next best thing you could be was a pimp. We
threw stones at sleeping winos and followed the vegetable wagon all the way
down to 140th Street waiting for the horse to move his bowels in the middle of
the street. Then we'd stay and watch the cars run over the large piles of dung.
Every time a tire scored a bull's eye we'd shout "Squish" and spin about with
glee. Don't let it be a truck that scored. Ecstasy. Sometimes we would run
straight across 148th Street to Colonial Park to play tag and rock fight and
climb the hill until the guilt snuck up on us one by one and then, each according to his conscience, we would begin to head for home.

From the very beginning my mother couldn't understand why it should   43
take me over an hour to walk less than four blocks, especially when it meant
showing up with my new jacket all muddy or my pants ripped at the knee, you
know, the kinds of things you never notice until your mother points them out.
And she made all her points clear with that belt. I tried telling her that the
clock on the kitchen wall must be broken or something because I always ran
straight home, but she wouldn't buy it. I eventually had to come around. And
that's when I really got jammed.

There was a substitute teacher for our class one day and she didn't know the   44
proper time to dismiss us. It must have been going on 12:30 and she was still reading us a story about Curious George. Our class was at the end of the hall, so when
the other classes let out we couldn't hear them. There was no impatient parent to
rescue us. The substitute just kept on and on about this wonderful monkey.

Finally she sensed something was wrong and asked us what time we were   45
supposed to let out.

"Twelve o'clock" we chorused.   46

"Oh no" she exclaimed. "Are you sure?"   47

"We get out twelve o'clock" some of us repeated, as general chatter erupted   48
about the room. Louis went up to her and said, "We get out when the two
hands is straight up. That's twelve o'clock right?" She ran out of the room.
When she returned a few moments later she was shouting "Hats and coats
everybody. Hats and coats now. We're late."

Late was the last word I needed to hear. She couldn't let us out of there fast   49
enough to suit me. I sprinted home as swiftly as possible, scaled the six flights of
stairs in record time, and as I burst into the apartment out of breath my mother,
as I knew she would be, was waiting for me belt in hand. She backed me up
against the door with her stern voice.

"Haven't I told you about not coming straight home from school?" I caught   50
my breath. I was sure glad I was armed with the truth.

"Ma we had a substitute. We had a substitute Ma and she didn't know what   51
time to let us out. I ran all the way home."

"Boy don't tell that barefaced lie. I'll take the skin off your backside for lyin   52
to me."

"But I ain't lyin Ma. I ain't.   53

"Shut up boy! Ain't no teacher can keep no class late like that."   54

"But she was readin us a story."   55

"Shut up I said. Don't be standin there and givin me no cold-ass argument."   56
She drew back the strap and I cringed in terror. I sidestepped her, as the first
blow crashed against my thigh, and took off for the living room. She was right
behind me. I dove to my knees and stuck my head under the couch. It was one
of the several defensive maneuvers I had developed by then. I was always mort-
gaging my rear to save my head. Wasn't going to let anybody beat me in the
head. Which was all right with Moms.

"You ain't accomplishin nothing by stickin that behind up there like that   57
boy. That's the part I want any old how. I'll teach you yet about not payin me no
mind." She had that talking-beating rhythm in high gear. You know how you had
to receive a lecture to go along with your whipping. And can't anyone on earth
hand out a more artistic ass whipping than a Black woman can. Syncopated whippings: Boy didn't I lash lash tell you about lash lash lying to me? Lash lash lash
lash hunh? Lash hunh boy? Lash lash lash hunh boy? Hunh? I was always supposed to answer these questions although my answering them never stopped anything and sometimes made matters worse, especially if I was giving the wrong
answers as I was that day. Although I was hollering my head off I still managed to

insist upon my innocence. To no avail. Lash lash lash I will break your behind lash if necessary lash boy. Do you hear me? Do you lash lash hear me?

I heard and I felt and it hurt both ways. After the beating I continued to   58
proclaim my innocence. Only stopped when she became angry all over again and threatened me with more punishment. Afterwards I complained to my sisters on occasion, but it was weeks before I mentioned the incident to my mother again. She just gave me a warm smile and said, "I'll tell you something Keith. It all evens out."

Sibling rivalry stalked me from behind. I was getting intensive reading les-   59
sons from Sherry and had made progress to the point where I was ready to show off for Moms. We had her cornered on the sofa and I was holding the book out in front of me. Sherry was on my right, ready to help if I faltered, so I started reading something like:

> "See here," said Don. "Here are blue flowers. We want blue flowers. Let us
> get blue flowers."

It was something along those lines, you know, and I was performing well.   60
My mother was beaming and I had her undivided attention until Judy came out of somewhere, slid the edge of a razor blade into the side of my face clear to the bone, narrowly missing my eye, and ripped a deep diagonal clean past my ear.

Blood popped out everywhere. I spent what seemed like hours with my   61
head ducked under a running faucet. Towels. Compresses. Mercurochrome. Bandages. Then my mother seized a high-heeled shoe and beat Judy worse than she had beaten me for almost getting myself killed out on the Avenue.

My little sister never apologized. In fact she used to taunt me about this   62
incident as she was later becoming a favorite target for my aggression. No matter what I did to her. Kick her, trip her, whatever. She would just keep repeating, "So I cut you in the face."

"Do it again" I would retort most angrily.   63
"I did it already."   64
"I dare you to do it again. I'll push you out the window."   65
"No you won't."   66
"Yes I will."   67
"No you won't."   68
"I will so."   69
"Then I'll cut you in your face again."   70
"Then come on. Come on if you still think you so big and bad."   71
"I ain't scared."   72
"Come on then sucker."   73

"I'll cut you right in the face again."   74

"What you waitin for then fraidy cat?"   75

"I did it already."   76

She was about as mean a three year old as you will ever find.   77

Actually I had my hardest battles with Sherry. She was good for teaching me   78
things but when her mood shifted I had to watch out. She gave me my next permanent scar by pressing a hot steam iron to the back of my hand. Burned off a circle of
flesh. I later shattered a light bulb against the bridge of her nose but she escaped
unharmed. I think you can say we were taking this rivalry thing a bit too seriously.

At times my sisters would double-team me. We were heavily into words   79
now and when my sisters discovered that to stifle mine was the best weapon
they could use against me, it led to some of the unhappiest moments I can
recall. They had found my fledgling sensitivity, clutched it about the windpipe,
and squeezed. They teased me and baited me but whenever I began to reply they
would shout as loudly as they could to obscure what I was saying. Their favorite
lines were "Am sam sam sam sam. Am sam sam sam sam." As soon as I parted
my lips they would start chanting and send me straight to tears. I would wipe
aside the water, swallow hard to compose myself, and fall apart all over again. I
could rumble and accept insults but I couldn't ever deal with not being allowed
to speak. Their am sam curse was too devastating. I had neither the sense to
ignore nor the strength to attack.

I don't recall much about a whole pregnancy, but when my mother left for   80
the hospital one night in June of '58 there was only a single wish ringing in my
consciousness: BOY. And I knew I would get a brother because it was the only
thing that could even the score. He would be my guarantee to be heard because
wasn't anybody going to brainwash little brother but me. I alone would teach
him how to bound down the stairs two at a time and sneak to the park. And
he'd be the real thing. No imitation like Judy. No turncoat like Sherry. I knew I
would have to handle his fights for him but that was fine as long as he listened
to me and helped me beat the am sam curse. We'd start our own "Ooma booma
booma booma" or something like that. Fix them good.

When the phone rang my grandmother, who was up from Alabama,   81
reached it first. I watched her smile as she spoke. As she turned toward me she
was saying, "Yeah he standin right here. You know he can't wait to hear the
news." She handed me the receiver.

"Hi Ma."   82

"Hi" she answered dreamily. "You finally have another sister."   83

I was condemned. I dropped the receiver and walked out of the room in a   84
daze. Debra Lynn showed up a few days later with a head full of wild hair. She

was a beauty, and from that day to this she has never been out of my heart. But she couldn't be a brother.

I had just one more summer to pass on 146th Street. Farmer Gray cartoons   85
in the morning. The Jocko Show in the afternoon. Sit down and rock Debra Lynn for a spell or jump up and go wild to the rhythm of my first favorite record, "Tequila," by the Champs. And I was beginning to tread more lightly about the apartment, trying to avoid all scars and bruised feelings, overjoyed at any opportunity to go outside. Just give me the playground or send me to the corner grocery so I can squeeze in as much Eighth Avenue as possible before I have to hurry back. I couldn't shoot a basketball high enough to make a goal but I began learning how to dribble and saw my first pair of dead wide open eyes on a fat man lying amid a crowd in front of the fish market with a thin jagged line of blood across the width of his throat.

On Sundays, for religion, we went up on the hill. Skipping along the hexagon-   86
shaped tile in Colonial Park. Darting up the steps to Edgecomb Avenue. Stopping in the candy store on St. Nicholas to load up. Leaning forward for leverage to finish the climb up to the church. I was always impressed by this particular house of the Lord. Tremendous gray and white cinder blocks. Polished maple pews in the main service room. Red carpet, stained windows, and gigantic organ pipes. And the Lord, he owned the best singers available. There was nothing like a gorgeous soprano wailing and sweating under influence of the spirit and a hot wig. There were always old women with blue dye in their hair shrieking and swooning during the sermon as folks around them grabbed hold of them while exclaiming, "Yes Lord. I see you done come to us." With women like that falling out in droves you had to believe. And Pops was up in the front row with the rest of the deacons. A broad-shouldered frame in a gray or blue suit. Sometimes wore white gloves to serve communion. He always winked at us when he passed by.

The first grade brought a teacher, Miss Novick, who we thought was the top   87
genius on the planet. She was going to turn us all into little scientists she would say. And there was invariably one experiment or another for us to observe.

She placed a glass jar, two small candles in holders, and a box of matches   88
on her desk. She raised the jar and candles over her head and waved them slowly for all to see.

"I have here a glass jar and two simple candles. Can everyone see them?"   89

"Yes Miss Novick" we replied, speaking as everyone.   90

"See them James?"   91

"Yeah."   92

"See them Karen?" 93

"Uh hunh." 94

"See them John?" 95

"I sees it." 96

"Okay." She returned the objects to her desk, lit the candles and held them 97
overhead. Our eyes were transfixed with magic show expectations.

"Now the candles are lit. You see? Rosanne? Ryan? Keith?" I gave a nod of 98
affirmation. Then she lowered the candles to the desk and lifted the jar, upside
down, as we inched forward in our seats.

"Now who can tell me what will happen if I set this jar down over one of 99
these flames? Can anyone tell me? James?" He could not. He was smart but
stumped. Sat looking dumb with his face greased and his eyes bulged and his
index finger glued to his chin.

"How about you Barbara?" 100

"You gonna catch the des' on fire Miss Novick." 101

"YEAAHHHHHHHH. . . ." 102

"No, little scientists. No. No. No. We will not harm the desk. Anyone 103
else?. . . No?. . . Well let us observe."

She placed the jar over one of the candles and we stared eagerly at both 104
flames until the one inside the jar died out. Miss Novick surveyed our puzzled
faces and smiled.

"Now why did that happen class?" 105

"You mean why it went out?" 106

"Yes Harold. Can you tell me why?" 107

"Because you put that jar on there. You made it go out Miss Novick. You 108
did it."

"Sure Harold. But how could I do it with only the jar?" 109

"I don't know. Was there some water in there?" 110

"There wasn't Harold. We all looked at the jar together, remember?" 111

"Oh yeah." 112

"Anyone else?" Miss Novick was extremely patient and thoroughly flus- 113
tered us all before giving us our first formal explanation concerning oxygen.

I liked the prospect of becoming a resident scientist up at P.S. 90 (strange 114
what faith I had in the public school system up there), and when the announcement came later that fall that we were moving into a house out in Queens I
was, at first, a bit disheartened. I knew there were scientific experiments elsewhere but I wasn't so sure I could get another Miss Novick or even more important, in a related field, another Eighth Avenue.

I wasn't anti-Queens; all I knew about the place was that it was over a   115
bridge somewhere. But I surely had no beef with Harlem. I didn't recoil at the
sight of its streets as I would at other times later in life. I had no sense of society
being so terrible. I was there and I fit.

On another level, however, I guess I did welcome a chance to leave the   116
apartment I was associating more and more with misunderstanding and pain.
House sounded like more space to stay out of the way of others.

So at the age of six it was time for a crossing. My young mind poised for any   117
game that came along. Could play the middle or skirt the fringe as I saw fit. Just
come out stepping light and easy, you know, and if it gets hectic remember to
cover in the clinch. The point was to hold the defense together while all about
me from complex fabrics of frustration and rejection and sensitivity and conflict
and hope and loneliness and resignation and reticence and wonderment and
bewilderment and romantic notions and romantic disappointments, from all
this and more, the imposing offense was being woven.

And the bridge bowed gracefully and beckoned. Bore me upon its majestic   118
back and arched me high above the cold and swirling dark waters of that
November toward another shore, and another truth, which all should know:
Most times a bridge is just another two-way street.

Keith Gilyard (1952–) received an M.F.A. from Columbia University and a doctor-ate of education at New York University. He is a poet, essayist, and editor, and a Distinguished Professor of English at Pennsylvania State University. Known for his research on language and literacy instruction for people of color and his emphasis on language's interrelation with social conscience and politics, he has been in demand as a writer and lecturer for three decades. The most recent of his five books is *Rhetoric and Ethnicity* (2004), and he has edited and co-edited another four. In 1992, his memoir *Voices of the Self: A Study of Language Competence* won an American Book Award. He was inducted into the International Literary Hall of Fame for Writers of African Descent in 2002.

RAPPING, READING AND ROLE-PLAYING

Keith Gilyard

Early Language

The speech of a large group of African-Americans has been given many labels, including Ebonics, Black English Vernacular, and just plain Black English. The last term is by far the most popular. I will use it throughout this text to refer to my native tongue, that is, the language variety I first acquired and the one I have always been able to use with greatest facility.   1

The idea of Black English is still controversial despite research dating back three decades, which documents that it is a legitimate linguistic system and not merely a collection of verbal aberrations arrived at by the reckless violation of the rules of a so-called superior variety of English. But let us presently make an end run around that debate. The intent here is not to argue the existence or overall merits of Black English. The case has been made quite well by scholars such as Smitherman (1977), Dillard (1973), and Haskins and Butts (1973). The most pressing purpose at this point is to demonstrate how the dialogue of the Keith character (me) is reflective of that language variety.* The analysis is meant to be indicative rather than exhaustive. As such, a thorough review of the rules of Black English will not be required. Structural explanations will be offered only to further illuminate the specific portions of the text being considered. Perhaps it is instructive, however, to include a general definition. Smitherman's should suffice: "Black Dialect is an Africanized form of English   2

---

*Again, the premise is that these sequences, while not actual, are certainly plausible.

reflecting Black America's linguistic-cultural heritage and the conditions of servitude, oppression and life in America" (p. 2).

In "First Lessons," as the four youngsters are engaged in the Peeping Tom   3
scene, we find the following snatches of dialogue.

(1) "What is they doin Sherry?" (Keith speaking)

(2) "Oh you so stupid Keith." (Sherry speaking)

(3) "Then why you laughin?" (Darnell speaking)

(4) "They doin nasty." (Darnell speaking)

The *is they* combination in sentence 1 would be identified as an error in noun-verb agreement under the rules of Standard English; however, this construction exemplifies the Black English convention of simplifying the conjugation of the verb *to be*. Smitherman again explains: "When the forms of *be* are used, they are simplified so that *is* and *was* usually serve for all subjects of sentences, whether the subjects are singular or plural, or refer to *I, you, we* or whatever" (p. 21).

Skeptics may suggest that this speech is not an example of some Black En-   4
glish rule but simply the utterance of a child who has yet to master this element of agreement. After all, the speaker in this case is only five, an age at which noun-verb agreement errors are likely still to be numerous for any speaker of English. However, I must counter that the type of noun-verb error committed by a five year old in the process of acquiring Standard English is of a different nature than constructions like *is they*. Consider the description by Beck (1979) of the language of the five- to six-year old child relative to noun-verb combinations:

> The child should be advancing in use of the full verb system, although errors, particularly in noun and verb number agreement, are still prevalent. . . . The kindergarten child is as likely to say "There is flowers" as to say "There are flowers," the head word sounding singular to the child, who incorrectly anticipates the major noun's number. (p. 96)

The puzzlement that exists for the child in Beck's presentation is not to be   5
found in the case of *is they* or, by transformation to the declarative form, *they is*. Here there is no question that the noun, *they*, is plural. The choice of the accompanying verb, *is*, is definitely not based on a perception of singularity as opposed to plurality and thus cannot be said to epitomize number confusion. Furthermore, and a more obvious rebuttal, I made *they is* "mistakes" long past the age that the speaker of strictly Standard English eventually masters even the most difficult aspects of noun-verb agreement. In fact, I am still making them. But my *they is* type of talk is not merely a transitory stage in the acquisition of Standard English. It clearly points to a deeply held rule, one I already was adhering to at the age of five. The simplification of the verb *to be*, like several

other features of Black English, can only erroneously be viewed as representing a stage, or worse, an arrest in the acquisition of an alternate linguistic system.

Operative in sentences 2, 3, and 4 is the much discussed zero copula rule, that is, the omission of *be* when it would only refer to events fixed in time and nonrepeating (Smitherman, p. 21). Thus we get in sentence 2 *you so* and not *you are so*; in 3, *why you* and not *why are you*; in 4, *they doin* and not *they are doin*. Although these lines are not exact quotations, it is obvious that, as a member of that peer group, I produced these types of utterances. This is not, by the way, to suggest that language learning is solely an imitative activity. We understand from Kelly (1963) that the essential nature of human learning lies not in imitating but in active construing. Fortunately, I speak so many zero copula phrases, both real and literary, that the claim above does not have to be based solely on the evidence so far chosen. I have opted to make the case at this juncture for purposes of organization.

6

Let us look at sentence 1 from another angle. Although the speaker of *is they* conforms to a rule of Black English, he ignores the zero copula rule, which he also uses on occasion. The zero copula rule is a non-obligatory rule, whereas the simplification of *to be* is required. Put another way, one may use a form of *to be* and still be speaking Black English, but that form must be *is* or *was*. It is interesting enough to ponder why he chose to bypass the zero copula rule while his sister and friends were using it. But matters become even more intriguing when one is aware that yet another rule of Black English was bypassed, that of question formation. Questions in Black English can be asked by means of rising intonation (Burling 1973). Thus one could hear "What they is doin?" as well as "What is they doin?" So the issue now is to determine what significance can be attached to sentence 1 in light of the fact that it reflects two choices to ignore certain rules of Black English. More on this a little later.

7

In the haircut scene, there is a two-sentence response to an inquiry by Judy.

8

(5) "Yeah you'll be one."
(6) "It gon be more fun too."

Note the use of the auxiliary in sentence 5, *you'll*, while in 6 it is ignored (an instance of zero copula). Sentence 5 is not Black English at all, although we can discern from the grammar of the following sentence that the speaker surely had the ability to say, "Yeah you gon be one." The contrast is even greater than that spotted in the earlier dialogue. Also note that *gon* represents a strong Black English phonology pattern. The sound system of Black English is relatively difficult to capture in print, but the contraction *gon* in place of *going to* is, nevertheless, a stark indicator. Smitherman describes its formation: "Here the *to* is omitted altogether, and the nasal sound at the end is shortened, producing a sound

9

that is somewhat like an abbreviated form of *gone*" (p. 18). To reiterate though, this option was not chosen in Sentence 5.

In the whipping scene, we see that the mother initiates the dialogue with a   10
question that is clearly Standard English. The reply is equally standard. But when the story is flatly rejected and the physical threat becomes immediate, whatever coolness has been maintained gives way and the dialect changes.

(7) "Boy don't tell that barefaced lie."
(8) "I'll take the skin off your backside for lyin to me."
(9) "But I ain't lyin Ma."
(10) "I ain't."

In part the child, in sentences 9 and 10, is following the lead of his mother   11
who not only has added to his stress but has actually shifted, in 7 and 8, into an alternate vernacular. Great variance in grammatical structure is not apparent in this speech, nor is the huge phonological shift evident. However, the semantics are telling. This is clearly the talk of Black folks. And it is not at all surprising that very quickly we come across a multiple (triple or more) negation.

(11) "Ain't no teacher can keep no class late like that."

This pattern of negation, distinct from the double negatives that appear commonly in all nonstandard forms of English, occurs quite frequently in Black English and is perhaps the most noncontroversial marker of that language variety.

My mother is a bidialectal speaker, capable of producing Black English and   12
Standard English as well. And it should be obvious, with the examples so far adduced, that even in the preschool years my own move toward bidialectalism was well underway, made possible no doubt by my awareness of my mother's verbal maneuvering. I had seen how she could speak to a grocer, a salesman, a doctor, or a stranger in one manner (Standard), and then turn around, watch me carelessly knock a bowl of cereal on the floor, and exclaim, "Now look what you done did!" She was displaying and I was learning a technique linguists refer to as code-switching. Elgin (1979) defines this phenomenon as the "ability to move back and forth among languages, dialects, and registers with ease, as demanded by the social situation" (p. 109). Although this is a pretty fair description of the skill involved, the word *ease* is objectionable as it seems to imply that the whole process is somehow psychically neat. I have often chosen to switch, rather than fight, but the routine hasn't always implied any emotional ease. For a definition that is essentially similar yet allows the appropriate room for pain, one may consult Penalosa (1981). He defines code-switching as "a strategy by which the skillful speaker uses his knowledge of how language choices are interpreted in his community to structure the interaction so as to maximize outcomes favorable to himself" (p. 77).

That my mother was the chief agent helping me to learn to code-switch   13
should not raise any eyebrows. She was, after all, the dominant person in my life.
There appears, however, to have been some specific sociolinguistic principle
operative as well. Labov (1981) contends that women generally employ more
prestige forms than men and tend to exhibit much greater fluctuation in the
modes they employ. The fact that my mother achieved the status of number-one
role model for bidialectal speech patterns in both the text and in my present
recollection was only, as Labov indicates, the most likely outcome.

Despite this discussion of bidialectalism, bear in mind that such discourse   14
does no damage to the claim that Black English is my native tongue. It merely
demonstrates that I was not growing up as a speaker of the basilect or most
uncontaminated form of the language (see Stewart 1969). Relatively few Blacks
are. A child, indeed a whole community, would have to exist in extreme isolation for any language variety to remain pure. I would expect, therefore, most
Blacks to be bidialectal to some extent. But if we accept another contention of
Labov, that no one is ever perfectly bidialectal, that is, even-handed in a linguistic sense, I think we can safely assert, based on the evidence then and now,
that for me Black English was developing as the dominant tongue while Standard English, though quite significant, was not wielded as handily.

With this information to augment the text, we can return to the dialogue   15
cited earlier and more firmly avow that it is authentic in that it captures the
reality that forms of Standard English were also being acquired. What initially
may seem to be blundering manipulations of voice are better understood as
accurate portrayals of an emerging bidialectalism. To render the speech only in
Black English would not have been genuine. Therefore we should expect sentences like number 1. There is no doubt that this is Black English, but the use
of the auxiliary *is* and its placement immediately preceding the subject, *they*,
displays competence (subject-auxiliary inversion) in forming interrogatives
along the lines of Standard English. Similarly, the use of *you'll* in sentence 5
manifests mastery of the contraction system. Beck indicates that both of these
capabilities generally come to be distinct, indeed, in the speech of the five to
six year old.

With this in mind, it should startle no one that sentence 6, a decidedly   16
Black English sentence, follows sentence 5, for it highlights the juxtaposing of
dialects that was occurring. Of great importance, in addition, is that each case
of shifting or mixing happens as the child is experiencing conflicting social
demands. In the Peeping Tom scene, he must appear knowledgeable even while
being forced to ask a question of slightly older peers; the haircut scene requires
that he talk down to a three year old yet coax her into action; and in the whipping scene, it is necessary that he try to inject some special combination of

caution and urgency in his voice in an attempt to avoid physical punishment. This implies an awareness of the social relevance of dialects, a skill often assigned by scholars to a later stage of development. Smitherman, for example, indites that "among school-age blacks, one would find a greater degree of bi-dialectalism among older adolescents than among younger black children, for adolescents have begun to get hip to the social sensitivities associated with different kinds of languages and dialects" (pp. 31–32). I think folks get hip long before that age. The crucial dynamic is choice. Younger children, mostly out of self-defense, are not on the whole as willing to "play the game." But they can perceive much of the game and could play a lot of it if they so desired.

Troike (1972) asserts that even the youngest schoolchildren pay a great   17
deal of attention to the social significance of dialect differences. Speaking of the child's ability to alternate between linguistic systems, he reasons that "despite cultural beliefs to the contary, even very young children are often quite aware of the social relevance of stylistic and dialect differences" (p. 305). He proceeds to give the example of a first-grader who was given a picture in a magazine and asked to tell a story about it to a researcher.

> The girl drew herself up, began "Once upon a time, . . ." and launched into a very formal narrative which was notable for containing no contractions. At the end of the story, she visibly relaxed, and from there on freely used contractions for the remainder of the interview. The whole subject of the range of styles and dialects in the productive and receptive repertory of children is only just beginning to receive attention, and a great deal yet remains to be learned. Nevertheless, it is clear that even pre-first-graders are far from linguistically naive and have already learned a great deal about the adaptive significance of linguistic behavior within their own very real social world. (p. 309)

The whole question of the child's social awareness of dialect differences will be of major concern, of course, throughout this work. At present, the essential notion to understand is that this social awareness on my part was considerably sharpened even during the preschool years.

I carried with me a tremendously empowering repertoire of speaking and   18
listening skills when I shuffled off to public school and continued to expand it once I arrived. Included in my bag of communicative tricks were that prize strategem, Black English, a productive (speaking) biloquialism, and a broader receptive (listening) bidialectalism. There was also an adroitness at responding to the perceived need to match each dialect to different sets of social circumstances. All this achievement may appear quite marvelous and, I guess, actually is. But it represents nothing miraculous beyond the basic miracle of existing,

nothing special among Black children, nothing that should not be the case if a developing mind is pretty much left alone. Put more succinctly, it really ain't no new news.

Reading Acquisition

As the story indicates, I literally shed blood in the process of learning how to read. Such action should not become the basis for educational policy (though perhaps on a symbolic level it has), but it does indicate, in a way that only blood can, just how important I felt reading was. Being able to comprehend print allowed me to participate in my environment on yet another level; it was a skill I just had to have. Naturally, therefore, I kept close tabs on whatever progress my older sister was making toward literacy, and I was, in fact, doing a considerable amount of reading before I received any formal school instruction. (Such instruction could not have come before first grade, at which point I was already six and a half.) [19]

I will attempt here to sketch how this reading acquisition transpired. First I will speak about the reading process in broad, general terms; then I will pay particular attention to the controversy that inevitably surrounds a discussion of initial reading instruction. I will consider then the role that literature (such as the fairy tales mentioned three times in the text) played in my personal attempts to read. And finally I will elaborate on the notion, alluded to above, of literacy in the context of social relations. [20]

THE READING PROCESS

Frank Smith (1971, 1979) asserts that since there are no unique physical structures in the brain that specifically account for the ability to read, there is nothing special to say about reading once a correct assessment of human learning in general has been made (1979, p. 2). In his view, when we look at print we derive meaning from it in much the same way as we derive meaning from other objects in the world. We recognize it, which is an alternate way of saying that we reduce all our relevant uncertainty about what it is, and we make informed predictions as to its meaning, which rule out unlikely occurrences. Smith realizes that "prediction is not a new and artificial skill that has to be learned but the *natural* way to make sense of the world" (1979, p. 77). We will make mistakes of course, but the point is that the mistakes are insignificant if they don't interfere with actual meaning. Or as Smith himself asks, "If a mistake makes no difference, then what difference can it make?" (1979, p. 34). A fluent reader, he gathers, will probably bother with only one-fifth of the graphic information on the page. [21]

Smith further argues that if one, in fact, tries to make too precise an identi-   22
fication of individual words or letters while reading, this increases his or her
chance of error. By analogy he explains:

> The situation is rather similar for a sentry on duty on a dark night who
> hears approaching footsteps but who cannot reveal his own position by ask-
> ing questions. His alternatives are to shoot or hold his fire. If he shoots and
> the intruder is indeed hostile, then the sentry will get a medal. If he holds
> his fire and the stranger is friendly his decision is also commendable. But a
> miss (letting through an enemy) or a false alarm (shooting a friend) are less
> desirable consequences. Yet the nature of the world is such that sentries
> always have to settle for some level of probability for the undesirable conse-
> quences; the man anxious to stop every enemy is going to shoot a friend
> from time to time, while the sentry anxious not to shoot a friend is occa-
> sionally going to let an enemy slip through. . . . The skilled reader cannot
> afford to set his criterion too high for deciding on word or meaning identifi-
> cation; we see that if he demands too much visual information, he will
> often be unable to get it fast enough to overcome memory limitations and
> read for sense. (1971, pp. 24–25)

Making sense, of course, is the single most important thing about reading,   23
for it is the urge that motivates us to read in the first place. And within the limits of his general conception, which clearly argues the centrality of an anticipa-
tory psychology to an understanding of the reading process, Smith offers several
specific insights into the act of reading that merit attention here. First is that
efficient readers do not decode to sound. If this were not so, if they did decode
to sound, then they could read no faster than the rate of speech or the rate at
which they could hear the words inside their heads. It is known that skilled
readers (perhaps like yourself) can read several times faster than the average
rate of speech. So Smith's stance appears to be correct. A related insight is that
one cannot read one word at a time and read for sense. This is due, as alluded to
above, to the physical limitations of short-term memory. If a person is reading at
such a slow pace, he or she cannot hold enough strands of information in his or
her brain simultaneously in order to make necessary connections, to make
sense. A third belief that logically follows is that the most fluent readers are the
ones who require the least visual information. And fourth is the notion that
"meaningful language is transparent; we look through words for the meaning
beyond" (1979, p. 123).

Some affirmation of Smith's approach can be found in the work of Isakson   24
(1979). His research, in which the performances of college students on a reaction-
time test were measured, indicates that sense is indeed extracted directly from
print in meaning units as opposed to word units:

The reader seems to be searching actively for the information which, combined with his general world knowledge, will allow him to identify the structural relationships between the words he has encountered. When the information is sufficient for at least a tentative identification of structure, processing activity increases so as to integrate the words received up to that point. (p. 164)

Kenneth Goodman (1967) has offered a view of the reading process, which   25
he terms a "psycholinguistic guessing game," which also supports Smith's position. He specifically criticizes Spache (1964) and McCracken and Walcutt (1963) for having forwarded the notion of reading as a linear, cumulative process rather than as a selective leap toward meaning.

THE NOT-SO-GREAT DEBATE

Much has been made of the argument between those who favor a global (read-   26
ing for meaning) approach to reading instruction and those who favor a code approach (usually phonics). Scholars of the Smith-Goodman ilk favor the global method of course. Their view is a logical extension of the theoretical stance described above. Let us consider specifically how this conception informs their pedagogical position.

Smith (1980) asserts that the only basic insights necessary for learning how   27
to read are (a) print is meaningful and (b) print is different from speech. Once these two insights have been achieved and children are exposed to a variety of interesting and complex material, then reading acquisition should, Smith believes, proceed as naturally as oral language acquisition. As he states:

> I have argued that children need two basic insights to begin to learn to read. Also, I have implied that with these insights children can solve all the other problems associated with print by themselves provided that no extraneous confusion or hindrance is put in their way. They must be able to predict and make sense of language in the first place, and they can do this only by bringing meaning to it. This is certainly the way that all children learn spoken language and is probably the reason that many of them succeed in learning to read despite the instructional method used. (p. 423)

Smith's notions seem plausible, but they are totally rejected by prophets of   28
the "phonics first" approach. Chief among these individuals is Rudolf Flesch, author of *Why Johnny Can't Read* (1955) and *Why Johnny Still Can't Read* (1981). He advances an argument long on acerbic rhetoric but decidedly short on substance.

My first objection to Flesch's conception is that he misrepresents the position   29
of the psycholinguists, namely Smith and Goodman. He says that psycholinguistics

is only look-and-say in shiny new garments (1981, pp. 23–24). But look-and-say, in the sense of focusing on one word at a time, giving word lists to memorize, and restricting vocabulary development, is definitely *not* what psycholinguistics is about at all. So any attack on those methods, and they certainly are restrictive, cannot simultaneously be a criticism of say, Smith, who seems to be Flesch's favorite target.

Aside from this, Flesch's perception of reading failure is much too simplistic.   30
He analyzes the phenomenon without any regard to the surrounding social or social-psychological circumstances. His argument, simply put, is that reading failure is rampant because of look-and-say instruction and would be eliminated if everyone were taught by the "phonics first" method. The fallacy here, of course, is to think that any instructional method alone can guarantee students success, for any such method is but an abstraction in and of itself. Its worth can be ascertained only in a social arena of real teachers and real students. (Note that Smith's primary concern is with the nature of reading, not the teaching of reading.)

Flesch persists in his distortion by presenting the following picture of read-   31
ing acquisition. Before one learns to read, the argument goes, one must know the "mechanics" of reading. In the case of phonics, one must first learn all the rules for spelling-to-sound correspondences (roughly 180 of them). Once one knows the rules one can sound out, and therefore read, any print. Typically, then, after one or two years of instruction a child can read 24,000 words, whereas a child taught another way can only read 1,000 or so words.

Again, Flesch is a proponent of sophism. If one defines reading as making   32
sense of print, then the mere sounding out of words does not assure that such activity is taking place. But perhaps even more basic is the question of whether one can actually sound out words accurately on the basis of phonics alone. Smith submits that one cannot because the spelling-to-sound correspondences in English are not one to one, but many to many. In fact, Smith asserts, the chances of successfully sounding out a word phonetically is only one in four (1979, p. 55). He illustrates the problem.

> Here are eleven common words in each of which the initial *ho* has a different pronunciation—*hot, hope, hook, hoot, house, hoist, horse, horizon, honey, hour, honest.* Can anyone really believe that a child could learn to identify any of these words by sounding out the letters? (1979, p. 56)

He goes on to add that "phonics works if you know what a word is likely to be in the first place. . . . It is not surprising that children who are best at phonics are the best readers—they have to be" (1979, pp. 56–57).

Smith overstates his case somewhat by arguing that a program based on   33
phonics would be too complex for even a computer to read. Flesch has coun-

tered by citing that a Kurzweil Reading Machine can, in fact, "read" by using a phonics-based program fed into a computer. But I fail to see the relevance of this information. For, alas, children are not Kurzweils, and the machine is doing what machines are made for: to do work that humans cannot do efficiently. Reading by phonics is some of that work.

The last problematic claim by Flesch is that other children will be severely limited in the number of words they can read as opposed to phonics-first readers. He has reached this conclusion by inspecting the word lists of non-phonics reading books. But I know of no evidence to show that children read only the words in their readers. Counting word lists, therefore, is by no means an accurate measure of how many words children know. If children have it set in mind to read and are actually reading in some instances, they will not allow themselves to be restricted to any reading book. Nor, I hope, will they be constrained by any teacher. Any method that tries to force them to focus on only one aspect of the reading process is harmful.

All this is not to say that phonics is irrelevant. It is one strategy for figuring out text and, as a child assembles a repertoire of strategies, there is some place for it. The essential point, however, is that a child is searching for sense and at no point should that search be hindered by dogmatic instruction. Just as one learns spoken language by total immersion in it, so it must be with reading. And so it was, I am sure, for me. Bissex (1980) has made a similar discovery. Reporting on her assiduous observation of her son she writes:

> Development—and Paul's development in particular—is not evenly paced. There is more rapid movement through the earlier strategies and concepts because these are more limited and incomplete in relation to the demands of the tasks. Especially at the beginning, quite drastic change seems essential for progress. It may not matter so much where a child begins in reading (phonics, sight words, language experience) as that he begins *somewhere* that works for him and soon moves somewhere *else*. Later strategies, being more inclusive and complex, allow room for more extended development. (p. 168)

Bissex, as is proper, sees a child's active intellect in control of the reading acquisition process. It is a blessing that children have such intellects, as well as the strength to persevere in the face of all the not-so-great debates around them.

OF LITERATURE

> Sentimental things are said about the magical world of literature and the imagination, but few think of applying this driving force to the basic learning of literacy tasks. Nor do they think of remedying the situation for those children who have not learned to operate imaginatively. For such children, half their motivation for becoming literate is paralyzed, and so learning to read must be like learning to walk with one leg. (Holdaway 1979, pp. 55–56)

Don Holdaway understands that the story, the poem, address and in turn   36
spur our curiosity in ways more powerful than our own immediate experience.
The world of fantasy opens to us whole new vistas. This is particularly true of
small children, always our most eager seekers. The lure of the story is what kept
me and my kindergarten class transfixed when we should have been on our way
home. In listening to *Curious George* we all wanted to know what this monkey
could encounter in the way of adventure, of ups and downs. Most important, we
wanted to find out what we could make of his ups and downs, for by then we, of
course, were having a few ups and downs ourselves. It is in such a way that literature can enlighten young lives, in fact, all lives. As Rouse (1978) tells us, "life
will never be a substitute for literature, it's not long enough" (p. 92).

When listening to a story and thus expanding the limits of their concep-   37
tion, children receive valuable assistance in their own quests to apprehend
print. Britton (1972) develops this idea:

> The children who listen are gaining experience of written forms of the Eng-
> lish language, and this aspect of the process is of particular importance to
> those who cannot yet read for themselves. There is an art of listening to
> reading that is very different from the process of listening to somebody talk-
> ing to you—and this art contributes to the art of reading. (p. 150)

The young listener even before attending school can put together, in Hold-   38
away's terms, a literacy set (p. 62). On an emotional level this involves having a
high expectation of print, of viewing it as a source of pleasure and fulfillment.
Linguistically the child is picking up on the types of intonation patterns,
idioms, and vocabulary that are found more in print than in speech. On an
operational level, the child has become aware of such predictive operations as
using the context to fill in particular language slots and can also follow plot and
other logical arrangements. Concerning the conventions of print itself, the
child may know that it is composed from left to right, from top to bottom, left
page before right page. The child may also know some letters, some phonetic
principles, and may have some concept of "words" and "spaces."

Looking back at "First Lessons," we see every indication that the develop-   39
ment of a literacy set as described above was well underway. I mentioned earlier
that I was reading before formal school instruction. By doing so I probably saved
myself, in a sense, from such instruction. With respect to reading I had a little
edge on the school, a leg up if you will. You might even say that up there on
146th Street I had a "head start."

OF FAMILY

Denny Taylor (1983), in describing her approach to ethnographic literacy   40
research, reports: "my task was to develop systematic ways of looking at reading

and writing as activities that have consequences and are affected by family life" (p. xiii). The implication is that much literacy acquisition (like mine) goes on in the home for which the home is not given proper credit. That oversight will not be a problem here.

If I ever had a true reading teacher, it was my older sister. If anyone were   41
explicitly manipulating my attempts to comprehend print, it was mainly she. Or perhaps I was manipulating her (probably both). For as determined as she was to show off what she knew, I was just as determined to make her display it. She was not going to leave me behind, participate on a broader level than I, share anything, especially with our mother, that I could not share. So apart from any incentive a school might provide, reading took on great significance within the confines of our very own family. It was a way not only of widening and deepening perspectives through a self-regulated encounter with story; it was a way of enhancing social status. This use of reading as a tool of social growth is seen by Taylor to be essential:

> The question emerges of whether we can seriously expect children who have never experienced or have limited experience of reading and writing as complex cultural activities to successfully learn to read and write from the narrowly defined pedagogical practices of our schools. Can we teach children on an individual level of intrapersonal processes what they have never experienced on a social level as interpersonal processes of functional utility in their everyday lives? I would submit that we cannot. (pp. 90–91)

It is clear that my early reading skills, like my oral ones, developed largely   42
within a family context. Familial relations dictated that these skills were to be regarded as cherished possessions. My younger sister at three, poised with blade in hand, obviously understood a great deal about the social value of reading.

Impression Management

On one level this entire chapter has been about linguistic role-playing, the use   43
of certain conventions of language to sustain various relationships. I have discussed my doing what we all do: using language as a way of adapting to situations and, to some extent, as a means of defining and controlling situations. We all practice, in Goffman's (1959) terms, the art of impression management. It is important to realize, however, that such a display of verbal ability as described above grows directly out of and then evolves alongside a general social competence. Or as Byers and Byers (1972) indicate:

> And when we examine a human relationship such as a simple conversation between two people, we almost immediately discover that there are multiple modalities or channels operating in addition to language. We discover that the modalities, verbal and nonverbal, are learned as patterns of the culture (as language is learned) and that they are systematic (as language

has grammar, for example). Furthermore we discover that they all fit together: they are systematically interrelated. (p. 6)

What we see, therefore, is that there is a nonverbal grammar (or grammars) to be acquired. More will be made of this later on. But even with respect to the character we have been considering thus far, the conception is certainly convenient, and it should not be surprising that I have made quite specific remarks in the narrative about this particular set of skills.

At the close of "First Lessons," I assert that I "could play the middle or skirt the fringe as I saw fit." It was easier written than done, of course, but it is evident that I had some idea of how much an actor I had to be and had confidence that I could handle the part. I had a clear (we might even say conscious) notion of how important even nonverbal adaptation or impression management was in protecting my own developing identity. If I had landed in Rome, I certainly would have been about the business of doing as the Romans were doing—if I had thought it would help matters. I later took this heightened awareness into a dominant White environment and, because I was afforded a certain measure of participation, I picked up certain elements of the grammar of White, middle-class, particularly Jewish, nonverbal communication (such as when to make eye contact and when not to), which I in turn used to guide the impressions the residents of that environment formed (while they were of course trying to figure out and outmaneuver me). It may be an open question as to who acted better, but I undoubtedly did all right. 44

"All the world," Goffman writes, "is not, of course, a stage, but the crucial ways in which it isn't are not easy to specify" (p. 72). He does, nevertheless, proceed to detail the most significant difference. "An action staged in a theater is a relatively contrived illusion and an admitted one: unlike ordinary life, nothing real or actual can happen to the performed characters" (p. 254). Art may imitate life, then, but it is not nearly as difficult. The curtain was always up for me, as for most, and I was a young lad as busy as the next child learning lines, mastering gestures, working on all levels to manage impression. 45

While I am being so direct about impression management let me offer, in closing out this chapter, a few more phrases in trying to shape yours. The home in Harlem from which I was catapulted into the larger world was one that was, in a sociolinguistic sense, enabling—not disabling. Tensions existed that obviously helped to shape my personality in ways I have yet to fully understand, but such tensions alone did not, in fact could not, impede the acquisition of the sociolinguistic ability that has been examined in this chapter. There was a consistency in that habitat and, I submit, it is the apprehension of consistency that is the cognitive key to communicative development. The prime affective 46 requirement, of course, is that the use of such skills helps to establish some social relation that is gratifying. My home, no matter what else it was, took care of me on both counts.

REFERENCES

Beck, M. S. 1979. *Baby talk: How your child learns to speak.* New York: Plume.

Bissex, G. L. 1980. *Gnys at wrk: A child learns to write and read.* Cambridge, MA: Harvard University Press.

Britton, J. 1972. *Language and learning.* Harmondsworth: Penguin. Originally published 1970.

Burling, R. 1973. *English in black and white.* New York: Holt, Rinehart and Winston.

Byers, P. & Byers, H. 1972. Nonverbal communication and the education of children. In Cazden et al., 3–31.

Dillard, J. L. 1973. *Black English: Its history and usage in the United States.* New York: Vintage. Originally published 1972.

Elgin, S. H. 1979. *What is linguistics?* 2d ed. Englewood Cliffs, NJ: Prentice-Hall.

Flesch, R. 1955. *Why Johnny can't read—And what you can do about it.* New York: Harper & Row.

Flesch, R. 1983. *Why Johnny still can't read: A new look at the scandal of our schools.* New York: Harper Colophon.

Goffman, E. 1959. *The presentation of self in everyday life.* Garden City, NY: Doubleday Anchor.

Goodman, K. S. 1967. Reading: A psycholinguistic guessing game. *Journal of the Reading Specialist* 4: 126–135.

Haskins, J. & Butts, H. F. 1973. *The psychology of Black language.* New York: Barnes & Noble.

Holdaway, D. 1979. *The foundations of literacy.* Sydney: Ashton Scholastic.

Isakson, R. L. 1979. Cognitive processing in sentence comprehension. *Journal of Educational Research* 72: 160–165.

Kelly, G. A. 1963. *A theory of personality: The psychology of personal constructs.* New York: Norton.

Labov, W. 1981. *The study of nonstandard English.* Rev. ed. Urbana: NCTE.

McCracken, G., & Walcutt, C. C. 1963. *Basic reading: Teacher's edition for the pre-primer and primer.* Philadelphia: Lippincott.

Penalosa, F. 1981. *Introduction to the sociology of language.* Rowley, MA: Newbury.

Rouse, J. 1978. *The completed gesture: Myth, character and education.* NJ: Skyline Books.

Smith, F. 1971. Understanding reading. New York: Holt, Rinehart and Winston.

Smith, F. 1979. Reading without nonsense. New York: Teachers College Press.

Smith, F. 1980. Making sense of reading—And of reading instruction. In *Thought & language/language and reading,* ed. M. Wolf, M. McQuillan, & E. Radwin, 415–424). Cambridge, MA: Harvard Educational Review. Reprinted from *Harvard Educational Review,* 1977.

Smitherman, G. 1977. *Talkin and testifyin: The language of Black America.* Boston: Houghton Mifflin.

Spache, G. 1964. *Reading in the elementary school.* Boston: Allyn and Bacon.

Stewart, W. A. 1969. Urban negro speech: Sociolinguistic factors affecting English teaching. *Florida FL Reporter 7* (Spring/Summer): 50–53, 166. Reprinted from *Social Dialects and Language Learning,* 1965.

Taylor, D. 1983. *Family literacy.* Exeter, NH: Heineman.

Troike, R. C. 1972. Receptive bidialectalism: Implications for second-dialect teaching. In *Language and cultural diversity in American education,* ed. R. D. Abrahams & R. C. Troike, 301–310. Englewood Cliffs, NJ: Prentice-Hall.

Jennifer Lawler (1965–) received her Ph.D. in medieval English literature at the University of Kansas in 1996 and is the author of more than twenty-five books on martial arts, feng shui, travel, drug legalization, Internet safety, and other topics. Her first novel is *Then Will Come Night and Darkness* (2006). She has been a martial-arts competitor and judge, a self-defense instructor, and an adjunct English instructor. She is the co-chair of the Book Division of the National Writers Union.

THE SCREENWRITER'S TALE

Jennifer Lawler

Everything I have been doing lately has been contaminated by Hollywood. As contaminations go, I'll take Hollywood every time. I'm pretty content with the idea of letting fame and fortune go to my head. I'm looking forward to becoming shallow and superficial.   1

What actually happened was, I wrote a novel and my agent showed it to a producer—this is the only useful thing my agent has ever done—and said producer asked if I would adapt the novel to a screenplay. I said, "Hell, yes." I'd like to know who wouldn't. So I've been sitting around waiting to get corrupted and stuff, and it can't happen fast enough to suit me.   2

The problem with adapting a novel to a screenplay is that you can't do anything else. For instance, I have spent four months rewriting plot outlines, since I am in charge of pleasing everyone at the studio. I have revised the plot outline seventeen times, and the outline they finally approved looks exactly like the first one I sent them. I am so busy pleasing the producer that I am incapable of doing anything else. I cannot finish the novel I am currently working on, I cannot write a scholarly research paper, I cannot even finish a letter to my sister, I am losing my mind. Susan says no one's noticed the difference, as far as she can see. Susan is my friend. She's a real scholar. I mean, you ask her a question like, "Who was Sir Walter Raleigh's son's tutor?" and she knows the answer. I mean, without having to look it up.   3

Anyway. Everywhere I look, all I see are possible movie scenes. I can't write a line without thinking, "I wonder how this would sound if Mel Gibson were saying it." I want Mel to star in my movie. Whenever I read anything, I sit   4 there casting parts. I think Sean Connery would make a really good Green Knight. I wonder if Harrison Ford would be interested in doing *Beowulf*. I can't even go to the grocery store without making it a dramatic moment, fraught with significant silences and carefully crafted emotion: "You want *how* much for a grapefruit?" or I'm getting kissed by a guy and I'm wondering, Is this scene effectively conveyed to the audience?

Susan says it's unfortunate there was an audience to start with since kissing   5
should be done in private.

So you see how this screenplay has affected me.   6

Susan says, "Don't blame the screenplay. You lacked decorum long before   7
Hollywood ever got hold of you."

I keep waiting for all the sex scenes to happen, but unfortunately my life   8
gets a G rating. It's really depressing when you can tell your mother every single
intimate detail of your life and all she can say is, "That's nice, dear."

Do I look like I ever wanted to lead a NICE LIFE????   9

Ha.   10

I wanted to write mystery novels. Really incredibly good mysteries. I wanted   11
to be moderately successful at this so that I wouldn't have to hold down a real
job. I wanted to chain smoke Marlboro Reds and drink vodka straight from the
bottle and stare moodily at the ceiling, just like all good mystery novelists do.

So that's what I set out to do, and, as you can see, Fate intervened. Fate is   12
inevitable, according to most Anglo-Saxon poetry, and I've always thought that
was a slightly redundant statement. But then, most Anglo-Saxon poetry is
redundant. It's that oral-formulaic thing.

Anyway, Fate intervened and I ended up in graduate school, trying to be a   13
scholar.

This is not as easy as it sounds. Neither the getting here nor the being here. 14
It made sense at the time, you see; I wanted to write stories, but you have to eat
somehow, and I got through college for that reason. Afterwards I held jobs
where people criticized me for stupid things like keeping callers on hold too
long, and so one day I gave it all up. (It's easy when you have nothing to lose.) I
liked college the first time around and thought I'd give it another try. I could
eat on a teacher's salary (that's what English majors become), but of course I
never really had any say: it was all Fate.

And Fate is inevitable.   15

But graduate school has been nothing like college was the first time around,   16
and trying to be a scholar is harder on me than I ever thought it would be, especially this year. Ever since I started the screenplay, I haven't been worth a damn
as either a novelist or a scholar.

Susan says, "You weren't worth a damn as a novelist even before that pro-   17
ducer got hold of you."

All I can say is, What does Susan know? She's never had to wring a 357-   18
page novel from a six-word idea.

Susan says, "You weren't worth a damn as a scholar, either."   19

Susan is really a maternal person at heart, sort of like a mountain lion.   20
She's been in charge of me for about a year now, and she takes her responsibilities very seriously, except when there's a football game on.

One of Susan's responsibilities involves making me act like a scholar. This   21
consists of her saying, "You aren't wearing that to class, are you?" She reminds
me, fairly constantly, that the English Department is very conservative and that
I am not very conservative, and her conclusion is that one of us is going to lose.
She also gives good advice like, "If you want to be taken seriously, you will
never breathe the word *Hollywood* on campus. Never. And if I were you, thank
God I'm not, I would never say anything about writing popular fiction. Maybe if
you were capable of writing literature, that would be okay. But never say the
words *mystery novel* around here."

Then she always says, "Look, do you want a tenure-track position or not?"   22

Susan is a practical person. It's one of her more annoying traits. I'm putting   23
all this in so that you will realize that this essay is all Susan's fault. She didn't
stop me in time. Her other responsibility is putting a stop to me. She feels that
someone needs to, and maybe she's right.

Anyway, I'm going to talk about mysteries and Hollywood A LOT, see if I   24
care. Just imagine I'm being my usual self, the way I am when Susan isn't making me be a scholar. Let me help you out here. Visualize a short brunette with
delusions of grandeur who looks about ten years old but is really much older
than that with an Irish temper and a sense of humor that no one has ever in the
history of the world appreciated. I have a tiny scar on the left side of my face
from falling out an apple tree when I was twelve, trying to climb too high. I
inherited the Grecian nose from my father, who taught me how to think and
tried also to teach me what to think, but this last failed. He doesn't mind. And
the broad peasant cheekbones come from my mother, the merchant's daughter,
who learned to be a lady and passed this on to me; the things I know, should I
be in the presence of a king, I owe to her. I try not to forget them, and sometimes I practice when it is late at night. I balance the book on my head instead
of reading it because the magazines showed my mother how this improved posture, but the things she wanted for me were things I did not understand. There
is a whole history behind this face. It isn't just the twelve gray hairs and the
wrinkles at the corners of my eyes or the fact that my skin got over being way

too oily and now it's way too dry. It's the stories my aunts and uncles tell me when they look at me and say what I remind them of, and tangled up with the genealogy are memories of passion and love and hatred and leaving and "Ave Maria" and McCarthy and raising children and fixing cars and riding horses and prisoner-of-war camps and razor wire, things I make nightmares from. Things I make stories from, the stories that I tell, but I don't expect people to believe them, either.

If it were possible, I would describe myself, but I am far too tempted to lie. I   25
would give myself a house and a lover or maybe a husband and three children or maybe a place in Manhattan and say that I can afford to park my car there. But really, if I were from New York, I would be from the Bronx. I try never to talk about myself in the English Department because I would be horrified if they found me out. They expect people to be truthful there; they don't appreciate artistic embellishments. When I hang out at the English Department, I try never to actually say anything about myself, but it happened that I was in the English Department one day, just schlepping around, talking to a professor, a medieval-ist. (I try only to talk to other medievalists.) So he says, "How's the reading list coming?" and I say it's not. I make the mistake of saying that I am having trouble with a scene I am trying to write, and it's taking all my time and effort.

"What scene?" he wants to know.   26

"I'm writing a screenplay," I say, trying not to wince. It sounds so awful   27
when I say it out loud, especially in the middle of the English Department.

"You're doing WHAT?" he inquires.   28

"I've got a contract," I apologize.   29

"If I were you," he says, "I would never have done that."   30

"Oh," I say, or something like that.   31

He gives me a severe look and commences lecturing me on the duties and   32
obligations of a graduate student. When he's done with that, he lectures me on the duties and obligations of a graduate teaching assistant. What it boils down to is, graduate students shouldn't write screenplays. If you want to be taken seri-ously as a scholar, you don't write movies, especially if any car-chase scenes are involved.

So I stand there, dumbfounded, staring across the chasm that separates us.   33
What do you mean, I want to ask, what do you mean, not write? I do not think he understands about making things, about nails you put in boards and houses you make with your own hands. I think, you know, this is a guy who has to go to the gym to work up a sweat. I don't say this out loud.

I am a writer. He is a scholar. It's a distance between us. Sometimes it   34
seems impossible. Sometimes it seems I do all the compromising.

All right. No one said the rules would change for me. The only writers wel- 35
come here are dead ones. The live ones are shunted into the creative writing
program where they are never heard from again. They might as well be in
another department for all the connection they have with literature. At some
universities, they *are* in a different department.

A teacher I know says, "I get so irritated when my composition students 36
think that's what English is." She explains to her students that composition
classes are a service of the English Department and that composition is not
what we do. What we do is Literature.

Oh. I see. Of course, any idiot knows that reading and writing have noth- 37
ing to do with each other. Being a writer and being a student of literature are
completely unrelated. A mere coincidence. An accident. You can be a writer
and a scholar as long as your being a writer has no influence on your being a
scholar.

I know of someone else who tried to do this, be a writer and a scholar, and, 38
as Thomas Kirby remarked about him, "Surely there is at least something to be
said for the writer who is sometimes brightly wrong rather than always dully
right" (266). This, of course, after strongly cautioning that John Gardner was,
after all, a popular novelist and therefore his biography of Chaucer was apt to be
a little, oh . . . "abetted by imagination" (Kirby 265). Which I guess is a bad
thing. I will have to ask Susan. She will surely know. That's one of the things
Susan tells me. She says I sound like a writer, not a scholar. For instance, I
refuse to use the words *tautological* and *belletristic* because I always forget we have
them, and I use real words instead. This is WRONG of me, I know, and Susan has
been trying to teach me to write like a scholar, which seems to consist mostly of
obscuring ideas rather than communicating them. Susan has successfully failed
to put any content into every paper she's ever written. That fact impresses the
hell out of me. I wish I could do that. But no, I have spent my whole life developing this really great (okay, so *great* is a relative term) fiction style, and it just
won't do for scholarship. No. You have to take really really long words and
make them into really really long sentences, and then you take the really really
long sentences and you make them into really really long paragraphs, and then
you take the really really long paragraphs, and you arrange them in a closely
argued way, using logic and reason. But none of the words are supposed to be
yours, you have to borrow them from other people, because obviously your
words aren't good enough, and then you have to tell the whole universe that
you borrowed your words from other people, who presumably borrowed their
words from yet someone else, referred to as a "scholar." And then there's this
whole book on the proper way of borrowing words and also on how you admit

to it, and then the whole thing has to follow a certain manuscript format, and all of it depends on what style manual you are told to use, there are about nine hundred of them, AND FRANKLY I DON'T NEED THAT KIND OF PRESSURE!!!

Life in academia is very hard on me.   39

I remember being absolutely horrified when I found out that scholars spent   40
all this time borrowing other people's words and rearranging them into papers and then getting these papers published, and doing it for free. I mean, scholars don't get paid for publishing stuff. I think we need a union or something. I have never heard of this, you know; if my royalty checks are thirteen seconds late, I'm on the phone with my lawyer. But scholars, who are ladies and gentlemen, do these sorts of labors for love, not profit.

To which I always say, love is highly overrated.   41

Okay. Here's another true story. When I first spoke to my producer, she   42
wanted to write a bio sheet, and she asked me what I did for a living. I told her I was a graduate student.

She said, "Oh, God. Not an academic. I can't tell them you're an academic."   43

You know how academics feel about people who make movies for a living?   44
That's exactly the same way they feel about us.

So I said I also worked in a lumber yard, which was true at the time, and   45
she was all excited. "I can tell them you are a blue-collar worker."

This, it seems, makes my writing real. Scholars don't know, of course, what   46
the real world is like, the one that gives you calluses on your hands. I haven't had the nerve to tell her that I no longer work at the lumber yard. I'm not about to tell her I'm a teacher now. That would make everything worse. I'm not going to tell any of them. I may never own up. But I'm afraid someone's going to rat on me, do this big, startling exposé, and I'll never hear from my agent, editor, or producer again.

I am beginning to feel hunted.   47

I am in the middle of this war, you see, and when you are in the middle   48
of a war, you declare your allegiance, you say to whom you are loyal. I'd do this, I would take a side, I would say, "I'm a writer" or "I am a scholar." I would do this, I would give one of them up, if I could find a way to do so without dying of the loss. I don't know. I guess scholars don't go around, bleating, "I would just die if I didn't read *Morte d'Arthur* once a year." Scholars—real scholars, I mean, like my friend Susan—approach literature differently from the way I do.

Lots of writers question the literacy of scholars because they so often get it   49
wrong. Now, I study literature by reading it and saying, hey, that's pretty good.

This, also, is WRONG of me.   50

In the first place, I'm never entirely sure if it is appropriate for a scholar   51
to actually like literature. For instance, I like medieval literature. No. I *love*
medieval literature. Medieval literature is the only stuff I will read, unless I
am forcibly made to look at Dickens or someone, which happens every now
and then. Anyway, I read criticism on medieval literature because I am supposed to. You can't get a Ph.D. unless you do (there's something they don't
tell you up front) and there's some guy, a Scholar, explicating (what the hell
is wrong with the word *explaining?*), and he's helping me out by comparing
hypermetric Type D2 oral-formulaic alliterative verse, or something, and
I'm real thankful for that, you know, it really clarifies the whole thing
for me.

This is what I know: If you recite *Beowulf* in Old English, it sounds just like   52
the end of the world. You get some old Anglo-Saxon scholar to do it for you
and I swear you will be on your knees, begging forgiveness. This appeals to me.
You listen to *Beowulf* and you will hear doom. You are supposed to. That's what
Beowulf is about. Doom.

I have another favorite. "The Wanderer." This is the first part: 53

```
Oft him anhaga      are gebideth
Metudes miltse      theah the he modcearig
geond lagulade      longe sceolde
hreran mid hondum      hrimcealde sae
Swa cwaeth eardstapa      earfetha gemyndig
wrathra waelsleahta      winemaega hryre
Oft ic sceolde ana      uhtna gehwylce
mine ceare cwithan      Nis nu cwicra nan
the ic him modsefan      minne durre
sweotule asecgan.  . . .
```

(Cassidy and Ringler 324–25)

Isn't that the most beautiful poem in the whole world? Since my word   54
processor has no wynn, ash, edh, thorn, or that weird-looking "z" letter that I
can never remember the name of, I have transliterated them into their modern
English equivalents. The really great thing about Old English is that if you don't
know what the word means, it means "warrior."

All right, here's the translation into modern English: 55

Often, he who is the lone-dweller awaits grace,
the mercy of the Lord, even though for a long
time he, heart-anxious, over the waterway has
to stir up with his hands the ice-cold sea, to
journey the paths of exile: Fate is inevitable.

So spoke the earth-walker, mindful of hardship,
cruel slaughter, the fall of precious kinsmen:
"Often I must alone at each dawn my cares lament.
There is not now one living creature to whom I
dare openly tell my heart. . . ."[1]

If you know that a medieval warrior paid fealty to a lord and that if he   56
showed cowardice or his lord died he became an exile, doomed to wander without protection, at the mercy of any old Geat or Dane, you'll appreciate "The
Wanderer."

This is the kind of thing a scholar does know. A scholar knows about war-   57
riors and exile and the philosophy of the average Anglo-Saxon, and they (we,
God forbid?) nod wisely and say, yes, that's the old wandering-the-paths-of-
exile thing again.

The first time I read "The Wanderer," as a writer who liked the sounds of   58
the words, I didn't know about exiles. And I found that you don't need to know
about exiles to understand "The Wanderer." You need only have been lonely
once.

Every time I read "The Wanderer," I forget that I am a scholar who knows   59
about exiles. I forget, even, the long and arduous process of learning Old English. I forget about the oral-formulaic tradition, and the words "Fate is
inevitable" sound profound to me.

I know exactly how the Wanderer feels. I knew before I ever studied litera-   60
ture in a systematic, scholarly way, and sometimes I am afraid that all I will
eventually do is obscure the Wanderer from my sight. I worry about that. You'd
think I'd have enough to worry about.

The Seafarer says, "Let us consider where we may have a home and then   61
think how we may get there."

Why can I never say anything that well? I despair of ever saying anything   62
that well. When I read, I think, if I could only say it that well. That's exactly
right; if only I could say it like that.

My critical apparatus is pretty uncomplicated. If I envy it, it's good. If I envy it,   63
it is profound and beautiful and true. If I don't envy it, somehow it's not literature.

I am constantly comparing myself to other writers. And when I think I am   64
better than they, that should tell you something. It tells me something.

I have been reading the *Cursor Mundi*. That's the history of the world. The   65
definitive edition, from Genesis to Doomsday. I picked it up to read it because I
thought I might be in it and I have been wondering how all this turns out.

How can there be a history of the world till Doomsday? It's just the sort of   66
thing a medieval scribe would do. It's just the sort of thing I would do. Remem-

ber Revelations? That's how the scribe knew what happens. Of course, the Vulgate version is different from what we have, but you remember, "And behold a pale horse and him that sat upon it was Death and Hell followed with him."

I love reading stuff like that.   67

They were storytellers, that's all. The need to tell stories has always been a   68
human drive, ever since humans flopped out of the water and gasped on dry
land. I imagine they looked around, those prehumans, and said, "This would
make a really great story. Now if only we had hands to write it down with."

You know how the tribal storyteller would gather the people around and   69
begin: This is the history of our people. There has never been a generation into
which a storyteller was not born. It was a special position. Sometimes there
were omens. This child will hold the memory of our people.

After a while, the storytellers began making their stories up, and this was   70
usually okay with everyone because while only a few people are ever storytellers,
all people have the need to hear stories.

To me, medieval literature is a group of stories. Just wonderful stories about   71
some things. We have, I think, forgotten about storytelling. We have forgotten
why we tell stories.

I study medieval writers so that I will never forget why I tell stories. We tell   72
stories so that other people will hear them. I do, anyway. I don't worry about
writing literature. Lit-ra-chur. I worry about telling stories.

Chaucer didn't worry about writing literature. Shakespeare didn't. Dickens   73
didn't. They wrote stories for people, plain people, like the guys I used to work
with at the lumber yard. They wrote because they had to, being storytellers.
They wrote because they had to, and the rent was due. They managed to make
literature out of their stories because they were geniuses.

Sometimes I am sad that we have become so snobbish and elitist. It's why I   74
find Chaucer comforting. He told stories, just like a storyteller is supposed to.

Okay, okay. So maybe those stories aren't very realistic. Who cares? I've got   75
"real" right outside my front door, you should see it. But you read stories with a
willing suspension of disbelief. I hope you read my stories like that. I mean, in
my screenplay, everyone lives happily ever after.

Oh, please. We all know about how likely that is. But I, like Chaucer's   76
Knight, prefer happy endings. I always have happy endings when I am in charge
of telling the stories.

This is how I read medieval literature. It is how I can read sexism and reli-   77
gious dogmas I don't believe in. I don't dismiss it. I don't go around saying, oh,
that's so sexist. I read the damned story and I suspend my reality and I accept
that Gawain is going to have an antifemale tirade. When he does, he is merely

adding discourtesy to the long list of his flaws. (You think the Green Knight didn't know that?) I remember that these are just stories like the ones I tell, only better written.

I think I should probably be criticized for doing this. Probably a scholar   78
isn't supposed to read this way. Probably scholars are supposed to use various interpretive approaches; but I imagine they have to use various interpretive approaches because they have never told stories. Only listened to them.

Sometimes I wonder why they think they should be allowed to get away   79
with it, criticizing the storyteller. I think you should only be allowed to criticize the storyteller if you are a better storyteller. Anything else seems like armchair quarterbacking to me.

I know this is also WRONG of me. I know I don't sound like a serious scholar.   80
Who cares? I know it sounds like I study medieval literature because it passes the time when I'm in the middle of writer's block. But that's not why I study literature. I study literature because I connect with it. Just not the same way a scholar does.

For instance, I'm reading Layamon's *Brut,* and I'm thinking, you know, I'm   81
positive I am descended from the Picts. If I painted myself blue, I would look exactly like a Pict. I don't know that scholars are supposed to go around thinking things like that. I don't know how many scholars go, "Wouldn't it be cool if I were descended from the Picts?"

Sometimes I wonder what I am doing in academia. Sometimes I wonder what a   82
scholar is good for. I know what storytellers are good for. I know Chaucer told stories because he had to. I'll bet you he even had writer's block a couple of times. I think that's how he ended up translating *La Roman de la Rose.* Imagine that, having writer's block and thereby changing the course of history. I am hoping to change the course of history sometimes when I have writer's block.

People keep assuring me I would understand medieval literature better if I   83
approached it as a scholar, not as an envious writer, not as a kid from Kansas imagining how neat it would have been if only she could have been a Celtic warrior.

So I try. I try to understand what some scholars call the "peculiar character"   84
of medieval literature. The "peculiar character" of the medieval mind. Because, of course, you can't appreciate literature unless you understand all those things. I spend a lot of time visualizing myself as a medieval peasant. Trying to live on a GTA stipend, for instance, can give you some startling insights into the nature of poverty in the Middle Ages. I'd have killed the tax collector, too.

But most of the time, I am not exactly sure what I am supposed to do as a　85
scholar. When I quit work at the lumber yard, I told the foreman I would be
teaching part time and studying the rest of the time. He stared at me some and
moved the wad of tobacco around in his mouth and finally said, "That ain't
working." He gestured toward the loading dock where two semis were jockeying
for position. It was our task to unload those trucks.

"Now that," he said slowly, patiently, so that I could grasp the concept,　86
"*that's* workin'."

Sometimes I wonder if maybe that's why I am here, to get out of having to　87
hold down a real job. I never much liked unloading those damned trucks.
Sometimes I have the sneaking suspicion that that's why all of us are here. We
just love to read, and if we call ourselves "scholars" we can fool everyone into
thinking we are doing more than that, and we can get out of having to unload
the semis.

I am here because the only two things I have ever loved—literature and　88
writing—collided. I landed here writing creatively about Grendel, which, let it
be said, was not exactly what anyone wanted. But it is exactly what I wanted
because I labor under the assumption that, as a writer, I can share medieval literature with everyone in the world. I labor under the assumption that I can illuminate medieval literature, the way the monks once did.

This, I know, is WRONG of me.　89

I know that I put no less than twenty-three quotations from medieval liter-　90
ature into the screenplay, and the producer was "enchanted." Her word. The
hero's nickname is Beowulf, not Rambo. The screenplay is a chivalric romance;
the characters go on a crusade. The producer recognized that right off, even if
she didn't have the right term for it. Well, it's not quite a chivalric romance. It's
a chivalric romance the way Chaucer or the *Gawain* poet would write a chivalric romance. It's got satire and parody and irony and gallows humor. Chaucer
would be proud of me. I like to think so, anyway. I am hoping to contaminate
Hollywood the way Hollywood has contaminated me.

Sometimes after I have been studying all day, I indulge in a little fantasy.　91
I'm at Yale or somewhere, I'm chair of the department, and I go stand in the
middle of the campus and I shriek, "I write mystery novels! I write screenplays!
And you can't stop me!"

Susan says a real scholar would never act like that.　92

I'm going to do it anyway.　93

NOTE

1. I am indebted to S.A.J. Bradley, whose modern English translation of "The Wanderer" (in *Anglo-Saxon Poetry*, trans. and ed. S.A.J. Bradley [London: J. M. Dent and Sons, 1982]) has greatly influenced my own.

WORKS CITED

Cassidy, Frederic, and Richard N. Ringler, eds. *Bright's Old English Grammar and Reader*. 3d ed. 2d corrected printing. New York: Holt, 1971.

Kirby, Thomas. "The General Prologue." In *Companion to Chaucer Studies*, ed. Beryl Rowland. Rev. ed. New York: Oxford University Press, 1979. 243–70.

Geneva Smitherman (1940–), received her Ph.D. from the University of Michigan in 1969 and is currently a University Distinguished Professor at Michigan State University, where she joined the faculty as an instructor in 1966. She is known for a writing style that blends academic discourse and African American language. She was a public school teacher in Detroit before becoming an instructor at several universities and then a lecturer in Afro-American Studies for two years at Harvard. The author of seven books, including *Talkin That Talk: Language, Culture, and Education in African America* (2000), she has also edited and contributed chapters and essays to other works on related subjects. Among many honors, she won the 2001 David H. Russell Research Award from the National Council of Teachers of English and has won grants from the Rockefeller Foundation and the U.S. Department of Health and Human Services.

INTRODUCTION

From Ghetto Lady to Critical Linguist

Geneva Smitherman

I was born into a sharecropping community[1] in rural Tennessee and started school   1 at age four, quickly learning to read under the tutelage of "Miss Earline," a Black teacher with two years of college who had responded to DuBois's call to the Talented Tenth.[2] As Life would have it, Miss Earline was to be the *only* African American teacher in all my years of schooling, from "primer" (as we called it) through Graduate School. In those years, I was monolingual, speaking the Ebonics of my family, my Traditional Black Church, and my sharecropping community. Miss Earline had deep roots in our community; she understood the language of us kids, and sometimes she even spoke our language. After a few years, my family moved to the "promised land," first to Southside Chicago, then Black Bottom Detroit. It was here, "up South," as Malcolm X once called the North, that I had my first taste of linguistic pedagogy for the Great Unwashed. Teachers who didn't look like me and who didn't talk like me attacked my language and put me back one grade level. Back then, educators and others attributed "Black Dialect" to the South, although nobody ever satisfactorily accounted for the fact that Black Northerners used linguistic patterns virtually identical to those of Black Southerners.

    Thus effectively silenced, I managed to avoid these linguistic attacks and   2 to be successful in school by just keeping my mouth shut—not hard for a ghetto child in those days. I was eventually elevated to my right grade and even

Geneva Smitherman, "Introduction: From Ghetto Lady to Critical Linguist" from *Talkin That Talk: Language, Culture, and Education in African America* by Geneva Smitherman, pp. 1–11. © 1999 Geneva Smitherman. Reproduced by permission of Taylor & Francis Books UK.

advanced three years. My nonverbal strategy worked until one month after my fifteenth birthday. It was at that point in my life that I became a college student and was forced to take a speech test in order to qualify for the teacher preparation program. I flunked the speech test.

At that time, many teacher-training programs had such tests, and they were linguistically and culturally biased against all varieties of US English other than that spoken by those who, as linguist Charles C. Fries had put it back in 1940, "carry on the affairs of the English-speaking people." Although the overwhelming majority of those who failed these tests were People of Color, I recall that there were a couple of whites in my group. I said to myself, "Now, what dem white folk doing up in here?" As it turned out, one of "dem white folk" was a speaker of what we now call "Appalachian English." The other was from the Bronx in New York City!   3

It wasn't that young people of Color and whites from working-class backgrounds could not be understood. By this stage in our lives, we had developed adequate enough code-switching skills that we were intelligible to those who "carry on the affairs of the English-speaking people." Rather, the problem was that there existed a bias against this different-sounding American English emanating from the margins. Yet our sounds were as "American as apple pie," having been created as a result of the historical processes that went into the making of America—the African Holocaust, the conquest of Native American peoples, the disenfranchisement of Latinos in the Westward Movement and American expansionism, and the exploitation of people for profits.   4

As descendants of those caught up in these forces, we found ourselves in a classroom with a speech therapist who wasn't sure what to do with us. Nobody was dyslexic. No one was aphasic. There was not even a stutterer among us. I mean, here was this young white girl, a teaching assistant at the university, who was just trying to get her Ph.D., and she was presented with this perplexing problem of people who didn't have any of the communication disorders she had been trained to deal with. Her solution: she taught us the test. Each of us memorized the pronunciation of the particular sounds that we needed to concentrate on. I recall two of my key areas were the post-vocalic -r sound in words like "four" and "more" (which for me were "foe" and "mow"), and the final -th sound in words like "mouth" and "south" (for me, "mouf" and "souf"). These are patterns that I now know reflect West African language influence dating from the enslavement era. But there I was living in the hood trying to mouth sounds like "more" and "sore" when all my girls was sayin "mow" and "so."   5

To the extent that such a story can have a happy ending, I can tell you that we all memorized and passed the speech test. I can also report that in the aftermath of the social movements that raged across "America, the beautiful" during   6 the 1960s and 1970s, this oppressive language policy—once the requirement to enter the teaching profession in many states—no longer exists.

Ironically, that speech therapy experience rescued me from the ghetto streets (where, at the time, I was enjoying a high degree of success—details in my memoirs). It became a symbol of the social and historical forces confronting my community. It aroused the fighting spirit in me, sent me off into critical linguistics, and I eventually entered the lists of the language wars. However, for every African American student like me, who wasn't driven back to the streets, and who survived, not just to enter the System, but to come into the System and call the Question—for every Geneva Napoleon Smitherman, there are many thousands gone. Some of them was my girls that I used to kick it wit on the corner of 47th and Wabash in Chicago, one of whom was killed while out there hustlin on Chicago's Southside. Among the others who have fallen was the Brothas me and my girls sang doo-wap background for in the songs that was gon help them escape the broken-down front porches of Joseph Campau Street in Detroit.

Intellectual insight into this early experience with language oppression came from my baptism in the fire of the Black Intellectual Tradition. (There was no Critical Linguistics way back then when I was in that speech therapy class; it had yet to be named and codified.) Reading the works of the intellectually versatile W. E. B. DuBois, historian Carter G. Woodson, educator Horace Mann Bond, linguist Lorenzo Turner, psychiatrist Frantz Fanon, and—finally, a Sista!—linguist Beryl Bailey—reading the works of these Elders and then later discussing their work in study groups with other African Americans, I began to gain an understanding of language and power.

DuBois made me confront the question, "Whither the Black intellectual?" In his essay by that title, and in his turn-of-the-century book, *The Souls of Black Folk*, he argued that the Talented Tenth should commit itself to using its knowledge, research, and scholarship for the upliftment of the entire Black group. DuBois taught me that the role of the intellectual—*any* intellectual, not just the *Black* intellectual—is not just to understand the world but to change it. Because he well understood the far-reaching ramifications of the production of knowledge, DuBois taught that one should work like a scientist but write like a writer. On the language front, DuBois had proposed Mother Tongue instruction as long ago as 1933 when he laid out his pedagogical philosophy in "The Field and Function of the Negro College":

> the American Negro problem is and must be the center of the Negro university . . . A French university is founded in France; it uses the French language and assumes a knowledge of French history . . . In the same way,

7

8

9

a Negro university in the United States of America begins with Negroes. It uses that variety of the English idiom which they understand; and above all, it . . . should be founded on a knowledge of the history of their people in Africa and in the United States, and their present condition.

(p. 93)

It was Carter G. Woodson who gave me an understanding of the critical sig-   10
nificance of history. In 1926, Woodson, an avowed race man, established *Negro History Week*, which has evolved into *African American History Month*. His critique of the post-Emancipation education of Blacks in America blasted the ahistorical, Eurocentric focus of this education. It had become a blueprint for maintaining the "back door" status of Blacks. He decried the pathological consequences of this education, which was *away* from, rather than *toward* the culture of Africans in America. Reading and studying Woodson's *Mis-education of the Negro* (1933) alerted me to the origin of those linguistic patterns that had landed me in speech therapy back in the day—a therapy that was *not* designed to help me discover the wellspring of those linguistic patterns, nor, obviously to celebrate them. Rather, the therapy was a linguistic eradication program, designed around what white linguist James Sledd has called "the linguistics of white supremacy" (1969). Commenting on the matter of language in *Mis-education*, Woodson noted that

> In the study of language in school pupils were made to scoff at the Negro dialect as some peculiar possession of the Negro which they should despise rather than directed to study the background of this language as a broken down African tongue—in short to understand their own linguistic history, which is certainly more important for them than the study of French Phonetics or Historical Spanish Grammar.
>
> (p. 203)

Revolutionary psychiatrist Frantz Fanon introduced me to the psychologi-   11
cal aspects of race and racism. His studies of the colonized personality clarified the deep wounds to the Black psyche that had been caused by colonialism and enslavement. Like DuBois, he articulated the problem of the dual dimension of the Black personality, and as a psychiatrist devoted himself to understanding the source of this duality. As a healer, he sought ways to bring a wholeness to the divided Black self that imitated things European and attributed inferiority to Black Culture. Although the "subjects" of his clinical research were mainly Africans colonized by the French, he was cognizant that his work applied to Africans elsewhere around the globe, and in fact, as he put it, to "every race that has been subjected to colonization." Fanon ascribed a fundamental signifi-

cance to language. He viewed it as basic in deconstructing and healing the wounded complexity of the Black psyche. In "The Negro and Language," Fanon argued that:

> Every colonized people—in other words, every people in whose soul an inferiority complex has been created by the death and burial of its local cultural originality—finds itself face to face with the language of the civilizing nation; that is, with the culture of the mother country . . . The Negro of the Antilles will be proportionately whiter . . . in direct ratio to his mastery of the French language . . . the fact that the newly returned Negro [i.e., from school in France] adopts a language different from that of the group into which he was born is evidence of a dislocation, a separation . . . The middle class in the Antilles never speak Creole except to their servants. In school the children . . . are taught to scorn the dialect. . . . Some families completely forbid the use of Creole. . . The educated Negro adopts such a position with respect to European languages . . . because he wants to emphasize the rupture that has now occurred.
>
> (1967, pp. 18ff.)

Lorenzo Dow Turner's *Africanisms in the Gullah Dialect* (1949) brought the history and the language together for me. Gullah (also Geechee) is the language spoken by rural and urban Blacks who live in the areas along the Atlantic coastal region of South Carolina and Georgia. Years ago I had the rare opportunity of meeting Mrs. Turner at an Atlanta University conference organized by linguist Richard Long in honor of her husband. According to Mrs. Turner, the Gullah study took Lorenzo Turner nearly twenty years, during which he also spent time learning West African languages. He felt that knowledge of these languages was absolutely essential to understanding the origin of and countering the myths about the Gullah form of US Ebonics. Mrs. Turner also spoke about the technical problems involved in collecting speech samples in those early years, a problem Lorenzo Turner solved by making his own phonograph recordings of Gullah speakers. 12

Turner's work located the history of Gullah in the languages of West Africa and created the intellectual space to examine the African linguistic history of African American speech communities outside the Gullah areas. It was while studying Turner that I learned the names of African languages—like Yoruba, Ibo, Fula, and others, which are now almost as familiar to me as my own name, but which I had never heard of or been exposed to in my entire (mis)education. Turner opened his pioneering work with these words: 13

> The distinctiveness of Gullah . . . has provoked comment from writers for many years. The assumption . . . has been that the peculiarities of the

dialect are traceable almost entirely to the British dialects of the seventeenth and eighteenth centuries and to a form of baby-talk adopted by masters of the slaves to facilitate oral communication between themselves and the slaves . . . The present study, by revealing the very considerable influence of several West African languages upon Gullah, will, it is hoped, remove much of the mystery and confusion surrounding this dialect [. . .] These survivals are most numerous in the vocabulary of the dialect but can be observed also in its sounds, syntax, morphology, and intonation; and there are many striking similarities between Gullah and the African languages in the methods used to form words.

(1949, Preface, xiii)

I came to understand language and power through the work of linguist   14
Beryl Bailey, whom I had the special fortune to meet in my youth before her untimely death stilled the voice of a great scholar and cut short the contributions she was beginning to make to Black Language and Black education. It was this Sista—who doesn't get her props—who led the 1960s explosion of research on Ebonics with her ground-breaking article, "Toward a New Perspective in Negro English Dialectology" (1965), which reflected several years of research and teaching. Bailey analyzed the systematic syntax of her native Jamaican Creole—which surely would have landed her in speech therapy too had she done her teacher training in the US. She turned her Columbia University dissertation into a book, *Jamaican Creole Syntax* (1966), making it the first full description of a Creole syntax in scholarly literature. In doing this work, she became attuned to the linkage between her native Jamaican tongue and the Black speech she heard on the streets of New York where she taught in the Black and Puerto Rican Studies Department at Hunter College. In fact, it was Bailey who reintroduced the concept of a linguistic continuum from Africa to the Caribbean and North America in the Diaspora. (I say "reintroduced" because Turner's work had gone out of print amid attacks on the concept of African survivals in Black Culture, an attack led, unfortunately, by Black sociologist E. Franklin Frazier in the 1950s.)

Bailey's work gave me the idea of tapping into the Black literary tradition   15
to recover the authentic linguistic nuances reproduced by our writers crafting works of art in the Black Tradition. In the 1965 article, she had utilized the language of the novel, *The Cool World*, to argue that African American Language was an independent linguistic system and needed to be considered as such. Not only did Bailey do linguistic research, she immediately began to apply her theoretical knowledge to issues involved in language and literacy instruction for speakers of Ebonics, both at public school and college levels. She sought to

explode myths and misconceptions that teachers had about Black children's abilities and called for revisions of the language arts curriculum and Black Language-specific instructional strategies for Black children (see, for example, Bailey 1968; 1969). In her own quiet, firm, determined way, this Sista was bout it, bout it—the use of education for the empowerment of Africans in America.

Armed with this intellectual background from the Black Tradition, I read- 16 ily embraced Critical Linguistics when it arrived upon the scene in the late 1970s. Arriving, though, from Europe, not America. In *Language and Control*, British linguists Fowler and Kress called for a Critical Linguistics in this way:

> [Linguistics] has been neutralized . . . [there is need for a] critical linguis-
> tics . . . aware of the assumptions on which it is based . . . and prepared
> to reflect critically about the underlying causes of the phenomena it studies,
> and the nature of the society whose language it is.
>
> (1979, 186)

I believe with Fairclough that the interconnections of language and society "may be distorted out of vision," and therefore a critical approach to language study will "make visible the interconnections of things" (1985).

More recently, I found a kindred spirit in Austrian linguist, Wodak— 17 winner of the million-dollar Wittgenstein Award. She calls not only for Critical Linguistics (CL), but also Critical Discourse Analysis (CDA). The "critical" nature of this line of inquiry into language demands that one go beyond the immediacy of the linguistic text to consider matters of socio-political and eco-nomic subordination and language, the perpetuation of inequality through language, and the historical backdrop against which these linguistic power-plays are enacted. Addressing the reaction against "Labovian quantitative lin-guistics," Wodak argues that we have to go beyond quantifying and counting. She states:

> CL and CDA may be defined as fundamentally interested in analyzing
> opaque as well as transparent structural relationships of dominance, dis-
> crimination, power and control as manifested in language. In other words,
> CDA aims to investigate critically social inequality as it is expressed, sig-
> nalled, constituted, legitimized, etc., by language use (or in discourse) . . .
> Consequently, three concepts figure indispensably in all CDA: the concept
> of *power*, the concept of *history*, and the concept of *ideology*.
>
> ("Critical Linguistics and Critical Discourse," 1995)

Being a critical linguist means seeking not only to describe language and 18 its socio-cultural rules, but doing so within a paradigm of language for social transformation. Recognizing the limitations of the quantitative paradigm and number crunching does not mean abandoning research. By no means. For research expands our knowledge base, and without knowledge there is no power and no prospect for change. Being a critical linguist means recognizing that all research is about power—who has it, who doesn't—and the use of power to shape reality based on research. Which is to say that all research is political and derives from a certain ideological stance. After all, even the position that asserts that research should be "objective" is itself an ideological position. Speaking from the vantage point of an "octogenarian questioner" about the teaching of social grammatical rules (e.g., don't use "ain't," avoid double negatives), linguist James Sledd, surely deserving of membership in the contemporary Critical Linguistics camp, has argued that:

> Since the blood, sweat, and tears of generations have neither eradicated *aint* nor taught journalists either to forget *whom* or at least to use it in the proper places, teachers must ask not just the surface questions of what rules to teach and when and how to teach and test them but the deeper questions of the nature and right purpose of the whole undertaking . . . This article makes the obviously debatable suggestion that the best way to enable the teaching of grammar usage is first to learn and teach some harsh ways of the world we live in, so that eventually, political action may just possibly create the preconditions for more successful teaching.
>
> ("Grammar for Social Awareness in Time of Class Warfare," 1996, p. 59)

I am conscious that research, when filtered through the eyes of others, can [19] come out distorted and far from the researcher's original intent. This is, I think, what happened to the work of some sociolinguists and ethnographers working on Black Language in the 1960s. Their findings were disseminated to the lay public unacquainted with sociolinguistic theory, ethnography, or historical linguistics. Often "deviant" descriptions of Black Talk were passed on to the public, and speech events such as signifyin, were caricatured as "jive talk" and "ghetto speech" used by oversexed African Americans, thus reinscribing the worst stereotypes of Ebonics speakers and Black people generally as clowning, low-life, sex-crazed ghetto dwellers. In my own work I have very consciously sought to present the whole of Black Life, and the rich continuum of African American speech from the secular semantics of the street and the basketball court to the talkin and testifyin of the family reunion and the Black Church.

From the moment I came onto the language battlefield, I was acutely con- [20] scious that people outside linguistics thought it hypocritical for linguists to argue for the legitimacy of "Black English" without ever using any of its forms or flava. I stepped to this challenge and made a decision to mix the language of school and the language of home. Thus, in the first article I wrote (though not the first I published), I tried to capture the essence of Black Language, using a mixture of academic talk and Black Talk. I titled that article, "English Teacher, Why You Be Doing the Thangs You Don't Do?" (1972). That publication led to an invitation from then-editor Stephen Tchudi to write a column for *English Journal*, which I ended up doing over a period of three years. In those columns, entitled "Soul 'N Style," I took my code-shifting and mixing even further, trying to make my points with the language arts crowd in the same voice I used with my Black professional friends when they expressed dismay over "Black English." Finally, in *Talkin and Testifyin: The Language of Black America* (1977), I expanded my rhetorical experimentation to book form, taking it to the max, conflating the Language of Wider Communication (i.e., "Standard American English"), Academic Discourse, and my Mother Tongue. This work marks the height of my effort to represent (as the Hip Hoppers say). Mel Watkins, reviewing *Talkin and Testifyin* in the *New York Times* spoke on my rhetorical strategy:

> Smitherman uses many of the mannerisms of black dialect even as she explains them, a device that gives her prose a distinct and effective tone. This could be a problem for readers not familiar with black patois—somewhat like studying a French-language text in which parts of the exposition are given in French. But this lively, unorthodox approach helps make "Talkin and Testifyin" an entertaining book that persuasively extends the meaning of black English.
>
> (29 March 1978)

I confess now something I have never before put into print: this kind of writing was the hardest writing I have ever done, requiring draft after draft after draft to get it right. "Right" meaning representing Black linguistic authenticity and simultaneously making it intelligible for those lacking linguistic competence in Ebonics. Then after this Faulknerian outpouring of the agony and sweat of my human spirit, after the endless late night hours of struggle to bring forth this new Black scholarly aesthetic—after all this, on more than one occasion I would have to do battle with editors to keep the Ebonics flava in a piece. (Not Steve Tchudi though. He was very receptive to my evolving "soul 'n style." With props and thanks for his encouragement, I report with pride that I won a national award for "Soul 'N Style.")

Without reopening old wounds, let me just run one example of this linguistic gate-keeping. Publication of the first edition of *Talkin and Testifyin* in 1977 was held up for weeks while my editor duked it out with her boss, marketing folk, and some of her colleagues about leaving those "g's" off "talking" and "testifying." With the language of my title, I was making a statement, and I was adamant about the "talkin"—and the "testifyin." Over the years, I have been amused by the way references to this book are misrepresented: sometimes with both "g's"; other times with a "g" on "talking," but none on "testifyin"; and a couple of times with no "g's" followed by "sic" (like, hey, that's on Smitherman, it ain me). Exactly. Irrespective of your language politics you have to stop and think about the implications of those "g's."

In later publications, I eased up on using this rhetorical strategy because I   23
was anxious to spread the word. Writing in two languages simultaneously demands enormous time and energy. (It took me eight years to write *Talkin and Testifyin*.)

Sista Beryl Bailey foreshadowed today's Critical Linguistics. She seemed to   24
be speaking directly to me as she argued for research that would not bind a scholar slavishly and narrowly to one paradigm. Rather, she contended that there was a need to carve out new, uncharted routes in the quest for the truth about what we are these days calling Ebonics. Keepin it real, way back in 1965, she made the case for intellectual boldness in analyzing the speech not only of Blacks in Jamaica, but also those in the United States:

> I was compelled to modify the orthodox procedures considerably and even, at times, to adopt some completely unorthodox ones. The first problem that I had to face was that of abstracting a hypothetical dialect which could reasonably be regarded as featuring the main elements of the deep structure. This may sound like hocus-pocus, but indeed a good deal of linguistics is. A hocus-pocus procedure which yields the linguistic facts is surely preferable to a scientifically rigorous one which murders those facts.
>
> ("Towards a New Perspective in Negro English Dialectology," p. 173)

NOTES

1. The sharecropping system, which was instituted among newly-freed slaves after the Civil War, provided a share of a farm's crop in exchange for a Black family's labor to produce the crop. The family was allowed a portion—e.g., a third—of the crop (usually cotton) and provided with a house, sometimes food, and other necessities, all of which were deducted from the family's share of the crop at the end of the year. John Hope Franklin notes that the "cost of maintenance was so great that at the end of the year the freedman was indebted to his employer for most of what he

made, and sometimes it was more than he made" (1967, p. 311). As one ex-slave put it: "Dem sharecroppuhs is jes like slaves" (Gaspar and Hine, 1996, p. 29).

2. The concept of the "Talented Tenth" was put forth by W. E. B. DuBois in his ideological formulation for Black liberation (1903; 1968). It was his view that the upper 10 percent of the Black population—the intelligentsia, professionals, business people, etc.—should take leadership and responsibility for the other 90 percent—the masses—and be in the forefront of the Black Struggle. Otherwise, Blacks would have white leadership forced upon them. In this connection, DuBois also urged the higher education of this group who would be expected to return to the community and contribute their talents to the advancement of the entire race. Some Black political theorists have questioned the validity of this ideology given the context of Blacks in a quasi-colonial existence under American capitalism.

REFERENCES

Bailey, B. L. (1965), "Toward a New Perspective in Negro English Dialectology," *American Speech* 40, pp. 171–177.

Bailey, B. L. (1966), *Jamaican Creole Syntax,* Cambridge: Cambridge University.

Bailey, B. L. (1968), "Some Aspects of the Impact of Linguistics on Language Teaching in Disadvantaged Communities," in A. L.

Bailey, B. L. (1969), "Language and Communicative Styles of Afro-American Children in the United States," *Florida Reporter,* spring/summer.

Davis (ed.), *On the Dialects of Children,* Champaign/Urbana, IL: National Council of Teachers.

DuBois, W. E. B. ([1903] 1961), *The Souls of Black Folk,* New York: Fawcett.

DuBois, W. E. B ([1933] 1973), "The Field and Function of the Negro College," in Aptheker, H. (ed.), *The Education of Black People: Ten Critiques, 1906–60.* Amherst: University of Massachusetts Press, pp. 83–102.

DuBois, W. E. B. (1968), *The Autobiography of W. E. B. DuBois,* New York: International Publishers.

Fairclough, N. L. (1985), "Critical and Descriptive Goals in Discourse Analysis," *Journal of Pragmatics,* 9, pp. 739–763.

Fanon, F. (1967), "The Negro and Language," in Fanon, F. (ed.), *Black Skin, White Masks,* New York: Grove.

Fowler, R. and Kress, G. (1979), "Critical Linguistics," in Fowler, R. *et al.,* (eds.), *Language and Control,* London: Routledge & Kegan Paul.

Franklin, J. H. (1967), *From Slavery to Freedom: A History of Negro Americans,* New York: Alfred A. Knopf, Inc.

Fries, C. C. (1940), *American English Grammar*, New York: Appleton-Century.

Gaspar, D. B. and Hine, D. C. (1996), *More than Chattel: Black Women and Slavery in the Americas*, Bloomington: Indiana University Press.

Sledd, J. (1969), "Bidialectalism: The Linguistics of White Supremacy," *English Journal*, 1307–1329.

Sledd, J. (1996), "Grammar for Social Awareness in Time of Class Warfare," *English Journal*, November.

Smitherman, G. (1972), "English Teacher, Why You Be Doing The Thangs You Don't Do?" *English Journal*, January, pp. 59–65.

Smitherman, G. ([1977] 1986), *Talkin and Testifyin: The Language of Black America*, Boston: Houghton Mifflin; reissued, with revisions, Detroit: Wayne State University Press.

Turner, L. D. (1949), *Africanisms in the Gullah Dialect*, Chicago: University of Chicago Press.

Wodak, R. (1995), "Critical Linguistics and Critical Discourse," in Verschueren, J. Ostman, J. and Blommaert, J. (eds), *Handbook of Pragmatics*, (pp. 204–210), Philadelphia and Amsterdam: John Benjamins.

Woodson, C. G. ([1933] 1969), *The Mis-Education of the Negro*, Washington, DC: Associated Publishers.

Amy Tan (1952–   ) studied at San Jose State University, earning there a B.A. in 1973 and an M.A. in 1974. She did postgraduate work at the University of California–Berkeley from 1974 to 1976. From 1976 to 1987 she worked in San Francisco in various jobs: as a language consultant to programs for disabled children from 1976 to 1981; as a reporter, managing editor, and associate publisher for *Emergency Room Reports* from 1981 to 1983; and as a freelance technical writer from 1983 to 1987. Realizing that she had become a "workaholic," Tan began therapy to deal with the problem. Unfortunately (or perhaps fortunately), her therapist tended to fall asleep during their sessions. Disgusted, Tan turned to herself for therapy, taking jazz piano lessons and beginning to write fiction as a way to slow down. Her enormously successful novel *The Joy Luck Club* (1989) was the result of this "therapy" and the start of a literary career. Since then, Tan has published novels—*The Kitchen God's Wife* (1991), *The Hundred Secret Senses* (1995), and *The Year of the Flood* (1995)—and children's books—*The Moon Lady* (1992) and *The Chinese Siamese Cat* (1994). In addition, she has written short stories and essays for various magazines.

Mother Tongue

Amy Tan

I am not a scholar of English or literature. I cannot give you much more than personal opinions on the English language and its variations in this country or others.   1

I am a writer. And by that definition, I am someone who has always loved language. I am fascinated by language in daily life. I spend a great deal of my time thinking about the power of language—the way it can evoke an emotion, a visual image, a complex idea, or a simple truth. Language is the tool of my trade. And I use them all—all the Englishes I grew up with.   2

Recently, I was made keenly aware of the different Englishes I do use. I was giving a talk to a large group of people, the same talk I had already given to half a dozen other groups. The nature of the talk was about my writing, my life, and my book, *The Joy Luck Club*. The talk was going along well enough, until I remembered one major difference that made the whole talk sound wrong. My mother was in the room. And it was perhaps the first time she had heard me give a lengthy speech, using the kind of English I have never used with her. I was saying things like, "The intersection of memory upon imagination" and "There is an aspect of my fiction that relates to thus-and-thus"—a speech filled with carefully wrought grammatical phrases, burdened, it suddenly seemed to me, with nominalized forms, past perfect tenses, conditional phrases, all the forms of standard English that I had   3 learned in school and through books, the forms of English I did not use at home with my mother.

Just last week, I was walking down the street with my mother, and I again found myself conscious of the English I was using, the English I do use with her. We were talking about the price of new and used furniture and I heard myself saying this: "Not waste money that way." My husband was with us as well, and he didn't notice any switch in my English. And then I realized why. It's because over the twenty years we've been together I've often used that same kind of English with him, and sometimes he even uses it with me. It has become our language of intimacy, a different sort of English that relates to family talk, the language I grew up with.

So you'll have some idea of what this family talk I heard sounds like, I'll quote what my mother said during a recent conversation which I videotaped and then transcribed. During this conversation, my mother was talking about a political gangster in Shanghai who had the same last name as her family's, Du, and how the gangster in his early years wanted to be adopted by her family, which was rich by comparison. Later, the gangster became more powerful, far richer than my mother's family, and one day showed up at my mother's wedding to pay his respects. Here's what she said in part:

"Du Yusong having business like fruit stand. Like off the street kind. He is Du like Du Zong—but not Tsung-ming Island people. The local people call putong, the river east side, he belong to that side local people. That man want to ask Du Zong father take him in like become own family. Du Zong father wasn't look down on him, but didn't take seriously, until that man big like become a mafia. Now important person, very hard to inviting him. Chinese way, came only to show respect, don't stay for dinner. Respect for making big celebration, he shows up. Mean gives lots of respect. Chinese custom. Chinese social life that way. If too important won't have to stay too long. He come to my wedding. I didn't see, I heard it. I gone to boy's side, they have YMCA dinner, Chinese age I was nineteen."

You should know that my mother's expressive command of English belies how much she actually understands. She reads the *Forbes* report, listens to *Wall Street Week*, converses daily with her stockbroker, reads all of Shirley MacLaine's books with ease—all kinds of things I can't begin to understand. Yet some of my friends tell me they understand 50 percent of what my mother says. Some say they understand 80 to 90 percent. Some say they understand none of it, as if she were speaking pure Chinese. But to me, my mother's English is perfectly clear, perfectly natural. It's my mother tongue. Her language, as I hear it, is vivid, direct, full of observation and imagery. That was the language that helped shape the way I saw things, expressed things, made sense of the world.

Lately, I've been giving more thought to the kind of English my mother speaks.   8
Like others, I have described it to people as "broken" or "fractured" English. But I
wince when I say that. It has always bothered me that I can think of no way to describe
it other than "broken," as if it were damaged and needed to be fixed, as if it lacked
a certain wholeness and soundness. I've heard other terms used, "limited English,"
for example. But they seem just as bad, as if everything is limited, including people's perceptions of the limited English speaker.

I know this for a fact, because when I was growing up, my mother's "limited"   9
English limited *my* perception of her. I was ashamed of her English. I believed that
her English reflected the quality of what she had to say. That is, because she expressed
them imperfectly her thoughts were imperfect. And I had plenty of empirical evidence to support me: the fact that people in department stores, at banks, and at restaurants did not take her seriously, did not give her good service, pretended not to
understand her, or even acted as if they did not hear her.

My mother has long realized the limitations of her English as well. When I   10
was fifteen, she used to have me call people on the phone to pretend I was she. In
this guise, I was forced to ask for information or even to complain and yell at people who had been rude to her. One time it was a call to her stockbroker in New York.
She had cashed out her small portfolio and it just so happened we were going to
go to New York the next week, our very first trip outside California. I had to get
on the phone and say in an adolescent voice that was not very convincing, "This
is Mrs. Tan."

And my mother was standing in the back whispering loudly, "Why he don't send   11
me check, already two weeks late. So mad he lie to me, losing my money."

And then I said in perfect English, "Yes, I'm getting rather concerned. You had   12
agreed to send the check two weeks ago, but it hasn't arrived."

Then she began to talk more loudly. "What he want, I come to New York tell   13
him front of his boss, you cheating me?" And I was trying to calm her down, make
her be quiet, while telling the stockbroker, "I can't tolerate any more excuses. If I
don't receive the check immediately, I am going to have to speak to your manager
when I'm in New York next week." And sure enough, the following week there we
were in front of this astonished stockbroker, and I was sitting there red-faced and
quiet, and my mother, the real Mrs. Tan, was shouting at his boss in her impecca-
ble broken English.

We used a similar routine just five days ago, for a situation that was far less humor-   14
ous. My mother had gone to the hospital for an appointment, to find out about a
benign brain tumor a CAT scan had revealed a month ago. She said she had spoken very good English, her best English, no mistakes. Still, she said, the hospital
did not apologize when they said they had lost the CAT scan and she had come for

nothing. She said they did not seem to have any sympathy when she told them she was anxious to know the exact diagnosis, since her husband and son had both died of brain tumors. She said they would not give her any more information until the next time and she would have to make another appointment for that. So she said she would not leave until the doctor called her daughter. She wouldn't budge. And when the doctor finally called her daughter, me, who spoke in perfect English—lo and behold—we had assurances the CAT scan would be found, promises that a conference call on Monday would be held, and apologies for any suffering my mother had gone through for a most regrettable mistake.

I think my mother's English almost had an effect on limiting my possibilities   15 in life as well. Sociologists and linguists probably will tell you that a person's developing language skills are more influenced by peers. But I do think that the language spoken in the family, especially in immigrant families which are more insular, plays a large role in shaping the language of the child. And I believe that it affected my results on achievement tests, IQ tests, and the SAT. While my English skills were never judged as poor, compared to math, English could not be considered my strong suit. In grade school I did moderately well, getting perhaps B's, sometimes B-pluses, in English and scoring perhaps in the sixtieth or seventieth percentile on achievement tests. But those scores were not good enough to override the opinion that my true abilities lay in math and science, because in those areas I achieved A's and scored in the ninetieth percentile or higher.

This was understandable. Math is precise; there is only one correct answer.   16 Whereas, for me at least, the answers on English tests were always a judgment call, a matter of opinion and personal experience. Those tests were constructed around items like fill-in-the-blank sentence completion, such as, "Even though Tom was _____ , Mary thought he was _____ ." And the correct answer always seemed to be the most bland combinations of thoughts, for example, "Even though Tom was shy, Mary thought he was charming," with the grammatical structure "even though" limiting the correct answer to some sort of semantic opposites, so you wouldn't get answers like, "Even though Tom was foolish, Mary thought he was ridiculous." Well, according to my mother, there were very few limitations as to what Tom could have been and what Mary might have thought of him. So I never did well on tests like that.

The same was true with word analogies, pairs of words in which you were sup-   17 posed to find some sort of logical, semantic relationship—for example, "*Sunset* is to *nightfall* as _____ is to _____ ." And here you would be presented with a list of four possible pairs, one of which showed the same kind of relationship: *red* is to *stoplight*, *bus* is to *arrival*, *chills* is to *fever*, *yawn* is to *boring*. Well, I could never think that way. I knew what the tests were asking, but I could not block out of my mind the images already created by the first pair, "*sunset* is to *nightfall*"—and I would see a burst of colors against a darkening sky, the moon rising, the lowering of a curtain of stars. And all the other pairs of words—red, bus, stoplight, boring—just threw up a mass of confusing images, making it impossible for me to sort out something as logical as saying: "A sunset precedes nightfall" is the same as "a chill precedes a fever." The only way I would have gotten that answer right would have been to imagine an associative situation, for example, my being disobedient and staying out past sunset, catching a chill at night, which turns into feverish pneumonia as punishment, which indeed did happen to me.

I have been thinking about all this lately, about my mother's English, about   18
achievement tests. Because lately I've been asked, as a writer, why there are not more Asian Americans represented in American literature. Why are there few Asian Americans enrolled in creative writing programs? Why do so many Chinese students go into engineering? Well, these are broad sociological questions I can't begin to answer. But I have noticed in surveys—in fact, just last week—that Asian students, as a whole, always do significantly better on math achievement tests than in English. And this makes me think that there are other Asian-American students whose English spoken in the home might also be described as "broken" or "limited." And perhaps they also have teachers who are steering them away from writing and into math and science, which is what happened to me.

Fortunately, I happen to be rebellious in nature and enjoy the challenge of dis-   19
proving assumptions made about me. I became an English major my first year in college, after being enrolled as pre-med. I started writing nonfiction as a freelancer the week after I was told by my former boss that writing was my worst skill and I should hone my talents toward account management.

But it wasn't until 1985 that I finally began to write fiction. And at first I wrote   20
using what I thought to be wittily crafted sentences, sentences that would finally prove I had mastery over the English language. Here's an example from the first draft of a story that later made its way into *The Joy Luck Club*, but without this line: "That was my mental quandary in its nascent state." A terrible line, which I can barely pronounce.

Fortunately, for reasons I won't get into today, I later decided I should envision   21
a reader for the stories I would write. And the reader I decided upon was my mother, because these were stories about mothers. So with this reader—in mind—and in fact she did read my early drafts—I began to write stories using all the Englishes I grew up with: the English I spoke to my mother, which for lack of a better term might be described as "simple"; the English she used with me, which for lack of a better term might be described as "broken"; my translation of her Chinese, which could certainly be described as "watered down"; and what I imagined to be her translation of her

Chinese if she could speak in perfect English, her internal language, and for that I sought to preserve the essence, but neither an English nor a Chinese structure. I wanted to capture what language ability tests can never reveal: her intent, her passion, her imagery, the rhythms of her speech and the nature of her thoughts.

Apart from what any critic had to say about my writing, I knew I had succeeded 22 where it counted when my mother finished reading my book and gave me her verdict: "So easy to read."

Deborah Tannen (1945–), was born in Brooklyn, New York, and earned a Ph.D. from the University of California at Berkeley. She has been a professor at Georgetown University since 1979 and writes poetry and short stories in addition to non-fiction. Her ten books on conversational styles and their impact on personal and professional life include the bestsellers *You Just Don't Understand: Women and Men in Conversation* (1990) and *You're Wearing That?: Understanding Mothers and Daughters in Conversation* (2005).

FIGHTING FOR OUR LIVES
Deborah Tannen

This is not another book about civility. "Civility" suggests a superficial, pinky-in-the-air veneer of politeness spread thin over human relations like a layer of marmalade over toast. This book is about a pervasive warlike atmosphere that makes us approach public dialogue, and just about anything we need to accomplish, as if it were a fight. It is a tendency in Western culture in general, and in the United States in particular, that has a long history and a deep, thick, and far-ranging root system. It has served us well in many ways but in recent years has become so exaggerated that it is getting in the way of solving our problems. Our spirits are corroded by living in an atmosphere of unrelenting contention—an argument culture.   1

The argument culture urges us to approach the world—and the people in it—in an adversarial frame of mind. It rests on the assumption that opposition is the best way to get anything done: The best way to discuss an idea is to set up a debate; the best way to cover news is to find spokespeople who express the most extreme, polarized views and present them as "both sides"; the best way to settle disputes is litigation that pits one party against the other; the best way to begin an essay is to attack someone; and the best way to show you're really thinking is to criticize.   2

Our public interactions have become more and more like having an argu-   3
ment with a spouse. Conflict can't be avoided in our public lives any more than
we can avoid conflict with people we love. One of the great strengths of our
society is that we can express these conflicts openly. But just as spouses have to
learn ways of settling their differences without inflicting real damage on each
other, so we, as a society, have to find constructive ways of resolving disputes
and differences. Public discourse requires *making* an argument for a point of
view, not *having* an argument—as in having a fight.

The war on drugs, the war on cancer, the battle of the sexes, politicians'   4
turf battles—in the argument culture, war metaphors pervade our talk and
shape our thinking. Nearly everything is framed as a battle or game in which
winning or losing is the main concern. These all have their uses and their place,
but they are not the only way—and often not the best way—to understand and
approach our world. Conflict and opposition are as necessary as cooperation and
agreement, but the scale is off balance, with conflict and opposition over-
weighted. In this book, I show how deeply entrenched the argument culture is,
the forms it takes, and how it affects us every day—sometimes in useful ways,
but often creating more problems than it solves, causing rather than avoiding
damage. As a sociolinguist, a social scientist, I am trained to observe and
explain language and its role in human relations, and that is my biggest job
here. But I will also point toward other ways for us to talk to each other and get
things done in our public lives.

The Battle of the Sexes
My interest in the topic of opposition in public discourse intensified in the years   5
following the publication of *You Just Don't Understand,* my book about communication between women and men. In the first year I appeared on many television
and radio shows and was interviewed for many print articles in newspapers and
magazines. For the most part, that coverage was extremely fair, and I was—and
remain—indebted to the many journalists who found my ideas interesting enough
to make them known to viewers, listeners, and readers. But from time to time—
more often than I expected—I encountered producers who insisted on setting up
a television show as a fight (either between the host and me or between another
guest and me) and print journalists who made multiple phone calls to my colleagues, trying to find someone who would criticize my work. This got me thinking about what kind of information comes across on shows and in articles that
take this approach, compared to those that approach topics in other ways.

At the same time, my experience of the academic world that had long been   6
my intellectual home began to change. For the most part, other scholars, like

most journalists, were welcoming and respectful in their responses to my work, even if they disagreed on specific points or had alternative views to suggest. But about a year after *You Just Don't Understand* became a best-seller—the wheels of academia grind more slowly than those of the popular press—I began reading attacks on my work that completely misrepresented it. I had been in academia for over fifteen years by then, and had valued my interaction with other researchers as one of the greatest rewards of academic life. Why, I wondered, would someone represent me as having said things I had never said or as having failed to say things I had said?

The answer crystallized when I put the question to a writer who I felt had   7
misrepresented my work: "Why do you need to make others wrong for you to be right?" Her response: "It's an argument!" Aha, I thought, that explains it. When you're having an argument with someone, your goal is not to listen and understand. Instead, you use every tactic you can think of—including distorting what your opponent just said—in order to win the argument.

Not only the level of attention *You Just Don't Understand* received but, even   8
more, the subject of women and men, triggered the tendency to polarize. This tendency to stage a fight on television or in print was posited on the conviction that opposition leads to truth. Sometimes it does. But the trouble is, sometimes it doesn't. I was asked at the start of more than one talk show or print interview, "What is the most controversial thing about your book?" Opposition does not lead to truth when the most controversial thing is not the most important.

The conviction that opposition leads to truth can tempt not only members   9
of the press but just about anyone seeking to attract an audience to frame discussions as a fight between irreconcilable opposites. Even the Smithsonian Institution, to celebrate its 150th anniversary, sponsored a series of talks billed as debates. They invited me to take part in one titled "The Battle of the Sexes." The organizer preempted my objection: "I know you won't be happy with this title, but we want to get people interested." This is one of many assumptions I question in this book: Is it necessary to frame an interchange as a battle to get people interested? And even if doing so succeeds in capturing attention, does it risk dampening interest in the long run, as audiences weary of the din and begin to hunger for more substance?

Thought-Provoking or Just Provocative?

In the spring of 1995, Horizons Theatre in Arlington, Virginia, produced two   10
one-act plays I had written about family relationships. The director, wanting to contribute to the reconciliation between Blacks and Jews, mounted my plays in repertory with two one-act plays by an African-American playwright, Caleen

Sinnette Jennings. We had both written plays about three sisters that explored the ethnic identities of our families (Jewish for me, African-American for her) and the relationship between those identities and the American context in which we grew up. To stir interest in the plays and to explore the parallels between her work and mine, the theater planned a public dialogue between Jennings and me, to be held before the plays opened.

As production got under way, I attended the audition of actors for my plays. After the auditions ended, just before everyone headed home, the theater's public relations volunteer distributed copies of the flyer announcing the public dialogue that she had readied for distribution. I was horrified. The flyer announced that Caleen and I would discuss "how past traumas create understanding and conflict between Blacks and Jews today." The flyer was trying to grab by the throat the issue that we wished to address indirectly. Yes, we were concerned with conflicts between Blacks and Jews, but neither of us is an authority on that conflict, and we had no intention of expounding on it. We hoped to do our part to ameliorate the conflict by focusing on commonalities. Our plays had many resonances between them. We wanted to talk about our work and let the resonances speak for themselves.   11

Fortunately, we were able to stop the flyers before they were distributed and devise new ones that promised something we could deliver: "a discussion of heritage, identity, and complex family relationships in African-American and Jewish-American culture as represented in their plays." Jennings noticed that the original flyer said the evening would be "provocative" and changed it to "thought-provoking." What a world of difference is implied in that small change: how much better to make people think, rather than simply to "provoke" them—as often as not, to anger.   12

It is easy to understand why conflict is so often highlighted: Writers of headlines or promotional copy want to catch attention and attract an audience. They are usually under time pressure, which lures them to established, conventionalized ways of expressing ideas in the absence of leisure to think up entirely new ones. The promise of controversy seems an easy and natural way to rouse interest. But serious consequences are often unintended: Stirring up animosities to get a rise out of people, though easy and "provocative," can open old wounds or create new ones that are hard to heal. This is one of many dangers inherent in the argument culture.   13

For the Sake of Argument

In the argument culture, criticism, attack, or opposition are the predominant if not the only ways of responding to people or ideas. I use the phrase "culture of   14 critique" to capture this aspect. "Critique" in this sense is not a general term for analysis or interpretation but rather a synonym for criticism.

It is the *automatic* nature of this response that I am calling attention to— 15 and calling into question. Sometimes passionate opposition, strong verbal attack, are appropriate and called for. No one knows this better than those who have lived under repressive regimes that forbid public opposition. The Yugoslavian-born poet Charles Simic is one. "There are moments in life," he writes, "when true invective is called for, when it becomes an absolute necessity, out of a deep sense of justice, to denounce, mock, vituperate, lash out, in the strongest possible language." I applaud and endorse this view. There are times when it is necessary and right to fight—to defend your country or yourself, to argue for right against wrong or against offensive or dangerous ideas or actions.

What I question is the ubiquity, the knee-jerk nature, of approaching 16 almost any issue, problem, or public person in an adversarial way. One of the dangers of the habitual use of adversarial rhetoric is a kind of verbal inflation— a rhetorical boy who cried wolf: The legitimate, necessary denunciation is muted, even lost, in the general cacophony of oppositional shouting. What I question is using opposition to accomplish *every* goal, even those that do not require fighting but might also (or better) be accomplished by other means, such as exploring, expanding, discussing, investigating, and the exchanging of ideas suggested by the word "dialogue." I am questioning the assumption that *everything* is a matter of polarized opposites, the proverbial "two sides to every question" that we think embodies open-mindedness and expansive thinking.

In a word, the type of opposition I am questioning is what I call "agonism." 17 I use this term, which derives from the Greek word for "contest," *agonia*, to mean an automatic warlike stance—not the literal opposition of fighting against an attacker or the unavoidable opposition that arises organically in response to conflicting ideas or actions. An agonistic response, to me, is a kind of programmed contentiousness—a prepatterned, unthinking use of fighting to accomplish goals that do not necessarily require it.

How Useful Are Fights?

Noticing that public discourse so often takes the form of heated arguments—of 18 having a fight—made me ask how useful it is in our personal lives to settle differences by arguing. Given what I know about having arguments in private life, I had to conclude that it is, in many cases, not very useful.

In close relationships it is possible to find ways of arguing that result in bet- 19 ter understanding and solving problems. But with most arguments, little is resolved, worked out, or achieved when two people get angrier and less rational by the minute. When you're having an argument with someone, you're usually not trying to understand what the other person is saying, or what in their experience leads them to say it. Instead, you're readying your response: listening for weaknesses in logic to leap on, points you can distort to make the other person look bad and yourself look good. Sometimes you know, on some back burner of your mind, that you're doing this—that there's a kernel of truth in what your adversary is saying and a bit of unfair twisting in what you're saying. Sometimes you do this because you're angry, but sometimes it's just the temptation to take aim at a point made along the way because it's an easy target.

Here's an example of how this happened in an argument between a couple   20
who had been married for over fifty years. The husband wanted to join an HMO by signing over their Medicare benefits to save money. The wife objected because it would mean she could no longer see the doctor she knew and trusted. In arguing her point of view, she said, "I like Dr. B. He knows me, he's interested in me. He calls me by my first name." The husband parried the last point: "I don't like that. He's much younger than we are. He shouldn't be calling us by first name." But the form of address Dr. B. uses was irrelevant. The wife was trying to communicate that she felt comfortable with the doctor she knew, that she had a relationship with him. His calling her by first name was just one of a list of details she was marshaling to explain her comfort with him. Picking on this one detail did not change her view—and did not address her concern. It was just a way to win the argument.

We are all guilty, at times, of seizing on irrelevant details, distorting some-   21
one else's position the better to oppose it, when we're arguing with those we're closest to. But we are rarely dependent on these fights as sources of information. The same tactics are common when public discourse is carried out on the model of personal fights. And the results are dangerous when listeners are looking to these interchanges to get needed information or practical results.

Fights have winners and losers. If you're fighting to win, the temptation is   22
great to deny facts that support your opponent's views and to filter what you know, saying only what supports your side. In the extreme form, it encourages people to misrepresent or even to lie. We accept this risk because we believe we can tell when someone is lying. The problem is, we can't.

Paul Ekman, a psychologist at the University of California, San Francisco,   23
studies lying. He set up experiments in which individuals were videotaped talking about their emotions, actions, or beliefs—some truthfully, some not. He has shown these videotapes to thousands of people, asking them to identify the liars and also to say how sure they were about their judgments. His findings are chilling: Most people performed not much better than chance, and those who did

the worst had just as much confidence in their judgments as the few who were really able to detect lies. Intrigued by the implications of this research in various walks of life, Dr. Ekman repeated this experiment with groups of people whose jobs require them to sniff out lies: judges, lawyers, police, psychotherapists, and employees of the CIA, FBI, and ATF (Bureau of Alcohol, Tobacco, and Firearms). They were no better at detecting who was telling the truth than the rest of us. The only group that did significantly better were members of the U.S. Secret Service. This finding gives some comfort when it comes to the Secret Service but not much when it comes to every other facet of public life.

Two Sides to Every Question

Our determination to pursue truth by setting up a fight between two sides leads   24
us to believe that every issue has two sides—no more, no less: If both sides are given a forum to confront each other, all the relevant information will emerge, and the best case will be made for each side. But opposition does not lead to truth when an issue is not composed of two opposing sides but is a crystal of many sides. Often the truth is in the complex middle, not the oversimplified extremes.

We love using the word "debate" as a way of representing issues: the abor-   25
tion debate, the health care debate, the affirmative action debate—even "the great backpacking vs. car camping debate." The ubiquity of this word in itself shows our tendency to conceptualize issues in a way that predisposes public discussion to be polarized, framed as two opposing sides that give each other no ground. There are many problems with this approach. If you begin with the assumption that there *must* be an "other side," you may end up scouring the margins of science or the fringes of lunacy to find it. As a result, proven facts, such as what we know about how the earth and its inhabitants evolved, are set on a par with claims that are known to have no basis in fact, such as creationism.

The conviction that there are two sides to every story can prompt writers or   26
producers to dig up an "other side," so kooks who state outright falsehoods are given a platform in public discourse. This accounts, in part, for the bizarre phenomenon of Holocaust denial. Deniers, as Emory University professor Deborah Lipstadt shows, have been successful in gaining television airtime and campus newspaper coverage by masquerading as "the other side" in a "debate."

Appearance in print or on television has a way of lending legitimacy, so   27
baseless claims take on a mantle of possibility. Lipstadt shows how Holocaust deniers dispute established facts of history, and then reasonable spokespersons use their having been disputed as a basis for questioning known facts. The actor Robert Mitchum, for example, interviewed in *Esquire*, expressed doubt about

the Holocaust. When the interviewer asked about the slaughter of six million Jews, Mitchum replied, "I don't know. People dispute that." Continual reference to "the other side" results in a pervasive conviction that everything has another side—with the result that people begin to doubt the existence of any facts at all.

The Expense of Time and Spirit

Lipstadt's book meticulously exposes the methods used by deniers to falsify the overwhelming historic evidence that the Holocaust occurred. That a scholar had to invest years of her professional life writing a book unraveling efforts to deny something that was about as well known and well documented as any historical fact has ever been—while those who personally experienced and witnessed it are still alive—is testament to another way that the argument culture limits our knowledge rather than expanding it. Talent and effort are wasted refuting outlandish claims that should never have been given a platform in the first place. Talent and effort are also wasted when individuals who have been unfairly attacked must spend years of their creative lives defending themselves rather than advancing their work. The entire society loses their creative efforts. This is what happened with scientist Robert Gallo.   28

Dr. Gallo is the American virologist who codiscovered the AIDS virus. He is also the one who developed the technique for studying T-cells, which made that discovery possible. And Gallo's work was seminal in developing the test to detect the AIDS virus in blood, the first and for a long time the only means known of stemming the tide of death from AIDS. But in 1989, Gallo became the object of a four-year investigation into allegations that he had stolen the AIDS virus from Luc Montagnier of the Pasteur Institute in Paris, who had independently identified the AIDS virus. Simultaneous investigations by the National Institutes of Health, the office of Michigan Congressman John Dingell, and the National Academy of Sciences barreled ahead long after Gallo and Montagnier settled the dispute to their mutual satisfaction. In 1993 the investigations concluded that Gallo had done nothing wrong. Nothing. But this exoneration cannot be considered a happy ending. Never mind the personal suffering of Gallo, who was reviled when he should have been heralded as a hero. Never mind that, in his words, "These were the most painful years and horrible years of my life." The dreadful, unconscionable result of the fruitless investigations is that Gallo had to spend four years fighting the accusations instead of fighting AIDS.   29

The investigations, according to journalist Nicholas Wade, were sparked by an article about Gallo written in the currently popular spirit of demonography: 30 not to praise the person it features but to bury him—to show his weaknesses, his villainous side. The implication that Gallo had stolen the AIDS virus was created to fill a requirement of the discourse: In demonography, writers must find negative sides of their subjects to display for readers who enjoy seeing heroes transformed into villains. The suspicion led to investigations, and the investigations became a juggernaut that acquired a life of its own, fed by the enthusiasm for attack on public figures that is the culture of critique.

Metaphors: We Are What We Speak

Perhaps one reason suspicions of Robert Gallo were so zealously investigated is   31
that the scenario of an ambitious scientist ready to do anything to defeat a rival appeals to our sense of story; it is the kind of narrative we are ready to believe. Culture, in a sense, is an environment of narratives that we hear repeatedly until they seem to make self-evident sense in explaining human behavior. Thinking of human interactions as battles is a metaphorical frame through which we learn to regard the world and the people in it.

All language uses metaphors to express ideas; some metaphoric words and   32
expressions are novel, made up for the occasion, but more are calcified in the language. They are simply the way we think it is natural to express ideas. We don't think of them as metaphors. Someone who says, "Be careful: You aren't a cat; you don't have nine lives," is explicitly comparing you to a cat, because the cat is named in words. But what if someone says, "Don't pussyfoot around; get to the point"? There is no explicit comparison to a cat, but the comparison is there nonetheless, implied in the word "pussyfoot." This expression probably developed as a reference to the movements of a cat cautiously circling a suspicious object. I doubt that individuals using the word "pussyfoot" think consciously of cats. More often than not, we use expressions without thinking about their metaphoric implications. But that doesn't mean those implications are not influencing us.

At a meeting, a general discussion became so animated that a participant   33
who wanted to comment prefaced his remark by saying, "I'd like to leap into the fray." Another participant called out, "Or share your thoughts." Everyone laughed. By suggesting a different phrasing, she called attention to what would probably have otherwise gone unnoticed: "Leap into the fray" characterized the lively discussion as a metaphorical battle.

Americans talk about almost everything as if it were a war. A book about   34
the history of linguistics is called *The Linguistics Wars.* A magazine article about claims that science is not completely objective is titled "The Science Wars." One about breast cancer detection is "The Mammogram War"; about competi-

tion among caterers, "Party Wars"—and on and on in a potentially endless list. Politics, of course, is a prime candidate. One of innumerable possible examples, the headline of a story reporting that the Democratic National Convention nominated Bill Clinton to run for a second term declares, "DEMOCRATS SEND CLINTON INTO BATTLE FOR A 2D TERM." But medicine is as frequent a candidate, as we talk about battling and conquering disease.

Headlines are intentionally devised to attract attention, but we all use military or attack imagery in everyday expressions without thinking about it: "Take a shot at it," "I don't want to be shot down," "He went off half cocked," "That's half the battle." Why does it matter that our public discourse is filled with military metaphors? Aren't they just words? Why not talk about something that matters—like actions?   35

Because words matter. When we think we are using language, language is using us. As linguist Dwight Bolinger put it (employing a military metaphor), language is like a loaded gun: It can be fired intentionally, but it can wound or kill just as surely when fired accidentally. The terms in which we talk about something shape the way we think about it—and even what we see.   36

The power of words to shape perception has been proven by researchers in controlled experiments. Psychologists Elizabeth Loftus and John Palmer, for example, found that the terms in which people are asked to recall something affect what they recall. The researchers showed subjects a film of two cars colliding, then asked how fast the cars were going; one week later, they asked whether there had been any broken glass. Some subjects were asked, "About how fast were the cars going when they bumped into each other?" Others were asked, "About how fast were the cars going when they smashed into each other?" Those who read the question with the verb "smashed" estimated that the cars were going faster. They were also more likely to "remember" having seen broken glass. (There wasn't any.)   37

This is how language works. It invisibly molds our way of thinking about people, actions, and the world around us. Military metaphors train us to think about—and see—everything in terms of fighting, conflict, and war. This perspective then limits our imaginations when we consider what we can do about situations we would like to understand or change.   38

Even in science, common metaphors that are taken for granted influence how researchers think about natural phenomena. Evelyn Fox Keller describes a case in which acceptance of a metaphor led scientists to see something that was not there. A mathematical biologist, Keller outlines the fascinating behavior of cellular slime mold. This unique mold can take two completely different forms: It can exist as single-cell organisms, or the separate cells can come together to   39 form multicellular aggregates. The puzzle facing scientists was: What triggers aggregation? In other words, what makes the single cells join together? Scientists focused their investigations by asking what entity issued the order to start aggregating. They first called this bosslike entity a "founder cell," and later a "pacemaker cell," even though no one had seen any evidence for the existence of such a cell. Proceeding nonetheless from the assumption that such a cell must exist, they ignored evidence to the contrary: For example, when the center of the aggregate is removed, other centers form.

Scientists studying slime mold did not examine the interrelationship   40
between the cells and their environment, nor the interrelationship between the functional systems within each cell, because they were busy looking for the pacemaker cell, which, as eventually became evident, did not exist. Instead, under conditions of nutritional deprivation, each individual cell begins to feel the urge to merge with others to form the conglomerate. It is a reaction of the cells to their environment, not to the orders of a boss. Keller recounts this tale to illustrate her insight that we tend to view nature through our understanding of human relations as hierarchical. In her words, "We risk imposing on nature the very stories we like to hear." In other words, the conceptual metaphor of hierarchical governance made scientists "see" something—a pacemaker cell— that wasn't there.

Among the stories many Americans most like to hear are war stories.   41
According to historian Michael Sherry, the American war movie developed during World War II and has been with us ever since. He shows that movies not explicitly about war were also war movies at heart, such as westerns with their good guy—bad guy battles settled with guns. *High Noon*, for example, which became a model for later westerns, was an allegory of the Second World War: The happy ending hinges on the pacifist taking up arms. We can also see this story line in contemporary adventure films: Think of *Star Wars*, with its stirring finale in which Han Solo, having professed no interest in or taste for battle, returns at the last moment to destroy the enemy and save the day. And precisely the same theme is found in a contemporary low-budget independent film, *Sling Blade*, in which a peace-loving retarded man becomes a hero at the end by murdering the man who has been tormenting the family he has come to love.

Put Up Your Dukes

If war provides the metaphors through which we view the world and each other,   42
we come to view others—and ourselves—as warriors in battle. Almost any human encounter can be framed as a fight between two opponents. Looking at it this way brings particular aspects of the event into focus and obscures others.

Framing interactions as fights affects not only the participants but also the   43
viewers. At a performance, the audience, as well as the performers, can be transformed. This effect was noted by a reviewer in *The New York Times*, commenting on a musical event:

> **Showdown at Lincoln Center.** Jazz's ideological war of the last several
> years led to a pitched battle in August between John Lincoln Collier, the
> writer, and Wynton Marsalis, the trumpeter, in a debate at Lincoln Center.
> Mr. Marsalis demolished Mr. Collier, point after point after point, but what
> made the debate unpleasant was the crowd's blood lust; humiliation, not
> elucidation, was the desired end.

Military imagery pervades this account: the difference of opinions between Collier and Marsalis was an "ideological war," and the "debate" was a "pitched battle" in which Marsalis "demolished" Collier (not his arguments, but him). What
the commentator regrets, however, is that the audience got swept up in the
mood instigated by the way the debate was carried out: "the crowd's blood lust"
for Collier's defeat.

This is one of the most dangerous aspects of regarding intellectual inter-   44
change as a fight. It contributes to an atmosphere of animosity that spreads like
a fever. In a society that includes people who express their anger by shooting,
the result of demonizing those with whom we disagree can be truly tragic.

But do audiences necessarily harbor within themselves a "blood lust," or is   45
it stirred in them by the performances they are offered? Another arts event was
set up as a debate between a playwright and a theater director. In this case, the
metaphor through which the debate was viewed was not war but boxing—a
sport that is in itself, like a debate, a metaphorical battle that pitches one side
against the other in an all-out effort to win. A headline describing the event set
the frame: "AND IN THIS CORNER . . .," followed by the subhead "A Black Playwright and White Critic Duke It Out." The story then reports:

> the face-off between August Wilson, the most successful black playwright
> in the American theater, and Robert Brustein, longtime drama critic for
> The New Republic and artistic director of the American Repertory Theatre
> in Cambridge, Mass. These two heavyweights had been battling in print
> since last June. . . .
>   Entering from opposite sides of the stage, the two men shook hands
> and came out fighting—or at least sparring.

Wilson, the article explains, had given a speech in which he opposed Black performers taking "white" roles in color-blind casting; Brustein had written a column disagreeing; and both followed up with further responses to each other.

According to the article, "The drama of the Wilson-Brustein confrontation   46
lies in their mutual intransigence." No one would question that audiences crave
drama. But is intransigence the most appealing source of drama? I happened to
hear this debate broadcast on the radio. The line that triggered the loudest
cheers from the audience was the final question put to the two men by the mod-
erator, Anna Deavere Smith: "What did you each learn from the other in this
debate?" The loud applause was evidence that the audience did not crave intransigence. They wanted to see another kind of drama: the drama of change—
change that comes from genuinely listening to someone with a different point of
view, not the transitory drama of two intransigent positions in stalemate.

To encourage the staging of more dramas of change and fewer of intransi-   47
gence, we need new metaphors to supplement and complement the pervasive
war and boxing match metaphors through which we take it for granted issues
and events are best talked about and viewed.

Mud Splatters

Our fondness for the fight scenario leads us to frame many complex human   48
interactions as a battle between two sides. This then shapes the way we understand what happened and how we regard the participants. One unfortunate
result is that fights make a mess in which everyone is muddied. The person
attacked is often deemed just as guilty as the attacker.

The injustice of this is clear if you think back to childhood. Many of us still   49
harbor anger as we recall a time (or many times) a sibling or playmate started a
fight—but both of us got blamed. Actions occur in a stream, each a response to
what came before. Where you punctuate them can change their meaning just as
you can change the meaning of a sentence by punctuating it in one place or
another.

Like a parent despairing of trying to sort out which child started a fight,   50
people often respond to those involved in a public dispute as if both were
equally guilty. When champion figure skater Nancy Kerrigan was struck on the
knee shortly before the 1994 Olympics in Norway and the then-husband of
another champion skater, Tonya Harding, implicated his wife in planning the
attack, the event was characterized as a fight between two skaters that obscured
their differing roles. As both skaters headed for the Olympic competition, their
potential meeting was described as a "long-anticipated figure-skating shootout."
Two years later, the event was referred to not as "the attack on Nancy Kerrigan"
but as "the rivalry surrounding Tonya Harding and Nancy Kerrigan."

By a similar process, the Senate Judiciary Committee hearings to consider the   51
nomination of Clarence Thomas for Supreme Court justice at which Anita Hill

was called to testify are regularly referred to as the "Hill-Thomas hearings," obscuring the very different roles played by Hill and Thomas. Although testimony by Anita Hill was the occasion for reopening the hearings, they were still the Clarence Thomas confirmation hearings: Their purpose was to evaluate Thomas's candidacy. Framing these hearings as a two-sides dispute between Hill and Thomas allowed the senators to focus their investigation on cross-examining Hill rather than seeking other sorts of evidence, for example by consulting experts on sexual harassment to ascertain whether Hill's account seemed plausible.

Slash-and-Burn Thinking

Approaching situations like warriors in battle leads to the assumption that   52
intellectual inquiry, too, is a game of attack, counterattack, and self-defense. In this spirit, critical thinking is synonymous with criticizing. In many classrooms, students are encouraged to read someone's life work, then rip it to shreds. Though criticism is one form of critical thinking—and an essential one—so are integrating ideas from disparate fields and examining the context out of which ideas grew. Opposition does not lead to the whole truth when we ask only "What's wrong with this?" and never "What can we use from this in building a new theory, a new understanding?"

There are many ways that unrelenting criticism is destructive in itself. In   53
innumerable small dramas mirroring what happened to Robert Gallo (but on a much more modest scale), our most creative thinkers can waste time and effort responding to critics motivated less by a genuine concern about weaknesses in their work than by a desire to find something to attack. All of society loses when creative people are discouraged from their pursuits by unfair criticism. (This is particularly likely to happen since, as Kay Redfield Jamison shows in her book *Touched with Fire,* many of those who are unusually creative are also unusually sensitive; their sensitivity often drives their creativity.)

If the criticism is unwarranted, many will say, you are free to argue against   54
it, to defend yourself. But there are problems with this, too. Not only does self-defense take time and draw off energy that would better be spent on new creative work, but any move to defend yourself makes you appear, well, defensive. For example, when an author wrote a letter to the editor protesting a review he considered unfair, the reviewer (who is typically given the last word) turned the very fact that the author defended himself into a weapon with which to attack again. The reviewer's response began, "I haven't much time to waste on the kind of writer who squanders his talent drafting angry letters to reviewers."

The argument culture limits the information we get rather than broadening   55
it in another way. When a certain kind of interaction is the norm, those who

feel comfortable with that type of interaction are drawn to participate, and those who do not feel comfortable with it recoil and go elsewhere. If public discourse included a broad range of types, we would be making room for individuals with different temperaments to take part and contribute their perspectives and insights. But when debate, opposition, and fights overwhelmingly predominate, those who enjoy verbal sparring are likely to take part—by calling in to talk shows, writing letters to the editor or articles, becoming journalists—and those who cannot comfortably take part in oppositional discourse, or do not wish to, are likely to opt out.

This winnowing process is easy to see in apprenticeship programs such as   56
acting school, law school, and graduate school. A woman who was identified in her university drama program as showing exceptional promise was encouraged to go to New York to study acting. Full of enthusiasm, she was accepted by a famous acting school where the teaching method entailed the teacher screaming at students, goading and insulting them as a way to bring out the best in them. This worked well with many of the students but not with her. Rather than rising to the occasion when attacked, she cringed, becoming less able to draw on her talent, not more. After a year, she dropped out. It could be that she simply didn't have what it took—but this will never be known, because the adversarial style of teaching did not allow her to show what talent she had.

Polarizing Complexity: Nature or Nurture?

Few issues come with two neat, and neatly opposed, sides. Again, I have seen   57
this in the domain of gender. One common polarization is an opposition between two sources of differences between women and men: "culture," or "nurture," on one hand and "biology," or "nature," on the other.

Shortly after the publication of *You Just Don't Understand*, I was asked by a   58
journalist what question I most often encountered about women's and men's conversational styles. I told her, "Whether the differences I describe are biological or cultural." The journalist laughed. Puzzled, I asked why this made her laugh. She explained that she had always been so certain that any significant differences are cultural rather than biological in origin that the question struck her as absurd. So I should not have been surprised when I read, in the article she wrote, that the two questions I am most frequently asked are "Why do women nag?" and "Why won't men ask for directions?" Her ideological certainty that the question I am most frequently asked was absurd led her to ignore my answer and get a fact wrong in her report of my experience.

Some people are convinced that any significant differences between men   59
and women are entirely or overwhelmingly due to cultural influences—the way

we treat girls and boys, and men's dominance of women in society. Others are convinced that any significant differences are entirely or overwhelmingly due to biology: the physical facts of female and male bodies, hormones, and reproductive functions. Many problems are caused by framing the question as a dichotomy: Are behaviors that pattern by sex biological or cultural? This polarization encourages those on one side to demonize those who take the other view, which leads in turn to misrepresenting the work of those who are assigned to the opposing camp. Finally, and most devastatingly, it prevents us from exploring the interaction of biological and cultural factors—factors that must, and can only, be understood together. By posing the question as either/or, we reinforce a false assumption that biological and cultural factors are separable and preclude the investigations that would help us understand their interrelationship. When a problem is posed in a way that polarizes, the solution is often obscured before the search is under way.

Who's Up? Who's Down?

Related to polarization is another aspect of the argument culture: our obsession   60
with ratings and rankings. Magazines offer the 10, 50, or 100 best of everything: restaurants, mutual funds, hospitals, even judges. Newsmagazines tell us Who's up, Who's down, as in *Newsweek's* "Conventional Wisdom Watch" and *Time's* "Winners and Losers." Rankings and ratings pit restaurants, products, schools, and people against each other on a single scale, obscuring the myriad differences among them. Maybe a small Thai restaurant in one neighborhood can't really be compared to a pricey French one in another, any more than judges with a vast range of abilities and beliefs can be compared on a single scale. And timing can skew results: Ohio State University protested to *Time* magazine when its football team was ranked at the bottom of a scale because only 29 percent of the team graduated. The year before it would have ranked among the top six with 72 percent.

After a political debate, analysts comment not on what the candidates said   61
but on the question "Who won?" After the president delivers an important speech, such as the State of the Union Address, expert commentators are asked to give it a grade. Like ranking, grading establishes a competition. The biggest problem with asking what grade the president's speech deserves, or who won and who lost a campaign debate, is what is not asked and is therefore not answered: What was said, and what is the significance of this for the country?

An Ethic of Aggression

In an argument culture aggressive tactics are valued for their own sake. For   62
example, a woman called in to a talk show on which I was a guest to say,

"When I'm in a place where a man is smoking, and there's a no-smoking sign, instead of saying to him 'You aren't allowed to smoke in here. Put that out,' I say, 'I'm awfully sorry, but I have asthma, so your smoking makes it hard for me to breathe. Would you mind terribly not smoking?' Whenever I say this, the man is extremely polite and solicitous, and he puts his cigarette out, and I say, 'Oh, thank you, thank you!' as if he's done a wonderful thing for me. Why do I do that?"

I think this woman expected me to say that she needs assertiveness training 63 to learn to confront smokers in a more aggressive manner. Instead, I told her that there was nothing wrong with her style of getting the man to stop smoking. She gave him a face-saving way of doing what she asked, one that allowed him to feel chivalrous rather than chastised. This is kind to him, but it is also kind to herself, since it is more likely to lead to the result she desires. If she tried to alter his behavior by reminding him of the rules, he might well rebel: "Who made you the enforcer? Mind your own business!" Indeed, who gives any of us the authority to set others straight when we think they're breaking rules?

Another caller disagreed with me, saying the first caller's style was "self- 64 abasing" and there was no reason for her to use it. But I persisted: There is nothing necessarily destructive about conventional self-effacement. Human relations depend on the agreement to use such verbal conventions. I believe the mistake this caller was making—a mistake many of us make—was to confuse *ritual* self-effacement with the literal kind. All human relations require us to find ways to get what we want from others without seeming to dominate them. Allowing others to feel they are doing what you want for a reason less humiliating to them fulfills this need.

Thinking of yourself as the wronged party who is victimized by a lawbreak- 65 ing boor makes it harder to see the value of this method. But suppose you are the person addicted to smoking who lights up (knowingly or not) in a no-smoking zone. Would you like strangers to yell at you to stop smoking, or would you rather be allowed to save face by being asked politely to stop in order to help them out? Or imagine yourself having broken a rule inadvertently (which is not to imply rules are broken only by mistake; it is only to say that sometimes they are). Would you like some stranger to swoop down on you and begin berating you, or would you rather be asked politely to comply?

As this example shows, conflicts can sometimes be resolved without con- 66 frontational tactics, but current conventional wisdom often devalues less confrontational tactics even if they work well, favoring more aggressive strategies even if they get less favorable results. It's as if we value a fight for its own sake, not for its effectiveness in resolving disputes.

This ethic shows up in many contexts. In a review of a contentious book,   67
for example, a reviewer wrote, "Always provocative, sometimes infuriating, this
collection reminds us that the purpose of art is not to confirm and coddle but to
provoke and confront." This false dichotomy encapsulates the belief that if you
are not provoking and confronting, then you are confirming and coddling—as if
there weren't myriad other ways to question and learn. What about exploring,
exposing, delving, analyzing, understanding, moving, connecting, integrating,
illuminating . . . or any of innumerable verbs that capture other aspects of
what art can do?

The Broader Picture

The increasingly adversarial spirit of our contemporary lives is fundamentally   68
related to a phenomenon that has been much remarked upon in recent years: the
breakdown of a sense of community. In this spirit, distinguished journalist and
author Orville Schell points out that in his day journalists routinely based their
writing on a sense of connection to their subjects—and that this sense of connection is missing from much that is written by journalists today. Quite the contrary, a spirit of demonography often prevails that has just the opposite effect: Far
from encouraging us to feel connected to the subjects, it encourages us to feel
critical, superior—and, as a result, distanced. The cumulative effect is that citizens feel more and more cut off from the people in public life they read about.

The argument culture dovetails with a general disconnection and break-   69
down of community in another way as well. Community norms and pressures
exercise a restraint on the expression of hostility and destruction. Many cultures
have rituals to channel and contain aggressive impulses, especially those of adolescent males. In just this spirit, at the 1996 Republican National Convention,
both Colin Powell and Bob Dole talked about growing up in small communities
where everyone knew who they were. This meant that many people would look
out for them, but also that if they did something wrong, it would get back to
their parents. Many Americans grew up in ethnic neighborhoods that worked
the same way. If a young man stole something, committed vandalism, or broke a
rule or law, it would be reported to his relatives, who would punish him or tell
him how his actions were shaming the family. American culture today often
lacks these brakes.

Community is a blend of connections and authority, and we are losing   70
both. As Robert Bly shows in his book by that title, we now have a *Sibling Society*: Citizens are like squabbling siblings with no authority figures who can command enough respect to contain and channel their aggressive impulses. It is as if
every day is a day with a substitute teacher who cannot control the class and
maintain order.

The argument culture is both a product of and a contributor to this alien- 71
ation, separating people, disconnecting them from each other and from those
who are or might have been their leaders.

What Other Way Is There?

Philosopher John Dewey said, on his ninetieth birthday, "Democracy begins in 72
conversation." I fear that it gets derailed in polarized debate.

In conversation we form the interpersonal ties that bind individuals 73
together in personal relationships; in public discourse, we form similar ties on a
larger scale, binding individuals into a community. In conversation, we
exchange the many types of information we need to live our lives as members of
a community. In public discourse, we exchange the information that citizens in
a democracy need in order to decide how to vote. If public discourse provides
entertainment first and foremost—and if entertainment is first and foremost
watching fights—then citizens do not get the information they need to make
meaningful use of their right to vote.

Of course it is the responsibility of intellectuals to explore potential weak- 74
nesses in others' arguments, and of journalists to represent serious opposition
when it exists. But when opposition becomes the overwhelming avenue of
inquiry—a formula that *requires* another side to be found or a criticism to be
voiced; when the lust for opposition privileges extreme views and obscures complexity; when our eagerness to find weaknesses blinds us to strengths; when the
atmosphere of animosity precludes respect and poisons our relations with one
another; then the argument culture is doing more damage than good.

I offer this book not as a frontal assault on the argument culture. That 75
would be in the spirit of attack that I am questioning. It is an attempt to examine the argument culture—our use of attack, opposition, and debate in public
discourse—to ask, What are its limits as well as its strengths? How has it served
us well, but also how has it failed us? How is it related to culture and gender?
What other options do we have?

I do not believe we should put aside the argument model of public dis- 76
course entirely, but we need to rethink whether this is the *only* way, or *always*
the best way, to carry out our affairs. A step toward broadening our repertoires
would be to pioneer reform by experimenting with metaphors other than
sports and war, and with formats other than debate for framing the exchange
of ideas. The change might be as simple as introducing a plural form. Instead
of asking "What's the other side?" we might ask instead, "What are the other
sides?" Instead of insisting on hearing "both sides," we might insist on hearing
"all sides."

Another option is to expand our notion of "debate" to include more dia-   77
logue. This does not mean there can be no negativity, criticism, or disagreement. It simply means we can be more creative in our ways of managing all of
these, which are inevitable and useful. In dialogue, each statement that one person makes is qualified by a statement made by someone else, until the series of
statements and qualifications moves everyone closer to a fuller truth. Dialogue
does not preclude negativity. Even saying "I agree" makes sense only against the
background assumption that you might disagree. In dialogue, there is opposition, yes, but no head-on collision. Smashing heads does not open minds.

There are times when we need to disagree, criticize, oppose, and attack—to   78
hold debates and view issues as polarized battles. Even cooperation, after all, is
not the absence of conflict but a means of managing conflict. My goal is not a
make-nice false veneer of agreement or a dangerous ignoring of true opposition.
I'm questioning the *automatic* use of adversarial formats—the assumption that it's
always best to address problems and issues by fighting over them. I'm hoping for a
broader repertoire of ways to talk to each other and address issues vital to us.

Cultural Literacies

Adam J. Banks was born in Cleveland, Ohio, and received his B. A. in 1992 from Cleveland State University. He earned his Ph.D. in English in 2003 at Pennsylvania State University. Since then, he has been an assistant professor of writing and rhetoric in the writing program of the Arts and Sciences College at Syracuse University in New York. He teaches African American rhetoric, technology theory, and technical communication and is the author of *Race, Rhetoric, and Technology: Searching for Higher Ground* (2005). He has also published in *Black Issues in Higher Education*.

TAKING BLACK TECHNOLOGY USE SERIOUSLY: AFRICAN AMERICAN DISCURSIVE TRADITIONS IN THE DIGITAL UNDERGROUND

Adam J. Banks

The first, and perhaps most important element of a meaningful access is use— more than merely owning or being close to some particular technology, people must actually use it, and develop the skills and approaches to using it that are relevant to their lives. Unfortunately, we know almost nothing about the uses to which African Americans put digital technologies or the processes by which they develop the skills, abilities, and approaches that will enable them to use computers, the Internet, or any other related tool or process in culturally relevant, individually meaningful ways.   1

This chapter raises the issue of how African Americans use computer-related writing technologies, and tries to answer the specific question of how Black computer users engage African American language and discourse patterns in online spaces. I argue here that despite the prevalence of work on the oral elements of African American language and discourse, and the dominance of early cyberspace theory that dismissed race and culture as irrelevant online, at least in one space, African American community Web site BlackPlanet, African American language and discourse live, and even thrive in online spaces. The strength of the presence of Black language and discourse online speaks not only to the richness of Black linguistic and discursive traditions, but also to the ways African American technology users can change technologies and make them relevant through the uses to which they put them—even when   2 those technologies are not Black owned or controlled. Black participation on the Web site also begins to show the ways cyberspace can serve as a cultural underground that counters the surveillance and censorship that always seem to accompany the presence of African Americans speaking, writing, and designing in more public spaces—spaces that seem to consistently say to them that no matter what traditions they might bring to the classroom, the workplace, or to technologies—these spaces (and the written English that accompanies them) are, and will continue to be White by definition.

As much attention as people have paid to the structures, features, and func-   3
tions of African American varieties of English—whether those varieties are referred to as African American Vernacular English, Ebonics, a creole, or a complete language that is a member of the Niger-Congo language family, the great preponderance of that attention has focused on the "oral" elements of those language traditions. In fact, one might say that just as African American rhetorical scholarship has tended to focus on oratory or other orally delivered texts like song lyrics, African American language study has taken African and African-derived oral traditions as givens, at times seeming to concede written language to the domain of White culture. Of course, there are many African American language scholars who do not make such concessions, but the broader body of research would seem to make it for them.

Although there has been much work done examining the ways African   4
American language patterns are manifest in written texts, the fact that the focus of much of that study and most of the theory of those language patterns has been on oral language production is clear. Titles from two of the more prominent books on Black English tell the story: John and Russell Rickford's 2000 book, *Spoken Soul: The Story of Black English,* and Geneva Smitherman's compilation, also from 2000, *Talkin that Talk: Language, Culture, and Education in African America* begin to show that focus. The Rickfords take their title from the name Claude Brown gives Black English in an interview on language, and they point to several reasons for borrowing Brown's phrase: a desire to stay rooted in the vernacular tradition of African American English, its links to other forms of cultural production like music, and "the fact . . . that most African Americans *do* talk differently from Whites and Americans of other ethnic groups, or at least most of us can when we want to. And the fact is that most Americans, Black and White, know this to be true" (p. 4).

Smitherman's focus on orality in *Talkin that Talk* and her classic first book   5
Talkin and Testifyin: The Language of Black America (1986) exists for similar reasons, though she also pushes the discussion further to account for distinctively Black rhetorical strategies and discourse features that, although rooted in Black

oral traditions, are manifest in written texts as well. Her work also connects these specific discursive patterns and rhetorical features to African American epistemologies, or world views. As Smitherman shows in the essay "How I Got Ovuh: African World View and African American Oral Tradition," the point is not simply a linguistic one. In other words, simply arguing that African American English is, obviously (though not yet for many teachers), rule governed and systematic, and just as valid an organ for expressing the thoughts, ideas, passions, joys, pains, aspirations, and struggles of a people as any other is no longer news for those who study the language variety. A whole legion of linguists have been on that case since Lorenzo Dow Turner more than 50 years ago.

Smitherman goes beyond this point to show how Black English, as   6
expressed through its oral traditions, represents distinctively African American worldviews:

> the oral tradition has served as a fundamental vehicle for gittin ovuh. That tradition preserves the Afro-American heritage and reflects the collective spirit of the race. Through song, story, folk sayings, and rich verbal interplay among everyday people, lessons and precepts about life and survival are handed down from generation to generation. (p. 199)

The continued focus of many on the oral in Black English, then, is not a resignation that written English is somehow the exclusive domain of Whites— Smitherman herself offers masterful analysis of a wide array of written texts— but a matter of remaining true to the roots of the language, no matter what forms it might take now. Maintaining that focus is also an act of self-determination, of resistance, of keeping oppositional identities and worldviews alive, refusing to allow melting pot ideologies to continue to demand that Black people assimilate to White notions of language and identity as the cost for access to economic goods or a public voice in American society.

THE "UNDERGROUND" IN AFRICAN AMERICAN CULTURE: THRIVING AND EXTINCT

The underground in Black life that the oral tradition still dominates has   7
become so popular as to almost no longer be metaphorically underground. By "underground," I refer to those spaces and cultural practices that exist away from the policing gaze of mainstream culture. I use it to call attention to those spaces that, whether initially created as ways of resisting the segregation and racism that prevented Black people from participating in mainstream American society (and usually punished them for trying), or as refuges from the constant struggle in trying to swim that stream, are dominated by Black cultural norms, Black worldviews, and Black language practices. The most well-known of these

sites, and the source of the concept of a Black underground is the Underground Railroad, a network of people, organizations, communication technologies, and language practices that Black people used to resist and escape the horrors of slavery. The railroad and other spaces and practices are termed *underground* because it operates when and where others fail to notice, although often in plain view.

This tension, between maintaining distinct cultural practices, often in plain view of others, is important to bear in mind because many recent popular culture texts seem to suggest that there is no underground anymore. The traditional sites of the underground have all been exposed—the barbershop and beauty salon, the nightclub, the church, standup comedy, the radio show, the studio, the basement. Hardly a Black sitcom or movie appears on television or onscreen without pointing to these sites: Nipsey's Bar, and the radio show that employs the lead character on "Martin," BET and HBO comedy shows "Comic View," "Def Comedy Jam," and even music video shows like "Rap City: Tha Bassment." No matter how much exposure spaces like these receive, although, the underground still exists because the exclusions that foster such spaces still exist. It also still thrives because the underground is much more than the physical spaces of the church or barbershop or studio. The underground is also the specific discursive practices that determine who gets in and who does not, from the posters in Black communities advertising concerts to the "grapevine" that Patricia Turner examines in her book on rumor in African American communities. The underground is the particular technologies, tools, processes that make those discursive practices possible. The chitlin circuit of locations comics perform on while attempting to "make it," and mix CDs are two examples of how networks and technologies are sites of underground cultural practices in addition to the physical spaces that receive so much exposure. Technologies, discursive practices, and networks of people all come together with physical spaces to create any particular manifestation of the "underground."

Common to almost all of these sites is the African American oral tradition—not just in the sense of Ebonics (but that too, often), or linguistic notions of communication, but all of the rhetorical and discursive features Smitherman (2000) describes so fully in *Talkin that Talk*. Because these spaces exist outside of the official gaze of schools, workplaces, and governments, those who become part of them truly do have the right to their own language. The presence of such spaces online would mean three things: first, it would be a repudiation of much early cyberspace theory that insisted race is and should be irrelevant online, that it would be made irrelevant by the fluidity inherent in online

8

9

subjectivities. Second, it would confirm the importance of discursive and rhetorical features that Smitherman links to African oral traditions for the written discourse of African Americans. The implication of this point is that the wide body of research in composition that fails to take into account the power of these traditions and continues to view Black student writers as less prepared than others, merely "writing like they talk," needs to be questioned and ultimately repudiated as antithetical to both the field's stated goals of fostering inclusion in writing instruction and the actual practice of writers. Third, it would show Black people taking ownership of digital spaces and technologies and point to the importance of taking Black users into account in technology user studies.

An examination of African American discourse online, then faces two distinct problems from the outset. The first is the assumption that is incorrectly taken from the work of scholars like the Rickfords, Geneva Smitherman, Keith Gilyard, Elaine Richardson, Clinton Crawford, and many others, that African American English is merely or mostly about spoken language. This assumption often leads teachers and scholars to believe a corollary assumption, namely while Black oral traditions are rich and varied, those traditions are irrelevant to the study of written English, and therefore writing instruction should be strictly and only about the mastery of standardized English.

Just as many compositionists hold these assumptions that Black traditions are irrelevant to the study of written English, much cyberspace theory also holds that race is, and should be, irrelevant online. Fortunately, some have confronted such theorizing, like Beth Kolko, who argues in her essay "Erasing @race: going White in the interface" that it's not just cyberspace theory or discourse that assumes a White default user, but that this assumption is often programmed right into the interface of online environments like MOOs and MUDs, the older sisters and brothers of current chat spaces. Kolko contends that the elision of race that occurs in these design choices negatively affects communicative possibilities, but also that "the history of online communities demonstrates a dropping out of marked race within cyberspace" (p. 214). This problem is such a significant one, Kolko argues, because "interfaces carry the power to prescribe representative norms and patterns, constructing a self-replicating and exclusionary category of 'ideal' user," a user that is almost always a "definitively White user" (p. 218). The construction of Black people and other people of color as non-technological and therefore irrelevant in the design and construction of technological tools continues even into the era of the Internet, even as those selling new technologies are quick to market a world of multicultural possibility.

TALKIN B(L)ACK TO THE DIVIDE: BLACK AGENCY IN THE JIM CROW CYBER SOUTH

Even if the persistence of exclusion and racism online make cyberspace seem   12
more like the old Jim Crow south than the age of limitless possibilities it was
sold as, Black people also have agency online, and there is a critical need to pay
attention to the ways African Americans who have crossed the Digital Divide
talk b(l)ack—to postmodern theories of race, to ideas about the role of technology in African American life, and to thoughts about how to address problems of
systematically differentiated access. In at least one place on the web, a community Web site called BlackPlanet, African American internet users respond to
these issues. Race and voice come together to do what David Holmes suggests
in "Fighting Back by Writing Black:" race and voice "can be used to map territory, create community, and ensure an ongoing sense of self—and group—
affirmation" (p. 65). In the sections that follow, I examine how BlackPlanet's
users use both language and technology to these ends, how—in this space, at
least—"race as a way of writing affords the best historical, ideological, and pedagogical response" (p. 66) to the Digital Divide. BlackPlanet's users also make
important arguments for the roles of play, experimentation, and community
building in learning and technology use, offering important cautions against the
narratives of crisis that often accompany efforts toward literacy, writing instruction, and technology access.

"Sometimes I wish they didn't even have these things in here. Kids just have   13
no idea how powerful a tool they have in front of them. If we had something like
this when we were in school, hell, I would have graduated at 15 or 16." This
comment from a Cleveland Public Library employee, says a great deal about how
people who are charged with providing technology access understand technologies, understand access. I worked part-time for the library at this time, filling in
at neighborhood branches assisting patrons when the library system was just
beginning to make computers and Internet connections available to its patrons.
Their approach to this task was to outfit each branch with four to six computers
in the hope that patrons would become more technologically literate as a result.

And the patrons responded—especially children and young adults. Librari-   14
ans and other staff members at many branches became disillusioned, however,
because these children and young adults weren't making what they saw as "productive" uses of computers or the Internet. The most popular activities were
chatting on sites like BlackPlanet, Yahoo, BlackVoices and others, downloading
music lyrics (often the uncensored versions, which really frustrated the staff),
and viewing music-related Web sites. Some branches specifically prohibited
chatting and downloading music lyrics, and some branches have policies ban-
ning these activities at certain hours.

The Cleveland Public Library employee's comment points to several issues, from cultural nostalgia to the frustration librarians and library staff feel about not being able to do more to help young people, to the potential uses students and others might put computers. I include it here to show the ways recreational uses of technologies are often seen as problematic rather than valuable. There are many people for whom a study of African Americans' recreational uses of the Internet would seem odd, or even counterproductive. There would appear to be far more important sites in which to study African American technology use and far more important kinds of online communication to study—e-mail and other workplace documents, college student writing, online student-teacher interaction, political organizations' or grassroots activists' uses of digital technologies. But there is a case to be made that African Americans' recreational uses of the Web are just as important a subject of study as any other, because those uses occur in spaces that are removed from the disciplinary forces of schools, libraries, and other organizations where literacies are taught. Ironically, these recreational uses often occur in libraries and schools. 15

As genuinely committed as many in these institutions are to providing African Americans and other people of color with meaningful access to digital technologies, that commitment is often spooked by the ghost of Quintilian's "good man speaking well"—the rhetor trained for official or public discourse. Recreational spaces like BlackPlanet allow for a fuller, more organic view of African American rhetorical production: vernacular sites like this provide the opportunity to see what patterns emerge outside the prescriptions used to prepare speakers for public communication. This look for vernacular rhetorical practices on BlackPlanet show users have taken space online to develop the kind of raced voice David Holmes, in connection with Larry Neal, Nellie McKay, Henry Louis Gates, and an entire literary and literate tradition, argue is essential to resistance to, and participation in, unwelcoming or outright racist environments. The heavy use of Black linguistic, discursive, and rhetorical patterns one finds on the site connects those traditions to digital futures, connects access to resistance and transformation, no matter how small the scale. 16

Before one even examines the site, BlackPlanet's name unmistakably announces the site's intentions. Some recognize it as an appropriation of Public Enemy's 1990 album "Fear of a Black Planet." The name announces that it is not any other hybrid, fluid space online, but rather a separate space; a space where all are welcome to visit or become members, but a distinctively Black space nonetheless. Black people "live" here, and control at least some portion of the virtual space through their uses of the site. This notion of even partial control has to be complicated somewhat: while its expressed intent is to serve 17

African American computer users, and is run by an African American CEO, BlackPlanet is not Black owned. This clearly presents limitations, but these limitations do not entirely negate the importance of the practices users engage in on the site, just as African American musicians, DJs, and club and concertgoers often danced, played, and sang in spaces that were not Black owned. Ownership is clearly important, but the cultural dimensions of language and technology use emerge even through the material relationships that determine ownership of technology companies.

BlackPlanet's potential as an underground site and one that shows the possibility of transformations of individual spaces, then, is a potential that emerges from use rather than ownership, and these uses show the degree to which members have claimed the space as their own. Black discursive conventions are the default, rather than easily dismissed as other. Tricia Rose speaks to the implications of this resetting of the default for our understandings of technologies and rhetorics in a chapter bearing the same name "Fear of a Black Planet: Rap Music and Cultural Politics in the 1990s." For Rose, the resistance inherent in rap music 18

> involves the contestation over public space, expressive meaning, interpretation, and cultural capital. In short, it is not just what one says, it is where one can say it, how others react to what one says, and whether one has the means with which to command public space. Cultural politics is not simply poetic politics, it is the struggle over context, meaning, and public space. (p. 277)

Just like with early assessments of rap and HipHop culture, much of what we want to assume is just "noise" is connected intricately to ideological, political, and rhetorical struggle. This struggle is exactly what takes place on BlackPlanet.

Individual usernames begin to show this claiming of space: space for an individual identity on the Planet, a connection to African American and Afro-diasporic culture, and public space in broader online and real world discourse. It is sometimes easy to dismiss the importance of online nicknames as merely whimsical, but their importance is clear here on BlackPlanet for several reasons. One of those reasons is that they show the site's members embracing Blackness clearly and openly, and in rich complexity, in clear opposition to theories about computers and cyberspace that assumed fragmentation and "identity tourism" would be the norm, or those theories and technology practices that assumed Whiteness as a default, because after all, "it doesn't matter who you are online." These nicknames make connections to Black musical traditions (2in2Prince, MoreHouseBlues, old-schoolmusicman, kweli, methodwoman); they claim space and authority to speak on political, cultural, and technical subjects (BlackbyDesign, WebDesignTips, liberatedlady); they proclaim Black sexuality as healthy in spite of the power of stereotypes of that sexuality (SensualOne, 19 skillz); they show members' participation in African American organizations (Blackman_06, AKATude, EasternStar); they misbehave and poke fun at assumptions about "good" behavior (legitballin, oldskoolplaya, dpimptress); they resist monolithic beauty standards and identify Black aesthetics as the standards for beauty in this space (bmorelocs, chocolate-beauty, redbonenubian). These names and the names of other members reveal complexity and diversity in notions of exactly what constitutes a Black identity but all of the users—many overtly through their usernames—participate in and claim a Black identity for themselves. These names also call attention to online identities that are free to claim all of these qualities and connections even as they question or revise them.

In her account for the rarity of African American scientists, Lois Powell   20
makes the claim in an essay "Factors Associated with the Underrepresentation of African Americans in Mathematics and Science" that African American and Latino youth avoid majoring in science because their cultures have constructed negative images of scientists and believe careers in the sciences to be unrealistic goals (p. 292). Powell asserts that these unfavorable images include those of scientists as strange, unhappy, and iconoclastic, no matter how intelligent. Although Powell seems to be genuinely concerned with increasing the numbers of African Americans pursuing mathematics and science careers, the argument seems to follow the same old conservative diatribes launched against African Americans: namely, that the problem is cultural and not systemic.

BlackPlanet users respond to this perception, though, and show that Black   21
people do connect with technologies in meaningful ways when they have access. Members "talk b(l)ack to perceptions like this by refiguring both technology and the image of the computer geek, connecting both to Black culture. Some of the forums on the site show this redefinition at work, covering topics from Linux, IT certification, tips for web designers, and Internet entrepreneurship. The language of the prompts of others might demonstrate the degree to which BP members have made technology connect with Black identity: a forum titled "what works what doesn't?" offers the following question: "What makes a good personal page? When you look at other people's personal pages on BP, what stands out?" This question might not seem significant in a discussion of cultural identity and technology, but the prompt foregrounds what other members of BP have done in establishing criteria for the broader genre of the personal web page. Another forum, "you know you are hooked on the Net when . . ." begins "OK, chat heads, techies, geeks, 'puter lovers . . . let's get real. Y'all know you spend way too much time on the Net when . . ." Black people are techies and geeks in this forum, and their use of AAVE suggests how comfortably within Black culture.

And while the joke in the prompt might suggest that Net use is discouraged, the tone and appropriation of the longstanding "you know you ghetto when" jokes show that they are accepted in the forum and on the Planet, even if they do suggest a line between being involved with technology and being hooked.

A final forum is called "Triflin Personal Pages," and leads with this comment: "Okay, I have about had it with some of these pages that are about the equivalent of Mr. T's gold chains. Too much mess!! Does anybody feel me on here?" This is a normalizing move, in which the user posting to the forum is attempting to get the group to set some expectations for page design, but of course this call looking for a response is also laced with echoes of an entire oral tradition: holla!!! Ya heard? Nahmeen?

Cross-Town Routes: Site Design and the Problem of Access

BlackPlanet's design and architecture emphasize this claiming of a separate public space, but they make that space accessible to anyone who is a part of the Planet. Although it offers a wide range of activities—almost all writing spaces of some kind; and many of them dedicated to improving technological literacy—almost everything on the site is self-contained. There are links to advertisers, of course, including gateway ads that one must click through to get to the site when one signs in, and the infamous pop up ads that have become so prevalent, but the content itself remains insular. This range of activities includes online discussions on technology, employment, relationships, gender and other identity issues; chats divided into rooms based on interests, whether "intellectual," social/sexual—"hot girls (and boys) with pics to prove it," or age-based; a personal Web page; tutorials on how to improve one's page; e-mail; news; polls; writing contests; notes and a "pager" that members use to send messages to one another. The site also allows users to search for friends (whether they are online at the time or not) based on their member profiles—a common feature on community Web sites to be sure, but one that takes on added significance with a group of people like African Americans, one with a history of rupture and displacement over generations, and often separated from other African Americans in their schools and workplaces.

Unlike many sites, the design of the homepage and the architecture of the site emphasizes the importance of all these elements. The site's structure is broad and narrow, with every Planet function either on the homepage or within one click of it. Menu bars at the top of the page and just over the fold identify community and individual functions, respectively—chats, fora, events, channels, and games at the top; notes, e-mail, the member's personal webpage, a member find function, and the pager all at the bottom. Both menu bars are available no matter where one is in the site's structure, and remain in view even

22

23

24

as a user scrolls below the fold of the homepage. The middle portion of the page features information more than the interactive functions presented in the menu bars, including news and polls. It also highlights content from other sections of the site, with links to the best member-written tutorials on HTML, for example, and the most popular discussion fora at the time (in this case a forum on holiday giving, taking online acquaintances offline, and the stock market).

The design of BlackPlanet is important because of what it implies about access. There are no parts of the Planet that are inaccessible because they are too far from home, or reachable only by way of endless rides on convoluted, barrier-maintaining bus systems, to use an urban planning metaphor. Nor do users have to wander around the site aimlessly in order to discover its content or get involved or connected with other Planet members, a connection that is one of the site's main goals. 25

HOLLA! OR, I NEED THEM HITS: COMING TO VOICE THROUGH STRUCTURED FEEDBACK

That goal, of developing an online community through various kinds of member interaction, informs the design of the interfaces of other BlackPlanet spaces as well. The personal web page and the profile that goes on it—what might be the two most important features on the entire site, in terms of the development and uses of a Black online voice—are template-driven. BP members can choose backgrounds, text sizes and colors, and receive feedback on their pages without knowing a thing about how to design, write, or code a web page. The focus here is to get people to establish themselves online as easily as possible, and then help them learn what they want to know as they go. This approach to technical communication might irk some like Johndan Johnson-Eilola, given his irritation with tacky web pages and WYSIWYG (what you see is what you get—web page editors like Netscape Composer that don't require users to know how to code their own pages) application users who are clueless about the rhetoric of web pages, as he explains in "Little Machines: Rearticulating Hypertext Writing." 26

But BlackPlanet's approach to teaching users would meet the exact challenge he raises as well: namely, to reestablish the social element of online writing instruction (in his case, technical instruction). Users learn from interaction with and guidance from more experienced users rather than just using a product and never learning anything about what lies behind, or underneath, the interface. This socialized instruction also contributes to the creation of a community—the exchange of feedback and guidance about personal pages helps the millions of users (10,500,000 at the time of this writing) forge connections with each other that ensure the growth of the community and the discursive conventions that develop within it. 27

In addition to the direct instruction that the site gives, in the way of   28
member-written tutorials and tips on subjects like HTML, or incorporating
music on one's page, or how to actually describe one's interests in interesting
ways, BP members also get direct feedback on their pages from other members
through the notes and guestbook entries, and indirect feedback from the hit
counters on every member's page. The guestbook reinforces the metaphor that
the member's personal page is her or his home on the Planet, and members regularly ask each other to visit their pages and sign each others' guestbooks. They
sometimes initiate that contact by visiting random pages and leaving feedback
themselves, along with a request that the recipient return the favor; or including a "tag" next to their posts in the chats asking people to visit their pages,
and/or by advertising that they have pictures, tips, or other content that people
want to see. Visitors to someone's "home" on the Planet can sign the guestbook,
or "lick the g-spot" in the Planet's vernacular. Members crave those notes, those
licks, those hits, because they provide connection with other members, because
that "holla" signifies that other members were moved to respond to something
that member had to say about herself or her world. In addition to comments
reaffirming things a visitor liked about a particular member's page, guestbook
entries and notes are used to make suggestions about how to improve the page
or give technical advice on various coding tricks, or sources for graphics, links,
or other content relevant to the subjects the member is interested in.

Individual member pages are so important on the Planet because they are   29
available from everywhere else on the site. For example, when one enters a chat
room, the user will see a list of the members in that room, but will also be able to
link immediately to those members' pages while they chat. The discussion fora
operate in the same way: they allow members to link to the page of anyone who
has posted, rather than just show the username. Any search of member profiles
will allow one to go directly to member pages as well, instead of providing just a
profile as some sites like Yahoo! does. In other words, members' pages, their
homes and identities on the Web are always available to everyone else. One can
see the page of any member who has given advice on how to create a web page
and see how that member incorporates her or his own advice. Members get ideas
on everything from how a page should look, to the range of possibilities one has
in creating a page, to how to write about one's personality and interests, and give
feedback because of these mechanisms. Community works to reinforce individual
identity on BlackPlanet through these functions, however similar to, or different
from, members' real life identities they might be. The availability of the personal
pages, at all times, a page design that incorporates multiple levels of feedback,
and users who crave that feedback show that, in this online space, individual
voices are still created in distinctively Black community contexts.

GOING INTO THE UNDERGROUND: AFRICAN AMERICAN DISCURSIVE FEATURES ONLINE

Knowing that there is an African American discourse community online that
operates in something of an "underground" is one thing, as is to know that the
design of this community, the interaction within it, and individual members attitudes claim a distinct African American identity in the midst of theories of fragmentation and alienation are important, but that still leaves the question of the
specific characteristics of the discourse that is produced in that space, and the
relationship it holds with the oral tradition Smitherman (2000) describes: "as we
shall see in closely examining the many facets of the oral tradition, the residue of
the African world view persists, and serves to unify such seemingly disparate
Black groups as preachers and poets, bluesmen and Gospel-ettes, testifiers and
toast-tellers, reverends and revolutionaries. Can I get a witness?" (p. 201). Not
only are all the figures Smitherman lists present in this online community, but so
are all of the modes of discourse she develops in this article: call and response,
mimicry, signifyin', testifyin', exaggerated language, proverbial statements, pun-
ning, spontaneity, image-making, braggadocio, indirection, and tonal semantics
(pp. 217–222). The presence of these modes online show the ways that the
"structural underpinnings of the oral tradition remain basically intact even as
each new generation makes verbal adaptations within the tradition. Indeed the
core strength of this tradition lies in its capacity to accommodate new situations
and changing realities" (p. 199), but they are central to it—without these discursive practices from an African American oral tradition, BlackPlanet, a writing
space, an electronic writing space at that, could not exist.

    Given the fact that most attention paid to African American language and
discourse in Composition has focused around AAVE or Ebonics—the grammatical, phonological, and semantic features of African American English, it is safe
to assume that many interested in this subject would visit the Planet looking for
these features on the pages, chats, and fora. Those visitors would find plenty of
what they came for too: copula variation, distinctly African American lexical
items (including, but not limited to, slang), existential it, pronunciation variation, invariant be, the absence of third person singular—s—all those features
and more are present in many different places on the site. And they are often
celebrated, rather than disparaged in chats and on personal pages. In fact,
BlackPlanet would be an excellent linguistic site in which to study what exactly
what features of AAVE do appear, with what regularity, and under what circumstances. But this isn't the issue I'm concerned with here—what's fascinating
about BlackPlanet, for me, is the degree to which users have written an oral tradition into cyberspace. While I maintain that all of the modes of discourse that
Smitherman identifies are present on BlackPlanet, I focus on the presence of
two: tonal semantics and sermonic tone. These three features show most clearly

the degree to which African American oral traditions dominate discourse on BlackPlanet.

Tonal semantics refers to the ways that intonation in a word or a phrase   32
can change its meaning. The example Smitherman and others frequently give is of the differences that can occur in the meaning of the word police when pronounced in the typical iambic pattern of English (poLICE) and when dramatic emphasis is given to the first syllable, the POlice. Part of what's involved is changes in meaning of words or phrases, and part of it is the speaker's ability to "get meaning and rhetorical mileage by triggering a familiar sound chord in the listener's ear. The words may or may not make sense; what is crucial is the rapper's [in this case, the rapper that existed before rap music: anyone can be a rapper in this sense] ability to make the words sound good. They will use rhyme, voice rhythm, repetition of key sounds and letters" (p. 222). This is a good deal to ask someone to be able to represent in writing. While BlackPlanet users certainly don't use tonal semantics to the degree that two African American speakers would in conversation, or a preacher would in addressing an audience, what is potentially surprising is the degree to which it does exist. It is used very frequently in chat rooms, with possibly as much as 30% of all utterances containing some form of tonal semantics. It is used most often in the greetings extended to people entering or leaving the room. These greetings show which members are regular members and are liked, respected, disliked, ignored, as well as new members who have not become part of that section of the Planet yet. Tonal semantics is expressed by altering spellings of words to alter tone or pitch, by shortening or elongating them to affect duration and/or pitch, and sometimes (but less often) by even appropriating the real world voices of well known figures like James Earl Jones or 1990s rapper/singer Michele' (known to have a very high, squeaky, irritating voice). Other typographic features can be used as well, like parentheses, punctuation marks—especially exclamation points, question marks, periods, and ellipses—as well as the size of the type (BlackPlanet only allows two sizes in chat, small and large). Thus, someone named "rawdawg" might be greeted by several people at once: 'sup raw/rawwwwwwww/ RAWWWW whas poppin patna???? (((((((((((((raw))))))))))))))))))/ RAWWWWWWWWWWWW (((hugs))) hey baby!!!!!, where each would have different meanings and would suggest different connections between the greeter and rawdawg. Tonal semantics might also be used when one is having a semiprivate conversation with a person in the public context of the chatroom, or when one is trying to get the conversation of the group.

Sermonic tone is a relatively new trope in Smitherman's (2000) canon; it   33
refers to the ways in which plain statements are given a gravity similar to that of

Sunday morning homiletic: "ordinary statements take on the tone of pronounce-ments and are given the force of the moral high ground; they are proclaimed with the profundity and moral sobriety of divinely inspired truth. This gives Black speech its elevated, fancy talk quality" (p. 260). The sermonic tone can be like a hyperbolic parable or fable, but without any story to illustrate its moral. The moral is taken for granted and pronounced from on high, as it were, reiterat-ing both its simplicity and the exigence for its utterance, since obviously y'all ain't got it yet. Many times these statements are made in an elevated language register, heightening the effect but this is not a necessary condition, as much of this tone has to do with the attitude of the speaker. The speaker has become a self-anointed preacher in these moments having taken on the power to glorify or condemn. This connection with the church is crucial, as Smitherman points out, because it is the church that has developed—in some way—almost every African American leader in the public sphere (p. 260). Although Smitherman focuses on the figure of the preacher and points out that this leadership was largely male, this tone was available to everyone, especially outside the church.

This particular trope is very important in a discussion of African American   34
discourse online because that identification with the Black preacher and the adoption of the sermonic tone amounts to his or her assertively claiming authority, taking permission to speak, on a subject he or she has decided has larger importance. To do this in an online space given the conditions of tech-nology access and the ways technology and cyberspace are constructed as White, is a critical disruption of those constructions, and, again, reminders that both race and culture carry definite meaning online. And it happens all the time on BlackPlanet, both in users' own writing, and their appropriation of other texts on their behalf.

On her personal page, one user, Moonlyt1, invokes the sermonic tone in   35
both her own words and her use of those of others:

Be Strong.

We are not here to play, dream, or drift. We've got hard work to do and heavy loads to lift. Shun not the struggle, for it is God's gift.

Be Strong.

—*unknown*

Let's chat . . .

I have an appetite for more information about African Americans and our involvement in the political process. I don't believe our voice has been col-lectively strong enough to cut through the clutter and make a difference in our communities.

Cleveland just elected its first female mayor, who begins January 7. Our Black Congresswoman is considering a bid for governor, and we may not have someone to replace her if she wins . . .

*What can we as African Americans do to prepare our next generation of leaders?

*How do we even identify who those should be?

*How do we make our voices heard to the folks currently in office?

I welcome an open dialogue on the subject. Hit me up, tell me what you think, and let me know if you've come across interesting web sites, magazine articles, or books I should get at.

Peace and love ...

In this excerpt, Moonlyt1 identifies herself as someone interested in political issues facing Cleveland and African-Americans in general. But through her use of the short verse "Be Strong," her descriptions of her interests, and her questions, she becomes an exhorter, attempting to foster a different kind of conversation than what normally occurs on recreational chat-based websites. Moonlyt1's voice takes on the sermonic tone, with interesting adjustments for the site's audience. Her particular voice in this space is a hybrid of formal and informal registers: the best example of this is the last paragraph: "I welcome an open dialogue on the subject. Hit me up. . . ."

The section begins with a general pronouncement about the state of Black   36 involvement in politics, moves on to a specific discussion of the case in Cleveland, a city with a history of deeply-rooted involvement of its African American community and portending trouble in the future. It then moves on to questions used to make the exhortation more direct—Moonlyt1's page is not merely a pronouncement, but a call in the best of the preaching tradition. By this point the user has become the pastor issuing the conventional invitation to fellowship after the sermon: "won't you come?" Moonlyt1's invocation of the preacher's voice in her space on the Net is significant beyond the specific dialogue she hopes to spark. As important as the role of the preacher in Black culture has always been, that role has almost always been gendered as male, with women overtly prohibited from taking leadership in churches and in Black communities. Bettye Collier-Thomas (1998) provides a context for utterances like Moonlyt1's in her book *Daughters of Thunder: Black Women Preachers and Their Sermons,* noting that in spite of the obstacles to leadership in the church Black women have always "come forth to pursue the prize—the pulpit." Personal Web pages and other online writing spaces allow women to claim those pulpits and to assume the authority they seek, unfettered by the assumptions and processes that would silence that authority.

The existence of spaces where one can be comfortable with who she is and position herself as someone with something valuable to say on issues in which she has a stake—Compositionists have long made the argument that this is what matters most in developing students with strong writing, speaking, and designing voices. Although BlackPlanet is by no means an ideal site, even for African Americans, and there is much that might trouble some about the recreational uses to which people put computers and the Internet, still there is much to learn from the underground sites where people new to any discursive situation have a chance to "get their game tight:" to learn the conventions, to experiment with voice, and tone, and craft; to get feedback that they actually want from people they will listen to; while in an environment where simplistic judgments about grammatical features do not lead to their discursive and intellectual complexity being entirely dismissed and/or their continued segregation from others whose voices are often just as raw.

THE BLACKER THE DISCURSIVE BERRY, THE SWEETER THE RHETORICAL JUICE

While there is much to learn from this and other sites, the major implication of this look at BlackPlanet ought to be clear. Composition's stubborn, narrow focus on the grammatical features of a language, and insistence on waging a limiting debate on Ebonics do not work in theory or in writing practice. This stubbornness, in spite of Smitherman's (2000) own work focusing on discursive features and rhetorical traditions, and her study of nearly 3,000 student essays in the National Assessment of Educational Progress over a 20-year period showing that "the Blacker the berry the sweeter the juice"—that "the more discernibly African American the *discourse*, the higher the primary trait and holistic scores; the less discernibly African American the discourse, the lower the primary trait and holistic scores" (p. 184). Not just the sermonic tone, but African American discourse in general shows what can happen when students and other writers genuinely do have the right to their own language: they claim the right to speak, take the space to do it, and become invested in doing it thoroughly and effectively, and develop rhetorical savvy. As the field questions the roles new communication technologies will play in Composition theory and instruction, and begins to seriously examine questions of access, it has an opportunity to reexamine old assumptions about race, language, and technology. Neither technology, nor the English language, nor Composition *have* to continue to be White by definition.

Just as Composition needs far more study of African American discursive   39
practices that take those discursive practices seriously, in their own right,
untainted by deficit models of language use, it needs more careful consideration
of how its teachers and researchers will create spaces that serve students better
in a technological landscape that puts many more communicative demands on
both student and teachers. To this end, this study offers three areas we can use
to ask exactly how it is we want our courses to be "used" toward students' development of rhetorical and technological mastery:

1. Like the library employee, we might worry far too much about the negative
   results of student behavior in recreational spaces and not enough about how
   they might benefit from them. When we provide them with rich discursive
   spaces and multiple opportunities for feedback, they will often help each
   other come to voice, even if those spaces allow for some amount of play.
2. Related to our skittishness about student "play" is a need we still feel to
   control every aspect of student work and interaction. This need often
   results in courses that are still designed far more around surveillance and
   control, far more around a willingness to do the university's police work for
   it, than around help students gain access to the university. We can counter
   this impulse toward control by including richly conceived underground
   spaces that students control. These spaces have encouraging student writing and design as their goals, and should give students a chance to get varied kinds of feedback they actually want from each other.
3. We still need to be primarily about the business of improving access to our
   courses and the university as best we can, and this is a design issue. We
   need to design courses students can actually navigate, with transparent
   organizing schemes, interfaces that don't hide the codes that really determine how our courses work, and give students many ways to find their ways
   back "home," wherever they might find themselves at any given moment.

There are many other examples of potentially transformative uses African   40
Americans have made of different technologies; these uses suggest possibilities
for both making meaningful change in the designs of Rhetoric and Composition
courses, and offer a hint of the kinds of knowledge users—particularly African
American users—can contribute to that effort.

Rhetoric and Composition poses the exact same kind of challenge for stu-   41
dents and faculty who take, design, and teach its courses as BlackPlanet does for
its users—African Americans do not have real ownership or control in the field,
even as one accounts for the tremendous accomplishments of eight former
African American chairs of Conference on College Composition and Communi-

cation (CCCC). Just as African American users of BlackPlanet find ways to create underground spaces that honor and build on Black discursive practices toward larger goals of rhetorical and technological mastery, "users" of Rhetoric and Composition can focus on creating similar spaces outside the larger controls of the academy, the society, and the discursive practices that dominate the field. As this is only one exploration of one figurative planet in the digital universe, there is obviously much more work to be done before identifying specific pedagogical practices that can guide the field. But it suggests the most important work we can do on behalf of our students is not knowledge work or critical work, but design work, work in creating the spaces in which they will communicate.

This is not an argument that teachers' knowledge and composition's history   42
of critical engagement are not important. This is not an argument that teachers can best serve students by simply creating spaces and then getting out of the way, an argument whose strongest versions are profoundly irresponsible to me. But there are times we can get out of the way and share some control, are moments when we can provide students with underground spaces, both online and off that are theirs, as one of the many goals we pursue. Stephen Doheny-Farina (2000), in his work, *The Wired Neighborhood*, quotes Tom Grundner, creator of the Cleveland Free-Net, in a vision of the Internet that can also guide Rhetoric and Composition and the spaces it designs for students:

> America's progress toward an equitable Information Age will not be measured by the number of people we can make dependent on the Internet. Rather it is the reverse. It will be measured by the number of local systems we can build, using local resources, to meet local needs. Our progress will not be measured by the number of college educated people we can bring online—but by the number of blue collar workers and farmers and families we can bring online. It will not be measured by the number of people who can access the card-catalog at the University of Paris, but by the number of people who can find out what's going on at their kids' school, or get information about the latest flu bug which is going around their community. (p. 125)

Imagining Rhetoric and Composition as a kind of community network, or   43
even "freenet" would similarly avoid becoming lost in a notion of so-called Standard English as a mythical promised land that we must deliver students to and make them buy into. Instead, the field could be guided by a vision that makes its courses dependent on their responsiveness to the wide variety of local situations students bring to them, a vision of many different paths toward the freedom that rhetorical excellence can (but does not necessarily) provide. The next chapter offers some particular principles that can guide that design for those willing to commit to it.

REFERENCES

Collier-Thomas, B. (1998). *Daughter of thunder: Black women preachers and their sermons*. San Francisco: Jossey-Bass.

Doheny-Farina, S. (2000). *The wired neighborhood*. New Haven, CT: Yale University Press.

Holmes, D.G. (1999). Fighting back by writing Black: Beyond racially reductive composition theory. In K. Gilyard (Ed.) *Race, rhetoric, and composition* (pp. 53–56). Portsmouth, NH: Boynton/Cook.

Kolko, B.E. (2000). Erasing @race: Going White in the (inter)face. In B. E. Kolko, L. Nakamura, & G. B. Rodman (Eds). *Race in cyberspace* (pp. 213–232). New York: Routledge.

Powell, L. (1990). Factors associated with the underrepresentation of African Americans in mathematics and science. *Journal of Negro Education, 59*(3), 292–298.

Rickford, J. R., & John, R. (2000). *Spoken soul: The story of Black English*. New York: Wiley.

Rose, T. (1991). Fear of a Black planet: Rap music and Black cultural politics in the 1990s. *Journal of Negro Education, 60*(3), 276–290.

Smitherman, G. (1986). *Talkin and testifyin: The language of Black America*. Detroit, MI: Wayne State University Press.

Smitherman, G. (2000). *Talkin that talk: Language, culture, and education in African America*. New York: Routledge.

Dennis Baron (1944–) has been professor of English and Linguistics at the University of Illinois at Urbana-Champaign since 1975 and has written seven books and monographs on grammar, the English language, and medieval English, including *Guide to Home Language Repair* (1994).

FROM PENCILS TO PIXELS: THE STAGES OF LITERACY TECHNOLOGY

Dennis Baron

The computer, the latest development in writing technology, promises, or threatens, to change literacy practices for better or worse, depending on your point of view. For many of us, the computer revolution came long ago, and it has left its mark on the way we do things with words. We take word processing as a given. We don't have typewriters in our offices anymore, or pencil sharpeners, or even printers with resolutions less than 300 dpi. We scour *MacUser* and *PC World* for the next software upgrade, cheaper RAM, faster chips, and the latest in connectivity. We can't wait for the next paradigm shift.

Computerspeak enters ordinary English at a rapid pace. In 1993, "the information superhighway" was voted the word—actually the phrase—of the year. In 1995, the word of the year was "the World Wide Web," with "morph" a close runner-up. The computer is also touted as a gateway to literacy. The Speaker of the House of Representatives suggested that inner-city school children should try laptops to improve their performance. The Governor of Illinois thinks that hooking up every school classroom to the Web will eliminate illiteracy. In his second-term victory speech, President Clinton promised to have every eight-year-old reading, and to connect every twelve-year-old to the National Information Infrastructure. Futurologists write books predicting that computers will replace books. Newspapers rush to hook on-line subscribers. The *New York Times* will download the Sunday crossword puzzle, time me as I fill in the answers from my keyboard, even score my results. They'll worry later about how to get me to pay for this service.

1

2

Dennis Baron, "From Pencils to Pixels: The Stages of Literacy Technologies" from *Passions, Pedagogies, and 21st Century Technologies*, ed. Gail E. Hawisher and Cynthia L. Selfe, pp. 15-33. Copyright © 1999 Utah State University Press. Reprinted by permission of Utah State University Press. Figure 1: Illustrations by Alan D. Iselin, appeared originally in Denise Schmandt-Besserat, "The Earliest Precursor of Writing," *Scientific American*, June 1978. Figure 5: Digital image created by Jack Harris/Visual Logic from *Scientific American*, February 1994. © 1994 by Jack Harris/Visual Logic. Reprinted with permission; original photograph of Marilyn Monroe courtesy of Personality Photos, Inc., www.personalityphotos.com; original photograph of Abraham Lincoln by Alexander Gardner (1863). Cartoon reprinted by permission of Dennis Baron.

I will not join in the hyperbole of predictions about what the computer will   3
or will not do for literacy, though I will be the first to praise computers, to
acknowledge the importance of the computer in the last fifteen years of my own
career as a writer, and to predict that in the future the computer will be put to
communication uses we cannot now even begin to imagine, something quite
beyond the word-processing I'm now using to produce a fairly conventional
text, a book chapter.

I readily admit my dependence on the new technology of writing. Once,   4
called away to a meeting whose substance did not command my unalloyed
attention, I began drafting on my conference pad a memo I needed to get out to
my staff by lunchtime. I found that I had become so used to composing virtual
prose at the keyboard I could no longer draft anything coherent directly onto a
piece of paper. It wasn't so much that I couldn't think of the words, but the
physical effort of handwriting, crossing out, revising, cutting and pasting (which
I couldn't very well do at a meeting without giving away my inattention), in
short, the writing practices I had been engaged in regularly since the age of four,
now seemed to overwhelm and constrict me, and I longed for the flexibility of
digitized text.

When we write with cutting-edge tools, it is easy to forget that whether it   5
consists of energized particles on a screen or ink embedded in paper or lines
gouged into clay tablets, writing itself is always first and foremost a technology,
a way of engineering materials in order to accomplish an end. Tied up as it is
with value-laden notions of literacy, art, and science, of history and psychology,
of education, of theory, and of practicality, we often lose sight of writing as
technology, until, that is, a new technology like the computer comes along and
we are thrown into excitement and confusion as we try it on, try it out, reject it,
and then adapt it to our lives—and of course, adapt our lives to it.

New communications technologies, if they catch on, go through a number   6
of strikingly similar stages. After their invention, their spread depends on acces-
sibility, function, and authentication. Let me first summarize what I mean, and
then I'll present some more detailed examples from the history of writing or literacy technologies to illustrate.

The Stages of Literacy Technologies

Each new literacy technology begins with a restricted communications function   7
and is available only to a small number of initiates. Because of the high cost of
the technology and general ignorance about it, practitioners keep it to themselves at first—either on purpose or because nobody else has any use for it—and
then, gradually, they begin to mediate the technology for the general public. The

technology expands beyond this "priestly" class when it is adapted to familiar functions often associated with an older, accepted form of communication. As costs decrease and the technology becomes better able to mimic more ordinary or familiar communications, a new literacy spreads across a population. Only then does the technology come into its own, no longer imitating the previous forms given us by the earlier communications technology but creating new forms and new possibilities for communication. Moreover, in a kind of backward wave, the new technology begins to affect older technologies as well.

While brave new literacy technologies offer new opportunities for produc- 8
ing and manipulating text, they also present new opportunities for fraud. And as the technology spreads, so do reactions against it from supporters of what are purported to be older, simpler, better, or more honest ways of writing. Not only must the new technology be accessible and useful, it must demonstrate its trust-worthiness as well. So procedures for authentication and reliability must be developed before the new technology becomes fully accepted. One of the great-est concerns about computer communications today involves their authentica-tion, and their potential for fraud.

My contention in this essay is a modest one: the computer is simply the latest 9
step in a long line of writing technologies. In many ways its development parallels that of the pencil—hence my title—though the computer seems more complex and is undoubtedly more expensive. The authenticity of pencil writing is still fre-quently questioned: we prefer that signatures and other permanent or validating documents be in ink. Although I'm not aware that anyone actually opposed the use of pencils when they began to be used for writing, other literacy technologies, including writing itself, were initially met with suspicion as well as enthusiasm.

Humanists and Technology

In attacking society's growing dependence on communication technology, the 10
Unabomber (1996) targeted computer scientists for elimination. But to my cha-grin he excluded humanists from his list of sinister technocrats because he found them to be harmless. While I was glad not to be a direct target of this mad bomber, I admit that I felt left out. I asked myself, if humanists aren't harmful, then what's the point of being one? But I was afraid to say anything out loud, at least until a plausible suspect was in custody.

Humanists have long been considered out of the technology loop. They use 11
technology, to be sure, but they are not generally seen as pushing the envelope. Most people think of writers as rejecting technological innovations like the com-puter and the information superhighway, preferring instead to bang away at manual typewriters when they are not busy whittling new points on their no. 2 quill pens.

And it is true that some well-known writers have rejected new-fangleness. 12
Writing in the *New York Times*, Bill Henderson (1994) reminds us that in 1849
Henry David Thoreau disparaged the information superhighway of his day, a
telegraph connection from Maine to Texas. As Thoreau put it, "Maine and
Texas, it may be, have nothing important to communicate." Henderson, who is
a director of the Lead Pencil Club, a group opposed to computers and con-
vinced that the old ways are better, further boasts that Thoreau wrote his anti-
technology remarks with a pencil that he made himself. Apparently Samuel
Morse, the developer of the telegraph, was lucky that the only letter bombs
Thoreau made were literary ones.

In any case, Thoreau was not the complete Luddite that Henderson would 13
have us believe. He was, in fact, an engineer, and he didn't make pencils for the
same reason he went to live at Walden Pond, to get back to basics. Rather, he
designed them for a living. Instead of waxing nostalgic about the good old days
of hand-made pencils, Thoreau sought to improve the process by developing a
cutting-edge manufacturing technology of his own.

The pencil may be old, but like the computer today and the telegraph in 14
1849, it is an indisputable example of a communications technology. Henderson unwittingly concedes as much when he adds that Thoreau's father founded
"the first quality pencil [factory] in America." In Thoreau's day, a good pencil
was hard to find, and until Thoreau's father and uncle began making pencils in
the New World, the best ones were imported from Europe. The family fortune
was built on the earnings of the Thoreau Pencil Company, and Henry Thoreau
not only supported his sojourn at Walden Pond and his trip to the Maine woods
with pencil profits, he himself perfected some of the techniques of pencil-making that made Thoreau pencils so desirable.

The pencil may seem a simple device in contrast to the computer, but 15
although it has fewer parts, it too is an advanced technology. The engineer
Henry Petroski (1990) portrays the development of the wood-cased pencil as a
paradigm of the engineering process, hinging on the solution of two essential
problems: finding the correct blend of graphite and clay so that the "lead" is not
too soft or too brittle; and getting the lead into the cedar wood case so that it
doesn't break when the point is sharpened or when pressure is applied during
use. Pencil technologies involve advanced design techniques, the preparation
and purification of graphite, the mixing of graphite with various clays, the bak-
ing and curing of the lead mixture, its extrusion into leads, and the preparation
and finishing of the wood casings. Petroski observes that pencil making also
involves a knowledge of dyes, shellacs, resins, clamps, solvents, paints, woods,
rubber, glue, printing ink, waxes, lacquer, cotton, drying equipment, impregnat-

ing processes, high-temperature furnaces, abrasives, and mixing (Petroski, 12). These are no simple matters. A hobbyist cannot decide to make a wood-cased pencil at home and go out to the craft shop for a set of instructions. Pencil-making processes were from the outset proprietary secrets as closely guarded as any Macintosh code.

The development of the pencil is also a paradigm of the development of literacy. In the two hundred fifty years between its invention, in the 1560s, and its perfection at John Thoreau and Company, as well as in the factories of Conté in France, and Staedtler and Faber in Germany, the humble wood pencil underwent several changes in form, greatly expanded its functions, and developed from a curiosity of use to cabinet-makers, artists and note-takers into a tool so universally employed for writing that we seldom give it any thought. 16

The Technology of Writing

Of course the first writing technology was writing itself. Just like the telegraph and the computer, writing itself was once an innovation strongly resisted by traditionalists because it was unnatural and untrustworthy. Plato was one leading thinker who spoke out strongly against writing, fearing that it would weaken our memories. Pessimistic complaints about new literacy technologies, like those made by Plato, by Bill Henderson, and by Henderson's idol, Henry David Thoreau, are balanced by inflated predictions of how technologies will change our lives for the better. According to one school of anthropology, the invention of writing triggered a cognitive revolution in human development (for a critique of this so-called Great Divide theory of writing, see Street 1984). Historians of print are fond of pointing to the invention of the printing press in Europe as the second great cognitive revolution (Eisenstein 1979). The spread of electric power, the invention of radio, and later television, all promised similar bio-cultural progress. Now, the influence of computers on more and more aspects of our existence has led futurologists to proclaim that another technological threshold is at hand. Computer gurus offer us a brave new world of communications where we will experience cognitive changes of a magnitude never before known. Of course, the Unabomber and the Lead Pencil Club think otherwise. 17

Both the supporters and the critics of new communication technologies like to compare them to the good, or bad, old days. Jay Bolter disparages the typewriter as nothing more than a machine for duplicating text, and as such, he argues, it has not changed writing at all. In contrast, Bolter characterizes the computer as offering a paradigm shift not seen since the invention of the printing press, or for that matter, since the invention of writing itself. But when the 18 typewriter first began to sweep across America's offices, it too promised to change writing radically, in ways never before imagined. So threatening was the typewriter to the traditional literatus that in 1938 the *New York Times* editorialized against the machine that depersonalized writing, usurping the place of "writing with one's own hand."

The development of writing itself illustrates the stages of technological   19 spread. We normally assume that writing was invented to transcribe speech, but that is not strictly correct. The earliest Sumerian inscriptions, dating from ca. 3500 BCE, record not conversations, incantations, or other sorts of oral utterances, but land sales, business transactions, and tax accounts (Crystal 1987). Clay tokens bearing similar marks appear for several thousand years before these first inscriptions. It is often difficult to tell when we are dealing with writing and when with art (the recent discovery of 10,000-year-old stone carvings in Syria has been touted as a possible missing link in the art-to-writing chain), but the tokens seem to have been used as a system of accounting from at least the 9th millennium BCE. They are often regarded as the first examples of writing, and it is clear that they are only distantly related to actual speech (see figure 1).

We cannot be exactly sure why writing was invented, but just as the gurus   20 of today's technology are called computer geeks, it's possible that the first writers also seemed like a bunch of oddballs to the early Sumerians, who might have called them cuneiform geeks. Surely they walked around all day with a bunch of sharp styluses sticking out of their pocket protectors, and talked of nothing but new ways of making marks on stones. Anyway, so far as we know, writing itself begins not as speech transcription but as a relatively restricted and obscure record-keeping shorthand.

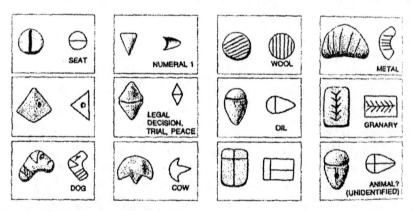

Figure 1   Clay Tokens and Sumerian Inscriptions

Clay tokens. Some of the commonest shapes are here compared with the incised characters in the earliest Sumerian inscriptions (only some of which have been interpreted) (Crystal 1987, 196).

As innovative uses for the literacy technology are tried out, practitioners   21
may also adapt it to older, more familiar forms in order to gain acceptance from
a wider group. Although writing began as a tool of the bean counters, it eventually added a second, magical/religious function, also restricted and obscure as a
tool of priests. For writing to spread into a more general population in the
ancient world, it had first to gain acceptance by approximating spoken language. Once writers—in a more "modern" sense of the word—discovered what
writing could do, there was no turning back. But even today, most written text
does not transcribe spoken language: the comparison of script and transcript in
figure 2 makes this abundantly clear.

Of course writing never spread very greatly in the ancient world. William   22
Harris (1989) argues convincingly that no more than ten percent of the classical
Greek or Roman populations could have been literate. One reason for this must
be that writing technology remained both cumbersome and expensive: writing
instruments, paints, and inks had to be hand made, and writing surfaces like clay
tablets, wax tablets, and papyrus had to be laboriously prepared. Writing therefore
remained exclusive, until cheap paper became available, and the printing press
made mass production of written texts more affordable and less labor-intensive.

Scripted dialogue:

Thersites: The common curse of mankind, folly and ignorance, be thine
in great revenue! heaven bless thee from a tutor, and discipline come not
near thee! Let thy blood be thy direction till thy death! then, if she that lays
thee out says thou art a fair corpse, I'll be sworn upon't she never shrouded
any but lazars. Amen.

Shakespeare, Troilus and Cressida, II, iii, 30.

Unscripted dialogue (Ostensibly):

Lt. Col. North: I do not recall a specific discussion. But, I mean. It was
widely known within the CIA. I mean we were tracking that sensitive intelligence. I—I honestly don't recall, Mr. Van Cleve. I mean it—it didn't seem
to me, at the time, that it was something that I was trying to hide from anybody. I was not engaged in it. And one of the purposes that I thought we had
that finding for was to go back and ratify that earlier action, and to get on
with replenishing. I mean, that was one—what I understood one of the purposes of the draft to be.

from Taking the Stand: The Testimony of Lt. Col. Oliver North, 15.

Figure 2   Script and Transcript

What Writing Does Differently

As a literacy technology like writing begins to become established, it also goes   23
beyond the previous technology in innovative, often compelling ways. For
example, while writing cannot replace many speech functions, it allows us to
communicate in ways that speech does not. Writing lacks such tonal cues of the
human voice as pitch and stress, not to mention the physical cues that accompany face-to-face communication, but it also permits new ways of bridging time
and space. Conversations become letters. Sagas become novels. Customs
become legal codes. The written language takes on a life of its own, and it even
begins to influence how the spoken language is used. To cite an obvious example, people begin to reject traditional pronunciations in favor of those that
reflect a word's spelling: the pronunciation of the "l" in "falcon" (compare the
l-less pronunciation of the cognate name Faulkner) and the "h" in such "th"
combinations as *Anthony* and *Elizabeth* (compare the nicknames *Tony* and *Betty*,
which reflect the earlier, h-less pronunciation).

In order to gain acceptance, a new literacy technology must also develop a   24
means of authenticating itself. Michael Clanchy (1993) reports that when writing was introduced as a means of recording land transfer in 11th-century England, it was initially perceived (and often rightly so) as a nasty Norman trick for
stealing Saxon land.

As Clanchy notes, spoken language was easily corroborated: human wit-   25
nesses were interactive. They could be called to attest whether or not a property
transfer had taken place. Doubters could question witnesses, watch their eyes,
see whether witnesses sank when thrown bound into a lake. Written documents
did not respond to questions—they were not interactive. So the writers and
users of documents had to develop their own means of authentication. At first,
seals, knives, and other symbolic bits of property were attached to documents in
an attempt to give them credibility. Medieval English land transfers also
adopted the format of texts already established as trustworthy, the Bible or the
prayer book, complete with illuminations, in order to convince readers of their
validity.

Questions of validity came up because writing was indeed being used to per-   26
petrate fraud. Monks, who controlled writing technology in England at the
time, were also responsible for some notorious forgeries used to snatch land from
private owners. As writing technology developed over the centuries, additional
ways of authenticating text came into use. Individualistic signatures eventually
replaced seals to the extent that today, many people's signatures differ significantly from the rest of their handwriting. Watermarks identified the provenance of paper; dates and serial numbers further certify documents, and in the

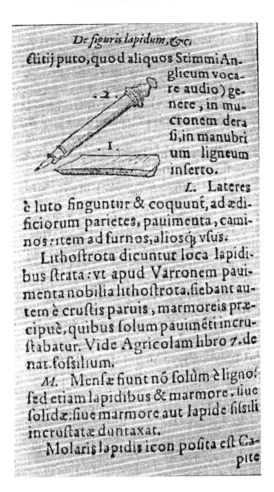

Figure 3 De Figuris Lapidum

Translation: "The stylus . . . is made . . . from a sort of lead (which I have heard some call English antimony), shaved to a point and inserted in a wooden handle." From *De rerum fossilium lapidum et gemmarum maxime, figuris et similitudinibus liber,* a book on the shapes and images of fossils, esp. those in stone and rock. Gesner wrote a Greek-Latin dictionary, was a doctor, lectured on physics, and, obviously, was a rock hound.

absence of other authenticators, stylistic analysis may allow us to guess at authorship on the basis of comparative and internal textual evidence. In the digital age, we are faced with the interesting task of reinventing appropriate ways to validate cybertext.

The Pencil as Technology

Just as writing was not designed initially as a way of recording speech, the pencil was not invented to be a writing device. The ancient lead-pointed stylus was used to scribe lines—the lead made a faint pencil-like mark on a surface, suitable for marking off measurements but not for writing. The modern pencil, which holds not lead but a piece of graphite encased in a wooden handle, doesn't come on the scene until the 1560s.

The 16th-century pencil consists of a piece of graphite snapped or shaved   28
from a larger block, then fastened to a handle for ease of use. The first pencils were made by joiners, woodworkers specializing in making furniture, to scribe measurements in wood. Unlike the traditional metal-pointed scribing tools, pencils didn't leave a permanent dent in the wood. By the time Gesner observed the pencil, it had been adopted as a tool by note-takers, natural scientists or others who needed to write, sketch, or take measurements in the field. Carrying pens and ink pots outdoors was cumbersome. Early pencils had knobs at one end so that they could be fastened with string or chain to a notebook, creating the precursor to the laptop computer.

Pencils were also of use to artists. In fact the word pencil means "little tail,"   29
and refers not only to the modern wood-cased pencil but to the artist's brush. Ink and paint are difficult to erase: they must be scraped off a surface with a knife, or painted over. But graphite pencil marks were more easily erased by using bread crumbs, and of course later by erasers made of rubber—in fact the eraser substance (caoutchouc, the milky juice of tropical plants such as ficus) was called rubber because it was used to rub out pencil marks.

Thoreau and Pencil Technology

It is true that Thoreau rejected modern improvements like the telegraph as   30
worthless illusions. In *Walden* he says, "They are but improved means to an unimproved end." Thoreau did not write much of pencils. He even omitted the pencil in his list of items to take into the Maine woods, though like naturalists before him, he certainly carried one on his twelve-day excursion in order to record his thoughts. Despite this silence, Thoreau devoted ten years of his life to improving pencil technology at his family's pencil factory. It was this pencil technology, not inherited wealth or publication royalties, that provided the income for one of the greatest writers of the American renaissance.

As Petroski tells it, the pencil industry in the eighteenth century was buf-   31
feted by such vagaries as the unpredictable supply of graphite, dwindling cedar forests, protective tariffs, and, for much of its history, an international consumer preference for British-made pencils. All of this affected John Thoreau and Co., manufacturers of pencils. Until the nineteenth century, the best pencil graphite (or plumbago, as it was often called), came from Borrowdale, in England. There were other graphite deposits around the world, but their ore was not particularly

pure. Impure ore crumbled or produced a scratchy line. In the later eighteenth century, the Borrowdale deposits began to run low, and exports were curtailed. After the French Revolution, with his supply of English graphite permanently embargoed, the French pencil-maker Nicholas-Jacques Conté learned to produce a workable writing medium by grinding the local graphite, mixing it with clay and water, and forcing the mixture into wooden casings.

This process allowed the French to produce their own pencils, and it also   32
permitted manufacturers to control the hardness of the lead, which in turn controlled the darkness of the mark made by the pencil. (The more clay, the harder the lead, and the lighter and crisper the mark; less clay gives a darker, grainier mark). So successful was Conté's process that Conté became synonymous with pencil, and Conté crayons are still valued by artists. In Nuremberg, Staedtler learned to mix ground graphite with sulfur. He and his rival, Faber, founded German pencil dynasties that also survive to this day.

The superiority of Borrowdale English graphite was evident to American   33
consumers as well, and they regularly preferred imports to domestic brands. American pencil manufacturers had a hard time convincing the public that they could make a good native pencil. In 1821 Charles Dunbar discovered a deposit of plumbago in Bristol, New Hampshire, and he and his brother-in-law, John Thoreau, went into the pencil business. By 1824 Thoreau pencils were winning recognition. Their graphite, however, was not as pure as Borrowdale, and since the Conté process was unknown in the United States, American pencils, though cheaper than imports, remained inferior.

Henry Thoreau set about to improve his father's pencil. According to Pet-   34
roski, Thoreau began his research in the Harvard Library. But then, as now, there was little written on pencil manufacture. Somehow, Thoreau learned to grind graphite more finely than had been done before and to mix it with clay in just the right proportion, for his improvements on the pencil-making process, combined with the high import duty imposed on British pencils after the War of 1812, led to great demand for Thoreau pencils.

Thoreau did not ascribe transcendent value to pencils. As Petroski sees it,   35
Thoreau's purpose was simply to make money. Once he developed the best pencil of the day, Thoreau saw no sense in trying to improve on his design. His pencils sold for seventy-five cents a dozen, higher than other brands, a fact which Emerson remarked on, though he still recommended Thoreau pencils to his friends. It is easy for us to think of Thoreau only as a romantic who lived deliberately, disobeyed civil authority, and turned Walden Pond into a national historic site. But to do these things, he was also an engineer and marketing expert. When pencil competition grew, shaving his profit margin, Thoreau

stopped pushing pencils and sold his graphite wholesale to electrotypers because this proved more lucrative (Petroski, 122).

Perhaps, then, Thoreau, despite his technological expertise, opposed   36
Morse's telegraph just to protect the family business. It is more likely, though, from the absence of references to pencil-making in any of his writings, that Thoreau honestly thought pencils were better for writing than electrical impulses, and he simply kept his business life and his intellectual life in separate compartments. In any case, Thoreau's resistance to the telegraph didn't stop the project.

The Telephone

The introduction of the telephone shows us once again how the pattern of com-   37
munications technology takes shape. The telephone was initially received as an interesting but impractical device for communicating across distance. Although as Thoreau feared, the telegraph eventually did permit Maine and Texas and just about everywhere else to say nothing to one another, Samuel F. B. Morse, who patented the telegraph and invented its code, saw no use for Alexander Graham Bell's even newer device, the telephone. Morse refused Bell's offer to sell him the rights to the telephone patent. He was convinced that no one would want the telephone because it was unable to provide any permanent record of a conversation.

Indeed, although we now consider it indispensable, like writing, the uses of   38
the telephone were not immediately apparent to many people. Telephone communication combined aspects of speaking and writing situations in new ways, and it took a while to figure out what the telephone could and couldn't do. Once they became established, telephones were sometimes viewed as replacements for earlier technologies. In some cities, news and sports broadcasts were delivered over the telephone, competing with the radio (Marvin 1988). Futurologists predicted that the telephone would replace the school or library as a transmitter of knowledge and information, that medical therapy (including hypnosis) could be delivered and criminals punished over the phone through the use of electrical impulses. The telephone even competed with the clock and the thermometer: when I was growing up in New York in the 1950s, my family regularly called MEridian 7-1212 to find out the time, and WEather 6-1212 for the temperature and forecast.

Of course the telephone was not only a source of information. It also   39
threatened our privacy. One early fear of putting telephones in people's homes was that strangers could call up uninvited; people could talk to us on the phone whom we would never wish to converse with in person—and no one predicted

then that people selling useless products would invariably call at dinner time. Today, as our email addresses circulate through the ether, we find in our electronic mailboxes not just surprise communications from long-lost acquaintances who have tracked us down using Gopher and other Web browsers, but also unwelcome communiqués from intruders offering get-rich-quick schemes, questionable deals, and shoddy merchandise. Even unsolicited religious messages are now circulating freely on net news groups.

The introduction of the telephone for social communication also required   40
considerable adaptation of the ways we talk, a fact we tend to forget because we think of the modern telephone as a reliable and flexible instrument. People had to learn how to converse on the telephone: its sound reproduction was poor; callers had to speak loudly and repeat themselves to be understood, a situation hardly conducive to natural conversation. Telephones were located centrally and publicly in houses, which meant that conversations were never private. Telephones emulated face-to-face communication, but they could not transmit the visible cues and physical gestures that allow face-to-face conversation to proceed smoothly, and this deficiency had to be overcome. Many people still accompany phone conversations with hand and facial gestures; very young children often nod into phone instead of saying "Yes" or "No," as if their interlocutor could see them.

Initially, people were unsure of the appropriate ways to begin or end phone   41
conversations, and lively debates ensued. The terms "hello" and "good-bye" quickly became standard, despite objections from purists who maintained that "hello" was not a greeting but an expression of surprise, and that "good-bye," coming from "God be with you," was too high-toned and serious a phrase to be used for something so trivial as telephone talk. As people discovered that telephones could further romantic liaisons, guardians of the public morality voiced concern or disgust that sweethearts were actually making kissing noises over the phone. Appropriate language during conversation was also an issue, and phone companies would cut off customers for swearing (like today's computer Systems Operators, or Sysops, the telephone operators, or *hello girls* as they were called in the early days, frequently listened in on conversations and had the authority to interrupt or disconnect calls).

While the telephone company routinely monitored the contents of tele-   42
phone calls, when transcripts of telephone conversations were first introduced as evidence in trials, phone companies argued that these communications were just as private and privileged as doctor-patient exchanges (Marvin, 68). Phone companies also tried to limit telephone access solely to the subscriber, threatening hotels and other businesses with loss of phone service if they allowed guests

or customers to make calls. Telephone companies backed down from their demand that phones only be used by their registered owners once another technological development, the pay telephone, was introduced, and their continued profits were assured (this situation is analogous to the discussions of copy protection and site licensing for computer software today).

The Computer and the Pattern of Literacy Technology

Writing was not initially speech transcription, and pencils were first made for woodworkers, not writers. Similarly, the mainframe computer when it was introduced was intended to perform numerical calculations too tedious or complex to do by hand. Personal computers were not initially meant for word-processing either, though that has since become one of their primary functions.   43

Mainframe line editors were so cumbersome that even computer programmers preferred to write their code with pencil and paper. Computer operators actually scorned the thought of using their powerful number-crunchers to process mere words. Those who braved the clumsy technology to type text were condemned to using a system that seemed diabolically designed to slow a writer down well below anything that could be done on an IBM Selectric, or even with a pencil. (Interestingly, when the typewriter was developed, the keyboard was designed to slow down writers, whose typing was faster than the machine could handle; initially computers too were slow to respond to keystrokes, and until type-ahead capability was developed, typists were frustrated by loud beeps indicating they had exceeded the machine's capacity to remember what to do.)   44

Early word-processing software for personal computers did little to improve the situation. At last, in the early 1980s, programs like Wordstar began to produce text that looked more like the typing that many writers had become used to. Even so, writers had to put up with screens cluttered with formatting characters. Word wrap was not automatic, so paragraphs had to be reformatted every time they were revised. Furthermore, printed versions of text seldom matched what was on the computer screen, turning page design into a laborious trial-and-error session. Adding to the writer's problems was the fact that the screen itself looked nothing like the piece of paper the text would ultimately be printed on. The first PC screens were grayish-black with green phosphor letters, displaying considerably less than a full page of text. When it came along, the amber screen offered what was seen as a major improvement, reducing eye strain for many people. Today we expect displays not only with black on white, just like real paper, and high resolution text characters, but also with color, which takes us a step beyond what we could do with ordinary typing paper.   45

If you type this:

^BCombining Special Effects^B. To combine special effects, simply insert one control character after another. For example, your ^BWordstar^B^VTM^V cursor may look like this: H^HI^HN^HZ.

| ^B a^B | = /(a^Vx^V^T2^T + a^Vy^V^T2^T + a^Vz^V^T2^T)

You (might) get this:

Combining Special Effects.   To combine special effects, simply insert one control character after another. For example, your **Wordstar**™ cursor may look like this: ■

a | = /(a_x^2 +a_y^2 + a_z^2)

Figure 4   Instructions from a Wordstar Manual

If the initial technical obstacles to word processing on a PC weren't enough   46
to keep writers away from the new technology, they still had to come up with the requisite $5,000 or more in start-up funds for an entry-level personal computer. Only die-hards and visionaries considered computer word processing worth pursuing, and even they held on to their Selectrics and their Bics just in case.

The next generation of word processors gave us WYSIWIG: "what you see   47
is what you get," and that helped less-adventurous writers make the jump to computers. Only when Macintosh and Windows operating systems allowed users to create on-screen documents that looked and felt like the old, familiar documents they were used to creating on electric typewriters did word-processing really become popular. At the same time, start-up costs decreased significantly and with new, affordable hardware, computer writing technology quickly moved from the imitation of typing to the inclusion of graphics.

Of course that, too, was not an innovation in text production. We've been   48
pasting up text and graphics for ages. The decorated medieval charters of eleventh-century England are a perfect parallel to our computerized graphics a millennium later. But just as writing in the Middle Ages was able to move beyond earlier limitations, computer word processing has now moved beyond the texts made possible by earlier technologies by adding not just graphics, but animation, video, and sound to documents. In addition, Hypertext and HTML allow us to create links between documents or paths within them, both of which offer restructured alternatives to linear reading.

The new technology also raises the specter of digital fraud, and the latest   49
literacy technology is now faced with the task of developing new methods of
authentication to ensure confidence and trust in its audience (see figure 5).

Over the years we have developed a number of safeguards for preventing or   50
detecting fraud in conventionally produced texts. The fact that counterfeit currency still gets passed, and that document forgeries such as the "Hitler Diaries" or
hoaxes like the physicist Alan Sokal's spoof of deconstruction, "Transgressing the
Boundaries: Toward a Transformational Hermeneutics of Quantum Gravity,"
come to light from time to time shows that the safeguards, while strong, are not
necessarily foolproof. The average reader is not equipped to detect many kinds of
document falsification, and a lot of text is still accepted on trust. A writer's repu-
tation, or that of a publisher, predisposes readers to accept certain texts as authoritative, and to reject others. Provenance, in the world of conventional documents,
is everything. We have learned to trust writing that leaves a paper trail.

Figure 5   Example of Digital Fraud

From Feb. 1994 *Scientific American*, William J. Mitchell, "When is seeing believing?" (68–73). Mitchell explains the
process used to create this photograph of Marilyn Monroe and Abraham Lincoln that never existed in the original. The
final result can be so seamless that the forgery is undetectable. Examples of the intrusion of such false images include
an ABC News broadcast in which correspondent Nina Totenberg was shown on camera with the White House in the
background. In actuality, she was miles away in a studio and the montage gave the impression she was reporting from
the field. Needless to say, fraudulent computer text is even easier to compose and promulgate across the bandwidth.

Things are not so black and white in the world of digital text. Of course, as   51
more and more people do business on the Internet, the security of transactions,
of passwords, credit card numbers, and bank accounts becomes vital. But the
security and authenticity of "ordinary" texts is a major concern as well. Anyone
with a computer and a modem can put information into cyberspace. As we see
from figure 5, digitized graphics are easy to alter. Someone intent on committing more serious deception can with not too much trouble alter text, sound,
graphics, and video files. Recently several former Columbia University students
were arrested for passing fake twenty-dollar bills that they had duplicated on
one of Columbia's high-end color printers. The Treasury Department reported
that while these counterfeits were easy for a non-expert to spot, some $8,000 to
$9,000 of the bad money had been spent before the counterfeiters attracted any
attention. Security experts, well aware of the problems of digital fraud, are
developing scramblers, electronic watermarks and invisible tagging devices to
protect the integrity of digital files, and hackers are probably working just as
hard to defeat the new safeguards. Nonetheless, once a file has been converted
to hard copy, it is not clear how it could be authenticated.

Digitized text is even easier to corrupt accidentally, or to fiddle with on   52
purpose. Errors can be inadvertently introduced when print documents are
scanned. With electronic text it may be difficult to recover other indicators that
we expect easy access to when we deal with print: the date of publication, the
edition (sometimes critical when dealing with newspapers or literary texts), editorial changes or formatting introduced during the digitization process, changes
in accompanying graphics (for example, online versions of the *Washington Post*
and the *New York Times* use color illustrations not found in the paper editions).
And of course digital text can be corrupted on purpose in ways that will not be
apparent to unsuspecting readers.

Electronic texts also present some challenges to the ways we attribute   53
expertise to authors. When I read newsgroups and electronic discussion lists, I
must develop new means for establishing the expertise or authority of a poster. I
recently tried following a technical discussion on a bicycle newsgroup about the
relative advantages of butyl and latex innertubes. I can accept the advice of a
bicycle mechanic I know, because we have a history, but posters to a newsgroup
are all strangers to me. They may be experts, novices, cranks, or some combination of the three, and in the case of the two kinds of tire tubes, I had difficulty
evaluating the often conflicting recommendations I received. After reading the
newsgroup for a while, becoming familiar with those who post regularly, and
getting a sense of the kinds of advice they gave and their attitudes toward the
subject, I began to develop a nose for what was credible. My difficulty was
compounded, though, because the most authoritative-sounding poster, in the

conventional sense of authoritative—someone who evoked principles of physics and engineering to demonstrate that flats were no more common or disastrous with latex than butyl tubes, and who claimed to have written books on bicycle repair—was clearly outshouted by posters attesting the frequency and danger of rupturing latex innertubes. In the end I chose to stay with butyl, since everyone seemed to agree that, though heavier than latex, it was certainly not the worst thing in the world to ride on.

My example may seem trivial, but as more and more people turn to the   54
World Wide Web for information, and as students begin relying on it for their research papers, verifying the reliability and authenticity of that information becomes increasingly important, as does revisiting it later to check quotations or gather more information. As anyone knows who's lost a file or tried to revisit a website, electronic texts have a greater tendency to disappear than conventional print resources.

Conclusion

As the old technologies become automatic and invisible, we find ourselves more   55
concerned with fighting or embracing what's new. Ten years ago math teachers worried that if students were allowed to use calculators, they wouldn't learn their arithmetic tables. Regardless of the value parents and teachers still place on knowing math facts, calculators are now indispensable in math class. When we began to use computers in university writing classes, instructors didn't tell students about the spell-check programs on their wordprocessors, fearing the students would forget how to spell. The hackers found the spelling checkers anyway, and now teachers complain if their students don't run the spell check before they turn their papers in.

Even the pencil itself didn't escape the wrath of educators. One of the   56
major technological advances in pencil-making occurred in the early twentieth century, when manufacturers learned to attach rubber tips to inexpensive wood pencils by means of a brass clamp. But American schools allowed no crossing out. Teachers preferred pencils without erasers, arguing that students would do better, more premeditated work if they didn't have the option of revising. The students won this one, too: eraserless pencils are now extremely rare. Artists use them, because artists need special erasers in their work; golfers too use pencils without erasers, too, perhaps to keep themselves honest. As for the no-crossing-out rule, writing teachers now routinely warn students that writers never get it right the first time, and we expect them to revise their work endlessly until it is polished to perfection.

The computer has indeed changed the ways some of us do things with 57 words, and the rapid changes in technological development suggest that it will continue to do so in ways we cannot yet foresee. Whether this will result in a massive change in world literacy rates and practices is a question even more difficult to answer. Although the cost of computers has come down significantly enough for them to have made strong inroads into the American office and education environment, as well as in the American middle class home, it is still the case that not every office or every school can afford to computerize, let alone connect to the World Wide Web. And it is likely that many newly computerized environments will not have sufficient control over the technology to do more than use it to replicate the old ways.

After more than a decade of study, we still know relatively little about how 58 people are using computers to read and write, and the number of people on-line, when viewed in the perspective of the total population of the United States, or of the world—the majority of whose residents are still illiterate—is still quite small. Literacy has always functioned to divide haves from have nots, and the problem of access to computers will not be easy to solve.

In addition, researchers tend to look at the cutting edge when they examine 59 how technology affects literacy. But technology has a trailing edge as well as a down side, and studying how computers are put to use raises serious issues in the politics of work and mechanisms of social control. Andrew Sledd (1988) pessimistically views the computer as actually reducing the amount of literacy needed for the low end of the workplace: "As for ordinary kids, they will get jobs at Jewel, dragging computerized Cheerios boxes across computerized check-out counters."

Despite Sledd's legitimate fear that in the information age computers 60 will increase the gap between active text production and routine, alienating, assembly-line text processing, in the United States we live in an environment that is increasingly surrounded by text. Our cereal boxes and our soft drink cans are covered with the printed word. Our televisions, films, and computer screens also abound with text. We wear clothing designed to be read. The new computer communications technology does have ability to increase text exposure even more than it already has in positive, productive ways. The simplest one-word Web search returns pages of documents which themselves link to the expanding universe of text in cyberspace.

Computer communications are not going to go away. How the computer 61 will eventually alter literacy practices remains to be seen. The effects of writing took thousands of years to spread; the printing press took several hundred years to change how we do things with words. Although the rate of change of

In the brave new world virtual text, if you chain an infinite number of monkeys to an infinite number of computers, you will eventually get, not Hamlet, but Hamlet BASIC.

computer development is significantly greater, it is still too early to do significant speculating.

We have a way of getting so used to writing technologies that we come to think of them as natural rather than technological. We assume that pencils are a natural way to write because they are old—or at least because we have come to think of them as being old. We form Lead Pencil Clubs and romanticize do-it-yourselfers who make their own writing equipment, because home-made has come to mean "superior to store-bought."

But pencil technology has advanced to the point where the ubiquitous no. 2 wood-cased pencil can be manufactured for a unit cost of a few pennies. One pencil historian has estimated that a pencil made at home in 1950 by a hobbyist or an eccentric would have cost about $50. It would cost significantly more nowadays. There's clearly no percentage in home pencil-making. Whether the computer will one day be as taken-for-granted as the pencil is an intriguing question. One thing is clear: were Thoreau alive today he would not be writing with a pencil of his own manufacture. He had better business sense than that. More likely, he would be keyboarding his complaints about the information superhighway on a personal computer that he assembled from spare parts in his garage.

WORKS CITED

Clanchy, Michael T. 1993. *From Memory to Written Record: England 1066-1307*. 2nd ed. Oxford: Blackwell.

Crystal, David. 1987. *The Cambridge Encyclopedia of Language*. Cambridge: Cambridge Univ. Press, p. 196.

Eisenstein, Elizabeth L. 1979. *The Printing Press as an Agent of Change*. Cambridge: Cambridge Univ. Press.

Harris, William V. 1989. *Ancient Literacy*. Cambridge: Harvard Univ. Press.

Henderson, Bill. 1994. No E-Mail from Walden. *New York Times* (March 16), p. A15. *New York Times*.

Marvin, Carolyn. 1988. *When Old Technologies Were New: Thinking about electric communication in the late nineteenth century*. New York: Oxford Univ. Press.

Petroski, Henry. 1990. *The Pencil: A History of Design and Circumstance*. New York: Alfred A. Knopf.

Sledd, Andrew. 1988. Readin' not Riotin': The Politics of Literacy. *College English* 50: 495-507.

Street, Brian V. 1984. *Literacy in Theory and Practice*. Cambridge: Cambridge Univ. Press.

Unabomber. 1996. Letter to the *San Francisco Chronicle* (April 25).

Bob Garfield is a critic, columnist, lecturer, and essayist who is the editor for *Advertising Age*, is the co-host of *On the Media* on National Public Radio, and is the advertising analyst for ABC News.

YOUTUBE VS. BOOB TUBE

By Bob Garfield

TV advertising is broken, putting $67 billion up for grabs. Which explains why Google spent a billion and change on an online video startup.

Look, before you even get to the second paragraph, try this: Go to   1
YouTube.com. In the search field, type in "boom goes the dynamite." A video thumbnail will pop up. Click on it and watch.

It's just a little outtake from a Ball State University campus TV newscast.   2
It features a courageous but overmatched freshman named Brian Collins presenting the worst sports-highlight rundown in human history, culminating in the worst sportscaster catchphrase ever conceived: "Boom goes the dynamite." It is horrifying. It is cruel. It is hilarious.

Search around some more. Type in "evolution of dance," which has got   3
nearly 35 million views in six months. You wouldn't think "Ohio motivational speaker's grand finale" would equal "mesmerizing," but Judson Laipply's seamless sampling of footwork to 30 songs, from Elvis to 'NSync, pretty much is.

Or try the accurately titled "Noah takes a photo of himself everyday for six   4
years." A time-lapse documentary of Noah Kalina over 2,356 days, it's a little thin on plot, but it nonetheless racked up more than 3 million views in six weeks.

You'd better also see "Numa Numa," which stars a chubby young man in   5
his New Jersey bedroom lip-syncing to an insipid but weirdly fetching Romanian pop song. Or, what the hell, live dangerously. Type in "sweet tired cat" and watch a drowsy kitten dozing off. The clip, which was viewed nearly 2 million times in two weeks, is 27 seconds of such concentrated cuteness that you might actually have a stroke and die. It's that excruciatingly adorable.

Bob Garfield, "YouTube vs. Boob Tube." © 2007 by Bob Garfield. Reprinted by permission of the author. Originally published in *Wired*, issue 14.12.

And, as it turns out, extremely valuable. Google—as you may have read in   6
every publication, online and off, in the entire freaking world—just paid $1.65 bil-
lion in stock to be the cute little kitty-cat's home.

The price tag for YouTube, just to put the investment in perspective, is   7
what Target paid for 257 Mervyns department stores and four distribution centers in 13 states, and just a bit more than WPP Group paid for the Grey Global
Group advertising network with 10,500 employees in 83 countries generating
$1.3 billion in revenue. Those, of course, are both profitable enterprises with
vast fixed assets. YouTube's fixed assets pretty much consist of a video interface
and a cool retro logo. So why is it worth nearly six times the gross domestic
product of Micronesia?

This story will definitively answer that question.   8

Well, maybe not exactly answer.   9

But explore.   10

OK, guess. But that guesswork begins in a very special, very poignant, and   11
potentially very lucrative place: the hitherto futile aspirations of the everyman
to break out of his lonely anonymous life of quiet desperation, to step in front of
the whole world and *be somebody*, dude. A recent Accenture study of 1,600
Americans found that 38 percent of respondents wanted to create or share content online. Aha! Suddenly the inexplicable "Numa Numa" begins to make
sense. He could, so he did. And so have lots like him. It's said that if you put a
million monkeys at a million typewriters, eventually you will get the works of
William Shakespeare. When you put together a million humans, a million cam-
corders, and a million computers, what you get is YouTube.

And there they are, in the bedrooms and dorms and cubicles of the world,   12
uploading their asses off, more than 65,000 times a day on YouTube alone.

"If you aren't posting, you don't exist," says Rishad Tobaccowala, CEO of   13
Denuo, a new media consultancy. "People say, 'I post, therefore I am.'"

Constituo, ergo sum. An interesting formulation that may well represent a   14
new rationalism for the digital age. But for the moment, let's not put Descartes
before the horse. Let's just get the measure of a phenomenon in progress—
because Google has recently bet the equivalent of 257 Mervyns stores that the
rise of video-sharing is more than just the latest rage. To YouTube's new owners, "Numa Numa" represents nothing less than cultural, sociological, and economic transformation—including, but not limited to, a reallocation of the
$67 billion that advertisers spent on TV in the U.S. last year.

That upheaval would require a couple of things to fall into place: (1) a   15
business model to convert what is basically an overgrown fan site into an actual
advertising medium and (2) a tectonic change in the worldwide media econ-

omy. But don't sell Google short. Not long ago, all *it* had was a search algorithm and a cool logo. Now, after reinventing online advertising, it has revenue of $9.3 billion a year and good reason to believe that neither of those daunting prerequisites is out of the question.

Until about five minutes ago, remember, almost all video-entertainment content was produced and distributed by Hollywood. Period. That time is over. There was a time when advertisers could count on mass audiences for what Hollywood thought we should be watching on TV. That time is all but over. There was a time when broadband penetration was too slight and bandwidth costs too prohibitive for video to be watched online. That time is *sooooo* over. "The era of the creepy blue light leaking out of every living room window on the block is now officially at an end," says my pal and occasional colleague Steve Rosenbaum, founder of video-sharing startup Magnify.net and one of the inventors a decade ago of citizen video. "The simple, wonderful, delirious fact is that people like you and me can now make and share content." 16

Delirious or not, it's a fact that Buzzmachine.com's Jeff Jarvis believes has changed the meaning of TV. "Just as our kids don't understand the difference between broadcast and cable," he says, "the line between TV and Internet TV is about to disappear." 17

Jarvis calls the phenomenon "exploding TV," and YouTube is exploding faster than anything else: from a standing start about a year ago to more than 100 million videostreams a day. It was on YouTube, not *Saturday Night Live,* that the world fell in love with "Lazy Sunday." It was there that we found ourselves smitten, intrigued, and ultimately betrayed by Lonelygirl15. And it is there that more than 65,000 videos go every day, their creators posting what they think are video clips but that are also improvised explosive devices laying waste to the old order. Hit Upload Video . . . 18

Boom goes the dynamite. 19

CHAD HURLEY SAYS HE DOESN'T REMEMBER. It's two weeks before the announcement of the Google acquisition, and he has just flown the red-eye to New York to make his case to Madison Avenue. He's turning right around in a few hours; he's stuck in yet one more conference room, and his eyes have the vacant look of someone whose body has a one-bar wireless connection to his nervous system. In a word, the dude is fried. Never mind that he's the cofounder of the Next Big Thing and poised to be a total tycoon; the question on the floor seems to have him stumped: What was the first video uploaded to YouTube by someone other than himself or YouTube cofounder Steve Chen? 20

He insists he can't quite recall, you know, the $1.65 billion moment. 21

"I think it was a few people from Stanford," Hurley offers. "People in a   22
dorm room doing weird things."

Weird things? What kind of weird things, Chad?   23

"I don't even remember," he says. "That was so long ago."   24

Yeah. Way back in May 2005. But you can scarcely blame the 29-year-old   25
if it's all a bit of a blur. In the intervening year and a half, YouTube has hosted
many millions of clips—all because Hurley and Chen wanted a utility like
Flickr for sharing videos. In a garage in Menlo Park, California, they built a simple interface and a one-click way to embed videos on other sites. It was a
serendipitous innovation, coinciding with the MySpace phenomenon and
yielding what Hurley calls "this"—as in, "It's all turned into this." Slouched
wearily in his stackable conference chair, he seems a little bewildered, but
maybe it's more like bemused. Ain't as though he has no explanation for all
this. You'll find it in the company slogan: "Broadcast Yourself."

"Everyone, in the back of his mind, wants to be a star," Hurley asserts for   26
probably the quadrillionth time, "and we provide the audience to make it
happen."

Lots of people can now watch themselves on sort-of TV, which is pretty fun   27
in itself. The bonus is that others want to watch them, too. Third-millennium
humanity has demonstrated an interest in sifting through millions of pieces of
crap produced by total strangers to discover a few gems—some accidentally
entertaining ("Boom Goes the Dynamite"), some breakout performances from
the previously obscure ("Treadmill Dance"), and some explorations of a new
art form crackling with genius (Ze Frank, Ask a Ninja, and the guys behind
Lonelygirl15.)

Throw in the uploaded TV commercials, such as Nike's Ronaldinho spot   28
showing the Brazilian soccer star miraculously volleying against the crossbar.
Add to that some professional content either stolen from or surrendered by Hollywood. Altogether, this stuff constitutes a bottomless reservoir of short-form
video content for others to siphon off if they choose. Which they do, millions of
times a day, from pages all over the Internet. That's the demand side of the
equation—monkey see, monkey use—foreshadowing the future of media,
already in progress.

Forget "exploding TV." The name for this thing is Monkeyvision.   29

EH? MONKEYVISION.   Pretty good, huh? How nice it must be to have big,   30
slick magazines coining catchwords for the phenomenon you created. Even
that's cold comfort, however, if you can't build an actual business around it.
Which is why Hurley went to New York: to explain to advertisers why they

should give him money to broadcast themselves. The bad news for his entourage is that advertisers *have* been broadcasting themselves for decades and would very much prefer the status quo. The good news is that the status quo isn't long for this world.

Without being overly simplistic or melodramatic, the state of the Old Commercial Broadcasting Model can be summarized like this: a spiraling vortex of ruin. Fragmentation has decimated audiences, viewers who do watch are skipping commercials, advertisers are therefore fleeing, the revenue for under-writing new content is therefore flatlining, program quality is therefore suffering (*Dancing With the Stars*. QED), which will lead to ever more viewer defection, which will lead to ever more advertiser defection, and so on.   31

In late October, NBC Universal announced a cut of 700 jobs as part of a $750 million retrenchment plan, which includes a moratorium on 8 P.M. come-dies and dramas due, presumably, to advertisers' waning interest. Nearly a year ago, perhaps reading the writing on the screen, Viacom spun off CBS Corp. to protect the growth of the parent company. And CBS itself, madly trying to cul-tivate new online distribution channels, put fall premieres of shows like *Smith* and *The New Adventures of Old Christine* on Google Video. NBC used Yahoo to premiere *Heroes* and AOL to offer sneak previews of its *Twenty Good Years* and *Studio 60 on the Sunset Strip*. And the brand-new CW Network celebrated its debut by posting for free *Runaway* and *Everybody Hates Chris* on MSN. Count-ing cable, dozens of networks are now making programs available online.   32

The networks say these are measures to promote the broadcast versions of their shows. The overwhelming probability is that the opposite is true, which bodes poorly for those invested in the status quo. One victim is local affiliates, which get a big chunk of their revenue from selling commercial space within network programs. The Internet, needless to say, bypasses them.   33

The digital revolution is equally terrifying to Madison Avenue, which has been footing the bill for *Gilligan's Island*, *The New Republic*, The Family Circus, Rush Limbaugh, *TRL*, and *The Wall Street Journal* forever. Until now, advertis-ers have underwritten mass media to reach mass audiences. Indeed, they've paid increasing premiums for the opportunity as audiences have shrunk, because even in a fragmented media world, the largest fragment—network TV—is the most valuable. But now they realize that they are losing not only mass but criti-cal mass.   34

They see the old model collapsing before them, and they have $67 billion to spend and no idea where to spend it. Because, at least until recently, the Internet has lacked both the riveting content and ad space inventory to absorb it. But what if there were a means to approximate the reach and mesmerizing   35 power of television online? What if there were a medium with not only the grip of TV but the vast scale to absorb all those ad dollars? And what if, as a bonus, the medium were able not merely to command eyeballs for marketers but to target content especially relevant to what the marketer is selling?

In short, what if there were a missing link between the old model and the glittering new one? What would happen then?   36

Actually, that's an easy one: Procter & Gamble would be ecstatic. Blood would flow in the gutters of Madison Avenue and Hollywood. And Regis Philbin would be out of our lives forever.   37

Oh, and someone would strike it filthy, stinking rich—and not the piddling few hundred million Hurley and Chen just earned, either. We're talking real money. Some of it would be dispersed along what somebody once referred to as the long tail of video-sharing Web sites: Bolt, Dailymotion, Grouper, Guba, iFilm, Magnify.net, Metacafe, Photobucket, Revver, Veoh, vidiLife, and many more. Presumably a chunk would be commanded by Yahoo, AOL, and MSN (which in September launched Soapbox in direct competition with YouTube). And, yes, as of October, YouTube is definitely the front-runner in the struggle to be the alpha male of Monkeyvision. But even 100 million daily streams and $1.65 billion into the evolution of this species, how it will actually thrive is a mystery.   38

"If anybody tries to answer that question, they are guessing," says Jennifer Feikin, director of video and multimedia search partnerships at Google. Before the YouTube acquisition, she says, Google Video was tinkering with ways to target ads to relevant content. In one approach, posters were asked to close-caption their videos using a Google tool, and the text was mined for metadata. It's an ingenious experiment—but only an experiment, because, after all, Feikin says, "we are at the very, very beginning of online video."   39

Yes, and so formidable are the challenges that it's not hard to make a case that the beginning is already the beginning of the end.   40

AS SOMEBODY ONCE SAID, 100 million people can't be wrong. They can, however, be useless. It turns out that success is 1 percent inspiration, 99 percent monetization. "They've got the audience," says John Montgomery, CEO of MindShare Interaction, a digital media arm of the WPP Group communications conglomerate. "In order now to monetize what they've got, they need to figure out a revenue model. But it's a very, very hard thing to do around user-generated media."   41

Of course, that's Google's problem now, and it's no easy banana to peel. Monkeyvision presents a terrifying list of unknowns: First, there's the basic   42 question of where, exactly, to put the ads. Prior to the acquisition, YouTube refused to sell ads appended to either end of a video—like a TV commercial—on the grounds of safeguarding the viewer experience. Indeed, many accept as an article of faith that a pre-video commercial is fatally intrusive. "There may be a user out there who likes a 30-second preroll," says Tod Sacerdoti of POSTroller. "If you find one, have him give me a call."

As for Sacerdoti's so-called postroll ads, even the most self-satisfied mar-   43
keter wants to know who in the world would stick around to watch—or, more to the point, who can prove that anyone did. This leaves as available ad real estate only the space adjacent to the video window—which is great for whoever is hosting the video. But, as Sacerdoti points out, a significant portion of YouTube videos are embedded elsewhere, mainly on individual MySpace pages. "Everyone talks about streams per day as YouTube's metric of success. But the vast majority of those streams are not on their Web site. In order for YouTube to monetize that traffic, it has to monetize those streams." Which YouTube (denying the "majority" characterization) also has insisted it will not do.

Advertisers do have another option: Wait until their commercials make it   44
onto YouTube and hope they go viral. YouTube actually encourages this—so long as the free posts are accompanied by paid versions. This, the company says, stimulates the viral effect. Perhaps. But as MindShare's Montgomery notes, for advertisers "the most successful way of using YouTube"—posting ads for free—"is a way in which YouTube doesn't make any money."

Which may suit the users just fine. One of the biggest obstacles to advertis-   45
ing success is the damage that success could inflict on the YouTube experience, till now an oasis of relative noncommercialism in a world of brand inundation. The Google deal has already spawned bitterness at the grass roots, where some are dubious that GooTube will retain its soul. "I think its the beginning of the end of youtube as we know it," wrote a poster named SamHill24. Another, Link420, declared simply, "ITS OVER!!!! youtube is screwed."

The second big issue is the nightmare of protecting intellectual property.   46
As eager as Madison Avenue is to push stacks of chips online, in the back of its mind is Napster. It, too, was a peer-to-peer revolutionary—one killed aborning by copyright infringement issues. Nobody wants to invest only to see the fledgling industry paralyzed with litigation, regulation, or legislation. And it is not an idle fear.

A lot of those upload monkeys have a nasty habit of posting clips from TV   47
shows or enhancing their clips by adding music tracks—which, of course, are somebody else's property. "When we started," says Steven Starr, founder and CEO of competing video-sharing startup Revver, "more than 90 percent of the

content was illegal. We took down many, many thousands of pieces of content." Revver's business model is as an oasis for original content, so it built into its infrastructure human and electronic means to sniff out copyright infringers. But thanks in part to its explosive growth and its free-for-all philosophy, YouTube had until recently been at a loss to manage the situation, relying on safe-harbor provisions of the Digital Millennium Copyright Act to insulate itself from liability. Until it actually installs a newly developed copyright infringement sniffer (coming soon, YouTube says), the best it can do is take down individual clips in response to a rights holder's complaint. And to demand—futilely—that users follow the rules.

So what about "Evolution of Dance," for instance? To put together this medley, did Laipply license 30 songs? "Don't know," replies YouTube senior marketing director Julie Supan. "You'd have to ask Judson." In the next breath, though, she suggests that the brief music excerpts fall within the bounds of fair use.

Indeed, thus far it appears that no record company has demanded the video be pulled down. But speculation abounds that copyright holders have just been waiting for someone with deep pockets, such as Google, to acquire YouTube, whereupon the lawsuits will fly.

Another possibility is that potential litigants are simply being patient. They understand YouTube's value to them as a marketing tool and are waiting for a technological solution. This fall, YouTube struck deals with Warner Music Group, CBS, Universal Music Group, and Sony BMG, not only to detect copyrighted material and, if necessary, remove it, but also to make much of it available to amateur video makers in exchange for a split of ad revenue.

So big media lawyers may or may not remain at bay. That has no bearing, however, on the potential grievances of the greater Monkeysphere.

"What about the rights of the content creators?" asks Max Kalehoff, blogger and vice president of marketing for Nielsen BuzzMetrics. "YouTube is basically going under the assumption that there's this community in place to blindly create content on YouTube's behalf without much in the way of compensation." Already, some of YouTube's most provocative creators—Ask a Ninja and the Lonelygirl15 team, to name two—have signed on with Revver, which shares ad revenue with content creators. Hurley acknowledges a similar arrangement could become part of the YouTube business model. In the meantime, will the hits keep coming? And once the ad revenue starts generating profits, will some aggrieved Monkeyvisionary file a class-action suit for a slice of the pie?

Let's just suppose that, contrary to Planck's Constant of American Economic Life over the last few decades, such litigation never happens. YouTube's problems are still far from over, for the greatest obstacle facing Monkeyvision isn't jurisprudence. It is prudence itself. Given the anything-goes nature of the Web, the 65,000-uploads-a-day question is: Will advertisers risk associating themselves with violence, pornography, hate speech, or God knows what lurks out there one click away? "Advertisers and brands are enormously risk averse," Magnify.net's Rosenbaum says. "The question now is how the raw and risky is made safe and comfortable. It's not a little question. It's a big question."

For instance, if you are, say, Meow Mix, and you bought ads adjacent to cat-   54
related videos, how surprised and disappointed you might be to learn you have sponsored a YouTube video uploaded by someone named mrwheatley and titled "exploding cat." Or the one from qu1rk89 titled "exploding cat." Or this one: "ma907h eats dead cat," which shows a guy . . . oh, never mind. As Cory Treffiletti, VP of media services for interactive agency Real Branding, grimly observes of the metadata describing a YouTube video, "Right now it consists of only a few key terms the user selects. And there's no blank to fill out for 'cat vivisection.'"

Magnify.net tries to address this problem by exploiting the distributive   55
quality of online video; it enables Web sites to build community channels—for, oh, say, cat lovers—that ask members to rate each video against various quality and suitability criteria. Advertisers could tap this data to place their ads alongside only appropriate clips.

YouTube, which has only the uploaders' descriptions of their videos to   56
work with, is so far standing pat. Supan insists that YouTubers have done an excellent job of policing their own space, although she acknowledges that one sketchy video can "rise up" to haunt all involved. "You know what?" she offers. "That is the nature of this environment. . . . The fact is, we cannot control content on our site."

Out-of-control content. That is hardly music—licensed or unlicensed—to   57
Madison Avenue's ears. And with a $177 billion total domestic ad budget at stake, nobody wants to be monkeying around. Which may be why the YouTube pilgrimage to Madison Avenue has so far not resulted in any sort of huge windfall. "They're not making fast decisions in some cases," Supan says. "They really have to develop a sort of new model for themselves."

So there you have it. For all the aforementioned reasons, you'd be forgiven   58
for wondering how clearly Google thought this thing through. The numbers do evoke a sort of '90s déjà vu. Could these guys have anted up nearly six times the GDP of Micronesia because they were *afflicted* with micronesia, a small case of memory loss about, say, the insane multiples squandered on fiber capacity just before the telecom crash? Eerily enough, $1.65 billion is just what Racal Telecom fetched from Global Crossing.

Ah, yes, the titans of yore. GeoCities. Prodigy. Netscape. But hold on;   59
we're speaking of the missing link here, and the defining nature of missing links
is that they go missing. They are, by definition, transitory. They evolve, change
the future, and disappear. Is YouTube some interim killer app, languishing on
Darwin's death row?

Nah. In one form or another, YouTube will survive. And prosper, despite   60
everything, for one overriding reason: 100 million streams a day. "The only bar-
rier to creating a YouTube competitor is that so many people are already on
YouTube," Denuo's Tobaccowala says. "What it has going for it is its sheer size.
In a fragmented world, there is a need for community and a need for massness."

Whoa. Massness? Could the irony be any thicker? The old model is a flam-   61
ing ruin, disintegrating into nothingness, and what rises from the ashes—in the
vast, distributed, exploded, long-tailed galaxy of the Internet—is a mass
medium? A general-interest destination? YouTube as the new boob tube?

That may not be Jarvis' idea of the glittering future, but it certainly is Hur-   62
ley's. "We think people want an entertainment destination," Hurley says, not
only without bombast but more or less listlessly as his latest interrogation winds
down. "Everyone else wants to see what everyone else is seeing and enjoying."

But of course. That. What Uncle Miltie and the Super Bowl and *Survivor*   63
have always offered is something to talk about at the water cooler, at the nail
salon, or on IM. "Did you see that horrible sportscast? 'Boom goes the dynamite!' What is that supposed to mean? . . . Wait. You haven't seen it? Ohhhh-
mygosh! I'll email you the link."

"It goes back to something primal," says Henry Jenkins, director of the   64
Comparative Media Studies program at MIT and the author of *Convergence
Culture: Where Old and New Media Collide*. "There's still a desire to have a
shared cultural context. We hunger for things we can discuss."

So if you're searching for the missing link, you need search no further. It   65
turns out to be the ability to fashion rudimentary (digital) tools to feed a not
merely national but global conversation, even if that conversation is about a
portly lip-syncing New Jerseyite. Why advertise next to some sad sack's weird
shenanigans?

Simple. Because it's not just shenanigans.   66

It's monkey business.   67

James Paul Gee is the Tashia Morgridge Professor of Reading in the Department of Curriculum and Instruction at the University of Wisconsin-Madison School of Education. He earned his Ph.D. in linguistics from Stanford University in 1975 and has published many articles on sociolinguistics and discourse analysis. He is also the author of *What Video Games Have to Teach Us About Learning and Literacy* (2003), which argues that thirty-six learning principles are a component of worthwhile video games and that playing video games is not a waste of time, and of *Situated Language and Learning* (2004), which discusses how video games might aid education reformers in re-envisioning schools. His latest work is *How Computer Games Help Children Learn* (2008), which he co-authored with David Williamson Shaffer.

CONCLUSION: DUPED OR NOT?

James Paul Gee

The argument in this book is not that what people are learning when they are playing video games is always good. Rather, what they are doing when they are playing good video games is often good learning. We can learn evil things as easily as we can learn moral ones. That's precisely why an organization like the neo-Nazi National Alliance wants to make a game like *Ethnic Cleansing*, a game in which the player kills African Americans, Latinos, and Jewish people, playing as a member of the Klu Klux Klan or a skinhead. However horrible its views, this organization realizes that video games are powerful learning devices for shaping identities. It realizes that they are even powerful learning devices for learning the *content* of the National Alliance's white power perspective on reality, ironically, given the grandfather's remark in chapter 2 that video games are a waste of time because children don't learn any content while playing them. 1

The power of video games, for good or ill, resides in the ways in which they meld learning and identity, a matter discussed throughout this book. If a player takes on what I called in chapter 3 a projective identity vis-à-vis the virtual character he or she is playing in a game, this constitutes a form of identification with the virtual character's world, story, and perspectives that become a strong learning device at a number of different levels. This is so because, in taking on a projective identity, the player projects his or her own hopes, values, and fears onto the virtual character that he or she is co-creating with the video game's 2 designers. Doing this allows the player to imagine a new identity born at the intersection of the player's real-world identities and the virtual identity of the character he or she is playing in the game. In turn, this projective identity helps speak to, and possibly transform, the player's hopes, values, and fears.

However, people are not dupes. They do not necessarily take from a video game, any more than they do from a book or movie, any one predictable message predetermined by the design of the game, movie, or text. It is quite possible that some people could play *Ethnic Cleansing* and form a projective identity that both lets them understand the sort of hate organizations like the National Alliance harbor and want to redouble their efforts to work for a world of peace, diversity, and tolerance. And, note, both these things are important: We cannot work for a world of peace, diversity, and tolerance while disdaining to understand those who resist, hate, and feel disenfranchised in such a world.

This certainly doesn't mean you should play *Ethnic Cleansing*. It does not mean you shouldn't despise neo-Nazi viewpoints. It doesn't mean you shouldn't protect yourself from neo-Nazis. It does mean that if you have no idea why people who would create or be drawn to such a game are so angry and filled with hate, then you are very unlikely to do anything more than recruit more members for organizations like the National Alliance by claiming your own moral superiority. However, to understand their rage means to understand the workings of history, economics, and culture. That is, it means gaining, in or out of school, an education, one that certainly goes far beyond what anyone can currently learn from video games. Sadly, this is not the sort of education usually offered in U.S. schools, least of all those driven back to passive learning and skill-and-drill by the current standardized-testing regime.

I am not here advocating any sort of "postmodernist" view that "anything goes" and all perspectives are simply sociocultural "constructions" and "culturally relative" (a very poor characterization of good work in postmodernism). Things can be "constructed" and still be true or false, solid or shabby. I certainly believe that we all need to defend ourselves from those who would disdain and even physically harm us. I don't advocate face-to-face dialogue with people pointing a gun at your head, either. What I do advocate is understanding the "play" of identities and perspectives as they work for and against each other in the world, now and throughout history. This is even a form of self-defense.

The left and right wings of the political spectrum have seriously misled us about how people learn from the cultural resources around us. For example, both sides tend to agree that canonical literature (the so-called Great Books) is indoctrinating. The right wing applauds the work the canon can do to align people with what it sees as mainstream and universal values, values that it also sees as already its own. The left wing decries this same thing, claiming that the values embedded in the canon are, far from being universal, just a historically and culturally specific instantiation of the values of certain sorts of western, "middle-class" white people, people who wish to use the canon to enshrine their values and perspectives as higher and better than those of other people and other cultures.

Both views show a woeful ignorance of—and even a certain disdain for—   7
how many people—especially many poor people, people who rarely get invited into academic debates about the canon, in any case—actually read and used, in the past, canonical works like those of Homer, Shakespeare, Milton, Carlyle, Arnold, Austen, Emerson, and a great many others. Of course, schools and churches have tried through the centuries, up to and including our own new century, to get people to read such literature—and the Bible—in *their* way, so as to enforce their values, values that, in many cases (certainly not all), stressed the subordination of women, nonwhites, and the poor. However, many a woman, nonwhite, or poor person actually read canonical works as empowering works that made them challenge the class hierarchy of their societies and the ways in which schools, churches, and rich people upheld this hierarchy in their own favor.

Jonathan Rose's massive tome, The *Intellectual Life of the British Working*   8
Classes, is chock full of stories from the eighteenth century through the twentieth of women, poor people, and nonwhite people who read canonical literature as representing their own values and aspirations and not those of the wealthy and powerful. For example, Mary Smith (b. 1822) was a shoemaker's daughter who had this to say: "For long years Englishwomen's souls were almost as sorely crippled and cramped by the devices of the school room, as the Chinese women's feet by their shoes." Here's what Smith had to say about reading Shakespeare, Dryden, and Goldsmith: "These authors wrote from their hearts for humanity, and I could follow them fully and with delight, though but a child. They awakened my young nature, and I found for the first time that my pondering heart was akin to that of the whole human race. . . . Carlyle's gospel of Work and exposure of Shams, and his universal onslaught on the nothings and appearances of society, gave strength and life to my vague but true enthusiasm."

Of course, the left wing will say that Mary Smith was a hegemonic dupe   9
moving to the dictates of the elites in her society without knowing it and mistakenly taking their values to be her own. But the only people who were duped by the canon were the right wing who thought it uncritically represented their viewpoints and the left wing who agreed with them. Mary Smith read what for us is "high literature" but what for her was "popular" enough, to say that even the daughter of a shoemaker was the equal, in intelligence and humanity, of any rich person.

So why did she read canonical works as empowering her humanity and rights   10
to equality in a hierarchical society? It's because she identified *herself* with the characters and viewpoints in these books. She projected herself into them. She didn't distance herself from the hero because he was a male and a king in a Shakespeare play, however much she might have wanted and certainly deserved female heroes.

Rather, she saw herself as projected into that powerful monarch. Perhaps   11
sometimes when she read Shakespeare, she was a king and other times a queen, just as, in playing *Arcanum*, I can make my female hero as strong as any male at melee fighting. Perhaps sometimes when she read Shakespeare, she was not a traditional monarch at all but a monarch shoemaker with the dignity and the human worth of a monarch. Perhaps sometimes she was all these and more at once. Remember, she was not just taking on the life of a virtual character in the book or play. She was also projecting herself into that character, creating something that both she and Shakespeare made, neither one of them alone.

Neither the right nor the left wing wrote the scripts for the plays in Mary   12
Smith's mind, no matter how influenced she, like all of us, was by the political and cultural factors of her time. Shakespeare was deeply influenced by his own times, but he wrote original scripts nonetheless. So did Mary Smith. She read books that today's students find boring, with the excitement that today's students find in video games, because, perhaps, she read them at least in part much like those students sometimes play video games—actively, critically, and projectively.

What Smith learned as she became these virtual characters in a projective   13
way was the values and perspectives of the various personae behind canonical literature. She did not see these values and perspectives as the preserve of only rich elites. They represented, in the form she gave them, her own values and aspirations. They made her see her equality to wealthy elites. She saw that, like all people, she had just as much capacity for greatness, truth, and morality as any hero, king, or rich person. And, of course, canonical works are full of people who are not males or kings, people acting out their true human worth in hierarchical worlds that hurt and disdain them. In the end, Mary Smith and many more like her believed that canonical literature, far from representing the values of wealthy elites, undermined their values and showed them for the hypocrites they were.

Right wingers and left wingers who argue over the canon tend to act as if peo-   14
ple like Mary Smith will read books realizing and accepting their "inferior station" and either want to emulate their "betters" (the right-wing perspective) or passively accept their inferiority as dupes of the elites in the society (the left-wing view). The Mary Smiths of the world need do no such thing. They already know that they are thinking, worthy beings. They sometimes see in canonical literature examples of who and what they could be, if others in society ceased to disdain them. And,

again, these examples are mutual creations they build with the authors of the book when they project themselves into the virtual creations of these authors.

Does all this mean I think there is some definitive list of "Great Books"? 15 No, by no means. For me, the canon is and was never a closed list. For me, any book is canonical if it lends itself to the powerful projective work in which Mary Smith engaged and leads people to desire not more hierarchy of the sort elites so often celebrate but more opportunities for the display of human worth and the greater development of human capacities for all people. Of course, that last statement is a value-laden one. A work is canonical, for me, if it gives people, in Kenneth Burke's phrase, new and better "equipment for living" in a harsh and unfair world. It is canonical if it allows them to imagine, and seek, in however small a way, to implement newer and better selves and social worlds.

In this sense, works like Ralph Ellison's *Invisible Man* and Gloria Naylor's 16 *Mama Day* are canonical for me and many other people. And, of course, there are a good many books written by women, nonwhite people, and poor people that never got on the "official" canon as a list due to the workings of racism and patriarchy but are most certainly, in my terms, canonical.

Traditional canonical works, like those of Homer, Shakespeare, Milton, and 17 Dryden, function today quite differently than they did in Mary Smith's day. Smith's society denied her any sort of schooling that gave her access to these books. In fact, her society felt it inappropriate for a shoemaker's daughter to be reading such books (which hardly comports well with the left's view that elites thought canonical literature would make people like Mary Smith quiescently accept their status). She picked them up anyway with defiance, and saw in them resonances with herself that just further proved her own intelligence and worth.

But schools have, by and large, tamed the canon. They have made it into 18 the stuff of tests, multiple-choice answers, and standardized responses. Everyone now, finally, has access to the canon at a time when schools have rendered it toothless and the left applauds ignoring it as a historical vestige of old, dead, western, aristocratic elites.

Furthermore, young people today have access to far more texts, images, and 19 diverse media, of far more kinds, than even the rich of Mary's Smith time had. Milton's *Paradise Lost* played a very different role in the textual ecology of Smith's world than it does for a young person today. For her it was a precious book, hard won through a great deal of physical labor (to buy it, if she didn't borrow it) and mental labor (to read it seriously). For a young person today, it is cheap to buy and the school tells them how to read it in the "right" way (or get a poor grade).

This is no plea for reading Milton, though I am sure many people still get a 20 great deal out of traditional canonical literature when they read it of their own choosing, usually outside of school. There is plenty of evidence that people still read and watch many things that serve some of the same purposes that canonical literature did for Mary Smith.

I am not pleading for the "canon" here, least of all as a list. Nor am I claiming that every poor person read like Mary Smith. I am claiming that elites can use anything—canonical literature, the Bible, biology, or any other sort of text—to attempt to dupe people by trying to force them to read it in the elite's way. I am claiming, as well, that there are plenty of Mary Smiths who are more than capable of saying "No, thank you" and reading it both *their way* and intelligently.

Video games are a new form of art. They will not replace books; they will sit beside them, interact with them, and change them and their role in society in various ways, as, indeed, they are already doing strongly with movies. (Today many movies are based on video games and many more are influenced by them.) We have no idea yet how people "read" video games, what meanings they make from them. Still less do we know how they will "read" them in the future. It won't do to start this investigation by assuming they are dupes of capitalist marketers—though, of course, some of them very likely are. But there will always be Mary Smiths out there who use cultural products, whether "high" or "low," for good purposes.

Video games are at the very beginning of their potential—"we ain't seen nothin' yet." They will get deeper and richer. Eventually some form of conversation between real people and computer-created characters will occur alongside the conversations among people in their virtual and real identities that already take place in Internet gaming. There are and will be vile games, and eventually there will be some "canonical" games, games that lend themselves powerfully to elevating the aspirations and imaginings of all people for better and more just worlds. These may be new aspirations and imaginings or ones that fill old visions with new meanings and hope.

But for now, video games are what they are, an immensely entertaining and attractive interactive technology built around identities. I have made but one claim for them here. They operate with—that is, they build into their designs and encourage—good principles of learning, principles that are better than those in many of our skill-and-drill, back-to-basics, test-them-until-they-drop schools. It is not surprising that many politicians, policymakers, and their academic fellow travelers who think poor children should be content with schooling for service jobs don't like video games. They say they don't like them because they are violent. But, in reality, video games do violence to these people's notions of what makes learning powerful and schools good and fair.

REFERENCES

Rose, J. (2001). *The intellectual life of the British working classes*. New Haven, Conn.: Yale University Press.

Horace Miner (1912–1993), a prominent American anthropologist, taught at Wayne State University in Detroit, Michigan and was a professor of sociology and anthropology at the University of Michigan. He also worked in, and wrote about, Canada, Africa, and South America. He wrote several books including *Culture and Agriculture* (1949) and *Primitive City of Timbuctoo* (1967).

BODY RITUAL AMONG THE NACIREMA[1]

Horace Miner

The anthropologist has become so familiar with the diversity of ways in which different people behave in similar situations that he is not apt to be surprised by even the most exotic customs. In fact, if all of the logically possible combinations of behavior have not been found somewhere in the world, he is apt to suspect that they must be present in some yet undescribed tribe. The point has, in fact, been expressed with respect to clan organization by Murdock (1949: 71).[2] In this light, the magical beliefs and practices of the Nacirema present such unusual aspects that it seems desirable to describe them as an example of the extremes to which human behavior can go.   1

Professor Linton[3] first brought the ritual of the Nacirema to the attention of anthropologists twenty years ago (1936: 326), but the culture of this people is still very poorly understood. They are a North American group living in the territory between the Canadian Cree, the Yaqui and Tarahumare of Mexico, and the Carib and Arawak of the Antilles. Little is known of their origin, although tradition states that they came from the east. . . .[4]   2

Nacirema culture is characterized by a highly developed market economy which has evolved in a rich natural habitat. While much of the people's time is devoted to economic pursuits, a large part of the fruits of these labors and a considerable portion of the day are spent in ritual activity. The focus of this activity is the human body, the appearance and health of which loom as a dominant concern in the ethos of the people. While such a concern is certainly not unusual, its ceremonial aspects and associated philosophy are unique.   3

The fundamental belief underlying the whole system appears to be that the human body is ugly and that its natural tendency is to debility and disease. Incarcerated in such a body, man's only hope is to avert these characteristics   4 through the use of ritual and ceremony. Every household has one or more shrines devoted to this purpose. The more powerful individuals in the society have several shrines in their houses and, in fact, the opulence of a house is often referred to in terms of the number of such ritual centers it possesses. Most houses are of wattle and daub construction, but the shrine rooms of the more wealthy are walled with stone. Poorer families imitate the rich by applying pottery plaques to their shrine walls.

While each family has at least one such shrine, the rituals associated with it are not family ceremonies but are private and secret. The rites are normally only discussed with children, and then only during the period when they are being initiated into these mysteries. I was able, however, to establish sufficient rapport with the natives to examine these shrines and to have the rituals described to me. 5

The focal point of the shrine is a box or chest which is built into the wall. In this chest are kept the many charms and magical potions without which no native believes he could live. These preparations are secured from a variety of specialized practitioners. The most powerful of these are the medicine men, whose assistance must be rewarded with substantial gifts. However, the medicine men do not provide the curative potions for their clients, but decide what the ingredients should be and then write them down in an ancient and secret language. This writing is understood only by the medicine men and by the herbalists who, for another gift, provide the required charm. 6

The charm is not disposed of after it has served its purpose, but is placed in the charm-box of the household shrine. As these magical materials are specific for certain ills, and the real or imagined maladies of the people are many, the charm-box is usually full to overflowing. The magical packets are so numerous that people forget what their purposes were and fear to use them again. While the natives are very vague on this point, we can only assume that the idea in retaining all the old magical materials is that their presence in the charm-box, before which the body rituals are conducted, will in some way protect the worshiper. 7

Beneath the charm-box is a small font. Each day every member of the family, in succession, enters the shrine room, bows his head before the charm-box, mingles different sorts of holy water in the font, and proceeds with a brief rite of ablution.[5] The holy waters are secured from the Water Temple of the community, where the priests conduct elaborate ceremonies to make the liquid ritually pure. 8

In the hierarchy of magical practitioners, and below the medicine men in prestige, are specialists whose designation is best translated as "holy-mouth-men." The Nacirema have an almost pathological horror of and fascination with the mouth, the condition of which is believed to have a supernatural influence on all social relationships. Were it not for the rituals of the mouth, they believe that their teeth would fall out, their gums bleed, their jaws shrink, their friends desert 9 them, and their lovers reject them. They also believe that a strong relationship exists between oral and moral characteristics. For example, there is a ritual ablution of the mouth for children which is supposed to improve their moral fiber.

The daily body ritual performed by everyone includes a mouth-rite. Despite the fact that these people are so punctilious[6] about care of the mouth, this rite involves a practice which strikes the uninitiated stranger as revolting. It was reported to me that the ritual consists of inserting a small bundle of hog hairs into the mouth, along with certain magical powders, and then moving the bundle in a highly formalized series of gestures.[7]

In addition to the private mouth-rite, the people seek out a holy-mouth-man once or twice a year. These practitioners have an impressive set of paraphernalia, consisting of a variety of augers, awls, probes, and prods. The use of these objects in the exorcism of the evils of the mouth involves almost unbelievable ritual torture of the client. The holy-mouth-man opens the client's mouth and, using the above mentioned tools, enlarges any holes which decay may have created in the teeth. Magical materials are put into these holes. If there are no naturally occurring holes in the teeth, large sections of one or more teeth are gouged out so that the supernatural substance can be applied. In the client's view, the purpose of these ministrations[8] is to arrest decay and to draw friends. The extremely sacred and traditional character of the rite is evident in the fact that the natives return to the holy-mouth-men year after year, despite the fact that their teeth continue to decay.

It is to be hoped that, when a thorough study of the Nacirema is made, there will be careful inquiry into the personality structure of these people. One has but to watch the gleam in the eye of a holy-mouth-man, as he jabs an awl into an exposed nerve, to suspect that a certain amount of sadism is involved. If this can be established, a very interesting pattern emerges, for most of the population shows definite masochistic tendencies. It was to these that Professor Linton referred in discussing a distinctive part of the daily body ritual which is performed only by men. This part of the rite includes scraping and lacerating the surface of the face with a sharp instrument. Special women's rites are performed only four times during each lunar month, but what they lack in frequency is made up in barbarity. As part of this ceremony, women bake their heads in small ovens for about an hour. The theoretically interesting point is that what seems to be a preponderantly masochistic people have developed sadistic specialists.

The medicine men have an imposing temple, or *latipso*, in every community of any size. The more elaborate ceremonies required to treat very sick patients can only be performed at this temple. These ceremonies involve not only the thaumaturge[9] but a permanent group of vestal maidens who move sedately about the temple chambers in distinctive costume and headdress.

The *latipso* ceremonies are so harsh that it is phenomenal that a fair propor-   14
tion of the really sick natives who enter the temple ever recover. Small children
whose indoctrination is still incomplete have been known to resist attempts to
take them to the temple because "that is where you go to die." Despite this fact,
sick adults are not only willing but eager to undergo the protracted ritual purification, if they can afford to do so. No matter how ill the supplicant or how
grave the emergency, the guardians of many temples will not admit a client if
he cannot give a rich gift to the custodian. Even after one has gained and survived the ceremonies, the guardians will not permit the neophyte to leave until
he makes still another gift.

The supplicant entering the temple is first stripped of all his or her clothes.   15
In everyday life the Nacirema avoids exposure of his body and its natural functions. Bathing and excretory acts are performed only in the secrecy of the
household shrine, where they are ritualized as part of the body-rites.
Psychological shock results from the fact that body secrecy is suddenly lost upon
entry into the latipso. A man, whose own wife has never seen him in an excretory act, suddenly finds himself naked and assisted by a vestal maiden while he
performs his natural functions into a sacred vessel. This sort of ceremonial treat-
ment is necessitated by the fact that the excreta are used by a diviner to ascertain the course and nature of the client's sickness. Female clients, on the other
hand, find their naked bodies are subjected to the scrutiny, manipulation and
prodding of the medicine men.

Few supplicants in the temple are well enough to do anything but lie on   16
their hard beds. The daily ceremonies, like the rites of the holy-mouth-men,
involve discomfort and torture. With ritual precision, the vestals awaken their
miserable charges each dawn and roll them about on their beds of pain while
performing ablutions, in the formal movements of which the maidens are
highly trained. At other times they insert magic wands in the supplicant's
mouth or force him to eat substances which are supposed to be healing. From
time to time the medicine men come to their clients and jab magically treated
needles into their flesh. The fact that these temple ceremonies may not cure,
and may even kill the neophyte, in no way decreases the people's faith in the
medicine men.

There remains one other kind of practitioner, known as a "listener." This   17
witch-doctor has the power to exorcise the devils that lodge in the heads of
people who have been bewitched. The Nacirema believe that parents bewitch
their own children. Mothers are particularly suspected of putting a curse on
children while teaching them the secret body rituals. The counter-magic of the
witch-doctor is unusual in its lack of ritual. The patient simply tells the "lis-

tener" all his troubles and fears, beginning with the earliest difficulties he can remember. The memory displayed by the Nacirema in these exorcism sessions is truly remarkable. It is not uncommon for the patient to bemoan the rejection he felt upon being weaned as a babe, and a few individuals even see their troubles going back to the traumatic effects of their own birth.

In conclusion, mention must be made of certain practices which have their base in native esthetics but which depend upon the pervasive aversion to the natural body and its functions. There are ritual fasts to make fat people thin and ceremonial feasts to make thin people fat. Still other rites are used to make women's breasts larger if they are small, and smaller if they are large. General dissatisfaction with breast shape is symbolized in the fact that the ideal form is virtually outside the range of human variation. A few women afflicted with almost inhuman hypermammary development are so idolized that they make a handsome living by simply going from village to village and permitting the natives to stare at them for a fee.   18

Reference has already been made to the fact that excretory functions are ritualized, routinized, and relegated to secrecy. Natural reproductive functions are similarly distorted. Intercourse is taboo as a topic and scheduled as an act. Efforts are made to avoid pregnancy by the use of magical materials or by limiting intercourse to certain phases of the moon. Conception is actually very infrequent. When pregnant, women dress so as to hide their condition. Parturition takes place in secret, without friends or relatives to assist, and the majority of women do not nurse their infants.   19

Our review of the ritual life of the Nacirema has certainly shown them to be a magic-ridden people. It is hard to understand how they have managed to exist so long under the burdens which they have imposed upon themselves. But even such exotic customs as these take on real meaning when they are viewed with the insight provided by Malinowski[10] when he wrote (1948: 70):   20

> Looking from far and above, from our high places of safety in the developed civilization, it is easy to see all the crudity and irrelevance of magic. But without its power and guidance early man could not have mastered his practical difficulties as he has done, nor could man have advanced to the higher stages of civilization.[11]

REFERENCES

Linton, Ralph. 1936. *The Study of Man*. New York, D. Appleton-Century Co.

Malinowsli, Bronislaw. 1948. *Magic, Science, and Religion*. Glencoe, The Free Press.

Murdock, George P. 1949. *Social Structure*. New York, The Macmillan Co.

ENDNOTES

1. From "Body Ritual among the Nacirema," *American Anthropologist* 58 (1956): 503–507. [Sourcetext as PDF: <*http://www.aaanet.org/pubs/ bodyrit.pdf*>.] Footnotes were added by Dowell.

2. George Peter Murdock (1897–1985), famous ethnographer.

3. Ralph Linton (1893–1953), best known for studies of enculturation (maintaining that all culture is learned rather than inherited; the process by which a society's culture is transmitted from one generation to the next), claiming culture is humanity's "social heredity."

4. Missing text as follows:
   According to Nacirema mythology, their nation was originated by a culture hero, Notgnihsaw, who is otherwise known for two great feats of strength— the throwing of a piece of wampum across the river Pa-To-Mac and the chopping down of a cherry tree in which the Spirit of Truth resided.

5. A washing or cleansing of the body or a part of the body. From the Latin *abluere*, to wash away.

6. Marked by precise observance of the finer points of etiquette and formal conduct.

7. It is worthy of note that since Prof. Miner's original research was conducted, the Nacirema have almost universally abandoned the natural bristles of their private mouth-rite in favor of oil-based polymerized synthetics. Additionally, the powders associated with this ritual have generally been semi-liquefied. Other updates to the Nacirema culture shall be eschewed in this document for the sake of parsimony.

8. Tending to religious or other important functions.

9. A miracle-worker.

10. Bronislaw Malinowski (1884–1942), famous cultural anthropologist best known for his argument that people everywhere share common biological and psychological needs and that the function of all cultural institutions is to fulfill such needs; the nature of the institution is determined by its function.

11. Did you *get* it? In any case, try analyzing Malinowski's statement in the context of what has come to be known as [Aurthur C.] "Clarke's Third Law": "Any sufficiently advanced technology is indistinguishable from magic."

Mike Rose graduated from Loyola University and the University of Southern California before receiving his Ph.D. from the University of California, Los Angeles in 1981. He is a professor of social research methodology at UCLA Graduate School of Education and Information Studies and former associate director of writing programs there. He has written four books, including *Possible Lives: The Promise of Public Education in America* (1995) and co-authored another with Malcolm Kiniry. He has published articles and essays in various periodicals including *Academic Medicine*, *College English*, and the *Los Angeles Times*.

A VOCABULARY OF CARPENTRY

Mike Rose

From the Renaissance through the nineteenth century, mechanics and engineers developed a variety of picture books, charts, and model displays that classified and illustrated basic mechanisms and mechanical movements: gear assemblies, for example, or ratchets, or levers and pullies. (Diderot's *Encyclopedia* contains a number of such illustrations, and we see descendants of them in vocational textbooks and on wall displays in trade school classrooms.) Reading about the history of these mechanical aids, I was curious about the way mechanisms were classified and the role such illustrated classification might play in developing a visual storehouse of devices (think here of Jon Guthier's library). And I was captivated by the names given to these aids: "theaters of machines" and "mechanical alphabet." The mechanical alphabet, especially, got me to think further, beyond the models to the words and metaphors we use, how much we could benefit from a richer alphabet, a vocabulary broad enough to accurately render physical work.   1

Looking at the old plates, thinking in terms of alphabets, ways to spell and depict, I wonder how many aspects of workplace intelligent behavior are underappreciated, or go unnoticed, because our occupational vocabularies are reductive or because we don't have a category for such behaviors in standard measures of intelligence. What testing vocabulary do we have, for example, to discern the making of judgments from the feel of things, or the strategic use of tool and body, or the rhythmic spacing of tasks, or the coordination of effort and material toward the construction of a complex object?   2

The display case sits in the back of the workshop like a monument. Lustrous   3
oak, glass shelves and doors, interior lights. Students walk by it, run a hand over
it, comment to visitors on its appearance. At the end of every day, they cover it
with brown wrapping paper, forming the paper into a protective cowl. At least
half of the students in Jerry Devries's wood construction class have worked on
the display case over the semester; it is now about a week or two from completion. A time of finishing touches.

Mr. Devries's workshop is one huge room, fifty feet by one hundred. If you   4
started at the display case and slowly walked toward the front of the room, looking about, you'd see wood and metal workstations and old and new power tools:
a band saw, a radial arm saw, a circular saw, a jointer, a belt sander as well as an
edgebander, a panel router, and a router controlled by computer. Various vent
pipes rise overhead, and yellow air compressor hoses coil down from the ceiling.
Against the middle of the west wall sits a large open cabinet with neat rows of
chisels and gouges, files, mallets, bit braces, awls, planes, spokeshaves, hand-
saws. Generation upon generation of woodworker's tools. This is the environment in which skill develops. Along the walls and resting above storage cabinets are models (a house frame, a chest of drawers) and displays of drawer
guides, miniature sliding cabinet doors, miter joints, and post and panel assemblies. At the very front of the room you'll find twenty-four student desks along
with Mr. Devries's own cluttered desk and podium. There is a blackboard covered with projects and the students assigned to them ("Wall Cabinet: Felipe,
Jesus, Gloria"), various sketches of these projects, some dimensions and calculations, and assorted announcements: "Habitat for Humanity job site visit Aug. 1."
The board extends around to a side wall by the door where the lists continue,
and there is a space where students write comments drawn from the chatter and
events of the day: "To sand or not to sand, that is the question."

Mr. Devries stands behind his podium, inching his index finger down a ros-   5
ter. He is 5'3", a solid man in his midforties with thinning red-brown hair. He is
an experienced cabinetmaker who has taught for twenty years, many of them
here at John Marshall High School in Northeast Los Angeles. Alternating
between comedy and drama as he finishes taking roll, he secures parental permission slips for that visit to the Habitat for Humanity construction site (where
the class volunteers their labor) and dispatches with the many microadministra-
tive tasks of the high school teacher. His students, twenty-three boys and one
girl, with one exception all Latino, are a mix of sophomores, juniors, and seniors. They sit postured in the angles and half-turns of variable attention, doo-
dling at arm's length, looking, in pairs, through fantasy art magazines, watching
Mr. Devries. In the rear corner seat, Louie, the class down, cracks a fairly audi-
ble joke about a guy chewing gum laced with Viagra.

Mr. Devries finishes up, closes his roll book, and with rising voice says,   6
"OK, let's *get to work*." And, in movement that is fluid, almost gentle, the students slide out of repose, up and out of their seats, and stream across the floor to
stations around the room: to the worktable by the radial arm saw, to the tool
cabinet, to the panel router, to wall racks in the far corner where they don
aprons and safety glasses. Within minutes the room is vibrant with the slam of
boards laid out to measure, the screech of the circular saw, the acrid smell of
blade on wood.

Some of the work the students do maintains the shop itself. They clean   7
machinery, cut and store wood stock, and make simple tools like sanding
blocks—the same activity you would have found in a nineteenth-century workshop. This work goes on continually, in between or during the primary projects
the students undertake. They can work on individual projects—a table or cabinet or bookcase for their homes—or work in teams on projects that flow into
the shop. After so many years of recognized achievement, Jerry Devries's classes
get requests from within the school and throughout the district to bid on larger
projects: storage cabinets, quantities of podiums, secretaries' stations, computer
tables, the majestic display case.

The majority of students, particularly at the sophomore and junior levels,   8
choose the team effort on these larger projects. Mr. Devries will select an older
student to supervise, thus providing extended experience in planning and delegating—and with the delegating comes a good deal of teaching, peer to peer.
For younger or less-experienced students, the team affords an apprenticing
structure in which to further develop the basic skills of woodworking and some
guided opportunity to plan, calculate, and think through a project. As you look
around the classroom, then, you'll see clusters of four and five students at various workstations, and an occasional lone student measuring, cutting stock, or
assembling—though even there, you'll often see someone assisting, for a cooperative spirit pervades the room.

I follow one of the sophomore boys back to the display case. Paul is a hand-   9
some kid whose usual dress is a black T-shirt adorned with bright and elaborate
fantasy art—cyborgs, aliens, cartoon characters, the sultry, exaggerated women
of car detailing—and baggy jeans cut at the cuff to form a floppy cover over running shoes. He smiles, sometimes laughs out loud, at the antics of the older,
rambunctious boys—hooting at Louie's Viagra joke—but tends toward a more
serious demeanor. He sits sidesaddle in his desk against the west wall, looking
out onto his classmates, looking across the room to Jerry Devries. It's common
that Paul will be the first at his workstation once Mr. Devries releases the class
from the preliminary business of the day. It is this blend of adolescent sociability
and focus that caught my eye—this boy who is laughing with everyone else

while tying his apron or reaching for a tape measure. He talks readily about the "integrity" of working with wood.

Paul enlists another boy to help him remove the paper covering from the display case. Then he grabs a framing square (an L-shaped metal ruler) off of a nearby table, pulls a stool over to the back of the display case, and begins the task assigned to him by Mr. Devries. Boards for support still need to be fastened to the back of the case, one along the top and one along the bottom. Paul's job is to draw the lines on the case that will mark the placement of the supports. Paul steps onto the stool, framing square in hand, pencil behind ear. He begins. I watch him for a long time.

Because the framing square is two feet long, Paul has to draw the lines in increments, steadying the framing square against several reference points, checking and double-checking each segment of each line. He has to be sure that each line is so many inches from the top or bottom and that each segment of each line is aligned with the other, and that the twin lines (across the top and across the bottom) are aligned.

Paul is cautious. Every time he slides the framing square from one increment of the line to another, he checks it at several points, his face turned slightly, eye close to the wood. Then he runs his pencil slowly along the rule, pulls his head back, and checks it again. This is a pretty basic task: Paul is using some fundamental measurement arithmetic and gaining practice with the framing square, aligning it on a surface, reading it. But he is also learning something, I think, about attending, summoning one's powers of concentration in the service of precision. We saw the role of attention in the waitress's work. Here we see it in a different context, and in a way that calls forth William James's classic discussion of attention: "Focalization, concentration of consciousness are of its essence." The exact placement of the supports matters, and it is one of the last tasks in the long life of this valued project. Paul focuses his efforts to get it right. I am drawn by his deliberateness, its development manifest in this task.

When we think about problem solving, creativity, acts of the mind, we tend to think of the grand moment, the clarifying insight, the breakthrough, the tough nut cracked. Fair enough. Such moments are worthy of acknowledgment. But I think it is also worth dwelling on the commonplace, ordinary expressions of mind that every day, a thousand times over, enable the work of the world to get done, and that, more than we think, are critical in solving the less common, more dramatic problems that face us. In his study of creativity, *The Mind's Best Work*, psychologist D. N. Perkins argues that creative ability, long studied as exceptional, can also be understood as "exceptional versions of familiar mental operations," such as perception and memory. The notion is

10

11

12

13

valuable here, for it encourages an appreciation of the significance of cognitive processes that, because of their frequency and familiarity, are taken for granted. Such an appreciation might provide one way to develop a vocabulary befitting the mind at work.

The more time I spend in Jerry Devries's workshop, the more I notice the   14
various ways this mix of attention and perception, knowledge of the field, and values plays out in the day-to-day routines of working with wood. Consider, for example, the sharpening of the senses that develops in the woodworking environment. "Use the eyes to test straightness, squareness, and symmetry," writes the author of an early-twentieth-century pedagogical tract, "before applying any other testing instruments." Jerry, like other expert carpenters I observed, is able to estimate length at a glance. He can eyeball a structure for misalignment, an angle that's off, gaps, bows, sags in an assembly. He troubleshoots the cause of problems through the look of things. He has an eye, and a touch, for texture. He scans for flaws, spotting a place high up on the interior wall of the display case where a screw has barely broken through the wood. This ability has been characterized by several cognitive researchers as *disciplined perception*—and we saw it in another kind of work with the hairstylists. It is disciplined because it emerges from one's training and depends on—and helps constitute—a body of knowledge. And what is perceived is connected to systematic action; here perception has meaning and consequence for assembly and repair.

The woodworker's visual skill is so much a part of the work that it's easy to   15
miss its special quality. Thus it was through a sense less identified with carpentry that the importance of disciplined perception first struck me.

We were at the Habitat for Humanity job site, Jerry and I talking. About fif-   16
teen yards away, a group of students was drilling holes in fence posts. Jerry suddenly turned around. "Hey," he yelled, "don't burn the motor out!" The students stopped, and he walked over. "Go slow," he said, and showed them how to handle the drill with more finesse. Earlier that day, another crew of Jerry's students had been cutting stock to length for the fence, and, this time, it was the sound of the saw that caught Jerry's ear. He made his way to the place where the students had set up the power miter box they were using—they had placed the tool on a sheet of plywood that rested on two sawhorses—and he moved the two sawhorses closer together. The weight of the miter box was causing the plywood to bend, and thus the stock that the students were cutting was bowing slightly, causing the saw to grab or bind into the wood. Jerry turned to Louie, of Viagra fame. "What'd I just do?" Louie explained the principle behind the action, using his hands to illustrate. As Jerry walked away, Louie leaned toward me and nodded at his teacher's retreating figure: "Interesting, huh?" Then, louder, for the

benefit of his peers, he said, "Devries tactics," a phrase the students use to label one of Mr. Devries's tricks of the trade, adjustments, or techniques.

As I walk around Jerry Devries's classroom or the Habitat for Humanity job   17
site, I too hear a range of sounds: the pounding of hammers, the squeal of power saws, the harsh router. But it's cacophonous, gross distinctions at best. I ask Jerry about the keenness of his ear. He laughs and says that he doesn't think he hears with particular acuity, that, in fact, he sometimes has trouble hearing what his students are saying. But he clearly has developed an ear for the sounds of trouble related to the use of power tools. In the first vignette with the drill, he hears a motor being pushed close to its limits. In the second, he hears something in the sound of the cut that suggests that the saw blade is binding into the wood. His is an ear trained to hear trouble, to perceive it amid all the other sounds of the workplace. This heightened perception enables him to protect against error or damage, and it also has pedagogic value, enabling him to intervene right at a strategic, teachable moment.

As with many work-related abilities, it's hard to trace specifically how this   18
skill develops, other than to say that it develops with experience, over time, and with certain motives and incentives—like protecting tools and teaching their proper use. But though difficult to trace, you can see moments of its development. Paul, whom we just met measuring the display case, is running a piece of stock through the jointer, to plane smooth its edge. He runs the board through three or four times, occasionally leaning back to look under the machine to see the shavings coming off. I ask him why he runs it through multiple times, and he explains that he had determined that it had a bow in the middle. (To check the evenness of the surface of an edge, Mr. Devries had shown the students how to set a board on the flat metal surface of the machine, then hunch down and look to see if any light comes through.) I then ask Paul how he decides on the number of times to put the board through—since he isn't stopping after every pass to perform the light test, and he explains that you can *hear* when the board is even, for the sound will continue without interruption, the blade will not be hitting any gaps in the surface of the wood. Paul seems to be on his way to developing the kind of trained ear that Jerry Devries has, an ear attuned to variation in the sound of a power tool on wood, and the potential meaning that sound may have.

I have been discussing the individual senses, but the integrated use of multiple senses—a long-standing curiosity to psychologists of perception—is also   19
commonplace in the shops I visited. I watched, for example, an auto mechanic use all of his senses but taste while repairing an engine—often using the senses in combination to "give [him] more information" or "to check one against the

other." A fascinating variation of this sensory integration is when a tradesperson uses one sense as a substitute for another, as when the plumber Jon Guthier reached up inside a wall to "help [him] see" the condition of the pipes hidden within. Here touch is used as a visualizing mechanism, to interpretive, diagnostic ends.

This focusing of attention and refinement of the senses occurs in the service of   20
assembly and repair, so they are intimately linked to the use of tools. And tools, of course, would be a key element in any vocabulary of work. The development of skill with tools involves, at the least, knowledge of a tool's purpose and function and competent use of the body: grip, stance, leverage, the efficient transfer of force. This attunement of body and tool is less foreign to me than Jerry's and Paul's refined ear. It was during one of my uncle Frank's visits to Los Angeles— the railroad had laid people off again, and he was looking out West for work— that he helped me build a storage box. I was hammering a panel onto the frame when he stopped me, moved my hand down to the base of the handle—I was "choking" it—and showed me how to swing the tool in a way that "let the hammer do the work." What struck me, I remember, was the surprise of the feel: the hammer seemed more powerful and my swing—from shoulder through wrist— increasingly fluid. And I got better at driving a nail.

Looking across Jerry Devries's workshop with a focus on movement, attend-   21
ing to biomechanics, I see a range of physical skill with a variety of tools and tasks: from one of the youngest boys struggling with the saw in a miter box, his strokes wobbly and uneven, to Louie on one knee, his torso turned into the tight space of a cabinet, working a chisel over a flaw in the frame. The biomechanical skills related to carpentry build on and enhance basic sensory, kinesthetic, and cognitive abilities that emerge through natural development, abilities that, themselves, as any neurologist will tell you, are wondrous: the ability to grasp, to pound, to attend to and track an object, to sequence movements. This is the endowment Mr. Devries's students bring with them and that, in his class or (often) earlier in fathers' or grandfathers' workshops, is further developed and channeled toward the skillful use of tools. His students' learning occurs continually and in multiple ways.

They learn how to effectively use their bodies by observing Mr. Devries's   22
demonstrations and the work of their peers. (Paul notes: "You see work going on all around you. You see people making small, small mistakes, and you learn from that.") Students learn through guided practice: Mr. Devries or an older student coaching or physically directing their movement. And they learn through their own trial and error, adjusting their stance and motion via the

visual and tactile feedback they get from tool and wood. Just about every photo-graph I have of Mr. Devries or a student using a tool catches several others looking on, gaze focused on the task. If we were to animate the photos, you'd commonly see those observers move from the periphery to take in hand the file, the nail punch, the bench plane. They would then mimic what they saw, get-ting the actual feel of it. Another thing you'd see is Mr. Devries or an older stu-dent moving into the frame to orally or physically guide the motion of hand and arm. Felipe, one of Mr. Devries's more competent juniors, comes over to the boy struggling with the backsaw in the miter box. Here, he tells him in Spanish, stand like this. And, look, this saw cuts going in, so push it all the way in, move your arm like this, now easy coming back. See?

Felipe's assist reveals something important—but often unsaid—about phys- 23
ical skill: that it's usually integrated with knowledge. His feel for the backsaw is combined with an understanding of how it works. I think of Willie, the expert mechanic in Douglas Harper's *Working Knowledge*, as he advises Harper on his misuse of the hacksaw: "A hacksaw *plays* its way through the metal. . . . If you lay on it too hard it will not cut on a straight line. Take your time—let it play." Willie and Felipe know things about the saws they're using and the materials they're using them on, and that knowledge informs their movement.

And students learn how to use a tool not only on the bench but in con- 24
strained space. Thus they learn how to maximize biomechanics, begin to develop the physical savvy that eventually yields the deft touch of the drywaller working overhead or the carpenter starting a nail with one hand. Gloria is standing with one leg inside and one leg outside the frame of a cabinet for the art department. She is attaching small boards under the base—these will protect the frame when it is stood upright—and has to lean out and over to get a clean swing of her hammer. She secures a board with her foot, angling the tip of her shoe in about forty-five degrees. She drives the nails. On the second board, she angles her foot differently, learning from the feel of her first attempt, and drives the nails home.

As with waitressing, many of these moves will become routine, but now, at 25
these freeze-frames of development, we see a conscious attending, mimicking, calibrating of the body. It is commonplace both in vernacular and in the psy-chological sciences to say that over time these physical skills become automatic, and to be sure, with practice, they require much less attention. But one of the professional carpenters I spoke to had an interesting take on this business of automaticity. He stopped me when I used the word *automatic*. It didn't feel right to him. "Confident," he said, after a moment, thinking out loud. Sure, your hammer strokes and sawing and all that, by now, are proficient, you do it right,

you do it once. But there's always some element of awareness to the work, for safety, but also because the task at hand will have its own demands, require its own minor adjustments. This calls to mind one of the conclusions in a recent study of blacksmithing: "Skilled performances [are] conceptually embedded even when immediate events press an agent to react seemingly without thinking." One's physical skills, then, though highly developed, will always be responsive to the environment, calling for a certain circumspection and adaptability. The hammer stroke becomes routinized but not mindless.

Let us now turn from a focus on body and hand to a consideration of tools themselves. Mr. Devries's students are surrounded by tools, both manual and power, and one of the significant things that will happen to these young people over their time with him and beyond is that their knowledge of tools, and the variations within kinds of tools—the crosscut saw, the ripsaw, the backsaw, the coping saw—will increase dramatically. They will be able to recognize these objects, name them, know what each can do—and as we just saw, they will learn how to manipulate them effectively. At the most fundamental level, clear in the human archaeological record, there are about a half-dozen things tools enable us to do, and to do profoundly better than by hand and arm alone: pound, cut, probe, scrape, join. But the variety of methods humankind has developed to perform these basic tasks, responses to emerging needs in assembly and repair, is staggering. Neuropsychologist Richard Gregory makes the nice observation that "tools contain ready-made answers to practical problems." Jerry Devries's students do not have to solve anew the problem of how to make an accurate forty-five-degree cut; they have the miter box and backsaw available, a set of devices that represents many generations of thought as well as advances in metallurgy and toolmaking. Tool as legacy. As Felipe helps that younger student use the miter box, he orients him to a historically embodied set of solved problems, and, in a sense, activates them, yielding the precise cut, the clean angle ready for joining.

Tools not only act on material but with experience become a vehicle for learning about the properties of materials themselves. As well, one learns about force and function, design and structure. Brain, hand, tool, wood become a complex cybernetic system, information flowing back and forth in action. We saw this feedback loop in play as students were learning to use their bodies in concert with tools. And, of course, tools like the tape measure, the framing square, and the spirit level provide data on length, angle, and tilt. Other tools, from the awl (that pointed tool that looks like an ice pick) to the crowbar, can be used inventively to help you determine and effect alignment. And, as Paul explains to me holding up, first, a piece of oak, then pine, different kinds of wood respond in different ways to nail, saw, plane, and sandpaper.

"The hammer," claims carpenter and writer Jeff Taylor, ". . . changes the   28
way you think." The use of tools over time contributes to a bodily, material
physics and mechanics, to a rich knowledge of assembly and repair, and to a
problem-solving orientation toward the built environment. This knowledge is
manifest in the workshop. I sensed it before I could put words to it—and
Richard Gregory's observation about tools embodying solutions to problems
helped guide my expression. There is intelligence in the surround, poised, so to
speak, for purposeful action. For the young person with an interest in woodworking, the shop must feel like a powerful invitation to competence, a path-
way to achievement. As I talk to Paul about the nearly completed display case,
he comments on its appearance and says how good it feels to see it through to
completion. He pauses, and shifts. "As time goes on," he says, gesturing, moving
his hand along an imaginary time line, "you get to use tools you haven't used
before. There's some tools here I haven't used yet." His eyes get big and he
smiles, "like the panel router," and he points across the room to a router on a
carriage that glides over a large, retaining frame. "That will enable me to do
some new things, and I'm excited. It gives you a good, nice cut."

Paul's comment brings us directly to the topic of power tools, which could be   29
seen to qualify much of what I've written about the development of physical
skill. With the advent of steam-powered (and, later, electrically powered) tools,
there has been a diminished need for the manual finesse of the preindustrial
craftsman. The band saw and jigsaw, for example, can quickly make all sorts of
irregular and curved cuts that took much longer, with much more adroit manipulation, when performed by hand. The use of power tools brought with it a
degree of de-skilling—and, some would say, a loss of craftsmanship. But what is
also true—immediately evident to anyone who tries to use a jig- or band saw—
is that power tools require a skill of their own. Also, as the historical record
shows, in domains such as furniture making, power tools were integrated into
craft traditions and practices, significantly altering the performance of many
operations but within the ethos and character of craft work.

Craft traditions are evident in the environment Jerry Devries provides.   30
And there is another, more personal, means of transmission. Some of the students I got to know had people in their families who worked with wood—
fathers, uncles, grandfathers—and these students, as youngsters, had spent time
in garages and workshops hanging around the older men. "Just seeing what he
could do," says one boy, "interested me." Craft traditions were manifest in this
work, transmitted and made immediate through bloodlines, through what one
group of educational researchers aptly calls a family's "funds of knowledge."

When I ask another boy why he's putting shelves in a bookcase with dowels—rather than with more expedient metal fasteners—he credits his grandfather, a master cabinetmaker, and says, "I just like to do it the old way." The use of dowels harkens back to, and honors, days in a grandfather's workshop and, as well, serves as an expression of who this boy wants to be.

I continually witnessed this dynamic relation between old craft and new   31
technology. Felipe had run one of the shelves of the wall cabinet he's building through the edge-bander, a machine that cuts and glues thin strips of decorative laminate along the edges of plywood or particleboard, and as he was inspecting the shelf, he noticed a small bubble of glue rising out of one of the seams. He is a deliberate and cautious worker and is a good teacher of his peers—as we saw in the miter box example. His grandfather and his uncles are cabinetmakers in Mexico, and they do their work by hand, with no power tools. As a boy, he would visit, watch, "help them a little, bring them their tools." But though he grew up around woodworkers, he says he's learned the skills and procedures of the trade primarily through the classes he's taken with Mr. Devries.

When we join Felipe—buzz-cut brown hair, a small stud on the top of each   32
ear—he has the shelf upright on a worktable, holding it with his right hand, a utility knife in his left, cutting in small, restricted motions at the bubble. Felipe moves here with a delicate touch. His face is right up on the seam, so close that the handle of the knife grazes his left cheek. He puts the knife down, taps the edge of the board with a small hammer, picks with thumb and forefinger at the remaining glue, then reaches for the knife and continues to trim the excess, face in close, eye fixed. With no direction from anyone, as a matter of course, it seems, Felipe scans the work of the edge-bander, detects a small flaw that disrupts the smooth line of the edge, and sets out to fix it. With careful and fine movement of the hand and the aid of tools that cut and compress, he continues the work of the edge-bander, completing the aesthetically clean line.

To be sure, the various cutting and routing power tools in Jerry Devries's   33
classroom remove some opportunity to develop hand and eye; they channel and in some ways limit Felipe's growth. Before the edge-bander was invented, a woodworker would have had to cut, align, and glue the laminate on that cabinet shelf, then trim and finish it. As well, the joints that hold the panels of the cabinet together would have been fashioned manually. In his celebration of hand tools, *Tools of the Trade: The Art and Craft of Carpentry*, Jeff Taylor provides eloquent commentary on the sense of craft such work develops: "At a certain point, upon a day, you almost become the work, a moving and cognitive part of the tool in your own hand."

With Taylor in mind, let me offer several interrelated observations based   34
on my time in Jerry Devries's workshop. First, Mr. Devries's curriculum, particularly for those students who work with him over time, includes considerable
instruction in the use of hand tools. And there are times when tasks like cutting
joints or affixing and trimming laminate must be done by hand: for example
where structural constraints are severe or where power tools fail—as when the
compressor attached to the edge-bander broke, forcing Felipe and his coworkers
to prepare another shelf by hand.

Second, the speed and precision of power tools does ease the work and free   35
up time—important motivations for those early tradespersons who adopted such
tools—time that can be spent on the planning and refinement of projects, on
assembly, on detail and repair. Electrical tools do not erase the need for thought
and care.

Furthermore, power tools, as the students continually tell me, bring their   36
own challenges, their own opportunities to master sequence and procedure and
physical skill. As I watch Paul use a table saw (a circular blade that comes up
through a slit in the table) to cut one-quarter of an inch off the width of a
board, he must first make sure one edge of the board is straight, so he had to
plane it by running it through the jointer. Then he must adjust the height and
angle of the saw blade, account for the width of the saw blade in his measurements, set the guiding or "rip" fence against the board appropriately, and control the wood through his own stance and movement—possibly with the aid of
a push stick. "It's the preparation that's hardest," he says, "remembering all the
steps and then doing them right." And once a student is actually operating the
tool, further knowledge and finesse are necessary. Felipe is using the band saw
to cut a half circle into a panel. The blade on a band saw is narrow and can
twist as it curves through the wood. To protect against this—and to assure a
smooth cut—Felipe, moving slowly and precisely ("you have to take your time
with the band saw"), makes a series of "relief cuts" into the section of the panel
that will be cut away, essentially breaking up the curve into smaller units, cutting each in turn.

Finally, though power tools "build the skill into the machine," the effective   37
use of such tools requires, at the least, some degree of that skill: in order to know
what the skill should yield, to adjust the machine accordingly, to troubleshoot
problems and repair them, and to judge the outcome. Paul and a senior named
Ricky are building an L-shaped secretarial workstation. Nine have been ordered,
and this is the prototype. Paul has prepared strips of alder molding for the edges
of the plywood top, and, upon affixing them, spies a tiny gap where two of the
strips meet. It's not sufficient to correct the problem here, for this is the first of

nine stations; if the cause of the problem isn't found, it will bedevil subsequent production. Over the next hour, with the more knowledgeable Ricky taking the lead, but with Paul participating fully as apprentice, the boys run through possible problems with the tools that fashioned the molding: perhaps the gauge on the power miter box is faulty; perhaps there is dirt or debris behind the fence on the router table. Or maybe the problem lies not with the molding but with the construction of the frame to which it is affixed. Did they make a mistake when assembling the frame? As they think the problem through, they also display knowledge of the way power tools work and of the physics they embody—as when Ricky discusses the "velocity and friction" of a sanding tool as a reason not to use it to remedy the kind of error they're confronting. This tool talk is coupled with a concern about the durability and appearance of the desk top, displaying, I think, an impressive integration of tool knowledge, troubleshooting, and craft values. And the entire event demonstrates something that we've been seeing in this workshop: a systematic approach to problems that would be useful in other academic and professional settings.

When I describe the above vignettes to expert carpenters, they comment   38
that as the students spend more time with power tools like these, their mastery of procedure will increase as will their feel for the tools, their finesse with them, and their capacity to express themselves through variations in design. As well, considering the wide range of ways one can cut and join, they will begin to make wiser decisions about which kind of saw or router or sander to use, given the materials and task at hand. They'll become adroit at adapting tool to need. It makes me think that someone, following Jeff Taylor's lead, should write a subsequent book on the "art and craft" of the power tool: an attempt to render the knack and judgment required for the router, the jointer, the band saw.

Before I leave this discussion of tool use, I want to consider a seemingly unre-   39
lated element of the vocabulary of work operating in Mr. Devries's classroom, one so familiar and ever-present that it frequently escapes mention: talk. Traditional discussions of technology tend, in various ways, to separate the technical and the social—and with the social, the play of language. What is so clear in this workshop setting, though, is the intimate interconnection of tool use, wood construction, and speech. Electrician and poet Susan Eisenberg captures the mix: "[W]ork and talk flowing like/wire through well-laid pipe."

Here is Jerry Devries showing Felipe and his peers how to make a "layout   40
stick," a long, thin piece of wood that has the measurements of the main components of their cabinet marked and labeled on it. As Mr. Devries demonstrates, he repeats for his students the names of new components (the *mullion* is

the center support of the front, or "face," frame of the cabinet); queries them on the functional justification for these components ("You're not gonna make a sixty-eight-inch cabinet without a mullion, why?"); informs them of pertinent codes ("Anything over thirty-six inches requires support"); asks them to think through the mathematical consequences of the interrelation of the cabinet's components ("How will you adjust for the presence of the two-inch mullion?"); voices functional or aesthetic biases ("Some cabinetmakers like a lot of face frame; I don't like as much face frame"); and has Felipe and company think about the physical context of their cabinet ("Is it going up to the height of the ceiling?"). The fashioning of the layout stick is surrounded by statements of fact, questions, opinions. All of Mr. Devries's instruction—before the whole class, in small groups, or individually—involves speech and gesture, and, as we've seen, peer-to-peer instruction is oral and gestural as well.

If we were able to record a day's worth of the more informal talk in Mr. Devries's classroom—or, for that fact, at a typical construction site—we'd get a wide range of types and topics: gossip, banter, commentary on the events of the day, declarations of things hoped for, plans and goals, chronicles of life on the home front. A lot of it would be crude and combative. What interests me, though, is the way this informal talk—as we saw with the hairstylists— functions as an open channel, rich in cognitive possibility; the way information, procedures, and tricks of the trade flow in and out of the banter, fantasy, and dirty jokes.   41

Mike, one of Mr. Devries's seniors, is showing Paul, who has been eager for this opportunity, how to use the panel router. Another senior, Ruben, takes a break from his work nearby and walks over, sparring lightly with Mike and Paul. The three gab a little, and Mike begins to clamp a small board over the panel he's placed on the frame of the router. Ruben asks what's with the board; Mike says it's to protect the panel and to stabilize it, fool. You don't need to do that, Ruben counters, unless the panel has been edge-banded—the small board will keep the router from stripping off the laminate. No, you do it anyway, says Mike, and the discussion goes back and forth around the panel router, Paul looking on, listening in.   42

Across the room, Felipe and his crew are working on the wall cabinet. Felipe, Gloria, and Jesus are double-checking the measurements for the cabinet when they run into some confusion about the length of the top panel. Felipe leaves to find Mr. Devries. Gloria and Jesus start exchanging flirtatious jabs, and as they do, they look at the sketches and lists on the table before them. Gloria points to the top panel, and they start calculating with pencil the measurements again, confirming the dimensions written on the plans for themselves.   43

During another part of the day, Mr. Devries is in the library with two   44
younger students, Ray and Billy, taking measurements for new doors on some
storage cabinets. Measuring the dimensions of the doors is a straightforward
task, but then Jerry begins to explain how the hinges they use may require that
they alter their measurements, for different hinges require different tolerances.
So given the kind of hinge currently used in the cabinets, they'll need to adjust
their measurement by one-half inch. Ray takes out a sheet of paper and writes
this down; Jerry leaves to check in on other students. Billy and Ray take the
measurements again, and, in the midst of gossip about school, in a mix of English and Spanish, Billy explains the concept of tolerance, placing his hand at
the edge of the door, turning his hand in and out, illustrating the function of
the hinge, and explaining the consequences for measurement.

And there are times when talk is not so directly purposeful, but still serves a   45
cognitive function. Ray, Billy, and I are walking back from the library. At some
point, it seems, the librarian described to Ray the kind of doors she wanted—
ones with ventilating holes along the bottom. As we walk, Ray is telling the
story of their encounter and laughing. Ray speaks English pretty well, but still
hesitates at times and can't find the right phrasing, particularly with idiomatic
speech. "She confused me," he says. "She wanted it like mouse cheese." He
laughs, and we do too. "Mouse cheese!" Ray continues and gestures with his right
hand by his head as he explains his puzzled reaction to what I assume was her
description of the ventilation holes being like Swiss cheese. We talk a few minutes more, until we arrive at the classroom, Ray and Billy still discussing the
doors and their function. Ray initiated the conversation to spark a laugh, but
also, I think, to clarify things in the safe conversational space created through
humor and with his friend Billy, in motion, outside the library. The comic story
becomes here a means to gain public consideration and assistance, to turn an
event over in one's mind and to think it through in the presence of others. And
it is one more reminder of the social and linguistic dimension of fashioning
things with tools.

As students take on projects like the display case or the kitchen cabinet, they   46
often find themselves at the current limits of their ability, and it is at those limits that further aspects of carpentry develop, both by instruction and guidance
and by assembly itself—through practice, peer interaction, trial and error. Three
of these aspects, interrelated ones, are planning the project and sequencing the
steps of assembly; conceptualizing and visualizing the project, both incremen-
tally and as finished object; and the use of what I'll call *material mathematics* to
facilitate planning and assembly. All the fundamental elements of carpentry

discussed earlier—from tool use to talk—are evident in these activities, both enable them and are further developed by them. Our expanded vocabulary of work would have to account for these activities, giving a sense of how they play out in practice.

Let me begin with planning and procedure. "Before a single piece of wood is cut," as Jerry Devries puts it, his students engage in the following planning processes. When a project is conceived or contracted, Mr. Devries breaks his class into small groups (composed of both more- and less-experienced students) and assigns to each a part of the project. In the case of the cabinet, one group has the face frame, another the shelves, another the doors. The groups draw up lists of the materials they think they'll need to make their part and the tools they'll use for preparation. Then the groups come together and write their lists on the chalkboard, and as a class revise them. These generic lists of procedures are compiled and further adapted to the specifics of a project—so for the shelves of Felipe's wall cabinet, you'd see: 47

Materials and Procedures	Tools
Select stock for 2 shelves (maple plywood)	
Ripcut [that is, lengthwise with the grain] to width 17″	circular saw
Crosscut to length 36 ¾″	panel saw

and so on.

In addition to a list of procedures, Jerry provides a general sketch of the project. On the front chalkboard, there is a three-dimensional drawing of a cabinet with some pieces and dimensions labeled. The team working on the cabinet has to adapt the sketch to their project. As the team begins the project, Jerry consults with them on the dimensions of the components. Usually this involves time spent filling out and verifying a list of exact measurements and the development of the layout stick, that handy, at-a-glance ruler. And as planning takes place, someone on the team (usually the more experienced member) fills out a "bill of materials," basically a price list of kinds of wood, dimensions, and expense.   48

Thus students specify and articulate in written lists and graphic representations the materials they'll need, their dimensions, and their cost; the procedures required to prepare and assemble them; and the way they'll look when assembled, their relation each to the other. Through his assignments, Mr. Devries makes these aspects of carpentry explicit, requiring students to think them through, talk them over. Not all teachers, not to mention apprenticeship arrangements, would initiate beginners in so systematic a fashion. There are other ways these skills can be learned—in some settings they are acquired primarily through observation and graduated participation—but Jerry Devries's   49 approach does enable us to get some sense of the complexity of these skills and their mastery, a sense of what gets absorbed into the expert's fluid practice.

The first thing to note is just how many sequential steps are involved in the   50
assembly of even a fairly simple structure. There are 125 steps enumerated in Felipe's list of procedures, and these lead only to the basic structure of the cabinet. And each step—crosscut door panels to 31¼"; edge-band the edge of the shelves—is, as we saw, composed of a number of more basic cognitive and biomechanical operations. The number of things to keep in mind—and the proper ordering of them—is, at Felipe's stage of development, overwhelming. (I saw evidence of the cognitive overload when he would, in addressing an item on the list of procedures, forget to do something—like plane an edge—that I saw him do routinely on simpler tasks.) Felipe notes that this cabinet "is the biggest thing I've been in charge of," and that the planning of it and keeping track of the procedures are the hardest aspects of the work. He is only able to do the job at all with a good deal of written and oral support. He follows his list of procedures carefully. My notes are full of moments when Felipe is looking over to his list (or to his sketch of the cabinet), or stopping work to fish the list out of his pocket or backpack. His activity is strongly coupled to these pieces of paper. As well, he draws on his peers when he can, though, because they are less experienced, they provide limited help with this aspect of the work. And, frequently, he consults with Mr. Devries, much of whose time is spent doing just this kind of checking in, verifying, guiding, instructing on the spot. This written and verbal assistance enables Felipe to move forward intellectually and functionally, learning and doing right at the brink of his ability.

As a long line of psychological studies—and our own commonsense experi-   51
ence—suggests, skilled routines develop with practice. ("You develop a sense of anticipation," a retired stonemason tells me. "The idea is to always think ahead, visualize where you'll end up, what you'll need next, and next after that.") As Felipe builds this and further cabinets, he will learn more about their structure and properties, and all the steps of preparation and assembly will become familiar, combined into meaningful units, executed more efficiently. He will need less support from his teacher and from his lists. It's as if his lists become abbreviated and internalized.

As this happens, the time required to complete a cabinet will decrease sig-   52
nificantly. Felipe will also be able to think ahead, anticipate subsequent procedures, and keep potential problems in mind. Eventually, the emerging structure of the object he is building will itself aid recall and proper sequencing of behaviors. I watched Felipe and his crew work on a second cabinet about five months after completing the first. They were fairly well along, inserting shelf standards into grooves they had cut into the interior of the side panels. (Standards are the

perforated metal strips onto which adjustable shelves are secured.) The exact placement and fastening of the standards is, in Felipe's words, "critical"; driving small nails into them, for example, can cause them to move slightly, leading to misalignment. I observed the installation of the standards in the first cabinet—a lengthy, painstaking affair—and in the second, which went more smoothly. As Felipe and his crew work with the standards for the second cabinet, Jesus, one of the younger boys, says that the first installation was harder, but now, pointing to the side of his head, they remember how to do it. "You get the experience," Felipe adds, "and you know what to do. Once you're building it, you see what's needed. You don't need the list of procedures." At about the midpoint of the construction of the first cabinet, Felipe, with several lists spread before him, bemoaned all this "paperwork," expressing a desire to "have things come back to you" as you do them. Already, it seems, he is moving in that direction, aided by memory, developing routines, and the object he and his coworkers are assembling.

Over time, Felipe will not only master routines of assembly, but, hand in glove, will acquire more knowledge about cabinets (and other wood furnishings), different types, different particulars of form and function, and an understanding of the range of possible configurations of parts to whole. At this point in his education, however, Felipe has built but one small, structurally simple cabinet, and the current, second, cabinet has a number of features the earlier project didn't. His storehouse of knowledge about cabinets, his "cabinet sense," is just developing, and the limits of his knowledge reveal themselves at various points throughout assembly. Like this one.

Felipe is trying to record final figures for all the components of the cabinet—he and his coworkers are eager to begin assembly. He is working with Gloria and Jesus, and he is sketching with them one more three-dimensional representation of the cabinet, using the layout stick, the list of procedures, and the bill of materials. When I come upon him, he is looking back and forth from the bill of materials to the sketch and talking to his peers. He seems puzzled. He asks Gloria to get the first sketch they made of the cabinet. She retrieves it from her backpack and unfolds it. They study it for a moment. He says something to Jesus, then takes a tape and measures—as if to confirm—the length of the cabinet. Sixty-eight inches. Felipe continues this way, double-checking, trying to verify, looking up occasionally to snag Mr. Devries who, however, is helping a group across the room. The source of this vexation, which lasts a good fifteen minutes, is a discrepancy that emerged as Felipe, Jesus, and Gloria were listing final numbers: the length of the sheet of plywood for the bottom of the cabinet—this is found on the bill of materials—is sixty-eight inches. But the length of the top panel—listed on another sheet—is sixty-seven inches. This makes no sense. As Felipe explains it, exhibiting a nice shift from numbers to their structural meaning, the top can't be shorter than the bottom, or the cabinet will look like this: and here he makes an abbreviated triangle in the air with his hands. What's going on?

Finally, Mr. Devries is free, Felipe goes to get him, and they confer. The   55
sketch Felipe has is inadequate, is not detailed enough to reveal that the top panel rests inside notches cut into the top of the side panels. These are called rabbit cuts. Felipe's discomfort resolves quickly into understanding. The bottom panel extends to the very ends of the side panels, but the top will be shorter by a half inch on each side, the dimensions of the rabbit cuts. Thus the mystery of the sixty-eight-inch bottom and the sixty-seven-inch top.

The depictions of the cabinet in Felipe's plans do not provide enough   56
information—through graphics or numbers—to enable him to figure out the discrepancy in measurement between top and bottom. Yet he must rely on these sketches—as he must depend on the list of procedures—for he does not yet know enough about cabinets to enable him to solve the problem readily . . . or not to assume that the discrepancy is a problem in the first place.

We get a sense of how powerful this kind of knowledge of the object is   57
when we watch an experienced carpenter confront the challenges of structure and assembly. One carpenter I observed was installing a set of sliding French doors into a constrained wall space. He stood back, chin in hand, surveying the frame, his eyes moving over it, occasionally nodding his head and saying something under his breath. When I asked him what he was doing, he said he was "picturing the door in my mind." Essentially, he was imagining the pieces as he would assemble them, thinking, for example, how the threshold will have to angle down, so that the rain will run off it, or picturing the sliding panels moving across the stationary ones, and where problems might develop with that. As well, he is imagining the look of the casings that came with the door, and realizing that they're too big, given the other woodwork in the room, and trying to visualize alternative casings he could fashion.

I find this intellectually rich. The carpenter is relying on a significant   58
knowledge base about doors, some of it generic, some specific to this uncommon structure. He is performing a number of mostly visual operations on this knowledge, operations documented in the research literature on mental imagery: he is examining and combining elements of the assembly, moving them, comparing, substituting, or transforming them. And there are not only structural and mechanical goals driving these operations but aesthetic ones as well—for example, the look of the casings. He is assembling the structure in his mind's eye and

is also reflecting on it. Thus, in fact, the task before this carpenter and what he does with it is more complex than the tasks involved in typical studies of mental imagery. The acquisition of such knowledge and the ability to use it this way is another sign of expertise. (This sense of the object has long been recognized as central to the expert's ability; I found crisp expression of it by a nineteenth-century shipbuilder: "[T]he most important part of the builder's craft [is] the carrying about the shape in his head as well as in the mould.") Felipe is at the beginning stages of developing a sense of cabinet structure. But watching him and his crew build their second wall cabinet, you see it developing.

There are some expected advances, of course. There is no confusion the 59 second time around about the length of the top and the bottom panels; that earlier episode taught Felipe a lot. And I saw other evidence of an emerging cabinet sense. Unlike the previous cabinet, this cabinet requires a plastic laminate over its surface. Felipe is laying the cabinet's face frame over a long sheet of plastic and tracing the outline of the frame onto it. This will give him the covering for the frame but leave two fairly large door-sized squares of the plastic. Felipe stops, takes a step back, looks the cabinet over, and then reaches for his list of measurements and a tape measure. I ask him what he's doing. We're short on laminate, he explains, and here you'll have these two excess pieces of it cut away from the frame. We'll need to use them. But, he realizes, they won't cover the doors themselves, because the doors will be larger than the opening; they'll attach onto and over the face frame. So, he's trying to think ahead and picture where the as-yet-uncut surplus might go. What other, smaller pieces of the cabinet could be covered. That's what he's about to check. When I describe this event to Jerry Devries he smiles and says, "That's how a cabinetmaker thinks."

Several times during the construction of the first wall cabinet—the one with 60 the puzzling sixty-seven-inch top—Felipe would comment on the mathematics involved in cabinet assembly. And I asked him about it myself. His comments were a bit contradictory, and the contradiction resonated with something that was vexing me as well. At times he would note that the math is "simple," "just numbers," "only fractions." At other times, though, even within the same few sentences, his face registering perplexity, he would observe that "a lot of math is involved" and that "it's difficult."

Felipe has taken algebra and is currently enrolled in college math; he 61 knows what more advanced mathematics looks like. On the face of it, the math involved in cabinet assembly is pretty simple: reading a ruler; adding and subtracting (and, less frequently, multiplying and dividing) whole numbers, mixed numbers, and fractions; working with the basic properties of squares and rectangles. Yet, he says, "there's so many pieces you need to take into consideration, otherwise, you'll mess up somewhere."

Felipe's puzzlement, I think, is located in the intersection of traditional math- 62 ematics, learned most often in school, and the mathematics developed in the car-penter's shop. Traditional mathematics is in evidence throughout Mr. Devries's workshop: from the calculations students do to determine cost per board foot to measurements scribbled on scraps of paper spread across the room. Considered from the perspective of school math—that is, if lifted from context and presented as problems in a textbook—the operations here would be, as Felipe observes, fairly rudimentary, grade-school arithmetic. But as these measures and calculations play out in assembly—particularly an assembly that is unfamiliar—things get more complex, and thus Felipe and his crew move slowly and with some uncertainty. With an incomplete sense of a cabinet's structure, Felipe must keep a number of variables in mind, arrayed in three-dimensional space, with each variable having consequences for the other. The top of the cabinet will be shorter in length by the sum of the two rabbit cuts in the side panels—but what about the width of the top? Will it rest in a cut in the back panel, and if so, what are the implications for the measurements of the back panel? Will the top extend into or onto the face frame? What does that mean for the face frame? And so on. In neurologist Frank Wilson's phrasing, this young carpenter is developing the ability to "spatialize" mathematics—and as Felipe notes, that means taking "so many pieces . . . into consideration." Jerry Devries tells me that he has students taking calculus who have a hard time with such tasks.

There is a small but growing research literature on mathematics in the 63 workplace—from the tailor's shop to the design studio—and a few of these stud-ies focus on carpentry. Listening to Felipe puzzle over the nature of the mathe-matics of assembly led me to look more closely at the math in Jerry Devries's shop, and what I saw matched earlier studies, some of which were conducted in other cultures, such as South Africa, suggesting some cognitive commonality to the way carpenters do the work they do.

One of the findings of this research is that a wide range of mathematical 64 concepts and operations is embodied in carpentry's artifacts and routines of practice, and in ways suited to the properties of materials and the demands of production. The carpenter's math is tangible and efficient. Take, for example, measurement. The ruler and framing square provide measurements, but so do objects created in the shop, like the layout stick, and one piece of wood, pre-cisely cut, then functions as the measure for another. Tools are also used as measuring devices. A sixteen-inch claw hammer laid sideways on a wall pro-vides a quick measure for the location of studs in a wall frame. And carpenters use their hands and fingers to measure and compare. ("I use my forefinger and thumb for calipers," reports master woodworker Sam Maloof.) They develop an eye for length and dimension, but also, my experts tell me, for relations and correspondences. Disciplined perception.

Working in the shop, the young carpenter learns a range of other mathematical concepts: symmetry, proportion, congruence, the properties of angles. Planing straight the edge of a board, cutting angles on the miter box, laying out the pieces of a cabinet's face frame to check for an even fit—through these activities, Mr. Devries's students see mathematical ideas manifested, and feel them, too, gaining a sense of trueness and error. Fractions were never more real to Felipe than during the episode with that cabinet top. We can return here to Richard Gregory's observation that tools embody solutions to past problems, and also note that tools—and other artifacts in the shop—contribute to a material understanding of mathematical abstractions. In fact, the abstractions can become, in a sense, tools themselves. I was watching a student installing a window frame into an unevenly cut opening; there was barely any wood along one side to take his nail. What to do? His teacher, who was watching, showed him how to "angle the nail in to find wood." With that, *angle* became another device in the student's repertoire. You can do things with an angle.

Abstraction is the essence of mathematics; the source of its power is its independence from the material world. What is worth considering, though, is the way this fact has been converted in our intellectual history into a series of judgments about the worth and status of kinds of mathematics—for example, that the more applied and materialized the mathematics is, the less intellectually substantial it is. (As schools of engineering were developing in the American research university, they were beset by such judgment.) Without disputing the conceptual power of abstraction, my time with Felipe left me wondering about this commonplace distinction between pure and applied, or abstract and concrete—and the problems with the distinction would intensify as I studied other kinds of work. When that carpenter visualizes the French doors and performs a number of cognitive operations on his mental image of them, his activity is directed by a general understanding of the basic geometry and physics of such structures. As routines of assembly, knowledge of structures, the ability to visualize, and material mathematics interact and develop in Felipe's practice, it would be difficult to mark exactly what is "concrete" and what is "abstract." Such distinction blurs in real-world problem-solving tasks. A proper vocabulary of work would need to include some means, some hybrid term perhaps, to render this complexity. "Tools are instruments," notes the early-twentieth-century educational tract cited earlier, "by which the hands give material expression to

65

66

thought." Felipe's cabinet is thought materialized, and as such embodies a record of the interplay of general principles, specific artifacts, and human need.

Felipe and I are standing in the small utility room attached to the school's main   67
office. There are old filing cabinets, a refrigerator, a sink and small service area, a microwave, a coffeemaker, stacks of paper cups. Standard fare. Above the sink is Felipe's cabinet. He and his crew installed it several weeks ago—without any help from Mr. Devries. Its shelves are becoming crowded: paper plates, baskets, a few pots, condiments, the secretaries' coffee cups. Mrs. Gutierrez is with us. She is the office supervisor who commissioned the cabinet. She just loves it, she says. We've needed something like this for a long time. Felipe and company used a natural stain on the pine, and the cabinet shines in fluorescence. I open the other door, smooth on its hinges.

A call comes in for Mrs. Gutierrez. Back she goes to the front office.   68
Silence. Then Felipe softly begins, "I didn't see it after we installed it, but, now, damn . . . I didn't know I could do that. Pretty nice. It looks nice." I close the door I opened. An easy click. I compliment Felipe, recalling Mrs. Gutierrez's praise, her words a measure of his achievement. "I feel good when people talk like that," he says. "The cabinet's not just there, and that's it. They're using it!"

There is a lovely poem of Marge Piercy's, "To Be of Use," in which she cel-   69
ebrates those who immerse themselves in "[t]he work of the world." I think of it here: "the thing worth doing well done/has a shape that satisfies, clean and evi-dent." The use of the cabinet offers Felipe, in this moment, a confirmation of the value of his effort—but in a way that goes beyond acknowledgment of his manual skill alone. The time he took, the uncertainties and revisions, the focus of his mind on the task—all of this now gains meaning from and locates Felipe in the sphere of social exchange. It is a heady thing to feel you can be of use.

Sylvia Scribner (1923–1991) received her Ph.D. from the New School for Social Research in New York in 1970 and was the co-author with Michael Cole of three books including *The Psychology of Literacy* (1981). She was also an editor of *Mind in Society* (1978). Among other achievements, she conducted psychological research in West Africa, was the associate director of the Mental Health Program in the National Institute of Labor Education, and was a psychology professor in the Graduate Center of the City University of New York. She was also a fellow of the American Association for the Advancement of Science and on the steering committee for New York Psychologists for Social Responsibility.

LITERACY IN THREE METAPHORS

Sylvia Scribner

Although literacy is a problem of pressing national concern, we have yet to discover or set its boundaries. This observation, made several years ago by a leading political spokesman (McGovern 1978), echoes a long-standing complaint of many policymakers and educators that what counts as literacy in our technological society is a matter "not very well understood" (Advisory Committee on National Illiteracy 1929).

    A dominant response of scholars and researchers to this perceived ambiguity has been to pursue more rigorously the quest for definition and measurement of the concept. Many approaches have been taken (among them, Adult Performance Level Project 1975; Bormuth 1975; Hillerich 1976; Kirsch and Guthrie 1977–78; Miller 1973; Powell 1977), and at least one attempt (Hunter and Harman 1979) has been made to put forward an "umbrella definition." Each of these efforts has identified important parameters of literacy, but none has yet won consensual agreement (for a thoughtful historical and conceptual analysis of shifting literacy definitions, see Radwin [1978]).

    The definitional controversy has more than academic significance. Each formulation of an answer to the question "What is literacy?" leads to a different evaluation of the scope of the problem (i.e., the extent of *il*literacy) and to different objectives for programs aimed at the formation of a literate citizenry. Definitions of literacy shape our perceptions of individuals who fall on either side of the standard (what a "literate" or "nonliterate" is like) and thus in a deep way

1

2

3

Sylvia Scribner, "Literacy in Three Metaphors," *American Journal of Education*, vol. 93, no. 1 (November 1984), pp. 6–21.

affect both the substance and style of educational programs. A chorus of clashing answers also creates problems for literacy planners and educators. This is clearly evident in the somewhat acerbic comments of Dauzat and Dauzat (1977, p. 37), who are concerned with adult basic education: "In spite of all of the furor and the fervor for attaining literacy . . . few have undertaken to say what they or anyone else means by literacy. Those few professional organizations, bureaus and individuals who have attempted the task of explaining 'what is literacy?' generate definitions that conflict, contradict but rarely complement each other. . . . These 'champions of the cause of literacy' crusade for a national effort to make literacy a reality without establishing what that reality is."

What lies behind the definitional difficulties this statement decries? The   4
authors themselves provide a clue. They suggest that literacy is a kind of reality that educators should be able to grasp and explain, or, expressed in more classical terms, that literacy has an "essence" that can be captured through some Aristotelian-like enterprise. By a rational process of discussion and analysis, the "true" criterial components of literacy will be identified, and these in turn can become the targets of education for literacy.

Many, although by no means all, of those grappling with the problems of   5
definition and measurement appear to be guided by such a search for the "essence"—for the "one best" way of conceptualizing literacy. This enterprise is surely a useful one and a necessary component of educational planning. Without denigrating its contribution, I would like to suggest, however, that conflicts and contradictions are intrinsic to such an essentialist approach.

Consider the following. Most efforts at definitional determination are based   6
on a conception of literacy as an attribute of *individuals*; they aim to describe constituents of literacy in terms of individual abilities. But the single most compelling fact about literacy is that it is a *social* achievement; individuals in societies without writing systems do not become literate. Literacy is an outcome of cultural transmission; the individual child or adult does not extract the meaning of written symbols through personal interaction with the physical objects that embody them. Literacy abilities are acquired by individuals only in the course of participation in socially organized activities with written language (for a theoretical analysis of literacy as a set of socially organized practices, see Scribner and Cole [1981]). It follows that individual literacy is relative to social literacy. Since social literacy practices vary in time (Resnick [1983] contains historical studies) and space (anthropological studies are in Goody [1968]), what qualifies as individual literacy varies with them. At one time, ability to write one's name

was a hallmark of literacy; today in some parts of the world, the ability to memorize a sacred text remains the modal literacy act. Literacy has neither a static nor a universal essence.

The enterprise of defining literacy, therefore, becomes one of assessing   7
what counts as literacy in the modern epoch in some given social context. If a nation-society is the context, this enterprise requires that consideration be given to the functions that the society in question has invented for literacy and their distribution throughout the populace. Grasping what literacy "is" inevitably involves social analysis: What activities are carried out with written symbols? What significance is attached to them, and what status is conferred on those who engage in them? Is literacy a social right or a private power? These questions are subject to empirical determination. But others are not: Does the prevailing distribution of literacy conform to standards of social justice and human progress? What social and educational policies might promote such standards? Here we are involved, not with fact but with considerations of value, philosophy, and ideology similar to those that figure prominently in debates about the purposes and goals of schooling. Points of view about literacy as a social good, as well as a social fact, form the ground of the definitional enterprise. We may lack consensus on how best to define literacy because we have differing views about literacy's social purposes and values.

These differing points of view about the central meaning of literacy warrant   8
deeper examination. In this essay, I will examine some of them, organizing my discussion around three metaphors: literacy as adaptation, literacy as power, and literacy as a state of grace. Each of these metaphors is rooted in certain assumptions about the social motivations for literacy in this country, the nature of existing literacy practices, and judgments about which practices are critical for individual and social enhancement. Each has differing implications for educational policies and goals. I will be schematic in my discussion; my purpose is not to marshal supporting evidence for one or the other metaphor but to show the boundary problems of all. My argument is that any of the metaphors, taken by itself, gives us only a partial grasp of the many and varied utilities of literacy and of the complex social and psychological factors sustaining aspirations for and achievement of individual literacy. To illustrate this theme, I will draw on the literacy experiences of a Third World people who, although remaining at an Iron Age level of technology, have nevertheless evolved varied functions for written language; their experience demonstrates that, even in some traditional societies, literacy is a "many-meaninged thing."

Literacy as Adaptation

This metaphor is designed to capture concepts of literacy that emphasize its sur-   9
vival or pragmatic value. When the term "functional literacy" was originally
introduced during World War I (Harman 1970), it specified the literacy skills
required to meet the tasks of modern soldiering. Today, functional literacy is
conceived broadly as the level of proficiency necessary for effective performance
in a range of settings and customary activities.

This concept has a strong commonsense appeal. The necessity for literacy   10
skills in daily life is obvious; on the job, riding around town, shopping for gro-
ceries, we all encounter situations requiring us to read or produce written symbols. No justification is needed to insist that schools are obligated to equip
children with the literacy skills that will enable them to fulfill these mundane
situational demands. And basic educational programs have a similar obligation
to equip adults with the skills they must have to secure jobs or advance to better ones, receive the training and benefits to which they are entitled, and
assume their civic and political responsibilities. Within the United States, as
in other nations, literacy programs with these practical aims are considered
efforts at human resource development and, as such, contributors to economic
growth and stability.

In spite of their apparent commonsense grounding, functional literacy   11
approaches are neither as straightforward nor as unproblematic as they first
appear. Attempts to inventory "minimal functional competencies" have floun-
dered on lack of information and divided perceptions of functionality. Is it realistic to try to specify some uniform set of skills as constituting functional literacy
for all adults? Two subquestions are involved here. One concerns the choice of
parameters for defining a "universe of functional competencies." Which literacy
tasks (e.g., reading a newspaper, writing a check) are "necessary," and which are
"optional"? The Adult Performance Level Project test (1975), one of the best
conceptualized efforts to specify and measure competencies necessary for success
in adult life, has been challenged on the grounds that it lacks content validity:
"The APL test fails to meet this [validity] criterion . . . not necessarily because
test development procedures were technically faulty, but because it is not logically possible to define this universe of behaviors [which compose functional
competence] without respect to a value position which the test developers have
chosen not to discuss" (Cervero 1980, p. 163).

An equally important question concerns the concept of uniformity. Do all   12
communities and cultural groups in our class-based and heterogeneous society
confront equivalent functional demands? If not, how do they differ? Some
experts (e.g., Gray 1965; Hunter and Harman 1979) maintain that the concept

of functional literacy makes sense only with respect to the proficiencies required for participation in the actual life conditions of particular groups or communities. But how does such a relativistic approach mesh with larger societal needs? If we were to consider the level of reading and writing activities carried out in small and isolated rural communities as the standard for functional literacy, educational objectives would be unduly restricted. At the other extreme, we might not want to use literacy activities of college teachers as the standard determining the functional competencies required for high school graduation. Only in recent years has research been undertaken on the range of literacy activities practiced in different communities or settings within the United States (e.g., Heath 1980, 1981; Scribner 1982*a*), and we still know little about how, and by whom, required literacy work gets done. Lacking such knowledge, public discussions fluctuate between narrow definitions of functional skills pegged to immediate vocational and personal needs, and sweeping definitions that virtually reinstate the ability to cope with college subject matter as the hallmark of literacy. On the other hand, adopting different criteria for different regions or communities would ensure the perpetuation of educational inequalities and the differential access to life opportunities with which these are associated.

Adapting literacy standards to today's needs, personal or social, would be shortsighted. The time-limited nature of what constitutes minimal skills is illustrated in the "sliding scale" used by the U.S. Bureau of Census to determine literacy. During World War I, a fourth-grade education was considered sufficient to render one literate; in 1947, a U.S. Census sample survey raised that figure to five years; and by 1952 six years of school was considered the minimal literacy threshold. Replacing the school-grade criterion with a functional approach to literacy does not eliminate the time problem. Today's standards for functional competency need to be considered in the light of tomorrow's requirements. But not all are agreed as to the nature or volume of literacy demands in the decades ahead. Some (e.g., Naisbitt 1982) argue that, as economic and other activities become increasingly subject to computerized techniques of production and information handling, even higher levels of literacy will be required of all. A contrary view, popularized by McLuhan (1962, 1964) is that new technologies and communication media are likely to reduce literacy requirements for all. A responding argument is that some of these technologies are, in effect, new systems of literacy. The ability to use minicomputers as information storage and retrieval devices requires mastery of symbol systems that build on natural language literacy; they are second-order literacies as it were. One possible scenario is that in coming decades literacy may be increased for some and reduced for others, accentuating the present uneven, primarily class-based distribution of literacy functions.

From the perspective of social needs, the seemingly well-defined concept of functional competency becomes fuzzy at the edges. Equally as many questions arise about functionality from the individual's point of view. Functional needs have not yet been assessed from the perspective of those who purportedly experience them. To what extent do adults whom tests assess as functionally illiterate perceive themselves as lacking the necessary skills to be adequate parents, neighbors, workers? Inner-city youngsters may have no desire to write letters to each other; raising one's reading level by a few grades may not be seen as a magic ticket to a job; not everyone has a bank account that requires the mastery of unusual forms (Heath 1980). Appeals to individuals to enhance their functional skills might founder on the different subjective utilities communities and groups attach to reading and writing activities.   14

The functional approach has been hailed as a major advance over more traditional concepts of reading and writing because it takes into account the goals and settings of people's activities with written language. Yet even tender probing reveals the many questions of fact, value, and purpose that complicate its application to educational curricula.   15

We now turn to the second metaphor.   16

Literacy as Power

While functional literacy stresses the importance of literacy to the adaptation of the individual, the literacy-as-power metaphor emphasizes a relationship between literacy and group or community advancement.   17

Historically, literacy has been a potent tool in maintaining the hegemony of elites and dominant classes in certain societies, while laying the basis for increased social and political participation in others (Resnick 1983; Goody 1968). In a contemporary framework, expansion of literary skills is often viewed as a means for poor and politically powerless groups to claim their place in the world. The International Symposium for Literacy, meeting in Persepolis, Iran (Bataille 1976), appealed to national governments to consider literacy as an instrument for human liberation and social change. Paulo Freire (1970) bases his influential theory of literacy education on the need to make literacy a resource for fundamental social transformation. Effective literacy education, in his view, creates a critical consciousness through which a community can analyze its conditions of social existence and engage in effective action for a just society. Not to be literate is a state of victimization.   18

Yet the capacity of literacy to confer power or to be the primary impetus for   19
significant and lasting economic or social change has proved problematic in
developing countries. Studies (Gayter, Hall, Kidd, and Shivasrava 1979; United
Nations Development Program 1976) of UNESCO's experimental world literacy program have raised doubts about earlier notions that higher literacy rates
automatically promote national development and improve the social and material conditions of the very poor. The relationship between social change and literacy education, it is now suggested (Harman 1977), may be stronger in the
other direction. When masses of people have been mobilized for fundamental
changes in social conditions—as in the USSR, China, Cuba, and Tanzania—
rapid extensions of literacy have been accomplished (Gayter et al. 1979; Hammiche 1976; Scribner 1982b). Movements to transform social reality appear to
have been effective in some parts of the world in bringing whole populations
into participation in modern literacy activities. The validity of the converse
proposition—that literacy per se mobilizes people for action to change their
social reality—remains to be established.

What does this mean for us? The one undisputed fact about illiteracy in   20
America is its concentration among poor, black, elderly, and minority-language
groups—groups without effective participation in our country's economic and
educational institutions (Hunter and Harman 1979). Problems of poverty and
political powerlessness are, as among some populations in developing nations,
inseparably intertwined with problems of access to knowledge and levels of literacy skills. Some (e.g., Kozol 1980) suggest that a mass and politicized
approach to literacy education such as that adopted by Cuba is demanded in
these conditions. Others (e.g., Hunter and Harman 1979) advocate a more
action-oriented approach that views community mobilization around practical,
social, and political goals as a first step in creating the conditions for effective
literacy instruction and for educational equity.

The possibilities and limits of the literacy-as-power metaphor within our   21
present-day social and political structure are not at all clear. To what extent
can instructional experiences and programs be lifted out of their social contexts in other countries and applied here? Do assumptions about the functionality and significance of literacy in poor communities in the United States warrant further consideration? Reder and Green's (1984) research and educational
work among West Coast immigrant communities reveals that literacy has different meanings for members of different groups. How can these cultural variations be taken into account? How are communities best mobilized for
literacy—around local needs and small-scale activism? or as part of broader

political and social movements? If literacy has not emerged as a priority demand, should government and private agencies undertake to mobilize communities around this goal? And can such efforts be productive without the deep involvement of community leaders?

Literacy as a State of Grace

Now we come to the third metaphor. I have variously called it literacy as salvation and literacy as a state of grace. Both labels are unsatisfactory because they give a specific religious interpretation to the broader phenomenon I want to depict—that is, the tendency in many societies to endow the literate person with special virtues. A concern with preserving and understanding scripture is at the core of many religious traditions, Western and non-Western alike. As studies by Resnick and Resnick (1977) have shown, the literacy-as-salvation metaphor had an almost literal interpretation in the practice of post-Luther Protestant groups to require of the faithful the ability to read and remember the Bible and other religious material. Older religious traditions—Hebraic and Islamic—have also traditionally invested the written word with great power and respect. "This is a perfect book. There is no doubt in it," reads a passage from the Qur'an. Memorizing the Qur'an—literally taking its words into you and making them part of yourself—is simultaneously a process of becoming both literate and holy.

The attribution of special powers to those who are literate has its ancient secular roots as well. Plato and Aristotle strove to distinguish the man of letters from the poet of oral tradition. In the perspective of Western humanism, literateness has come to be considered synonymous with being "cultured," using the term in the old-fashioned sense to refer to a person who is knowledgeable about the content and techniques of the sciences, arts, and humanities as they have evolved historically. The term sounds elitist and archaic, but the notion that participation in a literate—that is, bookish—tradition enlarges and develops a person's essential self is pervasive and still undergirds the concept of a liberal education (Steiner 1973). In the literacy-as-a-state-of-grace concept, the power and functionality of literacy is not bounded by political or economic parameters but in a sense transcends them; the literate individual's life derives its meaning and significance from intellectual, aesthetic, and spiritual participation in the accumulated creations and knowledge of humankind, made available through the written word.

The self-enhancing aspects of literacy are often given a cognitive interpretation (Greenfield and Bruner 1969; Olson 1977). For centuries, and increasingly in this generation, appeals have been made for increased attention to literacy as

22

23

24

a way of developing minds. An individual who is illiterate, a UNESCO (1972) publication states, is bound to concrete thinking and cannot learn new material. Some teachers of college English in the United States (e.g., Farrell 1977) urge greater prominence for writing in the curriculum as a way of promoting logical reasoning and critical thinking. Literate and nonliterate individuals presumably are not only in different states of grace but in different stages of intellectual development as well. Although evidence is accumulating (Scribner and Cole 1981) refuting this view, the notion that literacy per se creates a great divide in intellectual abilities between those who have and those who have not mastered written language is deeply entrenched in educational circles of industrialized countries.

The metaphor of literacy-as-grace, like the others, has boundary problems.   25
For one thing, we need to know how widely dispersed this admiration of book knowledge is in our society. To what extent are beliefs about the value of literateness shared across social classes and ethnic and religious groups? How does book culture—more accurately, how do book cultures—articulate with the multiple and diverse oral cultures flourishing in the United States? Which people value literacy as a preserver of their history or endow their folk heroes with book learning? Are there broad cultural supports for book learning among wide sectors of the population? McLuhan and others have insisted that written literacy is a vestige of a disappearing "culture." Is this point of view defensible? And if so, what implications does it pose for our educational objectives?

I have described some current views of the meaning of literacy in terms of   26
three metaphors. I have tried to indicate that each metaphor embraces a certain set of, sometimes unexamined, values; moreover, each makes assumptions about social facts in our society—the utilities of literacy and the conditions fostering individual attainment of literacy status. These metaphors are often urged on us as competitive; some choice of one or the other does in fact seem a necessary starting point for a definitional enterprise. But for purposes of social and educational planning, none need necessarily become paramount at the expense of the others; all may have validity. To illustrate this argument, I will briefly describe research on the social meaning of literacy among a West African people. Learning how literacy functions among a people far removed from us culturally and geographically may help us take a new look at its functions here at home.

Social Meaning of Literacy: A Case Study

My own consideration of the question "What is literacy?" was prompted by   27
research experiences in a traditional West African society. Together with colleagues, I spent five years studying the social and intellectual consequences of

literacy among the Vai people of West Africa (Scribner and Cole 1981). The material conditions of Vai life are harsh. Rural villages lack electricity and public water supplies; clinics and schools are scarce; dirt roads, often impassable in the rainy season, restrict social and economic exchanges. To the casual observer, Vai society is the very prototype of traditional nonliterate subsistence farming societies. Yet the Vai have practiced literacy for over 150 years, initially in a syllabic writing system of their own invention. The Vai script has been passed on from one generation to another in tutorial fashion without benefit of a formal institution such as a school and without the constitution of a professional teacher group. In addition to this indigenous script, literacy in the Arabic and Roman alphabets also flourishes in the countryside. The Vai are a Muslim people, and the Arabic script is the literacy for religious practice and theological learning. Missionaries and, more recently, the Liberian government have been disseminating English literacy, the official government literacy, through the establishment of Western-style schools. About one-third of the Vai male population is literate in one of these scripts, the majority in the Vai script. Many read and write both Vai and Arabic, and some outstanding scholars are literate in all three scripts. Since each writing system has a different orthography, represents a different language, and is learned in a different setting, becoming literate in two or more scripts is an impressive intellectual accomplishment. Why do people take the trouble to do it?

Certain obvious answers are ruled out. Literacy is not a necessity, for personal survival. As far as we could determine, nonliteracy status does not exclude a person from full participation in economic activities or in town or society life. As we look around Vai country and see major activities and institutions continuing to function in the traditional oral mode, we are at a loss to define the literacy competencies that might be useful in everyday life. But Vai literates have not been at such a loss and have found no end of useful functions for writing. Commonly they engage in extensive personal correspondence, which for some involves the composition of 30–40 letters per month. Since Vai society, like other traditional societies, maintains an effective oral grapevine system, reasons for the popularity of letter writing are not self-evident, especially since all letters must be personally sent and hand-delivered. Yet literates find the advantage of secrecy and guarantee of delivery more than compensation for the time and trouble spent in writing. Scholars (Hair 1963; Holsoe 1967) speculate that the usefulness of the Vai script in protecting secrets and allowing clandestine resistance to the central governing machinery of Liberia, whose official literacy was English, were important factors in its invention and longevity.

28

On closer study, we find that Vai script literacy also serves many personal   29
and public record-keeping functions. Household heads keep albums for family
births, deaths, and marriages; some maintain lists of dowry items and death feast
contributions that help to regulate kinship exchanges. Records also enlarge the
scope and planful aspects of commerical transactions. Artisans maintain lists of
customers; farmers record the yield and income from cash-crop farming. The
script also serves a variety of administrative purposes such as recording house
tax payments and political contributions. Some fraternal and religious organizations maintain records in Vai script. All of these activities fit nicely into the
metaphor of literacy as functional adaptation; the only surprising aspect is that
so many varieties of pragmatic uses occur in an economic and social milieu in
which modern institutions (schools, cash markets) still play a limited role.

Not all literacy uses are devoted to practical ends. Although the Vai script   30
has not been used to produce public books or manuscripts, in the privacy of
their homes, many Vai literates engage in creative acts of composition. Almost
everyone keeps a diary; some write down maxims and traditional tales in copybooks; others maintain rudimentary town histories; some record their dreams
and tales of advice to children; a few who might qualify as scholars produce
extended family and clan histories. Townspeople, when questioned about the
value of the script, will often cite its utilitarian functions, but will equally as
often speak about its importance for self-education and knowledge. Vai script
literates are known in the community, are accorded respect, and are sought out
for their information and help as personal scribes or as town clerks. A Vai parable about the relative merits of money, power, and book learning for success in
this world concludes with the judgment that the "man who knoweth book pas-
seth all."

Why this excursion into a case of African literacy after our metaphoric dis-   31
cussion of the goals of literacy education in a technological society? Perhaps
because Vai society, much simpler than ours in the range of literacy functions it
calls for, nonetheless serves to highlight unnecessary simplicities in our attempts
to define the one best set of organizing principles for literacy education. If we
were called on as experts to devise literacy education programs for the Vai people, which metaphor would dominate our recommendations? Would we emphasize the spread of functional competencies, urging all farmers to keep crop
records and all carpenters to list customers? This would be an effective approach
for some, but it would neglect the interests and aspirations of others. Should we
appeal to the cultural pride of the populace, suggesting Vai script literacy be
extended as an instrument for group cohesion and social change? We might

count on support for this appeal, but resistance as well; Qur'anic schools and the network of Muslim teachers and scholars are a powerful counterforce to the Vai script and a countervailing center for cultural cohesion. Moreover, families participating in the Vai script tradition do not necessarily repudiate participation in English literacy; some find it prudent to have one or more children in English school as well as Qur'anic school. As for literacy as a state of grace, aspirations for self-improvement and social status clearly sustain many aspects of Vai literacy both in the Arabic religious and Vai secular traditions. A diversity of pragmatic, ideological, and intellectual factors sustains popular literacy among the Vai.

The sociohistorical processes leading to multiple literacies among the Vai   32
are not unique. In their research in Alaska, Reder and Green (1983) found community members practicing literacy in any one (or, occasionally, a combination) of three languages. Some used the Cyrillic script, introduced by the Russian Orthodox Church, for reading and writing Russian; others used that script for literacy activities in their native Eskimo language; and still others participated in English literacy. Each of these literacies, they report, occurred through distinct socialization processes and in well-defined, nonoverlapping domains of activity, and each had a distinctive social meaning. Wagner (in press) similarly documents the multiple meanings of literacy in contemporary Moroccan society, and other reports might be cited.

This is not to suggest, of course, that all cultural groups have elaborated   33
rich functions for literacy, nor that all groups strive for participation in the official literacy of their state (as, for example, English in Alaska and throughout the United States). The value of the growing body of ethnographic studies for the "What is literacy?" question is twofold. First, it promotes skepticism of the "one best answer" approach to the improvement of literacy in our society. Second, it urges the need for understanding the great variety of beliefs and aspirations that various people have developed toward literacy in their particular historical and current life circumstances.

What implications does this analysis have for literacy policy and education?   34
This is a question that calls for the continued, sustained, and thoughtful attention of educators and others in our society. One implication that I find compelling is the need to "disaggregate" various levels and kinds of literacy. If the search for an essence is futile, it might appropriately be replaced by serious attention to varieties of literacy and their place in social and educational programs. In this disentangling process, I would place priority on the need to extricate matters of value and policy from their hidden position in the definitional enterprise and to address them head on. The International Symposium for Lit-

eracy, closing UNESCO's Experimental World Literacy Program, declared that literacy is a fundamental human right (Bataille 1976). Literacy campaigns need no other justification. Setting long-range social and educational goals, however, pushes us farther toward an inquiry into the standard of literacy that is a desirable (valued) human right in our highly developed technological society, whose policies have such a powerful impact on the world's future. What is *ideal* literacy in our society? If the analysis by metaphor presented here contributes some approach to that question, it suggests that ideal literacy is simultaneously adaptive, socially empowering, and self-enhancing. Enabling youth and adults to progress toward that ideal would be a realization of the spirit of the symposium in Persepolis reflective of the resources and literacy achievements already available in our society. This suggests that long-term social and educational policies might be directed at maximal literacy objectives; minimal literacy standards would serve a useful function, not as goals but as indicators of our progress in equipping individuals and communities with the skills they need for "takeoff" in continuing literacy careers.

Recognition of the multiple meanings and varieties of literacy also argues for a diversity of educational approaches, informal and community-based as well as formal and school-based. As ethnographic research and practical experience demonstrate, effective literacy programs are those that are responsive to perceived needs, whether for functional skills, social power, or self-improvement. Individual objectives may be highly specific: to qualify for a promotion at work, to help children with their lessons, to record a family history. Anzalone and McLaughlin (1982) have coined the term "specific literacies" to designate such special-interest or special-purpose literacy skills. The road to maximal literacy may begin for some through the feeder routes of a wide variety of specific literacies. 35

These are speculative and personal views; others will have different conceptions. The notions offered here of ideal and specific literacies do not simplify the educational issues nor resolve the definitional dilemmas. I hope, however, that these concepts and the metaphoric analysis from which they flowed suggest the usefulness of "dissecting literacy" into its many forms and, in the process, clarifying the place of fact and value in discussions of the social meaning of literacy. 36

NOTE

This paper is based on a planning document for research on literacy that I prepared when associate director of the National Institute of Education. Eugene Radwin made many helpful comments on that document and contributed a number of bibliographic references cited here.

REFERENCES

Adult Performance Level Project. *Adult Functional Competency: A Summary.* Austin: University of Texas, Division of Extension, 1975.

Advisory Committee on National Illiteracy. "Report." *School and Society* 30 (1929): 708.

Anzalone, S., and S. McLaughlin. *Literacy for Specific Situations.* Amherst: University of Massachusetts, Center for International Education, 1982.

Bataille, L., ed. *A Turning Point for Literacy: Proceedings of the International Symposium for Literacy, Persepolis, Iran, 1975.* Oxford: Pergamon Books, 1976.

Bormuth, J. R. "Reading Literacy: Its Definition and Assessment." In *Toward a Literate Society: The Report of the Committee on Reading of the National Academy of Education,* edited by J. B. Carroll and J. S. Chall. New York: McGraw-Hill Book Co., 1975.

Cervero, R. M. "Does the Texas Adult Performance Level Test Measure Functional Competence?" *Adult Education* 30 (1980): 152–65.

Dauzat, S. J., and J. Dauzat. "Literacy in Quest of a Definition." *Convergence* 10 (1977): 37–41.

Farrell, L. J. "Literacy, the Basics, and All that Jazz." *College English* 38 (1977): 443–59.

Freire, P. *Cultural Action for Freedom* (Monograph Series no. 1). Cambridge, Mass.: Harvard Educational Review, 1970.

Gayter, M., B. Hall, J. R. Kidd, and V. Shivasrava. *The World of Literacy: Policy, Research and Action.* Toronto: International Development Centre, 1979.

Goody, J., ed. *Literacy in Traditional Societies.* Cambridge: Cambridge University Press, 1968.

Gray, W. *The Teaching of Reading and Writing: An International Survey.* Chicago: Scott, Foresman & Co./UNESCO, 1965.

Greenfield, P. M., and J. S. Bruner. "Culture and Cognitive Growth." In *Handbook of Socialization: Theory and Research,* edited by D. A. Goslin. New York: Rand McNally & Co., 1969.

Hair, P. E. H. "Notes on the Discovery of the Vai Script." *Sierra Leone Language Review* 2 (1963): 36–49.

Hammiche, B. "Functional Literacy and Educational Revolution." In *A Turning Point for Literacy: Proceedings of the International Symposium for Literacy, Persepolis, Iran, 1975,* edited by L. Bataille. Oxford: Pergamon Press, 1976.

Harman, D. "Review of *The Experimental World Literacy Program.*" *Harvard Educational Review* 47 (1977): 444–46.

Heath, S. B. "The Functions and Uses of Literacy." *Journal of Communication* 30 (1980): 123–33.

Heath, S. B. "Toward an Ethnohistory of Writing in American Education." In *Writing: The Nature, Development and Teaching of Written Communication,* vol. 1, edited by M. F. Whiteman. Hillsdale, N.J.: Lawrence Erlbaum Associates, 1981.

Hillerich, R. L. "Toward an Assessable Definition of Literacy." *English Journal* 65 (1976): 50–55.

Holsoe, S. E. "Slavery and Economic Response among the Vai." In *Slavery in Africa: Historical and Anthropological Perspectives,* edited by S. Miers and I. Kopytoff. Madison: University of Wisconsin Press, 1977.

Hunter, C. S. J., and D. Harman. *Adult Illiteracy in the United States.* New York: McGraw-Hill Book Co., 1979.

Kirsch, I., and J. T. Guthrie. "The Concept and Measurement of Functional Literacy." *Reading Research Quarterly* 13 (1977–78): 485–507.

Kozol, J. *Prisoners of Silence: Breaking the Bonds of Adult Illiteracy in the United States.* New York: Continuum Publishing Corp., 1980.

McGovern, G. *Congressional Record* (September 1978), p. 14, 834.

McLuhan, M. *The Gutenberg Galaxy.* Toronto: University of Toronto Press, 1962.

McLuhan, M. *Understanding Media: The Extensions of Man.* New York: McGraw-Hill Book Co., 1964.

Miller, G. A., ed. *Linugistic Communication: Perspectives for Research.* Newark, Del.: International Reading Association, 1973.

Naisbett, J. *Megatrends: Ten New Directions Transforming Our Lives.* New York: Warner Books, 1982.

Olson, D. R. "From Utterance to Text: The Bias of Language in Speech and Writing." *Harvard Educational Review* 47 (1977): 257–81.

Powell, W. R. "Levels of Literacy." *Journal of Reading* 20 (1977): 488–92.

Radwin, E. "Literacy—What and Why." Unpublished manuscript, Harvard University, 1978.

Reder, S., and K. R. Green. "Literacy as a Functional Component of Social Structure in an Alaska Fishing Village." *International Journal of the Sociology of Language* 42 (1983): 122–41.

Resnick, D. P., ed. *Literacy in Historical Perspective.* Washington, D.C.: Library of Congress, 1983.

Resnick, D. P., and L. B. Resnick. "The Nature of Literacy: An Historical Exploration." *Harvard Educational Review* 47 (1977): 370–85.

Scribner, S. "Industrial Literacy" (Final Report to the Ford Foundation). New York: CUNY, Graduate School and University Center, 1982. (*a*)

Scribner, S. "Observations on Literacy Education in China." *Linguistic Reporter* 25 (1982): 1–4. (*b*)

Scribner, S., and M. Cole. *The Psychology of Literacy*. Cambridge, Mass.: Harvard University Press, 1981.

Steiner, G. "After the Book." In *The Future of Literacy*, edited by R. Disch. Englewood Cliffs, N.J.: Prentice-Hall, Inc., 1973.

United Nations Development Program. *The Experimental World Literacy Programme: A Critical Assessment*. Paris: UNESCO, 1976.

UNESCO. *Regional Report on Literacy*. Teheran: UNESCO, 1972.

Wagner, D. A., B. M. Messick, and J. Spratt. "Studying Literacy in Morocco." In *The Acquisition of Literacy: Ethnographic Perspectives*, edited by B. B. Schieffelin and P. Gilmore. Norwood, N.J.: Ablex, in press.

Beverly Daniel Tatum (1954–) was raised in Bridgewater, Massachusetts, and received a Ph.D. in clinical psychology in 1984 at the University of Michigan and an M.A. in religious studies at Hartford Seminary in Connecticut in 2000. In 1989, she joined the faculty of Mount Holyoke College in South Hadley, Massachusetts, as a psychology professor and went on to become dean of the college. In 2002, she assumed the presidency of Spelman College in Atlanta, Georgia. She is the author of *Why Are All the Black Kids Sitting Together in the Cafeteria?* (1997), which won the National Association of Multicultural Education Book of the Year Award, and of *Assimilation Blues: Black Families in a White Community* (1987). She has contributed chapters to many scholarly works and has been published in journals such as *Liberal Education* and *Educational Leadership*.

DEFINING RACISM: "CAN WE TALK?"

Beverly Daniel Tatum

1

Early in my teaching career, a White student I knew asked me what I would be teaching the following semester. I mentioned that I would be teaching a course on racism. She replied, with some surprise in her voice, "Oh, is there still racism?" I assured her that indeed there was and suggested that she sign up for my course. Fifteen years later, after exhaustive media coverage of events such as the Rodney King beating, the Charles Stuart and Susan Smith cases, the O. J. Simpson trial, the appeal to racial prejudices in electoral politics, and the bitter debates about affirmative action and welfare reform, it seems hard to imagine that anyone would still be unaware of the reality of racism in our society. But in fact, in almost every audience I address, there is someone who will suggest that racism is a thing of the past. There is always someone who hasn't noticed the stereotypical images of people of color in the media, who hasn't observed the housing discrimination in their community, who hasn't read the newspaper articles about documented racial bias in lending practices among well-known banks, who isn't aware of the racial tracking pattern at the local school, who hasn't seen the reports of rising incidents of racially motivated hate crimes in America—in short, someone who hasn't been paying attention to issues of race. But if you are paying attention, the legacy of racism is not hard to see, and we are all affected by it.

The impact of racism begins early. Even in our preschool years, we are exposed to misinformation about people different from ourselves. Many of us grew up in neighborhoods where we had limited opportunities to interact with people different from our own families.

2

When I ask my college students, "How many of you grew up in neighbor- 3
hoods where most of the people were from the same racial group as your own?"
almost every hand goes up. There is still a great deal of social segregation in our
communities. Consequently, most of the early information we receive about
"others"—people racially, religiously, or socioeconomically different from
ourselves—does not come as the result of firsthand experience. The secondhand
information we do receive has often been distorted, shaped by cultural stereotypes, and left incomplete.

Some examples will highlight this process. Several years ago one of my stu- 4
dents conducted a research project investigating preschoolers' conceptions of
Native Americans.[1] Using children at a local day care center as her participants, she asked these three- and four-year-olds to draw a picture of a Native
American. Most children were stumped by her request. They didn't know what
a Native American was. But when she rephrased the question and asked them
to draw a picture of an Indian, they readily complied. Almost every picture
included one central feature: feathers. In fact, many of them also included a
weapon—a knife or tomahawk—and depicted the person in violent or aggressive terms. Though this group of children, almost all of whom were White, did
not live near a large Native American population and probably had had little if
any personal interaction with American Indians, they all had internalized an
image of what Indians were like. How did they know? Cartoon images, in particular the Disney movie *Peter Pan*, were cited by the children as their number-
one source of information. At the age of three, these children already had a set
of stereotypes in place. Though I would not describe three-year-olds as prejudiced, the stereotypes to which they have been exposed become the foundation
for the adult prejudices so many of us have.

Sometimes the assumptions we make about others come not from what we 5
have been told or what we have seen on television or in books, but rather from
what we *not* been told. The distortion of historical information about people of color leads young people (and older people, too) to make assumptions that
may go unchallenged for a long time. Consider this conversation between two
White students following a discussion about the cultural transmission of racism:

"Yeah, I just found out that Cleopatra was actually a Black woman." 6
"What?" 7

The first student went on to explain her newly learned information. The sec- 8
ond student exclaimed in disbelief, "That can't be true. Cleopatra was beautiful!"

What had this young woman learned about who in our society is consid- 9
ered beautiful and who is not? Had she conjured up images of Elizabeth Taylor
when she thought of Cleopatra? The new information her classmate had shared

and her own deeply ingrained assumptions about who is beautiful and who is not were too incongruous to allow her to assimilate the information at that moment.

Omitted information can have similar effects. For example, another young woman, preparing to be a high school English teacher, expressed her dismay that she had never learned about any Black authors in any of her English courses. How was she to teach about them to her future students when she hadn't learned about them herself? A White male student in the class responded to this discussion with frustration in his response journal, writing "It's not my fault that Blacks don't write books." Had one of his elementary, high school, or college teachers ever told him that there were no Black writers? Probably not. Yet because he had never been exposed to Black authors, he had drawn his own conclusion that there were none.

Stereotypes, omissions, and distortions all contribute to the development of prejudice. *Prejudice* is a preconceived judgment or opinion, usually based on limited information. I assume that we all have prejudices, not because we want them, but simply because we are so continually exposed to misinformation about others. Though I have often heard students or workshop participants describe someone as not having "a prejudiced bone in his body," I usually suggest that they look again. Prejudice is one of the inescapable consequences of living in a racist society. Cultural racism—the cultural images and messages that affirm the assumed superiority of Whites and the assumed inferiority of people of color—is like smog in the air. Sometimes it is so thick it is visible, other times it is less apparent, but always, day in and day out, we are breathing it in. None of us would introduce ourselves as "smog-breathers" (and most of us don't want to be described as prejudiced), but if we live in a smoggy place, how can we avoid breathing the air? If we live in an environment in which we are bombarded with stereotypical images in the media, are frequently exposed to the ethnic jokes of friends and family members, and are rarely informed of the accomplishments of oppressed groups, we will develop the negative categorizations of those groups that form the basis of prejudice.

People of color as well as Whites develop these categorizations. Even a member of the stereotyped group may internalize the stereotypical categories about his or her own group to some degree. In fact, this process happens so frequently that it has a name, *internalized oppression*. Some of the consequences of believing the distorted messages about one's own group will be discussed in subsequent chapters.

Certainly some people are more prejudiced than others, actively embracing and perpetuating negative and hateful images of those who are different from themselves. When we claim to be free of prejudice, perhaps what we are really saying is that we are not hatemongers. But none of us is completely innocent. Prejudice is an integral part of our socialization, and it is not our fault. Just as the preschoolers my student interviewed are not to blame for the negative messages they internalized, we are not at fault for the stereotypes, distortions, and omissions that shaped our thinking as we grew up.

To say that it is not our fault does not relieve us of responsibility, however.   14
We may not have polluted the air, but we need to take responsibility, along with others, for cleaning it up. Each of us needs to look at our own behavior. Am I perpetuating and reinforcing the negative messages so pervasive in our culture, or am I seeking to challenge them? If I have not been exposed to positive images of marginalized groups, am I seeking them out, expanding my own knowledge base for myself and my children? Am I acknowledging and examining my own prejudices, my own rigid categorizations of others, thereby minimizing the adverse impact they might have on my interactions with those I have categorized? Unless we engage in these and other conscious acts of reflection and reeducation, we easily repeat the process with our children. We teach what we were taught. The unexamined prejudices of the parents are passed on to the children. It is not our fault, but it is our responsibility to interrupt this cycle.

Racism: A System of Advantage Based on Race

Many people use the terms *prejudice* and *racism* interchangeably. I do not, and I   15
think it is important to make a distinction. In his book *Portraits of White Racism*, David Wellman argues convincingly that limiting our understanding of racism to prejudice does not offer a sufficient explanation for the persistence of racism. He defines racism as a "system of advantage based on race."[2] In illustrating this definition, he provides example after example of how Whites defend their racial advantage—access to better schools, housing, jobs—even when they do not embrace overtly prejudicial thinking. Racism cannot be fully explained as an expression of prejudice alone.

This definition of racism is useful because it allows us to see that racism,   16
like other forms of oppression, is not only a personal ideology based on racial prejudice, but a *system* involving cultural messages and institutional policies and practices as well as the beliefs and actions of individuals. In the context of the United States, this system clearly operates to the advantage of Whites and to the disadvantage of people of color. Another related definition of racism, commonly used by antiracist educators and consultants, is "prejudice plus power." Racial prejudice when combined with social power—access to social, cultural, and economic resources and decision-making—leads to the institutionalization

of racist policies and practices. While I think this definition also captures the idea that racism is more than individual beliefs and attitudes, I prefer Wellman's definition because the idea of systematic advantage and disadvantage is critical to an understanding of how racism operates in American society.

17 In addition, I find that many of my White students and workshop participants do not feel powerful. Defining racism as prejudice plus power has little personal relevance. For some, their response to this definition is the following: "I'm not really prejudiced, and I have no power, so racism has nothing to do with me." However, most White people, if they are really being honest with themselves, can see that there are advantages to being White in the United States. Despite the current rhetoric about affirmative action and "reverse racism," every social indicator, from salary to life expectancy, reveals the advantages of being White.[3]

18 The systematic advantages of being White are often referred to as White privilege. In a now well-known article, "White Privilege: Unpacking the Invisible Knapsack," Peggy McIntosh, a White feminist scholar, identified a long list of societal privileges that she received simply because she was White.[4] She did not ask for them, and it is important to note that she hadn't always noticed that she was receiving them. They included major and minor advantages. Of course she enjoyed greater access to jobs and housing. But she also was able to shop in department stores without being followed by suspicious salespeople and could always find appropriate hair care products and makeup in any drugstore. She could send her child to school confident that the teacher would not discriminate against him on the basis of race. She could also be late for meetings, and talk with her mouth full, fairly confident that these behaviors would not be attributed to the fact that she was White. She could express an opinion in a meeting or in print and not have it labeled the "White" viewpoint. In other words, she was more often than not viewed as an individual, rather than as a member of a racial group.

19 This article rings true for most White readers, many of whom may have never considered the benefits of being White. It's one thing to have enough awareness of racism to describe the ways that people of color are disadvantaged by it. But this new understanding of racism is more elusive. In very concrete terms, it means that if a person of color is the victim of housing discrimination, the apartment that would otherwise have been rented to that person of color is still available for a White person. The White tenant is, knowingly or unknowingly, the beneficiary of racism, a system of advantage based on race. The unsuspecting tenant is not to blame for the prior discrimination, but she benefits from it anyway.

For many Whites, this new awareness of the benefits of a racist system elic-   20
its considerable pain, often accompanied by feelings of anger and guilt. These
uncomfortable emotions can hinder further discussion. We all like to think that
we deserve the good things we have received, and that others, too, get what
they deserve. Social psychologists call this tendency a "belief in a just world."[5]
Racism directly contradicts such notions of justice.

Understanding racism as a system of advantage based on race is antithetical   21
to traditional notions of an American meritocracy. For those who have internalized this myth, this definition generates considerable discomfort. It is more
comfortable simply to think of racism as a particular form of prejudice. Notions
of power or privilege do not have to be addressed when our understanding of
racism is constructed in that way.

The discomfort generated when a systemic definition of racism is intro-   22
duced is usually quite visible in the workshops I lead. Someone in the group is
usually quick to point out that this is not the definition you will find in most
dictionaries. I reply, "Who wrote the dictionary?" I am not being facetious with
this response. Whose interests are served by a "prejudice only" definition of
racism? It is important to understand that the system of advantage is perpetuated when we do not acknowledge its existence.

Racism: For Whites Only?

Frequently someone will say, "You keep talking about White people. People of   23
color can be racist, too." I once asked a White teacher what it would mean to
her if a student or parent of color accused her of being racist. She said she would
feel as though she had been punched in the stomach or called a "low-life scum."
She is not alone in this feeling. The word *racist* holds a lot of emotional power.
For many White people, to be called racist is the ultimate insult. The idea that
this term might only be applied to Whites becomes highly problematic for after
all, can't people of color be "low-life scum" too?

Of course, people of any racial group can hold hateful attitudes and behave   24
in racially discriminatory and bigoted ways. We can all cite examples of horrible
hate crimes which have been perpetrated by people of color as well as Whites.
Hateful behavior is hateful behavior no matter who does it. But when I am
asked, "Can people of color be racist?" I reply, "The answer depends on your
definition of racism," If one defines racism as racial prejudice, the answer is yes.
People of color can and do have racial prejudices. However, if one defines
racism as a system of advantage based on race, the answer is no. People of color
are not racist because they do not systematically benefit from racism. And
equally important, there is no systematic cultural and institutional support or

sanction for the racial bigotry of people of color. In my view, reserving the term *racist* only for behaviors committed by Whites in the context of a White-dominated society is a way of acknowledging the ever-present power differential afforded Whites by the culture and institutions that make up the system of advantage and continue to reinforce notions of White superiority. (Using the same logic, I reserve the word *sexist* for men. Though women can and do have gender-based prejudices, only men systematically benefit from sexism.)

Despite my best efforts to explain my thinking on this point, there are some 25 who will be troubled, perhaps even incensed, by my response. To call the racially motivated acts of a person of color acts of racial bigotry and to describe similar acts committed by Whites as racist will make no sense to some people, including some people of color. To those, I will respectfully say, "We can agree to disagree." At moments like these, it is not agreement that is essential, but clarity. Even if you don't like the definition of racism I am using, hopefully you are now clear about what it is. If I also understand how you are using the term, our conversation can continue—despite our disagreement.

Another provocative question I'm often asked is "Are you saying all Whites 26 are racist?" When asked this question, I again remember that White teacher's response, and I am conscious that perhaps the question I am really being asked is, "Are you saying all Whites are bad people?" The answer to that question is of course not. However, all White people, intentionally or unintentionally, do benefit from racism. A more relevant question is what are White people as individuals doing to interrupt racism? For many White people, the image of a racist is a hood-wearing Klan member or a name-calling Archie Bunker figure. These images represent what might be called *active racism*, blatant, intentional acts of racial bigotry and discrimination. *Passive racism* is more subtle and can be seen in the collusion of laughing when a racist joke is told, of letting exclusionary hiring practices go unchallenged, of accepting as appropriate the omissions of people of color from the curriculum, and of avoiding difficult race-related issues. Because racism is so ingrained in the fabric of American institutions, it is easily self-perpetuating.[6] All that is required to maintain it is business as usual.

I sometimes visualize the ongoing cycle of racism as a moving walkway at 27 the airport. Active racist behavior is equivalent to walking fast on the conveyor belt. The person engaged in active racist behavior has identified with the ideology of White supremacy and is moving with it. Passive racist behavior is equivalent to standing still on the walkway. No overt effort is being made, but the conveyor belt moves the bystanders along to the same destination as those who are actively walking. Some of the bystanders may feel the motion of the conveyor belt, see the active racists ahead of them, and choose to turn around, unwilling to go to the same destination as the White supremacists. But unless they are walking actively in the opposite direction at a speed faster than the conveyor belt—unless they are actively antiracist—they will find themselves carried along with the others.

So, not all Whites are actively racist. Many are passively racist. Some, though not enough, are actively antiracist. The relevant question is not whether all Whites are racist, but how we can move more White people from a position of active or passive racism to one of active antiracism? The task of interrupting racism is obviously not the task of Whites alone. But the fact of White privilege means that Whites have greater access to the societal institutions in need of transformation. To whom much is given, much is required.   28

It is important to acknowledge that while all Whites benefit from racism, they do not all benefit equally. Other factors, such as socioeconomic status, gender, age, religious affiliation, sexual orientation, mental and physical ability, also play a role in our access to social influence and power. A White woman on welfare is not privileged to the same extent as a wealthy White heterosexual man. In her case, the systematic disadvantages of sexism and classism intersect with her White privilege, but the privilege is still there. This point was brought home to me in a 1994 study conducted by a Mount Holyoke graduate student, Phyllis Wentworth.[7] Wentworth interviewed a group of female college students, who were both older than their peers and were the first members of their families to attend college, about the pathways that lead them to college. All of the women interviewed were White, from working-class backgrounds, from families where women were expected to graduate from high school and get married or get a job. Several had experienced abusive relationships and other personal difficulties prior to coming to college. Yet their experiences were punctuated by "good luck" stories of apartments obtained without a deposit, good jobs offered without experience or extensive reference checks, and encouragement provided by willing mentors.   29

While the women acknowledged their good fortune, none of them discussed their Whiteness. They had not considered the possibility that being White had worked in their favor and helped give them the benefit of the doubt at critical junctures. This study clearly showed that even under difficult circumstances, White privilege was still operating.   30

It is also true that not all people of color are equally targeted by racism. We all have multiple identities that shape our experience. I can describe myself as a light-skinned, well-educated, heterosexual, ablebodied, Christian African American woman raised in a middle-class suburb. As an African American woman, I am systematically disadvantaged by race and by gender, but I system-   31 atically receive benefits in the other categories, which then mediate my experience of racism and sexism. When one is targeted by multiple isms—racism, sexism, classism, heterosexism, ableism, anti-Semitism, ageism—in whatever combination, the effect is intensified. The particular combination of racism and classism in many communities of color is life-threatening. Nonetheless, when I, the middle-class Black mother of two sons, read another story about a Black man's unlucky encounter with a White police officer's deadly force, I am reminded that racism by itself can kill.

The Cost of Racism

Several years ago, a White male student in my psychology of racism course wrote in his journal at the end of the semester that he had learned a lot about racism and now understood in a way he never had before just how advantaged he was. He also commented that he didn't think he would do anything to try to change the situation. After all, the system was working in his favor. Fortunately, his response was not typical. Most of my students leave my course with the desire (and an action plan) to interrupt the cycle of racism. However, this young man's response does raise an important question. Why should Whites who are advantaged by racism *want* to end that system of advantage? What are the costs of that system to them?   32

A *Money* magazine article called "Race and Money" chronicled the many ways the American economy was hindered by institutional racism.[8] Whether one looks at productivity lowered by racial tensions in the workplace, or real estate equity lost through housing discrimination, or the tax revenue lost in underemployed communities of color, or the high cost of warehousing human talent in prison, the economic costs of racism are real and measurable.   33

As a psychologist, I often hear about the less easily measured costs. When I ask White men and women how racism hurts them, they frequently talk about their fears of people of color, the social incompetence they feel in racially mixed situations, the alienation they have experienced between parents and children when a child marries into a family of color, and the interracial friendships they had as children that were lost in adolescence or young adulthood without their ever understanding why. White people are paying a significant price for the system of advantage. The cost is not as high for Whites as it is for people of color, but a price is being paid.[9] Wendell Berry, a White writer raised in Kentucky, captures this psychic pain in the opening pages of his book, *The Hidden Wound:*   34

> If white people have suffered less obviously from racism than black people, they have nevertheless suffered greatly; the cost has been greater perhaps than we can yet know. If the white man has inflicted the wound of racism

upon black men, the cost has been that he would receive the mirror image of that wound into himself. As the master, or as a member of the dominant race, he has felt little compulsion to acknowledge it or speak of it; the more painful it has grown the more deeply he has hidden it within himself. But the wound is there, and it is a profound disorder, as great a damage in his mind as it is in his society.[10]

The dismantling of racism is in the best interests of everyone.   35

A Word About Language

Throughout this chapter I have used the term *White* to refer to Americans of   36
European descent. In another era, I might have used the term *Caucasian*. I have used the term *people of color* to refer to those groups in America that are and have been historically targeted by racism. This includes people of African descent, people of Asian descent, people of Latin American descent, and indigenous peoples (sometimes referred to as Native Americans or American Indians).[11] Many people refer to these groups collectively as non-Whites. This term is particularly offensive because it defines groups of people in terms of what they are not. (Do we call women "non-men?") I also avoid using the term *minorities* because it represents another kind of distortion of information which we need to correct. So-called minorities represent the majority of the world's population. While the term *people of color* is inclusive, it is not perfect. As a workshop participant once said, White people have color, too. Perhaps it would be more accurate to say "people of more color," though I am not ready to make that change. Perhaps fellow psychologist Linda James Myers is on the right track. She refers to two groups of people, those of acknowledged African descent and those of unacknowledged African descent, reminding us that we can all trace the roots of our common humanity to Africa.

I refer to people of acknowledged African descent as Black. I know that   37
African American is also a commonly used term, and I often refer to myself and other Black people born and raised in America in that way. Perhaps because I am a child of the 1960s "Black and beautiful" era, I still prefer Black. The term is more inclusive than *African American*, because there are Black people in the United States who are not African American—Afro-Caribbeans, for example—yet are targeted by racism, and are identified as Black.

When referring to other groups of color, I try to use the terms that the peo-   38
ple themselves want to be called. In some cases, there is no clear consensus. For example, some people of Latin American ancestry prefer *Latino*, while others pre-fer *Hispanic* or, if of Mexican descent, *Chicano*.[12] The terms *Latino* and *Hispanic* are used interchangeably here. Similarly, there are regional variations in the use of the terms *Native American*, *American Indian*, and *Indian*. *American Indian and*

Native people are now more widely used than *Native American*, and the language used here reflects that. People of Asian descent include Pacific Islanders, and that is reflected in the terms *Asian/Pacific Islanders* and *Asian Pacific Americans*. However, when quoting others I use whichever terms they use.

My dilemma about the language to use reflects the fact that race is a social   39 construction.[13] Despite myths to the contrary, biologists tell us that the only meaningful racial categorization is that of human. Van den Berghe defines race as "a group that is socially defined but on the basis of physical criteria," includ-ing skin color and facial features.[14]

Racial identity development, a central focus of this book, usually refers to the   40 process of defining for oneself the personal significance and social meaning of belonging to a particular racial group. The terms *racial identity* and *ethnic identity* are often used synonymously, though a distinction can be made between the two. An ethnic group is a socially defined group based on *cultural* criteria, such as language, customs, and shared history. An individual might identify as a member of an ethnic group (Irish or Italian, for example) but might not think of himself in racial terms (as White). On the other hand, one may recognize the personal significance of racial group membership (identifying as Black, for instance) but may not consider ethnic identity (such as West Indian) as partic-ularly meaningful.

Both racial and ethnic categories are socially constructed, and social defini-   41 tions of these categories have changed over time. For example, in his book *Eth-nic Identity: The Transformation of White America*, Richard Alba points out that the high rates of intermarriage and the dissolution of other social boundaries among European ethnic groups in the United States have reduced the signifi-cance of ethnic identity for these groups. In their place, he argues, a new ethnic identity is emerging, that of European American.[15]

Throughout this book, I refer primarily to racial identity. It is important,   42 however, to acknowledge that ethnic identity and racial identity sometimes intersect. For example, dark-skinned Puerto Ricans may identify culturally as Puerto Rican and yet be categorized racially by others as Black on the basis of physical appearance. In the case of either racial or ethnic identity, these identi-ties remain most salient to individuals of racial or ethnic groups that have been historically disadvantaged or marginalized.

The language we use to categorize one another racially is imperfect. These   43 categories are still evolving as the current debate over Census classifications indicates.[16] The original creation of racial categories was in the service of oppression. Some may argue that to continue to use them is to continue that oppression. I respect that argument. Yet it is difficult to talk about what is essentially a flawed and problematic social construct without using language that is itself problematic. We have to be able to talk about it in order to change it. So this is the language I choose.

ENDNOTES

1. C. O'Toole, "The effect of the media and multicultural education on children's perceptions of Native Americans" (senior thesis, Department of Psychology and Education, Mount Holyoke College, South Hadley, MA, May 1990).

2. For an extended discussion of this point, see David Wellman, *Portraits of White Racism* (Cambridge: Cambridge University Press, 1977), ch. 1.

3. For specific statistical information, see R. Farley, "The common destiny of Blacks and Whites: Observations about the social and economic status of the races," pp. 197–233 in H. Hill and J. E. Jones Jr. (Eds.), *Race in America: The struggle for equality* (Madison: University of Wisconsin Press, 1993).

4. P. McIntosh, "White privilege: Unpacking the invisible knapsack," *Peace and Freedom* (July / August 1989): 10–12.

5. For further discussion of the concept of "belief in a just world," see M. J. Lerner, "Social psychology of justice and interpersonal attraction," in T. Huston (Ed.), *Foundations of interpersonal attraction* (New York: Academic Press, 1974).

6. For a brief historical overview of the institutionalization of racism and sexism in our legal system, see "Part V: How it happened: Race and gender issues in U.S. law," in P. S. Rothenberg (Ed.), *Race, class, and gender in the United States: An integrated study*, 3d ed. (New York: St. Martin's Press, 1995).

7. P. A. Wentworth, "The identity development of non-traditionally aged first-generation women college students: An exploratory study" (master's thesis, Department of Psychology and Education, Mount Holyoke College, South Hadley, MA, 1994).

8. W. L. Updegrave, "Race and money," *Money* (December 1989): 152–72.

9. For further discussion of the impact of racism on Whites, see B. Bowser and R. G. Hunt (Eds.), *Impacts of racism on White Americans* (Thousand Oaks, CA: Sage, 1981); P. Kivel, *Uprooting racism: How White people can work for racial justice* (Philadelphia: New Society Publishers, 1996); and J. Barndt, *Dismantling racism: The continuing challenge to White America* (Minneapolis: Augsburg Press, 1991).

10. W. Berry, *The hidden wound* (San Francisco: North Point Press, 1989), pp. 3–4.

11. It is important to note here that these groups are not necessarily mutually exclusive. For example, people of Latin American descent may have European, African, and Native American ancestors. The politics of racial cate-

gorization has served to create artificial boundaries between groups with shared ancestry.

12. It is difficult to know which is the preferred term to use because different subgroups have different preferences. According to Amado Padilla, younger U.S.-born university-educated individuals of Mexican ancestry prefer Chicano(a) to Mexican American or Hispanic. On the other hand, Latino is preferred by others of Mexican ancestry or other Latin American origin. Those of Cuban ancestry may prefer Cuban American to Latino, whereas recent immigrants from Central America would rather be identified by their nationality (e.g., *Guatematecos or Salvadoreños*). A. Padilla (Ed.), *Hispanic psychology* (Thousand Oaks, CA: Sage, 1995).

13. For an expanded discussion of the social construction of race, see M. Omi and H. Winant, *Racial formation in the United States*, 2d ed. (New York: Roudedge, 1994),

14. P. L. Van den Berghe, *Race and racism* (New York: Wiley, 1967).

15. See R. Alba, *Ethnic identity: The transformation of White America* (New Haven: Yale University Press, 1990).

16. For a discussion of the census classification debate and the history of racial classification in the United States, see L. Wright, "One drop of blood," *The New Yorker* (July 25, 1994): 46–55.

Barry Wellman (1942–) is a professor of sociology at the University of Toronto, where he directs NetLab, the Centre for Urban and Community Studies. Chair–Emeritus of the Community and Urban Sociology section of the American Sociological Association and a member of the Royal Society of Canada, he studies the way people behave, communicate, and socialize in virtual networks. He has authored or co-authored over 300 articles and is an editor of three books on related subjects. He is also the North American Editor for the journal *Information, Communication and Society*.

COMPUTER NETWORKS AS SOCIAL NETWORKS

Barry Wellman

> Computer networks are inherently social networks, linking people, organizations, and knowledge. They are social institutions that should not be studied in isolation but as integrated into everyday lives. The proliferation of computer networks has facilitated a deemphasis on group solidarities at work and in the community and afforded a turn to networked societies that are loosely bounded and sparsely knit. The Internet increases people's social capital, increasing contact with friends and relatives who live nearby and far away. New tools must be developed to help people navigate and find knowledge in complex, fragmented, networked societies.

Once upon a time, computers were not social beings. Most stood alone, be they mainframe, mini, or personal computer. Each person who used a computer sat alone in front of a keyboard and screen. To help people deal with their computers, the field of human-computer interaction (HCI) developed, providing such things as more accessible interfaces and user-friendly software. But as the HCI name says, the model was person-computer.   1

Computers have increasingly reached out to each other. Starting in the 1960s, people began piggybacking on machine-machine data transfers to send each other messages. Communication soon spilled over organizational boundaries. The proliferation of electronic mail (e-mail) in the 1980s and its expansion into the Internet in the 1990s (based on e-mail and the Web) have so tied things together that to many, being at a computer is synonymous with being connected to the Internet.   2

Barry Wellman, "Computer Networks as Social Networks," *Science*, vol. 293, no. 5537 (September 14, 2001), pp. 2031–2034. Reprinted with permission from AAAS. Table 1 is from Barry Wellman, Anabel Quan Haase, James Witte, and Keith Hampton, "Does the Internet Increase, Decrease, or Supplement Social Capital?: Social Networks, Participation, and Community Commitment," *American Behavioral Scientist*, vol. 45, no. 3 (November 2001), pp. 436–455 (Tables 2 and 3). Copyright © 2001 by SAGE Publications, Inc. Reprinted by permission of SAGE Publications, Inc.

As a result, HCI has become socialized. Much of the discussion at current 3
HCI conferences is about how people use computers to relate to each other (1).
Some participants build "groupware" to support such interactions; others do
ethnographic, laboratory, and survey studies to ascertain how people actually
relate to each other. This work has slowly moved from the lone computer user
to dealing with (i) how two people relate to each other online, (ii) how small
groups interact, and (iii) how large unbounded systems operate—the ultimate
being the worldwide Internet, the largest and most fully connected social network of them all. Just one small portion of the Internet—Usenet members—
participated in more than 80,000 topic-oriented collective discussion groups in
2000. 8.1 million unique participants posted 151 million messages (2–4). This is
more than three times the number identified on 27 January 1996 (5).

Computer scientists and developers have come to realize that when com- 4
puter systems connect people and organizations, they are inherently social.
They are also coming to realize that the popular term "groupware" is misleading,
because computer networks principally support social networks, not groups. A
group is only one special type of a social network; one that is heavily intercon-
nected and clearly bounded. Much social organization no longer fits the group
model. Work, community, and domestic life have largely moved from hierarchi-
cally arranged, densely knit, bounded groups to social networks.

In networked societies, boundaries are more permeable, interactions are 5
with diverse others, linkages switch between multiple networks, and hierarchies
are flatter and more recursive (6–8). Hence, many people and organizations
communicate with others in ways that ramify across group boundaries. Rather
than relating to one group, they cycle through interactions with a variety of
others, at work or in the community. Their work and community networks are
diffuse and sparsely knit, with vague overlapping social and spatial boundaries.
Their computer-mediated communication has become part of their everyday
lives, rather than being a separate set of relationships.

When computer-mediated communication networks link people, institu- 6
tions, and knowledge, they are computer-supported social networks. Indeed, if
Novell had not gotten there first, computer scientists would be saying "netware"
instead of "groupware" for systems that enable people to interact with each other
online. Often computer networks and social networks work conjointly, with
computer networks linking people in social networks and with people bringing
their offline situations to bear when they use computer networks to interact.

The intersection of computer networks with the emerging networked soci- 7
ety has fostered several exciting developments. I report here on two developing
areas: (i) community networks on- and offline and (ii) knowledge access.

Community Networks On- and Offline

Community, like computers, has become networked. Although community was 8
once synonymous with densely knit, bounded neighborhood groups, it is now
seen as a less bounded social network of relationships that provide sociability
support, information, and a sense of belonging. These communities are partial
(people cycle through interactions with multiple sets of others) and ramify
through space [a low proportion of community members in the developed world
are neighbors (7)]. Where once people interacted door-to-door in villages (subject to public support and social control), they now interact household-to-
household and person-to- person (9).

Although the support of collaborative work was the initial purpose of the 9
Internet (both e-mail and the Web), it is an excellent medium for supporting far-
flung, intermittent, networked communities. E-mail transcends physical propin-
quity and mutual availability; e-mail lists enable broadcasts to multiple community
members; attachments and Web sites allow documents, pictures, and videos to be
passed along; buddy lists and other awareness tools show who might be available
for communication at any one time; and instant messaging means that simultaneous communication can happen online as well as face-to-face and by telephone.

Systematic research on what people actually do on the Internet has lagged 10
behind the Internet's development. After a long period of pundit supposition,
travelers' tales, and laboratory studies of computer-mediated communication,
survey-based and ethnographic research is now appearing.

These studies address a vigorous public debate about whether people can 11
find community online. Critics wonder whether relationships between people
who never see, smell, or hear each other can be the basis for true community
[reviewed in (10); examples include (11–13)]. Other detractors make an opposite argument: The Internet may be so immersive that it lures people away from
other pursuits (14) and involves them in online interactions that only reinforce
their existing opinions.

By contrast, enthusiasts see the Internet as extending and transforming 12
community. John Perry Barlow asserts that "with the development of the Internet . . . we are in the middle of the most transforming technological event since
the capture of fire" (15). They point to the ability of the Internet to span dis-
tances and time zones at low cost, to sustain relationships based on shared interests (even when the participants are residentially dispersed), and to provide
powerful links between people and dispersed knowledge (16).

Too often the debate has been (i) Manichean: The Internet is bringing 13
heaven or hell, but nothing in between. (ii) Unidimensional: The Internet is
such a powerful force that other considerations, such as gender and status in an

organization, are ignored. (iii) Parochial: The Internet should be considered as an entity in itself, rather than as fitting into the full range of work, community, and daily life. (iv) Presentist: The Internet is such a transforming force that long-term social trends, such as the pre-Internet move to networked communities, are irrelevant.

As the debate continues, the Internet is now used by a majority of North Americans, although its growth rate is slowing and may stabilize at about 60% of adults. The digital divide is decreasing rapidly in North America, although socioeconomic status (education, occupation, and income) remains an important differentiator (17–20). The digital divide is much more significant in two ways in less developed countries: (i) A much lower percentage of the population use the Internet and (ii) the users are predominantly well-connected elites (21). In the developed world, the amount of time spent online is increasing, per capita as well as overall. For example, the average AOL user spent 31 min per day online in the first quarter of 1997; in 4 years, this had more than doubled to 64 min online in the first quarter of 2001 (22). Nor does familiarity breed interpersonal contempt: The more contact people have online, the greater the impression they make on each other (23). 14

Survey-based evidence about the Internet's effect on community has been mixed. Most cross-sectional studies show that those frequently online are more involved in community (24–27). By contrast, one study (28) suggests that extensive online involvement took people away from interaction with household and community members. Moreover, the only true longitudinal study found that some "newbies" became more depressed, alienated, and isolated during the first 6 months of computer use (29). 15

Robust results indicating how the Internet fits into community life are now available (30–32). It is becoming clear that the Internet is not destroying community but is resonating with and extending the types of networked community that have already become prevalent in the developed Western world. Old ties with relatives and former neighbors are maintained; new ties are developed among people sharing interests. It is not only that time and space become less important in computermediated communication, but that it is easy to communicate with large groups of community members (using lists) and to bring unconnected community members into direct contact. The ease with which computer- mediated communication connects friends of friends can also increase the density of interconnections among clusters of network members within communities. 16

For one thing, as the newbies studied by Kraut *et al.* (33) gained more experience with the Internet, their depression and alienation disappeared, and their 17

social contact increased enough to have a positive impact on their overall interactions with community members. A comparative analysis found that social
support obtained online helped people to deal with depression (*34*).

Other studies have found that the Internet increased community interac-   18
tion (*35, 36*). For example, a large *National Geographic* Web survey found that
face-to-face visits and phone calls were neither more numerous nor fewer for
people who use e-mail a great deal. E-mail just added to the fund of contact, so
that the overall volume of contacts with friends and relatives through all media
was higher for people who use e-mail a lot (*27*) (Table 1).

However, another study found that e-mail use is displacing telephone use to   19
some extent (*37*). Perhaps there are differences in the kinds of communication

TABLE 1   E-mail use by total annual communication. [Source: Survey2000; see (*27*) for details]

E-mail use	Kin					Friends				
	F2F*	Phone	Letters	E-mail	Total	F2F	Phone	Letters	E-mail	Total
Within 50 km										
Never	77	117	6	1	201	104	136	6	1	247
Rarely	65	116	6	5	192	84	112	8	5	209
Monthly	61	113	6	7	187	74	98	5	9	186
Weekly	62	120	6	13	201	76	99	7	20	202
Few times/week	63	115	7	24	209	83	113	7	37	240
Daily	60	118	8	52	178	92	126	9	118	345
Total	61	117	7	39	224	88	120	9	86	303
Beyond 50 km										
Never	12	37	8	1	58	13	25	7	1	46
Rarely	10	36	8	5	59	11	19	7	4	41
Monthly	9	35	7	10	61	8	16	6	8	38
Weekly	9	36	9	19	73	8	17	6	16	47
Few times/week	10	39	9	35	93	9	19	7	30	65
Daily	10	43	10	72	135	10	25	8	85	128
Total	10	41	10	55	116	10	23	8	62	103
*F2F, face to face.										

that take place on the Internet or by telephone or face-to-face. Although one study of a dispersed work group found much similarity in what was said by means of each of these media (26), another found that among community members, e-mail is preferred more when people want to garner information efficiently.

The positive impact of the Internet on community ties is true for those liv-   20 ing both nearby and far away. The proportionate gain in contact is greatest for contact with friends and relatives living at a distance (9, 38), as one might expect from a system able to cross time zones at a single bound and in which there is no differentiation between short-distance and long-distance messages. Yet online as well as offline contact is highest with those living nearby (9, 38). Cyberspace does not vanquish the importance of physical space. For example, many e-mail and chat messages arrange face-to-face meetings (26, 39).

The recent case of "Netville" (a suburb of Toronto) is especially interest-   21 ing, because here neighborhood access to a high-speed Internet service helped bring neighborhood members together for face-to-face get-togethers, from visits in private homes to semipublic barbeques (40, 41). Those who were part of the high-speed service knew three times as many neighbors as the unwired and visited with 1.6 times as many. Nor was the Internet only used socially: Netville residents used their local discussion list to mobilize against the real estate developer and the local Internet service provider (40). To be sure, Netville may be a special case because the residents were newly arrived and excited to be part of an Internet experiment. Yet recent work in Michigan (42) and Los Angeles (43) shows how the Internet can reinforce traditional community development approaches.

Despite the past decade's excitement about the Internet, as it pervades life   22 it may become as taken for granted as that once transforming technology, the telephone (44). One indication is that those who have been on the Internet the longest and the most frequently are least apt to feel that they are a part of an online community, although their overall sense of community remains (27). This may reflect their greater likelihood of encountering distasteful situations, such as flaming, hacking into accounts, virus transmission, or unwanted junk mail "spam." Or it may mean that those with much Internet experience do not privilege it as a special form of community. Or it may support the fears of those who believe that computer-mediated communication is not a satisfactory surrogate for face-to-face contact.

Thus, preliminary findings create new questions. At present, Internet stud-   23 ies of community are in full swing: The Pew Internet and American Life project does a monthly tracking study (35). The Stanford Institute for the Quantitative

Study of Society is doing frequent surveys (14, 45). The U.S. General Social Survey, which is central to social science research, included an Internet module in 2000 and may do so again. The 2001 Canadian General Social Survey has an Internet module. The large-scale international National Geographic Survey2000 data are available for use [(27,46); see http://survey2000 .nationalgeographic.com]. The National Geographic Society (in conjunction with Clemson University and the University of Toronto) is doing an even larger and more comprehensive Web survey in fall 2001. A University of Maryland "Web institute" is archiving many surveys online with statistical software available for reanalysis (47). Along with such survey efforts, there is scope for ethnographic community studies [such as what Hampton and Wellman have done in Netville (38, 40, 47–49)].

Finding Knowledge in a Networked Society

Many organizations are similar to networked communities in having multiple   24
sets of work team members (including multiple superiors), physically dispersed relationships, and teams of co-workers shifting by the day and week as employees get involved in multiple projects. The situation is different from that dealt with by traditional organizational theory, which comprehends densely knit workgroups neatly structured in bureaucratic, hierarchical organizational trees (6, 50–52).

How do people work together in large, sprawling, networked organizations   25
where they are simultaneously members of multiple, transitory, physically dispersed teams? In particular, how do people in such organizations obtain knowledge from others when they do not know whom to ask?

These questions are of immediate practical importance for complex organi-   26
zations. Hence, computer-supported solutions are developing for working through trusted interpersonal relationships to identify, locate, and receive information within and between communities and organizations. It is not surprising that work in this area has been driven by computer scientists and communication scientists interested in building tools for knowledge access and management.

One issue is finding out who knows what; a more complex task in net-   27
worked organizations (53). Normally, one attempts to examine the documentation or other help sources and then wanders out into a hallway in search of friendly colleagues. The problem becomes acute, however, in distributed communities [(54), p. 97].

How do people wander the hallway when their team or other supports   28
are physically distributed? One approach is to build awareness tools (55). Two of these, Cruiser (56) and Postcards/Telepresence (57, 58), provided

low-resolution video pictures of offices or cubicles. The picture told others whether people were in their offices and perhaps available. The low resolution of the picture was not able to show what people were doing and afforded some privacy.

Another approach, Babble, builds on the traditional groupware approach, which facilitates a small defined group working together (59). Babble shows each person as an animated and colored circle that moves closer to the center as the person gets more involved in team activities. 29

When people are asked about the size of their networks, they consistently report them as smaller than the 1000 or more others that they probably know well enough to converse with (60–62). Rolodexes and their database equivalents are some help, but the listing can be computer-supported. ContactMap (52) looks at ongoing Internet exchanges to record a person's contacts. 30

Such memory aids typically record each person as a discrete entity. New developments record the connections of network members (63, 64). As such approaches develop, they have the potential to do primitive automated social network analysis—identifying clusters, boundaries, centrality, bridges, and blocks—by analyzing who jointly receives an e-mail and who forwards e-mails to whom. 31

Who holds the organizational or community memory, now that the veteran employee—the fount of work lore—is neither known nor accessible? Often people ask their workmates. But what if they do not know? People then wonder whether friends of friends know, yet most people do not possess a list of all of their friends' friends, much less are aware of what their friends' friends know. Yet it is reasonable to assume that the number of friends of friends is 100,000, assuming that each person knows approximately 1000 others and that 10 percent of each person's ties are unique. These are too many names to keep track of, yet people often want a personal touch when giving and getting information. They may want to talk to the information holder to supply a nuanced or confidential request; the information holder may only be willing to release such information to a friend or a friend of a friend. 32

IKNOW is software that stores information about friends of friends; not only who they are but what information they know (65). It seeks to answer the question: "Who knows who knows what?" The hope is that through the use of such indirect but personal ties, people will supply reliable and appropriate information. Issues remain. The first is about software that is scalable to map and supply such contact information for a large amorphous organization. The second is about data collection: How do systems compile information about who 33 knows what? The third is about privacy: Do people want to reveal their friends and their skill sets to strangers?

The Answer Garden *(54)* addresses such issues of data collection and pri- 34
vacy, although it does not deal with interpersonal connections. It provides tools for people to build repositories of commonly requested questions and answers, in part by building up these repositories from ongoing question-and-answer sessions. Thus, only the information that has been publicly provided is available. However, this provides only limited access to the files of each work team member. Good solutions are not yet available that balance team needs to have access to personal files with the needs of each person to limit a team's access to only the germane portions of his or her entire files.

With so much potential and need to connect, there is the need to prioritize 35
communication. Does my boss supersede my peers? Does my wife or husband have higher priority than my sister or brother? Dealing with such matters would be an advanced implementation for the simple filter rules now commonly available for e-mail. Important, as yet unpublished, work is being done to establish rules for prioritizing computer-mediated contact, both deductively setting a priori rules and inductively watching which messages a person takes first.

An Internet year is like a dog year, changing approximately seven times 36
faster than normal human time. Nevertheless, I expect the transition from a group-based to a networked society to continue *(66)*. Although technology does not change society—it only affords possibilities for change—powerful forces are shaping the Internet: increased broadband use, global ubiquity, portability, 24/7 availability, personalization, and the switch from place-to-place to person-to-person connectivity. These suggest the accelerating need for social network concepts and tools for engaging with the Internet.

REFERENCES AND NOTES

1. The key HCI conferences are sponsored by the Association for Computing Machinery. They are SIGCHI (Special Interest Group on Computer-Human Interfaces), SIGGROUP (groupware and group processes), and CSCW (Computer-Supported Cooperative Work).
2. M. A. Smith, personal communication.
3. M. A. Smith, in *Communities in Cyberspace*, M. A. Smith, P. Kollock, Eds. (Routledge, London, 1999), pp. 195–219.
4. M. Dodge, R. Kitchin, *Mapping Cyberspace* (Routledge, London, 2001).
5. S. Southwick, *Liszt: Searchable Directory of E-Mail Discussion Groups* (report to BlueMarble Information Services, Bloomington, IN, 1996).

6. B. Wellman, in *Culture of the Internet*, S. Kiesler, Ed. (Lawrence Erlbaum, Mahwah, NJ, 1997), pp. 179–205.

7. B. Wellman, in *Networks in the Global Village*, B. Wellman, Ed. (Westview Press, Boulder, CO, 1999), pp. 1–47.

8. M. Castells, *The Rise of the Network Society* (Blackwell, Malden, MA, ed. 2, 2000).

9. B. Wellman, *Int. J. Urban Reg. Res.* **25**, 227 (2001).

10. B. Wellman, M. Gulia, in *Networks in the Global Village*, B. Wellman, Ed. (Westview Press, Boulder, CO, 1999), pp. 167–194.

11. C. Stoll, *Silicon Snake Oil: Second Thoughts on the Information Highway* (Doubleday, New York, 1995).

12. M. Slouka, *War of the Worlds: Cyberspace and the High-Tech Assault on Reality* (Basic Books, New York, 1995).

13. V. Jergens, "Does the Internet Bring Us Down," *New York Times*, 3 September 1998 (online at www.nytimes.com).

14. N. Nie, *Am. Behav. Sci.*, in press.

15. J. P. Barlow, S. Birkets, K. Kelly, M. Slouka, *Harper's* **1995,** 40 (August 1995).

16. H. Rheingold, *The Virtual Community* (MIT Press, Cambridge, MA, ed. 2, 2000).

17. M. Kew, B. Wellman, *Curr. Sociol.*, in press.

18. A. Reddick, C. Boucher, M. Groseillers, *The Dual Digital Divide: The Information Highway in Canada* (Public Interest Advocacy Centre, Ottawa, Canada, 2000).

19. National Telecommunications and Information Administration (NTIA), *Falling Through the Net* (NTIA, Washington, DC, 2000).

20. E. Fong, B. Wellman, R. Wilkes, M. Kew, *Correlates of the Digital Divide: Individual, Household and Spatial Variation* (report to Office of Learning Technologies, Human Resources Development Canada, Ottawa, Ontario, June 2001).

21. W. Chen, J. Boase, B. Wellman, in *The Internet in Everyday Life*, B. Wellman, C. Haythornthwaite, Eds. (Blackwell, Oxford, in press).

22. A. Odlyzko, *The History of Communications and its Implications for the Internet* (AT&T Labs-Research, Florham Park, NJ, 2000).

23. Y. Liu, *The Effects of Frequency and Duration of Messaging on Impression and Relational Development in Computer-Mediated Communication: An Exploratory Study* (report presented at the Annual Conference of the International Communication Association, Washington, DC, 2001).

24. J. Katz, *Wired* **1997** 68, 76, 274 (December 1997).

25. J. Katz, R. Rice, P. Aspden, *Am. Behav. Sci.*, in press.

26. C. Haythornthwaite, B. Wellman, *J. Am. Soc. Inf. Sci.* **49,** 1101 (1998).

27. B. Wellman, A. Q. Haase, J. Witte, K. Hampton, *Am. Behav. Sci.*, in press.

28. N. Nie, L. Erbing, *Study Offers Early Look at How Internet Is Changing Daily Life* (Institute for the Quantitative Study of Social Science, Stanford, CA, 2000).

29. R. Kraut *et al.*, *Am. Psychol.* **53,** 1017 (1998).

30. P. DiMaggio, E. Hargittai, N. Russell, J. Robinson, *Annu. Rev. Sociol.* **27,** 207 (2001).

31. C. Haythornthwaite, B. Wellman, Eds., special issue on the Internet in everyday life, *Am. Behav. Sci.*, in press.

32. B. Wellman, C. Haythornthwaite, Eds., *The Internet in Everyday Life* (Blackwell, Oxford, in press).

33. R. Kraut *et al.*, *Internet Paradox Revisited* (Carnegie Mellon University, 2001).

34. R. LaRosa, M. S. Eastin, J. Gregg, *J. Online Behav.* **1** (2001) (see www .behavior.net/job/v1n2/paradox. html).

35. P. Howard, L. Rainie, S. Jones, *Am. Behav. Sci.*, in press.

36. B. Anderson, K. Tracey, *Am. Behav. Sci.*, in press.

37. J. Dimmick, C. J. Gade, C. Rankin, *A Niche of Microdimension Analysis of Displacement of Long Distance Phone Use by E-Mail* (paper presented at the International Communications Association Annual Meeting, Washington, DC, 2001).

38. K. Hampton, B. Wellman, *Am. Behav. Sci.*, in press.

39. R. Ling, B. Yttri, in *Perpetual Contact*, J. Katz, M. Aakhus, Eds. (Cambridge Univ. Press, Cambridge, in press).

40. K. Hampton, B. Wellman, *City and Community*, in press.

41. K. Hampton, thesis, University of Toronto (2001).

42. P. Resnick, *Who's That? Connecting Neighbors through Directories and Distribution Lists* (paper presented at CHI'99 Conference, Seattle, WA, May 1999).

43. S. J. Ball-Rokeach, Y.-C. Kim, S. Matei, *Commun. Res.* **28,** 429 (2001).

44. C. Fischer, *America Calling: A Social History of the Telephone to 1940* (Univ. of California Press, Berkeley, CA, 1992).

45. N. Nie, L. Erbing, *Study Offers Early Look at How Internet Is Changing Daily Life* (Stanford University, 2000; www.stanford.edu/groups/siqss/ Press_release. html).

46. J. C. Witte, L. M. Amoroso, P. E. N. Howard, *Social Sci. Comput. Rev.* **18,** 179 (2000).

47. The archive at www.webuse.umd.edu contains original data from more than 20 surveys in which behavioral questions about Internet usage were asked of nationally representative samples, including the Digital Divide surveys done by the U.S. Census Bureau for the NTIA, the 2000 U.S. General Social Survey, and national time use surveys. Users can directly analyze the data interactively using statistical software. In addition to the data archive, the Web site contains an annotated bibliography of behavioral research into more than 15 areas of Internet use (such as the digital divide, time displacement, and social networks), articles on Internet behavior, and links to other resources.

48. B. Hampton, B. Wellman, *Am. Behav. Sci.* **43**, 475 (1999).

49. N. K. Baym, in *Culture of the Internet*, S. Kiesler, Ed. (Lawrence Erlbaum, Mahwah, NJ, 1997), pp. 103–120.

50. N. S. Contractor, *Manage. Commun. Q.* **13**, 154 (1999).

51. N. Nazer, thesis, University of Toronto (2000).

52. B. A. Nardi, S. Whittaker, H. Schwartz, *First Monday* **5**, 30 (2000).

53. R. Cross, S. Borgatti, *The Ties that Share: Relational Characteristics that Facilitate Knowledge Transfer and Organizational Learning* (working paper of the Carroll School of Management, Boston College, Boston, MA, 2000).

54. M. Ackerman, D. McDonald, *Answer Garden 2: Merging Organizational Memory with Collaborative Help* (paper 97-105 presented at the Conference on Computer-Supported Cooperative Work, Cambridge, MA, December 1996).

55. O. Liechti, *SIGGROUP Bull.* **21**, 3 (2000).

56. R. Fish, R. Kraut, R. Root, R. Rice, *Commun. ACM* **36**, 48 (1993).

57. B. Buxton, *Telepresence: Integrating Shared Task and Person Spaces*, in proceedings of Graphics Interface '92, Vancouver, British Columbia, May 1992.

58. G. Moore, in *Video-Mediated Communication*, K. Finn, A. J. Sellen, S. Wilbur, Eds. (Lawrence Erlbaum, Mahwah, NJ, 1997), pp. 301–321.

59. E. Bradner, W. Kellogg, T. Erickson, *Social Affordances of BABBLE* (paper presented at the European Computer-Supported Cooperative Work Conference, Copenhagen, Denmark, November 1998).

60. J. Boissevain, *Friends of Friends: Networks, Manipulators, and Coalitions* (Blackwell, Oxford, 1974).

61. M. Kochen, Ed. *The Small World* (Ablex, Norwood, NJ, 1989).

62. D. J. Watts, *Small Worlds* (Princeton Univ. Press, Princeton, NJ, 1999).

63. W. Sack, *Mapping Conversations: Position Paper for the CSCW Workshop Dealing with Community Data* [paper presented at the Computer-Supported

Cooperative Work Conference (CSCW 2000), Philadelphia, PA, December, 2000].

64. Q. Jones, G. Ravid, S. Rafaeli, *Information Overload and Virtual Public Discourse Boundaries* (paper presented at CSCW 2000, Philadelphia, PA, December, 2000).

65. N. Contractor, D. Zink, M. Chan, in *Community Computing and Support Systems, Lecture Notes in Computer Science,* T. Ishida, Ed. (Springer-Verlag, Berlin, 1998), pp. 201–217.

66. M. Castells, *The Rise of the Network Society* (Blackwell, Malden, MA, ed. 2, 2000).

67. Research underlying this article has been supported by the Bell University Laboratories, Communications and Information Technology Ontario, Mitel Networks, the Office of Learning Technologies (Human Resources and Development Canada), the Social Science and Humanities Research Council of Canada, and at the University of Toronto: our NetLab at the Centre for Urban and Community Studies, Department of Sociology, and the Knowledge Media Design Institute. Discussions with NetLab colleagues have been invaluable, especially J. Boase, W. Chen, K. Hampton, C. Haythornthwait, A. Q. Haase, J. Salaff, and B. Wellman. M. Prijatelj and U. Quach provided valuable assistance.

Disciplinary Literacies

Robert G. Bringle is the Chancellor's Professor of Psychology and Philanthropic Studies in the School of Science of the University Graduate School at Indiana University–Purdue University in Indianapolis, where he has worked since 1974. He received his Ph.D. in Social Psychology from the University of Massachusetts-Amherst and is known in the social psychology field for his scholarship on love, envy, and attachment in close relationships. He began his work in service learning in 1981 and became the director for the Center for Service and Learning in 1994. He is the author of With Service in Mind: Concepts and Models for Service-Learning in Psychology (1998), Colleges and Universities as Citizens (1999), and The Measure of Service Learning: Research Scales to Assess Student Experiences (2003).

Julie A. Hatcher is associate instructor of education and the assistant director of the Center for Service and Learning at Indiana University–Purdue University in Indianapolis.

IMPLEMENTING SERVICE LEARNING IN HIGHER EDUCATION

Rober G. Bringle and Julie A. Hatcher

In a recent article, "Creating the New American College," Ernest Boyer challenges higher education to reconsider its mission to be that of educating students for a life as responsible citizens, rather than educating students solely for a career. By doing so, the "New American College" will take pride in connecting theory to practice in order to meet challenging social problems, particularly those faced by universities in urban settings. As Ira Harkavey of the University of Pennsylvania Center for Community Partnerships has noted, "Universities cannot afford to remain shores of affluence, self-importance and horticultural beauty at the edge of island seas of squalor, violence and despair" [5, p. A48]. Emphasizing service has the potential to enrich learning and renew communities, but will also give "new dignity to the scholarship of service" [5, p. A48].

Universities have valuable resources (for example, students, faculty, staff, classrooms, libraries, technology, research expertise) that become accessible to the community when partnerships address community needs. They also have a

Robert G. Bringle and Julie A. Hatcher, "Implementing Service Learning in Higher Education," *The Journal of Higher Education*, vol. 67, no. 2 (1996), pp. 221-239. Copyright 1996 The Ohio State University. Reproduced with permission.

We gratefully acknowledge the comments of Amy Driscoll, Catherine Ludlum, Keith Morton, William Plater, Tim Stanton, and Pam Velo on a draft of this article.

tradition of serving their communities by strengthening the economic development of the region, addressing educational and health needs of the community,
and contributing to the cultural life of the community [12, 23, 27]. Emphasizing
the value of community involvement and voluntary community service can also
create a culture of service on a campus [for example, 17, 26].

From a programmatic perspective there are two salient means through which   3
universities support and promote community partnerships: (a) extracurricular and
(b) curricular. On campus a significant number of college students actively participate in extracurricular community service through student organizations, the
activities of student service offices and campus-based religious organizations [for
example, 1, 24]. Many faculty, staff, and students, particularly those at urban campuses, are involved in their communities (for example, neighborhood development, community agencies, churches, youth work) independent of the university.

Academic programs can also engage students in the community. Profes-   4
sional schools in particular create a variety of experiential learning opportunities for their students (for example, clinicals, internships, co-op programs, field
experiences, practica, student teaching). However, the learning objectives of
these activities typically focus only on extending a student's professional skills
and do not emphasize to the student, either explicitly or tacitly, the importance
of service within the community and lessons of civic responsibility.

We view service learning as a credit-bearing educational experience in   5
which students participate in an organized service activity that meets identified
community needs and reflect on the service activity in such a way as to gain further understanding of course content, a broader appreciation of the discipline,
and an enhanced sense of civic responsibility. Unlike extracurricular voluntary
service, service learning is a course-based service experience that produces the
best outcomes when meaningful service activities are related to course material
through reflection activities such as directed writings, small group discussions,
and class presentations. Unlike practica and internships, the experiential activity in a service learning course is not necessarily skill-based within the context
of professional education.

Service learning provides an additional means for reaching educational   6
objectives, and academic credit is appropriate for service activities when learning objectives associated with the service are identified and evaluated. Faculty
who use service learning discover that it brings new life to the classroom,
enhances performance on traditional measures of learning, increases student
interest in the subject, teaches new problem solving skills, and makes teaching
more enjoyable. In addition, service learning expands course objectives to
include civic education. Benjamin Barber, of the Walt Whitman Center for the

Culture and Politics of Democracy, Rutgers University, considers service learning to be an indispensable method for citizenship education through which students learn the arts of democracy [2, 3].

Research has supported claims that have been made for the value of service   7
learning in higher education. Markus, Howard, and King [21], using procedures that closely approximated a randomized control-group design, found that students in service learning sections had more positive course evaluations, more positive beliefs and values toward service and community, and higher academic achievement as measured on mid-term and final examinations. Other research supports the contention that service learning has a positive impact on personal, attitudinal, moral, social, and cognitive outcomes [4, 7, 8, 15].

The recent interest in service learning has been strengthened by the work   8
of national organizations interested in combining service and education (for example, Campus Compact, American Association for Higher Education, Council of Independent Colleges, Council for Adult Experiential Learning, National Society for Experiential Education, National Youth Leadership Council, Partnership for Service-Learning), and the National Community Service Trust Act of 1993. Universities are particularly well suited to become national leaders in the development of service learning.

Indiana University–Purdue University Indianapolis is an urban university   9
that has invested resources and personnel to establish an Office of Service Learning. In doing so, we (a) participated in Campus Compact's Summer Institute for the Project on Integrating Service with Academic Study and the Stanford Summer Institute on Service Learning, (b) attended national and regional conferences on service learning and experiential education, (c) reviewed the extant service learning literature, (d) collected information from many programs which were in various stages of institutionalizing service learning, (e) reviewed materials from eight university-based centers focusing on service, and (f) participated on the University of Colorado at Boulder listserv on service learning (Internet: sl@csf.colorado.edu). On the basis of this work, we developed the following model for implementing and institutionalizing service learning within higher education.

Comprehensive-Action Plan for Service Learning (CAPSL)

Developing service learning at the institutional level has been characterized as a   10
cycle that includes awareness, planning, prototype, support, expansion, and evaluation [20, pp. 37–38]. This model of institutional change was based on the 44 institutions that participated in the three-year Campus Compact Project on Integrating Service with Academic Study. Based on our examination of service learning programs nationwide and our discussions with many more experienced

persons, we have expanded this model and have applied it to additional constituencies. The resulting model, the Comprehensive Action Plan for Service Learning (CAPSL), identifies four constituencies on which a program for service learning (for example, an office of service learning) needs to focus its principle activities: institution, faculty, students, and community. Although this is not an exhaustive list of constituencies to be considered in service learning programming, these four constituencies must be included for the initial efforts to be successful.

CAPSL also identifies a sequence of activities/tasks/outcomes to be pursued for each of the four constituencies (see Table 1). Following initial planning, activities need to increase awareness within each constituency concerning the general nature of service learning. This educational process is helped by having at least one concrete example or prototype course available. An office of service learning can then expand the development of service learning by gathering resources and designing activities for each constituency. The office also needs to document the implementation of service learning (monitoring) and the outcomes of service learning (evaluation). The results of all these efforts should be recognized publicly in the media and through scholarship and research published in professional journals. Finally, evidence of growth and maturity will be reflected in the degree to which service learning becomes institutionalized. 11

The sequence of activities identified by CAPSL represents a heuristic that can focus attention on important steps of planned change and the pattern will seldom be linear. Instead, there may be numerous cycles back and forth across activities. However, as Wood [33] observes, even though change is not linear or uniform, "what is important is to maintain the direction, to keep to the course" (p. 53). CAPSL provides that direction by identifying a sequence of actions for 12

TABLE 1 Comprehensive Action Plan for Service Learning (CAPSL)

	Institution	Faculty	Students	Community
Planning				
Awareness				
Prototype				
Resources				
Expansion				
Recognition				
Monitoring				
Evaluation				
Research				
Institutionalization				

strategic planning by prioritizing activities and providing a basis for monitoring progress. There is a rationale to the ordering of tasks in CAPSL which presumes that an activity may be premature if other previous tasks have been neglected. For example, faculty development efforts mentioned under expansion (for example, service learning course development stipends) will be of limited effectiveness if faculty do not understand service learning. Nor should the sequence of tasks be considered lock step such that an earlier step needs to be accomplished in its entirety before the next step is attempted (for example, all or most faculty do not need to understand service learning in order to proceed with expansion, only enough to justify those efforts). It is not assumed that progress across the constituencies goes at the same pace. Programmatic development will typically occur unevenly in a mix of small increments and a few big jumps.

Institutions

CAPSL describes a model for the development of service learning in universities at the institutional level (see Table 2 for examples). A small group of key individuals (administrators, faculty, students, staff, community leaders) with the appropriate interest, motivation, and skills is needed to execute the critical first steps. As Wood [33] points out, "Educational programs . . . need champions. Those champions must be found in the faculty if an innovation is to be profound and long-lasting. Administrators should not be shy about seeking out faculty champions" (p. 53). The planning stage needs to include a self-assessment on the following items: (a) where the institution is and where it is going; (b) the institutional, student, and faculty culture, climate, and values [31]; and (c) the resources and obstacles for developing service learning in the institution. Individuals in this group will benefit from discussions with individuals at institutions with more mature programs and at conferences that include service learning as a topic. A strategic action plan for implementing service learning can then be developed [for example, 19, 30] and institutional commitments (for example, budget, office space, personnel commitments) can be secured. As Schmidtlein [28] points out, the key to successful change is, "adapting planning practices to the institution's unique characteristics" (p. 85). One of the best ways for a university to do this is with the help of Campus Compact's regional institutes that target institutional development. 13

At some point in these early steps it is necessary to identify a person to assume leadership and administrative responsibility for subsequent program operations and to establish an office of service learning. The office of service learning will need to communicate to staff, students, faculty, and community 14

TABLE 2   Examples of Institutional Activities

	Institution
Planning	• Form a planning group of key persons • Survey institutional resources and climate • Attend Campus Compact Regional Institute • Develop a Campus Action Plan for service learning • Form an advisory committee
Awareness	• Inform key administrators and faculty groups about service learning and program development • Join national organizations (e.g., Campus Compact, National Society for Experiential Education, Partnership for Service-Learning) • Attend service learning conferences
Prototype	• Identify and consult with exemplary programs in higher education
Resources	• Obtain administrative commitments for an Office of Service Learning (e.g., budget, office space, personnel) • Develop a means for coordinating service learning with other programs on campus (e.g., student support services, faculty development) • Apply for grants
Expansion	• Discuss service learning with a broader audience of administrators and staff (e.g., deans, counselors, student affairs) • Support attendance at service learning conferences • Collaborate with others in programming and grant applications • Arrange campus speakers and forums on service learning
Recognition	• Publicize university's service learning activities to other institutions • Participate in conferences and workshops • Publish research • Publicize service learning activities in local media
Monitoring	• Collect data within institution (e.g., number of courses, number of faculty teaching service learning courses, number of students enrolled, number of agency partnerships)
Evaluation	• Compile annual report of Office of Service Learning • Include service learning in institutional assessment
Research	• Conduct research on service learning *within* institution and across institutions
Institutionalization	• Service is part of university mission statement and service learning is recognized in university publications • Service learning is an identifiable feature of general education • Service learning courses are listed in bulletins, schedule of classes, and course descriptions • University sponsors regional or national conferences on service learning • Hardline budget commitments to sustain service learning programs

agencies its mission and planned activities. As Rubin [26] notes, this is a more formidable task at a commuter university than at a small liberal arts college because of "the lack of personal relationships and informal networks" (p. 48).

Farmer [13] cautions that some educational change is ephemeral because "too often change agents focus too much on implementing change and too little on sustaining it" (p. 16). Thus, the efforts and investments devoted to initiating service learning must be complemented with the resources to sustain and expand the program. Institutions should examine their faculty reward structures and determine how they facilitate and inhibit faculty involvement in service learning. With development and maturity, service learning will become a significant component of the curriculum, and faculty and staff will participate in service learning organizations, share their success with other institutions, and contribute to professional conferences. 15

The university, as an institution, can be both the means of and the object of data collection that monitors program development, evaluates institutional outcomes, and publishes the results of this research in professional journals. The office of service learning should facilitate this research, which is critical to strengthening the knowledge base to promote and expand service learning within academia [16]. 16

Academically, the prevalence of service learning courses is initial evidence that service learning is important to the institution. An additional sign of growth and maturity occurs when service learning transcends a collection of courses. For example, coordinated course sequences in service learning, service learning being integral to general education, and an entire curriculum organized around service learning [for example, 22] reflect increasing levels of programmatic development and maturity. Administratively, evidence that service learning is institutionalized would include having service and service learning as explicit parts of the institution's mission, long-range plans, institutional assessment, and hard-line budget allocations. 17

Faculty

Faculty involvement is critical because service learning in its most common form is a course-driven feature of the curriculum. Therefore, the work of an office of service learning must focus on interesting faculty in service learning and providing them with support to make the curricular changes necessary to add a service learning component to a course. Some faculty may already be using experiential learning activities that are similar to service learning. Identifying and involving interested and experienced faculty in planning (for example, forming a faculty advisory committee) is important to later activities (see 18

Table 3 for examples). This needs to include formal and informal forums, for as Wood [33] points out, "the absence of such conversation virtually guarantees maintenance of the status quo" (p. 53).

Creating a common understanding of what constitutes service learning at a 19 particular institution will pay dividends later. This can be accomplished through brochures, news releases, faculty workshops, brown bag talks, and presentations at departmental meetings. These activities can be helped by having a prototype course that provides a local example which includes a syllabus to read, an instructor who can share wisdom and advice, examples for how course components such as reflection and evaluation can be structured, and a group of students who are advocates for service learning. In addition, syllabi that provide examples of service learning courses across the curriculum can be collected from other institutions.

A primary task of an office of service learning will be to facilitate course 20 development. As a change agent, the office of service learning can expect to play many of the multiple roles identified by Farmer [13]: (a) catalyst, (b) solution giver, (c) process helper, (d) resource linker, and (e) confidence builder. A particularly important role is providing the opportunity for experienced faculty to meet one on one with interested faculty. The office can also gather resources (for example, syllabi, literature), provide support (for example, grants, faculty stipends), and plan faculty development activities (for example, workshops, campus speakers) that lead to the expansion of service learning courses. The office should regularly publicize the successes on campus and in the community.

Beyond those faculty who are initially curious, how can additional faculty 21 be drawn to explore service learning? First, claims about service learning must be realistic, otherwise disenchantment and resentment will develop. Faculty are willing to explore change, including service learning, when the promise of the innovation leaves them feeling more efficacious and more competent as teachers [10] and when the investments to achieve these outcomes are modest. Therefore, effective faculty development must include presenting a clear understanding of service learning, the expected benefits from service learning for the faculty and student, and the requisite investments of time.

In addition, ways can be found to involve faculty in activities that are 22 related to service learning but fall short of developing a new course. For example,

TABLE 3 Examples of Faculty Activities

	Faculty
Planning	• Survey faculty interest and service learning courses currently offered • Identify faculty for service learning planning group and advisory committee
Awareness	• Distribute information on service learning (e.g., brochures, newsletters, and articles) • Identify a faculty liaison in each academic unit
Prototype	• Identify or develop prototype course(s)
Resources	• Identify interested faculty and faculty mentors • Maintain syllabus file by discipline • Compile library collection on service learning • Secure faculty development funds for expansion • Identify existing resources that can support faculty development in service learning • Establish a faculty award that recognizes service
Expansion	• Offer faculty development workshops • Arrange one-on-one consultations • Discuss service learning with departments and schools • Provide course development stipends and grants to support service learning • Focus efforts on underrepresented schools • Develop faculty mentoring program • Promote development of general education, sequential, and interdisciplinary service learning courses
Recognition	• Publicize faculty accomplishments • Include service learning activities on faculty Annual Report forms • Involve faculty in professional activities (e.g., publications, workshops, conferences, forums) • Publicize recipients of the faculty service award
Monitoring	• Collect data on faculty involvement (e.g., number of faculty involved in faculty development activities, number of faculty offering service learning courses)
Evaluation	• Provide assessment methods and designs to faculty (e.g., peer review, portfolios) • Evaluate course outcomes (e.g., student satisfaction, student learning)
Research	• Facilitate faculty research on service learning • Conduct research on faculty involvement in service learning
Institutionalization	• Service learning is part of personnel decisions (e.g., hiring, annual review, promotion and tenure) • Service learning is a permanent feature of course descriptions and the curriculum • Service learning is an integral part of the professional development of faculty

faculty can be asked to conduct reflection sessions for student groups who have completed service projects. This provides the opportunity for faculty to observe and guide some of the lessons learned from the students' service experience. Faculty can also be asked to participate in short-term community service projects so that they become more familiar with opportunities for learning from service in the community. Also, faculty can be asked to team-teach in an existing service learning course.

The office of service learning can also develop a program of faculty development in service learning. One such curriculum for faculty [6] offers a series of workshops on the general nature of service learning, reflection, building community partnerships, student supervision and assessment, and course assessment and research. These seminars can be presented over a semester, an academic year, a summer, or during an intensive period of instruction (for example, a week). Faculty development workshops can also be coupled with extrinsic incentives (for example, course development stipends) and support (for example, grants for student assistants, experienced faculty who serve as mentors) to overcome obstacles. Faculty are also sensitive to the value of enhancing student learning and satisfaction, recognition during personnel review, and publication of articles in scholarly journals about their work on service learning. Therefore, an office of service learning should help faculty to achieve these professional goals. 23

Our belief is that faculty respond best to these initiatives when the office reports directly to an academic officer (for example, academic dean, academic vice president) because such an arrangement provides academic leadership and academic integrity to service learning. However, regardless of the administrative arrangement, collaboration with an active student volunteer program within Student Affairs can facilitate the development of service learning. The successes of the Haas Center at Stanford, the Center for Social Concern at Notre Dame, and the Swearer Center at Brown University reflect the benefits of having both efforts (that is, service learning and student volunteer services) housed together in a central location. 24

An office of service learning will also be in a position to collect information that monitors faculty activities and the resulting growth in service learning courses on campus. As a service learning program matures, it will develop the means through which it can collect evaluation data that detail student and faculty outcomes resulting from service learning courses. The work by Barber [2] and Giles and Eyler [14] to develop scales specifically designed for service learning courses is an extremely important step in the evolution of research on service learning. Determining why particular outcomes occur requires, in addition to adequate outcome measures, sophisticated experimental designs and data analysis procedures. 25

Academically, service learning that is an integral part of the curriculum   26
and is not dependent upon a small group of faculty reflects institutionalization.
Administratively, institutionalization of faculty commitment to service learning
is demonstrated when service learning is recognized and used in personnel decisions (hiring, promotion and tenure, merit reviews).

Students

Students are in a paradoxical position with regard to service activities. On the   27
one hand, some students are involved in voluntary service through campus
organizations. Campus Compact provides ample evidence of the vigor that
student-initiated and student-led service programs can display. Furthermore,
students may be actively involved in their communities independent of the
campus, particularly nontraditional students at urban campuses. On the other
hand, students are dependent upon others for service learning opportunities.
Service learning typically occurs only if a faculty member develops a service
learning course, the course is approved, the course is offered, and the course is
appropriate for a student (for example, meets degree requirements, prerequi-
sites). Faculty are also dependent upon students in that a service learning course
will be successful and repeated if students enroll in the course and if it results in
a successful educational experience.

Astin's [1] research shows a sharp decline in student volunteer activities   28
between high school and college. Furthermore, in comparison to residential
campuses, nonresidential urban universities are learning environments that are
disproportionately classroom oriented, with fewer campus activities occurring
outside the classroom. As Schuh, Andreas, and Strange [29] note about urban
universities that are commuter campuses, "People can come and go so freely
that it is difficult for the institution to develop traditions, bonds with students,
and a sense of belonging" (p. 67). Our research [32] found that, for our commut-
ing students, academic credit related to service activities increased the attractiveness of students getting involved in service. Thus, service learning, with the
incentive of academic credit for service associated with the classroom, provides
an important means for increasing student participation in community service
and enhancing the community service experiences for those already involved.
Furthermore, service learning can provide an important function for students at
urban universities by integrating their multiple life role in the community [18]
with support services and academic credit.

As Schuh, Andreas, and Strange [29] point out, universities that "promote   29
students' involvement in out-of-class experiences that are educationally purposeful" (p. 66) create a powerful learning environment and a greater sense of

belonging. This is particularly important to a commuter campus, which can too easily regard students impersonally. Successful service programs, including both voluntary service and service learning, can build a greater sense of community on campus. This is consistent with Astin's [1] finding that rates of peer interactions and faculty/student interactions were both strongly related to participation in volunteer work.

It is important in planning a service learning program to know the nature   30 of the student climate and culture, including student attitudes toward voluntary service activities (individual or through student groups) and student attitudes toward service learning course development (for example, Is service learning more attractive in freshman courses, in the major, only in certain disciplines, only for additional credit?). In addition it is valuable to have students involved in planning activities (for example, as members of service learning advisory committees, writing grant proposals) in order to develop campus-wide support (see Table 4).

Although service learning is becoming more prevalent in K–12 curricula,   31 many students, and particularly nontraditional students, do not know about service learning. On small campuses, formal and informal communication can quickly and effectively solve this problem. However, at large universities, informing students about the nature of service learning courses is much more difficult. Providing information about course offerings to counselors, descriptions in course schedules, articles in school newspapers, and using students from past service learning classes as advocates can help inform others. As students become more experienced with service learning, some can assume leadership roles in courses as student assistants and site coordinators and participate in the design and execution of action research that focuses on needs assessment, program evaluation, and advocacy. Recognition of students' involvement in voluntary service and service learning is important. This recognition should start with designing effective service learning courses so that students have successful experiences that result in enhanced learning. In addition, recognition can include internal and external publicity, scholarships that reward past service or include a service requirement, nominations for regional and national service awards, and co-curricular transcripts that summarize service and service learning experiences that typically are not recorded on academic transcripts.

The office of service learning should collect information that reflects   32 growth in enrollment in service learning and its impact on students. In

TABLE 4   Examples of Student Activities

	Students
Planning	• Survey student involvement in service activities (e.g., individuals and student groups) • Survey student attitudes toward service and service learning • Identify students for service learning planning group and advisory committee
Awareness	• Distribute information about service learning (e.g., newspaper articles, posters, brochures, student orientation) • Inform counselors about service learning • Arrange presentations to student organizations
Prototype	• Recruit students for prototype course(s)
Resources	• Publicize service learning courses (e.g., class schedule, counselors) • Establish service learning scholarships • Secure money for service learning course assistants and site coordinators
Expansion	• Establish a broad offering of service learning courses, including required general education courses, sequential courses, and interdisciplinary courses • Include past students from service learning courses in the recruitment of new students • Create course assistant and site coordinator positions for students • Develop 4th credit option for students to design "independent" service learning components • Offer service learning minor • Involve students in the development of service learning courses and related activities (e.g., workshops, focus groups, state organizations, conferences)
Recognition	• Publicize recipients of student scholarships that recognize service • Write letters of recommendation for students involved in service • Nominate students for local, regional, and national recognitions and awards • Create co-curricular transcript
Monitoring	• Collect data on student involvement (e.g., enrollment, withdrawal rates)
Evaluation	• Evaluate service learning courses (e.g., student satisfaction, learning outcomes, retention)
Research	• Conduct research on student service learning experiences • Promote student involvement in action research
Institutionalization	• Consistently high enrollment in service learning courses • Widespread use of 4th credit option • Service learning is part of student culture

addition, research may also be directed at student outcomes (for example, cognitive, affective, behavioral, social) that document the impact of service learning.

One effective means for expansion of service learning is the "4th credit   33
option" implemented at Georgetown University and the Lowell Bennion Center at the University of Utah. This allows students to propose a contract with any instructor to do service learning for additional academic credit on an individual basis. This option empowers students to initiate service learning experiences and encourages faculty to experiment with service learning on a small scale.

Delve, Mintz, and Stewart [11] provide an example of a student develop-   34
ment model that identifies the following five phases of involvement in service learning: (a) exploration (naive excitement), (b) clarification (values clarification), (c) realization (insight into the meaning of service), (d) activation (participation and advocacy), and (e) internalization (the service experience influences career and life choices). A mature service learning curriculum will promote this type of student development through coordinated course sequences and assessment of student outcomes.

Institutionalization of service learning for students is reflected in extensive   35
use of the 4th credit option, widespread faculty interest in service learning and student enrollment in service learning classes, curricula integrated around service learning, student assessment related to service learning activities, service learning that is part of the institution's general education curriculum [22], student recruitment to the campus because of service learning curricula, increased retention of students due to service learning, and a student culture that accepts and promotes service and service learning.

Community

Although interactions between the university and their communities are inte-   36
gral to any university [9, 25], building these interactions into partnerships is a matter of time and commitment of resources [12]. According to Ruch and Trani [27], three characteristics identify effective university-community relationships: (a) the interaction is mutually beneficial to the university and the community, (b) the interaction is guided by institutional choice and strategy, and (c) the interaction is one of value and import to both partners. Universities must provide strong leadership, articulate clear goals, and maintain supportive institutional policies to develop these partnerships.

Community representatives need to be involved in planning service learn-   37
ing programs (see Table 5). However, representation is difficult because it prompts such questions as, "Who should be represented? Which communities?

Agencies? Funding sources? Clients? Neighborhoods? Government?" The appropriate constituencies may not be identifiable prior to program and course development. Under these circumstances, those who are planning service learning programs must choose their best approximation at representation and acknowledge that adjustments may be necessary as the program evolves. Staff

TABLE 5   Examples of Community Activities

	Community
Planning	• Survey existing university/community partnerships • Identify community representatives for service learning planning group and advisory committee
Awareness	• Distribute information on service learning (e.g., newsletter, brochure) • Initiate meetings and site visits with agency personnel • Educate agency personnel on differences between voluntary service and service learning
Prototype	• Collaborate with agency personnel to develop prototype course(s)
Resources	• Compile list of agencies interested in service learning • Compile community needs assessments (e.g., United Way community needs assessment) • Secure money for site-based student coordinators • Write a community agency resource manual on the university's policies and procedures for service learning courses
Expansion	• Initiate community workshops and discussions on service learning • Increase involvement of agency personnel in course design and university-level service learning activities • Explore new service learning opportunities • Collaborate with community agencies on programming, grant proposals, and conferences
Recognition	• Sponsor recognition events for agencies and agency personnel • Publicize community partnerships in local media
Monitoring	• Monitor training and supervision of students at agency • Maintain records of student and faculty involvement at agency
Evaluation	• Assess impact of service learning activities on meeting agency and client needs
Research	• Collaborate with agencies on action research projects
Institutionalization	• Faculty are formally involved with agency (e.g., consultant, board of directors) • Agency personnel are formally involved with university (e.g., team teach course, campus committees) • Agencies allocate additional resources to support and train student volunteers

from agencies with extensive volunteer support programs and with experience in service learning (for example, prototype course) may be good choices. Agency staff are assumed to be adequate representatives of the communities *and* clients served by that agency. However, if only agency personnel are represented, an additional concern is that there may not be adequate representation from clients and community members.

Even community agencies that have extensive experience with volunteers   38
may not know about the nature of service learning and how the differences between service learning and voluntary service are important to their responsibilities. Thus, formal and informal education about service learning is important for site supervisors, directors of volunteer services, and agency directors.

Communities need to participate in guiding the identification of service   39
activities at a macro level (for example, United Way community needs assessment) and a micro level (for example, a particular course). An office of service learning provides an important function of cataloging and linking constituencies and resources as service learning courses are developed. In turn, the office should monitor and evaluate community placements. As previously mentioned, the aspiration is that the university and segments of the community develop partnerships. Evidence that a stable, meaningful, and mature partnership is evolving would include continuity in the relationships across time, consensus that mutual needs are being met, collaboration in advocacy and grant proposals, formal and informal participation by the agency staff in the university context (for example, team teaching), and formal and informal participation by the faculty, alumni, and students in the agency (for example, advocacy, board of directors, etc.)

Conclusions

Virtually all universities are interested in committing their resources to develop   40
effective citizenship among their students, to address complex needs in their communities through the application of knowledge, and to form creative partnerships between the university and the community. Service learning provides one means through which students, faculty, and administrators can strive toward these aspirations.

The Comprehensive Action Plan for Service Learning (CAPSL) provides a   41
heuristic for guiding the development of a service learning program in higher education. It does so by concentrating efforts on four constituencies that must be considered in implementing a service learning program and by providing a means for developing strategic plans that address each constituency. In addition, CAPSL provides a means for assessing each constituency, the develop-

mental status of a service learning program. Although this agenda may appear daunting, assembling a team from the constituencies and prioritizing objectives can make the work more manageable.

As a general guide, CAPSL only specifies the goal at each step (for example, increase awareness among students). This is both an advantage and a disadvantage of the model. On the positive side, it is general enough that the execution of each cell can be tailored to local conditions. Unfortunately, for the same reason, it is not possible to detail how each step can be successfully accomplished at a particular university, although some suggestions and examples are provided. It is possible to take the sequence of activities from the whole CAPSL model (that is, planning through institutionalization) and apply it to any cell in the matrix (for example research by faculty). Regardless of how CAPSL is used it does provide guidance for planned development and evaluation of service learning programs.

NOTES

Campus Compact, c/o Brown University, Box 1975, Providence, Rhode Island 02912 (401) 863-1119.

REFERENCES

1. Astin, A. W. "Student Involvement in Community Service: Institutional Commitment and the Campus Compact." Paper presented at the meeting of the California Campus Compact, Los Angeles, December 1990.
2. Barber, B. R. "A Mandate for Liberty: Requiring Education-based Community Service." *The Responsive Community (Spring 1991).*
3. Barber, B. R., and R. M. Battistoni (Eds.). *Educating for Democracy.* Dubuque, Iowa: Kendall/ Hunt,1994.
4. Boss, J. A. "The Effect of Community Service Work on the Moral Development of College Ethics Students." *Journal of Moral Education,* forthcoming.
5. Boyer, E. "Creating the New American College." *Chronicle of Higher Education,* 9 March 1994, A48.
6. Bringle, R. G., and J. A. Hatcher. "A Service-Learning Curriculum for Faculty." *Michigan Journal of Community Service Learning,* forthcoming.
7. Bringle, R. G., and J. F. Kremer. "An Evaluation of an Intergenerational Service Learning Project for Undergraduates." *Educational Gerontologist, 19 (1993),* 407416.
8. Cohen, J., and D. Kinsey. '. . . Doing Good' and Scholarship: A Service-Learning Study." *Journalism Educator* (Winter 1994), 4–14.

9. Colon, M., M. Kennedy, and M. Stone. "A Metropolitan University and Community Development." Metropolitan Universities, 1 (1990–91), 61–74.

10. Deci, E. L., and R. M. Ryan. "Intrinsic Motivation to Teach: Possibilities and Obstacles in Our Colleges and Universities." In Motivating Professors to Teach Effectively, edited by J. L. Bess, pp. 27–35. San Francisco: Jossey-Bass, 1982.

11. Delve, C. I., S. D. Mintz, and G. M. Stewart. "Promoting Values Development through Community Service: A Design." In Community Service as Values Education, edited by C. I. Delve, S. D. Mintz, and G. M. Stewart, pp. 7–29. San Francisco: Jossey-Bass, 1990.

12. Dore, J. "A City and Its Universities: A Mayor's Perspective." Metropolitan Universities, 1 (1990), 29–35.

13. Farmer, D. W. "Strategies for Change." In Managing Change in Higher Education, edited by D. W. Steeples, pp. 7–17. San Francisco: Jossey-Bass, 1990.

14. Giles, D., Jr. "National Service-Learning Research Project." National Society for Experiential Education Quarterly (Spring 1994), 11.

15. Giles, D. E., Jr., and J. Eyler. "The Impact of a College Community Service Laboratory on Students' Personal, Social, and Cognitive Outcomes." Journal of Adolescence, 17 (1994), 327–339.

16. Giles, D., E. P. Honnet, and S. Migliore (Eds.). Research Agenda for Combining Service and Learning in the 1990s. Raleigh, N.C.: National Society for Internships and Experiential Education, 1991.

17. Golden, D. C., B. O. Pregliasco, and M. J. Clemons. "Community Service: New Challenges for a Metropolitan University." Metropolitan Universities, 4 (1993), pp. 61–70.

18. Jacoby, B. "Adapting the Institution to Meet the Needs of Commuter Students." Metropolitan Universities, 1 (1990), 61–71.

19. Keller, G. Academic Strategy: The Management Revolution in Higher Education. Baltimore, Md.: Johns Hopkins University Press, 1983.

20. Kupiec, T. Y. (Ed.). Rethinking Tradition: Integrating Service with Academic Study on College Campuses. Denver, Colo.: Education Commission of the States, 1993.

21. Markus, G. B., J. P. F. Howard, and D. C. King. "Integrating Community Service and Classroom Instruction Enhances Learning: Results from an Experiment." Educational Evaluation and Policy Analysis, 15 (1993), 410–419.

22. Mentkowski, M., and G. Rogers. "Connecting Education, Work, and Citizenship." Metropolitan Universities, 4 (1993), 34–46.

23. Muse, W. V. "A Catalyst for Economic Development." Metropolitan Universities, 1 (1990), 79–88.

24. O'Brien, E. M. "Outside the Classroom: Students as Employees, Volunteers, and Interns." Research Brief, 4 (1993), 1–12.

25. Perlman, D. H. "Diverse Communities: Diverse Involvements." Metropolitan Universities, 1 (1990), 89–100.

26. Rubin, S. G. "Community Service and Metropolitan Universities." Metropolitan Universities, 2 (1991), 47–57.

27. Ruch, C. P., and E. P. Trani. "Scope and Limitations of Community Interactions." Metropolitan Universities, 1 (1990–91), 27–39.

28. Schmidtlein, F. A. "Responding to Diverse Institutional Issues: Adapting Strategic Planning Concepts." In Adapting Strategic Planning to Campus Realities, edited by F. A. Schmidtlein and B. H. Milton (pp. 83–93). San Francisco: Jossey-Bass, 1990.

29. Schuh, J. H., R. E. Andreas, and C. C. Strange. "Students at Metropolitan Universities." Metropolitan Universities, 2 (1991), 64–74.

30. Steeples, D. W. Successful Strategic Planning: Case Studies. San Francisco: JosseyBass, 1988.

31. Tierney, W. G. (Ed.). Assessing Academic Climates and Cultures. San Francisco: Jossey-Bass, 1990.

32. Velo, P. M., and R. G. Bringle. "Matching Empathy with Concrete and Abstract Reasons to Promote Volunteerism." Paper presented at the 13th Mid-American Undergraduate Psychology Research Conference, Evansville, Ind., April 1994.

33. Wood, R. J. "Changing the Educational Program." In Managing Change in Higher Education, edited by D. W. Steeples (pp. 51–58). San Francisco: Jossey-Bass, 1990.

William A. Diehl received his doctorate in secondary and adult literacy from Indiana University, Bloomington's language education department in 1979. He has published over 25 articles, two textbooks, and several manuals on a variety of topics, including workforce literacy, at-risk youth, and developmental education. He is the education cluster lead and senior program manager at Commonwealth Corporation in Boston, Massachusetts.

Larry Mikulecky received his Ph.D. from the University of Wisconsin in 1976. Since then he has been a professor of education at Indiana University, Bloomington, where he has previously served as chair of the language education department and the director of the learning skills center. He conducts research and teaches on adolescent and adult literacy and on technology's role in language and literacy education. He has published widely on these topics in such journals as *Journal of Literacy Research*, *Peabody Journal of Education*, and *Reading Psychology*. He is the author of *Real World Literacy Demands: How They've Changed and What Teachers Can Do* (1996).

THE NATURE OF READING AT WORK

William A. Diehl
Larry Mikulecky

One of the roles of reading instruction receiving increased attention is that of preparing individuals for the literacy demands of occupations. This role has been highlighted in recent years as part of the controversies surrounding functional literacy and minimum competency testing in the U.S. Recent research in functional literacy (Louis Harris and Associates, 1970; Northcutt, 1975; Murphy, 1975; Gadway and Wilson, 1975) has indicated that large numbers of Americans may not have sufficient reading skills to function in common (including occupational) situations. While other researchers (Fisher, 1978; Kirsch and Guthrie, 1977–1978; Mikulecky and Diehl, 1979) have raised important questions about the extent of these findings, the findings have been used as evidence that the American educational system has been grossly negligent in preparing students to "function" in society (Copperman, 1978). The demand that reading educators teach the minimum literacy competencies necessary to function in various settings, including occupational settings, gives rise to the question of what, in terms of literacy, is required.

1

William A. Diehl and Larry Mikulecky, "The Nature of Reading at Work," *Journal of Reading*, vol. 24, no. 3 (December 1980), pp. 221–228. Copyright 1980 by International Reading Association. Reproduced with permission of International Reading Association in the format Textbook via Copyright Clearance Center.

Unfortunately, little research has been done to determine how literate a person should be to function in a particular adult situation. The nature of literacy demands in particular settings outside of schools has rarely been investigated. Instead, "representative" literacy tasks have traditionally been used in research as indicators of reading proficiency in various situations. Such tasks tend to be arbitrary, are not necessarily reflective of the real demands on individuals, and are completed in a testing situation that bears little resemblance to the setting in which the task is normally encountered. Since the settings differ, subjects do not have access to extralinguistic cues (e.g., machines, multiple materials, and advice of others) that they might normally use to help complete a functional reading task. In order to gain a more accurate picture of functional literacy demands and the abilities needed by people facing the demands, it is necessary to research the pragmatic demands within the context of actual situations.

One purpose of the study reported here was to specify the literacy demands encountered in a broad range of occupations. One hundred seven subjects from one-hundred occupations and twenty-six workplaces were interviewed and tested at their work sites. The subjects ranged from a lawyer and a vice-president of a large corporation to assembly line workers and stone cutters. The subjects were selected from workplaces chosen randomly in a seventy-mile radius of Bloomington, Indiana (thus including Indianapolis). Subjects represented a full range of the occupations listed in the *Dictionary of Occupational Titles* (U.S. Employment Service, 1977) and appeared to be representative of the adult working population on such variables as sex, race, income earned and occupational category (Diehl, 1980). The subjects were administered the Diehl-Mikulecky Job Literacy Survey (1980), which includes items assessing the literacy demands encountered in occupations and the strategies employed by subjects in meeting the demands. The survey, which takes approximately an hour to complete, collects data on a number of variables hypothesized to affect functional literacy. In addition to information on literacy demands, it collects information on attitudinal factors, ability factors, and extralinguistic factors.

A portion of the survey asked subjects to show and describe the reading tasks they had completed on the job within the previous month. These tasks were rated according to type of display, frequency of use, and importance to the job. Additionally, where possible, the actual job reading materials used by individuals were collected and a readability level determined using the FORCAST formula, developed by Caylor and Sticht (1973) specifically for use with occupational material. Data were also collected on the amount of time spent per day on reading job materials. Based on responses to a series of questions, each piece of reading material cited by subjects was also categorized according to the type of strategy employed in completing the task. Four general categories were used, based on field-testing and on earlier work by Sticht (1977). The categories were:

- "Reading-to-learn" in which the subject reads with the intention of remembering text information and applies some learning strategy to do so;
- "Reading-to-do with no learning" in which the subject uses the material primarily as an aid to do something else (e.g., fix a machine) and later reports not remembering the information; these materials thus serve as "external memories" (Sticht, 1977);
- "Reading-to-do with incidental learning" in which the subject uses the material primarily as an aid to do something else, but in the process learns (remembers) the information;
- "Reading-to-access" in which the subject quickly reads or skims material to determine its usefulness for some later task or for some other person; the material is then filed or passed on.

These four general strategies (or purposes) were further divided into 16,   5
specific strategies used with job materials. Diehl (1980) described these specific strategies.

Descriptive statistics on the "reading tasks" encountered on the jobs are   6
presented in Table 1.

Several striking results and conclusions can be drawn from the data   7
reported in the table. First, reading at work appears to be a ubiquitous activity. Close to 99% of the subjects reported doing some reading each day at work. They reported an average of 113 minutes a day spent in job reading. Although this figure is higher than that reported in some other studies (Sharon, 1973–1974; Mikulecky, Shanklin, and Caverley, 1979), it may be because reading is so closely related to other job tasks that it often is overlooked by subjects reporting on time spent reading unless it is specifically probed. There are indications from other job research (Sticht, 1975) that the figure of 113 minutes (or close to two hours) accurately reflects job reading time.

While the 113 minute results should not be generalized to the total popula-   8
tion, it does indicate that workers, overall, tend to read a great deal on the job, and probably read job materials more each day than any other type of material. This conclusion would suggest that job-related literacy is the most important type of functional literacy and should be stressed to a greater extent in functional literacy programs.

When the sample of subjects was divided into quartiles by variables that   9
indicate job success, *t* tests revealed few significant differences (p<.01) between groups on job reading time. The variables were income earned, job

TABLE 1 Descriptive Statistics on Reading Demands Reported

Reading tasks encountered on the job	Percent of total citations (339 tasks cited)
Type of display used	
Entire book	15%
Part of book: text	19
Part of book: chart, graph, etc.	12
1–3 page text	31
1–3 page chart	21
Other	2
Frequency of use	
Less than once a month	10%
Once a week to once a month	7
Two to four times a week	22
Daily	61
Importance to completing job task	
Not important	23%
Important, but not vital	56
Vital to job task completion	21
Type of general strategy employed	
Read-to-learn	11%
Read-to-do (no learning)	40 } 63% total.
Read-to-do (incidental learning)	23 } read-to-do
Read-to-assess	26
Readability of materials (measured by FORCAST, Caylor and Sticht, 1973)	
Mean grade equivalent for 106 pieces of material from 57 subjects = 10.9	
Standard deviation = 1.2 grade levels	
Range = level 8.4 to level 13.8	
Reported time spent per day reading job material	
Mean for 107 subjects = 112.5 minutes	
Standard deviation = 119 minutes	
Range = 0 minutes (10 subjects*) to 480 minutes (3 subjects)	
Median = 61 minutes	

*Although 10 subjects reported no reading, eight of them later in the interview cited reading materials they use "daily." Thus, only two subjects could be said to do no reading on the job.

prestige. (Hodge, Siegel, and Rossi, 1966, p. 286–93), and job responsibilities (as rated by the Dictionary of Occupational Titles). Higher level occupations tended to involve more job reading, but not significantly more, indicating that time spent reading job materials is an important component of jobs at almost all levels.

Subjects reported that in most cases (56%) the reading tasks were "impor-   10
tant, but not vital" to the completion of a job task. Information to be gained
from the reading, in other words, was viewed as helpful (but not necessary) to
completing a job task; either the same information could be gotten from another
source (e.g., a co-worker) or the job could be completed (perhaps less efficiently)
without the information. In 23% of the reading citations, subjects indicated the
reading was "not necessary" and only in 21% of the citations were the reading
tasks felt to be "vital" in completing a task. Overall, then, almost 80% of the
reading tasks cited were felt not to be necessary to completing job tasks.

These results suggest that many of the literacy "demands" of a job are not   11
really demands at all; rather, literacy materials are used, not so much out of
necessity as because they make the job task easier or more efficient. It has been
suggested that the literacy "demands" of the workplace are increasing with technological changes (Levin, 1975). It may be, instead, that demands are not
increasing; it may be that the opportunities to use print to help carry out a job
task are what is increasing. The distinction between "literacy demands" and
"literacy availability" is an important one. It may be, as some researchers
(Sticht, et al., 1972; Newman et al., 1978; Diehl, 1979) suggest, that some jobs
are closed unnecessarily to people with little education or poor reading abilities,
based on a false estimation of the "demands" of the job.

Results of this study indicate that reading tasks on the job tend to be highly   12
repetitive and are completed in conjunction with specific job tasks. The majority
(61%) of the 339 reading tasks cited by subjects were reported to be done "daily."
An additional 22% of the reading tasks were performed at least once a week.

Most of these tasks (63%) were reading-to-do tasks. In such tasks, the
material serves as a reference only—an external memory (Sticht, 1977)—and   13
the information is applied directly, and usually immediately, to a job task. In
some reading-to-do tasks (24% of the total), subjects learned the material—
usually because of a repetition of the task or because the single trial was sufficient for learning. In most cases (40% of the total), subjects did not learn the
material; they reported they would "read the material again tomorrow to do the
same task."

These results suggest some important aspects of functional literacy tasks   14
that may differ substantially from literacy tasks encountered in school and training settings. The job reading tasks appeared to be more integrated with other
job tasks, more immediately applied to situations, and more repetitious than
school reading tasks. These surface differences indicate the possibility that
major differences in information processing demands exist between job (mainly
reading-to-do) and school (mainly reading-to-learn) reading tasks. While the

current study does not attempt to define or investigate such differences, some conjectures can be made based on the available evidence.

In reading-to-do tasks, the reader has access to extralinguistic cues that are usually directly related to the reading material; a one-to-one correspondence often exists between aspects of the job environment (e.g., the parts of a lathe sitting on a table in front of the worker) and the text (e.g., a diagram with lathe parts laid out; a written description of each part and how it fits with the other; a parts list with identification numbers). The main task for the worker, then, is to "crack the code" of the particular graphic display—to match the visual objects in the work environment to the particular form of representation of them in the text. Once the representation is understood, the worker can easily go from environment to text, checking each in a search for particular information. 15

The same type of process would occur when a worker used text to follow directions; the environment includes the machine (or form, or whatever) to which the directions are to be applied. The worker's main task is to understand the correspondence and use a combination of information from the text and from the environment to complete the task. 16

The existence of an information-rich environment should enable workers to gain information from the text they would not have gained if they read the information in isolation. By using both textual and environmental cues, workers should be able to gain more information than their simple "reading ability" would suggest they could. In fact, studies (Sacher and Duffy, 1978; Diehl, 1980) indicate that workers can successfully read and apply information from job materials up to two grade levels above their assessed reading levels. These studies support the idea that an information-rich environment may make a significant difference in how well information is processed. 17

It may be argued, then, that "cracking the code" is the primary task for the job reader—a task that will then enable the worker to select and use appropriate cues from the environment to help with reading the text. The fact that job reading tasks are done repetitively then becomes significant. The code need only be cracked once; once the correspondence between the print and the environment is understood, it becomes far easier to quickly get the necessary information from the text. 18

For example, the first time a salesperson encounters a specialized order form s/he must not only locate specific information (e.g., prices quoted) but, in the process, must learn how the graphic display corresponds to the job tasks (e.g., where and how products are listed; where and how estimates are quoted). Once this correspondence is understood, the salesperson can proceed more rapidly, and with less attention, through subsequent forms. 19

The locating and application of information involves less cognitive pro-   20
cessing each time the information is used. In fact, the location and application
of information becomes so easy that it is often done with a minimum of attention (which may explain why some workers forgot about reading tasks that they
do daily, until probed, and which may explain why workers can use the same
material daily for the same purpose).

Reading-to-learn tasks (which are probably most typical in school and   21
training situations), on the other hand, are less related to an immediate context and require more attention than the reading-to-do tasks. Because the
environment provides far fewer relevant cues or bits of information that corre-
spond directly with the text, the reader probably must make many more infer-
ences, must draw more extensively on cues from the text in developing a sense
of meaning, must apply the information—if it is applied at all—in his/her own
imagination, and must store the information in memory for later possible use
or application. It would seem that the decontextualized nature of reading-to-
learn tasks requires different cognitive processes than are required in reading-
to-do tasks.

While the above discussion is conjecture, results from this study and others   22
lend some support to the hypothesis that reading-to-do and reading-to-learn (or
"functional" and "schooling") tasks differ from one another. Additional
research, such as is currently being conducted by Mikulecky may indicate that
in fact, reading tasks as done in school are different from functional reading
tasks. If this is true, it would question the premises on which "functional literacy" assessments are made (e.g., tests are given in a context different from that
in which tasks are actually encountered). Further, if functional and schooling
tasks are substantially different, and if functional tasks are indeed strongly influenced by context, the argument that schools do (or even should) prepare students to be functionally literate is questionable.

CONCLUSIONS

Five tentative conclusions about job literacy demands can be drawn from these
data.

1. Reading on the job is a ubiquitous activity and may be the most prevalent
   type of reading done by employed adults. This makes job-related reading an
   important part of functional literacy.
2. Reading materials on the job tend to be viewed as external memories. Subjects tend not to learn the material, because they treat the material as information continually available to them.

3. Literacy tasks on the job are completed in an information-rich context. Because most of the tasks involve the application of information to a particular job task, the job task itself provides a number of extralinguistic cues that may help the reader gain information quickly with a minimum of attention.

4. Because the reading materials are used in an information-rich context, the main task of the job reader is to determine the relationship between the graphic display and objects in the environment. Use of the context and the repetitious nature of job tasks probably enable many workers to read material on the job that they would not be able to read in isolation.

5. Reading at work and reading in school settings may be quite different from each other, in terms of extralinguistic cues available, cognitive demands, and uses of information gained. Additional research in this area is needed; if research supports these indications, it would have important implications for the design of functional literacy tests and programs, as well as implications for schools and job-training programs.

REFERENCES

Caylor, John S., and Thomas G. Sticht. *Development of a Simple Readability Index for Job Reading Material*. Alexandria, VA: Human Resources Research Organization, 1973.

Copperman, Paul. The *Literacy Hoax: The Decline of Reading. Writing and Learning in the Public Schools and What We Can Do about It*. New York: Morrow, 1978.

Diehl, William A., "The Variable and Symbolic Natures of Functional Literacy: An Historical Review and Critique of Research." Master's thesis. Indiana University, 1979.

Diehl, William A. "Functional Literacy as a Variable Construct: An Examination of Attitudes, Behavior, and Strategies Related to Occupational Literacy." Diss. Indiana University, 1980.

Diehl, William A., and Larry Mikulecky. The Diehl-Mikulecky Job Literacy Survey." *Job Literacy*. Bloomington: Reading Research Center, School of Education, Indiana University, 1980. pp. 65–78.

Fisher, Donald L. *Functional Literacy and the Schools*. Washington, DC: National Institute of Education, 1978.

Gadway, Charles, and H. A. Wilson. *Functional Literacy: Basic Reading Performance*. Denver: National Assessment of Educational Progress, 1975.

Hodge, Robert W., Peter M. Siegel, and P. H. Rossi. "Occupational Prestige in the United States. 1925–1963." *Class, Status, and Power*. Ed. Richard Bendix and Samuel Lipsett. 2nd ed. New York: Free Press, 1966. pp. 286–293.

Kirsch, I., and J. T. Guthrie. "The Concept and Measurement of Functional Literacy." *Reading Research Quarterly* 13 (1977–1978): pp. 485–507.

Levin, Beatrice. "Reading Requirements for Satisfactory Careers." *Reading and Career Education*. Ed. Duane Nielsen and Howard Hjelm. Newark, DE: International Reading Association, 1975. pp. 78–81.

Mikulecky, Larry J., Nancy L. Shanklin, and David C. Caverley. *Adult Reading Habits, Attitudes, and Motivations: A Cross-Sectional Study*. Monograph in Language and Research Studies No. 2. Bloomington: Indiana University School of Education, 1979.

Mikulecky, Larry J., and William Diehl. "An Examination of Work-Related Literacy and Reading Attitudes." Paper presented at the Functional Literacy Conference. Bloomington, IN, June 1979.

Murphy, Richard T. *Adult Functional Reading Study: Project 1: Targeted Research and Development Reading Program Objectives. Subparts 1, 2, 3*. Princeton: Educational Testing Service, 1975.

Northcutt, Norvell. "Functional Literacy for Adults." *Reading and Career Education*. Ed. Duane Nielsen and Howard Hjelm. Newark, De: International Reading Association, 1975. pp. 43–49.

Sacher, J., and Thomas Duffy. "Reading Skill and Military Effectiveness." Paper presented at the American Educational Research Association Conference. Toronto, Mar. 1978. ED 151 745.

Sharon, Amiel T. "Racial Differences in Newspaper Readership." *Public Opinion Quarterly* 37 (1973): 611–817.

Sticht, Thomas G., John Caylor, Richard Kern, and Lynn Fox. "Project REALISTIC: Determination of Adult Functional Literacy Skill Levels." *Reading Research Quarterly* 7 (1972): pp. 424–465.

Sticht, Thomas G., ed. *Reading for Working: A Functional Literacy Anthology*. Alexandria, VA: Human Resources Research Organization, 1975. ED 102 532

Sticht, Thomas G., "Comprehending Reading at Work." *Cognitive Processes in Comprehension*. Ed. M. A. Just and P. A. Carpenter. Hillsdale, NJ: Erlbaum, 1977.

U.S. Employment Service. *Dictionary of Occupational Titles*. 4th ed. Washington, DC: U.S. Employment Service, 1977.

Christina Haas is associate professor of English at Kent State University in Ohio. She received her Ph.D. in rhetoric at Carnegie Mellon University in 1987 and has published widely in the fields of rhetoric, composition, and communication in such journals as *Computers and Composition* and the *Journal of Business and Technical Communication*. She is the author of *Writing Technology: Studies on the Materiality of Literacy* (1995). Previously she was assistant professor of English at Pennsylvania State University and an instructor at the University of Wyoming and Central Wyoming College.

LEARNING TO READ BIOLOGY
One Student's Rhetorical Development in College

CHRISTINA HAAS

This longitudinal study examines the reading processes and practices of one college student, Eliza, through eight semesters of undergraduate postsecondary education. Specifically, the study traces the development of this student's beliefs about literate activity—focusing not only on changes in her reading and writing activities per se, but also on her views about those activities, her representations of the nature of texts, and her understanding of the relationship between knowledge and written discourse within her disciplinary field of biology. Multiple data sources— including extended interviews, reading/writing logs, observations and field notes, texts, and read-and-think-aloud protocols—were used to explore Eliza's rhetorical development over her 4 college years. Results of various analyses together suggest that Eliza's conceptions of the function of texts and the role of authors—both as authors and as scientists—grew in complexity. A number of possibly interrelated factors may account for Eliza's expanding notions of authors and of texts: increased subject matter knowledge, instructional support, "natural" development, and mentoring in an internship situation.

Christina Haas, "Learning to Read Biology: One Student's Rhetorical Development in College," *Written Communication*, vol. 11, no. 1 (January 1994), pp. 43-84, copyright © 1994 by SAGE Publications, Inc. Reprinted by permission of SAGE Publications, Inc.

Author's Note: I would like to thank John Buck, Davida Charney, Stephen Doheny-Farina, Rosa Eberly, Cheryl Geisler, Rich Haswell, David Kaufer, Marty Nystrand, Nancy Penrose, Jack Selzer, and Sandra Stotsky for provocative conversations which helped me think more clearly about many of the issues addressed here. Carrie Rose Haas of the Chemistry Department of the University of Washington, John Lowe of the Chemistry Department at Penn State, and Andy Stephenson of the Biology Department at Penn State provided technical assistance. My deepest debt is to Eliza, who opened her educational life to me for 4 years. Watching her grow in confidence, intellect, and ability was an exciting and humbling experience. Some of the data collection was supported by a grant to C. M. Neuwirth, J. R. Hayes, and C. Haas from the Fund for the Improvement of Post Secondary Education; the Information Technology Center at Carnegie Mellon University also provided partial support. A version of this article was given at a Writing Special-Interest-Group session at the 1992 American Educational Research Association meeting in San Francisco.

At the college level, to become literate is in many ways to learn the patterns of   1
knowing about, and behaving toward, texts within a disciplinary field (Bartholomae, 1985; Berkenkotter, Huckin, & Ackerman, 1988; Bizzell, 1982; Geisler,
1990; Herrington, 1985, 1992). Scholars from a wide variety of subject areas
have acknowledged that within their disciplines, texts are best seen not as static,
autonomous entities but as forms of dynamic rhetorical action: Authors create
texts and readers read texts in a complex of social relationships, motivated by
goals sanctioned (or not) by the surrounding culture, to achieve purposes that
are always in the broadest sense persuasive. Disciplinary texts, like all texts, are
intensely situated, rife with purpose and motive, anchored in myriad ways to the
individuals and the cultures that produce them. This is true not only for texts
within the humanities and softer social sciences (e.g., see Belsey, 1980; Fish,
1980; Tompkins, 1980, in literary theory; Geertz, 1983, in anthropology; Grice,
1975; Nystrand, 1986, in linguistics; Brown, Collins, & Duguid, 1989; Mishler,
1979, in psychology) but also those within "harder" disciplines such as economics (McCloskey, 1985), physics (Bazerman, 1988), and—more to my purposes
here—the life sciences (Gould, 1993; Latour, 1987; Latour & Woolgar, 1979;
Myers, 1985,1991; Selzer, 1993).

Bruno Latour (1987; Latour & Woolgar, 1979), in particular, has been con-   2
cerned with understanding how scientific facts (codified and reproduced as written texts) come to be seen as freed of the circumstances of their production. His
work, along with others' (Bazerman, 1988; Gilbert & Mulkay, 1984; Myers,
1985), has shown scientific activity, and its resultant facts and theory—presented
in the form of written texts—to be highly rhetorical and scientists themselves to
be motivated and committed agents in this enterprise.[1] A great number of studies
of science have focused on discourse—conversations and lab notes as well as conference presentations and formal articles—as both the means of scientific activity and
the best way to study the scientific enterprise (e.g., Blakeslee, 1992; Gragson &
Selzer, 1990; Herndl, Fennell, & Miller, 1991; Winsor, 1989). In short, much of
the real work of science is the creation and dissemination of texts, broadly conceived. In addition, other studies of scientific discourse (Fahnestock, 1986;
Gilbert & Mulkay, 1984) have suggested that scientists adjust the strength of
their claims depending on the audience: Texts meant for scientific insiders hedge
and qualify claims, while texts for lay persons and other outsiders strip out such
qualifiers, making claims seem more certain and less open to question. Experts
within scientific domains, then, draw upon rich representations of discourse as a
social and rhetorical act, what Geisler (1991) has called socially configured mental models, as they create and interpret texts and as they judge the validity and
usefulness of the information within them.

LEARNING ABOUT LITERATE ACTIVITY IN THE SCIENCES

One of the things students of science must become privy to, as part of their dis-   3
ciplinary education, is this rhetorical, contingent nature of written scientific
discourse. Science educators at every level have been concerned with fostering
students' cognizance of the contexts, conduct, and purposes of science as well as
its factual content (Fensham, 1985; Mitman, Mergendoller, Marchman, &
Packer, 1987; National Academy of Sciences, 1989). Mitman et al. (1987) have
defined the components of "scientific literacy" as not only the mastery of scientific facts and concepts, but an understanding of "the evolving contributions of
individual scientists and groups of scientists, . . . the social communities and
historical settings in which scientists work" (p. 630) and the place of science
within "the broader contexts of human endeavor" (p. 612). In general, these
educators have argued that in order to understand, use, and judge scientific
content—and, of course, scientific content remains of vital importance to science educators—students need a metaunderstanding of the motives of science
and scientists and the history of scientific concepts. That is, a rhetorical understanding of the human enterprise of science, as well as the texts that constitute
and reflect that enterprise should be bound to the learning of scientific facts.

The educational task of helping students recognize the human nature of   4
scientific activity and rhetorical nature of scientific texts may be part of a larger
problem in academic literacy for students: a "myth" of autonomous texts that
seems to operate in academic settings at every level. This myth has been well
described—and well critiqued—in other contexts by Nystrand (1987), Cazden
(1989), Brandt (1990), and Farr (1993). In general, the belief in autonomous
texts views written academic texts as discrete, highly explicit, even "timeless"
entities functioning without contextual support from author, reader, or culture.
Research studies by Applebee (1984), Geisler (1990), Haas and Flower (1988),
Hynds (1989), Nelson (1990), and Vipond and Hunt (1984), among others,
have suggested that beginning college students approach academic tasks as if
they believe that texts are autonomous and context free. Treating texts as if
they are autonomous may be facilitated both by features of academic discourse
itself (see Farr, 1993, for a review of linguistic research on academic discourse)
and by a culture of schooling that encourages students to see texts primarily as
repositories of factual information (Goodlad, 1984). Certainly a number of
school reading and writing tasks—in college as well as high school—seem to be
predicated on the doctrine of the autonomous text: strict new critical readings
of literary works; tests that ask students to recall and reiterate informational
content only; textbooks that always seem to be written by nobody and everybody, as if the information embodied in them was beyond human composition,

and beyond human question.[2] The educational problem, then, is this: Entering college students may hold an arhetorical or asituational theory of written discourse, a representation or model of discourse that precludes seeing text as motivated activity and authors as purposeful agents, when in fact discourse theorists and scientific educators agree that students would benefit from a more rhetorical model.

Do students' views of academic discourse change over the course of their college careers? Studies of development in the college years such as those by Perry (1970) and by Belenky, Clinchy, Goldberger, and Tarule (1986) have not specifically addressed issues of reading and writing, although I will return in my discussion to their relevance for the case I present here. In an ambitious and extensive set of studies, Haswell (1988a, 1988b, 1991) looked at growth in writing competence through college but did not explicitly address how students view texts or how disciplinary training and literacy instruction interact. This article, then, provides an initial exploration of one student's developing rhetorical understanding of texts. It details a longitudinal study, an extended 4-year examination of one student as she progressed during college, focusing primarily on how the student's views of, and interactions with, disciplinary texts changed through her postsecondary education. Although Eliza (a pseudonym) may have tacitly subscribed to the doctrine of autonomous texts early in her college career, by the time she left college she had come to a greater awareness of the rhetorical, contingent nature of both the activities and discourses she participated in within her chosen field, biology.

In order to track Eliza's developing notions of text, I focused primarily on her reading processes and practices, and on the various texts she read, rather than on her writing processes and products. This was done for several reasons. First, studying Eliza's reading allowed me to examine her interactions with a greater number of texts, since she read many more texts than she wrote through the 4 years. She also read many more types of texts—textbooks, research reports, articles, proposals, lab notes, data sheets—than she wrote, especially in her biology and chemistry courses. In addition, I hypothesized that in her reading practices, Eliza might demonstrate more rhetorical sophistication than she would in her writing, where many more production skills must be managed (Scardamalia, Bereiter, & Goelman, 1982). Indeed, in discussions of her reading, Eliza showed a level of awareness of the activity and agents of discourse that seldom was obvious in the texts she wrote. Finally, while a great number of recent studies (Berkenkotter et al., 1988; Herrington, 1985, 1992; McCarthy, 1987; McCarthy & Fishman, 1991; Nelson, 1990) have examined students' writing in academic disciplines, few have expressly looked at how students read specialized texts within the disciplines.

RHETORICAL READING

Before discussing Eliza's case in detail, it is important to examine more closely   7
the application of rhetorical theories of discourse to actual literate practice: how
might we expect contextually rich social theories of discourse to play themselves
out in the real-time practices and processes of actual readers? The beginnings of
an answer to this question can be found in recent work in three separate but
related disciplines—social psychology, linguistics, and rhetoric. In each of these
fields, theoretical accounts of the pragmatics of social situation have been developed, motivated by questions such as "What is the nature of social situations,
including discourse?" and "How are situations represented cognitively by individuals?" Three theories can serve as representatives of recent work in each field:
Argyle, Furnham, and Graham (1981) in social psychology, van Dijk (1987) in
linguistics, and Bitzer (1968) and his critics and correctors in rhetoric (Biesecker,
1989; Jamieson, 1973; Vatz, 1973). While these theorists have different foci, all
three theories are concerned with the nature of social, communicative acts and
how individuals participate in and understand those acts.

Drawing together common elements of these theories, I postulate a model or   8
representation of discourse situations, a *rhetorical frame*, that helps readers account
for the motives underlying textual acts and their outcomes. Elements of the
rhetorical frame include participants, their relationships and motives, and several
layers of context. For instance, when readers approach a discourse situation, they
presumably have some knowledge or representation of the participants, including
the identity, knowledge, and background of author and intended readers. While
van Dijk (1987) and Argyle et al. (1981) did not differentiate between the persons involved in the discourse situation, rhetorical theorists (e.g., Bitzer, 1968;
Vatz, 1973) named them as rhetor, or speaker, and audience. Readers may also
know of, or postulate, a certain kind of relationship between the participants,
what Argyle et al. (1981) labeled the participants' "roles and status." As examples
of status, the reader and author may share (or not) a number of assumptions, or
one participant may be in a position of greater power. Of the rhetoricians,
Biesecker (1989) was the most directly concerned with social relationships. Also
useful to the reader is some representation of the motives of the participants—
why the author wrote the piece, why she or he chose the form that was chosen,
why she or he used a particular structure or chose certain words. Van Dijk (1987),
with his cognitive emphasis, was especially concerned with motivation and with
the purposes, plans, and goals that are driven by motives.

Undergirding the settings of discourse participants are several layers of con-   9
text: A text is an utterance, part of an intertextual context consisting of closely
and distantly related texts, or what Jamieson (1973) called antecedent rhetorical forms. A text may draw upon, extend, or refute a myriad of other texts,

whether those texts are directly cited or not. Knowing something about this complex of related texts will certainly aid a reader's interpretation. A text may also be supported by situational, cultural, and historical contexts. Argyle et al. (1981) and van Dijk (1987) treated context mostly in terms of setting, but Bitzer (1968) (and, following him, Biesecker, 1989) went further in identifying systems of belief, traditions, and cultural attitudes as constraints which shape and determine discourse. Knowledge of contexts will aid a reader's interpretation, and indeed, knowing something about cultural and historical contexts can reveal a great deal about discourse participants, and vice versa.

Acknowledging or attempting to understand these elements of discourse— 10
constructing a rhetorical frame which includes authors, readers, motives, relationships, and contexts—is what I call the process of rhetorical reading. Although every text has an author, a context, and active readers, many texts are constructed in ways that downplay, hide, or strip away the rhetorical frame. Rhetorical reading—that is, recognizing the rhetorical frame that surrounds a text, or constructing one in spite of conventions which attempt to obscure it—is often crucial for understanding argument and other sophisticated forms of discourse. Indeed, information about discourse situations—including representations of authorship, authorial intention, and intertextuality—has been identified as an aid to successful interpretation in previous research (Beach, Appleman, & Dorsey, 1990; Geisler, 1990; Haas & Flower, 1988; Huckin & Flower, 1991; Tierney, LaZansky, Raphael, & Cohen, 1987; Vipond & Hunt, 1984).

What does the process of rhetorical reading look like? Examples drawn from 11
previous studies of readers reading both experimental and naturalistic texts, and thinking aloud as they did so (Haas, 1991, 1993; Haas & Flower, 1988), show some readers thinking about and using rhetorical elements of discourse, while others do not. For instance, one example of a rhetorical reader (from Haas & Flower, 1988) was an engineering graduate student reading a text, the source and author of which were not identified, in the experimental session. (The text was actually a psychology textbook preface.) During his reading, he assigned the author both a gender, "this guy," and a profession, "he's some kind of scientist." The reader also tried to account for the author's motives: "This guy is crying out for" a new kind of science. Later, the reader hypothesized a source for the text, at one point speculating that it came from a scholarly psychology journal and noting that the article "wouldn't work for the man-in-the-street."

Another rhetorical reader (from Haas, 1991) was a junior history major 12
reading a more "naturalistic" text, a section of a book-length, policy-oriented historical analysis assigned in an elective history course. While reading aloud, this reader identified characteristics of the authors, noting that the text was

written by "two men" who are "good writers." According to the reader, these authors wanted to encourage policymakers—the intended reader she constructs (based on her reading of the book itself and of prefatory material)—to think about faulty historical analogies. Further, she placed the text, its authors, and readers in a historical context (dealing with Korea after the Korean War).

Each of these readers moved beyond an "autonomous" text and tried to account for a number of situational or rhetorical elements—author, authorial intent, reader identity, and historical, cultural, and situational context—to "frame" or support the discourse. In short, these readers were not content simply to extract information or to accept the arguments of an autonomous text. Other readers, however, seemed to treat the text as more of an autonomous, context-less object. The protocols of these readers were characterized by the absence of the kinds of rhetorically based comments we saw above. In the face of confusion about the texts they were reading, these readers returned to the text itself, rereading sections of the text and making comments like, "I don't understand why he's saying that. Better reread it." Of course, rereading is often an appropriate and useful strategy for understanding difficult texts. My point here is that some readers seemed to rely overly on this strategy, invoking it again and again. They attempted to understand the text not by moving out from it to a rhetorical context, but by moving in, focusing ever more closely on the text as an object. 13

THE STUDY

This longitudinal case study used a variety of methods and data sources to track Eliza's developing rhetorical understanding of scientific texts and other scientific acts. Specifically, I wanted to explore these questions: Does Eliza believe that academic texts are autonomous, or does she recognize the rhetorical nature of scientific action and scientific texts? Do these beliefs change as she moves through 4 years of college science instruction? 14

The Subject/Participant

Eliza was 1 of a group of 6 randomly selected case study participants that I began to track in their freshman year at a private research university. Eliza grew up in a middle-class family in a large eastern city and attended a large parochial high school near her home. She was the youngest of four children and had a large extended family, with aunts, uncles, and cousins living nearby. Her parents' education ended with high school, as did her two older sisters', while Eliza and her brother completed college. Eliza reported that her parents were "very proud, very supportive" of her during college,[3] both financially and emotionally. Her postsecondary education was partially financed by federal grants and through work-study awards. 15

Eliza graduated 14th out of a class of 450 from her high school, where she   16
was in the upper tracks in English, math, and science. Eliza said she was
"brainy" in high school, but "not a bookworm—more like the class nerd." She
felt her high school education was "as good as any," and she was especially full
of praise for the math program there—"Sister Elise could teach anyone mathematics." The math club won citywide competitions for 3 straight years while
Eliza was in high school. The curriculum for science classes—1-year-long course
for each of 4 years—consisted mostly of lectures and textbook reading, with a
minimal amount of lab work. Students were evaluated almost exclusively
through objective tests in these science courses.

Eliza came to college interested in biology and later considered the possibil-   17
ity of pursuing a double major in biology and chemistry before finally deciding
(late in her sophomore year) to focus exclusively on biology. As a freshman, she
said she was majoring in biology "because I'm pretty good at it," but by the time
she graduated, her interest in the subject was much deeper and more committed. During her senior year, she made comments like, "I'm learning to be a scientist," or "I'm going to be a scientist," or even, "I am a scientist." College-level
reading and writing were time consuming for Eliza, as for many of her classmates, but she worked hard at both and was determined to do well. Her final
college grade point average was about 3.0.

Setting

The study took place from August 1986, 1 week after Eliza arrived at college, to   18
April 1990, a few weeks before she graduated with a BS in biology. The setting
was a private research university in a medium-sized eastern city. About 6,500
students, one third of whom are graduate students, attend the university, which
is predominately White. Males outnumber females by a ratio of about 3 to 1
among undergraduates.

Interviews took place in my office in a computer development center where I   19
was a part-time consultant. Because Eliza did not identify me with any department from which she was taking classes, I believe she felt free to give honest and
detailed descriptions of her teachers, assignments, and course work, and her feelings about them. At the same time, as Patton (1980) has suggested, I wanted Eliza
to see me as someone who "spoke her language," that is, as someone who had at
least a passing knowledge of the subjects in which she was interested. For the first
three semesters, I could use course notes and background knowledge from my own
upper-division undergraduate courses in biology to keep informed. Later, I relied
on a colleague in chemistry (who had an undergraduate degree in biology) and on
some outside reading to help me attain a cursory knowledge of some of the topics
Eliza was addressing in reading, writing, and lab work assigned in biology.

Type of data	Amount (and unit of measure)
Freshman year	
Three interviews	~6 hours; 2,428 words*
One interview with each teacher	45 minutes; not transcribed
Reading sessions observed	30 minutes total
Reading/writing logs, 2 classes	14 log pages
Texts written for one class	30 pages
Sample texts read for two classes	[examined and returned]
Sophomore year	
Four interviews	~7 hours; 3,345 words*
Reading session observed	20 minutes
Reading/writing logs, 8 classes	30 log pages
Texts written for two classes	39 pages (including figures)
Sample texts read for two classes	[examined and returned]
Junior year	
Two interviews	~5 hours; 2,925 words*
Texts written for two classes	[examined and returned]
Sample texts read for eight classes	[examined and returned]
Two read-and-think-aloud protocols	~30 minutes each
Senior year	
Two interviews	~4 hours; 4,250 words*
Texts written for two classes	[examined and returned]
Sample texts read for three classes	[examined and returned]
Two read-and-think-aloud protocols	~30 minutes each

FIGURE 1   Data sources for each year.
*Excluding interviewer questions

Data Sources

Qualitative case study methods were used to track Eliza through her 4 years of   20
college, and attempts were made to triangulate data sources. Figure 1 shows
types and amounts of data collected. Interviews (several each year) were supplemented with the examination of artifacts (texts written and read for classes),
reading/writing logs kept by Eliza (freshman and sophomore years), observations
by the researcher of classes and reading sessions, and the collection of several
read-and-think-aloud protocols (junior and senior years). As is often the case
with qualitative research, data sources and methods evolved as the study progressed (see Goetz & LeCompte, 1984, especially chapter 5, Data Collection
Strategies). For example, reading/writing logs were discontinued after the sophomore year because Eliza indicated that they were taking an inordinate amount
of her study time to complete. At this point, read-and-think-aloud protocols

were added (they were used in the junior and senior years only) as an alternative data source that could furnish some of the same kinds of information as the
logs. In addition, I terminated my concurrent interviews with Eliza's teachers
when she indicated that my talking to her teachers made her uncomfortable. (I
did talk with some of these teachers later.)

Interviews. Following Perry (1970) and Belenky et al. (1986), the most   21
important data source for the study was a series of 11 extended, minimally structured interviews with Eliza, a total of more than 21 hours over the course of
4 years. I often went into interviews with a loose script, but I also allowed interviews to develop naturally, with ample time for clarification and follow-up. I
made every attempt to make the interviews friendly, casual, and conversational.
We began with background questions, "Tell me a bit about your high school English class." "Can we start by just listing what [classes] you're taking this semester?"
Later in the interviews—and during later interviews—we focused on more complex issues, "How does this [lab report] compare with what you expect to do in
grad school?" "What sorts of difficulties do you have with these [journal articles]?"

Interviews consisted of five of the six types of researcher queries identified   22
by Patton (1980): background and demographic questions, "How many writing
classes did you have in high school?"; experience and behavior questions,
"What kinds of things are you reading for [the term paper]?"; opinion and value
questions "Is this [reading of texts in developmental biology] different from that
of the reading you did last year?" "How important will this [course] be [for the
work you are doing]?"; feeling questions, "Do you like [developmental biol-
ogy]?"; and knowledge questions, "What is [developmental biology]?" Few questions were of the type identified by Patton as sensory questions (describing sensory impressions).

Many of the interviews also included discourse-based questions. Eliza   23
brought materials she was reading (and sometimes writing) for her classes to the
interviews, and I asked her to tell me about the reading she was engaged with at
that point. She often illustrated her points about the texts by explicitly pointing
to the texts or parts of them: "See, these three are all related because they deal
with tyrosine phosphorylation." At no point did I query Eliza directly about
authors, their intentions, or contextual variables. What I learned about Eliza's
thinking about these rhetorical elements arose in the natural course of her
telling me about the texts she was reading and writing or about the classes. To
elicit as much detail as possible, I sometimes prompted her to continue with
neutral queries like, "What else?" or "Oh, really?" and "Can you say more about
that?" All interviews were audiotaped and later transcribed. I also took notes
during all interviews.

Reading/writing logs. During the freshman and sophomore years, Eliza kept 24
reading/writing logs of her activities in selected classes, two in freshman year and
eight in sophomore year. I did not ask Eliza to write a discursive narrative via journal entries in the logs. Rather, using specially prepared log sheets, she kept track of
dates and times of reading and writing, wrote a short characterization of the assignment (completed only in an initial entry about an assignment or when her thinking about the assignment was revised), provided a brief description of goals for the
session, made a detailed list of the activities she engaged in during each session,
and noted any problems or frustrations she encountered while working.[4] A sample
set of entries from a sophomore reading/writing log is shown in Figure 2.

Read-and-think-aloud protocols. A total of four read-and-think-aloud proto- 25
cols were collected during Eliza's junior and senior years. During the junior year,
one of the texts Eliza read aloud was an experimental text used in a previous
study (Haas & Flower, 1988); the other text in the junior year and both texts
read during the senior year were "naturally occurring" texts that Eliza was reading in the course of her studies, rather than texts I assigned her to read. For
these latter three read-aloud sessions, I asked Eliza to choose a text she planned
to read but had not read yet. In each case, she selected a published article that
she was assigned to read for a biology class. Protocols lasted approximately 30
minutes each; during this time, Eliza read about half of each article.

Date/Time	Assignment	Goals	Activities	Problems
11/26/87 4:00	Cell biology research paper*	Read articles and decide if they're relevant to my paper; relatively easy.	Starting to read first article. Taking notes on index cards—writing down experiments and some facts.	
4:37				Tired; 5 minute break.
4:50			Starting first article again.	Hard to understand—lots of technical words.
5:20			Finish first article.	
5:25			Found second article much shorter. Taking notes like before.	
6:00			Finish second article (not as complex).	

FIGURE 2 Example of reading/writing log entries from Eliza's sophomore year.
*Capitalization of initial word in each entry added in some cases.

The experimental text was partitioned into segments (from one to five sen-   26
tences each) with the question, "How do you interpret the text now?" presented
between segments (see Haas & Flower, 1988, for further details about this
experimental text). For the naturally occurring texts, I asked Eliza (before she
began reading) to stop every paragraph or so and answer the question, "How do
you interpret the text now?," which was typed on a card and put on the table in
front of her. Because the expert scientists studied by Bazerman (1985) and by
Charney (1993) often previewed, skimmed, and skipped parts of the articles
they read, I told Eliza to read the articles as she normally would: "Feel free to
skim, or skip around, or whatever you would like." In each case, however, she
read the text linearly. Eliza was allowed to practice the think-aloud procedure
on an unrelated text before each session began. Each session was tape-recorded
and later transcribed for analysis.

Observation of reading sessions. During the freshman and sophomore years, I   27
observed Eliza reading texts silently. These observation sessions usually followed
interviews. During Eliza's junior and senior years, observation sessions were not
a separate data source, but were collapsed into the read-and-think-aloud protocols (i.e., I observed her from across the room and took notes on her reading
aloud during the protocols).

Other data. I also examined many of the texts Eliza was reading and writ-   28
ing for her courses. Interestingly, although Eliza used an advanced computer
system being developed at the university for most of her writing, she always
read from hard copy, often going to the trouble of printing out copies of texts
that her teachers had taken the trouble to put on-line. I collected photo-
copied samples of some of the texts Eliza was reading and writing; others I
examined and returned. In the freshman year, I collected all writing she did
for her English class, as well as samples of the texts she was reading for that
class. In the sophomore year, I collected all of her writing for her cell biology
class (labs and a term paper) and samples of texts read in two other classes. In
the junior and senior years, I examined or collected samples of texts written
and read for two classes, both in her major field. Eliza and I also exchanged
numerous e-mail and handwritten messages. These texts and informal correspondence added to my understanding of Eliza's learning, but they were not
formally analyzed.

LONGITUDINAL NARRATIVE

In order to examine—and do justice to—the richness of Eliza's undergraduate   29
educational experience, I constructed a longitudinal narrative drawing on qualitative analysis of data from the sources described above.

Analysis

In constructing the narrative, I used the transcripts of the 11 interviews, Eliza's   30
reading/writing logs, the writing sessions I observed that involved reading, and
the read-and-think-aloud protocols. I focused on three aspects of Eliza's reading:
(a) the reading tasks she was given or assumed and her stated goals for these
reading tasks; (b) her practices and processes of reading; and (c) her views of
discourse and knowledge.

Reading tasks and goals. Information about Eliza's reading tasks and goals   31
were drawn from three sources: the interviews, the reading/writing logs, and the
read-and-think-aloud protocols. From those segments of the interviews in
which Eliza was discussing specific texts, I identified comments about reading
tasks (including both class reading assignments and other tasks Eliza assumed on
her own). These included such comments as, "I have to read about a hundred
pages a night," "We have this stuff on tests," and "I'm reading this to get an idea
of how to set up my own report." I also identified reading goals, which were
often tied to means of evaluation, as in "I need to read this really carefully,
because he's going to be picky about the details." In addition, I used stated goals
from Eliza's reading/writing logs (e.g., "Get a general knowledge of my topic").
Finally, task-level goals (e.g., "I better get this for the test") were identified in
the read-and-think-aloud protocols.

Reading practices. Observations of reading/writing sessions, interview tran-   32
scripts, reading/writing logs, and read-and-think-aloud protocols were analyzed
to characterize Eliza's reading practices during each of the 4 years. During
observed writing sessions and during the protocols, I took notes on how Eliza
interacted with the texts she read. These activities included linear reading,
skimming, skipping, outlining, highlighting, and note making. I identified segments of the interviews in which Eliza discussed her approach to or interactions
with specific texts (e.g., "I reread the intro several times" and "I looked first at
the figures and legends") as well as those segments in which she discussed her
search and note-taking strategies for research papers (e.g., "I just looked up
some sources from the back of the textbook and took notes on three of the articles"). In the reading/writing logs, I identified instances in which Eliza
described reading practices and activities (e.g., "took more notes on article,"
"skimmed first part," and "reread the methods section").

Views of discourse and knowledge. While the analysis of reading tasks and   33
goals and reading practices was fairly straightforward, identifying and characterizing Eliza's views of discourse and knowledge was more complicated; therefore,
a second reader assisted in this phase of the analysis. The interview transcripts
were the primary data source for identifying and characterizing Eliza's views of

discourse and knowledge and the analysis proceeded as follows: First, working closely with the interview transcripts, we used analytic induction (Goetz & LeCompte, 1984) to identify seven kinds of statements that could reveal something about Eliza's views of discourse. These were instances in which Eliza was discussing (a) the nature of reading and writing generally; (b) characteristics of specific texts; (c) characteristics of authors, either generally or specifically; (d) explicit mention of the nature of knowing and learning; (e) specific mention of her own knowing or learning; (f) task-level goals for reading specific texts; or (g) reading tasks she was assigned or assumed on her own.

I was not interested in these seven categories per se (i.e., I did not compare types of statements). Rather, the scheme was used as a tool to help identify relevant segments of the interviews. Using this scheme, we identified 81 interview segments, 72 of which we agreed revealed something about Eliza's views of discourse and/or knowledge. The other 9 segments were recountings of specific assignments, 3 from the freshman year and 6 from the sophomore year. We reasoned that these may have been more of a reflection of the instructor's views than of Eliza's, and therefore these recountings of assignments were omitted from further analysis. The 72 identified segments ranged in length from two to eight t-units (roughly, independent clauses and dependent clauses with subject and verb), excluding researcher discourse.

The second reader and I then determined that 30 of the 72 previously identified segments included some mention of one or more rhetorical elements— writer identity and purpose; intended or actual reader and motivation; and intertextual, situational, historical, and cultural context. Throughout this analysis, it was important to use the context surrounding segments (including interviewer questions and previous discussions) to determine whether a given segment could be used to infer Eliza's discourse views. Although the number of segments may seem low for interviews ranging in length from approximately 800 to approximately 2,000 words, recall that Eliza was not asked specifically about nor prompted for her views about discourse or about rhetorical concerns. Table 1 shows the number of the interview segments revealing discourse views for each of the 4 years and the number and proportion of these segments that included rhetorical concerns.

Results

As Table 1 shows, the number of interview segments identified as revealing something about Eliza's views of discourse were similar in freshman and sophomore years (10 and 13 respectively); in the junior and senior years, the number about doubled, to 24 and 25. The number of these identified segments that dealt with rhetorical concerns was 2 in the freshman year, 1 in the sophomore

TABLE 1 Interview Segments Revealing Views of Discourse and Rhetorical Concerns

Year	Total Interview Segments Identified as Revealing Views of Discourse	Number of Identified Segments Dealing With Rhetorical Concerns	Proportion of Identified Segments Dealing With Rhetorical Concerns
Freshman	10	2	.20
Sophomore	13	1	.07
Junior	24	13	.53
Senior	25	14	.56
Total	72	30	—

year. This number is markedly greater in the junior and senior years—13 and 14 respectively. And the proportions of segments dealing with rhetorical concerns to total segments show a similar trend, with proportions of over 50% in the junior and senior years.

The following narrative traces Eliza's interactions with and learning about texts through 4 years of college. For each of her 4 college years, I discuss first the kinds of reading tasks in which Eliza engages, drawing primarily on interviews and reading/writing logs. Next I describe Eliza's reading processes and practices, drawing from the read-and-think-aloud protocols, my observations of reading sessions, reading/writing logs, and interviews. The narratives for each year conclude with a longer section, which examines how Eliza's conceptions of the rhetorical nature of discourse and the contingent nature of scientific facts developed. Interviews (particularly the segments identified as revealing views of discourse) were the primary data source for these sections, and they were supplemented with data from reading/writing logs, read-and-think-aloud protocols, and teacher interviews. 37

Eliza as a freshman: "The book says." As a freshman, Eliza's academic work focused almost exclusively on preparing for tests in her biology, chemistry, and math courses. She also wrote a fairly extensive synthesis of various authors' positions papers in her English class. Her processes consisted of mostly linear reading of textbooks and, for the English class, essays. If she had trouble comprehending, her strategy was usually to reread, and she made extensive use of a highlighter, sometimes marking whole paragraphs with it. She also often took notes, usually verbatim, from her reading. According to statements made in interviews or entries in her reading/writing logs, Eliza's goals for most of her reading were "to learn it," "to understand it," or even "to memorize it." Understanding the book or what "the book says" was paramount at this point in Eliza's college career. Eliza viewed her role as a reader as one of extracting and retaining information, a not unsavvy approach, given the ways that she was held accountable for the reading. 38

In the reading for her English class, Eliza's goal was slightly different, stated most frequently as "to figure out what they're saying." The curriculum in her English class was built upon a recognition of authors and their claims and positions. Students in the class worked from a common corpus of texts on a single topic—animal experimentation—and produced progressively more difficult written texts based on readings: summary, synthesis, analysis, and original contribution. In addition, the instructor asked students to create visual representations—a path of argumentation, a synthesis tree—to help them visualize the conversation going on among the several authors. (This curriculum is illustrated in Kaufer, Geisler, & Neuwirth, 1989.) Possibly due to the emphasis in this class on authorial conversations, Eliza seemed to view the texts she read for her English class less as a source of information to extract and more of a place in which someone says something. That someone did not usually have an identity (beyond author) nor a motive, although "he" did have a gender: All references to authors used the masculine pronoun, even though some of the texts were written by women. In interviews and reading/writing logs, she stressed the importance of understanding the authors, as she often repeated statements like, "I'm trying to understand what he's saying" and "trying to figure out what he's *really* saying." "Trying to figure out what they're saying" was also stated as a goal in reading/writing logs. Whether due to the different kinds of texts she was reading for this class or to the instructor's emphasis on authorial claims, Eliza seemed to have a clearer sense that the essays were connected to human agents, and she even had some cognizance that the texts were connected: "He [the teacher] says it's like they're [the authors] having a conversation." However, the authors Eliza discussed often seemed synonymous with the book she described in her reading for other classes, with "the author says" equaling, in effect, "the book says." Nor during this year did she mention authors' motives or intentions, the multiple contexts surrounding the texts she read, or intended readers and their reactions.

As a freshman, then, Eliza seemed to have a bifurcated view about texts and authors: On the one hand, she talked as if both the texts for her biology and chemistry class and the information contained in them was unconnected to human agents—"understanding what the book says" or "understanding what it says" were frequently cited goals in the reading/writing logs. In the reading for her subject matter courses, she seemed to operate without a rhetorical frame, accepting the texts she read as autonomous. On the other hand, the curriculum in her English class seemed to be nudging her toward a more sophisticated conception of discourse, with at least some mention of authors and their relationship: Authors "have a conversation" (as in the example above) and "they were bothered by the same things that bothered me."

Two pairs of concepts developed by Belenky et al. (1986) are useful in fur-   41
ther examining Eliza's developing theories of knowledge. The notions of
received knowledge and procedural knowledge and of separate knowing and
connected knowing emerged at various points as Eliza's education progressed.
As a freshman, Eliza's epistemological theory seemed to be one of received
knowledge, and her role was receiver of that knowledge. Her goals were to learn
or understand or memorize what "the book says," or "figure out what he [the
author] is really saying." Tellingly, she described how her English teacher would
have to accept the claims of her paper if "I can prove it in writing from the
book." The book here was the ultimate authority—through which one received
knowledge and by which one's own contributions were judged.

Reading as a sophomore: Eliza encounters the research paper. During her soph-   42
omore year, Eliza's reading tasks and reading practices, and the means by which
she was evaluated, remained essentially the same. The one major change in her
reading, from her point of view at least, was that there was simply a lot more of
it. It was Eliza's and her classmates' impression that the department and the college attempted to "scare people away" with the amount of work that was
required in the courses that Eliza took during this year. She continued to have
hundreds of pages of textbook reading every week, frequent exams, and little
discussion in her classes. Eliza did have more lab courses during this year than
during the previous one, but these labs required little reading.

Eliza's reading practices showed an increased attention to the procedures of   43
knowing. According to Belenky et al. (1986), procedural knowers are "absorbed
in the business of acquiring and applying procedures of obtaining . . . knowledge" (p. 95). As a sophomore, Eliza seemed to view learning as the application
of certain procedures: Reading was always done with highlighter in hand, for
instance, and her notes (usually almost verbatim) were labeled and organized.

One interesting development during Eliza's sophomore year was the   44
research paper assigned in her cell biology course. The instructor gave the students little direction on the project, assigning a research paper that was to be
five or six pages long. In Eliza's words, "We're supposed to pick a topic that
interests us, and then just go more in depth with it, go in research books and
just write about it." The topic was selected from a list of cell structures provided
by the instructor. The paper was also to include a section on experimental
methods, but this section involved little reading and Eliza seemed to spend little
time on it. According to Eliza, the goal was to write "a paper that tells what's
known about our topic," and she did not attempt to develop a thesis or controlling idea, nor did she even see a need for one (cf. Stotsky, 1991).

Eliza located articles by using a reference list provided in the back of her cell   45
biology textbook, and she ended up reading three of these articles and taking

notes on them. Although the three articles varied in their relevance and usefulness for Eliza's paper, she noted in her log that the reading and note taking was
easy. In her log she said, "My goal is to prepare a general knowledge of my topic,
using papers listed in the book." Activities noted in her log included "reading,
taking notes," "writing down some relevant facts," and "pulling out" information.
For Eliza, writing the research paper seemed a matter of applying the appropriate
procedure (Belenky et al., 1986): If one finds the relevant articles and pulls out
the appropriate facts, then one "can make a research paper [oneself]." Eliza
talked as if a research paper was a simple task, and in fact, for her it was: She and
many of her classmates wrote their papers together in the library the night before
the papers were due. The following excerpt shows the almost casual way that
Eliza treated this assignment:

> I just took brief little notes, like types of drugs, or something about the
> experiment. And basically just sat down later on and just wrote the paper
> from there. I figure it was the next night. [Consults reading/writing log in
> front of her.] Yeah. Basically that's what everybody did, they waited—they
> just went and read the articles the night before, and got in groups or some-
> thing and wrote it, you know, to help each other out.

Eliza's strategy for the research paper resembled what Nelson (1990) identi-   46
fied as a "low investment" strategy in students performing similar tasks: She
waited until the last minute and then relied on a minimum number of sources,
sources selected mainly because they were easy to locate and convenient. But my
knowledge of Eliza even at this early point in her college career led me to believe
that she was in fact quite committed and "invested" in her education, her field of
study, and her future as a biologist. She approached classes with a real serious-
ness, and she spent a great deal of time and effort preparing for tests in her chemistry and cell biology and genetics courses. I believe Eliza's limited, even cavalier,
approach to the research paper assignment was due to the fact that it simply did
not occur to her that reading articles and writing a research paper had much at
all to do with her goal of becoming a biologist. Tasks like her chemistry lab or
genetics exams, or even her math homework, were obviously tied in her mind to
the work of biologists, and for these kinds of tasks Eliza had a very high investment approach. Writing a research paper may have seemed to her an exercise
that was quite unconnected to the real work of science.

Eliza seemed to view her own research paper and the articles she read as   47
unconnected to the field of biology as she construed it: autonomous information
embodied in textbooks, which she was required to learn. This notion is supported by the almost complete lack of reference in her interviews and logs to
rhetorical or contextual elements surrounding the texts she read. The attention

to authors, which surfaced during her reading for her English class in her fresh-man year, had disappeared. There was no evidence that she viewed any of the texts she read as the product of an individual author's motives or actions. Nor did she exhibit any cognizance of the texts she read as historically or culturally situated. Even the citation lists in the articles she read were used primarily as a convenient way to find other articles, not as an intertextual system tying separate texts together.

During her sophomore year, Eliza still seemed happy with her arhetorical, asituational approach to reading texts that she viewed primarily as autonomous. Certainly, it was an approach that was well rewarded. She got a good grade on her research paper, and she did well on exams in all of her classes. If Eliza operated without a rhetorical frame for much of her reading and writing during her sophomore year, there was nothing in her school environment to signal weakness or problems with that approach.

Eliza's junior year: Seeing authors as scientists. One important change in Eliza's life this year was her new work study job. Beginning this year, Eliza took a work study job growing protein mutants in a lab run by one of her professors. Eliza's direct supervisor in this work, a graduate student named Shelly, became an important mentor for her during the junior year and on into the senior year. She described the work this way:

> It [the lab job] gives me a lot of individual attention because I work side by side with Shelly, who's a graduate student in the lab, and like she's—well they gave me a project and when I need help or have problems, she guides me through it. Like an apprentice, I guess. . . . . I like it better [than classes] because it's more difficult. Well, not more difficult, exactly, but like nobody knows the end result, like [they would] in my bio lab.

As a reader, Eliza this year seemed much more sophisticated. In contrast to the methodical, linear reading she engaged in earlier, Eliza now exhibited a range of reading strategies—skimming, reading selectively, moving back and forth through texts, reading for different purposes at different times. In this way, she was beginning to look like the practicing scientists whose reading Bazerman (1985) and Charney (1993) have studied. She also read some texts not solely to glean information but to learn about conventions and structures: "I'm reading this to get an idea of how to set up my own report." She also made a distinction now between "just textbook reading" and reading journal articles, and she predicted (probably accurately) that "in grad school, all I'll read will be journal articles."

The academic tasks that Eliza faced still included a number of exams, although her classes tended to be smaller and some of these exams were what she called "essay exams," which meant that students answered questions in short paragraphs rather than through one word responses or multiple choice. Eliza also had a research paper to do this year in her virology class. But the assignment itself, or Eliza's representation of it, was more specific and complex and connected the research paper to the larger situational and cultural context of virology research. Rather than a goal of "prepar[ing] a general knowledge" of her topic, as in the sophomore year, Eliza's goal was now to "find out what people are doing" with a particular virus, look at "where the technology is going in the future," and to "think up some experiments" to do with the vaccinia (cowpox) virus. Implicit here was the notion that her work on the vaccinia virus would be tied to the work of others, via her text.

In both her reading for this particular research paper and her reading   52
more generally, Eliza exhibited a much greater awareness of the contexts surrounding the texts she read. This was reflected in the greater number of interview segments that dealt with rhetorical concerns (see Table 1). Her first-year attention to authors reemerged in the interviews during the junior year, but in a much more complex way. Whereas the authors she talked about as a freshman were writers only, the authors she talked about now were writers, certainly, but also scientists. She attributed motives to these authors, seeing them as making choices as researchers—"so they're using this as a prototype for the manipulation"—or as agents in an uncertain enterprise—"they're saying they're not sure if this is how it replicates" and "they don't know too much about the actual microbiology of the virus." She showed a cognizance of the activity of the field of virology, claiming that a particularly well-investigated virus is "like a beaten horse—they've studied it so much." When she encountered an article reporting what was to her a particularly esoteric and specialized kind of research, she asked somewhat sardonically, "What kind of people *do* research on this?" Now, texts were not autonomous objects, but manifestations of scientific action and human choices.

At this point, Eliza was also beginning to recognize a historical, situational   53
context surrounding and supporting the texts she read. In one interview, she went on at great length about how she selected articles to read: "First, of course, I see if the titles are relevant . . . but some of them, like from 1979, well, 1979 isn't that far back, but they weren't sure then if what they were seeing was true." Later, she claimed that "some of them were really old, like in the 70s," and were "getting me nowhere," so "I set a limit of like, maybe, 1980 to the present." In general, by her junior year, Eliza had a much more fleshed out representation of authors—authors as writers and as scientists, authors with motives and within circumstances—than she did earlier. And texts, the claims they make, and their truth value, were now seen as the product of a particular, historical time.

Reading contingent science as a senior: Increasing sensitivity to context. The 54
academic tasks she was required to complete had changed somewhat by Eliza's
senior year. She had exams now in only two of her courses, and other assignments included critical presentations of research articles and critiques of others'
interpretations of similar articles. She had extensive writing assignments based
on reading in two of her classes, but now she did not call these research papers;
rather, they were a review article and a model proposal.

Eliza's reading processes and practices also continued to grow in complex- 55
ity. She now spent a great deal of time and effort going over figures and tables
in texts she read, offering by way of explanation: "This is important. Most professors can readjust by looking at figures and their legends." She also exhibited a
greater awareness of the intertextual nature of discourse; texts were not isolated,
but linked. She still used citations to uncover relevant articles, but rather than
skimming the citation lists as she did the year before, she now examined how
particular sets of articles used and represented the claims of their sources (cf.
Latour, 1987), and she claimed that one can often "tell by the title if they build
on one another." The claims of another set of articles "are all related, indirectly," she said.

Eliza's attention to the rhetorical elements of discourse—authors, readers, 56
motives, contexts—also exhibited increased sophistication in her senior year.
For Eliza, as a senior, not all of an author's claims were equal. While the results
section may have been solid, the claims of a discussion may have been more
contingent, as illustrated in the following example, where Eliza demonstrated
her understanding of scientists' uncertainty and their commitment to theory
despite insufficient data and where she used a metaphorical term (handwaving)
for how this uncertainty is manifest in written discourse:

Eliza: There's a lot of handwaving in the discussion.
CH: What's that?
Eliza: Handwaving? They're not sure of their theory. They sort of have data
        which suggest it. But they can't come out and say that . . . You don't
        know what's happening first. Is it binding here first? Is it binding to an
        active enzyme? You're not sure.
CH: Do you think they're not sure?
Eliza: Yes. I'm sure they're not sure.

Eliza also had specific representations of different kinds of authors. Authors 57
who write journal articles were active scientists, "the people who actually did
the study," while authors of textbooks tended to be more senior with a great
deal of experience: "even older than my boss [an associate professor who runs

the lab where she works], because he's been around a long time but he's not qualified to do a textbook yet." Textbooks and journal articles were also seen in a certain historical context. Eliza recognized that one reads these texts with an eye toward this temporal aspect of their composition. She said, "By the time a textbook is written it's out of date. To really learn the stuff, you have to read the journals." This was a far different approach to text than the one she demonstrated as a freshman, when one simply memorized as best one could "what the book says."

Eliza's independent work with the graduate student Shelly continued in the   58
senior year. Although it is clear that Eliza's relationship with Shelly was not perfect—when asked if Shelly was easy to work with, Eliza hesitated, then said with a laugh, "Sometimes!"—she was proud of work she had done in the lab. Eliza observed, "I'm working for her, but I've created two mutants in a protein, on my own." Eliza said she had learned a lot from the experience: "Like when I started I was clueless. I really never could understand totally what they were talking about." However, she stressed that "Now when Shelly says something to me, I understand what she's talking about." And later: "I understand what they're [other professors and grad students on the project] talking about."

Eliza's work with Shelly in the lab may also have contributed to her aware-   59
ness of the social and rhetorical dimensions of discourse. This is suggested by the way she discussed her writing in conjunction with this work. She was concerned that readers of her lab journal be able to use the information there: "It [her writing] is important because somebody who comes when I leave is going to want to work with my mutants and they are going to want to understand how it works, how it grows." She was also beginning to understand how discourse fits into the larger culture of scientific research, recognizing how her own writing will help her make a place for herself within that culture. Regardless of her skill as an immunologist, she believed, without writing, "I'd never get my point across. I'd never get a grant. I'd never have any money, so forget it. I'd be out of luck." A text was now seen not as a storehouse of information but as a way to pursue one's scientific agenda; without it, the scientist is isolated, unable to do her work, "out of luck."

Despite her obviously greater sophistication, Eliza, as a senior, still exhib-   60
ited a certain tension in the way she talked about texts and the way she talked about facts and knowledge. Like the scientists studied by Gilbert and Mulkay (1984), Eliza seemed to move back and forth between two repertoires, the first a foundationalist view of texts, demonstrated by comments like the following from a senior-year interview: "The teacher will nail us if we're not perfectly factual," an example that suggests as well that Eliza's professor was concerned with

students factual understanding of course material. At other times, Eliza voiced a more contingent view of the texts she read, noting "handwaving" in the discussion of an article or mentioning that researchers may have been confused or mistaken in plotting their results. It seems unlikely, however, that Eliza was in control of these repertoires in quite the same way that the biochemists studied by Gilbert and Mulkay were. Further, this bifurcation in the way she viewed texts may have reflected her continuing dual roles, functioning both as a budding scientist taking her place in a research community and as a student, still responsible for learning course content and demonstrating her competence to her teachers and other authorities. Similarly, Eliza by turns exhibited characteristics of both "separate" knowing and "connected" knowing (Belenky et al., 1986). She sometimes separated herself from the knowledge or claims of a text, positioning herself above it, as when she described how "I started by just looking at the figures and legends to see what's wrong with them" or predicted that in grad school she will "just look at articles and tear them apart, say what's wrong with them." But she had also become somewhat more of a connected knower, seeing connections between her own uncertainty about scientific methods and findings and the uncertainty of the researcher/authors whose research she read. Eliza also described her connections to the mutants that were the object of her research, connections that Harding (1986) identified as one of the traits of feminist science. Eliza said she knows "what it [the mutant] likes to grow on, what it hates to grow on. . . . It really is like the baby that you have to watch out for." Eliza here echoed the now-famous anecdote of geneticist Barbara McClintock, describing herself as "part of the system . . . right down there with [the chromosomes]," and the chromosomes themselves as her "friends" (cited in Keller, 1983).

Discussion of the Narrative

Through her 4 years of college, Eliza's theory of discourse changed in important   61
ways. Early in her college career, the bulk of the texts she read for school were seen as sources of information, and her job as a reader was primarily to extract this information for use in tests or reports. For the most part, both texts and the information they contain seemed unconnected to the authors or the circumstances that produced them. Not that Eliza was unable to understand the concept of author or authorial claims: in the reading of essays for her English class, she became somewhat conversant with these notions. An English curriculum which stressed authorial conversations and encouraged students' graphic representations of authors' interactions may have contributed to Eliza's understanding of discourse during the freshman year. But, in the sophomore year, when the

"scaffolding" (Applebee, 1984) provided by Eliza's English class and instructor were withdrawn, she again seemed content to view texts as autonomous. As evidenced by her approach to the research paper in her sophomore year, Eliza seemed to view reading and writing as unconnected to the scientific work for which she was preparing herself. Rather, at this point, reading and writing were seen as the work of school, not the work of science.

Beginning in her junior year, we begin to see important changes in Eliza's views of discourse: She exhibited a growing cognizance of texts (and the science they report) as the result of human agency. Similarly, her representations of discourse seem to have expanded to include a notion of texts as accomplishing scientific and rhetorical action, fulfilling purposes and motives, as well as presenting facts and information. Her recognition of the rhetorical nature of discourse was somewhat uneven, of course: Sometimes she talked as if science and scientific texts were purely factual, set in stone; other times, she saw them as more contingent. By her senior year she often viewed texts as multiply connected—to authors and scientists, to other readers, and to historical circumstances—and even demonstrated some understanding of her own connections both to scientific texts (and, by implication, to their authors) and to the objects of her own research. 62

LINGUISTIC ANALYSIS OF INTERVIEW TRANSCRIPTS: ANALYSIS AND RESULTS

The following enumerative discourse analysis of interview transcripts adds to and supports Eliza's "story" as seen in the longitudinal narrative and provides triangulation of method and approach. Two linguistic examinations of the typed transcripts of the 11 interviews (3 in the freshman year, 4 in the sophomore years, and 2 each in the junior and senior years) were also conducted. In the first of these analyses, I looked for patterns in the verbs that Eliza assigned to written texts and to authors; in the second, I examined the number and kind of human agents that appeared in the interview discourse. 63

Being, saying, and doing verbs. In order to learn more about Eliza's conceptions of authors and discourse—specifically, whether she viewed texts and authors as primarily static or active—"being," "saying," and "doing" verbs attached to explicit mentions of authors and texts as subjects were identified and tallied for each 1,000 words in the interviews (following Geisler, 1991). The analysis proceeded as follows: In the interview transcripts for each of the 4 years, explicit mentions of texts and authors in clausal subject position were first identified. (Only Eliza's speech was analyzed; interviewer questions were not included.) Explicit mentions of texts included "book," "article," "material," "text" and the pronoun "it" as referring to one of these nouns; explicit mentions of authors included "author(s)" and "he" and "they" as directly referring to 64 authors. Omitted were instances where "is about" followed the noun (as in "the book is about"), as these phrases usually signaled a paraphrasing of content rather than an explicit discussion of texts or authors per se. As Table 2 shows, in the freshman year there were 3.9 of these mentions per 1,000 words of interview transcript. There were 3.2 mentions per 1,000 words of interview data in the sophomore year, 22.6 per 1,000 in the junior year, and 12.8 per 1,000 in the senior year. These numbers reflect the fact that Eliza's discussion of texts as a freshman and sophomore often focused on the content of those texts; later, she talked more regularly about the texts as texts. Note that the number of mentions was highest in the junior year, then tapered off in the senior year. Other data support a difference between the sophomore and junior years, but do not explain why the authorial mentions were almost twice as high in the junior as the senior year.

Next, the verb attached to each of these text or author subject nouns was identified and coded as being (state) verbs, saying verbs, or doing (action) verbs. Examples of being or state verbs were, "The book is long," "The material was difficult," "It [an article] is technical," and "They're [author/scientists] not sure." Saying verb examples included, "The report mentioned the virus," "He [author] restates his position," and "They're [authors] talking about the procedures here." Verbs of action or doing included, "They [author/scientists] manipulated the variables," "They [author/scientists] came up with an experiment to test it," and "They [author/scientists] are preparing you for the results." Note that these last examples reflect a subtle difference between authors as scientists (conducting research) and authors as authors (constructing texts). Both were included in the analysis.

The presence of being verbs revealed no real trend, with proportions of .33, .45, .36, and .37 for each of the 4 years. The proportion of saying verbs was high in the freshman year (.66), and then diminished somewhat, with proportions of .45 in the sophomore year, .35 in the junior year, and .23 in the senior year. Doing verbs, which may have signaled a more complex understanding of the potential of texts to do things in the world (cf. Austin, 1962; Searle, 1979),

TABLE 2 Authorial Mentions (per 1,000 interview words) and Attached Verbs

Year	Explicit Mention of Text or Author (per 1,000 words)	Proportion of Authorial Mentions Attached to Verbs		
		Being	Saying	Doing
Freshman	3.9	.33	.66	[none]
Sophomore	3.2	.45	.45	.10
Junior	22.6	.36	.35	.29
Senior	12.8	.37	.23	.40

were completely absent in the freshman year and accounted for 10% of authorial and text mentions in the sophomore year. Fully 29% of these mentions in
the junior year and 40% of them in the senior year, however, were attached to
doing verbs. The difference is not simply one of agency (certainly saying verbs
attribute agency); rather, doing verbs signal some understanding that texts (and
authors) not only make statements but literally accomplish action. Together,
verbs of being and saying accounted for most of the authorial and text mentions
in the freshman and sophomore year (100% and 90%, respectively). However,
the proportions are much more evenly distributed among the three kinds of
verbs in the junior and senior years, possibly reflecting Eliza's growing cognizance that texts do things as well as say things and that authors are active scientists as well as writers.

Human agents. In order to understand who were the significant players in   67
Eliza's talk about her education, and specifically about the texts she read, I also
examined the human agents Eliza named in the interviews over 4 years. This
analysis revealed a growing cast of characters in the "drama" of her interaction
with texts. I identified all persons named in the subject position of clauses,
omitting those in which Eliza spoke of herself, those in which she spoke of me,
and those in which a pronoun (he or they) had an unclear referent. As Table 3
shows, Eliza's teachers played a significant role throughout her postsecondary
education. They were mentioned 10.6 times per 1,000 words of interview in the
freshman year, and their presence remained strong through the sophomore
(7 mentions per 1,000 words), junior (5 per 1,000 words), and senior (7 per
1,000 words) years. The presence of other students remained fairly constant as
well, with 3.7 mentions per 1,000 words in the freshman year, 3.3 per 1,000 in
the sophomore year, 2.8 per 1,000 in the junior year, and 2.4 per 1,000 in the
senior year. Another important presence was the female graduate student who
supervised Eliza's work in the lab. This graduate student mentor, Shelly, was
mentioned 1.3 times per 1,000 words in Eliza's junior year (a proportion of .05
of the human agents mentioned this year), and Shelly's importance increased in
the senior year, when she was mentioned 2.6 times per 1,000 words, accounting
for 10% of the human agents mentioned.

The biggest change was the increasing importance of authors over 4 years.   68
Authors were mentioned 3.1 times per 1,000 words in Eliza's freshman year,
accounting for 20% of the human agents mentioned in the freshman year interviews. In the sophomore year, authors diminished in importance, with less than
one mention per 1,000 words, or 6% of the human agents mentioned. However,
in Eliza's junior year, authors were mentioned 17.1 times per 1,000 words of
interview transcript, or 64% of the human agents mentions, and their presence

TABLE 3   Human Agents Named by Eliza in Interviews

Year and Agents	Human Agents in the Subject Position	
	Mentions (per 1,000 interview words)	Proportion
Freshman		
Teachers	10.6	.60
Other students	3.7	.20
Authors	3.7	.20
Sophomore		
Teachers	6.6	.62
Other students	3.3	.31
Authors	.5	.06
Others	.2	.01
Junior		
Authors	17.1	.64
Teachers	5.1	.19
Other students	2.8	.10
Mentor	1.2	.05
Others	.2	.01
Senior		
Authors	10.0	.40
Teachers	7.2	.31
Mentor	2.7	.10
Other students	2.4	.09
Other researchers	1.3	.05
Other lab workers	.7	.03
Others	.4	.01

remained high with 10 mentions per 1,000 words in the senior interview transcripts, or 40% of the human agents mentioned that year. This analysis supports the story told in the longitudinal narrative: There, authors (and other rhetorical concerns) appear in the freshman year, fade somewhat in the sophomore year, then reemerge in a much stronger way in the junior and senior years.

These linguistic analyses of Eliza's interview discourse point to her developing understanding of texts and authors as doing things as well as saying things and to the growing presence of authors in Eliza's interactions with texts. Other results support the notion of linguistic development within specialized communities; for example, Penrose and Fennel (1992) found junior and senior science majors more closely approximating the linguistic choices of expert scientists.

69

The analysis of Eliza's interview discourse suggests that Eliza was coming to understand that science is the result of human action and that texts are an important way in which the work of science gets done. The increasing number of people that appeared in the interviews in the junior, and especially the senior, year may also reflect that Eliza was beginning to understand that many people (authors, mentors, researchers, and lab workers, as well as teachers and students) are involved in the work of science.

GENERAL DISCUSSION

We have seen how Eliza developed as a reader in a number of ways through her   70
4 years of college. Her reading practices became more sophisticated as she moved away from the linear reading and verbatim-note taking strategies of her freshman year to the skimming, selective reading, and in-depth attention to tables and legends in the senior year. Her goals for reading changed as well. In the freshman year she was primarily concerned with "figuring out what the book says"—understanding and memorizing scientific concepts. As a senior, Eliza was trying to find or make a place for herself within an academic community, and she used reading to help her reach that goal—although reading continued to function, as it had throughout her college career, as a way to become conversant with scientific concepts. Arguably, the most important change in Eliza's reading of texts, however, was in her growing awareness of the rhetorical frame supporting written discourse—including a representation of authors as active, motivated agents and a cognizance of the historical, situational, and intertextual contexts supporting both readers and writers. As a senior reading the texts of her major field, Eliza resembled expert readers in her attention to rhetorical concerns. To my mind, this change constituted the beginnings of a new theory of discourse for Eliza. She began to see texts as accomplishing scientific action as well as embodying scientific knowledge: She recognized that behind scientific texts are human authors with motives, authors who are also interested, but sometimes uncertain, scientists; she started to see that scientific facts are contingent and historically bound. The changes in Eliza's use of verbs to talk about texts and authors and the growing presence of human agents in her interview discourse suggest, as well, that important changes were going on in Eliza's view of the scientific enterprise. Possibly most importantly, Eliza began to see her own role as not simply learning the facts but of negotiating meaning—that is, doing her work—amidst the many voices of her discipline.

What kinds of factors and events may have led to Eliza's growth and devel-   71
opment as a reader? Of course, a longitudinal case study does not allow strong causal arguments, but I would like to suggest four somewhat interrelated expla-

nations. Teasing out how the factors described below, and others, influenced Eliza's rhetorical growth is beyond the scope of this study. Further qualitative and quantitative studies, as well as meta-analyses of existing research, will be necessary in order to begin to understand the complex of factors contributing to the rhetorical development, in reading and in writing, of students like Eliza.

Increased domain knowledge. A strong knowledge explanation for Eliza's 72 development would maintain that her increased facility with the terms and concepts of biology (and its subfields of immunology and molecular biology) led to her increased rhetorical sophistication. In this view, the "world of domain content" precedes and supports the "world of rhetorical process" (cf. Bereiter & Scardamalia, 1987; Geisler, in press). Research in areas as diverse as the cognition of chess playing, in which Chase and Simon (1973) found expert players to have huge numbers of domain-specific patterns in memory, and sociolinguistic studies of literacy by Scribner and Cole (1981), which showed Vai villagers able to perform logical operations in known but not unknown domains, support the strong knowledge explanation. In fact, this explanation was one that Eliza herself offered for her increased facility with reading academic articles. In her junior year, she noted that "it [the article] was really technical, but I understood a lot more than if I had been a sophomore reading it, [because] I've been exposed to a lot of terms." One possible drawback to the knowledge explanation is that it rests on a conception of domain knowledge as static, fixed, and necessarily prior to rhetorical knowledge, a conception that has been questioned by recent advances in the philosophy of knowledge (e.g., Rorty, 1979).

Instructional support. A second explanation would hold that, as Eliza's edu- 73 cation proceeded, she was exposed to different kinds of classes and assignments, and that this instructional support, provided by her teachers and by the curricula within the biology department, was responsible for Eliza's rhetorical development. Indeed, as we have seen, there were vast differences in class structure, assigned texts, and reading and writing assignments as Eliza's college education progressed. Some credence is added to this explanation by the fact that when Eliza was given explicit support for thinking about authorial claims and other rhetorical elements—through the texts, assignments, and interactive framework of her freshman English class—she seemed able to invoke and use at least some rhetorical knowledge.

A variant of the instructional support explanation would hold that it was the 74 different kinds of texts that Eliza read that invited or required different strategies, goals, and views of discourse from her. Eliza certainly did read different kinds of texts later in her college years, as primarily textbook reading gave way to research reports and published articles. Analyses like those of Fahnestock (1986) and

Gilbert and Mulkay (1984) have demonstrated that the texts scientists write for "outsiders" (like entry-level textbooks) are quite different than those they produce for "insiders" (like theoretical and experimental journal articles). And in some ways, Eliza was a different reader—with different goals, strategies, knowledge, and rhetorical sophistication—when she read these different kinds of texts.

"*Natural" development.* To students of life-span studies or developmental psychology, Eliza's growth in rhetorical sophistication echoes other studies of college-age adults, most notably that of Perry (1970) and of Belenky et al. (1986). We have already seen some of the ways that the changes in Eliza's views about facts and discourse in science illustrate various positions in the Belenky et al. scheme: As a freshman she seemed to view knowledge as something to be received—therefore her almost overriding attention to "what the book says." Later, she exhibited characteristics of the procedural knower, and as a senior she looked, at times, like a separate knower and at other times like a connected knower. While Belenky et al. were careful to caution that the positions of knowing that they described are not stages or part of a developmental progression, at least in Eliza's case, one way of knowing did seem to give way to others.

Perry's (1970) study of Harvard undergraduate males (to which Belenky et al. [1986] provided something of a corrective) more explicitly chronicled a movement by undergraduates in how they view knowledge and authority, especially in terms of their schoolwork. According to Perry, there are nine positions in the developmental scheme, as students move from dualism to multiplism to relativism and finally to commitment. Like the current study, Perry was especially interested in the outlook which "perceives man's [sic] knowledge and values as relative, contingent, and contextual" (p. 57). Early in her college career, Eliza, like Perry's dualist, viewed knowledge as information, correct and incorrect information, with authorities (in Eliza's case, textbooks) embodying correct or true information. As a multiplist, she began to see that authors hold various positions on values (in the English class) and later, that different biologists hold different views of nature. As a senior, Eliza exhibited characteristics of the contextual relativist (who understands that truth depends on context) and even of commitment, as she more closely identified herself with a field of study and indirectly with the values of that field. Interestingly, I saw little evidence that Eliza ever held the extreme relativist position Perry described (in which no truth or values exist) or the extreme subjective position Belenky et al. described (in which all knowledge is personal and private). Possibly, as a member of a culture that highly esteems science and as an individual who never really questioned the value and contributions of science, Eliza found these positions simply untenable.

It is possible, then, to see Eliza moving through various positions in the 77
Perry (1970) and Belenky et al. (1986) schemes. However, as Bizzell (1984) has forcefully argued, Perry's scheme (and, I would argue, the scheme of Belenky et al. as well) does not in fact describe strictly "developmental," that is, natural or inevitable, stages. Rather, Perry's work described the results of a certain kind of education or enculturation—and the philosophical assumptions that Perry's subjects acquired were often ones they chose, not ones that were genetically preprogrammed. Similarly, while I would not claim that Eliza set out with the goal of viewing science rhetorically, she clearly did want to emulate the graduate students and professors with whom she worked—recall the statements that "I'm learning to be a scientist," "I'm becoming a scientist," and "I am a scientist." Interestingly, Perry attributed his subjects' development to the classics-based liberal arts education at Harvard. Although Eliza, as a senior, ended up resembling subjects at the upper ends of the Perry scheme, her education was quite different, a classically scientific one, with minimal exposure to humanities or liberal arts courses.

Mentoring in a sociocultural setting. Seeing education as the process of 78
becoming an insider leads to the fourth possible explanation, namely, that the context of Eliza's work experience directly supported her education in biology. Beginning in the summer between her sophomore and junior years, Eliza began to work as an assistant performing routine tasks in the lab of one of her professors, under the direct supervision of one of the professor's graduate students. As the linguistic analysis of human agents mentioned in the interviews revealed, Shelly became quite important to Eliza, making up a full 10% of the mentions of human agents in the interviews from Eliza's senior year. Other studies have suggested that the mentoring that Shelly provided for Eliza may be very important for students entering academic disciplines. Theorists of education like Brown et al. (1989) have postulated that "cognitive apprenticeship" is one mechanism by which students acquire complex skills, while feminist theorists have suggested that a strong (female) mentor can help women achieve in university settings (Belenky et al., 1986; Rich, 1979). The National Academy of Sciences (1989), in a document for students called *On Being a Scientist*, has stressed the importance of the mentor-student relationship, and a recent study by Blakeslee (1992) has shown this scientific mentoring in action in one physics research lab.

Eliza also worked within a larger team of scientists as she participated in the 79
day-to-day work of the lab. Some of her responsibilities were tedious and mundane—keeping records and cleaning equipment—but she was also responsible for other, more complex tasks, such as creating and monitoring the growth

of several protein mutants in the lab and attending staff meetings of lab personnel, including the professor. By late in her senior year, she was able to say that
"When I go to lab meetings now, I understand what they're talking about. And
it's not just Shelly's work either. It's other people who are working on the same
project. I *understand what they're saying* [emphasis hers]. It's great because I never
understood before."

Eliza's experiences in the real world setting of a lab, where students, profes-   80
sors, and other technicians worked together in the conduct of research, probably
taught her a great deal about the actual, contingent nature of much scientific
activity. Indeed, in one sense Eliza was much like Gilbert and Mulkay (1984) or
Latour and Woolgar (1979): These researchers, like Eliza, were "students" of scientific activity, and they learned a great deal about the very human enterprise of science, and its social and discourse-based nature, by watching the day-to-day operation of a research lab. Eliza may have learned the same lessons about the rhetorical
nature of science in her observations of and work in the cell biology lab.

A biologist and a chemist with whom I consulted on the project both   81
believed that, for many science students, extended experience working in a lab
(beyond class labs) is of paramount importance in facilitating a growing understanding of the scientific enterprise, describing the experience as "like a light
bulb going on" for students (J. P. Lowe, personal communication, 23 January,
1993; A. G. Stephenson, personal communication, 21 January, 1993). In fact,
the chemistry department at my own university attempts to make this experience happen sooner for students than it did for Eliza through a freshman semi-
nar, a one-credit optional course for freshman majors. Students meet one
evening a week with one or two professors, tour their labs, meet graduate students, and "learn that this world of science exists," as the coordinator of the
program, John Lowe, put it (personal communication, 23 January, 1993).

CONCLUDING COMMENTS

This study offers a detailed, fine-grained look at one student's development over   82
time, something we could not see in a study designed to address similar questions with groups of students of different ages. Another of the real benefits of
this kind of research—longitudinal, in-depth case study—is that it allows a
richer picture of an individual. Multiple data sources enrich our view of Eliza
and her learning, and observing her over time cautions us against making gener-
alizations about her abilities or her thinking. Because many of Eliza's teachers
knew her for only a semester or possibly a year, they may have had limited
knowledge of her long-term educational and career goals and of her history as a
learner. Indeed, it is interesting to contemplate how different our views of stu-

dents might be, and how our teaching might differ as well, if we were able to learn about our students over a period of years rather than weeks.

As I suggested in the opening paragraphs of this article, we are beginning to understand a great deal about expert literate practice in a number of domains, both within and beyond the academy (Bazerman & Paradis, 1991; Geisler, in press; Nelson, Megill, & McCloskey, 1987; Simons, 1990). Our students, however, may not approach academic reading and writing with the same theories that disciplinary insiders do about how discourse works. We need to know more about the kinds of theories of discourse that students hold when they arrive in college, and how these theories are reinforced or challenged by the instruction they receive across the university. And, if students do approach academic texts as autonomous rather than rhetorically and socially configured, it may be because such theories have served them well in a culture of schooling that emphasizes the retention of information. As I have suggested, one of the tasks of disciplinary education at the postsecondary level may be to help students move beyond theories of texts as autonomous to richer, more complex rhetorical theories of discourse. We need to know more, as well, about the complex of social, institutional, and cognitive factors that support this kind of learning, because to be literate involves not only attaining the skills to perform complex acts of reading and writing, but developing the rhetorical knowledge to understand and use the myriad contexts surrounding, supporting, and linking texts. Longitudinal studies provide one rewarding way to read students' stories of rhetorical development, reminding us that the stories of students' learning are not simple ones, and neither will be the theories that account for those stories.

NOTES

1. Scholars of the rhetoric of science are not in complete agreement about the precise relationship between science and rhetoric, however. A range of positions—from "science *uses* rhetoric" to "science is rhetoric"—are possible. See Simons (1990) for an overview of some of these controversies.

2. My comments here should not be construed as an indictment of teachers—within the sciences or elsewhere—or of secondary schools in general. As we shall see later, Eliza was in many ways very well-served by her previous science education. My claim (and it is not original) is that the myth of the autonomous text grows out of an entire *culture* of schooling, illustrated most powerfully for me by Goodlad's (1984) book *A Place Called School*. For a variety of reasons, many of them discussed by Goodlad, this culture often strips human context and rhetorical motive away from the learning of facts and concepts.

3. Currently, Eliza is less than 2 years away from a PhD in biology, conducting immune-system research in cell biology and coauthoring papers with her major professor. Her family continues to be supportive, says Eliza: "I'll be the first doctor—well, Ph.D.—in the family!"

4. For writing sessions, Eliza also noted whether she used a computer or pen and paper for composing. This data was used for a separate study (see Haas, 1989).

REFERENCES

Applebee, A. N. (1984). *Contexts for learning to write*. Norwood, NJ: Ablex.

Argyle, M., Furnham, A., & Graham, J. A. (1981). *Social situations*. London: Cambridge University Press.

Austin, J. L. (1962). *How to do things with words*. Oxford: Clarendon Press.

Bartholomae, D. (1985). Inventing the university. In M. Rose (Ed.), *When a writer can't write* (pp. 134–165). New York: Guilford.

Bazerman, C. (1985). Physicists reading physics: Schema-laden purposes and purpose-laden schema. *Written Communication, 2*, 3–23.

Bazerman, C. (1988). *Shaping written knowledge: The genre and activity of the experimental article in science*. Madison: University of Wisconsin Press.

Bazerman, C., & Paradis, J. (Eds.). (1991). *Textual dynamics of the professions*. Madison: University of Wisconsin Press.

Beach, R., Appleman, D., & Dorsey, S. (1990). Adolescents' use of intertextual links to understand literature. In R. Beach & S. Hynds (Eds.), *Developing discourse practices in adolescence and adulthood* (pp. 224–245). Norwood, NJ: Ablex.

Belenky, M. F., Clinchy, B. M., Goldberger, N. R., & Tarule, J. M. (1986). *Women's ways of knowing*. New York: Basic Books.

Belsey, C. (1980). *Critical practice*. London: Methuen.

Bereiter, C., & Scardamalia, M. (1987). *The psychology of written composition*. Hillsdale, NJ: Lawrence Erlbaum.

Berkenkotter, C., Huckin, T., & Ackerman, J. (1988). Conversation, conventions, and the writer. *Research in the Teaching of English, 22*, 9–44.

Biesecker, B. A. (1989). Rethinking the rhetorical situation from within the thematic of *differance*. *Philosophy and Rhetoric, 22*, 110–130.

Bitzer, L. F. (1968). The rhetorical situation. *Philosophy and Rhetoric, 1*, 1–14.

Bizzell, P. (1982). College composition: Initiation into the academic discourse community. *Curriculum Inquiry, 12*, 191–207.

Bizzell, P. (1984). William Perry and liberal education. *College English, 46*, 447–454.

Blakeslee, A. M. (1992). *Inventing scientific discourse: Dimensions of rhetorical knowledge in physics*. Unpublished doctoral dissertation, Carnegie Mellon University, Pittsburgh.

Brandt, D. (1990). *Literacy as involvement: The acts of writers, readers, and texts*. Carbondale: Southern Illinois University Press.

Brown, J. S., Collins, A., & Duguid, P. (1989). Situated cognition and the culture of learning. *Educational Researcher, 18*, 32–42.

Cazden, C. (1989). The myth of autonomous text. In D. M. Topping, D. C. Crowell, & V. N. Kobayashi (Eds.), *Thinking Across Cultures: Third International Conference on Thinking* (pp. 109-122). Hillsdale, NJ: Lawrence Erlbaum.

Charney, D. (1993). A study in rhetorical reading: How evolutionists read "The spandrels of San Marco." In J. Selzer (Ed.), *Understanding scientific prose* (pp. 203–231). Madison: University of Wisconsin Press.

Chase, W. G., & Simon, H. A. (1973). Perception in chess. *Cognitive Psychology, 4*, 55–81.

Fahnestock, J. (1986). The rhetorical life of scientific facts. *Written Communication, 3*, 275–296.

Farr, M. (1993). Essayist literacy and other verbal performances. *Written Communication, 8*, 4–38.

Fensham, P. J. (1985). Science for all: A reflective essay. *Journal of Curriculum Studies, 17*, 415–435.

Fish, S. (1980). *Is there a text in this class? The authority of interpretive communities*. Cambridge, MA: Harvard University Press.

Geertz, C. (1983). *Local knowledge: Further essays in interpretive anthropology*. New York: Basic Books.

Geisler, C. (1990). The artful conversation: Characterizing the development of advanced literacy. In R. Beach & S. Hynds (Eds.), *Developing discourse practices in adolescence and adulthood* (pp. 93–109). Norwood, NJ: Ablex.

Geisler, C. (1991). Toward a sociocognitive model of literacy: Constructing mental models in a philosophical conversation. In C. Bazerman & J. Paradis (Eds.), *Textual dynamics and the professions* (pp. 171–190). Madison: University of Wisconsin Press.

Geisler, C. (in press). *Academic literacy and the nature of expertise*. Hillsdale, NJ: Lawrence Erlbaum.

Gilbert, G. N., & Mulkay, M. (1984). *Opening Pandora's box: A sociological analysis of scientists' discourse*. Cambridge: Cambridge University Press.

Goetz, J. P., & LeCompte, M. D. (1984). *Ethnography and qualitative design in educational research*. Orlando, FL: Academic Press.

Goodlad, J. I. (1984). *A place called school: Prospects for the future*. New York: McGraw-Hill.

Gould, S. J. (1993). Fulfilling the spandrels of world and mind. In J. Selzer (Ed.), *Understanding scientific prose* (pp. 310–336). Madison: University of Wisconsin Press.

Gragson, G., & Selzer, J. (1990). Fictionalizing the readers of scholarly articles in biology. *Written Communication, 7*, 25–58.

Grice, H. P. (1975). Logic and conversation. In P. Cole & J. Morgan (Eds.), *Syntax and semantics. Vol. 3. Speech acts* (pp. 41–58). New York: Academic Press.

Haas, C. (1989). "Seeing it on the screen isn't really seeing it": Computer writers' reading problems. In G. E. Hawisher & C. L. Selfe (Eds.), *Critical perspectives on computers and composition instruction* (pp. 16–29). New York: Teachers College Press.

Haas, C. (1991, March). *Learning to read in college: Case studies of college readers in history and biology*. Paper presented at the Conference on College Composition and Communication, Boston.

Haas, C. (1993). Beyond just the facts: Reading and writing as rhetorical action. In A. Penrose & B. Sitko (Eds.), *Hearing ourselves think: Cognitive research in the college writing classroom* (pp. 19–32). New York: Oxford University Press.

Haas, C., & Flower, L. (1988). Rhetorical reading strategies and the construction of meaning. *College Composition and Communication, 39*, 167–183.

Harding, S. (1986). *The science question in feminism*. Ithaca, NY: Cornell University Press.

Haswell, R. H. (1988a). Dark shadows: The fate of writers at the bottom. *College Composition and Communication, 39*, 303–315.

Haswell, R. H. (1988b). Error and change in college student writing. *Written Communication, 5*, 479–499.

Haswell, R. H. (1991). *Gaining ground in college writing: Tales of development and interpretation*. Dallas: SMU Press.

Herndl, C. G., Fennell, B. A., & Miller, C. R. (1991). Understanding failures in organizational discourse. In C. Bazerman & J. Paradis (Eds.), *Textual dynamics and the professions* (pp. 279–304). Madison: University of Wisconsin Press.

Herrington, A. (1985). Writing in academic settings: A study of the contexts for writing in two college chemical engineering courses. *Research in the Teaching of English, 19*, 331–359.

Herrington, A. (1992). Composing one's self in a discipline. In M. Secor & D. Charney (Eds.), *Constructing rhetorical education* (pp. 91–115). Carbondale: Southern Illinois University Press.

Huckin, T., & Flower, L. (1991). Reading for points and purposes. *Journal of Advanced Composition, 11*, 347–362.

Hynds, S. (1989). Bringing life to literature and literature to life. *Research in the Teaching of English, 23*, 30–61.

Jamieson, K. H. (1973). Generic constraints and the rhetorical situation. *Philosophy and Rhetoric, 6*, 162–170.

Kaufer, D. S., Geisler, C., & Neuwirth, C. M. (1989). *Arguing from sources: Exploring issues through reading and writing*. San Diego: Harcourt Brace Jovanovich.

Keller, E. F. (1983). *A feeling for the organism*. San Francisco: Freeman.

Latour, B. (1987). *Science in action*. Cambridge: Harvard University Press.

Latour, B., & Woolgar, S. (1979). *Laboratory life: The social construction of scientific facts*. Beverly Hills, CA: Sage.

McCarthy, L. P. (1987). A stranger in strange lands: A college student writing across the curriculum. *Research in the Teaching of English, 21*, 233–265.

McCarthy, L. P., & Fishman, S. (1991). Boundary conversations: Conflicting ways of knowing in philosophy and interdisciplinary research. *Research in the Teaching of English, 25*, 419–468.

McCloskey, D. N. (1985). *The rhetoric of economics*. Madison: University of Wisconsin Press.

Mishler, E. G. (1979). Meaning in context: Is there any other kind? *Harvard Educational Review, 49*, 1–19.

Mitman, A. L., Mergendoller, J. R., Marchman, V. A, & Packer, M. J. (1987). Instruction addressing the components of scientific literacy and its relation to student outcomes. *American Educational Research Journal, 24*, 611–633.

Myers, G. (1985). The social construction of two biologists' proposals. *Written Communication, 2*, 219–245.

Myers, G. (1991). Stories and style in two molecular biology review articles. In C. Bazerman & J. Paradis (Eds.), *Textual dynamics and the professions* (pp. 45–75). Madison: University of Wisconsin Press.

National Academy of Sciences. (1989). *On being a scientist*. Washington, DC: National Academy of Sciences Press.

Nelson, J. (1990). This was an easy assignment: How students interpret academic writing tasks. *Research in the Teaching of English, 24*, 362–396.

Nelson, J. S., Megill, A., & McCloskey, D. N. (1987). *The rhetoric of the human sciences*. Madison: University of Wisconsin Press.

Nystrand, M. (1986). *The study of written communication: Studies in reciprocity between writers and readers*. New York: Academic Press.

Nystrand, M. (1987). The role of context in written communication. In R. Horowitz & J. Samuals (Eds.), *Comprehending oral and written language* (pp. 197–212). New York: Academic Press.

Patton, M. Q. (1980). *Qualitative evaluation methods*. Beverly Hills, CA: Sage.

Penrose, A. M., & Fennell, B. A. (1992, April). *Agency and proof in scientific prose*. Paper presented at the annual meeting of the American Educational Research Association, San Francisco.

Perry, W. G., Jr. (1970). *Forms of intellectual and ethical development in the college years: A scheme*. New York: Holt, Rinehart & Winston.

Rich, A. (1979). Toward a woman-centered university. In *On lies, secrets, and silence* (pp. 125–155). New York: Norton.

Rorty, R. (1979). *Philosophy and the mirror of nature*. Princeton, NJ: Princeton University Press.

Scardamalia, M., Bereiter, C., & Goelman, H. (1982). The role of production factors in writing ability. In M. Nystrand (Ed.), *What writers know* (pp. 173–210). New York: Academic Press.

Scribner, S., & Cole, M. (1981). *The psychology of literacy*. Cambridge, MA: Harvard University Press.

Searle, J. (1979). *Speech acts*. Cambridge: Cambridge University Press.

Selzer, J. (1993). Introduction. In J. Selzer (Ed.), *Understanding scientific prose*. Madison: University of Wisconsin Press.

Simons, H. W. (1990). The rhetoric of inquiry as an intellectual movement. In H. Simons (Ed.), *The rhetorical turn: Invention and persuasion in the conduct of inquiry* (pp. 1–34). Chicago: University of Chicago Press.

Stotsky, S. (1991). On developing independent critical thinking: What we can learn from studies of the research process. *Written Communication, 8*, 193–212.

Tierney, R. J., LaZansky, J., Raphael, T., & Cohen, P. (1987). Authors' intentions and readers' interpretations. In R. Tierney, P. L. Anders, & J. Mitchell (Eds.), *Understanding readers' understanding* (pp. 205–226). Hillsdale, NJ: Lawrence Erlbaum.

Tompkins, J. P. (1980). *Reader-response criticism: From formalism to poststructuralism*. Baltimore: Johns Hopkins.

van Dijk, T. (1987). Episodic models in discourse processing. In R. Horowitz & J. Samuals (Eds.), *Comprehending oral and written language* (pp. 161–196). New York: Academic Press.

Vatz, R. E. (1973). The myth of the rhetorical situation. *Philosophy and Rhetoric, 6*, 154–161.

Vipond, D., & Hunt, R. A. (1984). Point-driven understanding: Pragmatic and cognitive dimensions of literary reading. *Poetics, 13*, 261–277.

Winsor, D. A. (1989). An engineer's writing and the corporate construction of knowledge. *Written Communication, 6*, 270–285.

Mark Sagoff is a senior research scholar at the Institute for Philosophy and Public Policy at the University of Maryland and the author of two books: *The Economy of the Earth: Philosophy, Law, and the Environment* (1988) and *Price, Principle, and the Environment* (2004). He has also published over 100 articles on a range of subjects including the environment, biotechnology, morality, and economics. He previously taught at Cornell, Princeton, and the University of Wisconsin at Madison and has won grants from various foundations, including the National Endowment for the Humanities. He is a former president of the International Society for Environmental Ethics, has been a member of the Science Advisory Board of the Committee on the Valuation of Ecosystem Services in the Environmental Protection Agency since 2003, and has been a fellow of the American Association for the Advancement of Science since 2000.

ZUCKERMAN'S DILEMMA: A PLEA FOR ENVIRONMENTAL ETHICS

Mark Sagoff

Many of us recall from childhood—or from reading to our own children— E. B. White's story of the spider Charlotte and her campaign to save Wilbur, a barnyard pig.[1] Charlotte wove webs above Wilbur's sty proclaiming the pig's virtues in words—"TERRIFIC," "RADIANT," and "HUMBLE"—she copied from newspaper advertisements salvaged by a helpful rat. Wilbur won a special prize at the county fair. Moved by these events, Zuckerman, the farmer who owned Wilbur, spared him from being sent to market. Charlotte saved Wilbur's life.   1

"Why did you do all this for me?" the pig asks at the end of Charlotte's Web. "I don't deserve it. I've never done anything for you."   2

"You have been my friend," Charlotte replied. "That in itself is a tremendous thing. I wove my webs for you because I liked you. After all, what's a life, anyway? We're born, we live a little while, we die. A spider's life can't help being something of a mess, what with all this trapping and eating flies. By helping you, perhaps I was trying to lift up my life a little. Heaven knows, anyone's life can stand a little of that" (p. 164).   3

Charlotte's Web illustrates three ways we value nature. First, nature benefits us. Nature is useful: it serves a purpose, satisfies a preference, or meets a need. This is the instrumental good. Traders have this kind of value in mind when they bid on pork belly futures. Price is the usual measure of the instrumental good.   4

Mark Sagoff, "Zuckerman's Dilemma: A Plea for Environmental Ethics." © The Hastings Center. Reprinted by permission. This article originally appeared in *The Hastings Center Report*, vol. 21, no. 5 (1991).

Second, we may value nature as an object of knowledge and perception.   5
This is the aesthetic good.[2] While the basis of instrumental value lies in our
wants and inclinations, the basis of aesthetic value lies in the object itself—in
qualities that demand an appreciative response from informed and discriminat-
ing observers. The judges who awarded Wilbur a prize recognized in him superb
qualities—qualities that made him a pig to be appreciated rather than a pig to
be consumed.

Third, we may regard an object (as Charlotte did Wilbur) with love or   6
affection. Charlotte's love for Wilbur included feelings of altruism, as we would
expect, since anyone who loves a living object (we might include biological systems and communities) will take an interest in its well-being or welfare. Love
might also attach to objects that exemplify ideals, aspirations, and commitments that "lift up" one's life by presenting goals that go beyond one's own welfare. We might speak of "love of country" in this context. Objects of our love
and affection have a moral good, and, if they are living, a good of their own.

Aesthetic value depends on qualities that make an object admirable of its   7
kind; when these qualities change, the aesthetic value of the object may change
with them. With love, it is different. Shakespeare wrote that love alters not
where it alteration finds, and even if this is not strictly true, love still tolerates
better than aesthetic appreciation changes that may occur in its object.

Although love is other-regarding in that it promotes the well-being of its   8
object, it does not require actions to be entirely altruistic. Only saints are completely selfless, and it is hardly obvious that we should try to be like them.[3]
Nevertheless, anyone's life can stand some dollop of idealistic or altruistic
behavior, as Charlotte says.

When we regard an object with appreciation or with love, we say it has   9
intrinsic value, by which we mean that we value the object itself rather than just
the benefits it confers on us. This essay concerns the intrinsic value of nature in
its relation to environmental policy. The two forms of intrinsic value—aesthetic
and moral—differ in important ways, as one would expect, since moral value
arises in the context of action, while aesthetic value has to do with perception. I
shall touch on these differences, but I do not have space to explicate them here.
Those of us who wish to protect estuaries, forests, species, and other aspects of
nature may give any of three kinds of arguments—instrumental, aesthetic, or
moral—to support our conviction. We might argue on instrumental grounds, for
example, that we should save species for their possible medicinal applications, or
rain forests because they add to global oxygen budgets. An aesthetic argument,
in contrast, would point to the magnificent qualities a ten-thousand-year-old forest or estuary may possess. In nature we find perhaps for the last time in history
objects commensurate with our capacity to wonder.

A moral argument describes obligations we have toward objects of nature   10
insofar as we regard them with reverence, affection, and respect. Such an argument may contend that humanity confronts a great responsibility in learning to
share the world with other species. Love of or respect for the natural world
increases our stature as moral beings, and it may teach us to be critical of and to
change our preferences and desires. By taking an interest in the welfare of some
creature beside herself, Charlotte too found there is more to life than "all this
trapping and eating flies."

Within the next decade or two, we shall decide the fate of many estuaries,   11
forests, species, and other wonderful aspects of the natural world. How can we
justify efforts to protect them? Will instrumental or prudential arguments do the
trick? If not, how will we justify the sacrifices we must make to save our evolutionary and ecological heritage?

Why Save the Whales?   Consider, as a real-world example, whales. Two centuries   12
ago, whale oil fetched a high price because people used it in lamps. Whales had
instrumental value. Electric lights are better and cheaper than oil lamps;
accordingly, there is little or no market for whale oil today.

Why, then, do so many people care about saving whales? Is it for instru-   13
mental reasons? Are they concerned about maintaining a strategic reserve of
blubber? Do they worry that the seas might fill up with krill? No; as whales have
lost their instrumental value, their aesthetic and moral worth has become all
the more evident.

Whale oil has substitutes in a way that whales do not. We get along easily   14
without whale oil because electricity lights our lamps. The extinction of whales,
in contrast, represents an aesthetic and moral loss—something like the destruction of a great painting or the death of a friend. Life goes on, of course, but we
mourn such a loss and, if we caused it, we should feel guilty or ashamed of it. No
one cares about the supply of whale oil, but we do care about the abundance of
whales. Aesthetic and moral value attaches to those animals themselves rather
than to any function they serve or benefit they confer on us. When they perish,
all that was valuable about them will perish with them.

Fungibility as the Mark of the Instrumental.   Insofar as we care about an object for   15
instrumental reasons, we would accept a substitute—for example, ball point
pens in place of quills—if it performs the same function at a lower cost. The
market price of any object should in theory not exceed that of the cheapest
substitute.

With intrinsic value, it is different. When we see, for example, a Jacques   16
Cousteau film about the ability of humpback whales to communicate with each
other over hundreds of miles, we are properly moved to admire this impressive

species. That we can fax junk mail faster and farther is irrelevant. We admire the ability of these whales to do what they do. It is this species we admire; its qualities demand admiration and attention.

Similarly, love is not transferable but attaches to the individuals one hap-   17
pens to love. At one time, people had children, in part, because they needed them as farm hands. Today, we think the relation between parents and children should be primarily moral rather than instrumental. One can purchase the services of farmhands and even of sexual partners, but our relationship to hired labor or sex is nothing like our relationship to children or spouses. We would not think of trading a child, for example, for a good tractor.

Technology, though still in its infancy, promises to do for many aspects of   18
nature what it has done for whales and for children, namely, to make us economically less dependent on them. This need not concern us. That we no longer require whales for oil or children for tending bobbins does not imply that we cease to value them. The less we depend on nature economically, the more we may find that the reasons to value species, forests, estuaries, and other aspects of nature are not instrumental but aesthetic and moral.

Why Protect the Natural Environment?   We undertake many environmental programs   19
primarily to protect the well-being of nature, even if we defend them as necessary to promote the welfare of human beings. Why, for example, did the Environmental Protection Agency ban DDT in the 1970s? The pesticide killed pelicans and other wildlife; that was the reason to prohibit its use. EPA banned it, however, as a human carcinogen—which it is not.[4] Today we should make no such pretense.[5] The new Clean Air Act undertakes an expensive program to control acid rain. The law does not pretend that acid rain causes cancer. It answers directly to moral and aesthetic concerns about what coal-burning power plants are doing to trees and fish.

We environmentalists often appeal to instrumental arguments for instru-   20
mental reasons, i.e., not because we believe them, but because we think that they work. I submit, however, that advances in technology will continue to undermine these arguments. The new biotechnologies, for example, seem poised to replace nature as the source of many cultural commodities. As one environmentalist observes: "In the years to come, an increasing number of agricultural activities are going to be taken indoors and enclosed in vats and caldrons, sealed off from the outside world."[6]

When machinery replaced child labor in mills and mines, people did not   21
stop raising children. Society found it possible to treat children as objects of love rather than as factors of production. As biotechnology industrializes agriculture, we may protect farmland for its aesthetic and symbolic value rather than for its

products. We may measure wealth not in terms of what we can consume but in terms of what we can do without—what we treasure for its own sake.

Poverty is one of today's greatest environmental and ecological problems. This is because people who do not share in the wealth technology creates must live off nature; in their need to exploit the natural commons, they may destroy it. Analogously, in an urban context, poor people have had to send their children to work in sweat shops—to survive. The problem, of course, is not that poor people have the wrong values. Extreme and deplorable inequalities in the distribution of wealth lead to the mistreatment of children and to the destruction of the environment.   22

Accordingly, I question the adequacy of the argument environmentalists often make that we must protect nature to provide for the welfare of human beings. I think it is also true that we must provide for the welfare of human beings if we are to protect the natural environment.   23

Zuckerman's Dilemma

Zuckerman faced a dilemma. He had to choose whether to butcher Wilbur (the slaughterhouse would have paid for the pig) or on moral and aesthetic grounds to spare his life.   24

What reasons have we to preserve biodiversity, protect rain forests, and maintain the quality of lakes, rivers, and estuaries? I should like to suggest that we confront Zuckerman's dilemma with respect to many of the most wonderful aspects of nature. As we come to depend on nature less and less for instrumental reasons, we may recognize more and more the intrinsic reasons for preserving it.   25

Water Pollution.   Consider, as an example, the problem of water pollution. The question I wish to ask here is whether instrumental arguments would justify the expenditure of the roughly $200 billion Americans invested between 1970 and 1984 in controlling water pollution.[7] Did this investment pay off in terms of our health, safety, or welfare? Could we conclude that, in this instance, instrumental as well as intrinsic values justify the protection of the environment?   26

I think it fair to say that the large public investment in water pollution control cannot be justified on instrumental grounds alone. The same money put into public clinics, education, or antismoking campaigns might have led to greater improvements in public safety and health. This is true in part because the major uses of water—commercial, industrial, agricultural, and municipal—are not very sensitive to water quality. Drinking water can be treated very cheaply and thus can tolerate many common pollutants. "Much of what has been said about the need for high quality water supplies," two experts write, "is more a product of emotion than logic . . . [A] plant at Dusseldorf, Germany,   27 withdraws water from the Rhine River, which is of far lower quality than the Delaware, the Hudson, or the Missouri, treats it . . . and produces quite potable drinking water."[8]

The Value of an Estuary. In the Chesapeake Bay, as in other prominent aquatic ecosystems, pollution must concern us deeply for moral and aesthetic reasons. It is not clear, however, that the harm pollution does to nature translates into damage to human health, safety, or welfare. Indeed, more pollution might be better from a strictly instrumental point of view.   28

The reason is that the major uses of the Bay are fairly insensitive to water quality. The Chesapeake possesses instrumental value as a liquid highway (Baltimore is a major port), as a sewer (tributaries drain several major cities), and as a site for a huge naval base (Norfolk). These uses affect but are not greatly affected by water quality or, for that matter, by the biological health, integrity, richness, or diversity of the Chesapeake ecosystem.   29

How does pollution affect the health of commercial and recreational fisheries in estuaries? Consider rockfish (striped bass). Environmentalists for many years deplored the pollution of the Hudson off Manhattan; they pronounced that portion of the estuary—one of the most degraded in the world—biologically dead. Developers of the Westway Project, who wished to fill the offshore waters to build condos, hired scientists who confirmed that rockfish did not and probably could not visit the polluted lower Hudson.   30

Environmentalists were able to stop the project, however, by arguing in the nick of time that even though the "interpier" area may be the most polluted ecosystem in the world, it functions as perhaps the most important, healthy, and thriving hatchery for rockfish on the Atlantic coast. The well-being of fish populations—at least as we view it—can have more to do with politics than with pollution.[9]   31

In the Chesapeake, rockfish populations rebounded after a moratorium on fishing. One might surmise, then, that while fisheries have been hurt by overharvesting, the effects of pollution are harder to prove. Bluefish, crabs, and other "scavengers" abound in polluted waters, including the Chesapeake. And organic pollutants, primarily compounds of nitrogen and phosphorus, could support oysters and other filter feeders if their populations (depleted by overfishing and natural disease) returned to the Bay.   32

Maryland's former director of tidal fisheries, recognizing the benefits of genetic engineering, argued that the Chesapeake Bay "should be run more like a farm than a wilderness."[10] He believed that the state should subsidize efforts to fabricate fish the way Frank Perdue manufactures chickens. Many experts agree that industrial mariculture, by pushing fish populations far beyond the carrying capacity of ecosystems, will render capture fisheries obsolete.[11]   33

Pollution at present levels hardly bothers boaters, which is why there are so 34
many "stinkpots" out there. Even in a "sick" estuary, a 347 Evinrude outboard
gives people what they apparently want: plenty of noise and plenty of wake.
Many recreational fish remain plentiful, and biotechnologists are engineering
others to withstand pollutants to which they now succumb. They have perfected a nonmigrating rockfish that need not transit the anoxic stem of the Bay.
(They have also perfected an acid-tolerant trout that does well in acidified
lakes.) It may not be efficient to regulate pollution to accommodate species. It
may be cheaper to regulate species to accommodate pollution.

Since a nasty jellyfish occurring naturally in the Bay makes swimming too 35
painful, recreational interest in the Chesapeake is limited in any case. Most
vacationers experience the Bay from bridges, where they sit in terrific traffic
jams on their way to resorts on the Atlantic shore. They seem willing to pay a
lot to visit the Ho Jos, discos, go gos, peep shows, and condos that stretch from
Atlantic City to Virginia Beach. If you are looking for recreational benefits people are willing to pay for, look for them there.

Why Not Pollute? We may find acts of environmental destruction to be aestheti- 36
cally and morally outrageous even if they do no damage to human health,
safety, or welfare. News reports tell us that Prince William Sound, now
"sparkling with sea life and renewed health," has produced a record salmon
catch a little more than a year after the tragic Valdez spill.[12] From a strictly
instrumental point of view, that spill was not nearly so detrimental as many
environmentalists thought. The immediate victims, more than 36,000 water-
fowl, at least 1,016 sea otters, and 144 bald eagles, have no commercial value.
Populations of wildlife will be detrimentally affected probably forever. These
animals have enormous aesthetic and moral—but little instrumental—worth.

I do not mean to suggest that water pollution, especially when it is illegal or 37
careless, is anything but morally and aesthetically outrageous. I do not mean to
minimize the harm it does. I am arguing only that pollution may represent a
failure in aesthetic appreciation and moral responsibility without representing a
market failure, that is, without impairing any of the uses we make of an estuary.
The Chesapeake will perform its major economic tasks: to function as a sewer, a
liquid highway, and a place for boating. If it were only the beneficial use rather
than the intrinsic value of the Bay that concerned us, controlling pollution further might not be worth the cost.

The Problem of Scale

"What's wrong with this argument," a reader might object, "is that it leaves out 38
the question of scale. We can get away with polluting an estuary here and there

if elsewhere healthy ecosystems support the global processes essential to life. At a local scale, an instrumental calculus may argue for industrializing a particular environment. The problem, though, is that when we apply the same calculus to every ecosystem, we end up by destroying the crucial services nature provides."

This argument has weight with respect to activities that affect the atmosphere. Scientists have shown a connection between the use of CFCs and changes in stratospheric ozone. Likewise, the excessive combustion of coal and oil threatens to change the world's climate. That we should follow policies that prudence recommends, I have no doubt. The Montreal Protocol concerning CFCs represents an important first step. Prudence also recommends that we reach similar international agreements to decrease the amount of fuel we burn and, perhaps, to increase our reliance on those forms of energy that do not involve combustion.   39

While it is urgent that we limit atmospheric pollution, this does not give us a reason to protect intrinsically valuable species or ecosystems. The pollution, degradation, and exploitation of the Chesapeake Bay, for example, has no cognizable effect on global biochemical processes. One may argue, indeed, that the more eutrophic the Bay becomes, the more carbon it will store, thus helping to counter the "greenhouse" effect. By solving the problems of the Chesapeake, we do little to solve the problems of the atmosphere. The two sets of problems arise from different causes, involve different sorts of values, and require different solutions.   40

Rain Forests.   Consider the rain forests, which seem doomed by economic progress. One can argue persuasively that humanity has no more important ethical or aesthetic task than to keep these magnificent ecosystems from being turned into particle boards and disposable diapers. Popular arguments to the effect that rain forests store net carbon or add to global oxygen budgets, however, may not be convincing.   41

Since rain forests are climax ecosystems, they absorb through the cold burning of decay as much oxygen as they release through respiration; thus the popular belief that these forests add to global oxygen budgets betrays a naivete about how climax ecosystems work.[13] One way to get a rain forest to store net carbon may be to chop it down and plant instead of trees fast-growing crops genetically designed to do very nicely in the relevant soil and climatic conditions. (The biologist Dan Janzen has described this dreadful possibility.)[14] The trees could be used to make disposable diapers which, after use, would go to landfills where they would store carbon nearly forever.   42

Biodiversity.   Anyone with any moral or aesthetic sense must agree that another of humanity's greatest responsibilities today is to arrest shameful and horrendous rates of extinction. Yet one is hard pressed to find credible instrumental argu-   43 ments for protecting endangered species in their habitats. The reason that we produce Thanksgiving turkeys by the millions while letting the black-footed boobie become extinct is that one bird has instrumental value while the other has not. The boobie had no ecological function; it was epiphenomenal even in its own habitat. Its demise in no way contributed, for example, to the loss of stratospheric ozone or to the "greenhouse" effect.

Environmentalists, to justify their efforts to protect biological diversity, sometimes speculate that exotic species might prove useful for medical purposes, for instance. No public health professional, as far as I know, has vouched for this proposition. Pharmaceutical companies are not known for contributing to the Nature Conservancy or for otherwise encouraging efforts to preserve biodiversity. They are interested in learning from folk medicine, but they cannot even think of tracking down, capturing, and analyzing the contents of millions of species (many of them unidentified) each of which may contain thousands of compounds. 44

If pharmaceutical companies wanted to mine exotic species, they would not preserve them in their habitats. They might trap and freeze them or sequence their genes for later reconstruction. Seed companies would likewise store germ tissue in banks, not leave it in the wild. Capturing and freezing specimens, not preserving habitats, would be the way to go, to make biodiversity benefit us. 45

Even a single endangered species enlists our respect and admiration, since (as one observer has said) it would require another heaven and earth to produce such a being. The grand diversity of life, particularly the existence of rare and exotic species, presents a profound moral obligation for civilization, which is to share the earth peaceably with other species. This obligation exists whether or not we can defend the preservation of species on grounds of self-interest rather than morality. The destruction of biodiversity may be immoral, even sinful, without being irrational or imprudent. 46

A Plea for Environmental Ethics

In an old movie, a character played by W. C. Fields, having, it appears, negligently killed a baby, confronts its hysterical mother. Eyeing her youthful figure, he says: "No matter, madam; I would be happy to get you with another." 47

What we find chilling in this scene is Fields's appeal wholly to instrumental value. He sees nothing wrong with killing a baby as long has he can "get" its mother with another child who, one day, will be equally capable of supporting her in her old age. To Fields, objects have only instrumental value; we can evaluate all our actions in terms of costs and benefits. They have no other meaning. 48

Moral Value—a Benefit or Cost? The scene in the movie might remind us of the way the EXXON Corporation dealt with public outrage over the recent 49 unpleasantness in Prince William Sound. The corporation assured everyone that the salmon fishery would bounce back. If anyone was out of pocket, EXXON would lavishly compensate them. EXXON said to the outraged public: "No matter, madam; we will be happy to make you at least as well off."

From the point of view of instrumental value alone, both Fields and EXXON   50
were correct. They could replace whatever was lost with equally beneficial or useful substitutes. Another baby could grow up to plow land or tend bobbins as well as the first. The mother's income in old age would not decrease. EXXON too would make up lost income. Isn't it irrational, then, for people to complain when children are killed or wildlife is destroyed? From the point of view of instrumental value, they aren't worth much. They may have meaning, but they confer few benefits on us. They make demands on us. They are mostly costs.

Indeed, raising children, preserving nature, cherishing art, and practicing   51
the virtues of civil life are all costs—the costs of being the people we are. Why do we pay these costs? We can answer only that these costs are benefits; these actions justify themselves; these virtues are their own reward.

I wonder, therefore, whether we environmentalists do well to argue for   52
environmental protection primarily on instrumental rather than on moral and aesthetic grounds. Are the possible medicinal or agricultural uses of rare and endangered species really what we care about? We might as well argue that we should protect whales for the sake of their oil or sea otters to harvest their teeth. I think the destruction and extinction of wildlife would horrify us even if we knew sea otter, murres, and eagles would never benefit us. How do we differ from Charlotte, then, who saved Wilbur even though he did nothing for her?

Preference versus Judgment.   "The distinction between instrumental and intrinsic   53
value," someone may object, "lies beside the point of environmental policy, since a cost-benefit analysis, based in willingness-to-pay estimates, can take both sorts of preferences into account. Whether people are willing to pay to protect wildlife for moral, aesthetic, or self-interested reasons (hunting, for example) is their business; all the policy maker needs to know is what their preferences are and how much they are willing to pay to satisfy them."

This objection misses the crucial importance of the way we choose to make   54
decisions. Consider, for example, how we determine whether a person is innocent or guilty of a crime. We might do this by sending questionnaires to a random sample of citizens to check off whether they prefer a guilty or innocent verdict and, perhaps, how much they are willing to pay for each. This method of reaching a verdict would be "rational" in the sense that it aggregates "given" preferences (data) to mathematical principles laid down in advance. The

method is also "neutral" in that it translates a data set into a social choice without itself entering, influencing, or affecting the outcome.

On the other hand, we may trust the finding of innocence or guilt to a jury 55 who are steeped in the evidence, who hear the arguments, and then, by deliberation, reach a collective judgment. This procedure, since it involves discussion and even persuasion, would not proceed from "given" preferences according to rules laid down in advance. The process or method itself is supposed to affect the result.

Which model would be most appropriate for environmental policy? Consider erosion. Public officials must assess instrumental reasons for protecting soil: they must determine how much arable land we need for crops, how much we are losing, and how best to conserve what we have. They also weigh intrinsic values, for example, what soil and its protection expresses about us or means to us as a community. Our policy, presumably, should be based not on the revealed or expressed preferences of a random sample of people, no matter how rigorous our techniques of sampling and aggregating may be, but on the judgment of responsible authorities after appropriate public consideration and debate.

Similarly, policies for civil rights, education, the arts, child labor, and the 57 environment depend on judgment—often moral and aesthetic judgment—concerning facts about the world and about ourselves, that is, about our goals and intentions as a community. People who believe we ought to save the whales, for example, do not tell us simply what they prefer; rather, they call for the reasoned agreement or disagreement of others. That is why public policy is always argued in public terms—in terms of what we ought to do, not what I happen to want.

With respect to aesthetic experience, anyone can tell you what he or she 58 likes, but not everyone can tell you what is worth appreciating. A person judges aesthetically not for himself or herself only but on the basis of reasons, arguments, or ideas that he or she believes would lead others to the same conclusion. Knowledge, experience, sensitivity, discernment—these distinguish judgments of taste from expressions of preference.

To be sure, we enjoy objects we appreciate, but we do not value these 59 objects because we enjoy them. Rather, we enjoy them because we find them valuable or, more precisely, enjoyment is one way of perceiving their value. To enjoy ecological communities aesthetically or to value them morally is to find directly in them or in their qualities the reasons that justify their protection. This is not a matter of personal preference. It is a matter of judgment and perception, which one might believe correct or mistaken, and thus argue for or against, within an open political process.

The contrast I have drawn between instrumental and intrinsic value borrows   60
a great deal, of course, from Kant, who summed up the distinction as follows.
"That which is related to general human inclination and needs has a market
price . . . But that which constitutes . . . an end in itself does not have a mere
relative worth, i.e., a price, but an intrinsic worth, i.e., a dignity."[15] Kant believed
that dignity attaches to objects because of what they are and, therefore, how we
judge them. The discovery of what things are—whether it is their moral, aesthetic, or scientific properties—has to do with knowledge. Like any form of
knowledge it is inter-subjective: it represents not the preference of individuals but
the will, the perception, or the considered opinion of a community.

Are Values Relative?   While many Americans may share an environmental   61
ideology—the United States has been described as Nature's Nation[16]—this does
not apply everywhere. Even if the love of nature belongs to most cultures, moreover, it might express itself in different ways. The Japanese may not experience
whales as we do; *Moby Dick* is one of our classics. Italians, who treasure their
artistic heritage, might as soon eat as listen to a song bird. How can we expect
other cultures to respond to nature in the ways we do?

This kind of question may lead environmentalists to suppose that instru-   62
mental arguments for protecting nature have a universality that intrinsic arguments do not. Yet instrumental arguments depend on interpretations of fact—
models of climate change, for example—that invite all kinds of disagreement.
And ethical issues arise, moreover, even when instrumental concerns are paramount, such as when determining how much industrialized and developing
nations should cut back combustion to counter global warming. It may be easier
to persuade, attract, or cajole other nations to cooperate (if not agree) with our
moral and aesthetic concerns than with our reading of prudence or self-interest.
The process of reaching agreement is the same, however, whether instrumental
or intrinsic values are at stake.

Living with Nature.   I have argued that we ought to preserve nature for its sake and   63
not simply our benefit. How far, however, should we go? The Chesapeake Bay
commends itself to us for intrinsic but also for instrumental reasons. How can
we balance our need to use with our desire to protect this ecosystem?

We confront this kind of question, I believe, also in relation to people   64
whom we love and whose freedom and spontaneity we respect but with whom
we have to live. Children are examples. We could treat our children—as we
might treat nature—completely as means to our own ends. We would then simply use them to take out the empties, perform sexual favors, tend bobbins, or
whatever it is that benefits us. This would be despicable as well as criminal. We

know that morality requires that we treat our children as ends in themselves and not merely as means to our own ends.

At the same time, we have to live with our kids, and this allows us to make 65 certain demands on them, like not to wake us up too early in the morning, no matter how much we love them for their own sake. While we insist on protecting our children's innate character, independence, and integrity, we have to socialize the little devils or they will destroy us and themselves. I think this is true of nature: we can respect the integrity of ecosystems even if we change them in ways that allow us all to share the same planet.

No clear rules determine how far one should go in disciplining one's chil- 66 dren or in modifying their behavior; socialization may have fairly broad limits. But there are limits; we recognize child abuse when we see it. Have we such a conception of the abuse of nature? I think we need one. At least we should regard as signs of environmental abuse the typical results of egregious assaults on ecosystems, such as eutrophication, pandemic extinctions, and so on. We might then limit changes we make in nature by keeping this notion of ecological health—or disease—in mind.

Zuckerman's Response

William Reilly, administrator of the Environmental Protection Agency, 67 recently wrote: "Natural ecosystems . . . have intrinsic values independent of human use that are worthy of protection." He cited an advisory scientific report that urged the agency to attach as much importance to intrinsic ecological values as to risks to human health and welfare. Mr. Reilly added:

> Whether it is Long Island Sound or Puget Sound, San Francisco Bay or the Chesapeake, the Gulf of Mexico or the Arctic tundra, it is time to get serious about protecting what we love. Clearly we do love our great water bodies: . . . They are part of our heritage, part of our consciousness. Let us vow not to let their glory pass from this good Earth.[17]

In 1991 the State of Maryland offered anyone registering an automobile the 68 option of paying $20 (which would go to an environmental fund) to receive a special license plate bearing the motto: "Treasure the Chesapeake." A surprising number of registrants bought the plate. How many of us would have ponied up the $20 for a plate that read: "Use the Chesapeake Efficiently" or "The Chesapeake: It Satisfies Your Revealed and Expressed Preferences"?

To treasure the Chesapeake is to see that it has a good of its own—and 69 therefore a "health" or "integrity"—that we should protect even when to do so does not benefit us. "Why did you do all this for me?" Wilbur asked. "I've never done anything for you." Even when nature does not do anything for us—one might think, for example, of the eagles and otters destroyed in Prince William Sound—we owe it protection for moral and aesthetic reasons. Otherwise our civilization and our lives will amount to little more than the satisfaction of private preferences: what Charlotte described as "all this trapping and eating flies."

In this essay, I have proposed that we may lift up our lives a little by seeing   70
nature as Charlotte did, not just as an assortment of resources to be managed and consumed, but also as a setting for collective moral and aesthetic judgment. I have also suggested that our evolutionary heritage—the diversity of species, the miracle of life—confronts us with the choice Zuckerman had to make: whether to butcher nature for the market or to protect it as an object of moral attention and aesthetic appreciation.

If Zuckerman had not learned to appreciate Wilbur for his own sake, he   71
would have converted the pig to bacon and chops. Likewise, if we do not value nature for ethical and aesthetic reasons, then we might well pollute and degrade it for instrumental ones. If a spider could treat a pig as a friend, however, then we should be able to treat a forest, an estuary, or any other living system in the same way.

REFERENCES

1. E. B. White, *Charlotte's Web* (New York: Harper & Row, 1952).
2. In defining the instrumental and aesthetic good, I follow the analysis of Georg Henrik von Wright, *The Varieties of Goodness* (London: Routledge & Kegan Paul, 1963), pp. 19–40. Von Wright, however, uses the term technical good where I use the term aesthetic good.
3. See Susan Wolf, "Moral Saints," *Journal of Philosophy* 79 (1982): 419–39.
4. During the early 1970s an enormous investment in research led to completely inconclusive findings based on animal studies, although one prominent pharmacologist summed up the available evidence by saying that at then-current levels DDT was not a human carcinogen. For documentation, see Thomas R. Dunlap, *DDT: Scientists, Citizens, and Public Policy* (Princeton: Princeton University Press, 1981), esp. pp. 214–17. Oddly, there have been few epidemiological studies during the 1980s, but those that were ~one show no clear link between DDT exposure and cancer risk. For a review with citations, see Harold M. Schmeck, Jr., "Study Finds No Link Between Cancer Risk and DDT Exposure," *New York Times,* 14 February 1989, reporting a decade-long study of nearly 1,000 people with higher than average exposure to DDT; it found no statistically significant link between the amount of DDT in their bodies and the risk of death by cancer.

5. Scholars argue correctly, I believe, that "in the 1970s, the prevention of cancer risks was accepted as a proxy for all environmental damage." A. Dan Tarlock, "Earth and Other Ethics: The Institutional Issues," *Tennessee Law Review 56*, no. 1 (1988): 63 (citing the DDT controversy as an example). See also, Regulating Pesticides, National Academy of Sciences (Washington, D.C.: NAS Press, National Research Council, 1980), pp. 18–28.

6. Jeremy Rifkin, *Biosphere Politics: A New Consciousness for a New Century* (New York: Crown, 1991), p. 69.

7. Office of Policy Analysis, EPA, The Cost of Clean Air and Water, Executive Summary (1984), p. 3. For an overview of the disappointing results of water quality protection, see William Pedersen, "Turning the Tide on Water Quality," *Ecology Law Quarterly 15* (1988): 69–73.

8. A. Kneese and B. Bower, *Managing Water Quality: Economics, Technology, Institutions* (Baltimore: John Hopkins Press, Resources for the Future, 1968), p. 125.

9. For details about the Westway Project, see The Westway Project: A Study of Failure of Federal/State Relations, Sixty-Sixth Report by the Committee on Government Operations, 98th Cong. 2d Sess., HR 98–1166, Washington, D.C., U.S.G.P.O.,1984. See also Action for a Rational Transit v. West Side Highway Project, 536 F. Supp.1225 (S.D.N.Y.1982); Sierra Club v. U.S. Army Corps of Engineers, 541 F.Supp. 1327 (S.D.N.Y 1982) and 701 F.2d 1011 (2d Cir.1983). For another case history exemplifying the same point farther up the Hudson, see L. W. Barnhouse et al., "Population Biology in the Courtroom: The Hudson River Controversy," *BioScience 34*, no. 1 (1984): 14–19.

10. George Krantz is quoted in the *Washington Post*, 26 September 1984.

11. See, for example, Harold Webber, "Aquabusiness," in *Biotechnology and the Marine Sciences*, ed. R. Colwell, A. Sinskey, and E. Pariser (New York: Wiley, 1984), pp. 115–16. Webber believes we depend on traditional fisheries only because the "results of recent research and development in the biotechnological sciences have not yet been integrated into the broader context of large scale, vertically integrated, high technology, centrally controlled, aquabusiness food production systems." He calls the substitution of industrial for "natural" methods of fish production in aquatic environments "Vertically Integrated Aquaculture (VIA)."

12. Jay Mathews, "In Alaska, Oil Spill Has Lost Its Sheen," *Washington Post*, 9 February 1991.

13. For discussion, see T. C. Whitmore, "The Conservation of Tropical Rain Forests," in *Conservation Biology: An Evolutionary Perspective*, ed.

M. Soule and B. A. Wilcox (Sunderland, Mass.: Sinauer, 1980), p. 313: "The suggestion, sometimes made, that atmospheric oxygen levels would be lowered by the removal of tropical rain forests rests on a mistaken view of climax ecosystems."

14. See William Allen, "Penn Prof Views Biotechnology as Potential Threat to Tropical Forests," *Genetic Engineering News* 7, no. 10 (1987): 10. The article quotes a letter by Janzen: "Tropical wildlands and most of the earth's contemporary species still exist because humanity has not had organisms capable of converting all tropical land surfaces to profitable agriculture and animal husbandry. Within one to three decades, organisms modified through genetic engineering will be capable of making agriculture or animal husbandry, or both, profitable on virtually any land surface. Agricultural inviability, the single greatest tropical conservation force, will be gone."

Some commentators have speculated that transpiration from rain forests may play some role in the atmosphere. Since more that 85 percent of water absorbed into the atmosphere comes from the oceans, however, the marginal difference—if any—in transpiration between natural and biotech species in rain forests is unlikely to be consequential.

15. Immanuel Kant, *Foundations of the Metaphysics of Morals,* ed. R. P. Wolff, trans. L. W. Beck (Indianapolis: Bobbs-Merrill, 1959), p. 53. Emphasis in original.

16. Perry Miller, *Nature's Nation* (Cambridge, Mass.: Harvard University Press, 1967).

17. William K. Reilly, "A Strategy to Save the Great Water Bodies," *EPA Journal* 16, no. 6 (1990): 4.

J. Blake Scott received his Ph.D. in English: Rhetoric and Composition at Pennsylvania State University in 1999 and has been associate professor of English at the University of Central Florida since 2002. He teaches undergraduate courses in composition, technical and professional writing, and graduate courses in rhetoric and composition, texts and technology, and technical writing. He also assists university-wide service learning projects there. Scott has published a variety of articles in journals such as *Quarterly Journal of Speech* and *Technical Communication Quarterly*. He has co-edited a book on technical communication and cultural studies, co-authored a book on service-learning in technical and professional communication, and authored *Risky Rhetoric: AIDS and the Cultural Practices of HIV Testing* (2003). He won the National Council of Teachers of English Award for best Collection of Essays on Technical and Scientific Communication (2007).

REARTICULATING CIVIC ENGAGEMENT THROUGH CULTURAL STUDIES AND SERVICE-LEARNING

J. Blake Scott

Although service-learning has the potential to infuse technical communication pedagogy with civic goals, it can easily be co-opted by a hyperpragmatism that limits ethical critique and civic engagement. Service-learning's component of reflection, in particular, can become an uncritical, narrow invention or project management tool. Integrating cultural studies and service-learning can help position students as critical citizens who produce effective and ethical discourse and who create more inclusive forms of power. Rather than being tacked on, cultural studies approaches should be incorporated into core service-learning assignments.

A growing number of technical communication teachers and students have found service-learning projects to be fulfilling extensions of their real-world writing assignments. As Thomas Deans suggests, service-learning takes sociorhetorical pedagogies to the next logical step, providing students with wider, community-based audiences, contexts, discourse communities, and modes of collaboration (9). Service-learning also provides students opportunities to develop, reflect about, and enact civic responsibility. This emphasis on civic responsibility can be motivating to students, leading them to look beyond their career preparation or their success in the course, and prompting them to engage with others in community problem-solving.

1

J. Blake Scott, "Rearticulating Civic Engagement Through Cultural Studies and Service-Learning," *Technical Communication Quarterly*, vol. 13, no. 3 (Summer 2004), pp. 289–306. Reprinted by permission of the publisher (Taylor & Francis, http://www.informaworld.com).

Yet much of service-learning's promise, including its promise of civic   2
engagement, goes unrealized in many technical communication courses. This is
largely because such courses are driven by what I call a "hyperpragmatist" ideology and set of institutional practices and structures. The main goal of this ideology is ensuring students' professional success. Although service-learning comes
out of a more robust pragmatist tradition, it can be co-opted by a hyperpragmatism that moves past critique, overlooks broader power relations and textual circulation, and narrowly positions students and their praxis.

This article argues that integrating cultural studies methods into a service-   3
learning approach can ward off this co-option. Further, the integration of the
two approaches can bring out the best of each, leading to a robust critical pedagogy of civic engagement. In such a hybrid pedagogy, students engage various
community stakeholders as partners rather than follow the directives of
"clients," and they critique and intervene in community-based practices rather
than merely conform to them. Rather than positioning students only as prepro-
fessional or critical consumers, the hybrid pedagogy I propose positions them as
what Jim Henry calls "discourse workers" who channel their cultural critiques
into discursive efforts to reshape institutional policy (11). The cultural studies
concept of articulation refers to the ongoing process by which coherent structures are produced out of linkages of various elements, such as social formations,
ideologies, identities, and practices (Hall and Grossberg 53). This article calls
for a rearticulation of technical communication pedagogy through the linkage
of service-learning and cultural studies.

In what follows, I first review the legacy of hyperpragmatism, arguing that   4
this ideology and set of practices still permeates technical communication pedagogy, limiting the civic dimension of students' work. Next, I explain how service-
learning models have the potential to develop students' civic awareness and
engagement. The practical challenges of service-learning threaten to squelch its
critical and civic potential, however, especially by relegating reflection to an
uncritical, tacked-on exercise and by limiting the scope of students' collaboration with others. Then I argue that integrating cultural studies' emphases and
strategies into a service-learning pedagogy can enable it to better ward off
hyperpragmatism. After overviewing the contributions cultural studies can
make to a pedagogy of civic engagement, I discuss more specific ways I have
integrated it into my service-learning courses and assignments, particularly as a
way to rethink approaches to user engagement.

LIMITATIONS OF HYPERPRAGMATISM

In the United States, the technical communication course developed out of   5
what Teresa Kynell calls a "milieu of utility" that characterized the vocational

education of engineers. Although the earliest versions of the course were more current traditional (i.e., formalist) than vocational, the course gradually began to incorporate more practical elements, such as various types of engineering reports. In the 1940s and 1950s, when the course moved from engineering to English and the field of technical communication emerged, curricula began to consider audience and readability more but still emphasized technical forms, to which the technical article and manual were added (Connors 340–341). Driving this utilitarianism, of course, was World War II and the technology boom it created.

Utilitarian, instrumental approaches have continued to flourish, of course, as attested by the growing corporate influence on curricula and research. Some scholars in the field have even argued that rhetorical theory is counterproductive in the technical communication course—counterproductive, that is, to the goal of training students to succeed in industry. Elizabeth Tebeaux, for example, has argued for vocational (and somewhat current traditional) training that teaches students to "document information clearly, correctly, and economically" (822). Patrick Moore has categorically dismissed rhetorical approaches in favor of instrumental ones that more closely resemble industry skills-based training.   6

As more researchers and teachers turned to social constructionist approaches, technical communication pedagogy took a more fully sociorhetorical turn. Although early process theory was quite compatible with formalist and instrumental approaches, social process theory helped move the field beyond instrumental concerns to an emphasis on praxis or social, rhetorical action. This turn brought us the emphasis on disciplinary and workplace discourse communities and their writing conventions and processes and prompted us to view students' training as enculturation (C. Miller, "Humanistic"). Yet, even these developments have not shifted the dominant vocational orientation of the field. Most research and teaching still focuses on understanding the discursive practices of organizations or disciplines in order to more effectively adhere to them. Within this paradigm, cultural study is mostly limited to the descriptive (i.e., uncritical) study of organizational culture. As Ann Blakeslee explains in the recently published collection *Reshaping Technical Communication*, which largely overlooks cultural critique and civic engagement in its focus on academic-industry collaboration, "Academic researchers often look at and then *describe* the workplace, specifically its practices and genres. Some aim to convey and *emulate* these practices and genres in the classroom" (43; emphasis added).   7

Thomas Miller and Dale Sullivan have expanded Carolyn Miller's rearticulation of technical communication as social praxis by arguing that this praxis must be located in larger public contexts and must involve the cultivation of   8 phronesis or practical wisdom. As Thomas Miller explains, this cultivation requires ethical deliberation grounded in the shared knowledge of the community (see also Scott, "Sophistic"). As I will explain shortly, service-learning can embody this more critical and civic notion of praxis.

As an ideology and set of practices, hyperpragmatism is primarily concerned with helping students understand and successfully adapt to the writing processes, conventions, and values of disciplinary and workplace discourse communities. It seeks to help students "conform to the practical conventions of writing that their future employers value most" (France 20). In his advocacy of instrumentalist pedagogy, Moore reveals his primary goal as the following: "Students will *profit* from studying instrumental discourse because they will make the transition from college to the marketplace much more easily" ("Rhetorical" 173; emphasis added). Hyperpragmatism's main priority, then, is to prepare students for successful careers. Along with conformity and effectiveness, hyperpragmatism values efficiency (the smoother students' enculturation, the better). In its more extreme forms, hyperpragmatism can be driven by what Steven Katz calls an "ethic of expediency," where expediency becomes a virtue that subsumes other ethical considerations. Katz argues that our capitalist society privileges an ethic of economic expediency by measuring success and happiness monetarily (274).

Consider, as an example of hyperpragmatism's continuing dominance, common notions of usability in our field. As Barbara Mirel points out, most of our approaches to usability can still be captured by John Gould and Clayton Lewis's 1985 definition: "Any system designed for people to use should be easy to learn (and remember), useful, . . . contain functions people really need in their work, and be easy and pleasant to use" (300; quoted in Mirel 168). Carol Barnum's more recent book on usability (and the accompanying PowerPoint presentation on the book's website) similarly defines it primarily in terms of effectiveness, efficiency, and user satisfaction. Approaches to user testing and other usability measures are often touted as ways to make the design process more efficient, please users, and save money. Such views of usability are underpinned by what Bradley Dilger calls an ideology of ease, the "culturally constructed desirability of 'making it easy' or being 'at ease' " (2). We can contrast pragmatic views of usability—grounded in efficiency and ease—with the more critical ones offered by Robert Johnson and Michael Salvo. In *User-Centered Technology*, Johnson distinguishes between user-friendly design and user-centered design. Though more efficient in the short run, a user-friendly model of design, Johnson explains, can ultimately disempower users by failing to engage them as co-designers and by keeping them dependent on experts to understand larger systems and deeper functions (28). By inviting users to be

9

10

partners in technology design from the beginning of the process, a user-centered model produces technology that is more responsive to users, empowering them to adapt the technology to their complex, dynamic contextual needs. Building on Johnson's theory and Scandinavian design theory, Salvo advances the practice of "user participatory design," which similarly involves a "sustained dialogue between user and designer, when noise becomes the material for information feedback rather than a distressing problem to be avoided or solved" (289). Such reconceptions of usability make room for ethical deliberation and civic engagement in a way that their more pragmatic counterparts do not.

In its attention to the individual development of students based on their vocational goals, hyperpragmatism is politically liberal. It also values the liberal goal of consensus, played out in our field's emphasis on collaboration. Hyperpragmatism's values of conformity and expediency are primarily conservative, however. Carl Herndl and Dale Sullivan have pointed out the tendency of technical communication research and pedagogy to reinforce dominant power relations. Even some studies and pedagogies aimed at change define such change in terms of increasing efficiency and productivity (e.g., Spilka, "Influencing"; Bernhardt); they thereby stop short of challenging the politics of standard practices.

Hyperpragmatist pedagogy is attractive in several ways, not the least of which is its accommodation of students' attitudes about and expectations of their education. Our students increasingly measure their education in terms of economic expediency. Students' self-perception as consumers of professional training (rather than, say, civic training) is tied to the larger corporatization of our field and the university. The increasing corporate sponsorship of our field has its plus side; corporate connections, including those through our trade organizations such as STC, help fund research and curricular programs. Jack Bushnell observes that many technical and professional communication programs have become corporate training grounds to reap internships, fellowships, and good-paying jobs for students (175–76). Administrators advocate corporate sponsorship for these very reasons, of course. But the corporatization of technical communication can also work to reinforce hyperpragmatist values and practices that limit students' development as citizen-rhetors.

As others have pointed out before me, the overly pragmatic orientation of the field is problematic on several counts (Herndl; Longo; C. Miller, "What's"; D. Sullivan). Hyperpragmatism's valuing of conformity can work to reinforce dominant power relations and privilege corporate interests. As Charlotte Thralls and Nancy Roundy Blyler argue, "Uncritically importing into the classroom the communication processes and practices of industry reproduces private corporate interest, making students the tools of capitalist ideology" (15). Dominant power

relations and corporate interests are disempowering for many, including technical communicators themselves, many of whom are still marginalized in the corporate cultures of "fast" capitalism as information transmitters (Henry). Hyperpragmatism can also move past or co-opt ethical deliberation and critique, partly
by pretending to be practical but not political. Although more robust hyperpragmatist pedagogies teach technical communication as praxis, they often limit this
to the social communication practices of discrete organizations, disciplines, or
professions and stop short of asking students to critique these practices (T. Miller;
D. Sullivan). Herndl points out that moving past critique, pragmatic, social
constructionist pedagogy also limits "possibilities for dissent, resistance, and revision" (349); students may therefore see little transformative power in their work.
A related limitation of hyperpragmatism is its narrow focus on discrete rhetorical
situations and the production processes of specific discourse communities. This
focus can be a useful starting point, to be sure, but it also overlooks the broader
conditions, circulation, and effects of technical communication. These limitations work together to narrowly position students as preprofessionals. Although
students are sometimes taught to be citizens of their employers and perhaps the
profession, they are too seldom taught to connect their work (and that of their
employers) to larger social issues, too seldom pushed to critique the ethical implications of their work on various publics, too seldom encouraged to engage these
various publics as audiences and even partners, and too seldom asked to reflect on
their noncorporate social responsibilities.

PROMISE AND CO-OPTION OF SERVICE-LEARNING

In response to these limitations (among other reasons) a growing number of   14
technical communication teachers have been turning to service-learning. Service-learning shares the vocational emphasis on experiential, real-world learning. The service-learning models in which students write for or with their community sponsors most clearly embody this emphasis. Service-learning also
expands the contexts of real-world learning to community-based, usually nonprofit organizations and their writing exigencies, the ethical stakes of which can
be powerful motivators for students. Further, this learning must meet community
needs and must be accompanied by structured reflection about civic responsibility. Such reflection is meant to help students gain both civic awareness and a
long-term desire to serve their communities. Leigh Henson and Kristene Sutliff
hope service-learning will help their technical writing students "ultimately
develop reasonable goals for their own roles in improving the world in which
they live" (192). In these ways, certainly, service-learning departs from or at least
adds to pragmatic goals. Like others, David Sapp and Robbin Crabtree argue that

technical communication and service-learning can make an "ideal pairing." Although typical technical communication courses often function as laboratories for professional training, they explain, an added service-learning component could function as a "companion laboratory in citizenship" that prepares students for responsible participation in democratic life (412, 426).

It is important to distinguish between the hyperpragmatism that service-learning is meant to challenge and the American educational philosophy of pragmatism to which service-learning is theoretically indebted. The latter, most fully developed by John Dewey, acknowledged the political dimensions of discourse, valued the interplay of critical reflection and action, was civic rather than narrowly vocational in scope, and had the goal of social reform. Interestingly, these are also common elements of cultural studies approaches, especially the radical pedagogy of Henry Giroux and others. Indeed, cultural critics Lawrence Grossberg and James Carey describe Dewey as an important figure in American cultural studies.

Despite this partly critical heritage, service-learning approaches to technical communication can all too easily slide into hyperpragmatism. Just as current traditional rhetoric co-opted many process approaches to first-year composition pedagogy (Crowley), hyperpragmatism has co-opted service-learning and other sociorhetorical approaches to technical communication. Nora Bacon addresses this danger when she warns against using an apprenticeship model of service-learning, arguing that such a model uncritically assimilates students into organizational discourses ("Building" 607). The co-option of service-learning by hyperpragmatism is partly the result of the powerful institutional and cultural forces that maintain it and partly the result of the unique demands of a service-learning pedagogy.

For students, the pragmatics of developing, producing, and managing service-learning projects can be challenging, to say the least. As Bacon recognizes, service-learning projects often "introduce students to a community agency one week and expect them to write in its voice the next," thereby requiring a more rapid process of enculturation ("Community" 47). Students must analyze both their sponsoring organization and their text's targeted audience. They must learn and adapt to their organization's values and discourse conventions. They must negotiate their projects in collaboration with each other, their instructor, their project sponsor, and sometimes members of their targeted audience. As part of their larger projects, students' work often involves a proposal, progress report(s), and other documents. The complex, time-consuming tasks of a service-learning project thus leave little time for reflection, ethical intervention, or anything else, especially when the project is initiated and completed within a semester.

Students' excitement about gaining valuable real-world experience and   18
working on worthwhile community projects can prevent them from critiquing
the discursive practices that they observe and participate in. In my experience,
students can get so caught up in fulfilling their duties to the organization and
pleasing their project sponsors that they fail to engage their other audiences or
consider the ethical implications of their work for these audiences.

Teachers of service-learning, too, must negotiate the challenges of finding   19
(or helping students find) appropriate sponsors, facilitating an array of student
projects (often with different sponsors), teaching students about various genres
and conventions, and evaluating the rhetorical effectiveness of student work. In
the face of such challenges, it can be easy, to focus only on the practical dimensions of service-learning projects. In addition, teachers often face the pressure of
industry-minded administrators and students to emphasize the practical, vocational benefits of service-learning. In reflecting on his previous version of service-learning, Jim Dubinsky writes, "I looked at my course in the mirror. When I
did, I saw the reflection of someone who had focused far too much on the
instrumental sense of being practical by emphasizing experiential learning's
advantages in terms of future employability" (69). Dubinsky is certainly not
alone. Technical communication scholarship on service-learning often emphasizes the vocational benefits and practical challenges of this pedagogy for students (e.g., Huckin; Matthews and Zimmerman). One way service-learning
courses (including my own) privilege the vocational is by encouraging students
to view their sponsoring organizations as practice clients whose accommodation
is their main concern. Before he adjusted his pedagogy, Dubinsky observed that
his students often "talked about *working for* clients rather than *working with* partners" (69). Unless recognized and addressed, this framing of student roles limits
their civic engagement by discouraging them from developing more reciprocal
relationships with a wider array of community stakeholders.

Hyperpragmatism's potential to co-opt service-learning is perhaps most evi-   20
dent in approaches to reflection—the key means of fostering civic awareness and,
for many of us, the most difficult and vexed part of teaching service-learning. In
service-learning courses where reflection is a significant component (in some it
is not), it is sometimes relegated to record-keeping logs or personal discovery
journals that don't facilitate critical thinking. "Journal writing in many service
courses may serve the purpose of creating a log or record of experience," Chris
Anson explains, "but falls short of encouraging the critical examination of
ideas, or the sort of consciousness-raising reflection, that is the mark of highly
successful learning" (169). Journal writing that breaks from pragmatism to
encourage personal deliberation often problematically prevents students from

recognizing the complexity of civic problems and solutions, from moving beyond uncritical empathy, and from gaining critical self-consciousness (Herzberg 59).

Reflection can also be subsumed into pragmatic invention and project   21
management exercises. Students might be asked, for example, to reflect on the ways their values intersect with those of their organization and/or audience in a rhetorical analysis exercise. Or students might analyze the ethos and conventions of their sponsoring organization, as in James Porter's forum analysis, which examines the background, discursive conventions, and other characteristics of a discourse community. Although such activities qualify as reflection in that they help students connect their projects to course goals, they rarely ask students to critique or propose interventions; instead they aim to help students better understand and negotiate their rhetorical tasks. In addition, such reflection activities can be too focused on the production process, failing to consider the subsequent transformations and effects of students' work as it is distributed and taken up.

Hyperpragmatism can also limit reflection by turning it into a project man-   22
agement tool. Some service-learning courses ask students to reflect on their collaboration, for example, or specific project challenges and their responses to these challenges. Such reflection can be incorporated into more formal assignments, such as the progress report. This type of reflection, too, can be devoid of any critical edge and simply serve as just another tool for making the service-learning project run more smoothly and efficiently.

Some teachers of service-learning are more diligent about framing reflection   23
as critical deliberation. Thomas Huckin has his students discuss the social problems addressed by their community sponsors, answering such questions as "Why are these organizations needed?" and "Why do we have such problems in our society?" (58). Sapp and Crabtree similarly encourage their students to "get a sense of the [sponsoring] agency's 'big picture'" and to reflect on the "larger social issues that give rise to the need for service" (426). Even when reflection is more critical, however, it is often tacked on as tertiary to the project, just as many technical communication textbooks and curricula tack on discussions of ethics. In addition, such reflection often takes place toward the end of the project or course, perhaps in a final evaluation report, when it is too late to act on. Students might be asked to deliberate about their documents' strengths and weaknesses or what they learned from the project, but this amounts to little more than an exercise. Such an approach to reflection may encourage students to be critical of ethical problems but not invite them to intervene in them. The practical demands of a service-learning course can override this type of reflection as well.

Bruce Herzberg points out that service-learning does not necessarily "raise   24
questions about social structure, ideology, and social justice" (59). Several
scholars, including Matthews and Zimmerman as well as Henson and Sutliff,
have argued that service-learning fosters value development and even long-term
civic engagement in technical communication students, but they don't explain
how this happens, and they present little evidence to support this claim. In
prompting his students to critically examine their relationships with community
stakeholders, Dubinsky illustrates one way we can encourage students' civic
engagement. I fear that most service-learning courses, however, are closer to
previous versions of Dubinsky's (and my) course that privileged vocational values and facilitated praxis but not phronesis. Such courses end up providing
additional and perhaps more interesting contexts for teaching the sociorhetorical pragmatics of technical communication, but they don't adequately convert
these contexts into opportunities for teaching students to recognize, critique,
and respond to the ethical implications of their work.

CONTRIBUTIONS OF CULTURAL STUDIES

Like other critical-civic traditions, including classical rhetoric, cultural studies   25
offers heuristics for extending and challenging hyperpragmatist technical communication pedagogy, as a few scholars have begun to argue. Drawing on radical
pedagogy, Herndl, for one, has called for approaches that critique the broader
relations of power inherent in technical communication and that enable ethical, public action based on this critique. I have adapted Richard Johnson's
notion of the cultural circuit to develop a heuristic that helps students critique
and respond to the broader effects of their work as it circulates and is transformed (Scott, "Tracking"). Henry's authoethnography assignment asks students to critique the ways workplace cultures (and fast-capitalist culture more
generally) position them and also to strategize ways to revise problematic
notions of professional writing and writers.

I've increasingly turned to cultural studies in particular, to ensure the criti-   26
cal and civic potency of student's service-learning work. Like service-learning,
cultural studies comes out of multiple traditions and can take various forms.
Some of these forms bear little resemblance to service-learning and its emphasis
on rhetorical production. In his argument for instilling in technical communication students an "aptitude for cultural criticism," Henry critiques some versions of cultural studies for their "insistence on forming students as critical discursive consumers, all the while wholly ignoring their formation as critical
discursive producers in any genre other than the academic essay" (10–11). In
contrast, other models of cultural studies, such as those developed by Michel

Foucault and Stuart Hall, share with service-learning a commitment to both critical awareness and ethical action.

Rather than teasing out the differences of various models, I'll offer the   27 working definition that has guided my pedagogy. As I'm defining it, cultural studies involves an ethical engagement with, critique of, and intervention into the conditions, functions, and effects of value-laden practices (including discursive ones). Also, cultural studies is as much interested in the circulation and rearticulations of cultural discourses as it is in their generic features. In contrast to approaches that stop at critical awareness or that dance around specific ethical imperatives, the main aim of the model I use is to revise problematic practices to create more egalitarian power relations and more widely beneficial effects. If it is to be effective, such intervention requires civic engagement, especially with those whom it is designed to help.

Cultural studies theory and heuristics can be especially useful to service-   28 learning projects, as such projects have the goal, however unfulfilled, of critical reflection and civic engagement. In addition, such projects require work that has explicit ethical implications and often present students with various ethical dilemmas, including how to negotiate organizational politics or how to balance their duties to their instructor, their organization, and their audiences. At the same time, service-learning can enhance a cultural studies pedagogy by providing a compelling context for students' self-critique and ethical action. A recursive loop of reflection and action is a key element of the Deweyian pragmatism on which service-learning is partly based (Deans 31).

Herndl, Scott, Henry, and others suggest several ways that cultural studies   29 can keep service-learning from lapsing into hyperpragmatism. First, a cultural studies approach requires students to assume a critical stance toward technical communication (especially their own) and the ideological systems of power that regulate it. Beyond learning to produce rhetorically effective texts, students learn to critique their texts' broader conditions and effects. Students might critique, for example, the ways their texts' production processes excludes some perspectives and privileges some values at the expense of others. Or they might interrogate spatial and other boundaries maintained by institutional structures.

Ideally, students' critique would come out of their engagement and deliber-   30 ation with community partners. Students' civic engagement might draw on Salvo's notion of user participatory design or on the similar impulses of the intercultural inquiry developed by Linda Flower, Elenore Long, and Lorraine Higgins. Flower et al. call for a community problem-solving dialogue that invites community stakeholders to be "partners in inquiry" and offer rival perspectives on the problem and its possible solutions. Such a dialogue values the unique perspectives of all participants and avoids a rush to consensus. Students engaged in intercultural inquiry might also enlist community stakeholders in assessing the effects of their work. This assessment could be based on a broader notion of accommodation that includes responsiveness (i.e., sustained, attentive engagement) and long-term empowerment as well as immediate satisfaction.

On a related note, cultural studies can also enhance service-learning by   31
expanding its sometimes narrow foci on immediate rhetorical situations, discrete discourse communities, and production processes to account for the larger cultural conditions and circulation of discourse. Although typical pragmatic heuristics such as the rhetorical triangle and forum analysis can be useful starting points, they can also lead students to overlook other conditions shaping their discourse and its transformations. In their article outlining an activist approach to service-learning, Donna Bickford and Nedra Reynolds similarly advocate helping students "make connections beyond the site of their encounter" (241). The model of the cultural circuit—which prompts students to track the trajectory of their texts' production, subsequent revision, distribution, reception, and incorporation into people's lives—can help students extend their analysis and build in ways to ensure their texts' ethical sustainability (Scott, "Tracking").

Finally, cultural studies-inflected versions of service-learning can help stu-   32
dents channel their critical engagement into discourses calling for ethical revision (Herndl 349). Such revision might occur in the students' projects themselves, particularly in their relations with others. Bickford and Reynolds pose what I think should be a central question for students in a service-learning course: How can we enter relationships "in ways that help destabilize hierarchical relations and encourage the formation of more egalitarian structures" (241)? Students might also direct their revisions—perhaps in the form of the "action plans" described by James Porter et al.—to their teachers, sponsoring organizations, and/or other community stakeholders ("Institutional"). Students might begin to create their action plan by engaging in what Patricia Sullivan and James Porter call "advocacy charting," which can help them strategize their action based on their situated relationships with others involved (Sullivan and Porter, *Opening* 183).

These cultural studies extensions of service-learning will likely complicate   33
students' service-learning projects. If we take students' civic development as seriously as their professional development, however, we will welcome such complication. To make the hybrid pedagogy I'm proposing more feasible, we might first acknowledge that most service-learning projects will not solve community problems or radically redistribute power relationships. Students will not

always be in positions of influence. This does not mean that we can't encourage students to address problems in modest ways, however. To make more time for expanded critique and engagement, we might encourage students to take on smaller technical communication projects, remembering as Dubinsky does to treat students' conduct or service as a major text of the course (64, 69). Another way to facilitate students' civic engagement is to, as Sapp and Crabtree recommend, "develop long-term relationships with the cosponsoring organizations" and other stakeholders (426). Larger service-learning projects could be broken up over multiple semesters, each set of students building on (and complicating) the work of the previous set. Students' action plans at the end of the course, for example, might be written to future students who will take up the next phase of the project. I now turn to a more sustained discussion of how I've begun to merge the pragmatic and cultural studies elements of my courses.

SPECIFIC INTEGRATIONS

I began to integrate cultural studies into my own service-learning courses, in which students produce technical or professional communication projects for nonprofit community and campus organizations, first by having students respond to critical reflection questions at different points in the semester but especially in a final evaluation report, where I asked them to critique their documents and the process that produced them. Huckin also describes structured, in-class reflection as something that happens mostly at the end of his courses (58), and Louise Rehling has her service-learning students write a final reflection essay not unlike my evaluation report. But I found that tacking on such reflection to the end of the course left critical reflection secondary to practical production and prevented students from acting on this reflection over the course of their projects.

Lately I've begun to experiment with ways to more fully integrate critical reflection, civic engagement, and ethical intervention into my service-learning courses. Following the model that Melody Bowdon and I propose in our textbook, most of my courses require semester-long projects that involve documents produced for a sponsoring organization as well as several invention and project management assignments, including a discourse analysis, a project proposal, a progress report, user testing, and a final report. These assignments, three of which I expand on below, can be revised to provide contexts for cultural critique, engagement, and action, especially with a focus on the ethics of usability.

My recent experimentation has led me to shift from requiring user testing toward the end of the project to having students consider and enact usability measures throughout the course, even before the project proposal. To make this possible, I help students choose organizations and projects that will enable easy access to their audiences and other community stakeholders. Instead of positioning users as passive subjects of testing and relegating their involvement to the end of the project, a cultural studies approach, informed by intercultural inquiry, would engage users as partners from the problem-defining stage onward. In more recent courses, I've asked students to supplement user testing and the user-test report with other mechanisms that engage stakeholders earlier in the project. A group of students producing brochures for the university's Counseling Center formed focus groups with students living in the dorms—one of their primary audiences—at the beginning of the project. The students then continued to work with the focus group throughout the project, seeking its feedback as they developed the texts' design, language, and so forth. I've had other student groups administer questionnaires to potential users and invite community stakeholders to informal proposal planning meetings.

Like many other teachers of service-learning projects, I begin with a project   37
proposal assignment. The main purpose of this assignment in a pragmatic service-learning course is to provide a blueprint of the project for the instructor, organization, and students themselves. To get to the actual projects, students are tempted to rush through the proposal writing process, which causes them to gloss over the problem and quickly decide on a solution and plan for implementing it. Some savvy students might consider their organization's definition of the problem; many, however, will not incorporate alternative perspectives on the problem and the larger conditions that make it possible.

When students form focus groups or other mechanisms for stakeholder   38
involvement early in the course, these stakeholders can help students and the organization define the problem, its significance, and its underlying causes. Flower et al. call this "getting the story behind the story." Instead of waiting until the end of the course, students can at this point deliberate about the larger cultural and institutional conditions that created and that maintain the problems addressed by their projects. In their proposal for an operations manual, a group working with a nonprofit agency promoting music education wrote about the lack of fine arts funding in U.S. education and about widespread ignorance of the benefits of music education. A group producing a leadership training video for a local Boys and Girls Club chapter considered the larger need for more community-based youth leadership programs and opportunities. A group producing job search materials for a halfway house for federal inmates connected the inmates' rhetorical situation to the institutional restraints imposed by the Federal Bureau of Prisons and to other obstacles to reentering society successfully.

Students can also ensure the responsiveness of their projects by inviting   39
stakeholders to help them brainstorm possible objectives and solutions as well
as assess the desirability and feasibility of these solutions. For example, a group
of students producing a website for a campus organization e-mailed a questionnaire to members and potential members asking them to identify what they'd
like to see the website include and do. If they do nothing else at this stage, I
require student groups to seek feedback about their project objectives from the
organization and at least a few of its clients. This feedback can help ensure that
these objectives reflect civic as well as academic and organizational goals.

In its emphasis on cultural circulation, a cultural studies approach to the   40
proposal assignment requires students to think through the changes their texts
will undergo after they are submitted to the organization; students consider not
only the life cycles of their texts but also how these texts will be transformed
along their trajectories. The organization will likely revise and distribute the
texts before they are taken up by various users, for example. This type of cultural analysis can help students plan ways to ensure the sustainability of their
texts. They could make the texts' design and delivery flexible enough to be distributed in multiple ways. In its proposal, the website group mentioned earlier
planned to make the website dynamically updateable and include help documentation on the site itself. To enable flexibility in revision and distribution,
the group producing the video planned to produce their text in various formats
(VHS, mini-DVD) and submit the raw footage.

In *Service-Learning in Technical and Professional Communication*, Bowdon   41
and I outline a progress report assignment that is somewhat informed by cultural studies. Instead of just reporting their progress in an effort to expedite
their project, students discuss a major ethical dilemma they've faced, perhaps
involving their conflicting values with the organization, instructor, or each
other. A cultural studies-inflected progress report might ask students to assess
shifts in power dynamics among project participants or to assess the usability
(in the fuller ethical sense of that word) of their emerging drafts. How do these
drafts interpellate their audiences, they might consider, and to what possible
effects? How well do they account for their users' contexts? Critical assessment
at this stage enables students to take action and make changes before submit-
ting their final products. After writing their progress reports, the brochure
group decided to form another focus group of students living off campus, and
the video group took measures to better incorporate the voices and stories of
youth leaders.

I call the final cultural studies-inspired assignment that I will discuss   42
here an action plan (following Porter et al.), but it could also be classified as

a recommendation report with an activist slant. As mentioned before, I used to have students write an evaluation report to me and their classmates as the final reflection assignment. In this report, students assessed their project's process and products in light of their objectives and the course's and organization's expectations. Although this assignment asked students to evaluate their work, it mostly led them to reflect on how this work could make a difference for the organization and local community, hopefully inspiring them to get involved in future projects. In addition to being mostly celebratory in nature, this assignment seemed like an afterthought, a final "exhale" after the real exertion of the actual project.

Rearticulating the evaluation report as an action plan with a wider audience (including decision-makers at the organization) gave it more purpose and punch. In the new assignment, students turn their critiques into plans of action for the organization, the instructor, and possibly other stakeholders. The action plan gives students a chance to recommend future courses of action to ensure the long-term benefits of their work and to otherwise address the community problem. Students can recommend that the organization revise, distribute, and assess their texts in certain ways. The brochure group suggested distributing their brochures at new student orientation and in the student union, for example. A group producing a website for a social service agency submitted as part of its action plan user testing directions and materials so that the agency could test the website once it was fully online. I've had students help their organizations set up postproduction focus groups as well. 43

Students can also use the action plan to recommend alternative or supplementary solutions such as new approaches to producing texts. Students who face difficulties involving users in the organization's text production process can recommend changes to this process. As Jeffrey Grabill's study of a local AIDS planning council demonstrates, the clients of some nonprofit and government organizations face substantial barriers to participation. As supplements to their brochures, the group working with the counseling center recommended fact sheets and new pages on the center's website. It also suggested that the center hold "question and answer" sessions with students (and possibly their families) at the beginning of each semester to inform them of the center's services and to seek their input. This group got some of these ideas from their focus group. Like the project proposal, the action plan can be codeveloped by the students' community partners, the product of civic engagement. Grabill's study illustrates this partnership nicely, as his activist recommendations were based on client input via "involvement meetings" and a questionnaire. 44

ENHANCED CIVIC ENGAGEMENT

The transformed assignments just discussed are certainly not the only avenues   45
for integrating cultural studies and service-learning. After all, one of the hall-
marks of cultural studies is its heterogeneity and adaptation to specific problems
and contexts. Other promising avenues include the authoethnographies of
workplace cultures taught by Henry and the more activist projects proposed by
Bickford and Reynolds. Student activism was a major contributor to the formation of service-learning in the United States (Liu). Others have drawn on cultural studies in fashioning new theories of discourse and research methods that
hold promise for service-learning pedagogy. We might draw on the methods of
institutional critique, for example, to help students critique "institutions as
rhetorical systems of decision making that exercise power through the design of
space (both material and discursive)" (Porter et al. 621). This critique could, in
turn, lead to proposals for changes in organizational or institutional policies,
processes, and spaces. Or we might draw on theories of ecocomposition to help
students develop a more nuanced and expansive awareness of the impact of
their texts on environments that include but are not limited to humans; in this
way, ecocomposition can help us develop a posthuman ethics for service-learning.
The next big challenge of implementing service-learning is sustainability, and
to this ecocomposition promises to make important contributions. Hopefully
this article will inspire others in the field to experiment in the intersection of
cultural studies and service-learning.

Both service-learning and cultural studies offer us exit ramps off the high-   46
way of hyperpragmatism, a highway that bypasses critical reflection and ethical
action and that fails to account for the surrounding conditions and relations
through which it runs. Taken together, however, service-learning and cultural
studies form an even more promising detour. Cultural studies can keep service-
learning from merging back onto the hyperpragmatist highway, a tempting
move given its practical demands and the institutional forces driving it. Service-
learning can ensure that the use of cultural studies doesn't stop with critical
awareness, becoming a dead end. Some versions of cultural studies, especially
those influenced by structuralism, start and stop with analysis or position students as critical consumers but not the "discourse workers" Henry describes. If
guided by an ethic of engagement and responsiveness, service-learning can also
combat the tendency of the cultural critic to determine the needs of subjects for
them. As Grossberg argues, some cultural studies approaches problematically
assume that the critic "already understands the right skills that would enable

emancipatory and transformative action" (385). An approach that draws on the best of service-learning and cultural studies has the potential to rearticulate the technical communication course into a training ground for critical citizens who produce effective and ethical discourse and who work to create more inclusive forms of power.

WORKS CITED

Anson, Chris M. "On Reflection: The Role of Logs and Journals in Service-Learning Courses." *Writing the Community: Concepts and Models for Service-Learning in Composition*. Ed. Linda Adler-Kassner, Robert Crooks, and Ann Watters. Washington, DC: American Association for Higher Education and NCTE, 1997. 167–80.

Bacon, Nora. "Building a Swan's Nest for Instruction in Rhetoric." *College Composition and Communication* 51.4 (2000): 589–609.

———. "Community Service Writing: Problems, Challenges, Questions." *Writing the Community: Concepts and Models for Service-Learning in Composition*. Ed. Linda Adler-Kassner, Robert Crooks, and Ann Watters. Washington, DC: American Association for Higher Education and NCTE, 1997. 39–55.

Bernhardt, Stephen A. "Improving Document Review Practices in Pharmaceutical Companies." *JBTC* 17.4 (2003): 439–73.

Bickford, Donna M., and Nedra Reynolds. "Activism and Service-Learning: Reframing Volunteerism as Acts of Dissent." *Pedagogy* 2.2 (2002): 229–52.

Blakeslee, Ann M. "Researching a Common Ground: Exploring the Space Where Academic and Workplace Cultures Meet." *Reshaping Technical Communication: New Directions and Challenges for the 21st Century*. Ed. Barbara Mirel and Rachel Spilka. Mahwah, NJ: Lawrence Erlbaum Associates, Inc., 2002. 41–56.

Bowdon, Melody, and J. Blake Scott. *Service-Learning in Technical and Professional Communication*. New York: Longman, 2003.

Bushnell, Jack. "A Contrary View of the Technical Writing Classroom: Notes Toward Future Discussions." *TCQ* 8.2 (Spring 1999): 175–88.

Carey, James W. "Overcoming Resistance to Cultural Studies." *What Is Cultural Studies?* E. John Storey. London: Arnold, 1996. 61–74.

Connors, Robert J. "The Rise of Technical Writing Instruction in America." *JTWC* 12.4 (1982): 329–51.

Crowley, Sharon. *Composition in the University: Historical and Polemical Essays*. Pittsburgh: U of Pittsburgh P, 1998.

Deans, Thomas. *Writing Partnerships: Service-Learning in Composition*. Urbana, IL: NCTE, 2000.

Dilger, Bradley. "The Ideology of Ease." *Journal of Electronic Publishing* 6.1 (Sept. 2000) <http://www.press.umich.edu/jep/06–01/dilger.html>.

Dubinsky, James M. "Service-Learning as a Path to Virtue: The Ideal Orator in Professional Communication." *Michigan Journal of Community Service Learning* 8 (Spring 2002): 61–74.

Flower, Linda, Elenore Long, and Lorraine Higgins. *Learning to Rival: A Literate Practice for Intercultural Inquiry.* Mahwah, NJ: Erlbaum, 2000.

France, Alan W. *Composition as a Cultural Practice.* Westport, CT: Bergin and Garvey, 1994.

Grabill, Jeffrey T. "Shaping Local HIV/AIDS Services Policy through Activist Research: The Problem of Client Involvement." *TCQ* 9.1 (2000): 29–50.

Grossberg, Lawrence. *Bringing It All Back Home: Essay on Cultural Studies.* Durham, NC: Duke UP, 1997.

Hall, Stuart, and Lawrence Grossberg. "On Postmodernism and Articulation: An Interview with Stuart Hall." *Journal of Communication Inquiry* 10.2 (1986): 45–60.

Henry, Jim. "Writing Workplace Cultures." *CCC Online* 53.2 (2001): <http://www.ncte.org/ccc/2/53.2/henry/article.html>.

Henson, Leigh, and Kristene Sutliff. "A Service Learning Approach to Business and Technical Writing Instruction." *JTWC* 28.2 (1998): 189–205.

Herndl, Carl G. "Teaching Discourse and Reproducing Culture: A Critique of Research and Pedagogy in Professional and Non-Academic Writing." *CCC* 44 (1993): 349–63.

Herzberg, Bruce. "Community Service and Critical Teaching." *CCC* 45.3 (1994): 307–19.

Huckin, Thomas N. "Technical Writing and Community Service." *JBTC* 11.1 (1997): 49–59.

Johnson, Richard. "What Is Cultural Studies Anyway?" *Social Text* 6 (1987): 38–80.

Johnson, Robert R. *User-Centered Technology: A Rhetorical Theory for Computers and Other Mundane Artifacts.* Albany: State U of New York P, 1998.

Katz, Steven B. "The Ethic of Expediency: Classical Rhetoric, Technology, and the Holocaust." *CE* 54.3 (1992): 255–75.

Kynell, Teresa C. *Writing in a Milieu of Utility: The Move to Technical Communication in American Engineering Programs, 1850–1950.* Norwood, NJ: Ablex, 1996.

Liu, Goodwin. "Origins, Evolution, and Progress: Reflections on a Movement." *Metropolitan Universities: An International Forum* 7.1 (1996): 25–38.

Longo, Bernadette. "An Approach for Applying Cultural Study Theory to Technical Writing Research." *TCQ* 7.1 (1998): 53–73.

Matthews, Catherine, and Beverly B. Zimmerman. "Integrating Service Learning and Technical Communication: Benefits and Challenges." *TCQ* 8.4
(1999): 383–404.

Miller, Carolyn R. "A Humanistic Rationale for Technical Writing." *CE* 40.6
(1979): 610–17.

———. "What's Practical About Technical Writing?" *Technical Writing: Theory
and Practice.* Ed. Bertie E. Fearing and W. Keats Sparrow. New York: MLA,
1989. 14–24.

Miller, Thomas P. "Treating Professional Writing as Social *Praxis.*" *JAC* 11
(1991): 57–72.

Mirel, Barbara. "Advancing a Vision of Usability." *Reshaping Technical Communication: New Directions and Challenges for the 21st Century.* Ed. Barbara
Mirel and Rachel Spilka. Mahwah, NJ: Lawrence Erlbaum Associates, Inc.,
2002. 165–87.

Mirel, Barbara, and Rachel Spilka, eds. *Reshaping Technical Communication:
New Directions and Challenges for the 21st Century.* Mahwah, NJ: Lawrence
Erlbaum Associates, Inc., 2002.

Moore, Patrick. "Rhetorical vs. Instrumental Approaches to Teaching Technical Communication." *Technical Communication* (1997): 163–73.

Porter, James E. *Audience and Rhetoric: An Archaeological Composition of the Discourse Community.* Englewood Cliffs, NJ: Prentice Hall, 1992.

Porter, James E., Patricia Sullivan, Stuart Blythe, Jeffrey T. Grabill, and Libby
Miles. "Institutional Critique: A Rhetorical Methodology for Change."
CCC 51.4 (2000): 610–42.

Rehling, Louise. "Doing Good While Doing Well: Service-Learning Internships." *BCQ* 63.1 (2000): 77–89.

Salvo, Michael J. "Ethics of Engagement: User-Centered Design and Rhetorical
Methodology." *TCQ* 10.3 (2001): 273–90.

Sapp, David Alan, and Robbin D. Crabtree. "A Laboratory in Citizenship: Service Learning in the Technical Communication Classroom." *TCQ* 11.4
(2002): 411–31.

Scott, J. Blake. "Sophistic Ethics in the Technical Writing Classroom: Teaching Nomos, Deliberation, and Action." *TCQ* 4.2 (1995): 187–99.

———. "Tracking Rapid HIV Testing Through the Cultural Circuit: Implications for Technical Communication." *JBTC* 18.2 (2004) 198–219.

Spilka, Rachel. "Influencing Workplace Practice: A Challenge for Professional
Writing Specialists in Academia." *Writing in the Workplace: New Research
Perspectives.* Ed. Rachel Spilka. Carbondale. IL: Southern Illinois UP, 1993.
207–19.

Sullivan, Dale L. "Political-Ethical Implications of Defining Technical Communication as a Practice." *JAC* 10.2 (1990): 375–86.

Sullivan, Patricia, and James E. Porter. *Opening Spaces: Writing Technologies and Critical Research Practices*. Greenwich, CT: Ablex, 1997.

Tebeaux, Elizabeth. "Let's Not Ruin Technical Writing, Too: A Comment on the Essays of Carolyn Miller and Elizabeth Harris." *CE* 41.7 (1980): 822–25.

Thralls, Charlotte and Nancy Roundy Blyler. "The Social Perspective and Professional Communication: Diversity and Directions in Research." *Professional Communication: The Social Perspective*. Ed. Nancy Roundy Blyler and Charlotte Thralls. Newberry Park, CA: Sage, 1993. 3–34.

Wei Zhu is an associate professor of applied linguistics and interim director of the Second Language Acquisition/Instructional Technology program at the University of South Florida in Tampa. Zhu completed a Ph.D. in Applied Linguistics in 1994 at Northern Arizona University and has published book chapters and articles on a variety of composition-related subjects, including peer revision and second-language writing.

FACULTY VIEWS ON THE IMPORTANCE OF WRITING, THE NATURE OF ACADEMIC WRITING, AND TEACHING AND RESPONDING TO WRITING IN THE DISCIPLINES*

Wei Zhu

Abstract

This study examined faculty views on academic writing and writing instruction.   1
Data reported in this article came from ten qualitative interviews with business and engineering faculty members. Transcripts of the interviews were analyzed inductively and recursively, and two views on academic writing and writing instruction were identified. One view held that academic writing largely involved transferring general writing skills, and writing instruction would be most effectively provided by writing/language teachers. The other view recognized the unique thought and communication processes entailed in academic writing and the role of both content course faculty and writing instructors in academic writing instruction. However, content course faculty and writing instructors each assumed a different set of responsibilities. Implications of the findings for academic writing research and instruction are discussed.

1. INTRODUCTION

The last two decades have witnessed a steady growth in research on academic   2
writing. One of the most significant findings of this body of research is that "students entering academic disciplines need a specialized literacy that consists of the ability to use discipline-specific rhetorical and linguistic conventions

*This article is a revised version of a paper that was presented by the author at the Annual Conference of American Association for Applied Linguistics in Arlington, Virginia, March 22–25, 2003.

This article was published in *Journal of Second Language Writing,* vol. 13, no. 1: Wie Zhu, "Faculty Views on the Importance of Writing the Nature of Academic Writing, and Teaching and Responding to Writing in the Disciplines,: pp. 29–41, Copyright Elsevier 2004, reprinted with permission.

Keywords: Faculty views on academic writing; Writing in content courses; Disciplinary writing and instruction.

to serve their purposes as writers" (Berkenkotter, Huckin, & Ackerman, 1991, p. 19). This body of research highlights a sociocultural dimension of academic literacy and reveals that writing in academic contexts is governed by the communicative purposes shared, and communicative conventions sanctioned, by members of specific discourse communities (Berkenkotter & Huckin, 1995; Geisler, 1994; Hyland, 2000; Swales, 1990). A significant amount of research has focused on academic genres, particularly on generic structure and features. Research findings show that structural and textual features of genres vary both within and across academic disciplines and that such variation embodies different social relationships between the reader and the writer as well as different values and beliefs underlying discursive practices in various discourse communities (Chang & Swales, 1999; Conrad, 1996; Hyland, 1997, 1999a, 1999b).

In addition to professional genres, academic writing research has also examined the genres/tasks students are expected to perform in university content classrooms (Braine, 1989, 1995; Bridgeman & Carlson, 1984; Canseco & Byrd, 1989; Carson, 2001; Hale et al., 1996; Horowitz, 1986; West & Byrd, 1982; Zhu, 2004). In one of the first studies on student writing tasks, Horowitz (1986) analyzed 54 writing assignments from one graduate and 28 undergraduate courses taught in 17 departments of an American university. Horowitz identified seven categories of writing tasks expected of students: summary of/reaction to a reading; annotated bibliography; report on a specified participatory experience; connection of theory and data; case study; synthesis of multiple sources; and research project. While Horowitz's study did not have a particular disciplinary focus, other studies examined written genres required of students in specific disciplines (e.g., Braine, 1989, 1995; Canseco & Byrd, 1989; West & Byrd 1982; Zhu, 2004). One finding is that much of what students need to write, particularly in upper division undergraduate and graduate level courses, is specifically tied to their disciplines.

Academic writing research that has examined writing in specific disciplinary courses indicates that writing serves different purposes in different courses and requires students to assume different social roles, and that communicative conventions are intricately intertwined with the content for, the aims of, and student roles in writing. More specifically, academic readers approach student writing with different sets of expectations, depending on the goals of writing, the perceived roles of the student writers, and the academic readers' own disciplinary expertise. Herrington's studies (1985a, 1985b) in two chemical engineering courses, Laboratory and Design, showed that students assumed different social roles in their writing in the two courses and were expected to use different lines of reasoning and provide different types of evidence depending on their roles. Faigley and Hansen's study (1985) of writing in a psychology course

and a sociology course showed different reactions to student writing from readers with different degrees of disciplinary expertise and different aims for writing.
Kathy's paper, written in the psychology course, was ranked highly by the
teaching assistant because of its adherence to organization, style, and format
requirements of experimental reports but not by the professor, who detected
problems with research design and discussion. Linda's paper, written for both
her sociology course and a writing course designed to teach writing in the social
sciences, received quite different grades and feedback from the sociology professor and the English professor teaching the writing course. While the English
professor was largely concerned with the surface features in Linda's paper, the
sociology professor paid more attention to "what knowledge the student had
acquired than in how well the report was written" (p. 147).

Research on academic discourse communities, student tasks/genres, and   5
reader expectations has both provided valuable information for and raised questions about academic writing instruction. An important issue concerns the role
of writing instructors and content course professors in helping students develop
academic literacy. Faigley and Hansen (1985), based on the findings of their
study, pointed out that "both the professional and liberal arts aims for teaching
writing pose major difficulties for a writing teacher from outside the student's
discipline" (p. 141). In the field of English for Academic Purposes, a debate has
centered on to what extent EAP writing teachers should socialize students into
disciplinary discursive practices and address specific aspects of disciplinary discourse. Spack (1988) argues that

> English teachers cannot and should not be held responsible for teaching
> writing in the disciplines. The best we can accomplish is to create programs
> in which students can learn general inquiry strategies, rhetorical principles,
> and tasks that can transfer to other course work. (pp. 40–41)[1]

Other researchers, however, argue that language teachers should and can play a
role in assisting students to acquire academic literacy through integrating authentic academic writing tasks in writing courses (e.g., Braine, 1988; Johns, 1988).
Johns, in particular, argues that "'general' academic English, employing artificially
constructed topics and materials, is insufficient for students who are exposed daily
to the linguistic and cultural demands of authentic university classes" (p. 706).

Whether some common academic literacy skills are transferable and what   6
the place is of these skills in the EAP writing curriculum has been discussed in
publications concerning EAP writing theories and instructional approaches
(e.g., Dudley-Evans, 1995; Johns, 1988, 1990, 1997). More recently, Hyland
(2002) argues that addressing specificity is an essential task of EAP/ESP writing
instructors. Hyland (2002) warns against the adoption of an "autonomous"

view of literacy, which "misleads learners into believing that they simply have to master a set of rules which can be transferred across fields" (p. 392). Hyland sees teaching specificity as a good starting point.

Much discussion in this debate, thus far, has focused on the role of the language/writing teachers in teaching academic literacy and justifiably so. Yet, given that much academic writing occurs in content courses, and given that the changing demographic profile of the student population in many institutions makes it necessary that responsibility "be extended to all faculty for improving the academic literacy skills of our language minority students" (Snow, 1997, p. 292), it is important to examine faculty views on academic literacy and on faculty role in literacy instruction. Several studies have examined faculty views on academic literacy. For example, Johns (1991) interviewed two experienced political science professors, who identified six factors that they believed contributed to academic "illiteracy": lack of disciplinary schemata; weakness in identifying the larger purposes of texts; little planning when reading and producing texts; inability to connect concepts with examples or facts; limited disciplinary vocabulary; and "unwillingness" on the part of the students to be objective when approaching texts or topics representing conflicting values or beliefs.

An examination of content course professors' views on academic writing and writing instruction could shed light on some of the beliefs underlying writing practices and instruction in content courses, which in turn could provide useful information for academic literacy instruction in the EAP context. This is the rationale for the study reported below.

2. METHODOLOGY

2.1. Context and Participants

The data reported here were collected as part of a larger study designed to examine several aspects of writing across disciplines. An essential goal of the larger study is to understand ESL students' target academic writing needs by examining the writing demands and instruction available in university content classrooms. The study took place at a large, public research university in the Southeast of the United States. The university offers various bachelor's, master's, and doctoral programs and enrolled about 35,000 students at the time of the study. The larger study collected data from several sources, including interviews of 23 faculty members from various disciplines. I report below the interview data from 10 business and engineering professors. I chose to focus on business and engineering here because they represent disciplines that are most attractive to international students (Davis, 1998). Examining business and engineering faculty's views on academic writing and writing instruction could contribute to an understanding of various aspects of writing in the content classrooms many ESL students will enter.

Six business and five engineering faculty members were interviewed. I con-   10
sidered knowledge and willingness, two important requirements for interviewees
(Rubin & Rubin, 1995), when selecting the initial interviewees. I contacted via
e-mail a few faculty members who were experienced and who I believed had
knowledge of writing in their program and field (e.g., tenured faculty members
and assistant professors in their later years on tenure-track, program directors,
dissertation advisers, and faculty with numerous publications). Interviews were
then set up when the persons contacted were willing to be interviewed. The
interview sample then "snowballed" as those interviewed mentioned or recommended colleagues who were perceived to be able to provide more information
or have knowledge of a particular area. To maximize the possibility that the sample represented different points of view, a third consideration in selecting interviewees according to Rubin and Rubin (1995), I contacted and interviewed faculty teaching at the undergraduate as well as graduate levels. Four faculty
members interviewed were teaching at the graduate level only, two at the undergraduate level only, and five at both undergraduate and graduate levels.[2] The
interviews were tape-recorded with permission; one interview with a business
professor could not be recorded due to technical difficulties. Because I would
not be able to offer quotes representing the professor's own voice from the
unrecorded interview, I did not include it in this article. Thus, the present article is based on the ten recorded interviews.

2.2. Qualitative Interviews

"Qualitative interviews" (Rubin & Rubin, 1995) were used because the purpose   11
of the study was to understand "people's more personal, private, and special
understandings" (Arksey & Knight, 1999, p. 4) of academic writing. Specifically, semi-structured interviews were used in this study, with an interview
guide prepared in advance (see Appendix A for the interview guide). Compatible with the central goal of the study, to assess students' target writing needs,
questions in the interview guide focused on the types of writing assignments
required of students; faculty perception of student writing skills; faculty role in
helping students develop academic writing skills; and the importance of writing.
As is often the case with semi-structured interviews, the order of the questions
was not fixed during the interviews, nor was the exact phrasing of the questions.
The general, lead questions in the interview guide were asked first and were
often followed by more specific questions to elicit further information. For
example, the question on faculty perception of student writing skills was followed by more specific questions concerning writing performance by undergraduate versus graduate students and by ESL students. Interviewees were also asked
questions pertaining specifically to their disciplines and programs and were

asked to share anything that they believed to be relevant to issues of academic writing at the end of the interview. Many interview questions focused on aspects of writing relevant to both native and nonnative English speaking students (e.g., faculty views concerning the importance and nature of academic writing and writing instruction). Nevertheless, insight can be gained specifically about ESL students' target writing needs and about EAP writing instruction from these interviews, although we cannot assume that the needs of native and nonnative English speaking students are always identical.

The interviews ranged from about 30 to 60 minutes, and my role during the   12
interviews was to raise questions, rephrase the questions if necessary, listen to the responses, prompt for further information, ask for clarifications, check with the interviewees my interpretation of their responses, and answer faculty questions. Faculty interviewees also raised questions about academic writing, which I answered. For example, during one interview, an engineering professor raised several questions, one of which concerned the use of peer feedback. We then spent a few minutes discussing how peer feedback might be used in engineering classrooms.

2.3. Data Analysis

The tape-recorded interviews were then transcribed. Informal analysis of the   13
interviews started at the transcribing stage where summaries and notes were written about some of the interviews. Formal analysis began when the transcripts, totaling 77 single-spaced pages, were coded. Procedures utilized to analyze the interview data were compatible with those recommended for analyzing qualitative interviews (Arksey & Knight, 1999; Rubin & Rubin, 1995). First, two interviews from business and engineering each were examined and preliminary coding categories developed and defined. The coding categories were then applied to the rest of the transcripts, and brief phrases describing the categories were written beside the interview segments that illustrated the categories. New categories were added as the interview transcripts were coded and were applied to interviews previously coded; several categories were combined. Thus, coding was very much a recursive process. To enhance consistency of coding, I kept notes which contained, among other things, definitions of the categories and decisions made for segments to which more than one category seemed to apply. I referred back to the notes frequently throughout the coding process. Once coding was completed, the coded transcripts were set aside and then reviewed. A few parts were recoded at this point. After this, the coded segments were cut out of the transcripts, with interviewee codes and brief notes referring to the context of the segments. Segments with the same codes were grouped and placed in a folder. Then, the interview segments were compared both within

and across categories for similarities and differences and for links among themes identified.

3. RESULTS

The faculty members discussed a variety of issues during the interviews. Due to   14
the scope of this paper, I share below only faculty comments concerning the
importance of writing, the nature of academic writing, and faculty roles in
teaching and responding to writing in the disciplines. Ample quotes from the
interviews are shared to illustrate the views expressed.

3.1. Importance of Writing

Both the business and engineering faculty emphasized the importance of writing.   15
They highlighted the role of writing as an important communication tool for
business people and engineers in the real world. The importance of writing for
career success in the business world was emphasized by the business professors:

> We demand that students be able to create papers, reports; they have to do
> this all the time; they do it all the time in business administration, in the
> real world, and it's one of the things you are most highly visible for to the
> people above you. (Business 2, p. 5)
>
> It is very important . . . most of our world is based on requests for pro-
> posals, being able to circulate white papers on ideas and comments. (Busi-
> ness 1, p. 4)

Comments from the engineering faculty echoed those given by the business   16
professors, again emphasizing how important writing skills are for career success,
particularly in terms of "selling ideas":

> In my discipline, writing is very important because engineers in the work
> place are considered professional people. Many engineers are in jobs work-
> ing either as consultants or high level professionals within their companies,
> and they'll all be writing reports, formal reports that will be going to clients
> or to upper management of their own company. They'll be writing business
> letters and memos, and engineers, unlike a lot of other professionals, I think
> are almost always trying to sell their own ideas. They are not just reporting
> results of something that is going on but they design things, collect and
> analyze data and try to draw conclusions from it. And so to me, it [writing]
> is critical for the engineer to be a success, not in every job but a large num-
> ber of engineering jobs. (Engineering 1, p. 1)
>
> Critical. If they want to be successful, written communication skills,
> communication skills in general, are critical . . . If they are in any job envi-
> ronment where they interact with people, clients whatever, communication
> skills are critical. (Engineering 2, p. 3)

Very important. Actually to find a job later on, more depends on English actually. (Engineering 6, p. 7)

Interestingly, while writing was perceived to be a critical skill for profes- 17
sional success in both fields, the emphasis given to it in the academic curriculum seemed to differ in the two disciplines. This was reflected in faculty comments concerning the place of writing in the business and engineering curricula. Comments from the business faculty indicated that the importance of writing was recognized at the policy level, and there were some concerted efforts to integrate writing into the business curriculum, although the success of policy implementation may not always be known:

> We have a college wide requirement that all classes are to have evaluated written work in them. I am not promising you that it's actually done every single time, but that's the college policy, and as far as I know, it's pretty much universal. We actually do require writing and we think people should have it. (Business 2, p. 1)

> So now what we are trying to do is to integrate that [writing] into all of the courses so faculty are encouraged to assign writing and have students make presentations. Not everybody does it, but at least we are trying to get at it . . . (Business 3, p. 7)

Compared to comments from the business faculty, those from the engineer- 18
ing professors suggested that integration of writing into the engineering curriculum was more limited, as reflected in comments such as "I can say that it is a part of many courses but only a small part" (Engineering 1, p. 2). The more limited integration of writing was also indicated in one engineering faculty member's comment, which contrasted the attention given to writing in the curriculum with the importance of writing in the real world:

> In school, they [students] don't see it [writing] as a necessary skill. When they get out to work, they'll change their mind on that. They'll tell you it's an important skill. But when they are in school, they don't see it as an important skill, and professors don't present it as an important skill. (Engineering 2, p. 3)

The faculty members accounted for the place of writing in the academic 19
curriculum by referring to disciplinary culture. Two engineering professors made this particularly clear. One said that there was little practice on writing in engineering because of the quantitative nature of the discipline:

> But we tend to be as a discipline very quantitative. We are more interested in the math, the graphs, the tables, and not so much in the texts. (Engineering 2, p. 1)

Later in the interview, this professor related lack of writing practice in   20
engineering to disciplinary culture again:

> But in the engineering culture, there is very little emphasis on the educa-
> tional environment on writing skills . . . when it comes down to practice, very
> little emphasis. And I don't think that's any big secret. (Engineering 2, p. 5)

Another engineering professor mentioned student major as a reason for   21
moderating writing assignments, indicating a relationship between the amount
of writing practice and the nature of the discipline. This professor mentioned
that he required short essays in his undergraduate classes, and when I asked him
how long the essays were, he responded,

> Maybe 500 words. That's two pages. Again, remember we are engineers, we
> are not English majors. So I have to moderate what I ask because not every-
> one is interested. (Engineering 4, p. 2)

Note that the different disciplines (Engineering vs. English) were given as   22
the reason for making the essay relatively short for the engineering students.

Comments from the business professors, however, indicated that writing   23
skills were considered essential in the business curriculum. In fact, writing skills
were considered business skills:

> We happen to think of it [writing] in the College of Business Administra-
> tion as a business skill. Obviously, it's a communication skill. Being good at
> communication is important to business. (Business 2, p. 1)

According to one business professor, an emphasis on communication, both   24
oral and written, characterized Business Information Systems as a unique discipline and separated it from other similar fields (e.g., Computer Sciences). This
professor contrasted assignments required in Computer Sciences with those
required in Business Information Systems and pointed out that assignments in
Computer Sciences "are more mathematically oriented. They are more programming oriented" (Business 1, p. 4). According to this professor, discussing
how information technology projects would be managed constituted an important feature of the assignments in his courses:

> whereas in my course I ask 'how would you manage this project?' and you
> can't do that in a mathematical equation. You have to say that is how I
> would treat my people, this is how I would schedule them, here is the
> budget I would need, which has to be a written assignment, so I think that
> is what a College of Business Information Systems program is all about. It is
> combining the technical with the managerial with the human aspects of
> the problem and bringing them all together. (Business 1, p. 4)

The professor added that an emphasis on writing "is what I think differentiates   25
us from the College of Engineering and Computer Sciences" (Business 1, p. 4).

To some extent, the attention accorded to writing in business could be seen   26
as a reflection of the discipline's desire to respond to the needs and expectations
of the business world, particularly the prospective employers, who were perceived to be the "customers" of business programs.[3] During the interviews, two
business faculty members mentioned prospective employers' needs when discussing the place of writing in the business curriculum. Their comments
revealed that communication skills, spoken and written, were on the very top of
the list of skills prospective employers desire, and this was one reason for
emphasizing writing in business course work. One of the professors said,

> We try to present a consistent message. They [students] know . . . our
> majors understand we talk to each other about what's important in our
> courses and we go in and say 'here is what they [employers] want. They
> want communication skills.' See, this is ranked in the order of importance
> [the faculty member showed me a list of skills]. Communication skills, then
> they look at work experience, then they look at interpersonal skills. What
> do they want? They want somebody who is smart, who is motivated, who is
> competent, and the academic credentials come down last, but it's more
> important to be a good communicator. (B6, p. 1)

3.2. Nature of Academic Writing

The faculty members shared their views on academic writing in the interviews.   27
Their comments indicated two related views concerning the nature of academic
writing.

3.2.1. Academic writing largely entails the transfer of general writing skills to different contexts.   28
This view held that success in academic writing largely depended on a set of
well-developed general skills which could be transferred to different contexts.
The general skills that faculty mentioned often in the interviews included audience awareness, logical organization, paragraph development (e.g., a paragraph
should have one main idea only), clarity, sentence structure, grammar, and
mechanics. This view, however, acknowledged that students would need to
grasp discipline-specific terminology. Responding to the question concerning
similarities and differences between writing in the interviewee's discipline and
other disciplines, one business professor emphasized the similarities in terms of
good organization and clarity:

> Economics as with other disciplines has its own jargon. Other than that, I
> don't think so. I think the goal would be to organize something well and

present the results with clarity and with good grammar and punctuation. (Business 3, p. 4)

One engineering professor emphasized the common need to consider the audience: 29

> You know it's like anything. Your reader is not going to be that technical. So it has to be a general audience. When you write a journal paper, people reading it are practicing engineers, so you have an obligation to write in a style and manner so that what you did and what you found can be easily understood. Otherwise, it serves no purpose. So I think that is true in any subject. (Engineering 4, p. 6).

The emphasis on general skills was further reflected in the belief that writing skills did not have to be developed in particular disciplinary context: 30

> I don't think we need necessarily business examples if we want to learn critical thinking, organization, writing for argumentation, writing for persuasion, writing for agreement. It doesn't matter what the topic is. I'll take the topic the professor gives me and work on the skill. (Business 2, p. 10)

3.2.2. Academic writing involves knowledge of unique thought and communication processes;   31
basic/general writing skills, however, serve as the foundation. This view recognized the uniqueness of writing in diverse disciplinary contexts with respect to thought processes and ways of communication. One engineering professor commented on the uniqueness of engineering writing because of the design and experimental processes involved:

> I think it's a bit different just because of the nature of our work and the way we traditionally have organized our processes, our design processes, our experimental processes, and so on. I think there is some uniqueness there. I think anybody who tries to teach English writing to engineering students should spend some time looking at engineering reports, published papers, engineering memos, and things like that. I think it would help them target the students better. (Engineering 5, p. 7–8)

A business faculty member described a business writing style that values briefness and simplicity: 32

> If you write these huge volumes, like you do in your English class or whatever, you are going to bore your audience to tears and you are not going to be effective . . . You have to write in such a way as to gain attention and keep attention, and has to be short, sweet and simple. On the other hand, it

has also to lead them by the hand through every aspect of the business. (Business 5, p. 3)

Thus, this view saw that academic writing involved more than the simple transfer of general writing skills and would require writers to have specific knowledge about disciplinary thought and communication processes. However, it considered the general skills as the foundation. In fact, this view implied a layered model of academic writing, with the disciplinary thought and communication processes built on a foundation laid by well-developed general writing skills. This view, for example, was reflected in comments given by the business faculty member quoted above on business writing style. When asked about how business writing skills could be developed, the faculty member said, "Number 1, you should learn proper English" (Business 5, p. 4). In a similar vein, an engineering professor mentioned three skills that students would need in order to write successfully in engineering: the skill to present ideas concisely; the skill to use a "somewhat" engaging style; and the skill to "condense, summarize technical literature." The professor described the last one as "kind of discipline specific" but believed that "if they [students] can't do the first two, then they won't be able to do the third one" (Engineering 2, p. 3). 33

3.3. Faculty Role in Teaching and Responding to Writing in the Disciplines

The business and engineering faculty interviewed believed that they had a role to play in helping students develop academic writing skills. This belief was expressed in comments such as "all professors are obligated at all times to try to help students develop writing skills" (Business 2, p. 1). One engineering professor in fact indicated that content course professors would have a more important role to play, given their knowledge of writing in their disciplines: 34

> First of all, I would agree that the professors in all disciplines have a role to play. I believe that their role is more important than the role of the English professors simply because in the discipline we all should have a good understanding of the kinds of writing the students will be expected to do, you know, when they are practicing in their field later on . . . (Engineering 1, p. 6)

Perhaps not surprisingly, faculty members interviewed saw their role in teaching academic writing as secondary to teaching content and technical skills. One business professor put it this way, "I think it [teaching writing] is secondary to the technical skills for the particular course that they are in, but if you can see how to help them, you should" (Business 2, p. 1). One engineering 35 professor shared this view and said that "I see my role more as helping them become better designers than writers. So if it is mentioned, it's tangential. It's never the main part" (Engineering 4, p. 10).

During the interviews, some faculty members described their role in help-   36
ing students develop academic writing skills more specifically in terms of providing writing opportunities and feedback. Two faculty members defined their role as providers of opportunities for writing:

> And so definitely I try to play a critical role in giving them the practice. I don't know whether I give them enough feedback, but I try to give them the experience of different types. (Engineering 5, p. 7)
> We would all say we do that [teaching writing]. I would say I doubt we know whether we succeed or not. Our implication is that because you do the task, you get better at it. (Business 2, p. 6)

Faculty comments indicated that the focus was on content and accuracy of   37
information when faculty members provided feedback on student writing although spelling and grammar errors were corrected or identified when necessary. One business professor said:

> I see my role as when I am handed something in, I read it for content first. I don't read it for grammar or punctuation. Is the person bringing the right facts together to draw the right conclusions to go to the next step in the problem? If I see that, then, I am pleased. I am not going to critique the writing skills of the project. It is where I see the writing or the ESL hindering the person from getting the content that . . . If I see that, I'll circle paragraphs, I'll draw lines of logic flow, saying basically there is a gap in the logic here or your understanding is not clear in this part of the paper. Now once I give it back to them, I sort of leave it up to them as to whether they want to come back and say, "help me do that better." I would say that not all of them do that. (Business 1, p. 3)

An engineering professor said that his chief goal was to help students in the   38
technical area when providing feedback:

> Actually, I don't try to improve their writing because I feel their writing is pretty good but their technical problems, for example, if they couldn't analyze, I try to help to improve . . . more in the technical area, not in the actual writing of the report. (Engineering 6, p. 4)

Later on, this professor said,   39

> I certainly would like to point it out if I discovered something wrong in the writing. I would certainly point it out to them. (Engineering 6, p. 6)

Two faculty members (B3 and B5) reported that they allowed students 40
opportunities to revise based on feedback they provided.[4] One professor said that
graduate students in his class would do a number of article synopses and were
given opportunities for revision if a paper was rejected. The decision for rejecting
a paper, however, was made based on the content rather than the writing:

> I should clarify that. I either accept or don't accept the paper. When I
> accept the paper, that means that they convey to me that they understood
> the main thrust of the article. When I don't accept the paper, that means
> that . . . I never reject a paper because of the grammar and the writing style.
> I would reject it because they didn't understand the article . . . Now, if a
> student has turned in the paper on time, and I reject it, then they rewrite it
> and get it back to me. They have the option of doing that. They can do
> that as long as they want. They keep rewriting and getting it back to me
> until I accept it. (Business 3, p. 4)

Although this professor primarily evaluated the papers on content, "the 41
things that I find I spend most time on is correcting their grammar and English
usage" (Business 3, p. 3). This professor mentioned that he even wrote students
little notes sometimes about the differences between "that" and "which," "further" and "farther," and "affect" and "effect." The professor reported that he
noticed improvement in his students' writing during the semester.

During the interviews, the faculty expressed two views on academic writing 42
instruction. The first view, consistent with the view that academic writing
largely involved the transfer of general writing skills, held that academic writing
instruction would be most effectively provided by the writing instructors
although content course faculty should help the students as much as possible,
through, for example, providing opportunities for writing and providing guidelines for and feedback on student writing.

Faculty comments indicated that this view was rooted in notions of disci- 43
plinary specialization and expertise. A business professor's comment illustrated
this view and its source:

> We should stick to the applied stuff we are experts at, and if there are other
> experts in the college, let's let the other professionals do the teaching [of
> writing]. It would be presumptuous for me to think that I can teach commu-
> nication better than you. You had better be better at it than me. It's your
> Ph.D. It's your life, and your application of skill goes to that. I want to see
> the result. But to think that I can generate the results better than the out-
> siders, there is no reason to believe that. (Business 2, p. 10)

The second view suggested a process of academic writing instruction jointly 44
undertaken by language/writing and content course instructors. Consistent with

the layered model of academic writing, which saw general skills as the foundation upon which discipline-specific literacy could be built, this view of writing instruction held that language/writing teachers ought to be responsible for helping students develop basic/general writing skills, and content course instructors would assume a leading role in teaching aspects of writing specific to a discipline. This view was presented elaborately by an engineering professor. This professor did not seem to see the need for offering writing courses specifically designed for engineering majors (he referred to this type of courses as "some kind of a course on report writing"), and emphasized the role of content course professors in teaching discipline-specific writing:

> I think I see the role as splitting. As a sort of customer of the English professors, what I would like to get from them, I would like for the English professors to show my students proper vocabulary, proper punctuation and still be able to instill creativity. I would also like to see them helping the student to develop the ability of expressing some logic, logical steps or whatever. That kind of background, good vocabulary, good punctuation skills and good grammar skills and some good creativity and good logic. Then our work will be pretty simple in the sense that we can help them to plan and express the kinds of information to people in the discipline. Like in engineering, for example, I don't think that it is so important that our students get some kind of a course on report writing but that they be able to get all of the other stuff so that when they get here in our classes we can begin the second half 'here's what you need to include in your report.' Give them perhaps an outline, 'do your report by this outline.' Classes will review drafts of reports, comment on them and send them back to our students for a final draft. We could focus then not so much on finding grammatical errors but really on the completeness with which they express various topics and looking at the organization and flow and looking at the content. The student will have the ability to throw out any kind of proofreading mistakes they might have and if they went and rewrote a section, it would come back well written. So that seems to me that if you think about it, almost the English professors and all of the other professors are almost all partners where the English professors take the lead in developing the basic skills of the students; in the discipline, the professor comes in and shapes the student into the way we do things because certainly the writing of an engineer and a psychologist and a historian are to be very different. I don't think they expect the English Department people to be responsible for all those different disciplines. The professors in the disciplines need to do that. (Engineering 1, p. 6)

The idea that content course professors ought to be responsible for teaching discipline-specific writing was reiterated by another engineering professor. Earlier in the interview, this professor mentioned three skills that students would

45

need in order to perform writing successfully in engineering, one of which was considered discipline specific (i.e., "condense, summarize technical literature"). Later in the interview, the professor commented on the teaching of these skills:

> It's only a technical writer that can help them [students] with the third one. But I think any writing environment, any communication environment would be very helpful. I don't think you actually have to focus on technical writing per se; the fact is that many students couldn't write a letter. (Engineering 2, p. 3)

Thus, the second view of academic writing instruction represented a model   46
of "division of labor" between language/writing instructors and content course professors.

4. DISCUSSION AND CONCLUSION

This study examined 10 business and engineering faculty members' views on the   47
importance of writing, the nature of academic writing, and faculty roles in teaching and responding to writing in the disciplines. Both the business and engineering faculty interviewed emphasized the importance of writing as a communication tool in the real world; however, their comments indicated that the emphasis given to writing in the academic curriculum differed in the two disciplines and that the differing place of writing in the curriculum reflected differences in disciplinary cultures. Faculty members expressed two views on academic writing and writing instruction. The first view held that academic writing entailed the transfer of a set of generalizable writing skills across contexts, and as such its development would be most effectively addressed by the writing/language instructors. This view reflected an "autonomous" view of literacy, a view shared by discipline faculty members in other studies (e.g., Lea & Street, 1999, cited in Hyland, 2002). Faculty who expressed this view, however, did indicate that they had a role to play in helping students develop academic writing ability. The second view expressed by the faculty interviewed held that academic writing involved particular disciplinary thought and communication processes, but that basic/general writing skills served as the foundation for the development of discipline-specific processes. The accompanying view of writing instruction held that content and writing instructors ought to be both involved in developing student academic writing skills, but each would play a different role: the writing/language instructors would be charged with the task of teaching basic/general writing skills, and the content course professors would assume responsibility for teaching those aspects of writing related to a specific discipline. Interestingly, those comments that academic writing involved unique

thought processes and that the unique processes needed to be taught by faculty in the disciplines came from the engineering faculty, although not all engineering faculty members shared this view. This suggests that faculty in a particular discipline do not all share a particular view of academic literacy and that it is important to examine the diverse views held by the faculty.

Faculty comments concerning their role in academic writing instruction 48 indicated that the faculty saw themselves largely as providers of writing opportunities and as providers of content-related feedback on student writing. Although the professors interviewed reported that some feedback on organization, grammar, and usage was offered in the form of notes, corrections, and identification of errors, the faculty focused on content when commenting on student writing, and opportunities for students to act upon the feedback and revise were not common. Thus, the feedback provided on student writing was largely summative than formative. The greater emphasis on providing opportunities for writing (than on providing feedback) by some faculty members and on content (than on the writing) when commenting on and evaluating student writing suggests an approach which values "writing to learn" (Griffin, 1985; Herrington, 1981) and in which writing is used as a means to help students acquire content knowledge and to meet the pedagogical needs of content area professors and programs (e.g., assessment of learning). While "writing to learn" could provide a good rationale for integrating writing into content courses because of its emphasis on content learning (Herrington, 1981), how it can lead to "learning to write" in university content classrooms is not entirely clear, particularly given the frequent absence of formative feedback and opportunities for revision. The emphasis on "writing to learn" and the view that writing and communication skills are most effectively addressed by the writing instructors suggest that in university content classrooms many second language learners may not always receive the kind of systematic feedback important for writing development. Therefore, EAP writing classrooms constitute an extremely important place for students to improve writing skills through instruction, feedback, and practice. Of particular importance seems to be formative feedback that can help students internalize the revision and editing processes so that students can initiate the revision and editing processes when necessary in the content classrooms. In addition, EAP writing instructors can familiarize students with various resources (e.g., handbooks, dictionaries, websites, writing centers, and tutoring services) available for revision and editing and help students develop strategies for seeking and attending to feedback. Preparing students in this fashion is not simply to "accommodate students to the content and pedagogy of mainstream academic classes" (Benesch, 1993, p. 711); rather, it is providing tools which

ESL students can use in the content classrooms so that they can more effectively and independently deal with content in the subject area.

Faculty comments concerning the nature of academic literacy and faculty   49
role in academic writing instruction indicate the need for teaching specificity in the EAP context. The view that academic writing largely entails the transfer of general writing skills reflects an "individual skill perspective" on literacy (McKay, 1993), and such a view may prevent content area faculty from effectively teaching disciplinary discourse. This view may also prevent content area faculty from effectively addressing ESL students' writing difficulties and needs as ESL students' difficulties with academic writing may be perceived simply in terms of lack of general rhetorical and language skills. A few faculty members expressed a view of academic writing that recognized specific disciplinary thought and communication processes, but even for these faculty members, it is not clear to what extent they were involved in teaching those processes. For example, one engineering professor (E5), who commented on the unique processes involved in writing in engineering, perceived his role in helping students develop academic writing skills mainly as the provider of opportunities for writing. Thus, we cannot assume that academic literacy instruction will always take place in content courses, and we need to play a role in teaching specificity. However, the view that unique thought processes are embodied in academic writing, and that these processes need to be taught by content area professors (as expressed in E1 and E2), also poses the familiar perplexing question for teaching specificity in the EAP context: Can EAP writing instructors, not being members of other disciplinary communities, teach the unique thought processes and the conventions used to express them? This is the question that triggered the initial debate on whether or not EAP instructors should initiate students into disciplinary discourse communities (Spack, 1988), and one that seems to continue to present difficulties for the argument for teaching specificity.

Given the socially situated nature of academic literacy (Berkenkotter &   50
Huckin, 1995; Berkenkotter et al., 1991; Swales, 1990), teaching specificity is a necessity in the EAP classrooms if we want to effectively prepare our students for academic writing. To address the difficulty posed by the question concerning whether or not EAP writing instructors have the expertise to teach discipline-specific thought and communication processes, we may want to consider more carefully what constitutes teaching specificity, and what are our specific roles in it. Does teaching specificity involve presenting to students specific discourse conventions, along with teaching the related content, values, and thought processes of the target discourse communities? Or does it involve raising students' awareness that there are multiple literacies through using various authentic tasks and texts? Or does it involve providing opportunities "for students to

conduct their own explorations of the discourse they hope to gain control of"
(Hirvela, 1997, p. 83), for example, through analysis and reflection in the form
of disciplinary portfolios? These all represent efforts to teach specificity, albeit
in different ways, but require EAP writing instructors to play different roles. For
example, the first conceptualization of teaching specificity would require EAP
writing instructors to possess disciplinary knowledge of the target discourse
communities and assume the role of experts in the disciplines. The third conceptualization, however, sees EAP instructors as facilitators and perhaps co-
investigators of discursive practices in the target communities. In this role, EAP
instructors can teach specificity without expert knowledge of the discourse communities whose discursive practices the students are hoping to acquire. In the
debate on whether or not to teach specificity, it is the first conceptualization
that seems to pose difficulties for teaching specificity with respect to EAP writing instructors' knowledge of the various discourse communities. This is not to
suggest that these are the only roles that EAP writing instructors may play or
that EAP instructors cannot teach disciplinary discourse conventions but that it
may be useful to consider what constitutes teaching specificity and what are our
specific roles in teaching specificity.

Perhaps we may also want to consider what constitutes the specificity we   51
want to teach. To what extent does specificity consist of disciplinary discourse
conventions and features, and to what extent can it be defined based on the
notion of disciplinary discourse community? Academic writing research has
indicated that disciplinary communities are not monolithic and has revealed
the "local contextual dimensions" (Casanave, 1995) of disciplinary communities. In addition, academic writing tasks are highly situated (Prior, 1995, 1998),
and what are perceived to be appropriate discourse conventions vary within the
same discipline, depending on the specific contexts and roles students are
expected to assume (Herrington, 1985a, 1985b; Samraj, 2002). Thus, a part of
the specificity we need to teach deals with the context for writing (Hyland,
2002; Johns, 1997), and recent research indicates that the context surrounding
writing in university classrooms is quite complex.

Samraj (2002) provides a useful framework for depicting the context for   52
writing in university content courses which captures the complexity and
interaction of various factors influencing the production of texts in university classrooms. Five contextual variables are identified: academic institution,
discipline, course, task and student, and these variables are arranged as layers
"to depict how various contextual elements may be related to one another"
(p. 165). The most general element, academic institution, is placed at the
top, and increasingly more specific elements of the academic discipline, the
course, the task, and the student, form layers below it. Each layer is con-

nected to and influenced by but does not completely overlap with the layer(s) above it. Samraj examined graduate student writing in two courses in a Master's program in environmental science and found that the contextual elements influenced student writing to various degrees and that "features of different contextual layers can be in dissonance" (p. 173). This dissonance and students' lack of consideration of certain layers of context explained some unsuccessful features in students' texts. Samraj's work shows that consideration of the disciplinary context alone is not sufficient and suggests that an understanding of the "layers of context" and their influence on student roles and texts produced should constitute an important part of the specificity we want to teach.

Academic writing is highly complex and is influenced by "layers of context." Successful academic writing instruction depends on a sound understanding of the complexity of writing in university content classrooms, and investigating faculty views on academic writing and writing instruction represents efforts to understand one aspect of the complexity. Future studies could examine how faculty views on academic writing actually influence instructional practices in content classrooms. Future studies could also examine how faculty members actually comment on student writing and how students perceive and use the feedback. Through continued research, we can gain a better understanding of writing in content courses, which should enable us to better prepare our students for academic writing.

ACKNOWLEDGEMENTS

I would like to thank Diane Belcher, Jun Liu, and two anonymous reviewers for their insightful comments on an earlier version of the paper. I am grateful to the Research Council of the University of South Florida for a research grant that supported this study. I would like to thank Ms. Lisana Mohamed for her assistance with transcribing a few of the interviews.

APPENDIX A. INTERVIEW GUIDE

1. What type(s) of writing assignments are required in your courses and discipline? What guidance do you provide on student writing? How do you comment on and evaluate student written work?

2. What do you think about your students' writing? What kinds of strengths and/or weaknesses do you see in your students' writing? What aspects of writing do you think your students need to work on?

3. How important is writing in your courses, program, and field?

4. What do you think is the role of content course instructors such as yourself in helping students develop academic writing skills, i.e., writing for [insert discipline] purposes? What are some of the things that you can help your students improve in terms of their writing? How can writing courses (e.g., composition courses) better prepare students for writing tasks in content courses? How do you think writing for [interviewee's discipline] is similar to or different from writing in another discipline?

5. Is there anything that I did not ask but you would like to add?

REFERENCES

Arksey, H. & Knight, P. (1999). *Interviewing for social scientists*. Thousand Oaks, CA: Sage Publications. The Association to Advance Collegiate Schools of Business. (1998). *Standards for Business Accreditation. AACSB International*. Retrieved January 29, 2003 from http://www.aacsb.edu/accreditation/standards.asp.

Benesch, S. (1993). ESL, ideology, and the politics of pragmatism. *TESOL Quarterly, 27*, 705–717.

Berkenkotter, C., & Huckin, T. (1995). *Genre Knowledge in disciplinary communication*. Hillsdale, NJ: Lawrence Erlbaum Associates, Publishers.

Berkenkotter, C., Huckin, T., & Ackerman, J. (1991). Social context and socially constructed texts: The initiation of a graduate student into a writing research community. In C. Bazerman & J. Paradis (Eds.), *Textual dynamics of the professions* (pp. 191–215). Madison, WI: University of Wisconsin Press.

Braine, G. (1988). A reader reacts. . . . *TESOL Quarterly, 22*, 700–702.

Braine, G. (1989). Writing in science and technology: An analysis of assignments from ten undergraduate courses. *English for Specific Purposes, 8*, 3–16.

Braine, G. (1995). Writing in the natural sciences and engineering. In D. Belcher & G. Braine (Eds.), *Academic writing in a second language* (pp. 113–134). Norwood, NJ: Ablex Publishing Corporation.

Bridgeman, B., & Carlson, S. (1984). Survey of academic writing tasks. *Written Communication, 1*, 247–280.

Canseco, G., & Byrd, P. (1989). Writing required in graduate courses in business administration. *TESOL Quarterly, 23*, 305–316.

Carson, J. (2001). A task analysis of reading and writing in academic contexts. In D. Belcher & A. Hirvela (Eds.), *Linking literacies: Perspectives on L2 reading–writing connections* (pp. 48–83). Ann Arbor, MI: The University of Michigan Press.

Casanave, C. P. (1995). Local interactions: Constructing contexts for composing in a graduate sociology program. In D. Belcher & G. Braine (Eds.), *Academic writing in a second language: Essays on research and pedagogy* (pp. 83–110). Norwood, NJ: Ablex Publishing Corporation.

Chang, Y. Y. & Swales, J. (1999). Informal elements in English academic writing: Threats or opportunities for advanced non-native speakers? In C. N. Candlin & K. Hyland (Eds.), *Writing: Texts, processes, and practices* (pp. 145–167). London and New York: Longman.

Conrad, S. (1996). Investigating academic texts with corpus-based techniques: An example from biology. *Linguistics and Education, 8*, 299–326.

Davis, T. M. (Ed.). (1998). *Open doors 1997/98: Report on international educational exchange.* New York: Institute of International Education.

Dudley-Evans, T. (1995). Common-core and specific approaches to the teaching of academic writing. In D. Belcher & G. Braine (Eds.), *Academic writing in a second language: Essays on research and pedagogy* (pp. 293–312). Norwood, NJ: Ablex Publishing Corporation.

Faigley, L., & Hansen, K. (1985). Learning to write in the social sciences. *College Composition and Communication, 36*, 140–149.

Geisler, C. (1994). *Academic literacy and the nature of expertise: Reading, writing, and knowing in academic philosophy.* Hillsdale, NJ: Lawrence Erlbaum Associates, Publishers.

Griffin, C. W. (1985). Programs for writing across the curriculum: A report. *College Composition and Communication, 36*, 398–403.

Hale, G., Taylor, C., Bridgeman, B., Carson, J., Kroll, B., & Kantor, R. (1996). *A study of writing tasks assigned in academic degree programs.* Princeton, NJ: Educational Testing Service.

Herrington, A. (1981). Writing to learn: Writing across the disciplines. *College English, 43*, 379–387.

Herrington, A. (1985a). Writing in academic settings: A study of the contexts for writing in two college chemical engineering courses. *Research in the Teaching of English, 19*, 331–361.

Herrington, A. (1985b). Classrooms as forums for reasoning and writing. *College Composition and Communication, 36*, 404–413.

Hirvela, A. (1997). "Disciplinary portfolios" and EAP writing instruction. *English for Specific Purposes, 16*, 83–100.

Horowitz, D. (1986). What professors actually require: Academic tasks for the ESL classroom. *TESOL Quarterly, 20*, 445–462.

Hyland, K. (1997). Scientific claims and community values: Articulating an academic culture. *Language & Communication, 17*, 19–31.

Hyland, K. (1999a). Talking to students: Metadiscourse in introductory course-books. *English for Specific Purposes, 18,* 3–26.

Hyland, K. (1999b). Disciplinary discourses: Writer stance in research articles. In C. N. Candlin & K. Hyland (Eds.), *Writing: Texts, processes, and practices* (pp. 99–121). London and New York: Longman.

Hyland, K. (2000). *Disciplinary discourses: Social interactions in academic writing.* Essex, England: Pearson Education Limited.

Hyland, K. (2002). Specificity revisited: How far should we go now? *English for Specific Purposes, 21,* 385–395.

Johns, A. (1988). Another reader reacts. . . . *TESOL Quarterly, 22,* 705–707.

Johns, A. (1990). Coherence as a cultural phenomenon: Employing ethnographic principles in the academic milieu. In U. Connor & A. Johns (Eds.), *Coherence in writing* (pp. 211–226). Alexandria, VA: Teachers of English to Speakers of Other Languages, Inc.

Johns, A. (1991). Faculty assessment of ESL student literacy skills: Implications for writing assessment. In Hamp-Lyons (Ed.), *Assessing second language writing in academic contexts* (pp. 167–179). Norwood, NJ: Ablex Publishing Corporation.

Johns, A. (1997). *Text, role, and context: Developing academic literacies.* Cambridge: Cambridge University Press.

Lea, M., & Street, B. (1999). Writing as academic literacies: Understanding textual practices in higher education. In C. N. Condlin & K. Hyland (Eds.), *Writing: texts, processes and practices.* London: Longman, 62–81.

McKay, S. L. (1993). *Agendas for second language literacy.* Cambridge: Cambridge University Press.

Prior, P. (1995). Redefining the task: An ethnographic examination of writing and response in graduate seminars. In D. Belcher & G. Braine (Eds.), *Academic writing in a second language: Essays on research and pedagogy* (pp. 47–82). Norwood, NJ: Ablex Publishing Corporation.

Prior, P. (1998). *Writing/disciplinarity.* Mahwah, NJ: Lawrence Erlbaum Associates, Publishers.

Rubin, H., & Rubin, I. (1995). *Qualitative interviewing: The art of hearing data.* Thousand Oaks, CA: Sage Publications.

Samraj, B. (2002). Texts and contextual layers: Academic writing in content courses. In A. Johns (Ed.), *Genre in the classroom: Multiple perspectives* (pp. 163–176). Mahwah, New Jersey: Lawrence Erlbaum Associates, Publishers.

Snow, M. A. (1997). Teaching academic literacy skills: Discipline faculty take responsibility. In M. A. Snow & D. M. Brinton (Eds.), *The content-based classroom: Perspectives on integrating language and content* (pp. 290–304). New York: Addison Wesley Longman.

Spack, R. (1997). The acquisition of academic literacy in a second language. *Written Communication, 14*, 3–62.

Spack, R. (1988). Initiating ESL students into the academic discourse community: How far should we go? *TESOL Quarterly, 22*, 29–51.

Swales, J. (1990). *Genre analysis: English in academic and research settings.* New York: Cambridge University Press.

West, G., & Byrd, P. (1982). Technical writing required of graduate engineering students. *Journal of Technical Writing and Communication, 12*, 1–6.

Zhu, W. (2004). Writing in business courses: An analysis of assignments types, their characteristics, and required skills. *English for Specific Purposes, 23*, 111–135.

NOTES

1. Spack, in her case study of Yuko published in *Written Communication* in 1997, pointed out that the realization that Yuko was not always able to transfer skills learned in her English courses to other settings challenged her assumptions previously held about general skills and strategies. Spack noted that "the present study reveals that our work in ESL courses is vulnerable, that academic skills are not fixed, that academic tasks can be understood only within specific contexts, that all academic work is socially situated" (p. 50).

2. Of the two faculty members who were teaching at the undergraduate level only, one was a full time instructor with years of teaching experience, and the other was a graduate teaching assistant. Both, however, were knowledgeable about various aspects of writing in the undergraduate courses in their respective programs.

3. Another influence on the integration of writing in business may be attributed to the accreditation criteria and standards set by the Association to Advance Collegiate Schools of Business (AACSB, 1998), which explicitly state that for undergraduate business studies "the business curriculum should include written and oral communication as an important characteristic" (C.1.2.c). For MBA and other general management master's programs, the standards state that "basic skills in written and oral communication, quantitative analysis, and computer usage, should be achieved either by prior experience and education, or as part of the MBA curriculum" (C.1.3.c). Here, written communication skills are accorded the same status as other skills essential for business, such as quantitative and computer

skills. Thus, an emphasis on writing at the policy level in business could be seen as a way to respond to the mandates of an important accreditation body.

4. Several professors mentioned that how they provided feedback varied, depending on the specific instructional role they assumed. For example, when they served as major professors on dissertation or thesis committees, they provided iterative feedback on content and on the writing of the dissertation or thesis.

Leah Zuidema received her Ph.D. in the Critical Studies in the Teaching of English program at Michigan State University in 2007 and is an assistant professor of English at Dordt College in Sioux Center, Iowa. Her teaching and research interests include English teacher education, composition-rhetoric, and teaching against language prejudice. She has published a variety of book chapters, has published articles in such journals as *English Education* and *English Journal*, and won a National Council of Teachers of English 2008 Promising Research Award.

MYTH EDUCATION: RATIONALE AND STRATEGIES FOR TEACHING AGAINST LINGUISTIC PREJUDICE

Leah A. Zuidema

"Language is a protective shield for prejudice—or ignorance."
—Robert MacNeil(2003)

Linguistic prejudice is one of the few "acceptable" American prejudices. In polite society, we don't allow jokes that we consider to be racist or sexist, and we are careful not to disparage a person's religious beliefs. Language is another matter. In *English with an Accent*, Rosina Lippi-Green (1997) writes that we regularly demand of people that they suppress or deny the most effective way they have of situating themselves socially in the world. *You may have dark skin, we tell them, but you must not sound Black. You can wear a yarmulke if it is important to you as a Jew, but lose the accent. Maybe you come from the Ukraine, but can't you speak real English? If you didn't sound so corn-pone, people would take you seriously. You're the best salesperson we've got, but must you sound so gay on the phone?* (pp. 63–64)

Many of us feel free to make judgments about others because of the ways that they use language. We make assumptions based on the ways that people speak and write, presuming to know about their intelligence, their competence, their motives, and their morality (Wolfram, Adger, & Christian, 1999, pp. 23, 27). As Vivian Davis (2001, p. 1) has explained, we assume that because we know a little about how people speak or write that we also understand "what they wear, what they eat, how they feel about certain things including birth, death, family, [and] marriage[,] and what they believe about the world and their place in it." We act as though dialects and accents are windows to people's

1

2

Leah Zuidema, "Myth Education: Rationale and Strategies for Teaching against Linguistic Prejudice," *Journal of Adolescent and Adult Literacy*, vol. 48, no. 4 (May 2005), pp. 668–675. Copyright 2005 by International Reading Association. Reproduced with permission of International Reading Association in the format Textbook via Copyright Clearance Center.

souls. And sometimes, we dare to ignore or dismiss entire groups of people because of what we assume their linguistic habits reveal about them.

Employers may assume, for example, that an employee who speaks American English with a Midwestern or Northern accent is more intelligent (and thus more competent) than an employee who uses Appalachian English. Teachers may assume that a student who uses so-called Standard English is more respectful of authority and more intelligent than a student who uses Ebonics. Landlords may assume that a person whose first language is English will take better care of a rental property than a tenant who speaks English with a Spanish accent.

These assumptions are not inconsequential thoughts. People act on their ideas, and as a result, prejudice becomes active discrimination. Employment, promotions, grades, recommendations, and business agreements are just a few of the things that may be affected (negatively or positively) by reactions to the ways a person uses language in speech or writing. Even people who live—by choice or by happenstance—in relative isolation from racial, ethnic, religious, or cultural diversity may engage in linguistic prejudice. Detrimental portrayals of language variation on the radio, on television, in films, and on the Internet all provide opportunities to cultivate negative attitudes, which can emerge as prejudicial judgments and behaviors when people encounter language variation in real life (whether on the telephone, in writing, or face-to-face). Individuals' private prejudices may move them to take public action, so that their condemning opinions are transformed into corporate policies, educational paradigms, and local, state, and federal laws—prejudice in practice, one might say.

Robert Phillipson calls this "practical" prejudice *linguicism,* and his definition encompasses the process I have outlined. *Linguicism* is the assembly of "ideologies, structures and practices which are used to legitimate, effectuate, and reproduce an unequal division of power and resources (both material and immaterial) between groups which are defined on the basis of language" (as cited in Daly, 1995, par. 4). The difficulty with fighting linguistic prejudice is that the general public may be slow to condemn it or may even be skeptical about its existence because linguicism is such an insidious process. Additionally, while most modern linguistics scholars acknowledge the existence of linguicism, their views have little influence on the general public (Smitherman, 2000, p. 81). The burden of preventing linguicism and countering its effects must fall elsewhere.

Some literacy educators have, appropriately, taken up the challenge of teaching against linguistic prejudice. As Lisa Delpit (1998) argues, it is "possible and desirable to make the actual study of language diversity a part of the curriculum for all students" (p. 19). IRA/NCTE *Standards for the English Language Arts* (1996) state that students should "develop an understanding of and respect for diversity in language use, patterns, and dialects across cultures, ethnic groups, geographic regions, and social roles.

Unfortunately, many schools and teachers have not incorporated such   7
study into their curricula. Perhaps this shouldn't surprise us; after all, even IRA and NCTE devote relatively little attention to the need for all students to study language variation. For example, while IRA and NCTE publications and position statements emphasize teachers' responsibilities to accept and accommodate diverse students' languages, no official statements have been made about teaching students themselves to be accepting of linguistic diversity. Even the frequently-cited (and recently reaffirmed) CCCC resolution "Students' Right to Their Own Language" (1974) stops short of declaring the need to teach students about others' rights to their own languages.

Similarly, a search of IRA's *Journal of Adolescent and Adult Literacy* issues   8
dating back to May 2000 uncovered no articles focused on students' attitudes toward or knowledge about linguistic diversity. The March 2001 themed issue of *English Journal* (entitled "And Language for All") includes several articles about teaching students whose own language is stigmatized, but it largely ignores the "mainstream" students. The exception is Marilyn Wilson's article on language study for preservice teachers. Wilson (2001) asserts, "Students who feel smug about their use of Standard English will benefit from understanding the linguistic strengths of speakers of other dialects" (p. 32). Aside from Wilson's article, the issue is devoted entirely to students whose use of stigmatized language in speech and writing often results in their own marginalization. These students are, of course, deserving of a themed issue dedicated to their educational needs. But to ignore the "smug" students is a grave mistake, for these are the people who hold—or, as adults, will hold—much of the power that allows linguistic stigmatization and discrimination to continue.

Teaching against Myths

If we really want to fight to eradicate linguicism—and what Harvey Daniels   9
(1983) refers to as "some of the basest hatreds and flimsiest prejudices" that linguicism masks—we cannot leave the task to urban or so-called multicultural schools (p. 9). All schools must heed the call to arms, and English language arts classrooms are among the most appropriate venues for taking action against linguicism. Because the classroom "is a major player in shaping language attitudes, and the classroom that is particularly crucial for the formation of ideas about language is that of the K-12 level," English language arts teachers should create opportunities to shape informed, positive student attitudes about language diversity—for all students (Smitherman, 2000, p. 396).

Helping adolescent learners to create informed opinions about language 10
diversity depends on educating against the misinformation about this topic that
many students believe. This misinformation can be divided into three broad
categories: myths about language, myths about others, and myths about the self.
These myths can and should be addressed across the curriculum; for instance,
social studies courses are well suited for confronting myths about others. Language
study, however, needs to be the starting point and primary focus in English
language arts courses. After all, studying language and its use (in writing,
literature, and speech) is the principal discipline of the English language arts
classroom. Dispelling some of the myths about language can lead to a resulting
change of attitude toward others and the self.

Following are clarifications of some of the most persistent misconceptions 11
about language, accompanied by strategies that can help students to learn
about the true nature of linguistic diversity. Instead of relying solely on lectures
and readings, the activities are designed so that students can act as "critical
co-investigators in dialogue with the teacher" (Freire, 1970, p. 68). To
facilitate this research process, students should collect samples of speech and
writing throughout their study, choosing specimens that demonstrate both
stigmatized and admired usages. Students can observe the language patterns of
amateurs as well as language professionals such as teachers, politicians, media
spokespersons, and published writers, and they can preserve their artifacts
with pen and paper and audio or video recorder. As learners confront new
ideas about language, they should examine their linguistic data collections in
order to verify the truth for themselves. Not all students will subscribe to all
language myths; it is important for teachers to discern which misconceptions
are most prevalent among particular student groups and to shape curriculum
accordingly.

Myth #1: English must obey the rules of grammar. Linguists would argue 12
that this statement could be either true or false, depending on one's definition
of grammar. If, by grammar, one means the internal patterns that a given language
naturally follows, or descriptions of these inherent patterns, then it is
true. In English, for example, it is breaking the rules to attach an article after a
noun (e.g., Cat _The_ in Hat _The_). Scholars did not gather at a conference to
decide on this arrangement; no government established this pattern as a law. It
is simply the way that English works, and when people ignore this or other
innate patterns of the language, it causes confusion. When we define *grammar*
as the organic patterns of a language, or descriptions of these patterns, it is correct
to state that English must obey grammatical rules.

Many non-linguists, however, define *grammar* as the rules of taste (which   13
linguists refer to as *usage*). Most people believe that observing the rules of taste is
the same as knowing the grammar of a language. These prescriptive rules of taste
assume great importance, so that many English speakers and writers are familiar
with admonitions such as "Don't say 'ain't,'" and "Ask '*may* I?'—I know that you
can," and "Don't end a sentence with a preposition." Most people will admit,
however, that breaking these kinds of socially-imposed rules does not actually
impede anyone's understanding of the message a person is attempting to communicate. When we define *grammar* as prescriptive standards of taste, it is possible
to say that English does not need to obey the rules in order to be effective.

Helping students to distinguish between the two definitions of grammar   14
can be difficult, but I find that using an analogy is often effective. I prefer to use
a discussion starter such as this one paraphrased from Lippi-Green (1997,
p. 15): "A taxi must obey the laws of physics, but it can disobey state laws. How
is English like a taxi?" Some students see the analogy right away; to help the
others, I ask as many of the following questions as necessary:

- Is it possible for a taxi to disobey the laws of physics? What are the consequences of trying to break these laws? Who makes the laws of physics? How
  can these laws be changed?
- How is it possible for a taxi to disobey our state laws? Why might this happen? What are the consequences? Who makes our state laws? For what purposes? How can these laws be changed?
- How do state laws (as they pertain to taxicabs) differ from the laws of
  physics? Why are they different?
- In the English language, what are some rules that work in the same way
  that the laws of physics work for taxis? (We call these rules *grammar*.) What
  are the consequences of trying to break these grammar rules? Who makes
  the grammar rules of English? How can these grammar rules be changed?
- What are some English language rules that work in the same way that state
  laws work for taxis? (We call these rules *usage*.) How is it possible to disobey these usage rules? Why might this happen? What are the consequences? Who makes usage rules? For what purposes? How can usage rules
  be changed?
- How does the analogy work? Is the analogy completely parallel? What are
  the limitations to the analogy?

A follow-up question such as "Who decides what is 'good' or 'Standard' En-   15
glish?" helps students to consider the authority and motivations of those who
control—or seek to control—language use.

It is important to introduce students to the distinctions between natural   16
grammar and taste-based grammar early in efforts to teach against linguicism.
Understanding that English must obey some kinds of grammar rules while having
the freedom to disregard others is key to correcting other common misconceptions about language variation. Students must also recognize the falsehood of:

Myth #2: Some dialects and languages don't have grammatical rules. This is   17
an argument that is frequently used to disparage stigmatized language systems
such as Ebonics, Appalachian English, and Hawaiian Creole English. Instead of
viewing these systems as patterned and rule-governed, many people call them
"slang" or "street talk" or resort to cruel labels that show blatant disrespect for
the speakers themselves. The best way for students to learn that stigmatized languages and dialects really are rule-governed is to discover it for themselves
through a series of guided activities.

Wolfram, Adger, and Christian (1999) have developed an excellent   18
sequence, "Illustrative Exercises of Grammatical Patterning," to help adolescent
learners to ascertain the logical, rule-governed nature of such configurations as
the "a-" prefix used in some Southern dialects and the invariant "be" from
Ebonics (pp. 196–200). For example, in exercises on the use of the "a-" prefix,
students examine matched sentence pairs and use their intuition to answer
questions such as, "Does it sound better to say, *A-building is hard work or He was
a-building a house?*" After analyzing a number of similar sentence pairs, learners
are prompted to determine which inherent patterns or rules govern the use of
the prefix. Whether students speak the mainstream English that some linguists
refer to as the Language of Wider Communication (LWC) or rely primarily on
stigmatized dialects or languages, exercises in grammatical patterning help them
to realize that all language systems are rule-governed. Understanding this concept helps students to see through false (but common) claims about the supposed stupidity or laziness of those who use stigmatized dialects and languages.
Additionally, realizing that speaking a prestigious variety (i.e., being a literal
smooth talker) does not make a person more intelligent or hard working reminds
learners about the folly of assigning credibility to a source based only on that
person's use of language. [See Appendix 1, "Recommended Readings on the
Grammar, Vocabulary, and Rhetoric of Ebonics and Other Stigmatized Language Systems."]

Language patterning exercises can convince students that systems such as   19
Appalachian English (AE) do indeed have organic grammatical rules, but some
learners may fail to realize that stigmatized languages and dialects also observe
their own taste-based rules of grammar. The challenge for us as teachers is find-

ing ways for students to observe or experience the rich complexities of dialects and languages that are unfamiliar to them. Ideally, students would interview speakers fluent in LWC as well as a stigmatized system such as AE, asking the speakers to provide examples of the ways that they adjust their AE pronunciation, vocabulary, and syntax when they are using the dialect for varied audiences and contexts.

Unfortunately, time, geography, and other factors frequently prevent such 20
interviews, but students can still have opportunities to see and hear the patterned, complex nature of several varieties of English in film documentaries such as *The Story of English* (Cran, 1996) or its sequel series, *Do You Speak American?* (Cran), which debuted on PBS television on January 5, 2005. The film *American Tongues* (Louis & Kolker, 1986) is nearly 20 years old, but it too engages students trying to understand that all American varieties of English are governed by natural as well as taste-based grammars. Teaching literature that incorporates accurate portrayals of specific dialects, particularly if they are used for a range of audiences and situations, is also an effective means for students to learn more about the grammaticality of stigmatized language systems and about the code-switching techniques employed by many speakers of stigmatized languages. For examples of literary characters discussing the ways they shift—or are expected to shift—their language use for various audiences, see chapter 6 of *A Lesson Before Dying* by Ernest Gaines (1993) or chapter 12 of *To Kill A Mockingbird* by Harper Lee (1988).

Helping students to understand that all language systems are governed by 21
two very different kinds of grammar rules is critical for success in wrestling with:

Myth #3: Standard English is better than other varieties. Learners who 22
understand the fallacies of the first two myths are also prepared to unpack this third myth. They acknowledge that judgments about "good" and "bad" language use are subjective social constructions. They recognize the falsehood in the argument that non-standard varieties are random or ruleless and therefore worthless. However, this complex myth also hinges on other misconceptions that need to be addressed.

One of these errors is the belief that "good" English is the everyday spoken 23
language of the most educated and intelligent people. Most LWC speakers recognize that their own language use does not often meet the ideals of so-called Standard English, but many of these same speakers also believe that with enough education and practice, they—like educated speakers "somewhere else"—will be able to let loose a flurry of grammatically perfect prose every time they open their mouths. In actuality, Standard English is an abstract ideal based not on speech but on the model of written language (Lippi-Green, 1997).

One way for students to investigate this idea is by analyzing their collected   24
speech and writing samples to determine which ones are most likely to show-
case formal Standard English. Learners soon discover that the "best" English is
usually found in writing and in speech based on writing, such as news broadcasts. Students should also analyze the differences between their own written
and spoken language patterns. These activities help students to understand that
most people, no matter how well educated, cannot hope to consistently speak
with the polish of revised and edited writing—the kind of language use which is
idealized as Standard.

Another problem with the "Standard English is good English" myth is that   25
Standard English is a moving target. Wolfram, Adger, and Christian (1999)
explain, "There is really no single dialect of English that corresponds to a standard English. . . . The norms for Standard English are not identical in all communities. Furthermore, there are two sets of norms—the informal standard and
the formal standard" (pp. 14–15). Students need to realize that no matter how
standard their English, all speakers are perceived by some listeners to have an
"accent." An interesting resource that helps to demonstrate this is the *Dialect
Survey* Web site at *http://cfprod01.imt.uwm.edu/Dept/FLL/linguistics/dialect/*
(Vaux, B., Golder, S. A., Star, R., & Bolen, B., 1999). Harvard linguists have
mapped dialect-related preferences so that one can see at a glance, for instance,
where in the U.S. it might be more acceptable to pronounce *poem* with two syllables than with one, and in what regions one should arrive for dinner at noon
rather than in the evening. Learners can also research the moving target concept by contrasting what a variety of sources (including dictionary and textbook
writers) mean when they refer to *Standard English*.

Most students know intuitively that formal Standard English is not the best   26
choice for every communicative situation, yet they are so used to having their
own grammar corrected that they cannot help but believe that non-standard
English is bad. Need evidence? Consider how often teens and even adults use
perfectly appropriate conventions of casual conversation and then, remembering they are speaking with English teachers, apologize in embarrassment for
their "bad grammar." Baron (1990) rightly states, "We must own up to the fact
that the teaching of English to speakers of English has promoted much of the
linguistic insecurity and fear of grammar that we observe today" (pp. 211–212).
It is important for students to hear English teachers acknowledging that a non-
standard register or even another dialect or language is sometimes the most
appropriate and effective choice. Hearing the message isn't enough; students
also need opportunities to consciously explore and reflect with their teachers
about effective uses of systems other than formal Standard English.

Detroit teacher Jerome Smith suggests an activity that is useful to this end.   27
Smith instructs his students to research and write about the unique vocabulary,
pronunciation, syntax, and other linguistic features of the speech communities
in which they participate. Students may choose communities defined by voca-
tion, age, interests, beliefs, gender, or other identifying features. Smith (2001)
explains that this assignment helps "students see that just because a speech
community is different or unique does not make it 'wrong,' dumb, or stupid. My
students discovered they all took part in different speech communities with special linguistic forms unique to their group, age, gender, occupation, geography,
situation, etc."

As they strive to appreciate the value of certain "non-standard" uses of lan-   28
guage, some learners also benefit from experiencing what it means for ideas to be
lost in translation. Students should select information that they would normally
discuss in their unique speech communities and "translate" the information into
the vocabulary, pronunciation, and syntax of another less-familiar speech community. To help LWC speakers gain an even greater appreciation for the pressures that speakers of stigmatized language systems face when they are pressured
to conform to unfamiliar varieties of English, student volunteers may attempt—
perhaps before an audience, if they are willing—to do their translating orally or
in a timed, unrevised writing. (For a less-intimidating approach, introduce students to literature that portrays the difficulties of learning and translating from
another language to English, such as An Na's young adult novel *A Step From
Heaven* (2001) or many of Pat Mora's poems in *My Own True Name: New and
Selected Poems for Young Adults* (2000)—particularly "Learning English: Chorus
in Many Voices.") Reflection upon these kinds of translating activities with ana-
lytical discussion helps students to recognize that the worth of a given language
system is tied to its appropriateness and effectiveness for a given context, purpose, and audience, not to inherent qualities such as syntax.

Some students may argue that acknowledging the value of stigmatized lan-   29
guage systems will change the English language, eventually resulting in its
decline or loss. These students believe:

Myth #4: English is not as good as it used to be, and it is getting worse.   30
"There seems to be a widespread feeling that the English language is a fragile
object and is constantly under siege," write Wolfram, Adger, and Christian
(1999, p. 100). Students are correct to notice that English—like other "live"
languages—is constantly changing. Some words or phrases become linguistic
fads; others fall into disuse or "misuse." Rules of taste change, and the pronunciations, uses, conjugations, and spellings of words are altered over time to adjust

to new contexts, speakers, purposes, and audiences. We call this adaptability *survival of the fittest* when we discuss other kinds of evolution; it is evidence of the resilience of language, not a matter for concern.

Students need to see for themselves that changes in language and language   31
standards are evidence of flexibility and no cause for worry. One way to make this possible is for learners to examine parallel texts in Old English, Middle English, and early and recent Modern English (Wolfram et al., 1999, p. 201). (See, for example, Catherine Ball's Web site tracing historical translations of "The Lord's Prayer" at *http://www.georgetown.edu/faculty/ballc/oe/pater_noster.html.*) Learning about the history of English, including its interaction with French, Latin, Ebonics, HCE, and Spanish, also helps students to understand how and why the language changes; the film series *The Story of English* is useful in this regard. Students who harbor doubts that English can survive change may be convinced by Harvey Daniels' humorous, instructive chapter "Something New and Ominous," which relates highlights from "the history of linguistic insecurity and intolerance and the periods of [erroneous] doomsaying which they regularly generate" (1983, p. 33). Examples from Daniels' chapter can help students to see that worries about language decline are not new, and that changes and flexibility are what help to keep English alive and thriving.

Teaching against the Miseducation of Myth Education

It is not enough to dispel widely held myths about language variation; we also   32
need to expose how myths and misconceptions are perpetuated so that students can participate in efforts to resist, subvert, and combat linguicism. Rosina Lippi-Green (1997) writes a blistering indictment of the powerful institutions that enable "language subordination": "Standard language ideology is introduced by the schools, vigorously promoted by the media, and further institutionalized by the corporate sector. It is underscored by the entertainment industry and underwritten in subtle and not so subtle ways by the judicial system" (p. 73). It is imperative that students learn to identify and critique prejudicial portrayals of languages, dialects, speakers, and writers. Projects such as the following provide opportunities for learners to conduct primary-source research and critical analysis of real-life attitudes toward linguistic diversity. Students can:

- Examine music lyrics, radio broadcasts, television shows, films, entertainment magazines, novels, Internet sites, and video games to uncover the prejudices of particular segments of the entertainment industry. Lippi-Green (1997) outlines her students' research of negative portrayals of language variation in Disney animated films in her chapter "Teaching Children How to Discriminate: What We Learn from the Big Bad Wolf." This chapter works well as a model for adolescent learners researching the ways in which pop culture sources link stigmatized as well as admired language varieties with people's abilities, morals, attractiveness, and so on.

- Collect samples of linguistic prejudice propagated by the news media in television, Internet, and radio news commentary as well as in printed editorials (Wilson, 2001). Students can also record instances when the news media present myths as truths instead of checking the scientific facts with actual linguists. I've found Barbra S. Morris's *English Journal* article "Toward Creating a TV Research Community in Your Classroom" (1998) to be an especially helpful resource for designing media-based, primary-source research projects with high school and college students.

- Interview employers and their employees, as well as "personnel officers in actual workplaces about their attitudes toward divergent styles in oral and written language" (Delpit, 1998, p. 44). Another option is for students to create written surveys that people can complete anonymously. Students can use their findings to debate the legality and implications of responses to linguistic diversity in the workplace. To complicate the debate, teachers may wish to share the results of research indicating that some listeners show a decreased ability to understand a person when they believe (based on appearance) that the speaker is of an ethnicity other than their own (Lippi-Green, 1997, p. 126–129). Students might also be surprised to learn that the EEOC's *Guidelines on Discrimination Because of National Origin* (*http://www.dol.gov/dol/allcfr/ESA/Title_41/Part_60-50/toc.htm*) outlaw "denial of equal employment opportunity" based on an individual's use of "linguistic characteristics of a national origin." The exception (per the Civil Rights Act of 1964) is when "an individual's accent . . . interferes materially with job performance" (as cited in Lippi-Green, 1997, p. 153–154). Also, students may be interested to know that workplace discrimination based on an individual's regional (vs. national) linguistic origin is not prohibited by law.

- Research court cases concerning discrimination that stems from linguistic prejudice. Lippi-Green (1997) outlines several of these cases in her chapter "Language Ideology in the Workplace and the Judicial System." She finds that the judges "were willing to depend on their own expertise in matters of language in a way they would never presume to in matters of genetics, or mechanical engineering, or psychology" (p. 160). Students can test Lippi-Green's claim about the behaviors of judges or look at the impact of judicial decisions on discrimination laws or employment and education policies. They might also investigate efforts to pass laws making English the official language of the United States, evaluating the rhetoric and rationale behind such policies as well as the implications of English Only legislation. Students can begin with an investigation into *U.S. English, Inc.*, one of the main proponents of the English Only movement, at *http://www.us-english.org/*. Counterarguments to the English Only movement are presented on the NCTE Web site in the CCCC Position Statement on the National Language Policy at *http://www.ncte.org/about/over/positions/category/div/107643.htm*.

- Consider the roles of schools in perpetuating linguistic prejudice. Opening our own practices for critique takes courage, trust, and careful leadership. If we partner with our students to go beyond critique, if we take action with them in changing our scholastic responses to language variation, we can communicate more clearly than in any other project we pursue together that we are committed to teaching and living against linguistic prejudice.

Students are sure to make disturbing findings in research projects such as these. We can help students to take positive action in response to their learning and make their research efforts more consequential by offering writing assignment options that work toward eliminating the propagation of linguistic prejudice and the practice of language-based discrimination. Students can compose fiction, poetry, and creative nonfiction that reflect on linguicism; they can write articles that expose linguistic prejudice, and they can write letters, proposals, public service announcements, and other documents that seek to combat linguicism. Publishing students' writings or delivering them to the intended audiences can empower students as activists in their world and make their learning meaningful in a way that writing for the teacher alone cannot do.   33

The ubiquitous problem of linguistic prejudice deserves significant attention in all schools. We ought to incorporate language study at all levels, in freestanding units or in partnership with literature, grammar, speech, and composition studies. While language study is not likely to eradicate language-based discrimination, it may serve to diminish our students' and our own willingness to use language "as both a channel and an excuse for expressing some of our deepest prejudices" (Daniels, 1983, p.5). Consistent, widespread education about the true nature of language may help to put an end to popular regard for linguicism as one of the last "acceptable" prejudices.   34

REFERENCES

Ball, C. N. (2000, July 1). The Lord's prayer in English. In *Old English pages.* Retrieved June 25, 2004, from *http://www.georgetown.edu/faculty/ballc/oe/ pater_noster.html*

Baron, D. (1990). Watching our grammar: The English language for English teachers. In G. Hawisher & A. Soter (Eds.), *On literacy and its teaching: Issues in English education* (pp. 208–223). Albany, NY: SUNY Press.

Conference on College Composition and Communication (1974, Fall). Students' right to their own language. *College Composition and Communication, 25.* Retrieved June 26, 2004, from *http://www.ncte.org/library/files/About_NCTE/ Overview/NewSRTOL.pdf*

Conference on College Composition and Communication (1988, March 16). The national language policy. CCCC position statement. Retrieved June 26, 2004, from *http://www.ncte.org/about/over/positions/category/lang/ 107643.htm*

Cran, W. (Director). (1996). *The story of English* [Documentary film]. MacNeil-Lehrer Productions and the British Broadcasting Corporation.

Cran, W. (Producer/ director). (2005). *Do you speak American?* [Documentary film]. MacNeil-Lehrer and Paladin InVision. *http://www.pbs.org/speak/*

Daly, M. (1995, September). The classic *Linguistic Imperialism. . .* being the book that all English speakers should read [Review of the book *Linguistic Imperialism*]. *New Internationalist Magazine, 271.* Retrieved June 25, 2004, from *http://www.newint.org/*

Daniels, H. (1983). *Famous last words: The American language crisis reconsidered.* Carbondale, IL: Southern Illinois University Press.

Davis, V. J. (2001, November 17). *Remembering the self in the academy: Rhetorical strategies for students of color.* Paper presented at National Council of Teachers of English Annual Convention, Baltimore.

Delpit, L. (1998). What should teachers do?: Ebonics and culturally responsive instruction. In T. Perry & L. Delpit (Eds.), *The real Ebonics debate: Power, language, and the education of African American children.* (pp. 17–26). Boston: Beacon Press. *http://www.beacon.org/k-12/real-ebonics-debate-detail.html*

Freire, P. (1970). *Pedagogy of the oppressed* (M. B. Ramos, Trans.). New York: Seabury.

Gaines, E. J. (1993). *A lesson before dying.* New York: Vintage. *http://www .randomhouse.com/vintage/catalog/display.pperl?isbn=9780375702709&view=tg*

International Reading Association & National Council of Teachers of English (1996). *Standards for the English language arts.* Retrieved June 26, 2004, from *http://www.reading.org/advocacy/elastandards/standards.html*

Lee, H. (1988). *To kill a mockingbird.* New York: Warner.

Lippi-Green, R. (1997). *English with an accent: Language, ideology, and discrimination in the United States.* New York: Routledge.

Louis, A., & Kolker, A. (Producers/directors). (1986). *American tongues.* [Documentary film]. United States: Center for New American Media. *http://www.cnam.com/flash/index.html*

MacNeil, R (2003, November 21). Keynote address presented at National Council of Teachers of English Annual Convention, San Francisco.

Mora, P. (2000). *My own true name: New and selected poems for young adults.* Houston: Arte Publico. *http://www.arte.uh.edu/view_book.aspx?isbn=1558852921*

Morris, B. S. (1998, January). Toward creating a TV research community in your classroom." *English Journal,* 87(1), 38–42.

Na, A. (2001). *A step from heaven.* New York: Speak. *http://www.frontstreetbooks.com/all_books.htm*

National Council of Teachers of English. *Our positions.* Retrieved June 26, 2004, from *http://www.ncte.org/about/over/positions*

Smith, J. (2001, Nov. 25). Re: [ncte-hs] against linguistic prejudice. Electronic mailing list message posted to ncte-hs in response to query from author. Retrieved June 26, 2004, from http://www.ncte.org/library/files/list_archive/ncte_hs/2001/nov2001/msg00217.asp (no longer available - full posting follows)

Subject: Re: [ncte-hs] against linguistic prejudice
From: "Jerome Smith"
Date: Sun, 25 Nov 2001 20:13:52 -0500

Dear Leah,

Years ago kids used to share "slam books" with each other. These were composition notebooks on which they listed names, questions, etc. and had each other fill in entries. These have varied and changed over the years, but form an interesting study. I related these to dialect geography, the change of language over time, and other linguistic issues, rather than scold kids for having them or filling them in.

I then went further and had kids do a project, trying to find an area of their own linguistic expertise about a unique "speech community." I recall one student wrote quite a paper on special terms used in his father's furniture business. I often do the same assignments that I give my students. This time, I myself wrote one about a university campus as a speech community (ran to over one hundred pages). All this, buttressed with reference to Martin Joos's *The Five*

Clocks, helped my students see that just because a speech community is different or unique does not make it "wrong," dumb, or stupid. My students discovered they all took part in different speech communities with special linguistic forms unique to their group, age, gender, occupation, geography, situation, etc. I could go on and on, but the assignment really worked well for me, and my students loved it.

I even had students volunteer to compile a dictionary of current teen terms and slang they figure Mr. Smith wouldn't know. Always helps my education to get fun lessons from my students.

Jerome Smith in Detroit

Smitherman, G. (2000) *Talkin that talk: Language, culture, and education in African America.* London: Routledge. *http://www.routledge-ny.com/shopping_cart/products/product_detail.asp?sku=&isbn= 0415208653&parent_id=&pc==*

U.S. English, Inc. (2004). U.S. English: Towards [sic] a united America. Retrieved June 26, 2004, from *http://www.us-english.org/*

Vaux, B., Golder, S. A., Star, R., & Bolen, B. (1999). *Dialect survey.* Retrieved June 26, 2004, from *http://hcs.harvard.edu/~golder/dialect/index.html*

Wilson, M. (2001, March). The changing discourse of language study." *English Journal,* 90(4), 31–36.

Wolfram, W., Adger, C. T., & Christian, D. (1999). *Dialects in schools and communities.* Mahwah, NJ: Lawrence Erlbaum Associates. *https://www.erlbaum.com/shop/tek9.asp?pg=products&specific=0-8058-2863-X*

APPENDIX 1: RECOMMENDED READINGS ON THE GRAMMAR, VOCABULARY, AND RHETORIC OF EBONICS AND OTHER STIGMATIZED LANGUAGE SYSTEMS

Gilyard, Keith and Elain Richardson. "Students' Right to Possibility: Basic Writing and African American Rhetoric." *Insurrections: Resistance in Composition.* Ed. Andrea Greenbaum. Albany, NY: State University of New York Press, 2001. 37-51. In addition to discussing strategies for teaching writing to Ebonics speakers, this chapter outlines 15 rhetorical features that occur frequently in Ebonics discourse. Examples of these rhetorical features include rhythmic language, proverbs, and sermonic tone.

Rickford, John Russell and Russell John Rickford. "Grammar." *Spoken Soul: The Story of Black English.* New York: John Wiley and Sons, Inc., 2000. 109–128. The authors systematically discuss the grammar of Ebonics, making frequent and helpful use of excerpts from actual conversations to explain the rules for plurals, possessives, pronouns, tense, and more.

————. "Vocabulary and Pronunciation." *Spoken Soul: The Story of Black English*. New York: John Wiley and Sons, Inc., 2000. 91–108. Rickford and Rickford study the historical roots and current vestiges of patterns in Ebonics vocabulary and pronunciation.

Smitherman, Geneva. *Black Talk: Words and Phrases from the Hood to the Amen Corner*. Revised Edition (with 300 new entries and new introduction). Boston & New York: Houghton Mifflin, 2000. Smitherman's dictionary goes beyond cataloging definitions: it also provides history, opinions about Ebonics' role in American education and culture, and an emphasis on the significance of the words and phrases that she highlights in Black Talk.

————. "Introduction to Ebonics." *Talkin That Talk: Language, Culture and Education in African America*. London & New York: Routledge, 2000. 19–40. Smitherman, a respected scholar of Ebonics who frequently uses Ebonics grammar, vocabulary, and rhetoric in her academic writing, argues for defining Ebonics as a language and traces its historical development.

Wolfram, Walt; Adger, Carolyn Temple; and Conna Christian. "Appendix: A Selective Inventory of Vernacular Structures." *Dialects in Schools and Communities*. Mahwah, NJ: Lawrence Erlbaum Associates, 1999. 203–223. The authors focus on pronunciation and grammatical structures, commenting on linguistic patterns and how they are manifested in a number of varieties of English. For example, in a section on "Final Cluster Reduction," the authors explain how and why "best apple" can become "bes' apple" in Ebonics as well as Hispanic English and Vietnamese English.

Robert Scholes (1929–) is the author of more than twenty books, most on genre elements, reading, writing, and author studies. After many years as a professor of English and comparative literature at Brown University, he is now a Research Professor there in the Department of Modern Culture and Media. His latest book is *Paradoxy of Modernism* (2006).

ON READING A VIDEO TEXT

Robert Scholes

The moments of surrender proposed to us by video texts come in many forms, but all involve a complex dynamic of power and pleasure. We are, for instance, offered a kind of power through the enhancement of our vision. Close-ups position us where we could never stand. Slow motion allows us an extraordinary penetration into the mechanics of movement, and, combined with music; lends a balletic grace to ordinary forms of locomotion. Filters and other devices cause us to see the world through jaundiced or rose-colored optics, coloring events with emotion more effectively than verbal pathetic fallacy and less obtrusively. These derangements of normal visual processing can be seen as either constraints or extensions of visual power—that is, as power over the viewer or as extensions of the viewer's own optical power, or both. Either way they offer us what is perhaps the greatest single virtue of art: change from the normal, a defense against the ever-present threat of boredom. Video texts, like all except the most utilitarian forms of textuality, are constructed upon a base of boredom, from which they promise us relief.

Visual fascination—and I have mentioned only a few of its obvious forms—is just one of the matrices of power and pleasure that are organized by video texts. Others include narrativity and what I should like to call, at least tentatively, cultural reinforcement. By narrativity, of course, I mean the pleasures and powers associated with the reception of stories presented in video texts. By cultural reinforcement, I mean the process through which video texts confirm viewers in their ideological positions and reassure them as to their membership in a collective cultural body. This function, which operates in the ethical-political realm, is an extremely important element of video textuality and, indeed, an extremely important dimension of all the mass media. This is a function performed throughout much of human history by literature and the other arts, but now, as the arts have become more estranged from their own culture and even opposed to it, the mass media have come to perform this role. What the epic poem did for ancient cultures, the romance for feudalism, and the novel for bourgeois society, the media—and especially television—now do for the commodified, bureaucratized world that is our present environment.

It is time, now, to look at these processes as they operate in some specific   3
texts. Let us begin with a well-known Budweiser commercial, which tells—most frequently in a format of twenty-eight seconds, though a longer version also exists—the life story of a black man pursuing a career as a baseball umpire. In this brief period of time, we are given enough information to construct an entire life story—provided we have the cultural knowledge upon which—this construction depends. The story we construct is that of a young man from the provinces, who gets his "big break," his chance to make it in the big city, to rise to the top of his profession. We see him working hard in the small-time, small-town atmosphere of the minor leagues, where the pace of events is slower and more relaxed than it is "at the top." He gets his chance for success—the voice-over narrator says, "In the minors you got to make all the calls, and then one day you get the call"—after which we see him face his first real test. He must call an important and "close" play correctly and then withstand the pressure of dispute, neither giving ground by changing his mind (which would be fatal) nor reacting too vigorously to the challenge of his call by an offended manager. His passing of this test and being accepted is presented through a later scene in a bar, in which the manager who had staged the protest "toasts" the umpire with a bottle of Budweiser beer, with a chorus in the background singing, "You keep America working. This Bud's for you." From this scene we conclude that the ump has now "made it" and will live happily ever after. From a few scenes, then, aided by the voice-over narration and a music track, we construct an entire life.

How do we do this? We draw upon a storehouse of cultural information   4
that extends from fairy tales and other basic narrative structures to knowledge about the game and business of baseball.

In processing a narrative text we actually construct the story, bringing a   5
vast repertory of cultural knowledge to bear upon the text that we are contemplating. Our pleasure in the narrative is to some extent a constructive pleasure, based upon the sense of accomplishment we achieve by successfully completing this task. By "getting" the story, we prove our competence and demonstrate our membership in a cultural community. And what is the story that we "get?" It is

the myth of America itself, of the racial melting pot, of upward mobility, of justice done without fear or favor. The corporate structure of baseball, with minor leagues offering a path for the talented to the celebrity and financial rewards of the majors, embodies values that we all possess, we Americans, as one of the deepest parts of our cultural heritage or ideology. It is, of course, on the playing field that talent triumphs most easily over racial or social barriers. Every year in baseball new faces arrive. Young men, having proved themselves in the minors, get their chance to perform at the highest level. Yale graduates and high-school dropouts who speak little or no English are judged equally by how well they hit, run, throw, and react to game situations. If baseball is still the national pastime, it is because in it our cherished myths materialize—or appear to materialize.

The commercial we are considering is especially interesting because it 6 shows us a black man competing not with his body but with his mind, his judgment and his emotions, in a cruelly testing public arena. Americans who attend to sports are aware that black athletes are just beginning to find acceptance at certain "leadership" positions, such as quarterback in professional football, and that there is still an active scandal over the slender representation of blacks at baseball's managerial and corporate levels. The case of the black umpire reminds viewers of these problems, even as it suggests that here, too, talent will finally prevail. The system works, America works. We can take pride in this. The narrative reduces its story to the absolutely bare essentials, making a career turn, or seem to turn, on a single decision. The ump must make a close call, which will be fiercely contested by a manager who is deliberately testing him. This is a story of initiation, in that respect, an ordeal that the ump must meet successfully. The text ensures that we know this is a test, by showing us the manager plotting in his dugout, and it gives us a manager with one of those baseball faces (Irish? German?) that have the history of the game written on them. This is not just partisan versus impartial judge, it is old man against youth, and white against black. We root for the umpire because we want the system to work—not just baseball but the whole thing: America.

For the story to work, of course, the ump must make the right call, and we 7 must know it to be right. Here, the close-up and slow motion come into play— just as they would in a real instant replay—to let us see both how close the call is and that the umpire has indeed made the right call. The runner is out. The manager's charge from the dugout is classic baseball protest, and the ump's self-control and slow walk away from the angry manager are gestures in a ritual we all know. That's right, we think, that's the way it's done. We know these moves the way the contemporaries of Aeschylus and Sophocles knew the myths upon which the Greek tragedies were based. Baseball is already a ritual, and a ritual we partake of mostly through the medium of television. The commercial has only to organize these images in a certain way to create a powerful narrative.

At the bar after the game, we are off stage, outside that ritual of baseball, but we are still in the world of myth. The manager salutes the ump with his tilted bottle of beer; the old man acknowledges that youth has passed its test. The sword on the shoulder of knighthood, the laying on of hands, the tilted Bud—all these are ritual gestures in the same narrative structure of initiation. To the extent that we have wanted this to happen we are gratified by this clos-ing scene of the narrative text, and many things, as I have suggested, conspire to make us want this ending. We are dealing with an archetypal narrative that has been adjusted for maximum effect within a particular political and social con-text, and all this has been deployed with a technical skill in casting, directing, acting, photographing, and editing that is of a high order. It is very hard to resist the pleasure of this text, and we cannot accept the pleasure without, for the bewildering minute at least, also accepting the ideology that is so richly and closely entangled with the story that we construct from the video text. To accept the pleasure of this text is to believe that America works; and this is a comforting belief, itself a pleasure of an even higher order—for as long as we can maintain it. Does the text also sell Budweiser? This is something only mar-ket research (if you believe it) can tell. But it surely sells the American way first and then seeks to sell its brand of beer by establishing a metonymic connection between the product and the nation: a national beer for the national pastime.

An audience that can understand this commercial, successfully construct-ing the ump's story from the scenes represented in the text and the comments of the narrative voice, is an audience that understands narrative structure and has a significant amount of cultural knowledge as well, including both data (how baseball leagues are organized, for instance, and how the game is played) and myth (what constitutes success, for example, and what initiation is). At a time when critics such as William Bennett and E. D. Hirsch are bewailing our igno-rance of culture, it is important to realize that many Americans are not without culture; they simply have a different culture from that of Bennett and Hirsch. What they really lack, for the most part, is any way of analyzing and criticizing the power of a text like the Budweiser commercial—not its power to sell beer, which is easily resisted, especially once you have tasted better beer—but its power to sell America. For the sort of analysis that I am suggesting, it is neces-sary to recover (as Eliot says) from the surrender to this text, and it is also nec-essary to have the tools of ideological criticism. Recovery, in fact, may depend upon critical analysis, which is why the analysis of video texts needs to be taught in all our schools.

Before moving on to the consideration of a more complex textual economy,   10
we would do well to pause and consider the necessity of ideological criticism.
One dimension of the conservative agenda for this try has been conspicuously
anticritical. The proposals of William Bennett and E. D. Hirsch, for instance,
different as they are in certain respects, are both recipes for the indoctrination
of young people in certain cultural myths. The great books of past ages, in the
eyes of Bennett, Hirsch, and Allan Bloom, are to be mythologized, turned into
frozen monuments of Greatness in which our "cultural heritage" is embodied.
This is precisely what Bloom does to Plato, for instance, turning the dialectical
search for truth into a fixed recipe for "greatness of soul." The irony of this is
that Plato can only die in this process. Plato's work can better be kept alive in
our time by such irreverent critiques as that of Jacques Derrida, who takes Plato
seriously as an opponent, which is to say, takes him dialectically. In this age of
massive manipulation and disinformation, criticism is the only way we have of
taking something seriously. The greatest patriots in our time will be those who
explore our ideology critically, with particular attention to the gaps between
mythology and practice. Above all, we must start with our most beloved icons,
not the ones we profess allegiance to, but those that really have the power to
move and shake us.

Revising
Literacies

J. Alison Bryant, who formerly taught at Indiana University Bloomington, now works for Nickelodeon/MTV Networks and is the editor of the essay collection, *The Children's Television Community* (2006).

Ashley Sanders-Jackson was a graduate student at Indiana University and is now a graduate student at the Annenberg School for Communication at the University of Pennsylvania.

Amber M. K. Smallwood was an associate instructor and doctoral student at Indiana University and is now an assistant professor of communication studies at Bridgewater College in Virginia.

IMing, TEXT MESSAGING, AND ADOLESCENT SOCIAL NETWORKS

J. Alison Bryant
Ashley Sanders-Jackson
Amber M. K. Smallwood

Abstract

Building on previous research in computer-mediated communication, social and communication networks, and adolescent development, this article raises three issues regarding adolescent use of socially interactive technologies (SITs) and their relationship to offline social networks: 1) whether adolescents are creating more, but weaker ties using SITs, 2) to what extent adolescent SIT-facilitated networks overlap with friendship networks, and 3) whether SIT relationships are important for adolescents who have fewer offline peer ties. In order to investigate these questions, network data collection and analysis were integrated with more traditional questionnaire methodology and statistical analysis. The results show that the adolescents in the study were not creating more ties using SITs, nor were they necessarily creating weaker SIT-based ties; that there was little overlap between SIT-facilitated and offline social networks; and that socially-isolated adolescents were less likely than other adolescents to use SITs.

J. Alison Bryant, Ashley Sanders-Jackson, and Amber M. K. Smallwood, "IMing, Text Messaging, and Adolescent Social Networks," *Journal of Computer-Mediated Communication*, vol. 11, issue 2 (2006). © 2006 Journal of Computer-Mediated Communication. Reprinted by permission of International Communication Association.

INTRODUCTION

Socially interactive technologies (SITs), such as instant messaging and text   2
messaging, are beginning to redefine the social networks of today's youth. By
offering fast-paced, inexpensive, online communication, SITs allow for new
online youth social networks to form and evolve. These online networks, in
turn, may affect the offline social and friendship networks in which youth are
immersed.

Much has been said about the prevalence of technology in the lives of ado-   3
lescents. Reports in the press and surveys from parents find points of view that
range from exuberant, discussing how socially-interactive technologies can save
youth from social isolation and depression, to alarming, focusing on how constant use of these technologies fosters anti-social behavior (Turow, 1999). The
reality, of course, lies somewhere in-between these two extremes. As with the
adoption and use of any other technology, there are a variety of factors that
affect how SITs are used on an individual level, as well as group dynamics that
come into play. This article focuses on both of these aspects of SIT use within
one of the most influential networks in youths' lives: the peer, or friendship,
network.

Previous research on youth and SITs has tended to focus on who is using   4
the technology and why, employing either in-depth ethnographic data with relatively small sample sizes (Eldridge & Grinter, 2001; Grinter & Eldridge, 2001,
2003; Grinter & Palen, 2002), or larger questionnaires focusing on basic user
data (Lenhart, 2003; Lenhart, Madden, & Hitlin, 2005; Lenhart, Rainie, &
Lewis, 2001). The main findings of such research have been threefold. First,
youth are using SITs to enhance communication among friends and family, to
make plans with one another, and to maintain social contact outside of their
day-to-day face-to-face conversations (Grinter & Eldridge, 2001, 2003; Grinter
& Palen, 2002; Lenhart, Madden, & Hitlin, 2005; Lenhart, Rainie, & Lewis,
2001; Schneider & Hemmer, 2005; Valkenburg & Peter, 2005). Second, these
technologies have been adopted by teens relatively quickly because IMing and
text messaging are more convenient, less expensive (especially in some countries), and faster than traditional technologies. The ability to time-shift and talk
at non-traditional times are added incentives (Grinter & Eldridge, 2001;
Kasesniemi & Rautianinen, 2002; Lenhart, Madden, & Hitlin, 2005; Lenhart,
Rainie, & Lewis, 2001; Ling & Yttri, 2002). Finally, research in this arena has
shown that although preference for using SITs to communicate is definitely on
the rise, and the use of SITs has surpassed that of email in the past year, youth
still tend to hold in-depth, important conversations offline (Grinter & Eldridge,
2003; Lenhart, Madden, & Hitlin, 2005).

Such research is vital to preliminary understandings of a new technol- 5
ogy's usage. However, it does not delve into the heart of some of the more
interesting questions, such as what group dynamics influence youth to adopt
particular technologies or to use them in a particular manner, or how using
these technologies actually affects how children and adolescents communicate
with one another. For example, do youth use these less-rich media technologies to obtain emotional, psychological, and other forms of support from their
peers? Do SITs reflect the same friendship networks that already exist? Part of
the issue is that although social groupings of adolescents are often mentioned
as being an important part of online and offline communication, research
looking at social networks is relatively uncommon. Moreover, the few studies
that have been conducted on the social networks facilitated by SITs have not
collected or analyzed social network data (Kavanaugh, Carroll, Rosson, Zin,
& Reese, 2005; Schneider & Hemmer, 2005); nor is there any network data
or analysis in research on adolescent use of these technologies. Network
approaches can be used to understand the communication dynamics of an
entire network (e.g., a group of friends at school or in a chat room), of subsets
of a network (e.g., a clique of "popular" kids at school and how they affect the
network as a whole), and of individuals within the networks (e.g., early
adopters of instant messaging). For this reason, network analysis is an important perspective to employ.

Another area of research that is under-developed concerns the effects of 6
socially interactive technologies on teen and pre-teen individuals (Livingstone &
Bober, 2005). The inclusion of pre-adolescents and adolescents is important
because they incorporate technology-mediated communication more strongly
into their social lives than do adults (Brown, Mounts, Lamborn, & Steinberg,
1993; Madden & Rainie, 2003). Moreover, although there has been considerable research about email communication and instant messaging, there has been
relatively little research on text messaging. This is surprising since the low-cost,
mobile nature of text messaging has made it very popular among adolescents in
many areas of the world (Eldridge & Grinter, 2001; Grinter & Eldridge, 2001,
2003; Grinter & Palen, 2002). It appears as though youth may have similar
social uses for text messaging as they have for instant messaging (IM), email,
and mobile phones; text messaging may often be used in conjunction with these
other technologies in multi-tasking (Lenhart, Madden, & Hitlin, 2005). The
Pew Internet & American Life Project identified text messaging as an important future direction for research (Lenhart, 2003); the most recent report issued
by the Project is the first to include this technology (Lenhart, Madden, &
Hitlin, 2005).

This article addresses each of these concerns by integrating network theory,   7
data collection, and analysis with research on adolescent SIT use to examine
the types of ties adolescents are creating online and offline, and how those two
types of relationships correlate. In order to address these issues, we build off of
previous research in computer-mediated communication, social and communication networks, and adolescent development to generate a set of research questions that we begin to address through the presentation of our research findings.
As one of the key thrusts of this article is to emphasize the need for network
research in the area of adolescent technology use, we conclude with a discussion
of the benefits and the challenges of this type of research.

Overlapping Networks: The Strength of Online Versus Offline Peer Ties

Young people's use of technology to communicate with one another is certainly   8
nothing new; consider the telephone in the 1950s and 1960s. What has changed
in the past decade, however, is the form that communication takes. New text-
based technologies are picking up where phones left off. Email and text messaging allow for rapid, asynchronous communication within one's peer network; IM
allows for synchronous communication among many friends at once. Moreover,
these SITs are relatively inexpensive, especially when used to contact friends
who would normally be a long distance or international call away.

Adoption of socially interactive technologies is high among adolescents.   9
Aside from email, the most often used Internet tool for peer communication is
instant messaging. This is also a youth-preferential activity, with 74% of online
adolescents in the U.S. having used instant messaging, compared with 44% of
online adults (Lenhart, Rainie, & Lewis, 2001). Research in the U.K has produced similar findings (Livingston & Bober, 2005). Moreover, those youth who
IM tend to do so regularly. In 2005, 65% of American teens, and 75% of
American teens who were online, used IM (Lenhart, Madden, & Hitlin, 2005).
Nearly half of teens who IM use it everyday. Most youth who IM use this application most regularly to maintain relationships, either with friends or family
members, especially those that do not live nearby (Lenhart, Rainie, & Lewis,
2001). Gender-wise, girls use IM as a venue for socializing more than do boys
(Jennings & Wartella, 2004). Moreover, although text messaging has been
gaining popularity with teens, only one-third of American teens report sending
text messages (although that number rises to 64% if one considers only teens
who have mobile phones) (Lenhart, Madden, & Hitlin, 2005).

Today's youth do not necessarily feel that using the Internet, email, IM,   10
and text messaging takes time away from their friendships. Instead, many consciously use these to influence their peer networks. According to a recent U.S.

Internet and SITs study, 67% of the youth surveyed felt that the Internet only helps "a little" or "not at all" when trying to make new friends (Lenhart, Rainie, & Lewis, 2001). In contrast, 48% of the respondents said that they use the Internet to improve their relationships with friends, and 32% said that they use the Internet to make new friends (Lenhart, Rainie, & Lewis, 2001). On the one hand, this supports the optimistic perspective that online communication promotes social support and expanded social interaction (Cole & Robinson, 2002; Katz & Rice, 2002; Kavanaugh, et al., 2005; Kestnbaum, Robinson, Neustadtl, & Alvarez, 2002) rather than isolation and depression (Kraut, Patterson, & Lundmark, 1998; Nie, Hillygus, & Erbring, 2002).[1] On the other hand, it may also support Ito and Daisuke's (2003) argument that adolescents are substituting poorer quality social relationships (weak ties) for better ones (strong ties).

There is some evidence to support this latter line of reasoning. Chan and   11
Cheng (2004) found significant differences between relationships that are formed through computer-mediated communication and relationships that are formed off-line, at least in the early stages. Online relationships are characterized by less depth, although this difference diminishes as the relationships continue to grow (Chan & Cheng, 2004). Moreover, if an individual belongs to an online or other community in which s/he forms computer-mediated relationships, s/he may eventually learn socially situated community norms that make the development of relationships easier and may increase the depth of relationships created online (Riva, 2002).

It seems likely that relationships that exist only over the Internet will have   12
less depth but will provide connections that are external to the participants' already existing social networks. In other words, people using the Internet will create less strong relationships, but there will be more of them. Two concepts in the existing social network literature that explain the existence of such ties are Granovetter's weak-tie relationships (1973, 1983) and the concept of bridging (as opposed to bonding) relationships (Lin, 2001). Weak ties are considered to be acquaintances, as opposed to strong ties that might be close friends or family members. People who have more weak ties as part of their social network are likely to have access to greater amounts of information, because the weak ties will bring in novel information (whereas their strong ties are likely to have duplicate information) (Grannovetter, 1973, 1983). Thus online relationships, which are generally less strong than offline relationships, could provide adolescents with increased information and may enlarge their perspective on the world around them. This, of course, could be both a positive and a negative experience.

A bridging relationship involves an individual who is outside an individ-   13
ual's usual interpersonal network. This relationship may involve a higher level
of heterogeneity (i.e., the person in the bridging position may not be as similar
to the individual as the individual's usual friends) and a lower level of emotional intensity than a bonding relationship, which involves a close interpersonal relationship with emotional intensity and sharing (Lin, 2001).

The concepts of weak ties and bridging relationships are similar to what   14
adolescents often experience in SIT-based relationships, at least according to
the anecdotal evidence put forth in the mainstream media. The concern often
expressed is that as adolescents spend more time using SITs to form relationships, they will create a greater number of relationships but these relationships
will not provide the social support that strong, offline relationships provide.
What has not been clear thus far is whether this trade-off between the number
and depth of relationships is occurring. We therefore ask the following research
question:

RQ1. Are adolescents creating more, but weaker, ties using SITs?   15

Do I Know You from Somewhere? How SIT and Offline Relationships Overlap

Another interesting, and thus far largely unaddressed, issue in the literature is   16
that of the relationship between offline and online friendships. If there is high
correlation between offline friendship networks and online SIT networks, we
can assume that the online ties are mapping onto and strengthening the offline
ties. If, however, there is not strong correlation between the networks, then
the adolescents are looking outside their friendship network for communication partners and possibly social support. Moreover, because we are interested
in the relative value of these ties (e.g., the closeness of friendship ties, the frequency of IM communication), we need to look at whether the ties are of corresponding strength. In this analysis, we examine the use of instant messaging
and text messaging (or short-message-service/SMS) and their correlation with
offline friendships.

Instant messaging and text messaging are both forms of technology-mediated   17
communication that provide a way for individuals to communicate with one
another and to create and reinforce social ties and friendships. Text messaging,
however, is different from IM and many other forms of CMC because it is not
anonymous. Because text messaging is usually facilitated through mobile phone
technology, it is difficult to obtain a telephone number from an individual without at least having met the person or knowing their first name. Additionally,
some research suggests that the use of text messaging may be perceived as a form
of socially acceptable gift (Taylor & Harper, 2003). This would imply that indi-

viduals who engage in this type of behavior share a set of norms that would indeed make the exchange of text messages a gift, thus reinforcing the idea that text messaging is generally utilized to strengthen the preexisting network of an individual.

How adolescents use these SIT relationships to broaden and/or deepen   18
their social networks remains unclear. Because it is common for adolescents to utilize SITs as a form of relationship maintenance and day-to-day communication (Gross, Juvonen, & Gable, 2002; Kreager, 2004; Wolak, Mitchell, & Finkelhor, 2003), we would expect users' friendship networks to overlap significantly with their SIT communication networks. On the other hand, if youth are using these technologies to develop new relationships and create romantic relationships (Gross et al., 2002; Kreager, 2004; Wolak et al., 2003), we may see less overlap between the two. In order to understand better the dynamics between these networks, we ask the following research question:

RQ2. To what extent do adolescent SIT communication networks overlap with   19
their friendship networks?

The Wallflower Becomes the Life of the Online Party?

Most of the previous discussion has focused on adolescents who have strong   20
offline relationships. However, there is a second group of adolescents who describe themselves as having fewer or less deep friendships (Kreager, 2004). These more isolated youth may utilize IMing and text messaging to fulfill different needs than individuals who utilize SITs to strengthen existing relationships. These SIT-based relationships may provide essential social support and camaraderie for otherwise isolated youth, which are particularly vital during this stage of social development. Whether or not such relationships are being formed, however, is not clear from the current literature. Therefore, we ask:

RQ3. Are SIT-based relationships important for adolescents who have fewer   21
offline peer ties?

DATA COLLECTION & ANALYSIS

The data for this article were collected from 7th-grade students at a middle school   22
in a midwestern college town in the United States. All of the students were given questionnaires about their use of different media, focusing on their use of instant messaging, text messaging, and other technology (computer, Internet, email, television, telephones, etc.). In addition, the questionnaires asked the students whom they consider to be their friends and, if they use SITs, with whom they IM and text message. There were 40 respondents to the questionnaire, all of them

between 11 and 13 years old. Eleven of the respondents were male and 29 were female.

For the open-ended friendship network questions, the participants were   23
asked to list up to 25 people and then to identify those people as "close friends," "good friends," or just "friends." For the IM and text message networks, they were asked to list up to 25 people with whom they communicate using each of these technologies and then to differentiate among those people with whom they communicated "most often," "often," or "occasionally." Finally, the questionnaire asked the participants how they view these SITs as fitting within the social and emotional spheres of their daily life. The questionnaires thus yielded three types of data: 1) a set of three self-report ego-networks (peer, IM, and text message networks) for each participant, 2) self-report data regarding media usage and adoption that was used as attribute data for each of the participants (or nodes in the networks), and 3) self-report data regarding feelings of social isolation/belonging and social support. These data were coded and analyzed using network analysis software (UCINet), as well as more traditional statistical analysis methods.

Results

General User Data   Although the primary focus of this analysis is on the network   24
data, it is important to understand the general media and SIT environment of the participants in this research. All participants indicated that they had a television at home, and 94.7% also had a computer at home. Participants spent, on average, over four more hours per week watching television (14.55 hours) than using a computer (10.37 hours). After home use, the most popular places for using the computer were school (90.0%), the library (42.5%), and at the home of a friend or family member (25.0%). While they are online, the participants in the study spend time surfing the Internet (87.5%), working on homework (85.0%), playing computer games (85.0%), sending and receiving email (80.0%), and instant messaging (60.0%), among other activities.

On average, study participants who IM spend 2.2 hours per day online with   25
this technology. Among the most popular reasons for IMing were to "keep in touch with friends" (92.0%), followed closely by to "make plans with friends" (88.0%). Other uses with more negative connotations included using IM to "play a trick on someone" (60.0%), to "write something you wouldn't say in person" (42.0%), and to "break up with someone" (24.0%). See Table 1 for the complete list of IM activities.

Text messaging was not as popular as IMing among our participants. Those   26
who text message average only 2.82 hours per week on this activity. Adoption

TABLE 1   What the Participants Do on IM

Keep in touch with friends	92.0%
Make plans with friends	88.0%
Play games with IM software	61.5%
Play a trick on someone	60.0%
Ask someone out	44.0%
Write something you wouldn't say in person	42.0%
Send non-text information	38.5%
Break up with someone	24.0%

rates were similar for both SITs, however. Over 65% of participants have been using both instant messaging and text messaging technologies for more than one year. Only 3.8% had adopted either technology within the past month.

Data on social isolation and belonging were also gathered. Ninety percent of the participants indicated that they have "lots of friends," while only 10.0% designated that they have "a few friends" or "no friends." When asked about the intensity of their friendships, 42.5% of participants indicated they have "lots of close friends," 52.5% have "a few close friends," and 5.0% listed having "no close friends." Mediated methods of communicating with friends, other than IMing and text messaging, included telephone (65.0%), email (35.0%), and chat rooms (10.0%).

Finally, participants reported a wide range of variation across all three forms of network data. When asked about friendship networks, the average number of friends listed was 17.33, with a range of 0 to 27,[2] and the average number of close friends was 6.23, with a range of 0 to 16. When asked about IM networks, the 23 youth who currently use IM had an average of 12.04 people with whom they IM, with a range from 1 to 25 (the maximum allowed by the questionnaire), and an average number of frequent IM partners of 2.39, with a range of 0 to 5. In addition, over 42% of IM users indicated between one and 20 people on their IM "buddy list," while 15.2% declared over eighty IM partners. Finally, when asked about text messaging networks, of the eight youth who currently text message, the average number of people with whom they do so was 8.63, with a range of 1 to 25 (the maximum allowed by the questionnaire), and an average number of frequent text message partners of 1.63, with a range of 0 to 5.

Network Data   In order to investigate the three research questions mentioned   29
above, we conducted three separate analyses.

RQ1. Are adolescents creating more, but weaker, ties using SITs? The first   30
part of this analysis looks at the total number of ties being created through the
various forms of communication. We performed a pair-samples t-test between
each pair of networks, looking at the total number of ties within the network
and different forms of communication. There was a significant difference
between total number of friends listed and total number of IM partners (t(df =
37) = 7.151, mean = 16.99, $p < 0.001$). There was also a significant difference
between total number of friends listed and total number of text messaging partners (t(df = 6) = 3.390, mean = 7.11, $p = 0.015$). In both cases, however, number of friends was greater than the number of SIT-based relationships. There
was no significant difference between total number of IM partners listed and
total number of text messaging partners. Thus there is a significant difference
between the two SIT forms of communication and interpersonal friendship networks, but not in the way previous research has suggested.

In order to address relational intensity of SIT communication relation-   31
ships as compared to offline relationships, a paired-sample t-test was run comparing the intensity between each of the three types of relationships.
Relationship intensity was defined as the average of the number of people the
participant listed as close friends (or communicated with most frequently via
IM or text messaging), divided by the total number of friends (or SIT partners) listed. This yielded a measure of intensity where participants' friendship
intensity or SIT intensity ranged from 0 to 1, with 1 being a very intense network where all friends were indicated to be close friends. There was no significant difference in relational intensity between friendship networks and text
messaging networks, between friendship networks and IM partner networks,
or between IM partner networks and text messaging networks. This implies
that there is no significant difference in intensity between any of the network
types.

RQ2: To what extent do adolescent SIT-facilitated networks overlap with   32
their friendship networks? In order to test the relationship between the social
networks with different forms of communication, we analyzed each participant's
valued ego-networks using quadratic assignment procedure (QAP) correlation
analysis. QAP analysis calculates inter-network comparisons using Pearson's
correlation coefficient between corresponding cells of two matrices. It then per-
mutes the rows and columns of one of the matrices and correlates it with the
other matrix, repeating this process hundreds of times to calculate how often

the random correlation is greater than (or equal to) the original correlation. A low proportion (< 0.05) indicates a strong relationship between the matrices (Borgatti, Everett, & Freeman, 2002).

Because we gathered valued network data, we were able to analyze these 33 data in two ways. First, we dichotomized the data and correlated the networks in order to see if there was general overlap between the people listed on the pairs of networks. Overall, there was little correlation between the dichotomized friendship network and the 2 SIT networks. Only nine significant relationships were found across 23 participants who use IM and have friendship networks. The average correlation was –0.249, with a range of correlations between –0.801 and 0.567. Among the eight participants who use text messaging, no significant relationships occurred between text messaging and friendship networks. The range of correlations between these relationships was –0.376 and 0.281, with the average correlation being –0.190. Finally, across the eight participants who use both text messaging and IM networks, there were two significant relationships, with a range of correlations between –0.354 and 0.659. The average correlation was 0.008. Therefore, there is little overlap among the three networks.

The second QAP analysis looked at the valued data for evidence of a corre- 34 lation between the strength of the relationships that participants had with each person in the different contexts. Again, we found little correlation between the strength of the online and offline relationships. Only four significant relationships were found across 23 participants who use IM and have friendship networks. The average correlation was 0.053, with a range of correlations between –0.674 and 0.529. Of those participants who text message, there was only one significant relationship with the friendship networks. The range of correlations between these relationships was –0.382 and 0.538, with the average correlation being –0.061. Finally, just as with the dichotomized data, there were two significant relationships between text messaging and IM networks, with a range of correlations between –0.278 and 0.924. The average correlation was 0.181. See Table 2 for a summary of these results.

RQ3: Are online relationships important for adolescents who have fewer 35 **offline peer ties?** The literature suggests that relatively isolated individuals might turn to SIT-based communication to augment their social interaction. Of the people who reported having friends, but have 10 or fewer friends, only 36% use IM, compared to 72% of people with more than 10 friends. For text messaging, 27% of the people who reported having friends, but have 10 or fewer friends, currently use text messaging, compared to 24% who have more than 10 friends. None of the adolescents who responded that they have few or no close

TABLE 2 Relationship between Friendship and SIT Networks

Networks correlated	Average dichotomized correlation	% of participants with significant dichotomized correlation	Average valued correlation	% of participants with significant valued correlation
Friend/IM	−0.249	39% (78% negatively correlated)	0.053	17% (25% negatively correlated)
Friend/txt	−0.190	0%	−0.061	13%
IM/txt	0.008	25%	0.181	25%

friends used instant messaging or text messaging. Therefore, IM does not seem to provide an alternative source of social support for people who are more isolated within their peer network.

Discussion

In response to research question 1, the participants in this research project do not seem to be creating either more or weaker ties using SITs. At first glance, this seems to contradict the literature on online relationships cited earlier, which says that people are substituting poorer quality online social relationships (weak ties) for better offline ones (strong ties). However, we first need to remember that the literature on online ties has thus far focused primarily on adults, not on youth, who may have integrated technology more seamlessly into their social lives. Second, when we look at how long the respondents have been using the technology, we see that 85% have been using IM for more than six months (and 65% have been using it for more than a year), and that 50% have been using text messaging for more than six months (with 30% using it for more than a year). The fact that the technology is no longer novel may mean that the desire to go online to create new relationships may also have dissipated. This finding is also supported by the finding of the Pew Internet Project that 67% of youth do not think that using the Internet is helpful in creating relationships (Lenhart, Rainie, & Lewis, 2001). 36

The analysis for research question 2 yielded similar results. For the participants in this study, very little overlap was found between their offline friendships and their SIT-based relationships. As regards whether the same ties existed in both the friend network and the IM communication network, only 39% of the participants had a significant correlation between the two networks. Looking at the similarity in the values of the relationships, we see an even 37 greater difference, with only 17% of the participants' networks significantly correlated. These results, considered together, show that even when there was overlap between the networks, which occurred relatively infrequently, the ties were of different strengths. Thus a respondent might list someone as a close friend, but only as an occasional IM partner.

In addition, it is interesting to note that although little significant difference was found between the networks, 78% of the significant dichotomous relationships were negative. This suggests that the participants in this study are unlikely to have the same friends online as offline. In conjunction with the low overlap found using the valued data, it suggests that they are more likely to spend time talking to acquaintances online. Although this may seem to be at odds with previous research on youth and SITs, it makes sense if one considers that youth still use technologies like the telephone to have in-depth conversations; presumably they would be more likely to have such conversations with their close friends. 38

An important issue to highlight regarding these results is that, particularly in this sample, the participants may be using IM but their friends may not. Although 60% of the participants who chose to complete the study use IM, the adoption rate may be lower in the general population. Without complete network data, which include attribute data as to whether the friends listed have adopted the same technology, we cannot know whether this is a mediating factor. 39

In the same way, the lack of correlation between friendship and text messaging networks suggests that the participants in this study are not text messaging their friends, and the slight overlap between IMing and text messaging suggests that they are using different SITs with different friends. This finding seems to be due primarily to the low adoption rate for the technology in this sample. Further research, possibly among older adolescents who are more likely to have their own mobile phones, should provide better data in these areas. 40

Coupled with the findings for research question 1, these network results indicate that the adolescents in this study were not creating more ties using SITs, were not necessarily creating weaker SIT-based ties, nor were they creating the same strength of tie across the three social networks. These findings point to a very complex set of social dynamics that requires further study. At the same time, they show that network data and analysis provide a useful lens for looking at teens' online and offline interactions that may reveal aspects of those interactions that are not otherwise evident. 41

Finally, the sample for this project included a group of adolescents who have been targeted in recent years by the media and mental health professionals 42 as being "at-risk" for anti-social (even violent) behavior: the loners (or social isolates). Social support perspectives on new technologies purport that those who have not found many or strong friendship ties in their everyday, offline life may use online communication as a way of increasing their social networks (and thereby increasing their level of social support). The findings of this study, however, call into question this scenario for this group of adolescents. Instead of creating new SIT-based relationships, the socially-isolated youth in this study are not creating any SIT relationships at all (or very few). This finding is in line with the results for research question 1, which show that the study participants are not creating more or stronger SIT-based ties, but the results for this particular group are especially stark. In particular, their text messaging relationships are similar to their more "popular" peers, but the IM relationships are markedly different. This may point to different uses for each of these technologies, but further research is necessary to understand the disparity between the relationships formed using them.

The data collection and analysis presented in this article are not without   43
limitations. The key limitation is the small number of participants, particularly those who use text messaging. The relatively low number of participants in this study is due to several factors. The first is that network data collection is more labor-intensive than traditional questionnaire data and that the collection of free recall ego network data, as were used in this study, is even more tedious for the participants. This inherent lack of user-friendliness in the methodology curtails response rates, particularly in populations that are not being coerced to participate by some higher authority. The students who participated in this study were eligible for a prize drawing for three $50 Best Buy gift certificates. In the future, it may generate more participation to offer a less valuable compensation that all respondents would receive, such as a movie pass.

In addition, the content of the questionnaire required participants to list   44
their friends by name, so that the researchers could then code the social network data across the three interaction types. Because peer pressures are so intense during adolescence, the possibility that someone might know who you listed as your friends may have discouraged people to participate. This issue was raised when the researchers received a phone call from a parent and an email from a prospective participant alluding to this concern.

Moreover, the process of completing the questionnaire was complicated by   45
the need to obtain parental consent. In order for students to fill out and return their questionnaire they had to take their questionnaire packets home for their parents to sign, fill them out, and then remember to bring them back to school to turn them in. This process, although necessary because the participants were

minors, created multiple opportunities for the questionnaire not to make it back to the researchers.

Finally, as mentioned above, our set of respondents included very few text message users. This may be because of the age group that was being targeted. Adolescents 11 to 13 years old may not have their own mobile phones, and therefore may not have access to text messaging capabilities. They are relatively likely, however, to have access to a computer and therefore to IM. Future research should increase the overall number of participants or focus on a slightly older cohort in order to gather more complete text message data. 46

Future Directions

The results of this research point to a very complex dynamic between offline and SIT-based friendships. In order to garner a more complete understanding of these interactions we need overtime network data from a complete adolescent network. The overtime aspect of the data would allow us to see how these networks interact and co-evolve. This may point to interesting and varying phenomena at different points in time, as well as yield some insight as to whether one network is the driving force for the other. Of course, the composition of the network of adolescents may change over time, complicating the data. 47

Moreover, we need to have access to complete network data. This is a particularly difficult issue. In the first place, friendships and SIT-based relationships are not geographically static; the people whom the adolescents will list as friends and SIT partners will not be contained within the population of participants. In preliminary data coding for this project, the ego-network from the 40 nodes garnered a complete network with over 500 nodes. If one were able to gather these data from an entire high school, one would have an unworkable number of nodes. Moreover, the sample would still not contain the ego network data for those friends and SIT partners who were not part of the population. 48

Another possibility would be to constrain the networks artificially. For example, one could create an online network data collection tool that would only allow participants to choose others within the population (e.g., all of the students at a high school) to list as part of their network. Although this would create a manageable set of network data, it would be artificial. In addition, part of the interest in the overlap between these networks is whether youth are going outside their everyday friendship networks for social support. Data for a constrained network would not provide information on those types of friendships. 49

This study was a first attempt to address these issues and to create a set of manageable, ego-network data for analysis. A vast amount of work remains to be done in this area. Technology is pervasive, and has become an integral, if 50 not overpowering, part of the lives of today's youth. By better understanding the interactions between the two, we can use these technologies more constructively to enhance the lives of young people.

NOTES

1. That is not to say that SIT use has no negative effects. Bullying via SITs has become a problem worldwide (Magid, 2001; National Children's Home, 2005), and SIT use in the classroom has become problematic, with students using the technologies to "pass notes" and cheat on exams (Bulliet, 2005; Magid, 2001).

2. Two participants listed more than the maximum number of friends (one listed 26 and the other 27).

REFERENCES

Borgatti, S. P., Everett, M. G., & Freeman, L. C. (2002). *Ucinet for Windows: Software for Social Network Analysis* (Version 6.15) [Computer software]. Harvard: Analytic Technologies.

Brown, B. B., Mounts, N. S., Lamborn, S. D., & Steinberg, L. D. (1993). Parenting practices and peer group affiliation in adolescence. *Child Development, 64* (2), 467–482.

Bulliet, M. (2005, March 30). School sneaks use gadgets to chat & cheat. *New York Post*, p. 3.

Chan, D., K.-S., & Cheng, G. H.-L. (2004). A comparison of offline and online friendship qualities at different stages of relationship development. *Journal of Social and Personal Relationships, 21* (3), 305–320.

Cole, J., & Robinson, J. P. (2002). Internet use and sociability in the UCLA data: A simplified MCA analysis. *IT & Society, 1* (1), 202–218.

Eldridge, M., & Grinter, R. (2001, April). *Studying text messaging in adolescents*. Paper presented to the Workshop on Mobile Communications: Understanding Users, Adoption & Design at the Conference on Human Factors in Computing Systems (CHI), Seattle, WA. Retrieved January 21, 2006 from http://www.cs.colorado.edu/~palen/chi_workshop/papers/ EldridgeGrinter.pdf

Granovetter, M. S. (1973). Strength of weak ties. *American Journal of Sociology, 78* (6), 1360–1380.

Granovetter, M. S. (1983). The strength of weak ties: A network theory revisited. *Sociological Theory, 1*, 201–233.

Grinter, R. E., & Eldridge, M. A. (2001). y do tngrs luv 2 txt msg? In W. Prinz, M. Jarke, Y. Rogers, K. Schmidt, & V. Wulf (Eds.), *Proceedings of the*

Seventh European Conference on Computer Supported Cooperative Work, *16–20 September 2001, Bonn, Germany* (pp. 219–238). Dordrecht, Netherlands: Kluwer Academic Publishers.

Grinter, R. E., & Eldridge, M. A. (2003). Wan2tlk?: Everyday text messaging. *Proceedings of the SIGCHI Conference on Human Factors in Computing Systems* (pp. 441–448). New York: ACM Press. Retrieved January 21, 2006 from http://delivery.acm.org/10.1145/650000/642688/p441-grinter.pdf

Grinter, R. E., & Palen, L. (2002). Instant Messaging in teenage life. *Proceedings of the ACM Conference on Computer Supported Cooperative Work* (pp. 21–30). NY: ACM Press. Retrieved January 21, 2006 from http://www.grinter.org/cscw02.pdf

Gross, E. F., Juvonen, J., & Gable, S. L. (2002). Internet use and well-being in adolescence. *Journal of Social Issues, 58* (1), 75–90.

Ito, M., & Daisuke, O. (2003). *Mobile phones, Japanese youth, and the replacement of social contact.* Retrieved January 21, 2006 from http://www.itofisher.com/PEOPLE/mito/mobileyouth.pdf

Jennings, N., & Wartella, E. (2004). Technology and the family. In A. L. Vangelisti (Ed.), *Handbook of Family Communication* (pp. 593–608). Mahwah, NJ: Erlbaum.

Kasesniemi, E.-L., & Rautianinen, P. (2002). Mobile culture of children and teenagers in Finland. In J. E. Katz & M. Aakhus (Eds.), *Perpetual Contact: Mobile Communication, Private Talk, Public Performance* (pp. 170–192). Cambridge: Cambridge University Press.

Katz, J. E., & Rice, R. E. (2002). *Social Consequences of Internet Use: Access, Involvement and Interaction.* Cambridge, MA: MIT Press.

Kavanaugh, A., Carroll, J. M., Rosson, M. B., Zin, T. T., & Reese, D.D. (2005). Community networks: Where offline communities meet online. *Journal of Computer-Mediated Communication, 10* (4). Retrieved January 21, 2006 from http://jcmc.indiana.edu/vol10/issue4/kavanaugh.html

Kestnbaum, M., Robinson, J., Neustadtl, A., & Alvarez, A. (2002). Information technology and social time displacement. *IT & Society, 1* (1), 21–37.

Kraut, R., Patterson, M., & Lundmark, V. (1998). Internet paradox: A social technology that reduces social involvement and psychological well-being? *American Psychologist, 52* (9), 1017–1031.

Kreager, D. A. (2004). Strangers in the halls: Isolation and delinquency in school networks. *Social Forces, 83* (1), 251–290.

Lenhart, A. (2003). *Adolescents, parents and technology: Highlights from the Pew Internet & American Life Project.* Paper presented to the Lawlor Group, Long Beach, CA. http://www.pewInternet.org/ppt/Adolescents,Parentsand Technology-Lawlor10.03.03a.nn.ppt [no longer available]

Lenhart, A., Madden, M., & Hitlin, P. (2005). *Teens and Technology: Youth are Leading the Transition to a Fully Wired and Mobile Nation.* Washington, DC: Pew Internet & American Life Project.

Lenhart, A., Rainie, L., & Lewis, O. (2001). *Teenage Life Online: The Rise of the Instant-Message Generation and the Internet's Impact on Friendships and Family Relationships.* Washington, DC: Pew Internet & American Life Project.

Lin, N. (2001). *Social Capital: A Theory of Social Structure and Action.* Cambridge: Cambridge University Press.

Ling, R., & Yttri, B. (2002). Hyper-coordination via mobile phones in Norway. In J. E. Katz & M. Aakhus (Eds.), *Perpetual Contact: Mobile Communication, Private Talk, Public Performance* (pp. 139–169). Cambridge: Cambridge University Press.

Livingstone, S., & Bober, M. (2005). *UK Children Go Online: Final Report of Key Project Findings.* London: Economic and Social Research Council.

Madden, M., & Rainie, L. (2003). *America's Online Pursuits: The Changing Picture of Who's Online and What They Do.* Washington, DC: Pew Internet & American Life Project.

Magid, L. (2001, December 13). Europe children cell use ahead of U.S.—for good, bad. *The Mercury News*, p. 3.

National Children's Home. (2005). *Putting U in the picture: Mobile bullying survey 2005.* London. Retrieved January 24, 2006 from http://www.nch.org.uk/uploads/documents/Mobile_bullying_%20report.pdf

Nie, N. H., Hillygus, D. S., & Erbring, L. (2002). Internet use, interpersonal relations, and sociability: A time diary study. In B. Wellman & C. Haythornthwaite (Eds.), *The Internet in Everyday Life* (pp. 215–243). Malden, MA: Blackwell.

Riva, G. (2002) The sociocognitive psychology of computer-mediated communication: The present and future of technology-based interactions. *Cyberpsychology and Behavior, 5* (6), 581–598.

Schneider, S., & Hemmer, K. (2005, May). *Telegraph lines in cyberspace? Identity, relationships, and group behavior in instant messaging communication.* Paper presented at the International Communication Association, New York.

Taylor, A. S., & Harper, R. (2003). The gift of the gab? A design oriented sociology of young people's use of mobiles. *Computer Supported Cooperative Work, 12* (3), 267–296.

Turow, J. (1999). *The Internet and the Family: The View From the Family, the View From the Press.* Philadelphia, PA: Annenberg Public Policy Center. Retrieved January 21, 2006 from http://www.annenbergpublicpolicycenter.org/04_info_society/family/rep27.pdf

Valkenburg, P., & Peter, J. (2005, May). *Adolescents' online communication and their closeness to friends*. Paper presented at the International Communication Association, New York.

Wolak, J., Mitchell, K. J., & Finkelhor, D. (2003). Escaping or connecting? Characteristics of youth who form close online relationship. *Journal of Adolescence, 26* (1), 105–119.

Lisa Nakamura received her Ph.D. in English at the City University of New York
Graduate Center in 1996 and is currently an associate professor in the department of
Communication Arts at the University of Wisconsin-Madison. She was the Illinois Program
for Research in the Humanities Fellow for the 2007–2008 academic year at the Institute of
Communications Research at the University of Illinois at Urbana-Champaign. She previously taught at Sonoma State University in northern California. She is the author of *Digitiz-
ing Race: Visual Cultures of the Internet* (2007) and co-editor of *Race in Cyberspace* (2000).

INTRODUCTION

Lisa Nakamura

The Internet is a place where race happens. In the early days of the Net, tech-   1
nological visionaries imagined the online world as a utopian space where
everything—even transcending racism—was possible. But now the Internet
"revolution" is over, a fact upon which nearly everyone, from hackers to academics to dot-com investors, agrees. This book looks at what happened to race
when it went online, and how our ideas about race, ethnicity, and identity continue to be shaped and reshaped every time we log on, even if we've just
entered the post-Internet "epoch."[1]

After years of idealistic technohype, David Brooks wrote, in the *New York*   2
Times Magazine,

> It's goodbye to the epoch—which must have lasted all of seven years—in
> which people chatted excitedly about free-agent nations, distance being
> dead, I.P.O.'s, the long boom and those dot-com ads during the Super Bowl
> that showed global children united by the wonders of instant communica-
> tion. One minute you've got zip-drive techies pulling all-nighters amid
> their look-at-me-I'm-wacky workstations, and the next moment—poof—it
> seems so stale. Suddenly, it doesn't really matter much if the speed of
> microprocessors doubles with the square root of every lunar eclipse (or
> whatever Moore's law was). And so just like a used-bong sale in 1978 or a
> yellow-tie auction in 1990, scenes like this [. . .] bring a psychological
> decade to a sobering close. What started out as the biggest revolution since
> Gutenberg ends up as a giant yard sale [. . .]. What's gone is the sense that
> the people who are using the stuff are on the cutting edge of history and
> everyone else is roadkill. (28)

I started the research that led to this book in 1995, a year after Brooks dates   3
the beginning of the Internet epoch, and completed it in 2001, the year he and
most pundits agree brought the end of the Internet's heyday. At three years shy
of a decade, it's a short-lived epoch indeed. Perhaps it succumbed to "Internet
time," that compression of time to which we've grown accustomed in our high-
tech lives.[2]

In these post-Internet times, it may be true that possessing access to the   4
Internet no longer guarantees one a place at the "cutting edge of history." However, *lack of access* to the Internet—often found along raced, classed, and still, to
a narrowing extent, gendered lines—continues to cut particular bodies *out* of
various histories in the making. The epochal terms used by Brooks to describe
the end of the "new economy" are characteristic of much popular intellectual
writing on the Internet: those people who were run over, routed around, or simply denied access to the Internet are characterized as "roadkill" on the information superhighway.[3] This online roadkill is, quite simply, the poor and people of
color.

Though Brooks writes that in 2001 there is no longer the sense that Inter-   5
net nonusers are roadkill (a debatable claim indeed, considering recent concern
over the "digital divide" that separates technology haves from have-nots), he
does acknowledge that it was once thought so during those crucial years in
which the discursive landscape of the Internet was being formed. Hence, people
of color were functionally absent from the Internet at precisely that time when
its discourse was acquiring its distinctive contours.

The repercussions of the discursive gap are immense, for, as I stated earlier,   6
the Internet is a place where race happens; even in the absence of users of color,
images of race and racialism proliferate in cyberspace. The ideological uses to
which race is put in this medium must be examined before we can even begin to
consider cyberspace's promise as a democratic and progressive medium. Daniel
Punday is one of many cyberculture scholars who pose the question, Can the
Internet propagate genuinely new and nonracist (and nonsexist and nonclas-
sist) ways of being, or does it merely reflect our culture at large? Punday identifies two phases of Internet scholarship, the first and most utopian of which
asserts that the former is true while the second asserts the latter. He writes that
"quite contrary to the early belief that cyberspace offers a way to escape gender,
race, and class as conditions of social interaction [. . .] recent critics suggest
that online discourse is woven of stereotypical cultural narratives that reinstall
precisely those conditions" (199).[4] In this passage, he claims that this second
phase of scholarship has become the dominant one: "these critics are debating
whether participants in online discourse are constructing coherent identities

that shed light on the real world or whether they are merely tacking together an identity from media sources. As critics have gradually begun to accept the latter, they have lost confidence in the socially transformative possibilities of online discourse" (204).

There is no doubt that the Internet is a "socially transformative" force; what seems to be at issue here is rather the specific nature of that ongoing transformation as well as its particular object. Rather than adopting a utopian or pessimistic view in which the Internet is viewed as either a vector for progressive change in the classical liberal tradition or as the purveyor of crude and simplistic "stereotypical cultural narratives," it seems crucial to first narrow the focus a bit and examine the specific means by which identities are deployed in cyberspace. Currently, "popular attitudes toward the Internet tend to be maddeningly bipolar—either the Net changes everything or the Net changes nothing" (Heilemann 138). Of course, the truth lies between these two poles: the Net changes *some* things. Images of race on the Net are both "stereotyped" at times, as in some chat rooms, cyberpunk fictions, and advertisements, and at other times, race is deployed in creative coalition building that creates a sense of community and racial identity online. As scholars become more sensitized to issues of diversity online,[5] there is a welcome shift in emphasis from simply recognizing that racial inequity does exist there to a growing concern with how race is represented in cyberspace, for the Internet is above all a discursive and rhetorical space, a place where "race" is created as an effect of the net's distinctive uses of language. Hence, it is crucial to examine not only the wide variety of rhetorical conditions of utterance, reception, audience, and user/speaker that create particular communicative situations in cyberspace, but also to trace the ways in which this array of situations creates "cybertypes," or images of racial identity engendered by this new medium. Only then will it be possible to assess the Net's potential for "social transformation."

What ideological and cultural work does race do in cyberspace? The question demands a number of different types of critical approaches and examples, since cyberspace makes so many different kinds of narrative possible: user-to-user narratives (such as those produced in chat rooms or e-mail) and user-to-interface narratives (that is to say, what happens when users encounter design issues and interact with them) constitute just two examples. There is also a formidable array of narratives about cyberspace, such as cyberpunk fictions and popular advertisements for the Internet, that inform the ways that users envision and interact with its racial terrain. Each chapter of this book addresses the question of racial cybertyping's operations (for better or worse) in the different rhetorical spaces of and around the Internet in an attempt to acknowledge their variety and particularity, for it makes no more sense to discuss the Net as one "thing" than it does to discuss literature without reference to period, genre, style, or audience.

Chapter 1, "Cybertyping and the Work of Race in the Age of Digital Reproduction," examines the ways that race gets coded for different kinds of work in the information economy, and traces the ways that cybertyping proliferates as part of a cultural matrix that surrounds the Internet. While foreign workers are often glorified as exemplary information workers (as in the case of immigrant Asian engineers with H1B visas), American racial minorities, in particular African Americans, are troped quite differently, as outsiders to digital economies and systems of representation. This permits a kind of cosmetic cosmopolitanism that perpetuates a digital divide that splits along the axis of racial representations as well as along patterns of computer access organized around racial difference. Racism in this country is ignored in favor of celebrating the diversity of "foreign" information workers, who are represented in advertisements as a Benetton-like rainbow of racial difference—decorative, exotic, and comfortably distant.

9

Chapter 2, entitled "Head-Hunting on the Internet: Identity Tourism, Avatars, and Racial Passing in Textual and Graphical Chat Spaces," focuses on user-to-user interactions in social role-playing spaces online. While these spaces could be categorized as "games," the MUDs, MOOs, and chat rooms that I examine,[6] specifically LambdaMOO and Club Connect, are also theatrical and discursive spaces where identity is performed, swapped, bought, and sold in both textual and graphic media. When users create characters to deploy in these spaces, they are electing to perform versions of themselves as raced and gendered beings. When users' characters, or "avatars," are differently raced from the user, the opportunity for online recreational passing or "identity tourism" arises; that is to say, users perform stereotyped versions of the "Oriental" that perpetuate old mythologies about racial difference. And as Caren Kaplan points out in *Questions of Travel*, tourists operate from a position of privilege and entitlement (62); to be a tourist is to possess mobility, access, and the capital to satisfy curiosities about "native" life. Chat-space participants who take on identities as samurai and geisha constitute the darker side of postmodern identity, since the "fluid selves" they create (and often so lauded by postmodern theorists) are done so in the most regressive and stereotyped of ways. These kinds of racial identity plays stand as a critique of the notion of the digital citizen as an ideal cogito whose subjectivity is liberated by cyberspace. On the contrary, only too often does one person's "liberation" constitute another's recontainment within the realm of racialized discourse. The socially marginalized have a different relation to postmodernity than do members of majority cultures or races. Hence, they have a different relation to cyberspace,

10

or to put it another way, they "do" virtuality differently. That is to say, the type of fragmentation of self or subjectivity they experience online (and as decentered subjects in postmodern culture) differs from that of "majority" users. Though Phillip Brian Harper doesn't look at the Internet specifically in *Framing the Margins: The Social Logic of Postmodern Culture*, he does cite technology as one of the forces engendering the fragmentation characteristic of life in postmodern times, and asserts that "what 'minority' subjects often experience as their primary source of disorientation—the social effects of their difference in contexts where it is construed as negative—will complicate their experience of what has heretofore been conceived as the 'general' disorientation characteristic of the postmodern condition" (29). In other words, being raced is in itself a disorienting position. Being raced in cyberspace is doubly disorienting, creating multiple layers of identity construction. While on the one hand people of color have always been postmodern (and by extension "virtual"), if postmodernism is defined as that way of seeing subjectivity as decentered, fragmented, and marginalized, on the other hand their lack of access to technology and popular figuration as the "primitive" both on- and offline (those virtual samurai and geisha are certainly not to be found in "modern," let alone postmodern, Japan) positions them simultaneously in the nostalgic world of the premodern. The Internet is certainly a place where social differences such as race are frequently construed as negative. While everyone in cyberspace is disoriented, people of color in cyberspace come to the medium already in this state, already marginalized, fragmented, and imbricated within systems of signification that frame them in multiple and often contradictory ways. The celebration of the "fluid self" that simultaneously lauds postmodernity as a potentially liberatory sort of worldview tends to overlook the more disturbing aspects of the fluid, marginalized selves that already exist offline in the form of actual marginalized peoples, which is not nearly so romantic a formulation. But then, this is symptomatic of both postmodern theory and cyberculture studies, neither of which wants to look at race critically. As Harper claims, "the experiences of socially marginalized groups implicitly inform the 'general' postmodern condition without being accounted for in theorizations of it" (4). Indeed, if we are all marginalized and decentered, or if we are all equally "virtual" when we are in cyberspace, what need is there to refer to race at all in discussions of identity online or in a postmodern world?

But, of course, we are not all equally on the margins in the world offline,   11
just as we are not all equally "virtual" in relation to the Internet. And as our culture's investment in computer gaming such as chat rooms and interactive social spaces only continues to grow, it becomes all the more important that we focus a critical gaze on the ways that race is played in these theaters of identity.

While chapter 2 identifies cybertyped versions of race enacted by users in   12
both graphical and textual chat spaces, chapter 3, entitled "Race in the Construct and the Construction of Race: The 'Consensual Hallucination' of Multiculturalism in the Fictions of Cyberspace," examines the source of these "types"
in popular narratives about cyberspace. The study of racial impersonation and
passing on MOOs and MUDs reveals a great deal about how people "do" race
online; this chapter locates the origin of some of these master narratives about
how race is done online in 1980s and '90s cyberpunk narratives. Close readings
of four influential cyberpunk texts—two from the 1980s (Ridley Scott's film
Blade Runner and William Gibson's novel *Neuromancer*) and two from the
1990s, (Neal Stephenson's novel *Snow Crash* and Andy and Larry Wachowski's
film *The Matrix*)—reveal the ways that cyberspace is racialized in popular narratives, and identify a progression from relatively simple and traditional forms of
techno-orientalism to a more nuanced vision of racial hybridity which nonetheless performs its own variety of cybertyping.

Chapter 4, " 'Where Do You Want to Go Today?': Cybernetic Tourism, the   13
Internet, and Transnationality," picks up where chapter 3 leaves off by extending
the range of inquiry to television and print advertisements produced by large
telephony and networking companies like IBM, Compaq, MCI, and Microsoft.
These advertisements, which appeared in mainstream and academic publications, are symptomatic of the ways that corporate discourse cybertypes use race as
a visual commodity for the user. Images of exotic travel in the "third world," and
"primitive" places and people, are part of a persistent pattern of signification that
reinforces the notion of the Western computer and network user as a tourist in
cyberspace. Earlier colonial discourses that privilege the Western gaze and the
sense of freedom, expansiveness, and mastery engendered by its deployment are
directly referenced in the quasi-anthropological visual language of these ads,
which often evoke images from *National Geographic* magazines of days gone by.

Chapter 5, "Menu-Driven Identities: Making Race Happen Online," exam-   14
ines the relationship between the user and the interface, in particular those
interfaces on the Internet such as website portals and e-mail programs, which
most users encounter on a daily basis, and traces the ways that interface design
can produce cybertyped versions of race. When interfaces present us with
menus that insist on a limited range of choices vis-à-vis race, this discursive narrowing of the field of representation can work to deny the existence of ways of
being raced that don't fit into neatly categorizable boxes. Registration pages on
websites that demand that users click a box describing them as "Asian,"
"African American," or "Hispanic" create a textual environment in which mix-
tures of or variations on these already contested categories are literally impossible to express using this interface. This kind of menu-driven racial identity not

only denies the possibility of a mestiza consciousness at a time when our social realities are bending to acknowledge the existence of various forms of racial and cultural hybridity, but also serves a racist ideology which benefits from retaining solid and simplistic notions of race. I juxtapose this reading of corporate interfaces that cybertype users in limiting and simplistic ways to another example, that of ethnic identity e-mail jokes that circulate between groups of users who can share a more fluid, less essentialized sense of racial identity. As John Heilemann notes,

> Andy Grove, C.E.O. of Intel, asserted in a 2001 interview with *Wired* that Internet penetration in the U.S. is substantially ahead of the rest of the world. In the next five years, one thing that is likely to happen is that Internet penetration in the rest of the world is going to replicate what's happened here. And that is going to let—Seattle-style protests notwithstanding—a globalization of culture, of business, of communications achieve a level of pervasiveness that in itself will change the world significantly. (139)

Grove is speaking from the point of view of a person who's been involved   15
in the Internet's infrastructure and commerce from the beginning, not as a scholar of critical theory, ethnic studies, or progressive politics. And in that sense he is typical of most of the captains of the Internet industry machine: his view is that "globalization of culture, of business, of communications" is an unambiguously good thing. Phallic metaphors of the Internet as a peculiarly "penetrative" medium sound patriarchal, as indeed they are. But more to the point, they figure globalization as the result of that penetration, a penetration that cannot be resisted, despite "Seattle-style protests." Clearly, there is a great deal at stake here. In *The Souls of Black Folk*, W. E. B. Du Bois writes that "the problem of the Twentieth Century is the problem of the color-line" (v). At the end of the Internet epoch and the advent of the twenty-first century, this is *still* the problem that haunts cyberspace. It is crucial that scholarly inquiry examine the ways that racism is perpetuated by both globalization and communications technologies like the Internet across a range of discursive fields and cultural matrices. This becomes all the more important as locales outside of the United States submit to "penetration" by the medium, and consequently undergo the sometimes-wrenching transformations that accompany such discursive shifts. This book examines the ways that race is configured in English-language based cyberspaces hosted in the United States. However, in the face of Grove's vision of Internet-driven globalization (which there is no reason in my mind to doubt) it is clear that more research needs to be done on the emerging terrain of race, ethnicity, and racism in non-American cyberspaces. America is not the only place where "digital divides" separate the "roadkill" from the digerati.

ENDNOTES

1. The penchant of theory to attach a *post* (like postmodernism and poststructuralism) to movements and theories appears to be alive and well.

2. See James Gleick's book *Faster* for a more sustained discussion of "Internet time" (83).

3. See David Silver's useful formulation regarding the ways that "the digital architecture of an online environment [can] influence or help to determine the kinds of cultural exchanges and interactions that take place" online. When interfaces not only ignore, but rather "route around" issues of race, gender, and sexuality, they "code its participants as the digital default: white, males, and heterosexual" (143).

4. The "recent critics" referred to by Punday are Shannon McRae, Stephen Shaviro, and myself.

5. There is still a huge amount of research to be done in this area: as Punday writes, "in contrast to gender issues, race online has received considerably less attention. When critics do address such issues, the emphasis is usually on access to the Internet rather than on how race is represented" (211).

6. MUDs (multiple-user dimensions, or multiple-user dungeons) and MOOs (multiple-user dimensions, object-oriented) are computer programs that numerous users can log into and explore while interacting with each other.

REFERENCES

Brooks, David. "The Day After." *New York Times Magazine* May 13, 2001:28.

Du Bois, W. E. B. *The Souls of Black Folk.* New York: Dover, 1903.

Gleick, James. *Faster: The Acceleration of Just about Everything.* New York: Vintage, 2000.

Harper, Phillip Brian. *Framing the Margins: The Social Logic of Postmodern Culture.* Oxford: Oxford University Press, 1994.

Heilemann, John. "Andy Grove's Rational Exuberance." *Wired* June 2001:137–147.

Kaplan, Caren. *Questions of Travel: Postmodern Discourses of Displacement.* Durham, NC: Duke University Press, 1996.

Punday, David. "The Narrative Construction of Cyberspace: Reading *Neuromancer*, Reading Cyberspace Debates." *College English* 63.2 (November 2000):194–213.

Silver, David. "Margins in the Wires: Looking for Race, Gender, and Sexuality in the Blacksburg Electronic Village." In *Race in Cyberspace.* Ed. Beth Kolko, Lisa Nakamura, and Gilbert B. Rodman. New York: Routledge, 2000.

CYBERTYPING AND THE WORK OF RACE IN THE AGE OF DIGITAL REPRODUCTION

Software engineers and academics have something in common: they both like to   1
make up new words. And despite the popular press's glee in mocking both com-
puter-geek and academic jargon, there are several good arguments to be made for
the creation of useful neologisms, especially in cases where one of these fields of
study is brought to bear on the other. The Internet has spawned a whole new set
of vocabulary and specialized terminology because it is a new tool for communicating that has enabled a genuinely new discursive field, a way of generating and
consuming language and signs that is distinctively different from other, older
media. It is an example of what is dubbed "the new media" (a term refreshingly
different from the all-purpose *post-* prefix so familiar to critical theorists, but destined to date just as badly). Terms such as *cybersex, online, file compression, hypertext link*, and *downloading* are now part of the Internet user's everyday vocabulary
since they describe practices or virtual objects that lack analogues in either
offline life or other media. The new modes of discourse enabled by the Internet
require new descriptive terminologies and conceptual frameworks.

Just as engineers and programmers routinely come up with neologisms to   2
describe new technologies, so too do academics and cultural theorists coin new
phrases and terms to describe concepts they wish to introduce to the critical
conversation. While these attempts are not always well advised, and certainly
do contribute at times to the impenetrable and unnecessarily confusing nature
of high theory's rhetoric, there are some compelling reasons that this move
seems peculiarly appropriate in the case of academic studies of the Internet. Lev
Manovich and Espen Aarseth both make a persuasive case for the creation and
deployment of a distinctively new set of terminologies to describe the new
media, in particular the Internet. In *The Language of New Media* Manovich
asserts that "comparing new media to print, photography, or television will
never tell us the whole story" and that "to understand the logic of new media
we need to turn to computer science. It is there that we may expect to find the
new terms, categories, and operations which characterize media which became
programmable. From media studies, we move to something which can be called
software studies; from media theory—to software theory" (65). This statement
calls for a radical shift in focus from traditional ways of envisioning media to a
new method that takes the indispensability of the computer-machine into

account. It truly does call for a reconceptualization of media studies, and constitutes a call for new terms more appropriate to "software studies" to best convey the distinctive features of new media, in particular the use of the computer.

Manovich identifies two "layers" to new media: the cultural layer, which is   3
roughly analogous to "content," and the computer layer, or infrastructure, interface, or other machine-based forms that structure the computer environment. His argument that the computer layer can be expected to have a "significant influence on the cultural logic of media" (63) is in some sense not original; the notion that form influences content (and vice versa) has been around since the early days of literary criticism. It has been conceded for some time now that certain forms allow or disallow the articulation of certain ideas. However, what is original about this argument is its claim that our culture is becoming "computerized" in a wholesale and presumably irrevocable fashion. This is a distinctively different proposition from asserting the importance of, say, electronic *literacy*, a paradigm that is still anchored by its terminology in the world of a very old medium: writing. Manovich calls for a new terminology, native to the computer: he goes on to write that

> in new media lingo, to "transcode" something is to translate it into another format. The computerization of culture gradually accomplishes similar transcoding in relation to all cultural categories and concepts. That is, cultural categories and concepts are substituted, on the level of meaning and/or language, by new ones which derive from the computer's ontology, epistemology, pragmatics. New media thus acts as a forerunner of this more general process of cultural re-conceptualization. (64)

If we follow this proposition, we can see that our culture is in the process of   4
being "transcoded" by the computer's "ontology, epistemology, pragmatics." While this statement has far-reaching implications, at the least it can be seen as an argument for a new openness in new media studies toward the adoption of a terminology that at least acknowledges the indispensable nature of the computer in the study of new media. This would be a transcoded kind of terminology, one that borrows from the language of the computer itself rather than from the language of critical theory or old media studies. In his article "The Field of Humanistic Informatics and its Relation to the Humanities," Espen Aarseth argues that the study of new media needs to be a "separate, autonomous field, where the historical, aesthetic, cultural and discursive aspects of the digitalization of our society may be examined [. . .]. We cannot leave this new development to existing fields, because they will always privilege their traditional methods, which are based on their own empirical objects" (n.p.).

In an attempt to transcode the language of race and racialism that I   5
observed online, I coined the term *cybertype* to describe the distinctive ways that the Internet propagates, disseminates, and commodifies images of race and

racism. The study of racial cybertypes brings together the cultural layer and the computer layer; that is to say, cybertyping is the process by which computer/human interfaces, the dynamics and economics of access, and the means by which users are able to express themselves online interacts with the "cultural layer" or ideologies regarding race that they bring with them into cyberspace. Manovich is correct in asserting that we must take into account the ways that the computer determines how ideological constructs such as race get articulated in this new medium.

Critical theory itself is a technology or machine that produces a particular kind of discourse, and I'd like to conduct a discursive experiment by poaching a term from nineteenth-century print technology. That term is *stereotype.*　6

The word *stereotype* is itself an example of machine language, albeit a pre-computer machine language; the first stereotype was a mechanical device that could reproduce images relatively cheaply, quickly, and in mass quantities. Now that computer-enabled image-reproducing technology like the Internet is faster, cheaper, and more efficient than ever before, how does that machine language translate into critical terms? Might we call new formulations of machine-linked identity *cybertypes*? This is a clunky term; in hacker-speak it would be called a "kludge" or "hack" because it's an improvised, spontaneous, seat-of-the-pants way of getting something done. (Critical theory, like the software industry, is a machine that is good at manufacturing linguistic kludges and hacks). I'd like to introduce it, however, because it acknowledges that identity online is still *typed,* still mired in oppressive roles even if the body has been left behind or brack-eted.[1] I pose it as a corrective to the disturbingly utopian strain I see embodied in most commercial representations of the Internet in general. Chosen identities enabled by technology, such as online avatars, cosmetic and transgender surgery and body modifications, and other cyberprostheses are not breaking the mold of unitary identity but rather shifting identity into the realm of the "virtual," a place not without its own laws and hierarchies. Supposedly "fluid" selves are no less subject to cultural hegemonies, rules of conduct, and regulating cultural norms than are "solid."　7

While telecommunications and medical technologies can challenge some gender and racial stereotypes, they can produce and reflect them as well. Cybertypes of the biotechnologically enhanced or perfected woman and of the Internet's invisible minorities, who can log on to the Net and be taken for "white," participate in an ideology of liberation from marginalized and devalued bodies. This kind of technology's greatest promise to us is to eradicate otherness—to create a kind of better living through chemistry, so to speak. Images of science freeing women from their aging bodies, which make it more difficult to conceive children and ward off cellulite, freeing men from the curse of hair loss,　8 and freeing minorities online from the stigma of their race (since no one can see them), reinforce a "postbody" ideology that reproduces the assumptions of the old one. In an example of linguistic retrofitting, I've termed this phenomenon an example of the "meet the new boss, same as the old boss" product line). In other words, machines that offer identity prostheses to redress the burdens of physical "handicaps" such as age, gender, and race produce cybertypes that look remarkably like racial and gender stereotypes. My research on cross-racial impersonation in an online community, described in chapter 2, reveals that when users are free to choose their own race, all were assumed to be white. And many of those who adopted nonwhite personae turned out to be white male users masquerading as exotic samurai and horny geishas.

Of course, this kind of vertiginous identity play, which produces and   9
reveals cybertyping, is not the fault of or even primarily an effect of technology. Microsoft's advertising slogan, "Where do you want to go today?" is another example of the discourse of technological liberation, and it situates the agency directly where it belongs: with the user. Though computer memory modules double in speed every couple of years, users are still running operating systems that reflect phantasmatic visions of race and gender. Moore's Law, which states that computer processing speeds double every eighteen months, does not obtain in the "cultural layer." In the end, despite academic and commercial discourses, to the contrary it does come down to bodies—bodies with or without access to the Internet, telecommunications, and computers and the cultural capital necessary to use them; bodies with or without access to basic healthcare, let alone high-tech pharmaceuticals or expensive forms of elective surgery.

Cybertypes are more than just racial stereotypes "ported" to a new medium.   10
Because the Internet is interactive and collectively authored, cybertypes are created in a peculiarly collaborative way; they reflect the ways that machine-enabled interactivity gives rise to images of race that both stem from a common cultural logic and seek to redress anxieties about the ways that computer-enabled communication can challenge these old logics. They perform a crucial role in the signifying practice of cyberspace; they stabilize a sense of a white self and identity that is threatened by the radical fluidity and disconnect between mind and body that is celebrated in so much cyberpunk fiction. Bodies get tricky in cyberspace; that sense of disembodiment that is both freeing and disorienting creates a profound malaise in the user that stable images of race work to fix in place.

Cybertypes are the images of race that arise when the fears, anxieties, and   11
desires of privileged Western users (the majority of Internet users and content producers are still from the Western nations) are scripted into a textual/graphical

environment that is in constant flux and revision. As Rey Chow writes in "Where Have All the Natives Gone?" images of raced others become necessary symptoms of the postcolonial condition. She writes that "the production of the native is in part the production of our postcolonial modernity" (30), and that "we see that in our fascination with the 'authentic native' we are actually engaged in a search for the aura even while our search processes themselves take us farther and farther from that 'original' point of identification" (46). The Internet is certainly a postcolonial discursive practice, originating as it does from both scientific discourses of progress and the Western global capitalistic project. When Chow attributes our need for stabilizing images of the "authentic native" to the "search for the aura," or original and authentic object, she is transcoding Walter Benjamin's formulation from "The Work of Art in the Age of Mechanical Reproduction" into a new paradigm. In a subsection to her essay entitled "The Native in the Age of Discursive Reproduction," Chow clarifies her use of Benjamin to talk about postcolonialism and the function of the "native." While Benjamin maintained that technology had radically changed the nature of art by making it possible to reproduce infinite copies of it—thus devaluing the "aura" of the original—Chow envisions the "native" himself as the original, with his own aura. When natives stop acting like natives—that is to say, when they deviate from the stereotypes that have been set up to signify their identities—their "aura" is lost: they are no longer "authentic." Thus, a rationale for the existence of racial cybertypes becomes clear: in a virtual environment like the Internet where *everything* is a copy, so to speak, and nothing has an aura since all cyberimages exist as pure pixellated information, the desire to search for an original is thwarted from the very beginning. Hence the need for images of cybertyped "real natives" to assuage that desire. Chow poses a series of questions in this section:

> Why are we so fascinated with "history" and with the "native" in "modern" times? What do we gain from our labor on these "endangered authenticities" which are presumed to be from a different time and a different place? What can be said about the juxtaposition of "us" (our discourse) and "them"? What kind of *surplus value* is created by this juxtaposition? (42)

The surplus value created by this juxtaposition (between the Western user and the discourses of race and racism in cyberspace) lies precisely within the need for the native in modern times. As machine-induced speed enters our lives—the speed of transmission of images and texts, of proliferating information, of dizzying arrays of decision trees and menus—all of these symptoms of modernity create a sense of unease that is remedied by comforting and familiar images of a "history" and a "native" that seems frozen in "a different time and a different place."

This is the paradox: In order to think rigorously, humanely, and imagina-   12
tively about virtuality and the "posthuman," it is absolutely necessary to ground
critique in the lived realities of the human, in all their particularity and specificity. The nuanced realities of virtuality—racial, gendered, othered—live in
the body, and though science is producing and encouraging different readings
and revisions of the body, it is premature to throw it away just yet, particularly
since so much postcolonial, political, and feminist critique stems from it.

The vexed position of women's bodies and raced bodies in feminist and   13
postcolonial theory has been a subject of intense debate for at least the past
twenty years. While feminism and postcolonial studies must, to some extent,
buy into the notion of there being such a thing as a "woman" or a "person of
color" in order to be coherent, there are also ways in which "essentialism is a
trap," (89) to quote Gayatri Spivak. Since definitions of what counts as a
woman or a person of color can be shifting and contingent upon hegemonic
forces, essentialism can prove to be untenable. Indeed, modern body technologies are partly responsible for this: gender reassignment surgery and cosmetic
surgery can make these definitions all the blurrier. In addition, attributing
essential qualities to women and people of color can reproduce a kind of totaliz-
ing of identity that reproduces the old sexist and racist ideologies. However,
Donna Haraway, who radically questions the critical gains to be gotten from
conceptualizing *woman* as anchored to the body, takes great pains to emphasize
that she does not "know of any time in history when there was greater need for
political unity to confront effectively the dominations of 'race,' 'gender,' 'sexuality,' and 'class'" (157). Though she replaces the formerly essential concept of
"woman" with that of the "cyborg," a hybrid of machine and human, she also
acknowledges that feminist politics must continue "through coalition—affinity,
not identity" (155). Both she and Spivak write extensively about the kinds of
strategic affinities that can and must be built between and among "women"
(albeit in quotation marks), racial and other minorities, and other marginalized
and oppressed groups.

Is it a coincidence that just as feminist and subaltern politics—built around   14
affinities as well as identities—are acquiring some legitimacy and power in the
academy (note the increasing numbers of courses labeled "multicultural," "ethnic," "feminist," "postcolonial" in university course schedules) MCI Worldcom,
and other teletechnology corporations are staking out their positions as forces
that will free us from race and gender? Barbara Christian, in her 1989 essay
"'The Race for Theory': Gender and Theory: Dialogues on Feminist Criticism,"
sees a similar kind of "coincidence" in regard to the increasing dominance of literary theory as a required and validated activity for American academics. She

asserts that the technology of literary theory was made deliberately mystifying and dense to exclude minority participation; this exclusionary language "surfaced, interestingly enough, just when the literature of peoples of color, of black women, of Latin Americans, of Africans, began to move 'to the center'" (278). The user-unfriendly language of literary theory, with its poorly designed interfaces, overly elaborate systems, and other difficulties of access happened to arise during the historical moment in which the most vital and vibrant literary work was being produced by formerly "peripheral" minority writers.

Perhaps I am like Christian, who calls herself "slightly paranoid" in this   15
essay (it has been well documented that telecommunications technologies encourage paranoia), but I too wonder whether cyberspace's claims to free us from our limiting bodies are not too well timed. Learning curves for Net literacy are notoriously high; those of us who maintain listservs and websites and multi-user domains (MUDs) learn that to our rue. Indeed, it took me a few years of consistent effort, some expensive equipment, and much expert assistance to feel anything less than utterly clueless in cyberspace. Rhetorics that claim to remedy and erase gender and racial injustices and imbalances through expensive and difficult-to-learn technologies such as the Internet entirely gloss over this question of access, which seems to me *the* important question. And it seems unlikely that this glossing over is entirely innocent. Cybertyping and other epiphenomena of high technologies in the age of the Internet are partly the result of people of color's restricted access to the means of production—in this case, the means of production of the "fluid identities" celebrated by so much theory and commerce today.

Increasing numbers of racial minorities and women are acquiring access to   16
the Internet—a hopeful sign indeed. Ideally, this equalizing of access to the dominant form of information technology in our time might result in a more diverse cyberspace, one that doesn't seek to elide or ignore difference as an outmoded souvenir of the body. Indeed, sites such as ivillage.com, Oxygen.com, Salon.com's Hip Mama webpages, and NetNoir, which contain content specifically geared to women and to African Americans, indicate a shift in the Internet's content that reflects a partial bridging of the digital divide. As women of color acquire an increasing presence online, their particular interests, which spring directly from gender and racial identifications (that is to say, those identities associated with a physical body offline), are being addressed.

Unfortunately, as can be seen from the high, and ultimately dashed, femi-   17
nist hopes that new media such as the Oxygen Network would express women's concerns in a politically progressive and meaningful way, gender and race can just as easily be co-opted by the e-marketplace. Commercial sites such as these

tend to view women and minorities primarily as potential markets for advertisers and merchants rather than as "coalitions." Opportunities for political coalition building between women and people of color are often subverted in favor
of e-marketing and commerce. (NetNoir is a notable exception to this trend. It
is also the oldest of these identitarian websites, and thus was able to form its
mission, content, and "look and feel" prior to the gold rush of dot-com commerce that brought an influx of investment capital, and consequent pressure to
conform to corporate interests, to the web).[2] Nonetheless, this shift in content
which specifically addresses women and minorities, either as markets or as political entities,[3] does acknowledge that body-related identities such as race and
gender are not yet as fluid and thus disposable as much cybertheory and commercial discourse would like to see them.

However, such is the stubborn power of cybertyping that even when sub-　18
stantial numbers of racial minorities do have the necessary computer hardware
and Internet access to deploy themselves "fluidly" online they are often rudely
yanked back to the realities of racial discrimination and prejudice. For example,
on March 13, 2000, in what was called "the first civil rights class action litigation against an Internet company," the Washington-based Equal Rights Center
and two African-American plaintiffs sued Kozmo.com for racial "redlining"
because of what was perceived as geographic discrimination (Katz n.p.).
Kozmo.com, an online service that delivers convenience foods and products,
claims to deliver only to "zip codes that have the highest rates of Internet penetration and usage" (Hamilton n.p.); however, the company's judgment of what
constitutes an Internet-penetrated zip code follows racial lines as well. African-
American Washingtonians James Warren and Winona Lake used their Internet
access to order goods from Kozmo, only to be told that their zip codes weren't
served by the company. Kozmo.com also refused to deliver to a neighborhood of
Washington, D.C., occupied primarily by upper-class African Americans with
equal "Internet penetration" as white neighborhoods (Prakash n.p.).[4] It seems
that these African-American Internet users possessed identities online that
were too firmly moored to their raced bodies to participate in the utopian ideal
of the Internet as a democratizing disembodied space. Unfortunately, it would
appear that online identities can never be truly fluid if one lives in the "wrong"
zip code.

As the Kozmo.com example shows, actual hardware access is a necessary　19
but not sufficient component of online citizenship. All of the things that citizenship implies—freedom to participate in community on an equal basis, access
to national and local infrastructures, the ability to engage in discourse and commerce (cyber- and otherwise) with other citizens—are abrogated by racist poli-

tics disguised as corporate market research. This example of online redlining, or "refusing to sell something to someone due to age, race or location" puts a new spin on cybertyping. Rather than being left behind, bracketed, or "radically questioned" the body—the raced, gendered, classed body—gets "outed" in cyberspace just as soon as commerce and discourse come into play. Fluid identities aren't much use to those whose problems exist strictly (or even mostly) in the real world if they lose all their currency in the realm of the real.

It is common to see terms such as "body," "woman," and "race" in quota-   20
tion marks in much academic writing today. The (after) images of identity that the Internet shows us similarly attempt to bracket off the gendered and raced body in the name of creating a democratic utopia in cyberspace. However, post-mortems pronounced over "the body" are premature, as the Kozmo.com lawsuit shows. My hope is that these discourses of cyber-enabled fluidity and liberation do not grow so insular and self-absorbed as to forget this.

In the mechanical age, technology was viewed as instrumental, as a means   21
to an end; users were figured as already-formed subjects who approach it, rather than contingent subjects who are approached and altered by it. However, this view has been radically challenged in recent years, in particular by the Internet and other telecommunications technologies, which claim to eradicate the notion of physical distance and firm boundaries not only between users and their bodies but between topoi of identity as well.

The Internet generates both images of identity and afterimages. The word   22
afterimage implies two things to me in the context of contemporary techno-science and cyberculture.

The first is its a rhetorical position as a "Y2Kism," part of the millennial   23
drive to categorize social and cultural phenomena as *post-*, as *after*. It puts pressure on the formerly solid and anchoring notion of identity as something we in the digital age are fast on our way to becoming "after." This notion of the posthuman has evolved in other critical discourses of technology and the body, and is often presented in a celebratory way.[5]

The second is this: the image that you see when you close your eyes after   24
gazing at a bright light: the phantasmatic spectacle or private image gallery that bears but a tenuous relationship to "reality." Cyberspace and the images of identity that it produces can be seen as an interior, mind's-eye projection of the "real." I'm thinking especially of screen fatigue—the crawling characters or flickering squiggles you see inside your eyelids after a lot of screen-time in front of a television, cathode ray tube (CRT) terminal, movie screen, or any of the sources of virtual light to which we are exposed every day. How have the blinding changes and dazzlingly rapid developments of technology in recent years

served to project an altered image or projection of identity upon our collective consciousness? This visual metaphor of the afterimage describes a particular kind of historically and culturally grounded seeing or misseeing, and this is important. Ideally, it has a critical valence and can represent a way of seeing differently, of claiming the right to possess agency in our ways of seeing—of being a subject rather than an object of technology. In the bright light of contemporary technology, identity is revealed to be phantasmatic, a projection of culture and ideology. It is the product of a reflection or a deflection of prior images, as opposed to afterimages, of identity. When we look at these rhetorics and images of cyberspace we are seeing an afterimage—both posthuman and projectionary—that is the product of a vision rearranged and deranged by the virtual light of virtual things and people.

Similarly, the sign-systems associated with advertisements for reproductive and "gendered" technologies reveal, in Valerie Hartouni's words, "the fierce and frantic iteration of conventional meanings and identities in the context of technologies and techniques that render them virtually unintelligible" (51). According to this logic, stable images of identity have been replaced by afterimages. When we look at cyberspace, we see a phantasm that says more about our fantasies and structures of desire than it does about the "reality" to which it is compared by the term *virtual reality*. Many of cyberspace's commercial discourses, such as the television and print advertisements I examine in closer detail in chapter 4, work on a semiotic level that establishes a sense of a national self. However, in a radically disruptive move they simultaneously deconstruct the notion of a corporeal self anchored in familiar categories of identity. Indeed, this example of "screen fatigue" (commercials are great examples of screen fatigue because they're so fatiguing) projects a very particular kind of afterimage of identity.

The discourse of many commercials for the Internet includes gender as only one of a series of outmoded "body categories" like race and age. The ungendered, deracinated self promised to us by these commercials is freed of these troublesome categories, which have been done away with in the name of a "progressive" politics. The goal of "honoring diversity" seen on so many bumper stickers will be accomplished by eliminating diversity.

It's not just commercials that are making these postidentitarian claims. Indeed, one could say that they're following the lead or at least running in tandem with some of the growing numbers of academics who devote themselves to the cultural study of technology. For example, in *Life on the Screen* Sherry Turkle writes,

When identity was defined as unitary and solid it was relatively easy to recognize and censure deviation from a norm. A more fluid sense of self allows for a greater capacity for acknowledging diversity. It makes it easier to accept the array of our (and others') inconsistent personae—perhaps with humor, perhaps with irony. We do not feel compelled to rank or judge the elements of our multiplicity. We do not feel compelled to exclude what does not fit. (261)

According to this way of thinking, regulatory and oppressive social norms   28
such as racism and sexism are linked to users' "unitary and solid" identities off-screen. Supposedly, leaving the body behind in the service of gaining more "fluid identities" means acquiring the ability to carve out new, less oppressive norms, and gaining the capacity to "acknowledge diversity" in ever more effective ways. However, is this really happening in cyberspace?

I answer this question with an emphatic no in chapter 2. I have coined the   29
term *identity tourism* to describe a disturbing thing that I was noticing in an Internet chat community. During my fieldwork I discovered that the afterimages of identity that users were creating by adopting personae other than their own online as often as not participated in stereotyped notions of gender and race. Rather than "honoring diversity," their performances online used race and gender as amusing prostheses to be donned and shed without "real life" consequences. Like tourists who become convinced that their travels have shown them real "native" life, these identity tourists often took their virtual experiences as other-gendered and other-raced avatars as a kind of lived truth. Not only does this practice provide titillation and a bit of spice; as bell hooks writes, "one desires a 'bit of the Other' to enhance the blank landscape of whiteness" (29), it also provides a new theater in cyberspace for "eating the Other." For hooks, "the overriding fear is that cultural, ethnic, and racial differences will be commodified and offered up as new dishes to enhance the white palate—that the Other will be eaten, consumed, and forgotten" (39). Certainly, the performances of identity tourists exemplify the consumption and commodification of racial difference: the fact that so many users are willing to pay monthly service fees to put their racially stereotyped avatars in chat rooms attests to this.

Remastering the Internet

The racial stereotype, a distinctive and ongoing feature of media generally, can   30
be envisioned in archaeological terms. If we conceive of multimedia, in particular what's been termed the "new media" engendered by the Internet, as possessing strata—layers of accretions and amplifications of imageries and taxonomies

of identity—then it is possible (and indeed, for reasons I will show shortly, *strategic*) to examine the structure of these layerings. Old media provide the foundation for the new, and their means of putting race to work in the service of particular ideologies is reinvoked, with a twist, in the new landscape of race in the digital age. Visions of a "postracial democracy" evident in much discourse surrounding the Internet (particularly in print and television advertisements), are symptomatic of the desire for a cosmetic cosmopolitanism that works to conceal the problem of racism in the American context.

I could put this another way: Where's the multi(culturalism) in multime-   31
dia? or Where is race in new media? What is the "work" that race does in cyberspace, our most currently privileged example of the technology of digital reproduction? What boundaries does it police? What "modes of digital identification" or disidentification are enabled, permitted, foreclosed vis-à-vis race? Has the notion of the "authentic" been destroyed permanently, a process that Benjamin predicted had begun at the turn of the century with the advent of new means of mechanical reproduction of images? How do we begin to understand the place of authenticity, in particular racial and cultural authenticity, in the landscape of new media? Digital reproduction produces new iterations of race and racialism, iterations with roots in those produced by mechanical reproduction. Images of race from older media are the analog signal that the Internet optimizes for digital reproduction and transmission.

On the one hand, Internet use can be seen as part of the complex of multi-   32
media globalization, a foisting of a Western (as yet) cultural practice upon "third world," minority, and marginalized populations. Recent protests in the Western world against the International Monetary Fund critique global capitalism and globalization as not only economically exploitative of the "third world," but also culturally exploitative as well, essentially creating a "monoculture of the mind."

A recent full-page advertisement in the *New York Times* (June 19, 2000)   33
uses the term *megatechnology* and superimposes it with an image of a television being carried on an African woman's head. (see fig. 1.1.) The ad copy reads, "Ours is the first culture in history to have moved inside media—to have largely replaced direct contact with people and nature for simulated versions on TV, sponsored by corporations. Now it's happening globally, with grave effects on cultural diversity and democracy." This advertisement, produced for the Turning Point Project, a coalition of more than eighty nonprofit organizations including Adbusters, the Media Alliance, the International Center for Technology Assessment, and the International Forum on Globalization, includes AOL Time Warner among the "biggest three global media giants" and explains

THE NEW YORK TIMES, MONDAY, JUNE 19, 2000   YME   A7

THIS ADVERTISEMENT IS #2 IN A SERIES ON
MEGATECHNOLOGY

Monocultures of the mind

*Ours is the first culture in history to have moved inside media—to have largely replaced
direct contact with people and nature for simulated versions on TV, sponsored by corporations.
Now it's happening globally, with grave effects on cultural diversity and democracy.*

*From New York to Africa, most people spend hours every day
watching TV. With global TV controlled by few companies,
people see lots of "Baywatch," "Jerry Springer" and CNN,
plus billions in advertising. It's a kind of mental re-training:
the cloning of cultures to all be alike.*

1. TV in the U.S.

2. Global TV

3. The Operators of the System

FIGURE 1.1   Monocultures of the Mind (Turning Point Project)

that cultural diversity cannot survive virtual reality, of which television is cited as the "earliest form."

It claims that global media, including (especially) the Internet, produce a   34
kind of "mental retraining; the cloning of all cultures to be alike." The positioning of this advertisement in a mainstream mass-media publication could seem to a cynical reader an exercise in bad faith, since the *New York Times* is itself a part of the global media complex the ad is critiquing. Nonetheless, the situatedness of this argument within a nonacademic publication demonstrates that concerns about "virtual reality" or cyberspace as a culturally imperialistic practice exist outside of the academy as well as inside.

Monocultures are posed here as the opposite of diversity. Ziauddin Sardar   35
characterizes cyberspace itself as a monoculture, the West's "dark side" and thus a powerful continuation of the imperialist project. The discourse of agribusiness and the bioengineering of crops is central here: monocultures are economies of scale, an erasure of diversity under current attack by the fashionable as offering little resistance to disease. But where does the hybrid, specifically the "hyphenated" American of color, stand in relation to this?

In this ad, the image of the African woman in native dress walking a dusty   36
road with a television balanced skillfully on her head is meant to be jarring, to operate as part of the argument against globalization, and against television watching in native cultures. Viewers are supposed to react with horror at the evil box contaminating her culture and the landscape. Yet, ought we (or do we) experience a similar horror when seeing a Filipino youth in Monterey Park, Los Angeles, carrying a boom box, break dancing, or eating a McDonald's hamburger? Or when we see a Chinese rock group performing in Britney Spears–type outfits? In the first example, vegetarians may well take offense, but the fact is that such sights are common, and are examples of what could be seen as resistant practices.

In the example with the African woman, the tourist gaze would like to see   37
her outside of time, protected from the incursions of digital "culture" (or monoculture) by Western intervention: the authenticity of the timeless primitive is threatened by the television set. In the second example, cultural appropriations and borrowings are commonly celebrated as hybridity and assimilation. In the culture of popular music, the productive samplings, mixings, and remasterings of hip-hop are envisioned as vital signs of a flourishing youth culture. The technologies of contemporary music create a space for these cultural mixings, scratchings, and bricolage.

How do these paradigms from music fit the Internet? Does the Internet   38
indeed create a monoculture? Is there space within it for the subaltern to speak?

How do representations of the subaltern in reference to the Internet preserve or deny diversity? How is the paradigm of tourism invoked to stabilize threatened ideas of the authentic native post-Internet?

The Internet has a global sweep, a hype (hysteria?) attached to it; it makes   39
distinctive claims to a radical postracial democracy that other media have failed to employ effectively. Racial cybertyping is at work on the Internet today, and its implications both *for* its "objects" and for the cultural matrix it is embedded in generally are far reaching. Groups such as racial and ethnic minorities, who are prone to being stereotyped in older media, are now being "remastered" to use more digital terminology, ported to cybertyping. Remastering, the practice of converting an analog signal—for instance, from a vinyl record, to a digital one like a digital video disc (DVD), or compact disk (CD), or to hypertext markup language (HTML)—preserves the "content" of the original piece while optimizing it for a new format. Remastering fiddles with sound levels and timbre, erases scratchy silences, smoothes roughnesses, and alters signal-to-noise ratios in such a way that the same song is made infinitely available for reproduction, replay, and retransmission. But with a difference: variations in tone, timbre, and nuance are detectable; while the song remains the same, some of its qualities are altered, as are the possibilities for different audiences, different occasions for capture, replay, and transmission. The weblike media complex of images of the racialized other as primitive, exotic, irremediably different, and fixed in time is an old song, one that the Internet has remastered or retrofit in digitally reproducible ways. I wish to get back in the studio, so to speak, and to see how this remastering happens and what its effects are upon social formations and readings of race in the age of digital reproduction. When you feed racism into this machine, what you get are images of "exotic" non-American racial minorities (but not American minorities) using technology.

The Internet is the fastest, most effective image-reproduction machine this   40
world has yet seen. Just as the stereotype machine, that clumsy mechanical device that produced multiple but imperfect copies of an original image, has been replaced by more efficient and clearer, cleaner modes of image reproduction, so too are racial stereotypes being replaced by cybertypes. While racial stereotypes can now be perceived by our ever more discerning eyes as crude and obvious, and have thus have been appropriated as camp (as in Bill Cosby's collection of racist black memorabilia), or parody (black humor, like Chris Rock's, turns upon this) or incorporated into a history of oppression, cybertypes have as yet managed to sneak under the radar of critical and popular scrutiny.[6] The digital images of natives, others, and the "raced" that proliferate on and around the Internet are clean, nonmechanical, and carried upon a beam of fiber-optic

light. Cybertyping's phantom track can be traced in a Cisco television advertisement, produced as part of a series entitled "The Internet Generation" that participates in a subtle blend of racism and racialism. Rather than stereotyping different races, it cybertypes them. The children in the first ad, "Out of the Mouths of Babes," repeat statistics about the Internet's improvements about older media (i.e., "The Web has [sic] more users in the first five years than television did in the first thirty") in distinctively accented voices while they are depicted in "native" dress in "native" settings, such as a temple pool, a mosque, and a rural schoolyard. In addition, their dialogue is fractured, as each sentence is continued or repeated by a different child in a different locale. Thus, the ad tries to literalize the smaller world that Benjamin predicted audiences accustomed to proliferating mechanical images, and, by extension, digital images, would come to desire and expect. One child tells us that "a population the size of the United Kingdom joins the Internet every six months. Internet traffic doubles every one hundred days." This depiction of the Internet as a population one joins, rather than a service one purchases and consumes or a practice one engages in, significantly uses the ur-imperial nation, the United Kingdom, as the yardstick of measurement here. This language of a "united kingdom" of multiracial "generations" seems utopian, yet polices the racial and ethnic boundaries of this world very clearly. Global capitalism is envisioned as a United Nations of users from different countries united in their praise of the Internet, yet still preserved in their different ethnic dress, languages, and "look and feel."[7] Despite the fact that international Internet users are likely to be city dwellers, these ads depict them in picturesque and idealized "native" practices uncommon even in rural areas.

Cybertyping's purpose is to representatively bracket off racial difference, to assuage fears that the Internet is indeed producing a monoculture. The greater fear, however, which cybertyping actively works to conceal, is the West's reluctance to acknowledge its colonization of global media, and ongoing racist practices within its own borders. The ad's claims that "soon, all of our ideas will be free of borders" tries to stake out the notion that America's responsibility for its own problems with race, the greatest problem of our age in W. E. B. Du Bois's terms, will be erased when "borders" (between nations, between the mind and the raced body) are figuratively erased. The subtlety of this argument is necessary in our postcolonial, postmodern age: scenarios that invoke the scramble for Africa, an emblematic episode of the West's division and exploitation of the non-Western world, just will not "play" anymore. However, porting the imperialist impulse to a commercial like Cisco's "Generations" series, which cybertypes race as useful rather than divisive sneaks it under the surveillance cameras.

This commercial remasters race. Remastering implies subjugation, the   42
recolonization of otherness in a "postcolonial" world, and its method rests
upon the ideological rock of cultural "authenticity." On the contrary, rather
than destroying authenticity, cybertyping wants to preserve it. Just as intellectuals in ethnic studies and women's studies are starting to radically question the
efficacy of "authenticity" as a flag to rally around, a way to gain solidarity, the
commercial discourse of the Internet (that is, the way it figures itself *to* itself)
scrambles to pick up that dropped flag.

The Internet must contain images of authentic natives in the service of   43
militating against particular images of cultural hybridity. The Internet functions
as a tourism machine; it reproduces digital images of race as other. Missing from
this picture is any depiction of race in the American context. The vexed question of racism here and now is elided. Racism is recuperated in this ad as cosmetic multiculturalism, or cosmetic cosmoplitanism. In this ad and others like
it, American minorities are discursively fixed, or cybertyped, in particular ways
to stabilize a sense of a cosmopolitan, digerati-privileged self, which is white and
Western.

Postracial Cosmopolitanism

In "The Unbearable Whiteness of Being: African American Critical Theory and   44
Cyberculture," Kalí Tal writes that "in cyberspace, it is possible to completely
and utterly disappear people of color," and that that the elision of questions of
race in cyberspace has led to its "whitinizing" (n.p.). On the contrary, race is far
from elided in these narratives; instead it is repurposed and remastered, made to
do new work. The following passage by James Fallows, taken from "The New
Poor," an article written for the *New York Times Magazine*, elucidates this:

> The tech establishment has solved, in a fashion, a problem that vexes the
> rest of America—and therefore thinks about it in a way that seems to pre-
> figure a larger shift. The hallway traffic in any major technology firm is
> more racially varied than in other institutions in the country. (It is also
> overwhelmingly male.) But the very numerous black and brown faces
> belong overwhelmingly to immigrants, notably from India, rather than to
> members of American minority groups. The percentage of African-Americans
> and Latinos in professional positions in booming tech businesses is
> extremely low, nearing zero at many firms. (95)
>   [. . .]
> People in the tech world inhabit what they know to be a basically
> post-racial meritocracy. I would sit at a lunch table in the software firm
> with an ethnic Chinese from Malaysia on one side of me, a man from
> Colombia across the table and a man born in India but reared in America
> next to him. This seems, to those inside it, the way the rest of the world

should work, and makes the entrenched racial problems of black-and-white American seem like some Balkan rivalry one is grateful to know is on the other side of the world. (95)

This article refers to the technological (and in this case Internet-driven) diaspora of brown, black, and yellow foreign high-tech workers into America's technology industry. This contributes to a cosmetic multiculturalism, a false sense of racial equality—or postracial cybermeritocracy—that I would term *cosmetic multiculturalism*. As Fallows notes, this cosmetic multiculturalism actively works to conceal "the entrenched racial problems of black-and-white America." The presence of black and brown faces from other countries, notably Asian ones, encourages white workers to inhabit a *virtually* diverse world, one where local racial problems are shuffled aside by a *global* and disaporic diversity created by talented immigrants as opposed to "hyphenated Americans." This is a form of tourism, benefiting from difference in order to make the American/Western self feel well-rounded, cosmopolitan, *postracial*. This is not digital identification, but digital *disidentification*—disavowal of the recognition of race in local contexts in favor of comfortably distant global ones. In the new landscape of cyberspace, other countries (i.e., markets, and sources of cheap expert immigrant labor in information fields) exist, but not American minorities. It only seems commonsensical, as Reed Koch, a manager at Microsoft, puts it, that "if you go ten years [in the high-tech corporate world] and extremely rarely in your daily life ever encounter an American black person, I think they disappear from your awareness" (Fallows 95). One of the symptoms of cybertyping is this convenient "disappearance from awareness" of American racial minorities, a symptom that "multiculturalist" Internet advertising and the discourse of technology work hard to produce.

Cybertyping and the American Scene

In Vijay Prashad's important work *The Karma of Brown Folk*, he poses a question to Asian readers: "How does it feel to be the solution?" In this volume, Prashad invokes Du Bois's rhetorical question to African Americans—"How does it feel to be a problem?"—and repurposes it in order to trace the construction of the Asian, in particular the South Asian, as a model minority. The figure of the Asian as model worker is inextricably tied to this stereotype, which has been reiterated as a particular cybertype of the Asian as an exemplary information worker. If one sees race as a major "problem" of American digital culture, an examination of these cybertypes reveals the ways in which Asians prove to be the "solution." Different minorities have different functions in the cultural landscape of digital technologies. They are good for different kinds of ideological work. And, in fact, this taxonomy of work and identity has been remastered: seeing Asians as the solution and blacks as the problem is and has always been a drastic and damaging formulation which pits minorities against each other and is evident in the culture at large.

On the contrary, in a fascinating twist, cybertyping figures both Asians and   47
blacks as the solution, but for different problems. While Asians are constructed as anonymous workers, an undifferentiated pool of skilled (and grateful) labor, African Americans serve as a semiotic marker for the "real," the vanishing point of cyberspace in particular and technology in general.[8]

The New New Thing: Head-Hunting the South Asian Cyborg

The issue of the *New York Times Magazine* that contains Michael Lewis's article   48
"The Search Engine" features a cover graphic that repeats the words "The New New Thing" hundreds of times. The subtitle is "How Jim Clark taught America what the techno-economy was all about." Clark, the founder of Netscape, Silicon Graphics, and Healtheon is described as "not so much an Internet entrepreneur as the embodiment of a new kind of economic man." This article reveals that the "new kind of economic man," specifically an American man, attains preeminence partly by his ability to repurpose the discourse of racism, to create new cybertypes of Asian technology workers, in ways which at first seem unobjectionable because they have become so common.

Clark spent a great deal of energy recruiting Indian engineers from Silicon   49
Graphics (like engineer Pavan Nigam) to work for his new start-up Healtheon. As Lewis writes, "Jim Clark [of Netscape] had a thing for Indians. 'The Indian outcasts of Silicon Valley,' he usually called them, 'my Indian hordes' in less sober moments. 'As a concentrated group,' he said, 'they were the most talented engineers in the valley . . . *And they work their butts off*'" (Lewis 82).

These "less sober moments" reveal cybertyping in action. This idea of Indi-   50
ans as constituting a horde devoid of individuality, a faceless mob, reveals both a fear of their numbers and a desire to become the head of the horde, their leader.[9] These "Indian outcasts" are seen as a natural resource to be exploited—valuable workers, like Chinese railroad laborers. What's more, they're a racial group characterized "naturally" as always-already digital, like Asians as a whole. In 1997, Bill Gates indulged in a moment of foot-in-mouth cybertyping when he declared during a visit to India that "South Indians are the second-smartest people on the planet (for those who are guessing, he rated the Chinese as the smartest; those who continue to guess should note that white people, like Gates, do not get classified, since it is the white gaze, in this incarnation, that is transcendental and able to do the classifying!)" (Prashad 70). Asian technology

workers are thought not to need a "personal life," just like Chinese railroad workers were thought to have nerves farther away from the skin. This characterization of Asians as being superior workers because of inherent, near-physiological differences, seeing them as impervious to pain, in their butts or elsewhere, places them squarely in a new, digital "different caste": the outcasts of Silicon Valley. This term repurposes the old language of caste, an ancient system that preserves hierarchical distributions of privilege and oppression, for use in the digital age. Keeping to this logic, no amount of work can make them a part of the digital economy as "entrepreneurs" or "new economic men"; they are figured as permanent outcasts and outsiders.[10] Yet, such is the power of cybertyping that Clark's and Gates's comments are not viewed as racist but as strategic, a canny recognition of the rightful work of race in the digital age: this is what makes Clark the "new economic man."

As Lisa Lowe writes, "stereotypes that construct Asians as the threatening 'yellow peril,' or alternatively, that pose Asians as the domesticated 'model minority,' are each equally indicative of these national anxieties" (18). Clark's figuration of South Indian engineers, his "thing," cybertypes them as simultaneously, rather than alternatively, the threatening horde *and* the model minority: both threatening as a quasi-conspiratorial "concentrated group" and enticing because of their engineering talents. This cybertype of the South Asian seeks to fix the "unfixed liminality of the Asian immigrant—geographically, linguistically, and racially at odds with the context of the 'national'—that has given rise to the necessity of endlessly fixing and repeating such stereotypes" (Lowe 19).

Indeed, the discourse of Internet technology has a "thing" for Asians. In the article noted above, Jim Clark describes himself as a *headhunter*, and the term is appropriate in at least two senses of the word. A headhunter, in the language of the cultural digerati, is an entrepreneur who locates professional "talent" and lures it away from one job to another. Much of the tension in this story has to do with Clark's quest to acquire Asian engineers he'd previously worked with for his new venture. A high-tech headhunter facilitates the flow of human capital and labor, often across national borders.[11] The term has roots in colonial discourse: a headhunter is a mythologized figure, like the cannibal, constructed by colonists to embody their notions of the native as savage, a creature so uncivilized and unredeemable that he cannot be broken of his habit of collecting humans as if they were trophies; thus he must be exterminated or civilized. The figure of the headhunter was a justification for colonization. Envisioning South Asians as if they were trophies, outcasts, or hordes, having a "thing for Indians," is a form of cybertyping; it homogenizes South Asians as a group in such a way that they constitute both the familiar model-minority para-

digm as well as a resource for global capital. And what's more, cybertyping permits this kind of speech, even allows it to signify as "cool," or "new" in a way
that Jimmy "the Greek" Synodinos's better-intentioned comments about the
superiority of black athletes could not be.

As Lewis writes, "By 1996 nearly half of the 55,000 temporary visas issued   53
by the United States government to high-tech workers went to Indians. The
definitive smell inside a Silicon Valley start-up was of curry" (82). This insistence upon the smell of curry in the context of global commerce and capitalism
works to discursively fix Asians as irredeemably foreign in order to stabilize a
sense of a national self. This smell, here invoked as a stereotyped sign of South
Asian identity, is figured as a benefit of sorts to white workers, a kind of virtual
tourism: they need never leave their start-up offices (a frowned-upon practice in
any event) yet can conveniently enjoy the exotic cuisine and odors of "another"
world and culture.

At the dawn of the twenty-first century, cultural digerati live lives com-   54
posed of these "less sober moments"; culturally and economically, Americans
are living in intoxicating times, a gold rush of sorts. The fever of acquisition,
creation, and entrepreneurship engendered by dot-com culture licenses specific
forms of racialism, if not overt racism, that are no more descriptive of the lived
realities of Asian immigrants or Asian Americans than earlier colonialist or
racist ways of speaking were. Just as the gold rush depended upon the exploited
labor of Chinese immigrants, black slaves, and Mexican workers and consequently created racial stereotypes to justify and explain their exploitation as
"Western expansion," so too does our current digital gold rush create mythologies of race that are nostalgic. That is, they hark back to earlier narratives of
race and racialism which were always-already "virtual" in the sense that they
too were constructed narratives, the product of representational labor and work.
As Susan Stewart defines nostalgia, it is a "sadness without an object." Nostalgia is "always ideological: the past it seeks has never existed except as narrative,
and hence, always absent, that past continually threatens to reproduce itself as a
felt lack" (23). The construction of postracial utopias enabled by the Internet,
and so prominently troped in television advertising for the Internet, seeks to fill
that "lack" by supplying us with new narratives of race that affirm its solidity in
the face of global culture, multiracialism, and new patterns of migration. Cybertyping keeps race "real" using the discourse of the virtual. The object of digital
nostalgia is precisely the idea of race itself. As Renato Rosaldo defines it, nostalgia is "often found under imperialism, where people mourn the passing of what
they themselves have transformed," and is "a process of yearning for what one
has destroyed that is a form of mystification" (quoted in hooks 25). Cybertyping

works to rescue the vision of the authentic raced "native" that, first, never existed except as part of an imperialist set of narratives, and second, is already gone, or "destroyed" by technologies such as the Internet.

African-American Digital Divides: Bamboozled by the Myth of Access

The year 2000 was a banner year, for "Web use became balanced between sexes   55
for the first time with 31.1 million men and 30.2 million women online in April, according to Media Metrix. In some months this year [. . .] female users have significantly outnumbered their male counterparts" (Austen D7). The digital divide between the genders is shrinking, which is not to say that there isn't gender cybertyping occurring online. (This contradicts prior predictions from the early and mid-1990s that a masculinist web would repel women from logging on: on the contrary, as in television, sexism didn't repel women from the medium). The hegemony of the web is still emphatically male. However, the article from which these statistics come, entitled "Studies Reveal a Rush of Older Women to the Web," also notes that "lost in the rush to use the Web, however, are the nation's poor."

While the article provides graphs and statistics to track web use by gender,   56
nationality, income, and whether users log on from home or work, it neglects to mention race as a factor at any point. This elision of race in favor of gender and class is symptomatic of what Radhika Gajjala sees as the tendency of "this upwardly mobile digiterati class to celebrate a romanticized 'multiculturalism' and diversity in cyberspace" (6).

It is widely assumed that the digital divide is created by inequities in access;   57
indeed, institutional efforts to address this divide seem solely focused on getting everyone online as quickly as possible. African Americans are cybertyped as information "have-nots," occupying the "wrong" side of the digital divide; it tropes them as the "problem." This fallacy—that access equals fair representation in terms of race and gender—can be traced by examining the ways that race has worked in other media.

No sane person would contend that once everyone has cable, television   58
will become a truly democratic and racially diverse medium, for we can see that this has not come to pass. Mainstream film and television depicts African Americans in consistently negative ways despite extremely high usage rates of television by African Americans.[12] Hence, the dubious goal of 100 percent "penetration" of African-American communities by Internet technologies cannot, by and of itself, result in more parity or even accuracy in representations of African Americans. How does the Internet perpetuate this myth of access-as-ultimate-equalizer? Cyberspace's rhetorics make claims that are distinctively different from those of other media: its claims to "erase borders" and magically pro-

duce equality simply via access can be seen nowhere else. However, Internet usage by racial minorities is a necessary, but not sufficient, condition of a meaningfully democratic Internet. As Spike Lee's brilliant film parody *Bamboozled* (2000) makes all too clear, even the presence of black writers or content producers in a popular medium such as television fails to guarantee programming that depicts "dignified black people" if audiences are unwilling to support the show in large numbers. In *Bamboozled*, the Harvard-educated black television writer Pierre Delacroix produces the most offensive, racist, "ignorant" variety show he can come up with as a form of revenge against his white boss. He fully intends that the show, which depicts blacks as Topsys, Aunt Jemimas, Sambos, and Little Nigger Jims, will be a resounding flop. He entitles it the *Man Tan New Millennium Minstrel Show* and requires the African-American performers to appear in authentic blackface made of burnt cork. Of course, it is a major hit with the networks and the audience. This can be seen as an object lesson to people interested in the Internet's potential as a space for activism and antiracist education: what needs to happen on the Internet to ensure that it doesn't become the newest of the new millennium minstrel shows? The film contains a clip from Lee's earlier film, *Malcolm X*, in which the protagonist addresses a crowd of African Americans, crying out, "You been hoodwinked, bamboozled." Until we acquire some insight into racial cybertypes on the Internet, we are quite likely to be hoodwinked and bamboozled by the images of race we see on the Net, images that bear no more relation to real people of color than minstrel shows do to dignified black people.

Due to the efforts of black activists and scholars working in older media studies, we can better see what's at stake in this limited range of representations of racial minorities. Studies of race and the Internet are just now beginning to catch up (which is not surprising, considering the familiar lag time in media criticism when it comes to critical readings of race).   59

We should wish Internet access for the betterment of material and educational conditions of African Americans, but ought not expect that the medium itself is going to represent them fairly without any strategies or plans put into place to encourage this direction.   60

Postracial Digerati? Cybertyping the Other

Some studies claim that the Internet causes depression. A 1998 Carnegie Mellon University study posits that this is so because the Internet reduces the number of "strong social ties" that users maintain in "real life" and replaces them with "weak" or virtual ties, which don't have the same beneficial psychological effects as face-to-face social interactions (Kraut and Lundmark 1029). The Internet's ability to produce depression in its users (at least in me) can be traced   61 at least in part to cybertyping, a kind of virtual social interaction that constructs people of color as "good" workers or "bad," on the "right" or "wrong" side of the digital divide. The Internet's claims to erase borders, such as gender, class, and racial divisions, and the ways in which public policy makers' attentions to bridging the "digital divide" that is erroneously attributed as being the source of these problems in representation, overshadow these more subtle varieties of cybertyping. This dynamic is indeed depressing, all the more so because largely silent and undiscussed.

Radhika Gajjala writes,

> Race, gender, age, sexuality, geographical location and other signifiers of "Otherness" interact with this class-based construction of "whiteness" to produce complex hierarchies and contradictions within the Digital Economy. While we can continue to call this[4] "whiteness" because the status quo is still based upon a cultural hegemony that privileges a "white" race, it might be more appropriate to refer to this upwardly mobile subject as a "privileged hybrid transnational subject" who is a member of the "digiterati" class. (6)

Here, Gajjala posits that "privileged hybrid transnational subjects" such as Clark's coveted South Asian programmers can be read, for all intents and purposes, as "white" since they participate in the "cultural hegemony that privileges a white race." While they are no doubt part of that hegemony, as is every person of color who consumes, produces, and becomes the object of representation of information technologies, I contend that they are put to work in that hegemony in distinctively raced ways. The "work" that they do in this hegemony, their value-added labor in the system of information practices dubbed "global capitalism," is this: their cybertypes work to preserve taxonomies of racial difference. The nostalgia for race, or visions of racial "authenticity" invoked by the Cisco advertisements, assuages a longing. The espoused public desire for technological uplift, in the discourse of science-fiction narratives, the desire to create a new class of "digiterati" that is in some sense postracial, is matched by a corresponding longing for "race" as a spectacle of difference, a marker to function as the horizon to the vanishing point of postmodern identities.

Contemporary debates about the digital divide tend to be divided roughly into two camps. The first of these maintains that the master's tools can never dismantle the master's house, to paraphrase Audre Lorde's formulation. In other words, if people of color rush to assimilate themselves into computer culture, to bridge the digital divide, they are simply adopting the role of the docile consumer of Microsoft, Intel, and other products, and are not likely to transform the cyberspace they encounter. Like feminists who adopt the values of the patriarchy, they may succeed as isolated individuals in what has thus far been a privileged white male's domain—technology and the Internet—but cannot bring about the kind of change that would bring about true equality. As Lorde writes, taking up the master's tools "may allow us to temporarily beat him at his own game, but they will never allow us to bring about genuine change. And this fact is only threatening to those women who still define the master's house as their only source of support" (99).

The second camp maintains that people of color can only bring about "genuine change" in the often imperialistic images of race that exist online by getting online. Envisioning cybertechnologies as less the master's tools than tools for discourse that can take any shape is an optimistic way of seeing things.   65

While it is impossible to say, definitively, which path is correct, there is no question that the digital divide is both a result of and a contributor to the practice of racial cybertyping. It is crucial that we continue to scrutinize the deployment of race online as well as the ways that Internet use can figure as a racialized practice if we are to realize the medium's potential as a vector for social change. There is no ignoring that the Internet can and does enable new and insidious forms of racism. Whether the master's tools present the best way to address this state of affairs has yet to be seen.   66

ENDNOTES

1. The amount of scholarship on embodiment and disembodiment in cyberspace is fairly substantial. See N. Katherine Hayles's *How We Became Posthuman* for a trenchant philosophical and literary approach to the issue, as well as Allucquère Stone's *The War of Desire and Technology*. Hayles covers a range of examples of body-techniques, while Stone is more Internet-specific. An article that addresses the issue of race and embodiment in cyberspace via an examination of digital art is Jennifer Gonzales's "The Appended Subject: Race and Identity as Digital Assemblage."

2. In an article entitled "Survivor: As Internet Industry Plays Survival of the Fittest, Netnoir.com celebrates 5th Anniversary," which appeared in Netnoir.com's online newsletter in 2000, the company announced that San Francisco mayor Willie Brown had proclaimed June 22 "Netnoir.com day in the city and county of San Francisco." In 1994, Netnoir.com's E. David Ellington received an award from the AOL Greenhouse Project to fund information technology entrepreneurs, and "soon after, AOL backed NetNoir with a 19.9 percent equity stake." Currently, NetNoir has partnered with AOL, Syncom Ventures, and Radio One. NetNoir's slogan— "Taking you there. Wherever there is"—stands as an interesting contrast to Microsoft's "Where do you want to go today?" in the sense that it is far more open-ended about the web's topography and structure.

3. Since the incredible dominance of the Internet by the World Wide Web in the 1990s, it has consistently supported this construction of women as bodies. The notion that the Internet is 90 percent pornography and advertising, while it may be a slight exaggeration, gestures toward the Internet's role as an extremely efficient purveyor of exploitative images of women. Similarly, the Internet's current bent toward merchandising and selling online constructs women as either "markets" or more commonly as scantily clad figures in commercials for products.

4. Kozmo.com has since gone out of business, for reasons unrelated to this lawsuit.

5. See *Posthuman Bodies*, edited by Judith Halberstam and Ira Livingston, as well as Scott Bukatman's *Terminal Identity: The Virtual Subject in Postmodern Fiction*.

6. Guillermo Gomez-Peña's work is a notable exception. In *Dangerous Border Crossers*, he describes how responses from live audiences and Internet users became the inspiration for a "series of performance personae or 'ethno-cyborgs' co-created (or rather 'coimagined') in dialogue with gallery visitors and anonymous net users" (49). These ethno-cyborgs are collaboratively constructed by canvassing and melding together Internet users' "projections and preconceptions about Latinos and indigenous people." (46) This performance project, *Mexterminator*, was constructed from the "majority of responses we received [that] portrayed Mexicans and Chicanos as threatening Others, indestructible invaders, and public enemies of American's fragile sense of coherent national identity" (49). Thus, these ethno-cyborgs are synthesized cybertypes of Mexican American identity.

7. Just as computer users become accustomed to the "look and feel" of particular interfaces (the loyalty of Macintosh users to the desktop metaphor is legendary), so too do consumers of popular discourse become strongly attached to particular images of race. As software designers and webmasters have learned, users are quick to protest when familiar websites, such as Amazon.com's are redesigned, and these designers have often responded to consumer protests by changing them back to their original appearance. This is also the case for the ways that the "native" is portrayed in popular culture.

8. See Alondra Nelson and colleague's essay collection *Technicolor: Race, Technology and Everyday Life* for a critique of this formulation; their work posits a reframing and redefinition of the "technical" to include sampling, sound technologies, and communications technologies such as the beeper, cellphone, and pager in ways that would "count" African Americans as innovators and users of note.

9. This is akin to Neal Stephenson's cyberpunk novel *The Diamond Age*, which represents Chinese girls as members of a faceless "horde" or model minorities.

10. Growing attention has been paid to the existence of a "glass ceiling" for Asian engineers in the high-technology industry, particularly in Asian-American publications and newspapers. However, despite this glass ceiling, R. Mutthuswami asserts that "highly educated Indians [. . .] serve as CEOs of 25 percent of the companies in Silicon Valley" (quoted in Kumar 81).

11. One can see the headhunter's analogue in the more down-market image of the "coyote." Coyotes are "smugglers of workers and goods . . . for the farms of South Texas, the hotels of Las Vegas and the sweatshops of Los Angeles" (Davis 27). They guide people across the U.S. Mexican border, and there are often casualties along the way.

12. Despite the existence of black-oriented programming on smaller cable networks such as the WB and UPN, the majority of African Americans, as well as Asians and Latinos (groups even less depicted on television as primary characters), understandably feel that their lived realities are entirely unrepresented on television. Of course the same is true for whites: few possess the limitless leisure and privilege enjoyed by the characters on the show *Friends*, for example; but they might at least aspire to these roles. What African-American woman truly would want to be the "hoochie mama" depicted on Ricki Lake's "reality" programming or the noble black mammy Oracle in the film *The Matrix?*

REFERENCES

Aarseth, Espen. "The Field of Humanistic Informatics and its Relation to the Humanities." Online at *http://www.hf.uib.no/hi/espen/HI.html*.

Austen, Ian. "Studies Reveal a Rush of Older Women to the Web." *New York Times*, June 29, 2000:D7.

Bukatman, Scott. *Terminal Identity: The Virtual Subject in Postmodern Fiction*. Durham, NC: Duke University Press, 1998.

Chow, Rey. *Writing Diaspora: Tactics of Intervention in Contemporary Cultural Studies*. Bloomington: Indiana University Press, 1993.

Christian, Barbara. "The Race for Theory." *Feminist Literacy Theory: A Reader*. Ed. Mary Eagleton. London: Blackwell, 1986.

Davis, Mike. *Magical Urbanism: Latinos Reinvent the U.S. Big City*. London: Verso, 2000.

Fallows, James. "The Invisible Poor." *New York Times Magazine*, March 19, 2000, 8–78, 95, 111–112.

Gajjala, Radhika. "Transnational Digital Subjects: Constructs of Identity and Ignorance in a Digital Enconomy." Paper presented at the Conference on Cultural Diversity in Cyberspace, College Park, MD, May 2000.

Gomez-Peña, Guillermo. *Dangerous Border Crossers*. London and New York: Routledge, 2000.

Gonzalez, Jennifer. "The Appended Subject: Race and Identity as Digital Assemblage." *Race in Cyberspace*. Ed. Beth Kolko, Lisa Nakamura, and Gilbert B. Rodman. New York: Routledge, 2000.

Halberstam, Judith and Ira Livingston, eds. *Posthuman Bodies*. Bloomington: Indiana University Press, 1995.

Hamilton, Martha. "Web Retailer Kozmo Accused of Redlining: Exclusion of D.C. Minority Areas Cited." *Washington Post*, April 14, 2000.

Haraway, Donna. *Simians, Cyborgs, and Women: The Reinvention of Nature*. New York: Routledge, 1991.

Hartouni, Valerie. "Containing Women: Reproductive Discourse in the 1980s." *Technoculture*. Ed. Constance Penley and Andrew Ross. Minneapolis: University of Minnesota Press, 1991.

Hayles, N. Katherine. *How We Became Posthuman*. Chicago: University of Chicago Press, 1999.

hooks, bell. *Black Looks: Race and Representation*. Boston: South End Press, 1992.

Katz, Frances. "Racial-Bias Suit Filed Against Online Delivery Service Kozmo.com." *KRTBN Knight-Ridder Tribune Business News: The Atlanta Journal and Constitution*, April 14, 2000.

Kraut, Robert and Vicki Lundmark. "Internet Paradox: A Social Technology That Reduces Social Involvement and Psychological Well-Being?" *American Psychologist*, 53.9 (1998):1017–1031.

Kumar, Amitava. "Temporary Access: the Indian H1-B Visa Worker in the United States." *TechniColor: Race, Technology, and Everyday Life*. Ed. Alondra Nelson and Thuy Linh N. Tu with Alicia Headlam Hines. New York: New York University Press, 2001.

Lewis, Michael. "The Search Engine." *New York Times Magazine*, October 10, 1999, 77–83+.

Lorde, Audre. "The Master's Tools Will Never Dismantle the Master's House." *This Bridge Called My Back: Writing by Radical Women of Color*. Eds. Cherrie Moraga and Gloria Anzaldúa. New York: Kitchen Table Press, 1981.

Manovich, Lev. *The Language of New Media*. Cambridge, MA: MIT, 2001.

Netnoir.com Newsletter. Online mailing list.

Prakash, Snigdha. *All Things Considered*. National Public Radio, May 2, 2000. *http://www.npr.org/templates/story/story.php?storyId=1073643*.

Prashad, Vijay. *The Karma of Brown Folk*. Minneapolis: University of Minnesota Press, 2000.

Sardar, Ziauddin. "Alt.Civilizations.FAQ: Cyberspace as the Darker Side of the West." *The Cybercultures Reader*. Ed. David Bell and Barbara Kennedy. New York: Routledge, 2000.

Spivak, Gayatri Chakravorty. *In Other Worlds: Essays in Cultural Politics*. New York: Routledge, 1988.

Stephensen, Neal. *The Diamond Age*. New York: Bantam, 1995.

Stewart, Susan. *On Longing: Narratives of the Minature, the Gigantic, the Souvenir, the Collection*. Durham, NC: Duke University Press, 1993.

Stone, Allucquère Rosanne. *The War of Desire and Techology*. Cambridge, MA: MIT Press, 1995.

Tal, Kalí. "The Unbearable Whiteness of Being: African American Critical Theory and Cyberculture."

Turkle, Sherry. *Life on the Screen: Identity in the Age of the Internet*. New York: Simon and Schuster, 1995.

Judith P. Nembhard was born in Jamaica and received a doctorate in English Education in 1978. She taught English in high school and college and has published work in journals including *College English, College Teaching,* and *Journal of Negro Education;* she was a contributing writer for *Adventist Review.* She was vice president for academic affairs and then dean of the college of arts and sciences at Northern Caribbean University. She founded *Sisters,* a Christian women's magazine. Currently retired, she teaches at Chattanooga State College in Tennessee as an adjunct English instructor and writes fiction and nonfiction concerned with spirituality.

A PERSPECTIVE ON TEACHING BLACK DIALECT SPEAKING STUDENTS TO WRITE STANDARD ENGLISH

Judith P. Nembhard

English departments nationwide are expending a great amount of energy and resources on developing methods to improve the writing skills of all students. A dramatic increase has occurred in the number of workshops, conferences, and institutes conducted to promote the teaching of writing. A highlight of this renewed emphasis on composition is in-service training programs, the best known of which is the National Writing Project, perhaps "the most successful large-scale plan for curriculum change in recent years."[1] Teachers are being retrained and equipped with the skills to help students become effective writers. But with this new thrust toward improving students' competence has come a nagging question either voiced directly or implied at gatherings of writing experts: Can black students be carried along on the wave of improvement?   1

The answer to the question often becomes lost in the mix of rhetoric and theorizing, but what eventually emerges is a disquieting suggestion that teaching black dialect speakers to write standard English poses almost insurmountable problems. Conference speakers often attach labels to these students, referring to them as "the nontraditional," "the culturally different," or "the linguistically different," and labels manifest a remarkable power in longevity and influence. However, if writing teachers are willing to deemphasize the labels and concentrate instead on teaching students, they will discover that preparing black students to write standard English, although somewhat difficult, is an attainable goal.   2

Judith P. Nembhard, "A Perspective on Teaching Black Dialect Speaking Students to Write Standard English," *The Journal of Negro Education*, vol. 52, no. 1 (1983), pp. 75–82. Reprinted by permission of the School of Education, Howard University.

Within the discipline, attitudes differ on teaching black students to write   3
standard English. To many, classroom teachers and scholars alike, the concept of
social dominance is implied in the requirement that black students become proficient in the use of standard English. They view the practice as evidence of one
social group asserting its superiority over another. Noted linguist James Sledd
observes that society uses differences in language to keep others "under control."[2]
Many white instructors assent to this viewpoint by lessening their demand for
proficiency among black students, treating their major syntactic and mechanical
infractions as "surface errors" to be mentioned by the way but not to be penal-
ized. Unwittingly, they are showing sympathy toward their black students for
perceived social injustices which they believe have limited the students' capacity
to perform on a level comparable to that of their white counterparts.

Moreover, such teachers may be a part of that group which Mina Shaugh-   4
nessy says rebels against the idea of error itself, arguing that all linguistic forms
are, after all, arbitrary. These teachers, according to Shaughnessy, point out that
conventions vary from dialect to dialect and, therefore, are not obligatory, "not
at least in those situations where variant forms can be understood by a reader or
where the imposition of new forms undermines the writer's pride or confidence
in his native language or vernacular."[3] But students who are dealt with in this
way later feel cheated of their right to be fully instructed in the standard dialect.
A case in point is the young woman who transferred from a highly regarded New
England university to a predominantly black university where instructors do take
note of students' writing errors. The student, after being shown the almost illiterate nature of her essay, asked plaintively, "Why didn't they tell me?"

Research conducted by such prominent linguists as Joan Baratz, Roger   5
Shuy, William Labov, and Ralph Fasold has established the validity of the black
dialect, with a highly developed and complex structure. They, along with other
linguists, also note that the black dialect differs from standard English. However, conflicting opinions exist concerning the demands that should be made
upon black dialect speakers regarding the use of standard English. According to
Margaret Yonemura, "children without standard American English are handi-
capped directly,"[4] and she asserts that teaching standard English is one of the
important acts which a school must perform.

But some educators are critical of the schools themselves, charging them with   6
requiring black students to disown their language and culture and learn an imposed
dialect. Allison Davis indicts the schools for demanding that black children learn
"to speak and understand a new language, 'standard' English."[5] The National
Council of Teachers of English Policy Statement "The Students' Right to Their
Own Language," issued in 1974, addresses this problem by asserting that black stu-

dents have a right to speak as they wish and to maintain their cultural linguistic heritage. David Dillon corroborates this view by emphasizing that "there is nothing inferior linguistically or cognitively about nonstandard usage, only different."[6]

To solve the problem of teaching standard English to black dialect speak- 7 ers, some educators advocate the principle of eradication, whereby, as a result of conscious effort on the part of the classroom teacher, the black dialect speakers' language is supplanted by the standard dialect, or what nearly approximates it. But this approach is viewed as neither effective nor desirable, particularly because of its negative effects on the self-concept of the students involved.[7]

Another approach which has the support of many linguists (Labov among 8 them) and classroom teachers is bidialectalism. Here the procedure is to allow students to retain their language but to enhance their linguistic range by acquiring the standard form as a second language, much as one would gain facility in using a foreign language. But James Sledd discounts this technique, calling it "a direct attack on minority language"[8] and urging that bidialectalism in the schools be abandoned. Instead, he calls upon the majority race to rid itself of prejudices. If the minority are given an education, he contends, "differences between dialects are unlikely to hurt anybody much."[9]

The object, then, of composition teaching to black dialect speakers is not 9 to eradicate the first-learned language, and thus, as Davis declares, destroy the "first-learned culture"[10]; neither is the goal the superimposing of a new language upon the language of unwilling subjects. Rather, the aim of teaching composition to black speakers should be to provide them with effective communication skills and to help them recognize that the individual who harbors any hope of ever being in a position to help influence change or correct social injustices must be able to make himself or herself understood to the educated people in the society. In addition, they must be made aware that limited language skills limit possibilities. Today's automated society does not have room for the man or woman who lacks skill in the language of education.

Thus, enlightened English instructors, cognizant of the importance of the 10 task of teaching black dialect speakers to write standard English, bring to the classroom appropriate attitudes and strategies to help build success. They do not spend an inordinate amount of class time trying to uproot impediments from black students' language. Instead, the time is more profitably devoted to teaching students the art of writing to make themselves understood to larger audiences and developing the qualities shared by good writers: clarity, convincingness, and originality. The ultimate criterion of good writing does not depend upon the dialect one speaks, but rather, as Dillon says, upon "whether or not someone has something worthwhile to say and how effectively it is said."[11]

The problems that black dialect speakers pose in a writing class have given   11
rise to a large volume of material on the subject, some of it the result of
research, much of it the product of speculation. P.A. Ramey views this array of
information as another form of racism, an attempt to support the "they're-so-
different-therefore-I-can't-teach-them attitude."[12] Looking at all the accumulated findings, some teachers may be intimidated and feel that they cannot do a
professional job of teaching black students to write well, but they can be
encouraged by one important fact: teaching black students to write involves
more than getting them to use plurals and to avoid double negatives.

In her observations about characteristic features of the work of inexperi-   12
enced writers, Shaughnessy notes that some non-black students share many of
the same errors—the omitted "ed" ending and the problematic "s" plural form,
for example—with the black dialect speaker. American-born Jewish, native-
American Irish, and Chinese-American students, she states, exhibit some of the
same linguistic features which clash "with many of the same stubborn contours of
formal English"[13] evident in the writing of black students. How do English
teachers treat the linguistic problems of these non-black students? They certainly
do not concentrate on dialect differences or attempt to stamp out the language
behaviors of a race. They take a positive approach, rightly emphasizing the
importance of clear communication. Whereas the teachers of the Irish or Jewish
students with linguistic differences approach the task of teaching them the standard forms with some degree of equanimity, teachers of black dialect speakers
oftentimes "cringe in disbelief and disgust" and may try "to forego as a wasted
effort any attempt to teach language."[14] Teaching black students to write neces-
sitates the same methods and attitudes employed in teaching non-blacks.

Black dialect speakers have been and are being taught to write effective   13
standard English. Joyce Armstrong Carroll describes a program which takes the
students through a process-centered writing strategy and helps them to become
confident users of standard English.[15] Prewriting, writing, and reformulating
techniques comprise the program. Students compose together, share their written work in class, and edit together. The teacher uses conferences to work on
individual writing problems and deals with widespread problems in the whole
class setting. The revision process receives the strongest emphasis. Students
write and rewrite with the goal of achieving clarity and specificity. Of course,
the need to edit out the nonstandard usage exists, but as Carroll points out,
"Accepting writing as a unique process makes it easier to deal with these [lin-
guistic] differences."[16] The constant writing and rewriting, with the students
focusing on voice, audience, and clarity, instead of on their grammatical deficiencies, leads to successful communication. Much time is spent refining sen-

tence structure and grammatical forms, but students are led to see this as part of the revision process, a necessary part in order to aid effective communication.

The writing program for the large black student population of Howard University has been successful, not because teachers have ignored research findings on black dialect, but because they have used this information to gain insights into the students' problems and have developed teaching practices that deemphasize the students' inadequacies. Freshmen in the Howard program write a diagnostic essay at the beginning of the semester. Based upon the results, the classroom instruction proceeds. The program provides extensive opportunity for the students to write, most of the time in class where they have the direct services of the teacher as consultant. The accent is on the process of writing, with all the phases—prewriting, planning, peer editing, and revising—coming into focus. Teachers closely monitor the students' growth in theme content, organization and development as well as grammar and mechanics. The program is a highly successful one for improving the writing competencies of black dialect speakers without damaging their self-esteem.   14

In view of the growing awareness of the importance of writing competence, the implications are that "administrators and supervisors are faced with the fact that teachers need additional training and support in order to meet the needs of nonstandard speaking students."[17] Professionals charged with developing a writing curriculum for black dialect speakers must understand that these students can be taught to write well only when both they and their teachers are freed from anxiety-laden black dialect concerns. In view of the prerequisite of a positive, workable approach to teaching writing to these students, programs aimed at this group must have the following essential components, among others, to ensure their success: 15

1. Teachers must demonstrate confidence in the students as potential learners. "When an individual works and studies in an environment in which . . . external appraisals judge him as adequate, he develops a general sense of adequacy—at least in connection with school activities."[18] Students' lack of knowledge about standard English is not a sign of their intellectual inferiority. Many black dialect speakers know little about standard English but a great deal about other subjects. Teachers can capitalize on this knowledge by showing them that facility in writing can be an asset in conveying this information to others.

2. Teachers must display high expectations for the students' success. It is essential that teachers convey to their students the expectation of quality work, a goal which not only should be spelled out in the syllabus but also implied in the teachers' attitude and demeanor. Once students perceive

that they are expected to succeed, they set about trying to measure up to the expectations.

3. Students must be aided in making the distinction between their oral speech and standard English. The differences can be explained on the basis of appropriateness and fit. Students need to know that each form of communication has its place and that it is to their advantage to become skilled in using the standard form. This approach couples frankness with understanding and concern, providing the framework for a cooperative effort between students and teachers.

4. Writing assignments must be graded fairly but thoroughly. No glossing over of errors should occur. Teachers (preferably an entire English department) should adopt an evaluation scale which takes into account all facets of a composition—content, organization, style, and grammar and mechanics. A useful grading scale assigns value and spells out the criteria which students must meet in each category of writing. Several reliable and satisfactory grading scales are currently in use.[19]

5. All English teachers must set aside time for conferences with students. Arbur states, "Except for our rather structured lectures and discussions in our classrooms, the private conferences we have with our students are our most important pedagogical activities."[20] It is during these private sessions that students ask about some of their most troublesome writing problems, some of which they may be too afraid or ashamed to mention in class. Conferencing provides an invaluable strategy for guiding students' writing progress.

6. Students must be required to do some of their writing in class. Inexperienced writers need opportunity to write in class[21] where the teacher can provide help during the actual writing, serving as guide and reference source. As students' writing matures, their dependence on the teacher diminishes. They continue to do some of their writing in class, but with more self-reliance.

7. Students must be provided with outside-of-class support, such as tutors and learning packages. Teachers should have available learning packages and exercise handouts on various topics in grammar and mechanics so that students can be given appropriate practice material at the conclusion of their conferences.

8. Teachers must not be afraid to give students failing grades when they are warranted. To a large percentage of black dialect speakers, writing standard English is a difficult undertaking; for some of them it will take extra time to achieve competence. Rationalizing students' deficiencies and giving them undeserved passing grades is not the way to help them to become good writers.

Requiring black dialect speakers to become proficient in using standard   16
English in the educational setting is not a denial of the reality of their background and heritage. Rather, it is an acknowledgment of a compelling reality
that can have lasting consequences for their future. Society uses language differences as markers of social status and power. Those educators in a position to
help black students prepare to assume responsible roles in the world must be
guided not by the students' differences from the norm but by their potential.
Writing teachers must focus less on dialect differences and more on the students' need to be linguistically competent to fill their roles in society. Indeed,
black students can and must be a part of the current emphasis on writing competence. If teachers first recognize the dignity and value of the students, the linguistic differences will then be placed in proper perspective, and the job of
teaching them to write will proceed unimpeded.

ENDNOTES

1. Zeni Flinn, "Curriculum Changes Through Staff Development," *Educational Leadership*, 40 (October 1982), 51.
2. James Sledd, "Bi-dialectalism: The Linguistics of White Supremacy," *English Journal*, 58 (December 1969), 1307.
3. Mina Shaughnessy, *Errors and Expectations: A Guide for Teachers of Basic
   Writing* (New York: Oxford University Press, 1977), p. 9.
4. Margaret Yonemura, *Developing Language Programs for Young Disadvantaged
   Children* (New York: Teachers College Press, 1969), p. 6.
5. Allison Davis, "Teaching Language and Reading to Disadvantaged Negro
   Children," *Dimensions of Dialect*, in Eldonna L. Evertts, ed. (Champaign,
   Illinois: National Council of Teachers of English, 1967), p. 58.
6. David Dillon, "Does the School Have a Right to Its Own Language?" *English Journal*, 69 (April 1980), 13.
7. Theodore Hipple, *Teaching English in Secondary Schools* (New York:
   Macmillan Co., Inc., 1973), p. 271.
8. Sledd, p. 1309.
9. Ibid.
10. Davis, p. 58
11. Dillon, p. 16.
12. P.A. Ramey, "Teaching the Teachers to Teach Black Dialect Writers," *Col-
    lege English*, 41 (October 1979), p. 199.
13. Shaughnessy, pp. 91, 92.
14. Hipple, p. 273.
15. Joyce Armstrong Carroll, "Minority Student Writers: From Scribblers to
    Scribes," *English Journal*, 69 (November 1980), 15.

16. Carroll, p. 16.

17. Elaine Wangberg, "Nonstandard Speaking Students: What Should We Do?" *The Clearinghouse*, 55 (March 1982), 305.

18. Benjamin Bloom, "Affective Outcomes of School Learning," *Phi Delta Kappan*, 59 (November 1977), p. 193.

19. See Charles R. Cooper and Lee Odell, *Evaluating Writing: Describing, Measuring, Judging* (Urbana, Illinois: National Council of Teachers of English, 1977) for a full discussion of grading.

20. Rosemarie Arbur, "The Student-Teacher Conference," in Richard Gebhardt (ed.), *Composition and Its Teaching* (Findley, Ohio: Ohio Council of Teachers of English, 1979), p. 96.

21. See Erika Lindemann's comments in *A Rhetoric for Writing Teachers* (New York: Oxford University Press, 1982), p. 239.

Vivian Sobchack (1940–) is professor emeritus of the University of California, Los Angeles's School of Theater, Film, and Television, and was associate dean of the School of Theater, Film, and Television there. A prolific author who has written on a wide range of subjects including film genre, philosophy, and theory, her essays have been published in *Body & Society*, *Film Quarterly*, and *Film Comment*, among others. She has edited two volumes of work on visual media and culture and authored five books, including *Screening Space: The American Science Fiction Film*, *The Address of the Eye: A Phenomenology of Film Experience*, and *Carnal Thoughts: Embodiment and Moving Image Culture*.

"SUSIE SCRIBBLES" ON TECHNOLOGY, TECHNË, AND WRITING INCARNATE

Vivian Sobchack

> *Il y a d'abord le moment où le désire s'investit dans la pulsion graphique, aboutissant à un objet calligraphique.*—Roland Barthes

> *Avoid haphazard writing materials.*—Walter Benjamin

The following phenomenological meditations on the carnal activity of writing were provoked by an electronic doll. A contemporary version of eighteenth-century anthropomorphic writing automata, "Susie Scribbles" appeared on the shelves of Toys R Us quite a number of Christmases ago and sold for $119. Unable to resist, I bought her. Susie and the peculiarities of her existence raised significant questions about writing bodies and writing technologies—not only because her automaton's instrumentalism interrogated what writing is and how it is accomplished but also because the form in which this instrumentalism was embodied interrogated what is—or is not—"human" about writing. Susie was a quite large female doll, about two feet high, meant to look (her brochure says) about five years old. She came with her own writing desk, a ballpoint pen (with four color ink cartridges for, one supposes, expressive purposes), a pad of paper, and a robotic arm—along with a tape cassette that fit in a player inserted in her back, which, under the overalls and pink polo shirt, gave her arm electronic instructions and enabled her to sing (albeit without moving her lips) about how much fun she and her consumer playmate were having. Aside from the very idea of her, as well as my curiosity about why—in this electronic

1

Vivian Sobchack, "'Susie Scribbles': On Technology, *Technë*, and Writing Incarnate" from *Carnal Thoughts: Embodiment and Moving Image Culture*, pp. 109–131. © 2004 by the Regents of the University of California. Reprinted by permission of the University of California Press.

moment—an anthropomorphic writing machine would still be fashioned to write with a pen rather than at a computer, what first really fascinated me about Susie was her comportment. A bit limp in body so that she could be positioned at her desk to appear as if she were really looking down at the paper, she had to be latched to her desk chair in back at her shoulders. Fair-skinned, blond, and blue-eyed, she had a facial expression that seemed to me somewhat anxious. Most disturbing, however, was her lack of neck muscle. Her five-year-old's head hung down over the writing pad abjectly at best, at worst as if her neck were broken. In sum, as both a "writing technology" and a simulacrum of the lived body, "Susie Scribbles" made substantial for me questions about the relations between technology and embodiment in the matter—and meaning—of writing. I will return to Susie and her accomplishments later, but first I want to explore the materiality of writing as it is more humanly experienced in its subjective and objective forms.

Within the context of phenomenological inquiry, Susie hyperbolizes—by hypostatizing—the material nature of both "writing bodies" and "bodies of writing" and thus reminds us that writing is never an abstraction. It is a concrete intentional *activity* as well as, in its various substantial forms, a concrete intentional *object*. Both activity and object, the phenomenon we call writing also sufficiently (if not necessarily) implicates an embodied and enworlded *subject*—the one who writes, and in writing, not only through labor brings some "thing" into material presence and social meaning that was not there before but also spatially and temporally lives the activity through her body in a specifically meaningful, because specifically material, way.[1] Which is to say that writing is as much about *mattering* as it is about *meaning*. Making things matter, however, requires both a *technology* and a *technique*. Although writing is itself a concrete as well as social mediation between subjective consciousness and the objective world of others, it is further mediated through the materiality of discrete instrumental forms. Although we may trace letters in the sand, chisel words into stone, or sign a childhood pact in the blood from our finger, today in our culture we usually write with pencils, pens, typewriters, and "word-processing" computers—technologies we differently (and to different degrees) *incorporate* into our bodies and our experience of writing.[2] These technologies not only demand different techniques to use them, but they also differently frame and transform the sense and matter of the activity, object, and subject of writing—and hence its experience and meaning. This is not to say that we all have the same experience of the use of a particular writing instrument, nor is it to say that our experience of a particular writing instrument is constant and may not vary with our task or our mood, nor is it to deny that our valuation of writing instruments and practices is always constituted

2

in history and culture. It is to say, however, that our carnal use of particular and material writing instruments informs and contributes to the structure of our thought and its concrete expression.

EMBODIED TECHNOLOGIES

In "A Phenomenology of Writing by Hand" Daniel Chandler points out that a   3
wide range of our experience of writing can be linked to five key features that inform the activity and product of writing but vary according to the substantial materiality of our writing implements: directness of inscription; uniformity of script; speed of transcription; linearity of composition; and boundedness of surface.[3] Glossing these features, Chandler writes:

> *Directness* refers to suspension in time and indirection in space. Clearly the pen and the pencil involve the most direct inscription; the typewriter involves spatial indirection and the word processor involves both this and temporally suspended inscription (making it the least direct). *Uniformity* refers to whether letters are shaped by hand (as with the pen and pencil) or pre-formed (as with the typewriter and the word processor). *Speed* refers to the potential speed of transcription relative to other tools. Clearly the typewriter and the word processor are potentially faster than the pen and the pencil, at least for longhand. *Linearity* refers to the extent to which the tool allows one to jump around in a text: here the word processor is far less linear than other media. By *boundedness* I refer to limits on the "frame-size" of a particular writing and reading surface. In the case of the typewriter, these bounds include the carriage width and the visibility of the text only above the typing line. In the case of the word processor this also includes the carriage width of the printer, but more importantly the number of lines and characters per line which can be displayed on the screen. Here the pen and the pencil are clearly less bounded. (72)

Although this may seem a dry reduction of what we already know (or think   4
we know), Chandler points out that these five features all "relate to the handling of space and time both by the tool and by the writer, and, since, as phenomenologists argue, such relationships are fundamental to our structuring of experience, it is hardly surprising that they may be experienced as transforming influences" (72). Thus, in "The Writer's Technique in Thirteen Theses," Walter Benjamin's quite serious dictum to the writer, Benjamin prescribes that writers "[a]void haphazard writing materials. A pedantic adherence to certain papers, pens, inks is beneficial. No luxury, but an abundance of these utensils is necessary."[4] And in an interview entitled "Un rapport presque maniaque avec les instruments graphique," Roland Barthes obsessed about his "problems in finding the right kind of pen."[5]

For example, now that I use the computer for writing anything more than   5
notes or lists, contemplation of the "bumpy" callus on the third finger of my
right hand fills me with a certain wonder. It brings back physical memories from
childhood and adolescence: of tightly gripping a pencil or pen, of writer's
cramp, of pressing into different textures of paper to meet various forms of
reception and resistance. Even at the moment of composing these present
thoughts on a computer (which demands only slight substantial bodily engagement, the light touch of my fingertips on the keys nearly overridden by the
intense concentration of my gaze), that callus reminds me of my earlier and
more physical connection with writing. Most particularly, I recall the specific
feeling of a vague thought gaining force and focus and momentum to take shape
and emerge through my arm and in the grip of my fingers in the material form
of words—which occasionally surprised even me with their sudden substance
and rare exactitude.[6] The callus on my finger also reminds me that there is a
reciprocity between our bodies and our various writing technologies that co-
constitute different experiences of *spatiality*. Unlike my upright posture at the
typewriter or computer, when I wrote with pencil or pen, I generally curled my
body forward toward the protective half-circle of my left arm—whether I was
sitting at a desk or table, sprawling on floor or bed, or propped up with a pad
resting against my knees, whether I was dreamily writing a poem or anxiously
taking a test at school. This bodily circumscription of a lived space made intimate not only points to my right-handedness in a way that my use of both
hands at the typewriter and computer keyboard does not, but it also suggests a
form of spatial privatization that my incorporation of pencil or pen inscribed
along with my meanings.[7] This is a space that Gaston Bachelard might have
described as shell-like: that is, a space constituted and inhabited in a dialectical
structure of intrusion and extrusion, a space that among other qualities allowed
for what Bachelard calls, as a characteristic of the *poiësis* of the shell, "the mystery of slow, continuous formation."[8] Thus, paradoxically, even in school, under
the monitoring eyes of others, writing by hand with pencil or pen was a private,
enclosed, and intimate experience of material and social emergence—one that
encompassed and protected a world from intrusion as it simultaneously extruded
and expressed it.

This lived space expanded but lost a certain intimate intensity when I   6
began to use a typewriter—although I was a good enough typist that, for the
most part, my experience of the machine, like that of my pencil or pen, was sufficiently transparent for me to incorporate and write through it. Writing at the
typewriter felt a less private experience; sitting at the machine somehow
demanded a correspondent spatial accommodation of the concrete and artifac-
tual quality of the room itself: the sheets of paper next to me, the furniture and

books surrounding me. These "things" became gently unfocused toward the horizons of my vision as I gazed at the paper in my typewriter, but they remained a very physical presence nonetheless, a complement to all of the concrete and often pleasurably resistant materials I was engaging: the striking keys, the keyboard, the paper to be inserted and pulled out and crumpled or laid on a growing pile of achievement, a bottle of "white out" for mistakes, and so on.

In contrast, when I sit at my computer, the space of my writing seems at once more intimate yet more immense than the shell-like experience of writing with a pen, and it also feels less physically grounded in the breadth of a world than the experience of writing at a typewriter. My experience at the computer is more tunnel-like than shell-like, more blindered, occluded, and abstract than expansively material and physical. Its intimate space is less one of intrusion and extrusion than of exclusion, its physical sense less that of impression and expression than of nearly effortless and immaterial exchange in which my body seems more diffuse—my head and the screen vaguely if intensely conjoined, my hands and fingers and the keyboard and mouse lightly felt peripherals to a less than solidly felt core. Even if, as Chandler notes above of writing through the computer, physical inscription is delayed and thus, as he puts it, "indirect," my sense of intense direct engagement with my words is enhanced if almost decorporealized—this proportionate to my spatial existence while writing, which seems in many ways to deny the limitations and resistances of my quotidian material world. Michael Heim describes this spatial experience in *Electric Language: A Philosophical Study of Word Processing*: "Words dance on the screen. Sentences slide smoothly into place, make way for one another, while paragraphs ripple down the screen. Words become high-lighted, vanish at the push of a button, then reappear instantly at will" in this "frictionless electric element."[9] (In this regard the callus on my finger also—and indelibly—reminds me that my body and the writing materials it engages are marked by different degrees of friction and resistance in the making of the mark. This is an issue even with "Susie Scribbles," who, although she will never get a callus, may "not work" since as her brochure notes, certain writing implements, "usually the markers with the broad cloth tips, . . . create too much friction for the hand.")

That callus, in calling me back from the computer into a more physical world of writing and writing instruments, reminds me also that my incorporation of pencil and pen and their particular materiality gives rise not only to particular *spatial forms* but also to particular *temporal forms*—for me marked at their limits, on the one side, by an aesthetic languor that locates its pleasure as much in the manual forging and visual sight of the letters and words as in their semantic and communicative value, and, on the other side, by a physical fatigue felt in the hand. Writing by hand seems slow and languorous or slow and laborious. Indeed, as Heim observes of writing by hand: "A certain amount of drudgery has always attached to the task of putting words on paper" (192). Yet the labor involved in handwriting also physically imprints and invests the subject in its object to constitute a particular *material value*. Thus, Heim also tells us: "The graphic stamp, or personal character, of the writer is more than a merely subjective component of the element of handwriting. . . . The graphic stamp is the subjective side of a process which includes the physical resistance of the materials and a respect for materials arising from this resistance" (193). For example, fascinated by watching his children use old-fashioned "dip pens" when they were in elementary school in France and compelled to try it out himself, philosopher Don Ihde comments on his perceived sense of "the slowness of the writing process" and the painfulness of rewriting. But, as he points out, this slowness has its correlated compensations: "I also discovered that while one's mental processes raced well ahead of the actual writing, (mental) editing could take shape while under way. One could formulate or reformulate a sentence several times before completion." Furthermore, Ihde notes how his "fascination with the actual appearance of the script, whose lettering could be quite beautiful in that the curves and varying scribing could attain aesthetic quality," led him to a rediscovery of the "art" of that style of writing we associate with belles lettres.[10]

Ihde describes and contrasts his own various experiences with different writing technologies ("the dip ink pen, a typewriter and the word processor") within a broader consideration of the phenomeno-logic of our embodied relations with, as he puts it, "technologies-in-use." Although he emphasizes that technologies (here, writing technologies) do not *determine* the subject's intentional behavior, he also emphasizes that technologies are never neutral, and thus, to varying degrees, they inform our behavior: "Technologies, by providing a framework for action, do form intentionalities and inclinations within which use-patterns take dominant shape." Thus, he tells us: "I could not claim that the use of the dip pen 'determined' that I write in the style of *belles lettres*, but the propensity or inclination was certainly there" (141). Certainly, the reason for writing is a cultural factor in qualifying any stylistic possibility or influence imposed by the specific materiality of writing. Nonetheless, inflected, of course, by their historical situation in various cultural contexts, different writing technologies, Ihde suggests, may "incline" us toward different compositional and stylistic possibilities "simply by virtue of which part of the writing experience is enhanced and which made difficult" (142). Heim notes this as well: "The manipulation of symbols, the arrangement of symbolic domains, has its own special time and motion" (138).

There are, then, even major differences between the material experience of   10
writing with a pencil or pen, since each possesses its own discretion, its own
spatial claims, temporal rhythms, and motions. I recall that, for me, writing
with a pencil involved a temporal rhythm rather different from writing with a
pen. It involved a freedom of scrawl nearly always informed by the possibility of
erasure. Indeed, erasure, itself part of the process, brought to writing with a pencil a particular temporal punctuation wrought by a hand gesture remarkably iso-
morphic, in this culture, with nodding one's head "no," followed by a motion
that brushed from the paper the rubbery remnants of words that no longer
mattered—at least not as written expression. Writing with pen rather than pencil, I recall a different rhythm: somewhat slower at first, when the page was
neat, so I wouldn't make the first nonerasable mistake, then gaining a freer, if
slightly hostile, momentum as the page became increasingly marked—and
measured—by the messiness of error and self-repudiation. Thus, as Ihde
remarks, "to actually rewrite was painful, and were the object to be a composed
letter, it would call for starting over, since there was no simple erasure" (141).
At the beginning (whether of a letter, a singular composition, or a fresh, new
school notebook whose blank white pages prompted my perfection and then
paled at my slips of hand or mind), I was more *thoughtful* writing with a pen,
more aware of the *permanent commitment* I was making—and marking. (This
experience was heightened in the few instances when, like Ihde, I tried to write
with a dip pen but was largely reduced with my use of a computer, where, until I
print them out, I can command words to move elsewhere or to vanish and do
not even have to brush or blow away their remains.) Using a pen, I had to *cross
out* mistakes rather than *erase* them, the rubbery pleasure of materially removing
them gone—replaced by (often angry) additive gestures that covered over their
worldly matter with slashes and black and blue marks so that, as if dead and
defaced bodies, later identification of the words would be impossible. When I
moved to the typewriter, however, these assaults on my mistakes were
transformed—on the one hand, by a careful and additive, brush-stroke coating
of Wite-Out that Heim calls "the industrial chore of correcting errors by imposing one material substance over another" (132) but that I found rather pleasura-
ble in its soothing and ritual antidote to my mistake; on the other hand, by the
typewriter's striking keys "x-ing" over a repudiated expression in a satisfyingly
brisk physical gesture and staccato rhythm: the rat-a-tat-tat (particularly of my
electric typewriter) evoking less a slashing or black-and-blue battery than an
efficient machine-gunning of the errant words into nonexistence.

As we incorporate writing technologies, we simultaneously excorporate and   11
give material form to our thoughts and feelings; and, as there is spatial reciprocity between the subjective and objective poles of this process, so also is there

temporal reciprocity. A journalist friend of mine who hates computers and almost always prefers to write with pencil or pen tells me that she feels not so much technologically challenged as *temporally challenged* by both electric and electronic writing technologies. "As it is," she says, "I can barely tolerate the impatient hum of the electric typewriter waiting for my fingers on the keys, a low insistent reminder that time is passing. How could I think at all with a hungry computer screen glaring at me all the time?"[11] The flashing or blinking computer cursor seems particularly insistent and demanding of a response. Thus, as Chandler notes, although "such a feeling of being pressured by the tool into behaviour with which one is uncomfortable is certainly not the experience of all writers . . . one must insist to those who dismiss it that it remains important for those who do experience it" (71). Furthermore, despite an occasionally broken pencil point or an empty ink cartridge, pencils and pens stay relatively unchanged and constant in their material instrumentality compared to computer word-processing programs and the temporal demands, distractions, and interruptions they impose on the writing process even as they make certain aspects of it "easier" and "faster."

"If our artifacts do not act on us," Elaine Scarry observes, "there is no point in having made them. We make material artifacts in order to interiorize them: we make things so that they will in turn remake us, revising the interior of embodied consciousness."[12] Thus, as writing technologies incorporated by my body, the pencil and pen in-formed not only the particular shape of my lived space and temporality but also the manner in which I approached my task of creating meaning and matter in the world. Here, as Ihde noted of his inclination to write belles lettres when he used the dip pen, the notion of *existential style* emerges—a style that "character-izes" the subject of writing as much as it does the written object. Writing's relation to existential style is, of course, most materially figured in the eccentricity and "personality" of one's handwriting. In this regard it is telling that the term *belles lettres* first emerged between 1630 and 1699, a period that marks the emergence of mechanical print culture. As Tamara Plakins Thornton notes: "Only at this point did script come to be defined as distinct from print. If print was the impersonal product of a machine, then script became the creation of the hand, physically—and conceptually—linked to the human being who produces it."[13]

Yet even so personal and nontechnological a matter as one's own handwriting may alter, along with one's manner, in response to a particular writing technology. Thus, although it has been hardly admitted in the discourse on writing, it is telling that along with Benjamin and Barthes a great many people favor certain kinds of writing instruments over others—even when several would seem to accomplish the same objective task equally well. When it comes to pencils, for example, I have always had a preference for those with no. 2 lead. A no. 1 pencil marks the page too lightly but not gently enough for me: it seems too hard and stingy and unforgiving at its tip. With pens, my range of preference (and desire) is broader—although, generally, whether fountain pen, ballpoint, or felt-tip, and whatever the color, I prefer a fine point. Only occasionally do these choices have something to do with my *objective* task. There's no discernible reason that I should prefer to take notes at a lecture with a ballpoint rather than a felt-tip pen, prefer a felt-tip for writing lists, reserve a fountain pen for special and more formal writing. I have no accountant's justification for seeking out a fine point. Nor, barring specific instructions on certain standardized tests or evaluation forms, does there seem to be any objective rationale for my preference of a no. 2 rather than no. 1 pencil—particularly when my choice in lead pencils seems in direct contradiction to my choice in fine-tipped pens (the softer, more expansive lead of a no. 2 pencil making thicker marks than a no. 1).

This apparent contradiction makes *existential* as well as *cultural* sense and, from a phenomenological perspective, is not a contradiction at all. It has direct bearing on the manufacture of my writing, the manner and style of my activity, the project that I am going about, and that objective matter called "writing" that I bring into being. As a child of my culture, with its sanctioned hierarchy of formality that begins with the pencil and moves from pen to typewriter/word processor to published print, I have always found writing with a pencil a relatively casual and dashing affair, writing with a pen relatively more committed and often even stately and formal.[14] Yet it is also materially and carnally true that the lighter imprint and stingy hardness of a no. 1 pencil does not coincide with the sloppy expansiveness and freeing allowance that, for me, is enabled by the softer lead and less resistant tip of a no. 2 pencil. (I have always tended to write theme outlines and impassioned poetry in pencil.) However, when I write more indelibly in ink, "committing" pen to paper (when do we ever use the term *commit* in relation to pencil, typewriter, or word processor?), I constitute the enabling possibility not only to physically *use* but also to materially *make* the "fine point." It is as though my thoughts go through an enhanced process of discrimination and refinement so that they are able to emerge physically through the precise and refined materiality of the pen nib. Indeed, before I switched to the typewriter and then to the computer, I preferred to write expository prose with a pen.

Now, of course, because of its ease, I write my essays and books on the computer—and, reminded by a certain quickening within my callus, I shudder at the thought of all the labor involved were I to have to use a pencil or pen or even my electric typewriter (which has been relegated for years now to somewhere in

14

15

the back of my hall closet). Indeed, much has been made of this "ease" in writing on the computer—particularly by critics who note that facilitation of the physical process of writing and the ability to easily manipulate and alter text encourage not only the sloppy expansiveness I associate with the casual impermanence of the pencil but also the endless qualifications that move toward the ever finer points that, for me, were first correlated to fine-point pens. Thus, there's a tendency to write "long" on the computer, to lose sight (literally) of how many "pages" (material sheets of paper) there are—or should be—in relation to a given project. In relation to this expanded capacity to write, O. B. Hardison Jr. notes that "the thrust of computer writing is continuous movement ('scrolling') from one screen to the next,"[15] and Heim points out that scrolling, however expansively openended, is also a mode of concealment that "hides the calculational capacity of computers which makes it possible to assign pages to the text in an infinite variety of formats, before or during the printout" (129).[16] And in regard to the way in which this expansiveness leads also to an increase in ever "finer points" of qualification, Ihde notes the reappearance of what he calls the "'Germanic tome,' the highly footnoted and documented scholarly treatise now made easier by the various footnoting programs favored by scholars already so inclined" (142). Ihde goes on to note that publishers increasingly complain about the growth of manuscript length over the contracted length since the advent of word processing. Writing on a computer, I find myself including more citations and adding more qualifying or expansive content footnotes than I would have before this technology—and this not because I am suddenly reading or thinking more than ever but because both writing and footnoting are easier to accomplish. Indeed, these days, how many of us who write on a computer no longer have a material sense of "the page" and, often writing over our assigned limits, practice a computational sleight of hand by reducing not the length of the essay but the size of the font?

In sum, my "style" of writing has correspondingly changed with the technologies of writing I have adopted or abandoned. Moving from pencil and pen to typewriter as my primary technology, I wrote more prose than poetry, and my prose became somewhat more staccato. Moving from typewriter to computer, I, too, tended to form lengthier sentences and found myself using a larger range of emphases—underlining, italics, boldface, different fonts—that corresponded to the inflections of my *voice* and *mood* in a way that neither handwriting nor the typewriter could so variously accommodate. Nonetheless, whereas these more modern technologies have amplified certain aspects of writing for me, such as the speed of composition or editorial freedom and fluidity, they have reduced others—particularly the *physical sense* of writing. The typewriter and, even more so, the computer have diminished my experience of language coursing through

16

my body to make both its—and my—mark on a resistant and resilient worldly surface.

Whatever particular aspects of experience are amplified or reduced through various writing technologies, the point to be made here is that my existential style and my writing style are correlated—and insofar as I incorporate different technologies of writing I am also incorporated by them. Chandler cites one writer who "goes so far as to suggest that he feels not simply that the pen is an extension of the hand, but that he himself becomes an extension of the pen: 'Words flow from a pen, not from a mind. . . . I *become* my pen; my entire organism becomes an extension of this writing instrument. Consciousness is focused in the point of the pen'" (69). Certainly I am not merely subjected to the material demands of pencil, pen, typewriter, or computer, and I can struggle against and override the responses they most easily provoke from me. Nonetheless, in what phenomenologists call the "natural attitude" (natural because it is historically and culturally "naturalized" into transparency—and, barring reflection—lived at a "zero-degree" of awareness), insofar as I privilege in practice a given writing technology, I will tend to succumb to its material demands and most likely form an existential habit of living according to its spatial, temporal, bodily, and technical coordinates.   17

EMBODIED TECHNIQUES

As these observations indicate, a phenomenology of the material and techno-logical experience of writing attempts to describe and bring to awareness the dynamic and essentially correlational structure of that experience as it entails the existential activity of writing, the intentional objects that emerge in mate-rial form as the means of writing and the written matter, and an embodied and enworlded subject who is the writer—activity, object, and subject all enabled and mediated through a particular writing technology that spatially and tempo-rally qualifies the embodied manner and objective style in which we write. However, given that phenomenological description of an existential kind recog-nizes that it is always also qualified by history and culture, it should further describe the ways in which the meaning of writing and its material technologies are historically and culturally enworlded—in particular embodied techniques and the meanings that in-form them.   18

Here, it is particularly telling and warrants further elaboration that the elec-tronic writing doll "Susie Scribbles" came in two other embodiments than a "five-year-old" Caucasian female: one an African American male child, the other a furry brown teddy bear. Insofar as we understand that writing by hand serves simultaneously as an indexical sign of subjectivity, a symbolic sign of class, and a pragmatic form of social empowerment, these selective embodiments of   19 writing automata are uncanny not only for their mechanical aptitude. They are also uncanny for their material revelation of certain kinds of beliefs about what (and who) constitutes appropriate writing and, as well, about the "inappropriate appropriation of writing"—beliefs that hold that certain writers, deemed lacking in significant (and therefore signifying) intentionality and subjectivity, are merely automatons engaged in appropriating and "aping" the appropriate writing of their accomplished betters. In this regard and in relation to those automaton scribblers who appeared on the toy store shelf—a female child, a black male child, and a culturally declawed animal—it is worth noting the unmarked absence of a white male child automaton. Thus, we might suppose that for the enlightened men at Wonderama Toys in (of all places) Edison, New Jersey, who conceived these writing automata, embodying the human ability to write not only in agencyless machines but also in the forms of supposedly less rational, less powerful, and inferior "others" both materializes an "uncanny" oxymoron and amplifies the very "not-human" nature of automatic writing.[17] It also functions, from the transparent perspective and legacy of Enlightenment (white male) humanism, as both self-aggrandizing and self-congratulatory. Indeed, as Annette Michelson writes of another and more "accomplished" female automaton "invented by Edison" in a fiction, the white girl, black boy, and furry teddy bear all sit at their writing desks as a "palimpsest of inscription"—each not only inscribing but also inscribed as both an "unreasoning and reasonable facsimile, generated by reason" itself.[18]

Thus far, I have scrupulously avoided discussion of writing as a discrete form of *symbolic* communication—nor have I yet discussed it as acculturated through an embodied *technique*. My emphasis has been instead on the radical physical activity and experience of the lived body in the act of writing and its entailment of material and technological means to make some "thing" that matters out of no "thing" at all. Indeed, closer phenomenological scrutiny reveals that the particular activity and thing we call writing and understand as a discrete order of symbolic communication is, in its very discretion, a secondary apprehension built on the primary ground of the material lived body making its meaningful mark on the world as a necessary condition of its very existence. This primary kind of symbolic activity is an activity more general than discrete, and it can be best described as a radical and emergent semiosis of the lived body that has, makes, and marks meaning in the world and to others. That is, always marking its existential situation by its punctual material presence and always in intentional movement that is tropic and choice-making, the lived body in its material presence and social existence constitutes the "original" diacritical mark and "magic" marker: it concretely and visibly produces in its very being the first formation of what we term—both humanly and alphabetically—"character."[19]

Some specific illustration might prove helpful here, and I will thus enlist   21
Sean, a five-year-old neighbor just beginning school at the time I interviewed
him. Accompanied by his younger brother, Sean stopped pedaling his tricycle
when I asked him what writing was. Not at all surprised by the question, he told
me that he knew—and then proceeded to arch and move his right arm in a set
of limited but fluid and morphologically regular curves across the air. "Does
your little brother write too?" I asked. "No," Sean said. "He's only three. He
scribbles." "Well, what's the difference between writing and scribbling?" I asked.
Sean then demonstrated scribbling—this time moving his arm back and forth
across the air in a more mechanical, rigid, and jagged fashion than he had
before.[20] I then asked Sean "what" he could write. He responded by telling me
first his name followed by a discrete pronouncement of its letters, and then he
announced a list of separate and disconnected words. After a brief moment of
silence he companionably offered up the fact that he had written *spiderwebs* the
other day. I am quite certain that he was not talking about the word as the sum
of its letters but rather that he had not as yet made a clear distinction between
writing and drawing.[21] Indeed, both Sean's sure distinction between writing and
scribbling and his confident conflation of writing and drawing raise a major
question about the general meaning and matter of writing: "Where does scribble
end and writing as communication, or drawing as representation, begin?"[22]
Finally, at the end of a lengthier conversation than I can recount here, I asked
Sean what writing was "good for," and, although he understood my question as
one about function and value, he groped for an answer he couldn't quite find.
Instead, he told me his little brother had a magic pencil that turned scribbling
into writing. "All you have to do," he told me, "is to scribble on this magic pad
with this magic pencil, say 'abracadabra,' and real writing will be there instead
of just squiggly lines." Definitely aware of the nature of writing as a bodily activity and a material object requiring a technique for its production, vaguely aware
of some kind of instant and magical material transformation accomplished by
writing, this five-year-old's concept of writing was founded—and, more significantly, focused—on its physical and material aspects.

Sean's initiation into writing, then, is grounded in bodily action and the   22
specific techniques involved in making material marks that matter—whatever
their vaguely apprehended use value or "reason" for being. On the one hand,
Sean illustrates the bodily *originality* of writing, of making one's mark, simultaneously in and on the world. On the other, his cultural initiation into the activity of writing came (just as mine had) by way of institutionalized instruction
and bodily imitation, an instruction and imitation focused on *technique*. That is,
the act of writing was brought into focus for Sean through a *bodily tuition*: a discrete set of objective steps that were to be physically followed prior to any clear

understanding he might have of what he was doing or why he was doing it (that is, why this particular mode of bringing matter into the world mattered). Thus, like all the writers who have come before him, Sean's generalized physical activity and pleasure of making and leaving any kind of marks on the world as an existential assertion of presence have been historically and culturally regulated into specific and highly objectified forms. Indeed, only with time and practice will Sean's larger inscriptional body movements become objectively contained by and regulated "in the hand."[23] The movements and techniques of "penmanship" will become incorporated into Sean's bodily schema and, once habituated, will eventually seem less alien and laborious than "natural."

In "Handwriting as an Act of Self-Definition" Thornton comments on the history and literature of techniques for writing by hand, pointing not only to "the exquisitely engraved penmanship manuals of the eighteenth century or the copybooks of the Victorian era" but also, of course, to the "Palmer method" that dominated the teaching of handwriting well into the twentieth century, articulating a mechanical and repetitive standard consonant with the Taylorism and Fordism that marked assembly-line production in the machine age. Thornton writes:

> Mr. Palmer promised to deliver a tireless arm that could compete with the typewriter, but what really attracted educators were his handwriting drills. . . . Sometimes they began with "preparatory calisthenics." Then, at the teacher's command, . . . students executed row after row of ovals and "push-pulls." School officials were blunt about the value of these drills. The lessons they conveyed—conformity to standard models, obedience to authority—would reform juvenile delinquents, assimilate foreigners, and acclimate working-class children to their futures in the typing pool or on the factory line.[24]

In this regard the brochure for the more contemporary "Susie Scribbles" is illuminating. Sitting at her desk with her "magic" pen and pad and her electronically controlled writing arm, Susie is regarded by those who made her not only as a play toy but also as "a learning assistant." Thus, the brochure first tells us (in somewhat righteous tones): "Remember that Susie Scribbles is about five years old and will write at that level by design. We would not want a toy writing better than a child." And then it continues (shades of Palmer embedded in its Montessori patience): "Susie Scribbles can assist your child in learning, but repetition is the key to learning, and always remember that each child learns at their own speed."

Monique Wittig's autobiographical novel *The Opoponax* wonderfully, meticulously, and painfully describes not only the young child's original focus on writing in its materiality and concrete grounding in bodily action rather

23

24

25

than in the symbolic meaning of what one is writing but also the culture's focus on the technology and techniques of writing as a form of social control rather than on writing as the matter of both personal and social expression. Wittig tells us of her young alter ego:

> Catherine Legrand can't write. She presses on the paper with the black pencil. She makes letters that stick out on both sides beyond the two lines you are supposed to write inside of, they stick out above and below, they touch the other lines, they are not straight. Mademoiselle says, Begin again. First you make d's and a's, then r's. The bellies of the s's are always too big, the r's fall forward on their canes.[25]

This description of the concrete (let alone bodily) shape of letters, as well   26
as a perceived sense of their objective recalcitrance, is extended in a later, and excruciating, passage that conjoins writing's concrete materiality with both technology and proscribed bodily technique:

> You write in your notebook with a pen which you dip into purple ink. The point scrapes the paper, the two ends come apart, it is like writing on a blotter, afterward the nib is full of little hairs. You take them off with your fingers. You start writing again. There are more hairs. You rub the pen on your smock. You wipe it on the skin of your hand. You separate the two parts of the nib so you can get your finger between them and clean them. The pointed ends do not go back together again, so that now you write double. . . . Mademoiselle gets mad. That makes the third [time] today, you must pay attention and hold your pen like this. . . . Mademoiselle leans over her shoulder to guide her hand. . . . You hold the pen between your thumb and index finger. Your index finger is bent at a right angle and presses against the round end the point is stuck into. Your thumb is a little less bent. The index finger is always sliding onto the inky point. . . . You have to press the index finger against the end of the pen with all your might so it won't slide off. The thumb is also pressed to the end to keep the pen tight between the fingers, which then you can't use. Your whole arm even hurts. . . . Anyway Catherine Legrand is a pig. Mademoiselle tells her so waving her notebook. . . . There are ink stains and fingerprints on the notebook. This is because when you dip the pen into the inkwell it either comes out full of ink or else without enough ink. In the first case the ink immediately drips onto the notebook just as you are getting ready to write. In the second case you press the nib of the pen onto the paper too hard and it makes holes. After this there is no point even trying to make the letters as you know how to do with a pencil. Françoise Pommier writes slowly and carefully. At the top of her notebook she pushes a clean blotter along the line, holding it in place with the hand that is not writing. She raises her head when she has finished the page. . . . Pascale Delaroche makes a blot. She gives a little cry. . . . Reine Dieu's notebook . . . has a lot of blots and holes like Catherine Legrand's. It also has doodles around

which Reine Dieu has written the letters as she was asked to do. She has tried to erase something here and there. This makes a funny mess with hills and valleys which you want to touch. Between the hills is dirty. Mademoiselle gets mad again and even throws Reine Dieu's notebook under the table.[26]

Catherine Legrand's (and Monique Wittig's) writing lessons with her dip   27
pen elaborately flesh out, yet also serve as ironic commentary on, Ihde's adult encounter with the same writing instrument when he is in France with his school-age children. Certainly, Catherine's writing lessons dramatize the materiality and technique that ultimately ground Ihde's adult understanding and valuation of the art and craft of belles lettres, but their extreme objectification (as well as hers by Mademoiselle) disallows her the pleasure of making her mark.[27] In *Electric Language* Heim writes: "The resistance of materials in handwriting enhances the sense of felt origination. . . . The stamp of characteristic ownership marks written thought as my own, acquired through the struggle with experience and with recalcitrant materials. Handwritten formulation thereby enhances a sense of personal experience or an integrity pertaining to the private, personal self" (186). Catherine Legrand's writing lessons would seem to counter this description—although Monique Wittig goes on to become "a writer" (albeit, in the context of her classroom experience, one who describes herself as an objectified third person).

Wittig's text also throws into relief the less restrictive penmanship lessons a   28
five-year-old American boy more recently gave me out of the classroom and against the empty slate of a spring sky. I remember his sure bodily distinction between writing and scribbling, his untroubled confusion of writing and drawing, and his inability to tell me what writing "was good for." It is not only in French schools that writing is first taught as a technology and technique, as a means of mattering rather than as a matter of meaning. Indeed, it is in this fact that our Enlightenment heritage might be made to seem strange. Although I can't quite think of how else to teach a child to write concretely, I can think how fundamental Enlightenment dualisms separated spirit and mind from the material body (figured now by Susie's effectively "broken" neck). Is it any wonder that this separation led to the objectification and mechanization of human subjectivity and greatly influenced the notion and instruction of writing as an objective technique? Furthermore, given this historical and cultural separation of meaning and matter, of consciousness and the body, insofar as it always also inscribes and makes matter an "existential style," I can understand how writing by hand would always also *confound* this objectification and remain, in a problematic way, *auratic*. [28] Thus, it is telling that in the mid-1700s, the period that marks the rise of scientific materialism and the move into mechanical typogra-

phy and print culture, we find both a complementarity and a contradiction in, on the one hand, the privilege enjoyed by belles lettres as a form of writing that embodies reflexive consciousness and individual sensibility and, on the other hand, a significant increase and interest in mechanical writing automata embodied as human beings.[29]

One particular example of such Enlightenment writing automata is worth considering in relation to "Susie Scribbles," the electronic doll who sits at her desk several centuries later. Invented by Pierre Jaquet-Droz and his son Henri-Louis and first exhibited in 1774 in Neuchâtel, Switzerland, where it is still in working order and exhibited today, Susie's Enlightenment equivalent was known as "The Scribe." Taking the form of a Caucasian boy aged about three, the mechanical child was accompanied and matched by a twin "brother" known as "The Draughtsman," who did not write but drew pictures. (Here, in an uncanny way, Sean's lingering confusion of writing and drawing is at once bifurcated and "twinned" as a difference that is, nonetheless, the same.) Gaby Wood describes the pair at the beginning of *Edison's Eve:*

> These prodigies, who look no older than toddlers, are dressed . . . in identical velvet jackets and silk pantaloons. Their faces are doll-like and blank; their bare feet dangle some way off the ground. The first boy begins by dipping his quill pen in a tiny ink well at the side of his desk. He shakes it twice, then methodically moves his hand across the paper and starts to trace the letters in his message. Meanwhile his twin works on a sketch. He slowly draws a head in profile, then drops his chin and blows away the dust from his pencil.[30]

A picture shows "The Scribe" seated like "Susie" at his own writing desk in a posture almost identical to hers; indeed, he looks amazingly like her—but for his differently fashioned clothing, his bare feet,[31] and the quill rather than ballpoint pen he holds in his fingers.

Such anthropomorphic automata were particularly valued for the exactitude of their lifelike qualities: for example, intricate mechanisms made "a girl's chest rise and fall at regular intervals in perfect imitation of breathing" and made "the eyes move and animate[d] the head," turning it round so it looked left and right and down and up again.[32] Correlatively, however, human beings of the period were often celebrated for their mechanical and autonomic "clockwork" qualities. Thus, philosopher Julien Offray de La Mettrie could write in 1748, "The human body is a machine which winds its own springs. It is the living image of perpetual movement."[33] This contradiction and complementarity between anthropomorphic automata and automated human bodies and the conundrum of their "reversibility" continues historically to the present day. In the context of a discussion on the bourgeois fascination with anthropomorphic automata in the nineteenth century, Susan Buck-Morss tells us: "This reversal epitomizes that which Marx considered characteristic of the capitalist-industrial mode of production: Machines that bring the promise of the naturalization of humanity and the humanization of nature result instead in the mechanization of both."[34] We are no less fascinated by notions of these human-machine exchanges, reversals, and reifications today—hence not only Susie in Toys R Us sold as an "interactive" teaching toy and fun-loving companion (with handwriting no better than a five-year-old's) but also, and more transparently, computers that catch viruses and humans who possess "artificial intelligence." Thus, how far have we come (or not) from de La Mettrie and the eighteenth century when our dominant techno-logic considers the human body, according to contemporary philosopher Jean-François Lyotard's provocative phenomenological critique, "as the *hardware* of the complex technical device that is human thought"?[35]

EMBODYING *TECHNĒ*

We can see in this historical and cultural trajectory how the matter of technology elides a humanly embodied meaning that matters and how mechanical technique becomes institutionalized and "industrialized" in penmanship classes where children learn to suppress the idiosyncrasies of their uniquely embodied "existential style," their very "originality." A paradox emerges, however: today, precisely because of this social suppression of writerly idiosyncrasy and the valuation of "originality" and "spontaneity" amidst the institutionalized and technological management of our lives, unlike some of our historical predecessors we tend to think that "painstaking penmanship betrays a deficient imagination."[36] Indeed, as Thornton suggests, since the onset of mechanical typography and print culture there has been an essential ambiguity about the relationship between the technological and mass production of writing and the lived body engaged in writing as an act of self-expression. Ever more troubling in highly technologized cultures that depend on standardization, an ongoing argument exists "between the forces of conformity and those of individuality" about "the nature of the self."[37]

In this sense, however much we may deny it, we are hardly yet post-Enlightenment or postindustrial, even as we are post-postmodern. "Susie Scribbles" is a concrete extension of the Enlightenment objectification of both writing and human being and the nineteenth century's valuation of assembly-line standardization, conformity, and repetition—which, among other things, gave us first the typewriter, then the word processor, and now "repetitive stress injury."[38] Susie is a specific anthropomorphic and electronic writing machine

aimed not at provoking intellectual reflection and amusing adults but at constituting "good parents" and at "engaging" and "instructing" children on what it is
to write. Materially, despite her Oshkosh B'Gosh overalls and her blonde pony-
tail, Susie bears great resemblance—if a different "clockwork"—to the automata
that have preceded her from the 1740s on. Indeed, if one looks at pictures and
diagrams of past automated writing dolls, Susie's robotic arm mechanism, albeit
directed electronically, is hardly that different from theirs. Yet, for all her similarity, Susie differs significantly from her forebears. It is not only that in a non-
philosophical culture she is not perceived as a philosophical toy or that her
cloyingly sweet voice and horrid taped laughter and song keep insisting aloud
how much "fun" she and the child-consumer will have writing "together."
Whereas the first thing written by her Enlightenment predecessor, "The
Scribe," was a provocative "I think, therefore I am," followed by "Our mechanisms defy time,"[39] the first thing Susie writes is the toll-free telephone number
of a "help line" in Edison, New Jersey, that one can call if she breaks down.
These things give one pause, of course, as does her drawing of the two "C" bat-
teries that give her the charge of her artificial life. Despite these differences,
however, it is the very *similarity* of Susie to her childish ancestors that marks her
real—and radical—*difference* from them. That is, it seems both culturally logical
and technologically natural that Enlightenment automata wrote with quill pens
in their mechanical hands. The dip pen was then a common writing technology. Thus we must ask, Why, in an electronically driven and obsessed culture,
does Susie write with a pen at all? Why is she not seated at a little word processor or computer? Why is a pen, even a plastic ballpoint with four color ink car-
tridges, the preferred instrument for an electronic doll in an electronic culture?
Indeed, if one thinks historically backward, we might ask if there have been any
writing dolls that, when it was a common mode of writing, sat at a typewriter?
Although I don't know for sure, I rather think not.

The answers to these questions lie, I believe, quite precisely, *in the hand.*   34
That Susie still writes with a pen in an electronic culture demonstrates that we
know deeply, and with the knowledge of the lived body, that writing is not
merely a learned mechanical technique. Rather, and more significantly, it is
always also *auratic* insofar as it is enabled not just by a material body but by a
lived body that, however regulated, cannot avoid inscribing its singular intentionality in acts and marks of *expressive improvisation.*[40] Even after years of discipline in penmanship classes, in that pen and pencil enable the broadest and
most idiosyncratic expression of the lived body making matter from "nothing"—that is, transforming meaning to matter and making matter mean—pen
and pencil are the technologies that best extend the idiosyncrasies of the *hand*
and most fully and materially mark the embodied, intentional, and contingent

excess of what writing is over its objectification, standardization, and mechanization. Although one might be mildly amused at its transparent social commentary, there would be no fascination, nothing *uncanny*, in seeing an anthropomorphic writing machine write *through* a nonanthropomorphic writing machine—particularly those like the typewriter or the computer, which have greatly reduced the unique *graphological excess* that brings into being and matter an embodied *existential style*.[41]

Thus, in a review of Thornton's *Handwriting in America*, although Thomas Mallon applauds the author's tracking of changes in methods and styles of penmanship, as well as her discussions of the history of handwriting analysis (which began in the romantic period) and the "twentieth-century showdown between characterological and physiological notions of handwritten individuality," he also chides Thornton for not considering the contemporary moment and "what has been lost or gained by our cultural shift toward mouse and screen." Mallon points out that although "the fax and E-mail have brought back letter-writing to an encouraging extent," they have marked the "limits of that revival, too." As both writers and readers, he says, we know that "you can't seal E-mail with a kiss, and the latest laptops protect us from even our own bodily fluids: the Macintosh Power Books have eliminated trackballs in favor of trackpads, so the sweat from one's thumb won't gum up the works." In contrast to electronic writing (even of an amorous kind), Mallon notes how the power and value of handwritten love letters emerge from the exchange of indexical signs of the physical proximity of the lovers' bodies to the page and from the graphological transfer and display of a "physical motion and intensity"—which does let them see you sweat or weep. Whatever an individual lover's method of penmanship, the embodied movement that made his or her expression matter was, as Mallon concludes, "connected to all those other movements that would make him, once he appeared in the flesh, yours truly."[42] (And, here, I might point out that Susie untruly—that is, mechanically albeit electronically—prints "I love you" on her writing pad to anyone and everyone who, dare I say it, turns her on.)

Our handwriting is singular—and it has taken on an increasingly auratic and precious quality as it has become increasingly scarce. Susie's difference from her mechanical ancestors is that, in an electronic culture, she further hyperbolizes the mystery not of writing as a technical enterprise but as an expression of the human hand. Thus, however hidden it is by her Oshkosh B'Goshes and saccharine songs and ignored by the adults who buy her, Susie is a philosophical toy after all. She and her forebears affirm across time that although writing is a technique and employs technology, it is always also something *more*. And in so doing, they charge us to reframe "the question concerning technology" to accommodate the intentional and lived body-subject in the act of writing not

35

36

only the word but also the world and herself. As Heidegger reminds us, technology consists not merely of objective tools, nor is technique merely their objective application. "Technology is . . . no mere means," he tells us. "Technology is a way of revealing." Thus, he returns us to the Greek notion of *technë*: "the name not only for the activities and skills of the craftsman, but also for the arts of the mind and the fine arts. *Technë* belongs to bringing-forth, to *poiësis*; it is something poetic."[43] Furthermore, *technë* is a way and manner of knowing. Making, bringing forth, and revealing are integral not only to the existence of matter but also to why and how some "thing" is known and understood as "mattering."

Necessarily and materially implicated in both this bringing forth and its particular modes of knowing is an embodied and intentional subject. Unlike Susie (the intentionless simulacrum who laughs without mirth and writes without mattering), this lived body subjectively incorporates and excorporates objective technologies and, in what Scarry calls a "consensual materialism," brings into material being both the variety of herself and multiple worlds.[44] Thus, even seated before a computer printing my thoughts in a tenpoint Geneva font that reveals nothing idiosyncratic of my hand, I am never reduced to a mere writing machine and never completely forget or forgo the mystery of the human hand's ability to reveal and bring forth an expression of human being. Even here, before my computer screen, even if in a relatively reduced way, my writing materially reveals itself as an existential style as well as a cultural habit. Indeed, my lived body is "continuous with the modes of reproduction that it also disrupts."[45] As I write, my choices of font and diacritical marks begin to signify something in excess of the digitized regularity of my words on the screen. (By the time you read this in a printed book, however, press editors surely will have further reduced my idiosyncrasies, pleading a "house style" that takes precedence over my original authorial style as it once was manifest in typographical and diacritical "preferences.") In sum, objectively material means (*technology*) and the tropology of subjective desire (*poiësis*) are bound in an irreducible intentional relation as a revelatory bringing forth (*technë*) that, in its diverse historical and personal practices, makes matter meaningful and meaning matter.

I have no idea whether, seated at their little desks and writing mechanically, historical versions of Susie provoked first in the children of their owners and later in their child owners an overwhelming urge to rip apart the "signifying scene." But I rather think so. Even though I am an adult who certainly respects a doll for which I paid $119 and who has read the brochure admonishing me to "remember that Susie is a machine" and, therefore, that I should not "abuse" her, I nonetheless admit to wanting to take off Susie's pink long-sleeved polo

37

38

shirt and to wrench her robotic writing arm from its socket "to see how it works." (I rather think, to the disappointment and horror of the adults who bought it for them, this is the only real interactivity the young owners of this supposedly "interactive" toy ever actually experience.) Although, on the surface, this urge "to see how it works" seems grounded in a sense of technology as mere *mechanical means*, I would suggest it reveals a much deeper curiosity about the radical *bringing forth* of both action and matter. Indeed, writing "by hand" (even, or especially, when it's mechanical) keeps alive the question of the animate and the inanimate, the lived body and the material "thing" that merely simulates a lived body, which is not only a material object but also an intentional and sentient subject. It is apposite here that "The Scribe" not only wrote the simulated assertion, "I think, therefore I am," but also wrote, as Wood tells us, "a more ironic tribute: 'I do not think . . . do I therefore not exist?' The writer, a mere machine, is able to communicate the fact that it cannot think. Clearly, however, it does exist: and if it is able to communicate that fact that it cannot think, is it possible that it can think after all? Might the machine be lying?"[46]

Given this question of the animate and the inanimate, the auratic lived body and its uncanny simulation, it is hardly surprising that children are usually so deeply disappointed after they have ripped apart their mechanical but animated playthings and found no *objective* and *technical* correlative to the *subjective* and deeply *poetic* curiosity they themselves have about the world and human being. Either in animatronic operation or dissected in a childish autopsy, Susie's robotic writing arm would tell us nothing *truly material* to either the meaning of writing or the matter of the hand. In fact, our fascination with the anthropomorphic writing machine lies precisely in its inability to tell us anything truly material to writing—even as it writes and "brings forth" meaning in material form. Ripping apart Susie's signifying scene would reveal nothing significant—either about signifying or about mattering. Susie is, after all, just a machine. Despite her technical facility for mechanical mimesis, she lacks precisely the ability to respond to what we really want to know: that is, how the intentionality, subjective desire, and existential style of the lived body come to materiality and matter through the *poiësis* of *technë* rather than the mechanics and automation of technique.

NOTES

1. In terms of material "things," the "matter" of writing does not necessarily entail an intentional subject. (Hence, as will be discussed later, the fascination with writing produced by automata.) But for the matter of writing to mean, for writing not only to necessarily "be" but for it to be sufficiently

"what" it is, it must entail an intentional subject. In this regard Margaret Morse, "Television Graphics and the Virtual Body: Words on the Move," in her *Virtualities: Television, Media Art and Cyberspace* (Bloomington: Indiana University Press, 1998), aptly points out that "much of the nomenclature of both writing and typographics—*hand, face, character*—are metonymies of the absent human body and of the subjectivity which we presume is responsible for them" (72).

2. I don't mention here the experience or techniques of writing with a brush in other cultures. Such an activity, with its particular materials and techniques, would have its own spatial, temporal, and bodily phenomeno-logic. Indeed, in contemporary Western culture writing has often been viewed by theorists (most male) as a form of sadistic incision, as violently aggressive; considering the use of a brush, one could understand its action on a surface as quite different: additive, caressive, nonviolent. See Andrew Brown, *Roland Barthes: The Figures of Writing* (Oxford: Clarendon Press, 1992), for discussion of this issue in relation to Barthes; Brown also mentions the felt-tipped pen as a writing instrument that does not aggressively scratch or impress the paper (170, 192–93).

3. Daniel Chandler, "The Phenomenology of Writing by Hand," *Intelligent Tutoring Media* 3, nos. 2/3 (May/Aug. 1992). Subsequent references will be cited in the text. See also Chandler's *The Act of Writing: A Media Theory Approach* (Great Britain: University of Wales, Aberystwyth, 1995), esp. chap. 6, "Writing Tools," 132–88.

4. Walter Benjamin, "One-Way Street," trans. Edmund Jephcott, in *Walter Benjamin: Selected Writings, Volume 1, 1913–1926*, ed. Marcus Bullock and Michael W. Jennings (Cambridge, MA: Harvard University Press, 1996), 458.

5. Brown, *Roland Barthes*, 192–93. Brown draws from an interview with Barthes—"Un rapport preseque maniaque avec les instruments graphique" [An Almost Maniacal Rapport with Writing Instruments], which was collected in the French edition of *Le Grain de la voix: Entretiens, 1962–1980* (Paris: Seuil, 1981), 170–74—to quote the epigraph that begins this essay: "Il y a d'abord le moment où le désire s'investit dans la pulsion graphique, aboutissant à un objet calligraphique" [There is a moment when desire infuses the graphic impulse, ending up in a calligraphic object] (translation mine). Brown also criticizes what he sees as an unfair reduction of this sentence by others to "J'aime écrire à la main" (193).

6. On writing as the movement of a thought through the body (albeit from a distinctively male perspective) see Charles Grivel, "Travel Writing," in *Materialities of Communication*, ed. Hans Ulrich Gumbrecht and K. Ludwig

Pfeiffer, trans. William Whobrey (Stanford, CA: Stanford University Press, 1994), 254–55.

7. Lisa Jensen, "Confessions of a Computer Phobe," *Santa Cruz (California) Good Times*, Dec. 13, 1990, writes: "Trying to coax inspiration from my own elusive muse is far too private a process to be scrutinized by the prying terminal eye" (23).

8. Gaston Bachelard, *The Poetics of Space*, trans. Maria Jolas (New York: Beacon, 1969), 106.

9. Michael Heim, *Electric Language: A Philosophical Study of Word Processing* (New Haven, CT: Yale University Press, 1987), 152. Subsequent references will be cited in the text.

10. Don Ihde, *Technology and the Lifeworld: From Garden to Earth* (Bloomington: Indiana University Press, 1990), 141. Subsequent references will be cited in the text.

11. Jensen, "Confessions of a Computer Phobe," 23.

12. Elaine Scarry, "The Merging of Bodies and Artifacts in the Social Contract," in *Culture on the Brink: Ideologies of Technology*, ed. Gretchen Bender and Timothy Druckrey (Seattle: Bay Press, 1994), 97.

13. Tamara Plakins Thompson, "Handwriting as an Act of Self-Definition," *Chronicle of Higher Education*, Aug. 15, 1997, B7. Although print has existed since the Gutenberg press, insofar as broad cultural understandings of writing by hand are concerned Thompson also points out: "As late as the 17th century, men and women hardly recognized an association between an individual and his or her script. Only in the early 18th century did the English legal authority Geoffrey Gilbert advance the new idea that 'men are distinguished by their handwriting as well as by their faces'" (B7).

14. Daniel Chandler, in an email to me (Aug. 7, 1997), mentions this notion of "the culturally-sanctioned hierarchy of formality" associated with these writing implements in Western culture.

15. O. B. Hardison Jr., *Disappearing through the Skylight: Culture and Technology in the Twentieth Century* (New York: Penguin, 1989), 259.

16. For a more "popular" discussion of scrolling see ibid., 259–346.

17. Mary Ann Doane, in "Technology's Body," in *Feminist Anthology in Early Cinema*, ed. Jennifer M. Bean and Diane Negra (Durham, NC: Duke University Press, 2002), aptly summarizes the "theory of evolution that opposes the more advanced, civilized, and neurotic exemplar of the human species to a primitive—that is, racial other—defined in terms of an immediacy of the body and unrestricted sexuality"; and she continues: "In Freud, a metonymic chain is constructed that links infantile sexuality, female sexuality, and racial otherness" (542). Also illuminating in this regard is

Donna J. Haraway, *Simians, Cyborgs, and Women: The Reinvention of Nature* (New York: Routledge, 1991).

18. See Annette Michelson, "On the Eve of the Future: The Reasonable Facsimile and the Philosophical Toy," in *October: The First Decade, 1976–1986*, ed. Annette Michelson, Rosalind Krauss, Douglas Crimp, and Joan Copjec (Cambridge, MA: MIT Press, 1987), 432. (In this brilliant essay about philosophical toys, cinema, and the bodies of women, Michelson writes of the android female Hadaly, invented by Thomas Alva Edison, in Villier de l'Isle-Adam's 1889 fiction, *L'eve future*.)

19. For further elaboration of the origins of semiosis in the lived body and its diacritical activity see my "The Lived Body and the Emergence of Language," in *Semiotics around the World: Synthesis in Diversity (Proceedings of the Fifth Congress of the International Association for Semiotic Studies, Berkeley, 1994)*, ed. Irmengard Rauch and Gerald F. Carr (Berlin: Mouton de Gruyter, 1997), 1051–54; and my *The Address of the Eye: A Phenomenology of Film Experience* (Princeton, NJ: Princeton University Press, 1992), 71–76.

20. On the possible meanings of scribbling at a much more sophisticated level than Sean's see Brown, *Roland Barthes*, esp. chap. 4, "The Scribbler," 152–209.

21. Régis Debray, in "The Three Ages of Looking," trans. Eric Rauth, *Critical Inquiry* 21 (spring 1995), notes "the ambiguity of *graphisme* itself [the translator retaining the French word 'because it signifies graphics or the graphic arts as well as handwriting or script'], which accounts for the double meaning of the Greek verb *graphein*, to draw and to write" (541). For extended discussion of the unclear distinction between writing and drawing see also James Elkins, *On Pictures and the Words That Fail Them* (Cambridge, UK: Cambridge University Press, 1998). Elkins asks: "How do we know when we are looking at writing, and not pictures? What criteria are brought into play, and how are they related to the more elaborate structures that preoccupy linguistics?" And he concludes: "Any picture can be understood as failed or incomplete writing, and the same is true of any writing" (130–31).

22. Brown, *Roland Barthes*, 178. Also of interest here is Barthes's wide-ranging work on the connection between the body and signification. In relation to the specific issue of writing, scribbling, and drawing see his essay, "Cy Twombly: Works on Paper," in *The Responsibility of Forms: Critical Essays on Music, Art, and Representation*, trans. Richard Howard (New York: Hill and Wang, 1985), esp. 158–62.

23. See Jonathan Goldberg, *Writing Matter: From the Hands of the English Renaissance* (Stanford, CA: Stanford University Press, 1990). Goldberg

traces a genealogy of the "relationship between the hand writing and hand-writing" in the Renaissance as an increasing separation and objectification of the hand from the whole—and subjective—body in relation to the instrumental production of script (236). I am grateful to Sarah Jain for directing me to this text.

24. Thornton, "Handwriting as an Act of Self-Definition," B7.

25. Monique Wittig, *The Opoponax*, trans. Helen Weaver (Plainfield, VT: Daughters, 1966), 24.

26. Wittig, *The Opoponax*, 31–33.

27. The exquisite torture of this objective technical training is contradicted by a simultaneous cultural belief in the value of the subjective idiosyncrasies of handwriting and graphology; on this contradiction see Roxanne Panchasi, "Graphology and the Science of Individual Identity in Modern France," *Configurations* 4, no. 1 (1996): 1–31.

28. Elaborating on Walter Benjamin's use of the term, Samuel Weber describes *aura* as "*the singular leave-taking of the singular*, whose singularity is no longer that of an original moment but of its posthumous aftershock." Certainly, writing by hand (the "singular leave-taking of the singular") and the hand-written object (the letter that stands as and for the "singular leave-taking of the singular" and is, in relation to the original moment of writing, its "posthumous aftershock") are auratic. See Samuel Weber, "Mass Mediauras, or: Art, Aura and Media in the Work of Walter Benjamin," in *Mass Mediauras: Form, Technics, Media*, ed. Alan Cholodenko (Stanford, CA: Stanford University Press, 1996), 104–5.

29. Although anthropomorphic automata date back to ancient Greek, Chinese, and Arabic cultures and, in Europe, to the medieval and Renaissance periods, the mid-1700s sees a marked proliferation of such fabrications. See, e.g., Jean-Claude Beaune, "The Classical Age of Automata: An Impressionistic Survey from the Sixteenth to the Nineteenth Century," trans. Ian Patterson, in *Fragments for a History of the Human Body, Part One*, ed. Michel Feher, Ramona Naddaff, and Nadia Tazi (New York: Zone, 1989), 430–80. For a recent history of these and later attempts at "mechanical life" see also Gaby Wood, *Edison's Eve: A Magical History of the Quest for Mechanical Life* (New York: Knopf, 2002).

30. Wood, *Edison's Eve*, xiii.

31. Wood, in *Edison's Eve*, writes: "The Jaquet-Droz figures conduct their marvellous activities barefoot, illustrating a belief, held by their contemporary Jean-Jacques Rousseau, that children would learn more freely if unhampered by shoes" (xx).

32. Jasia Reichardt, *Robots: Fact, Fiction, and Prediction* (London: Penguin, 1978), 14. For illustrations of writing automata see 13–15.

33. Quoted from his essay "L'Homme Machine," in Julie Wosk, *Breaking Frame: Technology and the Visual Arts in the Nineteenth Century* (New Brunswick, NJ: Rutgers University Press, 1992), 81. (I am indebted to Jennifer Gonzalez for this reference.)

34. Susan Buck-Morss, *The Dialectics of Seeing: Walter Benjamin and the Arcades Project* (Cambridge, MA: MIT Press, 1991), 363. Relevant here is Benjamin on late-nineteenth-century bourgeois culture: "You have no idea how these automatons and dolls become repugnant, how one breathes relief in meeting a fully natural being in this society" (363).

35. Jean-François Lyotard, "Can Thought Go On without a Body?" trans. Bruce Boone and Lee Hildreth, in *Materialities of Communication*, ed. Hans Ulrich Gumbrecht and K. Ludwig Pfeiffer, trans. William Whobrey (Stanford, CA: Stanford University Press, 1994), 291 (emphasis added). It is worth noting that the same technologic that informs Lyotard's description of the human body as the "hardware" of thought also informs its description as the completely disposable and despised "wetware" of "neuromancers." See, e.g., William Gibson's influential novel, *Neuromancer* (New York: Ace, 1984).

36. Thomas Mallon, "Minding Your 'P's' and 'Q's,' " review of *Handwriting in America: A Cultural History*, by Tamara Plakins Thornton, *New Yorker*, Feb. 3, 1997, 79.

37. Thornton, "Handwriting as an Act of Self-Definition," B7.

38. Writing of the historical recognition of "occupational diseases," Carolyn Steedman, in *Dust: The Archive and Cultural History* (New Brunswick, NJ: Rutgers University Press, 2002), notes the emergence of what we now call "repetitive stress injury" in the 1920s, when "the British Association of Women Clerks focused a century of complaints about writers' cramp among clerical workers, in their attempts to have it scheduled as an industrial sickness with no limit of compensation. But theirs were arguments about the physical effect of minutely repeated movements of hand and arm; the comparison was with telegraphists (telegraphists' cramp was a scheduled industrial disease for which benefit might be claimed indefinitely under the National Insurance legislation of 1911) and with comptometers" (33n14).

39. Wood, *Edison's Eve*, xiv, xvii.

40. This relation between various representational and expressive technologies and "the hand," between the mechanical and the improvisational, are quite wonderfully elaborated in two works by phenomenological sociologist David Sudnow. See his *Ways of the Hand: The Organization of Improvised Conduct* (Cambridge, MA: Harvard University Press, 1978); and *Talk's*

Body: A Meditation between Two Keyboards (New York: Knopf, 1979). In the latter Sudnow contrasts touch typing with jazz improvisation on a piano keyboard.

41. In regard to graphological excess and its marking of existential style, it bears noting that idiosyncrasies in typewriting usually belong less to the human user than to the machine (hence, police work occasionally involves finding a particular typewriter so as to find the person who might have composed something incriminating on it). In contrast, the computer as a writing machine is much more standardized: no keys to chip, no misalignments of letters, etc. However, as mentioned previously, writing on a computer "builds in" some small level of "personal choice" and "expressive potential" that exceeds the typewriter insofar as the writer can use a broader number and variety of typefaces, font sizes, and diacritical marks through which to express existential style. E-mail writers in particular have developed a novel mode of using diacritical marks to indicate existential tone: the ironic wink, peals of laughter, etc. Nonetheless, whatever graphological excess the computer allows over what the typewriter can provide, it still does not afford the personal expression of the "expressive hand" as do pencil and pen.

42. Mallon, "Minding Your 'P's' and 'Q's,'" 81.

43. Martin Heidegger, "The Question Concerning Technology," trans. William Lovitt, in *Martin Heidegger: Basic Writings*, ed. David Farrell Krell (New York: Harper and Row, 1977), 294.

44. Scarry, "Merging of Bodies," 97.

45. Brown, *Roland Barthes*, 185.

46. Wood, *Edison's Eve*, 8.

ISBN 978-0-697-78322-6
MHID 0-697-78322-7